The Guide to American Law

The Guide to American Law

Everyone's Legal Encyclopedia

Volume 1

West Publishing Company

St. Paul • New York • Los Angeles • San Francisco

In addition to the staff of West Publishing Company in St. Paul and New York, many other individuals and organizations contributed to the preparation of this work. In particular West Publishing Company thanks Scott Knudson and Arne Sorenson for writing many of the entries on international law as well as the following for their part in the production of these volumes:

Production Credits

Copy Editing: Carlisle Graphics
Composition: Carlisle Graphics
Photo Research: Carlisle Graphics
      Linda A. Kammer
      Susan Moore
      PICTURE RESEARCH
Editorial Research: Patricia A. Lewis

Photo Credits

Page 13   Courtesy of Sarah Weddington, Attorney
Page 13   Courtesy of Robert C. Flowers, Attorney
Page 13   Courtesy of Jay Floyd, Attorney

Copyright © 1983 By
    WEST PUBLISHING CO.
    50 West Kellogg Boulevard
    P.O. Box 64526
    St. Paul, Minnesota 55164-9979

Printed in the United States of America.

1st Reprint 1984

Library of Congress Cataloging in Publication Data

Main entry under title
  The Guide to American Law

  Bibliography: p
  Includes index
  I. Law United States-Dictionaries
KF156.E83 1983   348.73'6   83-1134
ISBN 0-314-73224-1 347.3086

Dedication

Harold W. Chase
1922–1982

We are fortunate, if once in a lifetime, we are privileged to be witness to a coming together of the ingredients necessary to produce a master work. Time and usage will tell us whether the educated world agrees with us that this work is a monumental achievement.

But we need not wait to assess the ingredients brought to us by Professor Harold Chase. Enthusiasm, dedication, generous spirit, wide knowledge of several disciplines were gifts from him to us. When we assembled to commiserate over his death, selfish sorrow and empty feelings for the future gave way to a renewed spirit to carry on as he would wish. We did carry on and we completed the job. We now want to dedicate it to him.

To Harold Chase:

a teacher
revered by his students
for his inspiration
and sense of fair play;

an author,
appreciated by his editors
for his professionalism and cooperation;

a marine general,
respected for placing his safety and life
where his words were;

a friend,
loved for his kindness,
patience, and gentle humor.

We hope this work is all you wanted it to be.

THE EDITORS

Volume 1

Contents

Signed Articles

Appendixes: Volume 1

Special Topics Lists

Indexes

A Complete List of Signed Articles

Abortion
Craig R. Ducat

Abrams v. United States (Justice Holmes's Dissent)
Richard G. Singer

Absolutes
Thomas I. Emerson

Absolutism
Craig R. Ducat

Activism
Louis Henkin

Act of State Doctrine
Charles H. McLaughlin

Adjudication
Glendon Schubert

Adjudicative Facts
Carl A. Auerbach

Administrative Agency
Carl A. Auerbach

Admission to Law School
John F. Dobbyn

Adversary System
Stephen A. Saltzburg

Advisory Opinions
Robert J. Harris

Affirmative Action
Arthur Larson

Age Requirement for Holding Office
Charles H. Backstrom

Alien
Charles Gordon

Alien and Sedition Acts
Stephen B. Presser

Alien Registration Act
Charles Gordon

Aliens, Admission and Exclusion
Charles Gordon

Aliens, Deportation
Charles Gordon

Aliens, Discrimination Against
Charles Gordon

Aliens, Registration
Charles Gordon

American Bar Association
Bernard G. Segal

American Civil Liberties Union
Norman Dorsen

American Law Book Publishing
Robert C. Berring

American Law Institute
Bernard G. Segal

Amicus Curiae
Erwin N. Griswold

Amnesty
Joseph L. Sax

Analytical Jurisprudence
Edgar Bodenheimer

Anarchy
Mulford Q. Sibley

Anglo-Saxon Law
Anthony D'Amato
Stephen B. Presser

Anthropological Jurisprudence
E. Adamson Hoebel

Apportionment
Robert B. McKay

Apprenticeship
Charles R. McKirdy

Arbitration, International
Charles H. McLaughlin

Armed Services
John De Barr

Attorney and Client
Francis H. Musselman

John Austin
Thomas M. Feldstein
Stephen B. Presser

"Automobile Exception" to Search Warrant Requirement
Joseph D. Grano

Avoiding Constitutional Questions
William M. Beaney

Sir Francis Bacon
J. H. Baker

Bail
Ronald L. Goldfarb

Baker v. Carr
Martin H. Redish

Bakke Case
J. Harvie Wilkinson III

Balancing
Louis Henkin

Bankruptcy
Marjorie Girth

Bay
Charles H. McLaughlin

Thomas Becket: Archbishop of Canterbury
Sue Sheridan Walker

Jeremy Bentham
Stephen B. Presser

Bible Reading
Eric L. Chase

Bill of Rights (English)
Peter R. Teachout

Bill of Rights (United States)
David Fellman

Birth Control
Susan M. Olson

Hugo Black
Thomas M. Feldstein
Stephen B. Presser

Sir William Blackstone
Stephen B. Presser

Boundaries
Charles H. McLaughlin

Henry de Bracton
Peter R. Teachout

Louis D. Brandeis
Thomas M. Feldstein
Stephen B. Presser

Brandeis Brief
Alpheus Thomas Mason

Color Plates

Space and the Law

Color plates 1–12 follow page 114.

Plates 1–12 are courtesy of the National Aeronautics and Space Administration.

Art and the Law

Color plates 13–20 follow page 338.

Plates 13–20 are courtesy of The West Collection, West Publishing Company, from annual West/ART AND THE LAW exhibitions. Copyright © 1979, 1980, 1981, 1982 West Publishing Company.

Preface

In the past decade, Americans in all walks of life have become increasingly affected by the law. Contributing factors include the extensive development and growth of Federal and state legislation as well as rules and regulations that have a far-reaching impact on everyday life. There has been a dramatic increase in administrative proceedings and litigation to interpret and enforce such measures. The public makes repeated demands for an effective and timely system of justice. An ever-growing number of students pursue an education to enter practice as attorneys. As a result, Americans need a readily available research source to consult to gain greater knowledge and understanding of the principles, institutions, and people that through the law provide stability and structure to daily life. *The Guide to American Law: Everyone's Legal Encyclopedia* presents in one reference set a panorama of the American legal system, which while comprehensive in scope is specific in its explanations of a cornucopia of legal topics. This unique multivolume work brings together diverse features and accurate text written in plain English that transcend the traditional format of legal encyclopedias and other secondary sources.

American Jurisprudence in the United States

The Guide encompasses not only legal principles and concepts, but also contains landmark documents and important acts, accounts of famous trials, historical movements and events, and biographies of prominent individuals. In addition, there are brief descriptions of legal organizations; information relating to key Federal regulatory agencies and departments; discussions of legal education, philosophies, and the legal profession; and legal maxims and famous quotations, all of which contribute to the highly developed and dynamic tableau of national jurisprudence.

International Law

Although its primary focus is on American law, *The Guide* discusses numerous principles, concepts, and treaties of international law which have ramifications upon the legal rights of American citizens, businesses, and private and public institutions, at home and abroad.

A Unique Publication

As a concise yet complete reference set on law, there is no other publication like *The Guide*. It is designed to meet everyone's needs for basic legal information and to make available a means of access to in-depth research through its various aids, such as case and statutory citations, cross references, tables of abbreviations, West publications used, selected sample legal forms and historical documents, and topical and general subject indexes. The inclusion of illustrations and famous quotations that reflect the pervasive influence of law on society makes *The Guide* a multidimensional record of American jurisprudence.

While neither a substitute for legal counsel nor the end of legal research for more sophisticated information needs, *The Guide* provides the groundwork upon which to formulate thoughtful questions and insights and to recognize the signposts leading to the ultimate goal of legal research.

HOW TO USE THIS REFERENCE SET

A to Z Format

The alphabetical arrangement of entries and signed articles and the diversity of features and research aids make *The Guide to American Law: Everyone's Legal Encyclopedia* an easy-to-use reference set.

Entries

Entries are explanations of the legal significance of a phrase, concept, topic, legal organization, individual, historical movement, or government agency. Although biographies have not been prepared on living persons, some brief biographical information is provided when integral to a comprehensive discussion in an entry, such as a famous trial, historical movement, or legal principle, or in a signed article.

Case and Statutory Citations   The text of an entry includes citations to important cases and statutes which elucidate abstract principles. Complete case citations to the official and West reporters follow the caption of the case and include the number of the volume of the reporter where the case is printed, followed by the abbreviation for the particular reporter, and the page number where the case appears. The use of an underscore where the volume and page number would normally appear in a case citation indicates that such information is currently unavailable because the official reporter has not yet been published. The date of the decision is designated within parentheses following the citation:

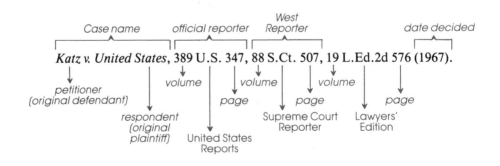

Statutory citation style varies slightly but usually includes the number of the title of the body of law to which such a statute is generally classified on the basis of its subject matter, the abbreviation of the name of the compilation of law, such as U.S.C. for the *United States Code* and U.S.C.A. for the *United States Code Annotated,* and the section sign and number which is assigned to the law.

For example, the statutory citation for the Department of Education Organization Act (93 Stat. 668; 20 U.S.C. 3401) means that the act is printed in volume 93 of the *Statutes at Large* beginning on page 668 and is also set out in Title 20 (dealing with Education) of the *United States Code* under section 3401.

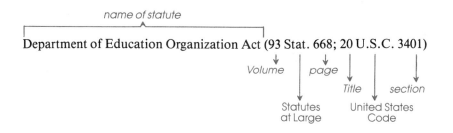

The Sherman Antitrust Act (15 U.S.C.A. §§ 1–7) means that the act is set out under Title 15 (dealing with Commerce and Trade) of the *United States Code Annotated* under sections one to seven.

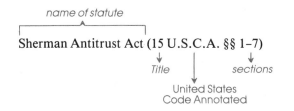

Open Boxes   As a convenience to the reader, an open box precedes the statement of a definition of various types of entries, such as legal terms, concepts, cases, statutes, and points of law. Where an entry has multiple definitions, each definition is preceded by an open box. Another open box follows the end of the last definition. This format allows for highlighting of definitions without ranking them. This feature is illustrated below:

> **AWARD** □ To concede; to give by judicial determination; to rule in favor of after an evaluation of the facts, EVIDENCE, or merits. □
> A jury awards DAMAGES; a municipal corporation awards a PUBLIC CONTRACT to a bidder.
> □ The decision made by a panel of arbitrators or commissioners, a jury, or other authorized individuals in a controversy that has been presented for resolution.
> □ A document that memorializes the determination reached in a dispute. □

Signed Articles

Signed articles, specially prepared for *The Guide* by some of America's foremost legal minds, offer unique insight into the featured material and reflect scholarly and thought-provoking analysis, often enhanced by the personal involvement of the author with the legal issues discussed.

Citations and Bibliographies   These incisive essays provide independent access to more rigorous research by their inclusion of case and statutory citations and bibliographic materials, such as law review articles, cited by author and the title of the article, the number of the volume where it appears, the title of the journal, its date, and its page number:

$$\overset{\textit{author}}{\overbrace{\text{Archibald Cox,}}} \quad \overset{\textit{title of article}}{\overbrace{\text{"Executive Privilege,"}}}$$

$$\overset{\textit{name of law review}}{122 \overbrace{\textit{University of Pennsylvania Law Review}} \text{ (June 1974): 1381–1438;}}$$

volume   date of publication   pages

or hornbooks or treatises, the titles of which are preceded by the names of their authors and followed by publication date:

$$\overset{\textit{names of editors}}{\overbrace{\text{Erica Dolgin and Thomas Guilbert, eds.,}}} \quad \overset{\textit{title of hornbook}}{\overbrace{\textit{Federal Environmental Law}}} \text{ (1974).}$$

date of publication

The inclusion of citations in both the entries and the signed articles attests to the professional quality and accuracy of the text and eliminates the need to undertake additional research to identify specific statutes or cases discussed.

Cross References

Two types of internal cross references demonstrate the interdependence and interrelationships among topics set out as entries and signed articles in *The Guide.* The cross reference indicated by the use of small capital letters in the text designates related terms, phrases, and concepts that are more completely defined and discussed elsewhere. For example, the text of the entry **Embezzlement** states: "There was no crime of embezzlement under the COMMON LAW." The cross reference indicates that an explanation of common law can be located under an entry of that name. The (See also,) form of cross reference is a statement that related material is treated in greater detail where indicated. The entry **Searches and Seizures** incorporates the cross reference "See also, Joseph D. Grano's essay on 'Automobile Exception' to Search Warrant Requirement." This cross reference directs the reader to a scholarly treatment of a specific subject by a legal expert.

Sample Forms

Specimens of selected forms which address recurring problems are included in the Appendix, not to replace consultation with an attorney, but to illustrate the application of law to everyday life. A table of sample forms appears in every volume of the set.

Excerpts of Landmark Documents

The inclusion of the text of selected historical documents, such as the Magna Charta and the Constitution, facilitates detailed examination and reference to their express language, which significantly contributed to the development of American jurisprudence. A table which enumerates the documents printed in the Appendix of *The Guide* is a feature in each volume.

Tables

Tables of abbreviations, cases and statutes cited, popular name acts, sample forms, historical documents, and West publications used appear in every volume to provide an immediate method of determining the availability of the relevant information.

Abbreviations   The table of abbreviations spells out abbreviations, particularly those used in international law that might be unfamiliar, such as *Dig. Intl. L.,* or *Digest of International Law.*

Cases, Statutes, and Popular Name Acts   The table of cases and statutes cited is a compilation of those in the text, and the table of the popular name acts cited provides an alternative means of pinpointing statutory inquiries.

Sample Forms   The table of specially selected sample forms indicates their ready location in the Appendix.

Landmark Documents   The table of historical documents excerpted in *The Guide* provides quick discovery of their inclusion in the Appendix.

West Publications   The list of West publications used in preparation of *The Guide* functions as a comprehensive bibliography for the entries, and supplies specific starting points for more intensive research.

General Subject and Topical Indexes

A general subject index permits a conventional search for information while a topical index allows focusing in on materials applicable to the specialized field of research. Each volume has its own subject index, permitting it to function either independently or as an integral part of the set.

Famous Quotations   In addition, famous quotations are indexed by both topic and author to facilitate their location.

International Law   International law topics also receive specialized topical treatment.

Multiresearch Tool

The diversity of these features enables *The Guide* to be used as a multiresearch tool. By checking the alphabetical listing of a subject or topic in the index or of an entry or signed article in a particular volume, a researcher can use *The Guide* as a dictionary, although it offers much more. As a result of its topical index which sets out main topics and subtopics, *The Guide* is a reference work that provides an outline to direct the course of more detailed research. The compilation of special subject features, such as an international law index and tables of cases and statutes cited, popular name acts, abbreviations, sample forms, and documents, makes *The Guide* a specialized resource, especially well-suited to particularized research needs.

Editorial Board

Contributing Authors

Aliotta, Jilda M.
B.A., 1974, Macalester College; Ph.D., 1982, University of Minnesota.
Visiting Assistant Professor of Political Science, Marquette University.

Auerbach, Carl A.
A.B., 1935, Long Island University; LL.B., 1938, Harvard University.
Professor, University of Minnesota Law School.

Backstrom, Charles H.
B.A., B.S., 1949, Moorhead State College; M.A., 1953; Ph.D., 1956, University of Wisconsin.
Professor of Political Science, University of Minnesota.

Baker, J. H.
LL.B., 1965; Ph.D., 1968, University of London; M.A., 1971, Cambridge University; Barrister at Law, 1966, Inner Temple.
Fellow of St. Catherine's College and University Lecturer, Cambridge University.

Bayles, Michael D.
B.A., 1962, University of Illinois; M.A., 1963, University of Missouri; Ph.D., 1967, Indiana University.
Director, Westminster Institute for Ethics and Human Values, Westminster College, London, Ontario.

Bazelon, David L.
B.S. (Law), 1931, Northwestern University.
Senior Circuit Judge, District of Columbia.

Beaney, William M.
A.B., 1940, Harvard University; LL.B., 1947; Ph.D., 1951, University of Michigan.
Professor, University of Denver College of Law.

Bedau, Hugo Adam
B.A., 1949, University of Redlands; M.A., 1951, Boston University; M.A., 1953; Ph.D., 1961, Harvard University.
Professor of Philosophy, Tufts University.

Berger, Raoul
B.A., 1932, University of Cincinnati; J.D., 1935, Northwestern University; LL.M., 1938, Harvard University.
Author of several books, including *Executive Privilege* (1974).

Berger, Vivian O.
B.A., 1966, Radcliffe College; J.D., 1973, Columbia University.
Professor, Columbia University School of Law.

Berring, Robert C.
B.A., 1971, Harvard University; J.D., 1974; M.L.S., 1974, University of California at Berkeley.
Librarian and Professor, University of California at Berkeley School of Law.

Blake, Harlan M.
B.A., 1946; M.A., 1947; J.D., 1954, University of Chicago.
Professor, Columbia University School of Law.

Blasi, Vincent A.
B.A., 1964, Northwestern University; J.D., 1967, University of Chicago.
Professor, Columbia University School of Law.

Blaustein, Albert P.
A.B., 1941, University of Michigan; J.D., 1948, Columbia University.
Professor, Rutgers, The State University of New Jersey School of Law, Camden.

Bodenheimer, Edgar
J.U.D., 1932, University of Heidelberg; LL.B., 1937, University of Washington, Seattle.
Professor Emeritus, University of California at Davis School of Law.

Bollinger, Lee
B.S., 1968, University of Oregon; J.D., 1971, Columbia University.
Professor, University of Michigan Law School.

Burns, Brian D.
A.B., 1971, New York University; J.D., 1974, Rutgers University.
Partner, Schenck, Price, Smith & King, Morristown, New Jersey.

Cantor, Norman L.
A.B., 1964, Princeton University; LL.B., 1967, Columbia University.
Professor, Rutgers, The State University of New Jersey, S.I. Newhouse Center for Law & Justice.

Chase, Eric L.
B.A., 1968, Princeton University; J.D., 1974, University of Minnesota.
Associate, Martin G. Margolis, Verona, New Jersey.

Chase, Harold W.
B.A., 1943; M.A., 1948; Ph.D., 1954, Princeton University.
Professor of Political Science, University of Minnesota.
Deceased.

Chisholm, Margaret
B.A., University of Pennsylvania; J.D., Harvard University.
Public Services Librarian, Yale Law School Library.

Christie, George C.
A.B., 1955; J.D., 1957, Columbia University; Dipl. Int'l. Law, 1962, Cambridge University; S.J.D., 1966, Harvard University.
James B. Duke Professor, Duke University School of Law.

Cohen, Julius
A.B., 1931; M.A., 1932; J.D., 1937, West Virginia University; LL.M., 1938, Harvard University.
Professor Emeritus, Rutgers, The State University of New Jersey, S.I. Newhouse Center for Law & Justice.

Cohen, Morris L.
B.A., 1947, University of Chicago; LL.B., 1951, Columbia University; M.L.S., 1959, Pratt Institute Library School.
Professor and Librarian, Yale Law School.

D'Amato, Anthony
A.B., 1958, Cornell University; J.D., 1961, Harvard University; Ph.D., 1968, Columbia University.
Professor, Northwestern University School of Law.

Danelski, David J.
LL.B., 1953, De Paul University; B.A., 1955, Seattle University; M.A., 1957; Ph.D., 1961, University of Chicago.
Professor of Political Science, Stanford University.

De Barr, John
A.B., 1947, Bucknell University; J.D., 1950, George Washington University.
Professor, California Western School of Law.

Dobbyn, John F.
A.B., 1959, Harvard University; J.D., 1965, Boston College; LL.M., 1969, Harvard University.
Professor, Villanova University School of Law.

Dolan, Paul
B.S., 1933; M.A., 1936, University of Pennsylvania; Ph.D., 1950, Johns Hopkins University.
Professor Emeritus of Political Science, University of Delaware.
Deceased.

Donovan, Dolores A.
J.D., 1970, Stanford University.
Professor, University of San Francisco School of Law.

Dorsen, Norman
B.A., 1950, Columbia University; LL.B., 1953, Harvard University.
Frederick I. & Grace A. Stokes Professor & Director, Arthur Garfield Hays Civil Liberties Program, New York University School of Law.

Ducat, Craig R.
B.A., 1966, Syracuse University; M.A., 1968; Ph.D., 1970, University of Minnesota.
Professor of Political Science, Northern Illinois University.

Elazar, Daniel J.
M.A., 1957; Ph.D., 1959, University of Chicago.
Professor of Political Science, Temple University.

Emerson, Thomas I.
B.A., 1928, LL.B., 1931; M.A., 1946, Yale University.
August E. Lines Professor Emeritus, Yale Law School.

Faw, Duane L.
J.D., 1947, Columbia University.
Professor, Pepperdine University School of Law.

Feeley, Malcolm
B.A., Austin College (Texas); M.A., 1967; Ph.D., 1969, University of Minnesota.
Professor of Political Science, University of Wisconsin.

Feerick, John D.
B.A., 1958; LL.B., 1961, Fordham University.
Dean and Professor, Fordham University School of Law.

Feldstein, Thomas M.
B.A., 1979, Stanford University; J.D., 1983, Northwestern University.

Fellman, David
B.A., 1929; M.A., 1930, University of Nebraska; Ph.D., 1934, Yale University.
Vilas Professor Emeritus of Political Science, University of Wisconsin.

Fisher, Louis
B.S., 1956, College of William and Mary; Ph.D., 1967, New School for Social Research.
Specialist in American national government, Congressional Research Service, Library of Congress.

Foster, Henry H.
A.B., 1933; J.D., 1936, University of Nebraska; LL.M., 1941, Harvard University; LL.M., 1960, University of Chicago.
Professor Emeritus, New York University School of Law.

Franklin, Mitchell
A.B., 1922; J.D., 1925; S.J.D., 1928, Harvard University.
Professor Emeritus and Professor Emeritus of Philosophy, State University of New York at Buffalo School of Law.

Freeman, Harrop A.
A.B., 1929; LL.B., 1930; J.S.D., 1945, Cornell University.
Professor Emeritus, Cornell Law School.

Friesen, Ernest
A.B., 1950, University of Kansas; J.D., 1955, Columbia University.
Dean and Professor, California Western School of Law.

Frisch, Morton J.
B.A., 1949, Roosevelt University; M.A., 1949, University of Chicago; Ph.D., 1953, Pennsylvania State University.
Professor of Political Science, Northern Illinois University.

Gaubatz, John T.
B.S., 1964, Colorado State University; J.D., 1967, University of Chicago.
Professor, University of Miami School of Law.

Gerald, J. Edward
B.A., 1927, West Texas State Teachers College; B.J., 1928; M.A., 1932, University of Missouri; Ph.D., 1946, University of Minnesota.
Professor Emeritus of Journalism, University of Minnesota.

Gerstein, Robert S.
B.A., 1961, University of California; Ph.D., 1967; LL.B., 1964, Harvard University.
Professor of Political Science, University of California at Los Angeles.

Gilbert, Catherine
B.A., 1983, Northwestern University.

Girth, Marjorie
LL.B., 1962, Harvard University.
Professor, State University of New York at Buffalo School of Law.

Goldfarb, Ronald L.
A.B., 1954; LL.B., 1956, Syracuse University; LL.M., 1960; J.S.D., 1962, Yale University.
Partner, Goldfarb, Singer & Austern, Washington, D.C.

Goldman, Sheldon
B.A., 1961, New York University; Ph.D., 1965, Harvard University.
Professor of Political Science, University of Massachusetts, Amherst.

Gordon, Charles
LL.B., 1927, New York University.
Adjunct Professor, Georgetown University Law Center.

Grano, Joesph D.
A.B., 1965; J.D., 1968, Temple University; LL.M., 1970, University of Illinois.
Professor, Wayne State University Law School.

Greenawalt, Kent
A.B., 1958, Swarthmore College; B. Phil., 1960, Oxford University; LL.B., 1963, Columbia University.
Cardozo Professor of Jurisprudence, Columbia University School of Law.

Greenfogel, Jane A.
B.S., 1970, University of Illinois; J.D., 1982, Rutgers University School of Law, Camden.

Griswold, Erwin N.
A.B., 1925; A.M., 1925, Oberlin College; LL.B., 1928; S.J.D., 1929, Harvard University.
Dean Emeritus and Langdell Professor Emeritus, Harvard University Law School.

Haddad, James B.
B.A., 1964, University of Notre Dame; J.D., 1967; LL.M., 1969, Northwestern University.
Professor, Northwestern University School of Law.

Hardeman, D. B.
B.A., 1933, University of Texas.
Former Texas state representative and administrative aide to Speaker of the House Sam Rayburn.
Deceased.

Harris, Robert J.
B.A., 1930, Vanderbilt University; M.A., 1931, University of Illinois; Ph.D., 1934, Princeton University.
James Hart Professor Emeritus of Government and Foreign Affairs and Former Professor of History, University of Virginia.

Hazard, John N.
B.A., 1930, Yale University; LL.B., 1934, Harvard University; certificate, 1937, Moscow Juridical Institute; J.S.D., 1939, University of Chicago.
Nash Professor Emeritus, Columbia School of Law.

Henkin, Louis
A.B., 1937, Yeshiva College; LL.B., 1940, Harvard University.
University Professor, Columbia University School of Law.

Hill, Larry B.
B.A., 1964, Cornell University; M.A., 1966; Ph.D., 1970, Tulane University.
Professor of Political Science, University of Oklahoma.

Hoebel, E. Adamson
B.A., 1928, University of Wisconsin; M.A., 1931, New York University; Ph.D., 1934, Columbia University.
Regents' Professor Emeritus of Anthropology, University of Minnesota.

Honnold, John O.
A.B., 1936, University of Illinois; J.D., 1939, Harvard University.
William A. Schnader Professor of Commercial Law, University of Pennsylvania Law School.

Hornstein, Elizabeth
A.B., 1966, Vassar College; J.D., 1969, Columbia University.
Lans Feinberg and Cohen, New York City.

Jackson, John H.
A.B., 1954, Princeton University; J.D., 1959, University of Michigan.
Professor, University of Michigan Law School.

Kapsch, Stefan J.
B.A., 1964; M.A., 1967; Ph.D., 1971, University of Minnesota.
Associate Professor of Political Science, Reed College.

Koenig, Louis W.
B.A., 1938, Bard College; M.A., 1940; Ph.D., 1944, Columbia University.
Professor of Government, New York University.

Konvitz, Milton R.
M.A., 1930; J.D., 1930, New York University; Ph.D., 1933, Cornell University.
Professor Emeritus, Cornell Law School.

Krislov, Samuel
B.A., 1951; M.A., 1952, New York University; Ph.D., 1955, Princeton University.
Professor of Political Science, University of Minnesota.

Lacovara, Philip A.
B.A., 1963, Georgetown University; J.D., 1966, Columbia University.
Partner, Hughes, Hubbard & Reed, Washington, D.C.

Larson, Arthur
B.A., 1931, Augustana College; B.A., 1935; M.A., 1938; B.C.L., 1957; D.C.L., 1957, Oxford University.
James B. Duke Professor Emeritus, Duke University Law School.

Lewis, Alfred J.
B.A., 1962; J.D., 1965, Temple University; M.A. in L.S., University of Michigan.
Assistant Law Librarian, University of California at Davis.

Lindsay, Robert
B.A., 1953; M.A., 1954, University of Wisconsin; Ph.D., 1965, University of Minnesota.
Professor of Mass Communications and International Relations, University of Minnesota.

Lusky, Louis
A.B., 1935, University of Louisville; LL.B., 1937, Columbia University.
Betts Professor, Columbia University School of Law.

McKay, Robert B.
B.S., 1940, University of Kansas; J.D., 1947, Yale University.
Professor, New York University School of Law.

McKirdy, Charles R.
B.A., 1965, State University of New York at Buffalo; M.A., 1969; Ph.D., 1969; J.D., 1974, Northwestern University.
Partner; Pope, Ballard, Shepard & Fowle, Chicago, Illinois.

McLaughlin, Charles H.
B.A., 1929; M.A., 1934, University of Denver; J.D., 1935, Harvard University; postgrad in public law, 1939–40, 1946, Columbia University.
Professor Emeritus of Political Science, University of Minnesota.

McLaughlin, Joseph M.
A.B., 1954; LL.B., 1959, Fordham University; LL.M., 1964, New York University.
Federal District Judge, Eastern District, New York.

Mason, Alpheus Thomas
B.A., 1920, Dickinson College; M.A., 1921; Ph.D., 1923, Princeton University.
McCormick Professor of Jurisprudence Emeritus, Princeton University.

Melli, Marygold S.
B.A., 1947; LL.B., 1950, University of Wisconsin.
Professor, University of Wisconsin Law School.

Moenssens, Andre A.
J.D., 1966, Chicago-Kent College of Law; LL.M., 1967, Northwestern University.
Professor & Director, Institute for Trial Advocacy, University of Richmond, The T. C. Williams School of Law.

Moreines, Sherri A.
B.A., 1978, University of Pennsylvania; J.D., 1983, Northwestern University.

Morrison, Fred L.
A.B., 1961, University of Kansas; B.A. (Juris.), 1963, Oxford University; Ph.D., 1966, Princeton University; J.D., 1967, University of Chicago.
Professor, University of Minnesota Law School.

Murphy, Paul L.
B.A., 1947, College of Idaho; M.A., 1948; Ph.D., 1953, University of California at Berkeley.
Professor of History and American Studies, University of Minnesota.

Musselman, Francis H.
B.A., 1950, Hamilton College, LL.B., 1953, Columbia University.
Resident Partner, Washington, D.C. office of Milbank, Tweed, Hadley & McCloy.

Nixon, Robert W.
B.A., 1961, Columbia Union College; B.S., 1964, Boston University; J.D., 1975, American University.
Associate, Office of General Counsel, General Conference of Seventh-day Adventists, Washington, D.C.

Noonan, John T., Jr.
A.B., 1947, Harvard University; Ph.D., 1951, Catholic University; LL.B., 1954, Harvard University.
Professor, University of California at Berkeley School of Law.

Olson, Susan M.
B.A., 1972, Pomona College; Ph.d., 1981, Syracuse University.
Assistant Professor of Political Science, University of Minnesota.

Pietris, Mary K. D.
B.A., 1963, Swarthmore College; M. Libr., 1965, University of Washington.
Chief, Subject Cataloging Division, Processing Services, Library of Congress.

Pollak, Louis H.
B.A., 1943, Harvard University; LL.B., 1948, Yale University.
Federal District Judge, Eastern District, Pennsylvania.

Presser, Stephen B.
A.B., 1968; J.D., 1971, Harvard University.
Associate Dean and Professor, Northwestern University School of Law.

Pritchett, C. Herman
B.A., 1926, James Millikin University; Ph.D., 1937, University of Chicago.
Professor of Political Science, University of California at Santa Barbara.

Raskind, Leo J.
Ph.D., 1952, London School of Economics; LL.B., 1955, Yale University.
Professor, University of Minnesota Law School.

Redish, Martin H.
A.B., 1967, University of Pennsylvania; J.D., 1970, Harvard University.
Professor, Northwestern University School of Law.

Reese, Willis L. M.
LL.B., 1938, Yale University.
Charles Evans Hughes Professor Emeritus and Special Services Professor, Columbia University School of Law.

Reitz, Curtis R.
A.B., 1951; LL.B., 1956, University of Pennsylvania.
Professor, University of Pennsylvania Law School.

Rheingold, Paul D.
B.A., 1955, Oberlin College; LL.B., 1958, Harvard University.
Individual practice and Counsel, Speiser & Krause, New York City.

Riggs, Robert E.
B.A., 1952; M.A., 1953, University of Arizona; Ph.D., 1955, University of Illinois; LL.B., 1963, University of Arizona.
Professor, Brigham Young University, J. Reuben Clark Law School.

Rosenblum, Victor G.
A.B., 1945; LL.B., 1948, Columbia University; Ph.D., 1953, University of California at Berkeley.
Professor, Northwestern University School of Law.

Rumble, Wilfrid E.
B.A., 1953; M.A., 1956, University of Minnesota; Ph.D., 1961, Johns Hopkins University.
Professor of Political Science on the Frederick Ferris Thompson Chair, Vassar College.

Saltzburg, Stephen A.
A.B., 1967, Dickinson College; J.D., 1970, University of Pennsylvania.
Professor, University of Virginia School of Law.

Sax, Joseph L.
A.B., 1957, Harvard University; J.D., 1959, University of Chicago.
Professor, University of Michigan Law School.

Schenk, Alan
B.S., 1961; LL.B., 1965, University of Illinois; LL.M., 1966, New York University.
Professor, Wayne State University Law School.

Schmidhauser, John R.
B.A., 1949, University of Delaware; M.A., 1952; Ph.D., 1954, University of Virginia.
Professor of Political Science, University of Southern California.

Schneider, Robert R.
B.S., 1979, University of Illinois; J.D., 1983, Northwestern University.

Schubert, Glendon
A.B., 1940; Ph.D., 1948, Syracuse University.
University Professor of Political Science, University of Hawaii at Manoa.

Segal, Bernard G.
B.A., 1928; J.D., 1931, University of Pennsylvania.
Partner, Schnader, Harrison, Segal & Lewis, Philadelphia, Pennsylvania.

Shapiro, Martin
B.A., 1955, University of California at Los Angeles; Ph.D., 1961, Harvard Institute of Political Science.
Professor, University of California at Berkeley School of Law.

Sherman, Edward F.
A.B., 1959, Georgetown University; LL.B., 1962, Harvard University; M.A., 1962, 1967, University of Texas.
Angus G. Wynne Professor, University of Texas School of Law.

Sibley, Mulford Q.
B.A., 1933, Central State College, Oklahoma; M.A., 1934, University of Oklahoma; Ph.D., 1938, University of Minnesota.
Professor Emeritus of Political Science and American Studies, University of Minnesota.

Sigler, Jay A.
B.A., 1954; J.D., 1957; M.A, 1960; Ph.D., 1962, Rutgers University.
Professor of Political Science, Rutgers University, Camden.

Singer, Richard G.
A.B., 1963, Amherst College; J.D., 1966, University of Chicago; LL.M., 1971; J.S.D., 1978, Columbia University.
Professor, Yeshiva University, Benjamin N. Cardozo School of Law.

Sorauf, Frank J.
B.A., 1950; M.A., 1952; Ph.D., 1953, University of Wisconsin.
Professor of Political Science, University of Minnesota.

Spear, Allan H.
B.A., 1958, Oberlin College; M.A., 1960; Ph.D., 1965, Yale University.
Associate Professor of History, University of Minnesota.

Speidel, Richard E.
A.B., 1954, Denison University; LL.B., 1957, University of Cincinnati; LL.M., 1958, Northwestern University.
Professor, Northwestern University School of Law.

St. Antoine, Theodore J.
A.B., 1951, Fordham University; J.D., 1954, University of Michigan.
James E. & Sarah A. Degan Professor, University of Michigan Law School.

Stein, Peter
B.A., 1949; LL.B., 1950; M.A., 1951, Cambridge University; graduate study, 1951–52, University of Pavia; Ph.D., 1955, University of Aberdeen.
Regius Professor of Civil Law, Queen's College, Cambridge University.

Sterk, Stewart E.
A.B., 1973; J.D., 1976, Columbia University.
Associate Professor, Yeshiva University, Benjamin N. Cardozo School of Law.

Stone, Victor J.
A.B., 1942, Oberlin College; J.D., 1948, Columbia University.
Professor, University of Illinois College of Law.

Sutton, John F., Jr.
J.D., 1941, University of Texas.
Dean and William Stamps Farish Professor, The University of Texas School of Law.

Sweeney, Joseph C.
A.B., 1954, Harvard University; J.D., 1957, Boston University; LL.M., 1963, Columbia University.
Professor, Fordham University School of Law.

Sweeney, Joseph M.
License, 1945, Grenoble University, France; LL.B., 1948, Harvard University.
Eberhard P. Deutsch Professor of Public International Law, Tulane University School of Law.

Swindler, William F.
B.A., B.S., 1935, Washington University; M.A., 1936; Ph.D., 1942, University of Missouri; LL.B., 1958, University of Nebraska.
John Marshall Professor Emeritus, College of William and Mary, Marshall-Wythe School of Law.

Teachout, Peter R.
B.A., 1962, Amherst College; J.D., 1965, Harvard University; M.A., 1967, University of Sussex, England.
Professor, Vermont Law School.

Tushnet, Mark
B.A., 1967, Harvard University; J.D., 1971; M.A., 1971, Yale University.
Professor, Georgetown University Law Center.

Ulmer, S. Sidney
B.A., 1952, Furman University; M.A., 1954; Ph.D., 1956, Duke University.
Professor of Political Science, University of Kentucky.

Vidal, Gore
Author of eighteen novels, including *Burr: A Novel* (1973).

Walker, Sue Sheridan
B.A., 1958, Loyola University; M.A., 1961; Ph.D., 1966, University of Chicago.
Professor of History, Northeastern Illinois University.

Ward, David
B.A., 1955, Colby College; Ph.D., 1960, University of Illinois.
Professor of Sociology, University of Minnesota.

Wasson, David F.
B.A., 1982, Northwestern University.

Wertheimer, Fred
B.A., 1959, University of Michigan; LL.B., 1962, Harvard University.
President, Common Cause, Washington, D.C.

Wilkinson, J. Harvie III
B.A., 1967, Yale University; J.D., 1972, University of Virginia.
Professor, University of Virginia School of Law.

Williams, Robert F.
B.A., 1967, Florida State University; J.D., 1969, University of Florida; LL.M., 1971, New York University; LL.M., 1980, Columbia University.
Associate Professor, Rutgers, The State University of New Jersey School of Law, Camden.

Wolff, Morris Hirsch
B.A., 1958, Amherst College; J.D., 1963, Yale University; M.A., 1978, Temple University.
Associate Professor, Delaware Law School, Widener University.

Zainaldin, Jamil S.
B.A., 1970, University of Virginia; Ph.D., 1976, University of Chicago.
Adjunct Professor of Law, Georgetown University.

Table of Abbreviations

Under each letter, abbreviations consisting of all capital
letters precede abbreviations containing both
capital and small letters.

A.	Atlantic Reporter
A. 2d	Atlantic Reporter, Second Series
AAA	American Arbitration Association
AAA-CPA	American Association of Attorney-Certified Public Accountants
AACP	American Association of Correctional Psychologists
AACSL	American Association for the Comparative Study of Law
AAFS	American Academy of Forensic Sciences
AAICJ	American Association for the International Commission of Jurists
AALL	American Association of Law Libraries
AALS	Association of American Law Schools
AAMC	American Association of Medico-Legal Consultants
AAPL	American Academy of Psychiatry and the Law
ABA	American Bar Association
ABC	American Bar Center
ABF	American Bar Foundation
ABLA	American Blind Lawyers Association; American Business Law Association
A/C	Account
A.C.	Appeal Cases
ACA	American Correctional Association
ACB	Association of the Customs Bar
ACJA-LAE	American Criminal Justice Association—Lambda Alpha Epsilon
ACJS	Academy of Criminal Justice Sciences
ACLU	American Civil Liberties Union
ACMS	Automated Career Management System
ACP	Agriculture Conservation Program
ACPL	American College of Probate Counsel
ACTL	American College of Trial Lawyers
ACYF	Administration for Children, Youth, and Families
A.D. 2d	Appellate Division, Second Series, N.Y.
ADAMHA	Alcohol, Drug Abuse, and Mental Health Administration
ADD	Administration on Developmental Disabilities
ADEA	Age Discrimination in Employment Act of 1967
ADP	automated data processing
ADPE	automatic data processing equipment
ADTS	Automated Data Telecommunications Service
AECB	Arms Export Control Board
AEDS	Atomic Energy Detection System
AEI	American Enterprise Institute for Public Policy Research
AELE	Americans for Effective Law Enforcement
A.E.R.	All England Law Reports
AFDC	Aid to Families with Dependent Children
AFIS	American Forces Information Service
AFL	American Federation of Labor
AFRes	Air Force Reserve
AFRRI	Armed Forces Radiobiology Research Institute
AIA	Association of Insurance Attorneys
AID	Agency for International Development
AILC	American Indian Law Center; Francis Deák, *American International Law Cases, 1783–1968* (1971).

AINL	Association of Immigration and Nationality Lawyers
AIPPI	International Association for the Protection of Industrial Property
AIUSA	Amnesty International, U.S.A. Affiliate
AJS	American Judicature Society
ALA	Association of Legal Administration
ALEC	American Legislative Exchange Council
ALI	American Law Institute
ALJ	Administrative Law Judge
ALO	Agency Liaison
A.L.R.	American Law Reports
AMS	Agricultural Marketing Service
ANA	Administration for Native Americans
ANZUS	Australia–New Zealand–United States Security Treaty Organization
AOA	Administration on Aging
APA	American Psychiatric Association
APHIS	Animal and Plant Health Inspection Service
APLA	American Patent Law Association
AP-LS	American Psychology–Law Society
ARS	Advanced Record System
ASCS	Agricultural Stabilization and Conservation Service
ASILS	Association of Student International Law Societies
ASLH	American Society for Legal History
ASM	available seatmile
ASPL	American Society for Pharmacy Law
ASPLP	American Society for Political and Legal Philosophy
ASQDE	American Society of Questioned Document Examiners
ATLA	Association of Trial Lawyers of America
AUL	Americans United for Life
AWSA	American Woman Suffrage Association
Act'g Legal Adv.	Acting Legal Advisor
aff'd per cur.	affirmed by the court
All E.R.	All England Law Reports
Am. Dec.	American Decisions
amdt.	amendment
Amer. St. Papers, For. Rels.	American State Papers, Legislative and Executive Documents of the Congress of the U.S., Class I, Foreign Relations, 1832–1859.
Amintaphil	American Section, International Association for Philosophy of Law and Social Philosophy
Ann. Dig.	Annual Digest of Public International Law Cases
App. Div.	Appellate Division Reports, N.Y. Supreme Court
Arb. Trib., U.S.– British Convention of 1853	Arbitration Tribunal, Claim Convention of 1853, United States and Great Britain
Art.	article
Asst. Att. Gen.	Assistant Attorney General
BALSA	Black American Law Students Association
BEA	Bureau of Economic Analysis
BFOQ	bona fide occupational qualification
BJS	Bureau of Justice Statistics
BLM	Bureau of Land Management
BLS	Bureau of Labor Statistics
BMP	Best Management Practices
BOCA	Building Officials and Code Administrators International
BPA	Bonneville Power Administration
BSC	Business Service Center
b.w.u.	blue whale unit
Bell's Cr. C.	Bell's English Crown Cases

Bevans	United States Treaties, etc. *Treaties and Other International Agreements of the United States of America, 1776-1949* (compiled under the direction of Charles I. Bevans) (1968-76).
Black.	Black's United States Supreme Court Reports
Blatchf.	Blatchford's United States Circuit Court Reports
Brit. and For.	British and Foreign State Papers
Burr.	James Burrows, *Report of Cases Argued and Determined in the Court of King's Bench during the Time of Lord Mansfield* (1766-1780).
c.	chapter
C.A.	Court of Appeals
CAB	Civil Aeronautics Board
CATV	cable television
CBO	Congressional Budget Office
CCA	Crop Condition Assessment
CCC	Commodity Credit Corporation
C.C.D. Pa.	Circuit Court Decisions, Pennsylvania
C.C.D.Va.	Circuit Court Decisions, Virginia
CCEA	Cabinet Council on Economic Affairs
CCH Trade Cases	Commerce Clearing House Trade Cases
CCR	Center for Constitutional Rights
C.C.R.I.	Circuit Court, Rhode Island
CD	certificate of deposit
CDC	Centers for Disease Control
CDC	Community Development Corporation
CDF	Children's Defense Fund
CDL	Citizens for Decency Through Law
CDS	Community Dispute Services
CENTO	Central Treaty Organization
CEQ	Council on Environmental Quality
CETA	Comprehensive Employment and Training Act
C & F	cost and freight
C.F. & I.	Cost, freight, and insurance.
CFNP	Community Food and Nutrition Program
C.F.R.	Code of Federal Regulations
CFTC	Commodity Futures Trading Commission
CGUSACE	Commanding General, United States Army Corps of Engineers
CHAMPVA	Civilian Health and Medical Program at the Veterans Administration
CHEP	Cuban/Haitian Entrant Program
CHINS	children in need of supervision
CHIPS	children in need of protection and services
CIA	Central Intelligence Agency
CID	Commercial Item Descriptions
C.I.F.	Cost, insurance, and freight.
CINCNORAD	Commander in Chief, North American Air Defense Command
C.I.O.	Congress of Industrial Organizations
C.J.	chief justice
C.J.S.	Corpus Juris Secundum
CLEO	Council on Legal Education Opportunity
CLS	Christian Legal Society
C.M.A.	Court of Military Appeals
CMEA	Council for Mutual Economic Assistance
C.M.R.	Court of Military Review
CNO	Chief of Naval Operations
C.O.D.	cash on delivery
COGP	Commission on Government Procurement
COMARC	Cooperative Machine-Readable Cataloging Program
COMCEN	Federal Communications Center
COMSAT	Communications Satellite Corporation

CONTU	National Commission on New Technological Uses of Copyrighted Works
COTP	Coast Guard Captains of the Port
CPA	Certified Public Accountant
CPI	Consumer Price Index
CRF	Constitutional Rights Foundation
C. Rob.	Christopher Robinson, *Reports of Cases Argued and Determined in the High Court of Admiralty* (1801–1808).
CRS	Community Relations Service
CSA	Community Services Administration
CSG	Council of State Governments
CSO	Consumer Services Organization
CSP	Center for the Study of the Presidency
CTA	*cum testamento annexo* (with the will attached)
CU	credit union
CWT	Consumers for World Trade
Cal. 2d	California Reports, Second Series
Cal. 3d	California Reports, Third Series
Cal. Rptr.	California Reporter
cert.	*certiorari*
Ch.	Chancery Division, English Law Reports
Ch.N.Y.	Chancery Reports, New York
Chr. Rob.	Christopher Robinson, *Reports of Cases Argued and Determined in the High Court of Admiralty* (1801–1808).
Claims Arb. under Spec. Conv., Nielsen's Rept.	Frederick Kenelm Nielsen, *American and British Claims Arbitration under the Special Agreement Concluded between the United States and Great Britain, August 18, 1910* (1926).
Coke Rep.	Coke's English King's Bench Reports
Comp.	Compilation
Conn.	Connecticut Reports
Conv.	Convention
Corbin	Arthur L. Corbin, *Corbin on Contracts: A Comprehensive Treatise on the Rules of Contract Law* (1950).
Cox's Crim. Cases	Cox's Criminal Cases (England)
Cranch	Cranch's United States Supreme Court Reports
Ct. Ap. D.C.	Court of Appeals, District of Columbia
Ct. App. No. Ireland	Court of Appeals, Northern Ireland
Ct. Cl.	Court of Claims, United States
Ct. Crim. Apps.	Court of Criminal Appeals (England)
Ct. of Sess., Scot.	Court of Sessions, Scotland
Cush.	Cushing's Massachusetts Reports
DARPA	Defense Advanced Research Projects Agency
DAVA	Defense Audiovisual Agency
D.C.	United States District Court
DCA	Defense Communications Agency
DCAA	Defense Contract Audit Agency
DCAR	Defense Contract Administration Services Region
DCII	Defense Central Index of Investigations
D.C. Del.	United States District Court, Delaware
D.C. Mass.	United States District Court, Massachusetts
D.C. Md.	United States District Court, Maryland
D.C.N.D.Cal.	United States District Court, Northern District, California
D.C.N.Y.	United States District Court, New York
D.C.Pa.	United States District Court, Pennsylvania
DCS	Defense Communications System
DCS	Deputy Chiefs of Staff
DCZ	District of the Canal Zone
DEA	Drug Enforcement Administration

DEPRA	Defense European and Pacific Redistribution Activity
DIA	Defense Intelligence Agency
DIPEC	Defense Industrial Plant Equipment Center
DIS	Defense Investigative Service
DLA	Defense Logistics Agency
D.L.R.	Dominion Law Reports (Canada)
DMA	Defense Mapping Agency
DMAAC	Defense Mapping Agency Aerospace Center
DMAHTC	Defense Mapping Agency Hydrographic/Topographic Center
DMAIAGS	Defense Mapping Agency Inter-American Geodetic Survey
DMAODS	Defense Mapping Agency Office of Distribution Services
DMS	Defense Mapping School
DNA	Defense Nuclear Agency
DOD	Department of Defense
DODDS	Department of Defense Dependents Schools
DOE	Department of Energy
DOT	Department of Transportation
DRI	Defense Research Institute
DRIS	Department of Defense Retail Interservice Support
DSAA	Defense Security Assistance Agency
Dall.	Dallas' Pennsylvania and United States Reports
Decl. Lond.	Declaration of London, February 26, 1909
Dev. & B.	Devereux & Battle's North Carolina Reports
Dig. U.S. Practice in Intl. Law	Digest of U.S. Practice in International Law
Dist. Ct. D.C.	United States District Court, District of Columbia
Dodson	Dodson's Reports, English Admiralty Courts
EBT	examination before trial
ECA	Educational and Cultural Affairs
ECOSOC	Economic and Social Council (United Nations)
EDA	Economic Development Administration
EDF	Environmental Defense Fund
E.D.N.Y.	Eastern District, New York
EDP	electronic data processing
E.D. Pa.	Eastern District, Pennsylvania
EDSC	Eastern District, South Carolina
E.D. Va.	Eastern District, Virginia
EEOC	Equal Employment Opportunity Commission
EFNEP	Expanded Food and Nutrition Education Program
EFTS	electronic fund transfer systems
EPA	Environmental Protection Agency; Equal Pay Act of 1963
ERA	Equal Rights Amendment
ERISA	Employee Retirement Income Security Act of 1974
ESF	Economic Support Fund
ESRD	End-Stage Renal Disease Program
ETA	Employment and Training Administration
ETS	Educational Testing Service
Eliz.	Queen Elizabeth (Great Britain)
Em. App.	Temporary Emergency Court of Appeals
Eng. Rep.	English Reports
et seq.	*et sequentes* or *et sequentia*; "and the following"
Eur. Ct. H.R.	European Court of Human Rights
Ex.	English Exchequer Reports, Welsby, Hurlstone & Gordon
Exch.	Exchequer Reports (Welsby, Hurlstone and Gordon)
F.	Federal Reporter
F. 2d	Federal Reporter, Second Series
FAA	Federal Aviation Administration
FAIR	Federation for American Immigration Reform
FAO	Food and Agriculture Organization of the United Nations

FAR	Federal Acquisition Regulations
FAS	Foreign Agricultural Service; free alongside
FBA	Federal Bar Association
FBI	Federal Bureau of Investigation
FCBA	Federal Communications Bar Association
FCC	Federal Communications Commission
FCIA	Foreign Credit Insurance Association
FCU	Federal credit unions
FDA	Food and Drug Administration
FDIC	Federal Deposit Insurance Corporation
FDPC	Federal Data Processing Center
FEC	Federal Election Commission
FEMA	Federal Emergency Management Agency
FFB	Federal Financing Bank
FGIS	Federal Grain Inspection Service
FHA	Federal Housing Administration
FHTNC	Fleet Home Town News Center
FHWA	Federal Highway Administration
FIA	Federal Insurance Administration
FIC	Federal Information Centers
FIC	Federation of Insurance Counsel
FICA	Federal Insurance Contributions Act
FIP	Forestry Incentives Program
FLETC	Federal Law Enforcement Training Center
FMCS	Federal Mediation and Conciliation Service
FMFLANT	Fleet Marine Force, Atlantic
FMFPAC	Fleet Marine Force, Pacific
FNS	Food and Nutrition Service
F.O.B.	free on board
FOIA	Freedom of Information Act
FPC	Federal Power Commission
FPMR	Federal Property Management Regulations
FPRS	Federal Property Resources Service
FR	Federal Register
FRA	Federal Railroad Administration
F.R.C. Ann. Rep.	Federal Radio Commission Annual Report
F.R.D.	Federal Rules Decisions
FSLIC	Federal Savings and Loan Insurance Corporation
FSQS	Food Safety and Quality Service
FSS	Federal Supply Service
FSTS	Federal Secure Telephone Service
FTC	Federal Trade Commission
FTS	Federal Telecommunications System
FUTA	Federal Unemployment Tax Act
F. Cas.	Federal Cases
Fed. Cas.	Federal Cases
F. Supp.	Federal Supplement
FmHA	Farmers Home Administration
GAFTA	Grain and Feed Trade Association
GAO	General Accounting Office
GAOR	General Assembly Official Records, United Nations
GA Res.	General Assembly Resolution (United Nations)
GATT	General Agreement on Tariffs and Trade
GNMA	Government National Mortgage Association
GNP	gross national product
GPA	Office of Governmental and Public Affairs
GPO	Government Printing Office
GRAS	generally recognized as safe
GRNL	Gay Rights National Lobby

GS	General Schedule
GSA	General Services Administration
Gen. Cls. Comm.	General Claims Commission, United States and Panama; General Claims Commission, United States and Mexico.
Geo. II	King George II (Great Britain)
Geo. III	King George III (Great Britain)
Gr. Br., Crim. Ct. App.	Great Britain, Court of Criminal Appeals
HCFA	Health Care Financing Administration
HCO	Harvard College Observatory
HDS	Office of Human Development Services
HELP	Homophile Effort for Legal Protection
HHS	Department of Health and Human Services
HIRE	Help through Industry Retraining and Employment
H.L.	House of Lords Cases (England)
HQDA	Headquarters Department of the Army
HUAC	House UnAmerican Activities Committee
HUD	Department of Housing and Urban Development
Hackworth	Green Haywood Hackworth, *Digest of International Law* (1940–44).
Hay and Marriott	Great Britain. High Court of Admiralty, *Decisions in the High Court of Admiralty during the Time of Sir George Hay and of Sir James Marriott, Late Judges of That Court* (1801).
H.Ct.	High Court
H. Lords	House of Lords (England)
Hen. & M.	Hening & Munford's Virginia Reports
Hill	Hill's New York Reports
Hong Kong L.R.	Hong Kong Law Reports
How.	Howard's United States Supreme Court Reports
How. St. Trials	Howell's English State Trials
Hudson, Internatl. Legis.	Manley O. Hudson, ed., *International Legislation: A Collection of the Texts of Multipartite International Instruments of General Interest Beginning with the Covenant of the League of Nations* (1931).
Hudson, World Court Reps.	Manley Ottmer Hudson, ed., *World Court Reports* (1934–).
Hun	Hun's New York Supreme Court Reports
Hunt's Rept.	Bert L. Hunt, *Report of the American and Panamanian General Claims Arbitration* (1934).
IAC	Interagency Council for Minority Business Enterprise
IACAC	Inter-American Commercial Arbitration Commission
IACP	International Association of Chiefs of Police
IAEA	International Atomic Energy Agency
IALL	International Association of Law Libraries
IBA	International Bar Association
ICAF	Industrial College of the Armed Forces
ICC	Interstate Commerce Commission
I.C.J.	International Court of Justice
ICLD	International Center for Law in Development
ICNAF	International Commission for the Northwest Atlantic Fisheries
ICNT	Informal Composite Negotiated Text
ICSID	International Centre for Settlement of Investment Disputes
IDA	International Development Association
IDCA	International Development Cooperation Agency
IES	intensive employment services
IFC	International Finance Corporation
IJA	Institute of Judicial Administration
ILC	International Law Commission
ILD	International Labor Defense
ILO	International Labor Organization

IMCO	Intergovernmental Maritime Consultative Organization
IMF	International Monetary Fund
INTELSAT	International Telecommunications Satellite Organization
IPDC	International Program for the Development of Communication
IPO	Intellectual Property Owners
IPTA	International Patent and Trademark Association
I.R.	Irish Reports
IRA	individual retirement account; Irish Republican Army
IRS	Internal Revenue Service
ISLLSS	International Society for Labor Law and Social Security
ISSN	International Standard Serial Numbers
ITA	International Trade Administration
ITO	International Trade Organization
ITU	International Telecommunication Union
IWC	International Whaling Commission
IWW	Industrial Workers of the World
Ill. Dec.	Illinois Decisions
Interpol	International Criminal Police Organization
Int'l. Law Reps.	International Law Reports
Intl. Legal Mats.	International Legal Materials
JCS	Joint Chiefs of Staff
JP	justice of the peace
John. Ch.	Johnson's New York Chancery Reports
Johns.	Johnson's Reports (New York)
K.B.	King's Bench Reports (England)
LAMP	Center for the Study of Legal Authority and Mental Patient Status
LC	Library of Congress
LCC	Life Cycle Costing
LDF	Legal Defense and Education Fund of the NAACP
LEAA	Law Enforcement Assistance Administration
LEAP	Law, Education and Participation (a project of CRF)
L.Ed.	Lawyers' Edition Supreme Court Reports
LMSA	Labor–Management Services Administration
LNTS	League of Nations Treaty Series
L.R.	Law Reports (English)
LSAC	Law School Admission Council
LSAS	Law School Admission Service
LSAT	Law School Aptitude Test
LSC	Legal Services for Children; Legal Services Corporation
LSCRS	Law School Candidate Referral Service
LSDAS	Law School Data Assembly Service
LTC	Long Term Care
Lofft's Rep.	Lofft's English King's Bench Reports
MAC	Military Airlift Command
MALDEF	Mexican American Legal Defense and Educational Fund
MAP	Media Access Project
MARC	Machine-Readable Cataloging
MBDA	Minority Business Development Agency
MBOC	Minority Business Opportunity Committee
MDB	multilateral development bank
M.D. Ga.	Middle District, Georgia
MEECN	Minimum Essential Emergency Communications Network
MGT	Management
MILSATCOM	Military Satellite Communications
MINS	minors in need of supervision
M.J.	Military Justice Reporter
MLAP	Migrant Legal Action Program
MPCAG	Military Parts Control Advisory Group
M.R.	Master of the Rolls

MSB–COD	Minority Small Business–Capital Ownership Development
MSHA	Mine Safety and Health Administration
MSPB	Merit Systems Protection Board
MSSD	Model Secondary School for the Deaf
MTB	Materials Transportation Bureau
MTMC	Military Traffic Management Command
Malloy	William M. Malloy, ed., *Treaties, Conventions, International Acts, Protocols, and Agreements between the United States of America and Other Powers* (1910–38).
Martens	Georg Friedrich von Martens, ed., *Noveau recueil général de traités et autres act es relatifs aux rapports de droit international* (Series I, 20 vols. [1843–75]; Series II, 35 vols. [1876–1908]; Series III [1909–]).
Mass.	Massachusetts Reports
Md. App.	Maryland, Appeal Cases
Metc.	Metcalf's Massachusetts Reports
Miller	David Hunter Miller, ed., *Treaties and Other International Acts of the United States of America* (1931–1948).
Minn.	Minnesota Reports
Misc.	Miscellaneous Reports, New York
Mixed Claims Comm., Report of Decs.	Mixed Claims Commission, United States and Germany, Report of Decisions.
Mo.	Missouri Reports
Mod.	Modern Reports, English King's Bench, etc.
Moore, Dig. Intl. Law	John Bassett Moore, *A Digest of International Law*, 8 vols. (1906).
Moore, Intl. Arbs.	John Bassett Moore, *History and Digest of the International Arbitrations to Which the United States Has Been a Party*, 6 vols. (1898).
Morison	William Maxwell Morison, *The Scots Revised Report: Morison's Dictionary of Decisions* (1908–09).
NAACP	National Association for the Advancement of Colored People
NALA	National Association of Legal Assistants
NALP	National Association for Law Placement
NALS	National Association of Legal Secretaries
NARF	Native American Rights Fund
NARS	National Archives and Record Service
NARUC	National Association of Regulatory Utility Commissioners
NASA	National Aeronautics and Space Administration
NATO	North Atlantic Treaty Organization
NAVINFO	Navy Information Offices
NAVPACEN	Navy Public Affairs Center
NAWSA	National American Woman's Suffrage Association
NBA	National Bar Association
NBS	National Bureau of Standards
NCA	National Command Authorities
NCAA	National Collegiate Athletic Association
NCBL	National Conference of Black Lawyers
NCCB	National Consumer Cooperative Bank
NCDC	New Community Development Corporation
NCI	National Cancer Institute
NCJA	National Criminal Justice Association
NCPC	National Capital Planning Commission
NCSL	National Center for Service Learning
NCUA	National Credit Union Administration
N.D. Ill.	Northern District, Illinois
N.D. Wash.	Northern District, Washington
NDU	National Defense University

N.E.	North Eastern Reporter
N.E. 2d	North Eastern Reporter, Second Series
NEH	National Endowment for the Humanities
NEPA	National Endowment Policy Act
NFIP	National Flood Insurance Program
NGTF	National Gay Task Force
NIEO	New International Economic Order
NIH	National Institutes of Health
NIJ	National Institute of Justice
NIRA	National Industrial Recovery Act
N.J.	New Jersey Reports
N.J. Super.	New Jersey Superior Court Reports
NLADA	National Legal Aid and Defender Association
NLM	National Library of Medicine
NLRA	National Labor Relations Act
NLRB	National Labor Relations Board
NLW	National Lawyers Wives
NMCS	National Military Command System
NOAA	National Oceanic and Atmospheric Administration
NOLA	National Association for Outlaw and Lawman History
NPI	National Paralegal Institute
NRA	National Recovery Act
NRC	Nuclear Regulatory Commission
NSC	National Security Council
NSCLC	National Senior Citizens Law Center
NSF	National Science Foundation
NTIA	National Telecommunications and Information Administration
NTID	National Technical Institute for the Deaf
NTIS	National Technical Information Service
NTS	Naval Telecommunications System
NTSB	National Transportation Safety Board
N.W.	North Western Reporter
N.W. 2d	North Western Reporter, Second Series
NWC	National War College
NWIP	Naval Warfare Information Publication
NWSA	National Woman Suffrage Association
N.Y.	New York Court of Appeals Reports
N.Y. 2d	New York Court of Appeals Reports, Second Series
N.Y.S.	New York Supplement Reporter
N.Y.S. 2d	New York Supplement Reporter, Second Series
N.Y. Sup.	New York Supreme Court Reports
Nielsen's Rept.	Frederick Kenelm Nielsen, *American and British Claims Arbitration under the Special Agreement Concluded between the United States and Great Britain, August 18, 1910* (1926).
No.	Number
OAS	Organization of American States
OASDI	Old-age, Survivors, and Disability Insurance Benefits
OASHDS	Office of the Assistant Secretary for Human Development Services
OCED	Office of Comprehensive Employment Development
OCHAMPUS	Office of Civilian Health and Medical Program of the Uniformed Services
OCS	Outer Continental Shelf
OCSE	Office of Child Support Enforcement
OEA	Organización de los Estados Americanos
OECD	Organization for Economic Cooperation and Development
OFPP	Office of Federal Procurement Policy
OICD	Office of International Cooperation and Development
OIG	Office of the Inspector General

OJARS	Office of Justice Assistance, Research, and Statistics
OJT	On-the-Job Training Program
OMB	Office of Management and Budget
ONP	Office of National Programs
OPD	Office of Policy Development
OPEC	Organization of Petroleum Exporting Countries
OPIC	Overseas Private Investment Corporation
OPM	Office of Personnel Management
OPNAV	Office of the Chief of Naval Operations
OPSP	Office of Product Standards Policy
O.R.	Ontario Reports
OR	Official Records
OSHA	Occupational Safety and Health Administration
OSHRC	Occupational Safety and Health Review Commission
OSM	Office of Surface Mining
OST	Office of the Secretary
OT	Office of Transportation
OTA	Office of Technology Assessment
OWL	National Order of Women Legislators
OWRT	Office of Water Research and Technology
Ops. Atts. Gen.	Opinions of the Attorneys-General of the United States
Ops. Comms.	Opinions of the Commissioners
P.	Pacific Reporter
P. 2d	Pacific Reporter, Second Series
PAC	political action committee
PADC	Pennsylvania Avenue Development Corporation
PASS	Procurement Automated Source System
PBGC	Pension Benefit Guaranty Corporation
PBS	Public Buildings Service
P.C.	Privy Council (English Law Reports)
PCIJ	Permanent Court of International Justice
	Series A—Judgments and Orders (1922–30)
	Series B—Advisory Opinions (1922–30)
	Series A/B—Judgments, Orders, and Advisory Opinions (1931–40)
	Series C—Pleadings, Oral Statements, and Documents relating to Judgments and Advisory Opinions (1923–42)
	Series D—Acts and Documents concerning the Organization of the World Court (1922–47)
	Series E—Annual Reports (1925–45)
P.D.	Probate Division, English Law Reports (1876–1890)
PDA	Pregnancy Discrimination Act of 1978
PD & R	Policy Development and Research
PGM	Program
PHA	Public Housing Agency
PHS	Public Health Service
PIC	Private Industry Council
PINS	persons in need of supervision
PIRG	Public Interest Research Group
P.L.	Public Laws
PLF	Pacific Legal Foundation
PLI	Practicing Law Institute
PLO	Palestine Liberation Organization
POC	Principal Operating Component
PPLC	Planned Parenthood League of Connecticut
PSE	Public Service Employment
PSI	Personnel Security Investigation
PSIP	Private Sector Initiative Program
PSRO	Professional Standards Review Organization
PTO	Patent and Trademark Office

PWA	Public Works Administration
Pa. Oyer and Terminer	Pennsylvania Oyer and Terminer Reports
Perm. Ct. of Arb.	Permanent Court of Arbitration
Pet.	Peters' United States Supreme Court Reports
Phila. Ct. of Oyer and Terminer	Philadelphia Court of Oyer and Terminer
Pick.	Pickering's Massachusetts Reports
Pratt	Frederic Thomas Pratt, *Law of Contraband of War, with a Selection of Cases from the Papers of the Right Honourable Sir George Lee* (1856).
Proc.	Proceedings
Q.B.	Queen's Bench (England)
RC	Regional Commissioner
RCWP	Rural Clean Water Program
RDS	Rural Development Service
REA	Rural Electrification Administration
RETORT	Reason and Equity in Tort
RFE	Radio Free Europe
RIT	Rochester Institute of Technology
RL	Radio Liberty
ROTC	Reserve Officers Training Corps
R.S.	Revised Statutes
RSVP	Retired Senior Volunteer Program
Ralston's Rept.	Jackson Harvey Ralston, ed., *Venezuelan Arbitrations of 1903* (1904).
Rec. des Decs. des Trib. Arb. Mixtes	G. Gidel, ed., *Recueil des décisions des tribunaux arbitraux mixtes, institués par les traités de paix* (1922–30).
Redmond	Vol. 3 of Charles I. Bevans, *Treaties and Other International Agreements of the United States of America, 1776–1949* (compiled by C. F. Redmond) (1969).
Roscoe	Edward Stanley Roscoe, ed., *Reports of Prize Cases Determined in the High Court of Admiralty before the Lords Commissioners of Appeals in Prize Causes and before the Judicial Committee of the Privy Council from 1745 to 1859* (1905).
SAO	Smithsonian Astrophysical Observatory
SASP	State Agencies for Surplus Property
SAT	Scholastic Aptitude Test
SBA	Small Business Administration
SCS	Soil Conservation Service
S.Ct.	Supreme Court Reporter
SCSCP	Senior Community Service Employment Program
S.D. Cal.	Southern District, California
S.D. Fla.	Southern District, Florida
S.D. Ga.	Southern District, Georgia
S.D. Me.	Southern District, Maine
S.D.N.Y.	Southern District, New York
SDS	Students for a Democratic Society
S.E.	South Eastern Reporter
S.E. 2d	South Eastern Reporter, Second Series
SEA	Science and Education Administration
SEAN	Scientific Event Alert Network
SEATO	Southeast Asia Treaty Organization
SEC	Securities and Exchange Commission
SEOO	State Economic Opportunity Office
SEP	simplified employee pension plan
SGLI	Servicemen's Group Life Insurance
SIFL	standard industry fare level

SIL	Smithsonian Institution Libraries
SLA	Symbionese Liberation Army
SIPC	Securities Investor Protection Corporation
SITES	Smithsonian Traveling Exhibition Service
SOS	Senior Opportunities and Services
SSA	Social Security Administration
SSI	Supplemental Security Income
SSIE	Smithsonian Science Information Exchange, Inc.
STIP	Skill Training Improvement Program
STS	Space Transportation Systems
S.W.	South Western Reporter
SWAPO	South-West Africa People's Organization
S.W. 2d	South Western Reporter, Second Series
SYEP	Summer Youth Employment Program
Sandf.	Sandford's New York Superior Court Reports
Sawy.	Sawyer's United States Circuit Court Reports
Scott's Repts.	James Brown Scott, ed., *The Hague Court Reports*, 2 vols. (1916–32).
Sec.	Section
Ser.	Series
Sess.	Session
So.	Southern Reporter
So. 2d	Southern Reporter, Second Series
Spec. Sess.	Special Session
Stat.	United States Statutes at Large
St. Tr.	State Trials, English
Sup. Ct. of Justice, Mexico	Supreme Court of Justice, Mexico
Supp.	Supplement
TDP	Trade and Development Program
TIAS	Treaties and Other International Acts Series (United States)
TOP	Targeted Outreach Program
TPUS	Transportation and Public Utilities Service
TRIMIS	Tri-Service Medical Information System
TRI-TAC	Joint Tactical Communications
TS	Treaty Series, United States
TVA	Tennessee Valley Authority
Tex. Sup.	Texas Supreme Court Reports
Tripartite Claims Comm., Decs. and Ops.	Tripartite Claims Commission (United States, Austria, and Hungary), Decisions and Opinions
U.C.C.	Uniform Commercial Code
U.C.C.C.	Uniform Consumer Credit Code
UCMJ	Uniform Code of Military Justice
UCPP	Urban Crime Prevention Program
UIS	Unemployment Insurance Service
UMTA	Urban Mass Transportation Administration
UN	United Nations
UNCITRAL	United Nations Commission on International Trade Law
UNCTAD	United Nations Conference on Trade and Development
UN Doc.	United Nations Documents
UNDP	United Nations Development Program
UNEF	United Nations Emergency Force
UNESCO	United Nations Educational, Scientific and Cultural Organization
UNICEF	United Nations Children's Fund
UNIDO	United Nations Industrial and Development Organization
UN Repts. Intl. Arb. Awards	United Nations Reports of International Arbitral Awards
UNTS	United Nations Treaty Series

UPU	Universal Postal Union
URESA	Uniform Reciprocal Enforcement of Support Act
U.S.	United States Reports
USAF	United States Air Force
USAMDW	United States Army Military District of Washington
U.S.C.C.A.N.	United States Code Congressional and Administrative News
U.S.C.	United States Code
U.S.C.A.	United States Code Annotated
USCMA	United States Court of Military Appeals
USDA	United States Department of Agriculture
USES	United States Employment Service
USFA	United States Fire Administration
USICA	International Communication Agency, United States
UST	United States Treaties
USTS	United States Travel Service
UYA	University Year for ACTION
Unif. L. Ann.	Uniform Laws Annotated
v.	*versus*
VA	Veterans Administration
VGLI	Veterans Group Life Insurance
VISTA	Volunteers in Service to America
V.L.A.	Volunteer Lawyers for the Arts
VM	Value Management
VOA	Associate Directorate for Broadcasting
VLA	Very Large Array
VMLI	Veterans Mortgage Life Insurance
Vict.	Queen Victoria (Great Britain)
WA	writing ability
WAPA	Western Area Power Administration
WBED	Women's Business Enterprise Division
WBP	Waterbank Program
W.D. Wash.	Western District, Washington
W.D. Wis.	Western District, Wisconsin
WEAL	Women's Equity Action League
WFAOSB	World Food and Agricultural Outlook and Situation Board
WHO	World Health Organization
WHS	Washington Headquarter Services
WIC Program	Special Supplemental Food Program for Women, Infants, and Children
WIN	Work Incentive Program
WIPO	World Intellectual Property Organization
W.L.R.	Weekly Law Reports, England
WPPDA	Welfare and Pension Plans Disclosure Act
WWMCCS	Worldwide Military Command and Control System
Wall.	Wallace's United States Supreme Court Reports
Wash. 2d	Washington Reports, Second Series
Wend.	Wendell's New York Reports
Wheat.	Wheaton's United States Supreme Court Reports
Wheel. Cr. Cases	Wheeler's New York Criminal Cases
Whiteman	Marjorie Millace Whiteman, *Digest of International Law*, 15 vols. (1963–73).
Will. and Mar.	King William and Queen Mary (Great Britain)
YCC	Youth Conservation Corps
YCCIP	Youth Community Conservation and Improvement Project
YETP	Youth Employment and Training Program
Yates Sel. Cas.	Yates' New York Select Cases

The Guide to American Law

ABANDONED BANK ACCOUNT

☐ A sum of money that had been deposited with a bank but has subsequently been given up by its owner. ☐

A bank account is considered abandoned when a depositor fails to present his or her passbook, the evidence of a person's account, to the bank for the posting of interest earned within a certain period of time specified by state law. When this occurs, that state is entitled to treat the account as its own, since in the eyes of the law, no one owns it any longer. The reversion of the ownership of abandoned property to the state is called ESCHEAT, but certain procedures must be observed before the funds actually become property of the state.

ABANDONMENT

☐ The failure to bring a civil lawsuit before the time limit set by law for bringing a suit, or to prosecute it once a complaint has been filed.

☐ The willful and intentional leaving of one spouse by another, which is a ground for DIVORCE, after the time period set by law has expired. The abandoning spouse must not have any intention of returning and must have left without the consent of the abandoned spouse. The ground of abandonment is commonly called DESERTION in state divorce statutes.

☐ The desertion or willful forsaking of a child by a parent who has foregone parental duties. When a child has been abandoned by a parent, that parent may lose the right to gain CUSTODY of the child at a later date. See also, Parent and Child.

☐ The voluntary relinquishment of all claims, rights, possession, or ownership of property with the intention not to reclaim it. A person who abandons property does so because he or she no longer wishes to have any interest in it. The first person who exerts control over the abandoned property with the intention to claim it becomes its owner. ☐

Library of Congress

Deteriorating fronts of abandoned stores in an Illinois town in 1939

1

By putting the chair, golf bag, and other belongings out with the rest of the trash, this householder has abandoned the property.

Property that can be abandoned Various types of PERSONAL PROPERTY—such as personal and household items—CONTRACTS, COPYRIGHTS, inventions, and PATENTS can be abandoned. Certain rights and interests in real property, such as EASEMENTS and LEASES, may also be abandoned. A ranch owner, for example, gives a shepherd an easement to use a path on her property so that the sheep can get to a watering hole. The shepherd later sells his flock and moves out of the state, never intending to return. This conduct demonstrates that the shepherd has abandoned the easement, since he stopped using the path and intends never to use it again. Ownership of real property cannot be obtained because someone else abandoned it but may be gained through ADVERSE POSSESSION.

Elements of abandonment Two things must occur for property to be abandoned: (1) an act by the owner that clearly shows that he or she has given up rights to the property; and (2) an intention that demonstrates that the owner has knowingly relinquished control over it.

The act Some clear action must be taken to indicate that the owner no longer wants his or her property. Any act is sufficient as long as the

property is left free and open to anyone who comes along to claim it.

Inaction—that is, failure to do something with the property or nonuse of it—is not enough to demonstrate that the owner has relinquished rights to the property, even if such nonuse has gone on for a number of years. A farmer's failure to cultivate his or her land or a quarry owner's failure to take stone from his or her quarry, for example, does not mean that either person has abandoned interest in the property.

The intention A person's intention to abandon his or her property may be established by express language to that effect or may be implied from the circumstances surrounding the owner's treatment of the property, such as leaving it unguarded in a place easily accessible to the public.

The passage of time, although not an element of abandonment, may illustrate a person's intention to abandon his or her property.

AB ANTE [*Latin, "Before; in advance."*]

For example, a legislature cannot agree *ab ante* to any modification or amendment to a law that a third party may make.

AB ANTIQUO
[*Latin, "Since ancient times."*]

ABATABLE NUISANCE ☐ A NUISANCE, an unreasonable or illegal use of property by one person that interferes with another person's use or enjoyment of his or her property or life, that can be easily stopped or made harmless. ☐

The term *abatable nuisance* usually refers to an action that can be stopped without resorting to a lawsuit. This right to help oneself to a solution is known as *summary abatement*. It can be used only in certain instances. For example, the limbs of a dead oak tree extend dangerously over the roof of a glass hothouse on adjoining land. This nuisance, which threatens to damage the hothouse, can be easily made harmless by cutting off the limbs. The owner of the hothouse may do this without having to go to court for permission. However, notification must be given to the owner of the nuisance before an attempt is made to abate it unless there is an immediate danger to health, life, or property. An electric company may, for example, remove the ice-laden branches of a tree without first giving notice to the owner of the tree when there is an excellent likelihood that the branches will pull down overhead power lines, causing a blackout in the area. The need for the removal of the branches would be considered urgent because of the danger they pose to public safety.

Anyone who tries to abate a nuisance summarily must not unnecessarily damage property, cause personal injuries, or disturb the peace—for example, burning down a house because it is used for prostitution. A neighbor who violates a law while abating a nuisance can be criminally prosecuted. For example, if something that is not legally a nuisance is removed, the neighbor may have to pay DAMAGES or even restore the property.

A *public nuisance,* one that causes damage or inconvenience to the general public, may be summarily abated by public officials, but procedural steps required by law must be followed.

The owner or the person responsible for an abatable nuisance will have to pay expenses incurred in the summary abatement, as long as it was proper.

A nuisance may be merely a right thing in the wrong place—like a pig in the parlor instead of the barnyard.

GEORGE
SUTHERLAND

James L. Shaffer

This homeowner's car blocking access to all the homes that share this common driveway creates an abatable nuisance.

ABATEMENT ☐ A decrease, reduction, or diminution; the suspension or cessation, complete or partial, of a continuing charge, such as rent. ☐

With respect to ESTATES, an abatement is a proportional diminution or reduction of the monetary LEGACIES, a disposition of property by WILL, when the funds or assets out of which such legacies are payable are insufficient to pay them in full. The intention of the testator, when expressed in the will, governs the order in which property will abate. Where the will is silent, abatement occurs in the following order: INTESTATE property, gifts that pass by the RESIDUARY CLAUSE in the will, general legacies, and specific legacies. See also, Wills.

In the context of TAXATION, an abatement is a decrease in the amount of tax imposed. Abatement of taxes relieves property of its share of the burdens of taxation after the assessment has been made and the LEVY of the tax has been accomplished.

ABATEMENT OF AN ACTION

☐ A mechanism of legal procedure that operates at the PLEADING stage of litigation to terminate or suspend a lawsuit for some reason other than the merits of the claim. ☐

The purpose of abatement is to save the time and expense of a trial when the plaintiff's suit cannot be maintained in the form originally presented. After an action abates, the plaintiff is ordinarily given an opportunity to correct errors in his or her pleading. If the plaintiff still is unable to allege the facts necessary to state a legal cause of action, then the action is terminated.

Not every possible reason for dissatisfaction with another person can be heard by a court. When the old common law FORM OF ACTION governed the procedure followed by courts, only legal wrongs that fit exactly into one of the allowed categories could be pleaded in court. If the defendant believed that the plaintiff's complaint did not fit one of these forms, the defendant could respond with a PLEA IN ABATEMENT. A plea in abatement was called a DILATORY PLEA because it delayed the time, if ever, when the court would reach the merits of the plaintiff's claim.

The rigid formality of common law pleading became less satisfactory as the world became more complicated. It has been replaced in each state by a procedure that allows the plaintiff to plead facts showing his or her right to legal relief. Modern systems of pleading retain a right for the defendant to seek abatement of the action when the plaintiff is not entitled to be in court. They allow a defendant to object to the court's JURISDICTION, the VENUE of the trial, the sufficiency of the

PROCESS or of the SERVICE OF PROCESS, the legal sufficiency of the plaintiff's claim, or the failure to include someone who must be a PARTY. A plea in abatement is made either in the defendant's ANSWER or by MOTION and ORDER—that is, an application to the court for relief and an order that can grant it. Abatement is usually granted in the form of a DISMISSAL of cause of action, and now the term *dismissal* is used more often than the term *abatement* for this procedure.

Today, the word *abatement* is most often used for the termination of a lawsuit because of the death of a party. Under the common law, a lawsuit abated automatically whenever a party died. This rule was considered a part of the substance of the law involved and was not merely a question of procedure. Whether the cause of action abated depended on whether or not the lawsuit was considered personal to the parties. For example, contract and property cases were thought to involve issues separate from the parties themselves. They were not personal and did not necessarily abate on the death of a party. Personal injury cases were considered personal, however, and did abate at death. These included claims not only for physical assault or negligent injuries inflicted on the body, but also for other injuries to the person—such as libel, slander, and malicious prosecution.

Today there are statutes that permit the REVIVAL OF AN ACTION that was pending when a party died. An executor or administrator is substituted for the deceased party and the lawsuit continues. A lawsuit may not be revived unless the underlying cause of action, the ground for the suit, continues to have a legal existence after the party's death. Revival statutes vary from state to state, but today most lawsuits do not abate.

This general rule does not apply to matrimonial actions. A lawsuit for divorce or separation is considered entirely personal and therefore cannot be maintained after the death of a party. Different states do make exceptions to this rule in order to settle certain questions of property ownership. An action for the annulment of a marriage after the death of an innocent spouse may be revived by the deceased spouse's personal representative if it is clear that the marriage was induced by fraud and the perpetrator of the fraud would inherit property to which he or she would otherwise not be entitled.

ABBOTT, Benjamin Vaughn Benjamin Vaughn Abbott (*b.* June 4, 1830 in Boston, Massachusetts; *d.* February 17, 1890 in Brooklyn, New York) graduated from New York University in 1850 and was admitted to the New York bar in 1852.

From 1855 to 1870 Abbott, in collaboration with his brother Austin, wrote a series of law treatises and reports, including *Digest of New York Statutes and Reports* (1860). The series led to *Abbott's New York Digest,* the most recent series of which has been renamed *West's New York Digest 3d.*

In 1864 Abbott became secretary of the New York Code Commission and was instrumental in the formulation of the New York Penal Code, much of which is still in use today.

From 1870 to 1872 he served as a commissioner to amend the statutes of the United States.

As an author, Abbott wrote several publications, including *Judge and Jury* (1880); *The Travelling Law School* (1884); and *Addison on Contracts* (1888).

ABDICATION

☐ Renunciation of the privileges and prerogatives of an office.

☐ The act of a sovereign in renouncing and relinquishing his or her government or throne, so that either the throne is left entirely vacant or is filled by a successor who is appointed or elected beforehand. ☐

National Archives

King Edward VIII abdicated his crown to marry Wallis Warfield Simpson. This is their wedding portrait.

INSTRUMENT OF ABDICATION

I, Edward the Eighth, of Great
Britain, Ireland, and the British Dominions
beyond the Seas, King, Emperor of India, do
hereby declare My irrevocable determination
to renounce the Throne for Myself and for
My descendants, and My desire that effect
should be given to this Instrument of
Abdication immediately.

In token whereof I have hereunto set
My hand this tenth day of December, nineteen
hundred and thirty six, in the presence of
the witnesses whose signatures are subscribed.

SIGNED AT
FORT BELVEDERE
IN THE PRESENCE
OF

King Edward VIII's instrument of abdication, which includes the signatures of his three brothers, Albert, Henry and George. Edward's brother, George, who was next in line to the British throne, succeeded him as King as George VI in 1936.

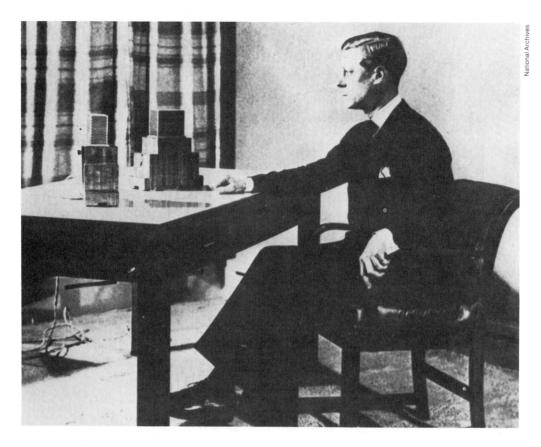

National Archives

David Windsor, the former King Edward VIII, preparing to speak over the radio to the British people.

A magistrate or public official may voluntarily renounce his or her office by giving it up before the time of service has expired. Abdication is the relinquishment of an office that was developed by an act of law. Once a person abdicates a position, he or she no longer has anything to do with it.

Abdication is not the same as resignation. Resignation is made when a person who has received an office from another returns it to him or her, as an inferior into the hands of a superior.

ABDUCTION

☐ The action of taking a person away by force and against his or her will, as in KIDNAPPING. When used in this manner, abduction is not a crime in itself but is one of the elements of the crime of kidnapping.

☐ The crime of illegally taking or detaining a female for purposes of MARRIAGE, concubinage, or PROSTITUTION. Unlike kidnapping, the criminal offense of abduction applies, in most cases, to females under a given age. ☐

Elements of offense   Although the laws defining the crime of abduction vary from state to state, abduction is made up of basic elements.

A female under a particular age as stated in the law must be taken somewhere or detained someplace by force or without her consent. The fact that the taking or detention is by force or without consent makes it unlawful. An example of force would be that of holding a person at gunpoint. Lack of consent may be demonstrated in different ways. A girl agrees to accompany an abductor under a false pretense. She is being detained without her consent if she would never have gone with her abductor had she known the truth. Sometimes the age of the female implies that she is not legally capable of giving consent because she is too young to know what she is doing and to understand the consequences of her act.

In order for a person to face criminal charges for abduction, that person must have taken the female for marriage, sexual intercourse, concubinage, or prostitution. If one of these reasons cannot be established, that person may not be prosecuted for abduction, but might be charged with kidnapping or FALSE IMPRISONMENT.

Persons who may be prosecuted   Anyone who abducts a female may be prosecuted. Even a husband who takes his wife to have sexual

Piratical Barbarity or the Female Captive recounts a case of abduction in 1825.

intercourse with another person may be charged with abduction if his wife is under the age specified in the abduction statute. Women who take, receive, or use a female who is a minor, usually under the age of eighteen or twenty-one, for prostitution or illicit sexual relations are also liable. In many states, people who AID AND ABET an abductor may be convicted. The owner of a small motel, for example, may be prosecuted for abduction if he or she knowingly provides shelter to an abductor and victim.

Defenses A person who has been charged with abduction cannot use as a defense the fact that the victim has been returned home. In cases where a female was abducted for marriage, it is no defense that the victim's previous marriage was void. Sometimes the statute that created the offense of abduction provides that if the victim forgives the abductor the offense will be dismissed. The pardon must be made by the victim verbally or impliedly, such as by marriage to the abductor. The charges against anyone else who assisted in the abduction would also be dropped once the marriage occurred.

Civil liability A female who has been abducted may sue her abductor in a civil lawsuit for the torts of ASSAULT AND BATTERY, FALSE IMPRISONMENT, or both for the damages and injuries she might have suffered.

ABET □ To intentionally encourage, incite, or help another person to commit a crime. □

For example, the manager of a jewelry store fails to turn on the store's silent alarm on the night she knows her cousin plans to rob the store. Her conduct is that of abetting the robbery. If, however, she merely forgot to turn on the alarm, she would not have abetted the crime.

The word abet is most commonly used as part of the comprehensive phrase AID AND ABET.

ABETTOR □ In criminal law, a person who intentionally commands, advises, instigates, or encourages another to commit a crime. □

A person who lends a friend a car for use in a robbery is an abettor even though he or she is not present when the robbery takes place. An abettor is not the chief actor, the PRINCIPAL, in the commission of a crime but must share the principal's criminal intent in order to be prosecuted for the same crime. An abettor may be guilty of a crime even though he or she is unable to actually commit the crime. Although a woman is legally and physically incapable of committing the crime of RAPE, she may be prosecuted for the crime if she has lured another woman to her

apartment so that the woman may be raped by someone else.

ABEYANCE □ A condition of being uncertain, suspended, or inactive, until an event occurs which resolves the matter. □

For example, until an order of foreclosure is granted by a court, a mortgagee does not have title to the property of a delinquent debtor which is the subject of a MORTGAGE in those jurisdictions which follow the lien theory of mortgages.

ABIDING CONVICTION □ A definite belief of guilt derived from a thorough examination of the whole case. □

This phrase is used commonly to instruct juries on the frame of mind required for guilt to be proved beyond a reasonable doubt.

AB INCONVENIENTI [*Latin, "From hardship or inconvenience."*] □ A description of an argument based upon the hardship of the case, and the inconvenient consequences that might follow from a different line of reasoning. □

AB INITIO [*Latin, "From the beginning."*] □ A description of a condition or thing that originally appears to be legal but becomes unlawful as a result of subsequent conduct or the disclosure of facts that were unknown when the situation began. □

The illegality of the conduct or the revelation of the real facts makes the entire situation illegal *ab initio* (from the beginning), not just from the time the wrongful behavior occurs. A person who enters property under the authority of law but who then by misconduct abuses his or her right to be on the property is considered a trespasser *ab initio*. If a sheriff enters property under the authority of a court order requiring him to seize a valuable painting, but instead he takes an expensive marble sculpture, he would be a trespasser from the beginning. Since the officer abused his authority, a court would presume that he intended from the outset to use that authority as a cloak under which to enter the property for a wrongful purpose. This theory, used to correct abuses by public officers, has largely fallen into disuse.

ABJURATION
□ A renunciation or abandonment by or upon oath.
□ The renunciation under oath of one's citizenship or some other right or privilege. □

[The Police are] . . . governed rather by regulations than laws; those who are subject to its jurisdiction are incessantly under the eye of the magistrate: it is therefore his fault if they fall into excess.

CHARLES DE MONTESQUIEU

James L. Shaffer

An abode—be it a
home in the
suburbs, a shack, or
a Navajo hogan—is
a place where one
lives.

Library of Congress

ABODE

☐ One's home or place of dwelling; residence of a legal voter.

☐ For the service of PROCESS, one's fixed place of residence for the time being; a person's *usual place of abode.* ☐

Abode is often used as a synonym for DOMICILE.

ABOLITION ☐ The destruction, annihilation, abrogation, or extinguishment of anything, but especially things of a permanent nature— such as institutions, usages, or customs, as the abolition of slavery. ☐

This illustration on the title page of *The Child's Anti-Slavery Book* (1860) was an effort by abolitionists to alert children to the horrors of slavery.

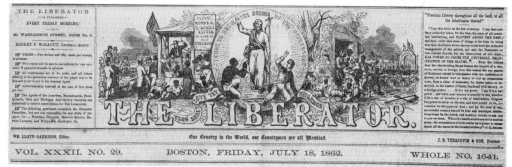

The Liberator, an abolitionist newspaper founded in 1831 and edited by William Lloyd Garrison, also carried articles promoting women's rights, racial equality, and temperance.

This engraving showing twelve leaders in the abolitionist movement fails to recognize the substantial contributions that women such as Sarah and Angelina Grimké, Harriet Beecher Stowe, and Harriet Tubman made to the defeat of slavery.

ABORTION □ The intentional expulsion or extraction of an unborn child from the uterus of its mother for a purpose other than causing a live birth or removing a dead fetus. □

History Abortion, except when deemed medically necessary to save the life of the woman, was a statutory crime in every jurisdiction of the United States until the 1973 landmark Supreme Court decision in *Roe v. Wade,* 410 U.S. 113, 93 S.Ct. 705, 35 L.Ed.2d 147. Prior to that time, anyone who administered a drug, whether directly or indirectly—such as by sending medicines and directions through the mails—or who used instruments or other means to intentionally induce an abortion, with or without the woman's consent, was guilty of the crime. If the methods used did not result in an abortion, the participant could be prosecuted for attempted abortion. If the woman died during the attempt or as a result of the abortion, the charge against the participant became murder.

ROE V. WADE

Jane Roe, an unmarried pregnant woman who could not get a legal abortion in Texas, brought a lawsuit in Federal court challenging Texas criminal legislation prohibiting abortions except when "procured or attempted by medical advice for the purpose of saving the life of the mother." She sought to have the law declared unconstitutional as an invasion of personal PRIVACY, protected by the First, Fourth, Ninth, and Fourteenth Amendments, on behalf of herself and other women similarly situated. She sought an INJUNCTION to prevent its enforcement. A licensed physician who had been arrested for violating the law was granted permission by the court to INTERVENE in the action. He claimed that the language of the law was unconstitutionally vague and that it violated his own and his patients' rights to privacy and his right to practice medicine as protected by the Constitution. A married, childless couple filed a companion complaint to that of *Roe,* which was dismissed for lack of STANDING because the woman was not pregnant. A three-judge district court agreed that the statute was unconstitutionally vague and overbroad, infringing upon the rights of privacy. It dismissed, however, the application for an injunction.

On appeal, the Supreme Court accepted the case but dismissed the physician's complaint. The Court agreed with the decision in *Roe* that a woman's constitutional right to privacy encompasses her decision to terminate her pregnancy. She does not, however, have an unrestricted right to do so. The state's interests in protecting health, medical standards, and prenatal life become dominant as the pregnancy progresses. The

state thereby has a greater right to regulate a decision on abortion during the later stages of pregnancy.

One of the arguments against abortion was that the fetus was a "person" whose life was guaranteed by the Fourteenth Amendment. The Court disagreed on the basis that the term *person* had been used only postnatally.

The Court divided pregnancy into three trimesters, three twelve-week periods, to provide a time frame to determine at what point the interests of the state begin to emerge. During the first trimester, the woman and her physician decide whether an abortion should be performed. This stage of pregnancy is not within the state's ambit of regulatory power, since until it ends, mortality in abortion might be less than mortality in childbirth; therefore, the health of the mother is not threatened. The abortion, however, must be performed by a licensed physician under medically safe conditions.

During the second trimester, the next twelve weeks of pregnancy, the state's interest in safeguarding the woman's health emerges. The state can regulate abortion procedures when reasonably related to the promotion of the health of the woman. Once the third trimester, or the last twelve weeks of the pregnancy, begins, the state has a dominant and legitimate interest in prenatal life, since the fetus is presumed to have a potential capability of meaningful life outside the womb. Once viable, a fetus is entitled to protection by the state by the proscription of abortion, except in cases where it is essential to preserve the life or health of the mother.

DOE V. BOLTON

When considering the legality of abortion, the Supreme Court also reviewed the companion case of *Doe v. Bolton,* 410 U.S. 179, 93 S.Ct. 739 35 L.Ed.2d 201 (1973), which challenged procedural requirements imposed by a Georgia statute that proscribed abortion in all but medically necessary cases. Mary Doe, a pregnant Georgia woman, challenged the constitutionality of the statute in Federal court, similar to the challenge made by Jane Roe in Texas. She also alleged that the procedural requirements—concerning hospital accreditation, committee approval, two-doctor agreement, and residence—that had to be met when an abortion was deemed medically necessary unduly restricted a woman's right to privacy and violated procedural DUE PROCESS OF LAW and EQUAL PROTECTION OF LAWS. The district court declared that the law was an unconstitutional infringement of privacy and personal liberty when it permitted abortion only in cases involving danger to the mother's life or health, the likelihood of a defective fetus, or a

Attorney Sarah Weddington, *top,* represented Roe while attorneys Robert C. Flowers, *middle,* and Jay Floyd represented Wade in the 1973 case of *Roe v. Wade.*

Pro-Life activists march in front of the Wisconsin State Capitol.

pregnancy resulting from rape. It upheld, however, the procedural requirements regulating the manner of performance and the quality of the ultimate decision to abort because of the state's legitimate interest in the protection of health and the preservation of a "*potential* of independent human existence."

On direct appeal, the Supreme Court ruled that the procedural requirements violated the Fourteenth Amendment. The state failed to prove that only hospitals could serve its interest in insuring the quality of the abortion procedure and in protecting the pregnant patient. A clinic or other health facility might similarly possess the personnel and equipment necessary for a safe abortion. The accredited hospital requirement was invalid in light of *Roe,* since it was a state regulation affecting the first trimester of pregnancy, a stage beyond state regulation.

The second requirement was for the approval of the abortion procedure by a designated committee of hospital staff members after the woman's personal physician had completed his diagnosis. The interests of neither the hospital nor the state were promoted by a merely repetitive review of the diagnosis. The hospital could fully protect itself—better serving its own interests than by a committee review—by refusing to admit a patient seeking an abortion. Since no other surgical procedure was shown to be subject to committee approval under state criminal law, no state interest in the committee requirement was demonstrated. The Court viewed the committee procedure as being unduly restrictive of the patient's rights.

The third requirement mandated the approval of the abortion decision by two licensed physicians other than the woman's personal physician. This was unconstitutional because it had no rational relationship to the patient's needs and unduly infringed upon the physician's right to practice medicine. The Court reasoned that the attending physician's best medical judgment that an abortion is necessary should be sufficient. No other statute required confirmation by two other doctors before an operation could be performed. A physician licensed by the state is recognized as able to make medical decisions without being forced to have his or her diagnosis confirmed in such a manner.

A requirement restricting abortions to state residents was also invalidated by the Court on the ground that a state must protect all persons who enter the state seeking medical services that are available there. See also, Residency Laws.

Constitutionality of other restrictions

After *Roe* and *Doe,* states began to liberalize their abortion laws in response to the decisions of the Supreme Court. The legislative imposition of various restrictions on the right to abortion became the subject of judicial scrutiny.

In the decision of *Planned Parenthood v. Danforth,* 428 U.S. 52, 96 S.Ct. 2831, 49 L.Ed.2d 788 (1976), the Supreme Court examined statutory provisions mandating that during the first twelve weeks of pregnancy a woman give written consent to have an abortion; and that a wife obtain her husband's consent and a minor, her parents' or guardian's consent—in writing—unless a medical necessity exists. In addition, the statute required physicians and health facilities responsible for the performance of abortion to maintain records. It also imposed criminal and civil liability upon a physician who failed to observe standards of professional care in performing abortions. Two physicians and Planned Parenthood, a family planning organization, initiated a lawsuit in Federal court to declare a Missouri abortion law unconstitutional and to ENJOIN its enforcement. A three-judge panel of the district court found the law valid except for the unconstitutionally vague provision concerning the standard of medical care to be met in the performance of an abortion. The plaintiffs appealed to the Supreme Court, which accepted the case.

The Court agreed with the lower court that the requirement of written consent by a woman planning to undergo an abortion during the first trimester was valid. The statement to be signed includes a provision requiring that the woman be informed of the nature of the procedure and a declaration that her consent is freely given. Since a decision to have an abortion is a significant and frequently stressful undertaking, it must be made with full knowledge of its nature and consequences. The consent requirement, similar to the INFORMED CONSENT to be given by any patient undergoing a medical or surgical procedure, is one method by which the state is assured of her rational decision to have an abortion.

The provision requiring that a husband give consent to his wife's abortion during the first trimester, unless it was deemed medically necessary

by a licensed physician, was considered unconstitutional. Since the state could not, in light of *Roe,* impose restrictions on the right to abortion during the first trimester of pregnancy, it was powerless to give a husband the authority to veto his wife's decision to have an abortion during that stage. Only a woman and her physician can decide whether an abortion should be performed during the first twelve weeks of pregnancy.

Requiring a minor to obtain parental consent for an abortion during the first trimester was likewise unconstitutional in light of *Roe's* first trimester prohibition.

The Court noted that minors, as well as adults, are protected by the constitutional right of privacy, although the scope of protection is not necessarily the same. It rejected that the state interest in regulating the access of minors to abortion by the need for parental consent would safeguard the family unit and parental authority. The Court did not, however, exclude the possibility that a statutory provision could be framed, consistent with *Roe,* that would require parental consent in cases where the minor is extremely young or immature.

The Court upheld the requirement that physicians and health facilities must keep records of abortions performed, as reasonably related to the preservation of maternal health. Such records provide information to be used in advancing medical knowledge. As long as the recording of such data is done in a confidential manner, which respects the woman's privacy, it is valid.

The provision that required a physician to exercise professional care to preserve the life and health of the fetus or face criminal or civil liability was unconstitutional, since it was vague and overbroad. It did not limit the required care to any particular stage of the pregnancy but required such lifesaving techniques to be employed during the entire pregnancy.

Parental consent   The requirement that a pregnant minor obtain parental consent for an abortion was invalidated by the Supreme Court in 1976 on the rationale that a state could not interfere with a woman's decision to have an abortion during the first trimester of her pregnancy. The Court noted, however, that this did not mean that a parental-consent provision could not be imposed in certain cases, such as extreme youth or immaturity, if the statute was properly drawn in accordance with the principles enunciated in 1973 in *Roe.* In the 1979 case of *Bellotti v. Baird,* 443 U.S. 662, 99 S.Ct. 3035, 61 L.Ed.2d 797, the Supreme Court struck down a statute that unconstitutionally infringed upon a minor's right to seek an abortion by requiring parental consent or judicial approval of her intention. A Massachusetts statute enacted in 1974 required an unmarried pregnant minor under age eighteen to obtain the consent of her parents for an abortion. If one or both parents refused, a court order of consent was necessary, but good cause had to be established. Physicians who proceeded with abortions on minors who did not obtain parental consent were subject to injunctions and criminal penalties.

William Baird who is the head of an organization that provides abortions, and Mary Moe—a pregnant minor who lived with her parents and wanted an abortion without notifying them—challenged the constitutionality of the law in district court. The court ruled that the statute was invalid because there was no justification offered for the need for parental consent. The attorney general of Massachusetts appealed to the Supreme Court but it remanded the case to the district court for certification of questions concerning the meaning of the statute to be answered by the highest state court. The questions were whether any minors—mature or immature—can obtain judicial consent without ever informing their parents, to which the court answered no; and whether a court can refuse consent to a mature minor who has made a decision to end her pregnancy because the court or the parent has decided otherwise, to which the court answered yes. In light of these answers, the district court invalidated the statute and enjoined its enforcement. On appeal, the Supreme Court affirmed the decision of the district court. The challenged statute required all minors to first inform their parents of their situation before they could seek court approval and did not make a distinction between mature and immature minors. The Court recognized that while a state has a significant interest in encouraging a family, as opposed to a judicial, resolution of a minor's decision to have an abortion, it must also provide an alternative procedure by which a minor can obtain authorization for an abortion. This would give a minor the opportunity to demonstrate that she is sufficiently mature to decide, regardless of her parent's wishes, or that if she is not capable of independently and maturely making such a decision, a court could decide that an abortion would still be in her best interests.

In the 1981 case of *H. L. v. Matheson,* 450 U.S. 398, 101 S.Ct. 1164, 67 L.Ed.2d 388, the Supreme Court upheld a Utah statute requiring under threat of criminal penalties that a physician notify, if possible, the parents of a minor before performing an abortion on her.

A physician advised an unmarried pregnant minor who still lived with, and was dependent upon, her parents that it was in her best medical interest to have an abortion. In compliance with the statute, he refused to perform one until he notified her parents. The minor brought an action in state court to have the statute declared unconstitutional and for an injunction to prevent its enforcement. She claimed to represent a class of unmarried pregnant minors who wanted abortions, but because of compliance with the statute by physicians, were effectively denied the right to end their pregnancies. The trial court and, on appeal, the Utah Supreme Court agreed that the statute did not unconstitutionally limit a minor's right of privacy to obtain an abortion or to enter a physician-patient relationship, and therefore refused to grant an injunction. The state courts reasoned that the notification of the minor's parents was "substantially and logically related" to the requirements set in *Doe.* Parents usually have information necessary for a physician to use his best medical judgment in the treatment of their child. The Utah statute also promoted the state interest in emphasizing the role of parents in the child-rearing process by requiring their notification whenever possible. The minor argued that the "if possible" qualification gave the physician discretion, but the court rejected this. "If possible" meant that whenever it was reasonable to make attempts to locate the parents and practical to give them notice, it must be done. If, however, it was not practical to do so, such as when the minor would lose the option of having an abortion because it would be medically infeasible if necessary to wait until the parents were notified, this requirement was no longer mandatory.

The Supreme Court affirmed the decision of the Utah courts. It reasoned that the statute was designated to protect minors, such as the appellant, by encouraging parental involvement in decisions with possibly traumatic and permanent consequences. The government interest in protecting potential life was reasonably related to a statute that, while encouraging childbirth, did not give anyone veto power over a minor's decision to have an abortion.

Federal financing   In 1976 Congress enacted the Hyde Amendment which restricted the availability of Medicaid funds for abortions for women who qualified as needy under Federal law. The later versions of the law provided that funds could be used for abortions only if the mother's life was threatened by a full-term pregnancy or when such a procedure was deemed necessary for a victim of RAPE or INCEST that was reported to the appropriate government agency. The 1976 version prohibited abortions except when necessary to save the mother's life. On the day the Hyde Amendment was enacted, Cora McRae—a New York Medicaid recipient in the first trimester of a pregnancy that threatened her health, but not her life—and the New York City Health and Hospital Corporations—a public corporation operating hospitals and abortion services—filed an action in Federal district court to prevent the enforcement of the 1976 funding restrictions. They claimed that the Hyde Amendment violated the First, Fourth, Fifth, and Ninth Amendments to the Constitution. The district court granted a preliminary injunction to prohibit the secretary of health, education, and welfare from enforcing the Hyde Amendment and to require Federal reimbursement for abortions performed under standards prior to the Hyde Amendment. The court also certified the case as a CLASS ACTION on behalf of all similarly situated women in New York State who are eligible for Medicaid and who decide to abort their pregnancy during the first twenty-four weeks, and of all qualified providers of abortion services. The secretary appealed to the Supreme Court which vacated the injunction and remanded the case to the district court to be evaluated in light of two decisions: *Beal v. Doe,* 432 U.S. 438, 97 S.Ct. 2366, 53 L.Ed.2d 464 (1977); and *Maher v. Roe,* 432 U.S. 464, 97 S.Ct. 2376, 53 L.Ed.2d 484 (1977). Those decisions held that the funding of nontherapeutic, medically unnecessary, abortions was not a condition of a state's participation in the Federal Medicaid program. States participating in the Medicaid program have broad discretion in determining what medical services would be covered by their own plans. The district court declared the Hyde Amendment unconstitutional and ordered the secretary to authorize the funding of all medically necessary abortions, not merely those essential for saving lives.

The secretary appealed to the Supreme Court, which in the case of *Harris v. McRae,* 448 U.S. 297, 100 S.Ct. 2671, 65 L.Ed.2d 784 (1980), upheld the constitutionality of the Hyde Amendment. The Court reasoned that Federal law does not mandate a state that participates in a medicaid program to fund medically necessary abortions if Federal reimbursement is not available under the Hyde Amendment. Medicaid is a cooperative effort by which the Federal government financially assists participating states by providing money to help them furnish health care to needy persons. The state assumes a certain percentage of the expenses not paid by the Federal government. The program was not designed to force a state to furnish services to an eligible individual that Congress itself refuses to fund. The enforcement of the Hyde Amendment, therefore, relieves the state of financial responsibility to pay for abortions no longer reimbursed by the Federal government.

The constitutionality of the Hyde Amendment was challenged as impinging upon the liberty aspect of the Due Process Clause, effectively depriving a poor woman of her right to decide upon an abortion. The Court rejected this argument; a woman is not deprived of her right to an abortion, but only of public financing of it. If the government has not created the difficulties—in this case, indigency—that prevent a woman from deciding upon an abortion, it is not the responsibility of the government to remove them. The liberty guaranteed by the Constitution does not mean that an individual is constitutionally entitled to government financing so that he or she can take advantage of all aspects of such liberty.

The amendment was also alleged to infringe upon religious freedom guaranteed by the First Amendment because of its prohibition of abortion, reflecting the thinking of the Roman Catholic Church. Based on its opinion in *McGowan v. Maryland,* 366 U.S. 420, 442, 81 S.Ct. 1101, 1113, 6 L.Ed.2d 393 (1961), the Court reasoned in the *Harris* case that merely because an enactment "happens to coincide or harmonize with the tenets of some or all religions" does not mean that it violates the Establishment Clause. See also, Religion.

The amendment was also challenged on equal protection grounds since it involved selective financing of medical treatments. Medicaid subsidizes, in general, all medically necessary services, but the amendment denies Federal reimbursement of all medically necessary abortions. The Court reasoned that the Equal Protection Clause gives a right to be free from invidious discrimination in statutory classifications and other governmental activity. Although the Hyde Amendment primarily affects the decision of a poor woman to have an abortion from a financial view, poverty is not a suspect classification that would invalidate a statute. A classification that does not impinge upon a right or liberty protected by the Constitution is valid only if rationally related to a legitimate governmental objective. The government argued, and the Court agreed, that the funding restriction was rationally related to its legitimate interest in protecting a potential life. By providing financial assistance to poor women who planned to have their children while refusing to financially aid women who planned on abortion, the Federal government made childbirth a more attractive alternative than abortion. The Court, therefore, upheld the Hyde Amendment as a constitutional exercise of the interest of the government in promoting potential life. See also, Craig R. Ducat's essay on Abortion and Susan M. Olson's essay on Birth Control.

Craig R. Ducat

Abortion

$\mathbf{R}$elying upon a constitutional right of privacy emanating from the word *liberty* in the Due Process Clause of the Fourteenth Amendment, the Supreme Court in *Roe v. Wade,* 410 U.S. 113, 93 S.Ct. 705, 35 L.Ed.2d 147 (1973), substantially restricted the use of the states' police power to criminalize the procurement and performance of abortions. At common law, abortion was not considered an indictable offense before "quickening" of the fetus (i.e., the first recognizable movement of the fetus in the uterus, usually occurring between the 16th and 18th weeks of pregnancy). After that point, it was generally treated as a misdemeanor, from the Victorian Age until the decision in *Roe.* However, the posture taken by state laws became much more severe, so that by the 1950s the vast majority of American jurisdictions forbade all abortions except those necessary to save or preserve the life of the mother (otherwise known as therapeutic abortions).

While recognizing in *Roe v. Wade* that "[t]his right of privacy . . . is broad enough to encompass a woman's decision whether or not to terminate her

An early exploiter of tabloid journalism—*The National Police Gazette*—printed in 1867 an account of an abortion accompanied by this engraving.

Library of Congress

18

pregnancy," the Court asserted that "this right is not unqualified and must be considered against important state interests in regulation." Those interests, the Court noted, must be "compelling" and "legislative enactments [furthering them] must be narrowly drawn to express only the legitimate state interests at stake." In applying this framework, the Court pointed out that "[t]hree reasons have been advanced to explain historically the enactment of criminal abortion laws in the nineteenth century and to justify their continued existence": (1) discouraging illicit sexual behavior; (2) restraining the pregnant woman from submitting to a medical procedure that jeopardizes her life; and (3) protecting prenatal life. The Court summarily rejected the first of these because it had not been advanced by the state in this case and because it had not been taken seriously by any court or commmentator. As to the last of these postulated justifications, the Court pointed out that such a blanket assertion could not constitutionally support a prohibition on all but therapeutic abortions from the point of conception since the fetus is not a "person" within the meaning of the Fourteenth Amendment—a conclusion drawn from the fact that the Constitution uses the word "person" only in the postnatal sense and because prevailing legal abortion practices at the time the Fourteenth Amendment was written were "far freer." While acknowledging "that at some point in time another interest, that of the health of the mother or that of potential human life, becomes significantly involved," the Court nonetheless took notice of the fact that even "those trained in the respective disciplines of medicine, philosophy, and theology . . . [were] unable to arrive at any consensus" as to when life begins. Speaking for the Court, Justice Harry A. Blackmun said: "In view of this, . . . we do not agree that, by adopting one theory of life, Texas may override the rights of the pregnant woman that are at stake. . . . [H]owever, . . . the State does have an important and legitimate interest in preserving and protecting the health of the pregnant woman, whether she be a resident of the State or a nonresident who seeks medical consultation and treatment there, and that it has still *another* important and legitimate interest in protecting the potentiality of human life." Observing that "[t]hese interests are separate and distinct," and that "[e]ach grows in substantiality" during pregnancy, and at some point "becomes 'compelling',," the Court concluded: "(a) For the stage prior to approximately the end of the first trimester, the abortion decision and its effectuation must be left to the medical judgment of the pregnant woman's attending physician. (b) For the stage subsequent to approximately the end of the first trimester, the State in promoting its interest in the health of the mother, may, if it chooses, regulate the abortion procedure in ways that are reasonably related to maternal health. (c) For the stage subsequent to viability, the State in promoting its interest in the potentiality of human life may, if it chooses, regulate, and even proscribe, abortion except where it is necessary, in appropriate medical judgment, for the preservation of the life or health of the mother." However, it should be noted that, as of this writing, resolutions are pending in Congress—and have been during every session since 1973—proposing a constitutional amendment that would include the fetus within the meaning of the word *person* in the Fourteenth Amendment, thus, defining life as beginning at conception and thereby overturning the Court's holding in *Roe v. Wade*.

Interstitial rulings since *Roe* have further defined the contours of the abortion prerogative. The state may not (1) confine the performance of abortions—and not at all during the first trimester—to only certain specially accredited hospitals without showing that such accreditation advances its interest in more ful-

Justice Harry A. Blackmun wrote the majority opinion in the case of *Roe v. Wade*.

The principle of liberty requires liberty of tastes and pursuits; of framing the plan of our life to suit our own character; of doing as we like, subject to such consequences as may follow: without impediment from our fellow creatures, so long as what we do does not harm them, even though they should think our conduct foolish, perverse, or wrong.

J.S. MILL

A Pro-Choice demonstration near the Capitol in Washington, D.C.

ly protecting the patient; (2) interpose examination by a hospital abortion committee; or (3) require additional approval of the abortion decision by two other physicians. State laws giving a spouse or parent (if the pregnant female is unmarried and underage) absolute veto power over the pregnant woman's abortion decision have also been declared unconstitutional, as have statutory provisions proscribing the use of saline amniocentesis as an abortion technique and imposing on the physician a duty to preserve the life of the fetus if possible whatever the stage of pregnancy on pain of civil or criminal liability. And, with respect to pregnant, unmarried, and unemancipated female minors, the Court has upheld a statutory regulation obliging a physician to "notify, if possible," the parents or guardian of such a minor prior to the performance of an abortion, at least where there has not been any showing as to her maturity. Finally, the Court has ruled that nothing in *Roe v. Wade* obligates the Federal government or the states to fund elective (as distinguished from therapeutic) abortions. In fact, the Court has said that a city may constitutionally refuse to permit the performance of elective abortions in city-owned hospitals while simultaneously providing hospital services to women carrying their pregnancies to term. And, of course, refusals by private hospitals, free of state influence and direction of their policies, are not "state actions" and therefore are not subject to constitutional challenge. In sum, then, although *Roe v. Wade* spells out a constitutional right, it does not obligate either the Federal or state government to encourage exercise of that right.

Following the decision in *Roe,* a so-called "right to life" movement has vigorously sought to "overturn" that decision by a constitutional amendment to make abortion illegal or by simple legislation that would state that life begins at conception. Should Congress pass such an act, it would still leave it to the courts to decide if such a law were constitutional. See also, Craig R. Ducat's essay on Privacy, Right of.

When those trained in the respective disciplines of medicine, philosophy, and theology are unable to arrive at any consensus, the judiciary, at this point in the development of man's knowledge, is not in a position to speculate as to the answer.

HARRY A. BLACKMUN

Bibliography: Germain G. Grisez, *Abortion: The Myths, the Realities, and the Arguments* (1970); John T. Noonan, Jr., *A Private Choice* (1979); "Symposium on the Law and Politics of Abortion," 77 *Michigan Law Review* (August 1979): 1569–1827.

ABOVE CITED OR MENTIONED
□ Quoted before, or appearing earlier, in the same publication. □

ABRAMS v. UNITED STATES
See Richard Singer's article on pages 22–23.

ABROGATION
□ The repeal or annulment of a former law by an act of legislative power, by constitutional authority, or by usage. □

For example, the abrogation of the Eighteenth Amendment to the Constitution, which prohibited the manufacture or sale of intoxicating liquors, was accomplished by the enactment of the Twenty-first Amendment. Implied abrogation takes place when a new law contains provisions that are positively contrary to a former law, without expressly abrogating such laws, or when the order of things for which the law has been made no longer exists.

ABSCOND
□ To flee from arrest or prosecution.
□ To hide out or conceal oneself from authorities, especially with the intention to avoid the service of legal PROCESS. □

When authorities from the Securities and Exchange Commission sought Robert Vescoe in 1976 for alleged stock manipulation, he absconded to Costa Rica.

ABSCONDING DEBTOR
□ One who flees or hides out in order to frustrate the just demands of his or her creditors. □

A person who moves out of the state may be an absconding debtor if it is that person's intention to avoid paying money that he or she owes.

It is difficult or impossible for a creditor to serve an absconding debtor with a SUMMONS in order to start a lawsuit and collect his or her money. Where a court is convinced that a debtor has absconded, it may permit the creditor to begin the lawsuit in some way other than PERSONAL SERVICE of a summons.

For example, a franchisee bought a doughnut franchise and opened up a small shop. He also bought a house for his family. Unfortunately, the business failed after a year, and he turned all of the equipment and materials back to the franchisor. The franchisor claimed that additional money was owed to him and decided to sue the former franchisee. A process server was sent to take a summons to the apartment which was listed as the address in the original application for the franchise. The landlord there told the process server that the former franchisee had moved and left no forwarding address. The franchisor applied to the court for permission to serve him as an absconding debtor. The court allowed the franchisor to publish notice of the lawsuit on three occasions in the legal section of the local newspaper. The franchisee did not see the notice and did not appear in court. The court entered a DEFAULT JUDGMENT against him without hearing his side of the story. After that, the franchisor began searching public records to see if the franchisee owned any property that could be seized to pay off the amount of the judgment. He discovered the recorded deed for the house and went back to court, seeking an order to have the house sold. This time the franchisee who was served personally with the court papers appeared with his attorney. He explained at the hearing that he had never intended to conceal himself or to avoid paying the money he owed. The court found that he had never been an absconding debtor who could be served merely by publication. The default judgment, therefore, could not be enforced, and the franchisor could not have the house seized and sold.

ABSENTEE
□ One who has left, either temporarily or permanently, his or her domicile or usual place of residence or business. □

An *absentee landlord* is an individual who leases real estate to another but who does not reside in the leased premises.
□ A person beyond the geographical borders of a state who has not authorized an AGENT to represent him or her in legal proceedings that may be commenced against him or her within the state. □

An *absentee corporation* is one which conducts business within a state other than the place of its incorporation but has not designated an agent for purposes of service of PROCESS, which might ensue from disputes involving its business transactions there.

Flight, or an escape from arrest for felony, is an acknowledgment of guilt . . . every man, who is accused, is bound to submit himself to the judgment of the law; and, whether it be a trespass, or whether it be a felony with which he is charged, it may, with truth, be said of him who shrinks from trial—facinus fatetur qui judicium fugit. [One who flees from trial admits a crime.]

J. DAY

Richard G. Singer

Abrams v. United States
(Justice Holmes's Dissent)

Few jurists have had the impact on American, and indeed international, legal thought as United States Supreme Court Justice Oliver Wendell Holmes, known as "The Great Dissenter." Few of these dissents were more powerful, or more influential, than his dissent in *Abrams v. United States,* 250 U.S. 616, 40 S.Ct. 17, 63 L.Ed. 1173 (1919). In this case several persons had been convicted of conspiring against the form of government of the United States during wartime and of seeking to thwart the war effort against Germany by distributing a political pamphlet that by modern standards would be classified mild in both tone and rhetoric but which, at that time, was perceived as radical and crude.

In a vibrant dissent, Justice Holmes declared that speech could be restricted only when it created a "clear and imminent danger" to the war effort. Although these words were common in cases involving other criminal attempts, the application to a case involving speech, the requirement that the danger be of the most extreme type, and that the speaker intend to bring about that danger were new. No longer, according to Holmes, should mere "concern" or disagreement with speech be the basis of governmental restriction or regulation.

In addition to setting the test for restriction of speech exceptionally high, Holmes articulated the philosophy behind such a position:

> Persecution for the expression of opinions seems to me perfectly logical. If you have no doubt of your premises or your power and want a certain result with all your heart you naturally express your wishes in law and sweep away all opposition. To allow opposition by speech seems to indicate that you think the speech impotent, as when a man says that he has squared the circle, or that you do not care whole-heartedly for the result, or that you doubt either your power or your premises. But when men have realized that time has upset many fighting faiths, they may come to believe even more than they believe the very foundations of their own conduct that the ultimate good desired is better reached by free trade in ideas[,]—that the best test of truth is the power of the thought to get itself accepted in the competition of the market[;] and that truth is the only ground upon which their wishes safely can be carried out. That[,] at any rate[,] is the theory of our Constitution. It is an experiment, as all life is an experiment.

Few notions in America's constitutional history have had as vital a life as that of the "marketplace of ideas." With sweeping phrases, Holmes both adopted and adapted the concept of laissez-faire into the First Amendment. In later decisions by the United States Supreme Court, these words would echo consistently,

The most stringent protection of free speech would not protect a man in falsely shouting fire in a theater and causing a panic. . . . The question in every case is whether the words used are used in such circumstances and are of such a nature as to create a clear and present danger that they will bring about the substantive evils that Congress has a right to prevent.

OLIVER WENDELL HOLMES, JR.

and the Court would broaden the scope of free speech, to the point that in the 1970s, again in the midst of another war, the Court held that a person could not be criminally liable for wearing a jacket upon which there was an otherwise profane reference to the war and its unpopularity (*Cohen v. California*, 403 U.S. 15, 91 S.Ct. 1780, 29 L.Ed.2d 284 [1971]).

It is possible, of course, that even without Justice Holmes the Supreme Court might have eventually reached the position of "free trade in ideas" that he defended in *Abrams*. But it is important to remember that prior to the *Abrams* case and *Schenck v. United States,* 249 U.S. 47, 39 S.Ct. 247, 63 L.Ed. 470 (1919), the Court had rarely had occasion to consider the First Amendment's power, since by its words it restricted only the Federal government from prohibiting speech. (It was not until the late 1920s that the Supreme Court accepted the view that the First Amendment also restricted state governments by incorporation into the Fourteenth Amendment.) Justice Holmes, therefore, was the first judicial spokesperson for the idea of virtually unlimited speech including, as he said, "the expression of opinion that we loathe and believe to be fraught with death. . . ." His defense of this position gave free speech a powerful judicial ally and articulator, and his position eventually became the law of the land. It is surely the genesis of the view that the First Amendment embodies "preferred freedom." See also, Stephen B. Presser's essay on Oliver Wendell Holmes, Jr.; Martin Shapiro's essay on Freedom of Speech; and Norman Dorsen's essay on Clear and Present Danger.

Bibliography: T. Emerson, *Toward a General Theory of the First Amendment* (1966); M. Lerner, *The Mind and Faith of Justice Holmes* (1943).

Dissents such as the one Justice Holmes wrote in the *Abrams* case demonstrated his power as a legal thinker.

Brown Brothers

In 1944 the U.S. armed forces made great efforts to encourage personnel serving overseas to vote by absentee ballot.

ABSENTEE VOTING □ Participation in an election by qualified voters who are permitted to mail in their ballots because they cannot appear at the polls in person on election day. □

A voter must show a valid reason for voting by absentee ballot, such as a serious illness, a military service obligation, or a business commitment that keeps him or her out of town on election day.

ABSOLUTE □ Complete; final; unconditional; not depending upon or relating to any other person or thing in order to be effective. □

For example, a *simple bond* is an absolute bond and can be distinguished from a *conditional bond*. Absolute can be used to describe DIVORCE, ESTATES, OBLIGATION, and TITLE.

ABSOLUTE CONTRABAND
See Neutrality.

ABSOLUTE DEED □ A document used to transfer unrestricted title to property. □

An absolute deed is different from a *mortgage deed,* which transfers ownership back to the mortgagee when the terms of the mortgage have been fulfilled.

ABSOLUTE NUISANCE □ The use of one person's property that substantially interferes with another person's right to use or enjoy his or her property, or life. □

An absolute nuisance differs from a NUISANCE in that it is determined by the significance of the interference with another's rights in light of the effect on the public rather than by the legality of the defendant's conduct or negligence in using his or her property in such a manner.

Generally, there are three kinds of absolute nuisances. Certain public nuisances—conduct, things, or places that obstruct or cause inconvenience or damage to the public—are designated by statute as absolute nuisances. A house of prostitution, for instance, is generally considered an absolute nuisance because it attracts suspicious people for immoral and unlawful practices, and therefore poses a threat to peace and public morals. By doing so, its presence substantially interferes with the rights of the neighborhood property owners to enjoy their land. The mere fact that such an establishment exists makes it an absolute nuisance.

An act, thing, or condition is an absolute nuisance if it is clearly unreasonable in view of the surrounding neighborhood, such as when a person builds and operates a fertilizer plant in a residential neighborhood. Neighbors of the plant would be prevented from using their backyards and might suffer nausea and other physical side effects. A court considers the type of activity, its location, and its method of operation before deciding whether such an activity significantly affects others' rights to use their property.

Abnormal and unduly hazardous activities, such as the manufacture and storage of explosives, are also absolute nuisances since they create a danger to public health and safety. These activities might be reasonable in certain situations, however, so as not to be absolute nuisances.

Thomas I. Emerson

Absolutes

The term *absolute* refers to a legal status or legal rule that is without exception, qualification, or condition. Thus *absolute liability* means liability or responsibility for conduct or for an event regardless of fault, intention, or accident. Similarly, *absolute privilege* in libel law protects the speaker, such as a legislator in performance of an official function or a judge presiding over a trial, irrespective of the truth or falsity of the statement or the motive of the speaker. Likewise an *absolute title* to land is a title that is exclusive, unconditional, and unencumbered.

The concept of a legal status or rule that is absolute is useful in the law in that it establishes a fixed principle, automatically applied, without need for an interpretation or separate decision in each case. It thus attempts to introduce clarity, certainty, and efficiency into the legal process. Usually this objective cannot be fully attained. Ambiguity often reenters with the necessity of defining the behavior or events that come within the absolute rule. And most absolutes sooner or later need qualification.

One of the best-known and most controversial uses of the absolute concept in law concerns the First Amendment. The absolutist position holds that the freedom of *speech, press, assembly,* and *petition* guaranteed by the First Amendment means that any behavior embraced by these terms should be protected against government prohibition or other interference, regardless of the nature of the communication or its consequences. The first major proponent of the absolutist interpretation of the First Amendment was Dr. Alexander Meiklejohn. Its principal advocate came to be Justice Hugo L. Black. Justice William O. Douglas in his later opinions also adhered to the absolutist position. It was never accepted by any other Supreme Court justice, and much less by the majority of the Court.

Dr. Meiklejohn justified his absolutist position on the ground that under our Constitution the people were sovereign, and in exercising this sovereign power, they needed to know and consider all facts, ideas, and opinions pertaining to the subject under consideration. Justice Black, while not rejecting the Meiklejohn view, primarily felt that the language of the First Amendment, in stating that *no law* may deny or abridge freedom of speech, precluded any exceptions. Other commentators stressed the importance of establishing a flat rule that would bind legislators, executive officials, and courts—particularly in periods of political stress. Opponents insisted that the absolute position was impossible both in theory and in practice, pointing out that some forms of speech—such as libel—had always been subject to restriction, and that others—such as threats of physical violence—could not be tolerated in a democratic society.

In actuality, the argument over the absolutist interpretation of the First Amendment has in large part missed the mark. Dr. Meiklejohn and Justice Black even admitted to some qualifications, such as regulations controlling the time,

[T]he [First] Amendment embraces two concepts,— freedom to believe and freedom to act. The first is absolute but, in the nature of things the second cannot be. Conduct remains subject to regulation for the protection of society.

OWEN J. ROBERTS

place, and manner—as distinct from the content—of speech. Moreover, it is clear that the absolute rule has no relevance in some areas of First Amendment law, such as the power of government to subsidize election campaigns. On the other hand, the fundamental idea underlying the concept of an absolute rule—the establishment of effective and binding limitations on government interference with freedom of expression—does have important applications in formulating First Amendment doctrine. In those areas the problem becomes one of defining as precisely as possible the forms of communication, whether verbal or nonverbal, which should be given special protection in light of the values served by the First Amendment. Once that has been done, it is entirely possible to adopt a rule that gives such behavior full, or absolute, protection. See also, Craig R. Ducat's essay on Absolutism.

Bibliography: Hugo L. Black, *A Constitutional Faith* (1969); Thomas I. Emerson, *The System of Freedom of Expression* (1970); Alexander Meiklejohn, *Political Freedom* (1960).

Craig R. Ducat

Absolutism

Absolutism is the name given to a particular approach to interpreting provisions of the Constitution. The hallmark of this school of thought is its reading of constitutional provisions as rules to be construed strictly by relying upon the plain meaning of the words or the intention of the framers so as to minimize the discretion of the judges. Although examples of the absolutist position can be drawn from many areas of constitutional law, absolutism has been used most frequently to characterize the stance taken by U.S. Supreme Court Justice Hugo Black in reading the First Amendment, notably with respect to the freedoms of speech, press, and association.

Justice Black's absolutist position was premised on the paramount importance of a *written* Constitution; for an application of legal rules to the powerful and the powerless alike was the only guarantee against tyranny and oppression. He emphasized that the American system was a constitutional, and not a parliamentary, system. By this he meant that although, in a democratic system, elected legislators might be the chief policymakers, their enactments were always subordinate to the Constitution, which was a compact among the sovereign people. Because courts were charged with the duty of adjudicating legal cases and controversies, it was their obligation to say what the law was when a statute appeared to conflict

Alabama Senator Hugo L. Black in 1937 before he became a justice on the Supreme Court

National Archives

27

with the Constitution. Like legislators, judges also were bound by the rules contained in the Constitution, and Black took care to point out that judges were obligated to accept the plain meaning of constitutional provisions and the intentions of the framers in writing them. Since judges were equally bound by and subordinate to the Constitution, there was never any warrant for them to rule on the basis of their personal political values.

Justice Black's view of the First Amendment presented with particular force this notion that constitutional provisions were rules that reflected an already-agreed-upon balance of competing political values which judges were duty bound to honor and apply. To Justice Black, the provision of the First Amendment that "Congress shall make no law . . . abridging the freedom of speech, or of the press . . ." meant precisely what it said. It contained a rule that *absolutely* precluded congressional legislation regulating the rights of speech and press. This same guarantee, he argued, was equally binding on the states, because First Amendment freedoms were included within the meaning of the word *liberty* in the Due Process Clause of the Fourteenth Amendment which the states were constitutionally bound to respect.

The emphasis Justice Black placed within the phrase "Congress shall make *no* law" often seemed, however, to obscure the real limitation contained in his simultaneous regard for the plain meaning of the word *speech*. Justice Black was "always . . . careful to draw a line between speech and conduct." Absolute protection extended only to pure speech, which meant that government could not impose "punishment of a person because he says [or writes] something, believes something or associates with others who believe the same thing . . ." The First Amendment, then, protected all speech—not just political speech—and protected it absolutely. Consequently, Justice Black repeatedly voted to declare unconstitutional all obscenity and libel laws as well as legislation that made it a crime to *advocate* the forcible overthrow of the government.

Picketing, marching, and demonstrating, however, mixed elements of conduct with speech and thus fell outside the absolute protection of the First Amendment. Speech plus, he said, "by its very nature tends to infringe the rights of others." Reasonable government regulation of conduct (as distinguished from speech) was constitutional, he argued, because there was a time and a place for such behavior. The recognition of this distinction between speech and conduct led Justice Black to uphold governmental prohibitions on flag and draft-card burning, on the wearing of black arm bands by protesting school children, and on the wearing of black leather jackets in public on the back of which was emblazoned the message "Fuck the Draft."

While the First Amendment absolutely guaranteed the right to speak, write, or associate, Justice Black was quick to point out that it did not obligate government to furnish places to speak, write, or associate. The right to petition the government was limited to communications addressed to the government and was not a license to address the public in general. And, he argued, that the First Amendment certainly did not give people a right to speak on private property. See also, Thomas I. Emerson's essay on Absolutes; Thomas M. Feldstein and Stephen B. Presser's essay on Hugo Black; and Martin Shapiro's essay on Freedom of Speech.

Bibliography: Hugo L. Black, *A Constitutional Faith* (1968); Craig R. Ducat, *Modes of Constitutional Interpretation* (1978).

Freedom to publish means freedom for all and not for some.

HUGO L. BLACK

It is a prized American privilege to speak one's mind, although not always with perfect good taste, on all public institutions.

HUGO L. BLACK

ABSQUE HOC [*Latin, "Without this."*]
☐ Technical words used in common law PLEAD-ING that meant that the pleader was denying all of the statements that followed. ☐

ABSQUE IMPETITIONE VASTI [*Latin, "Without impeachment of waste."*]
☐ A clause that long ago was used in leases to show that a tenant was not to be liable to suit (*impetitione*), or called to account, for committing WASTE. ☐

ABSTENTION DOCTRINE ☐ The concept under which a FEDERAL COURT exercises its discretion and equitable powers and declines to decide a legal action over which it has jurisdiction pursuant to the Constitution and statutes where the state judiciary is capable of rendering a definitive ruling in the matter. ☐

A Federal court invokes the abstention doctrine when the resolution of a case can be reached by the application of state law, thereby avoiding the unnecessary decision of constitutional questions also raised by the facts of the case. A Federal court can even be ordered to invoke the abstention doctrine by a superior Federal court. In the 1941 case of *Railroad Commission of Texas v. Pullman Company*, 312 U.S. 496, 61 S.Ct. 643, 85 L.Ed. 971, the Supreme Court recognized the doctrine when it reversed an injunction prohibiting enforcement of a Commission order that only white Pullman conductors could be in charge of sleeping cars and ordered the Federal trial court to abstain from deciding the case pending a dispositive ruling on the issues of state law by the Texas state court. If, however, the relevant state law is unambiguous or egregiously unconstitutional, a Federal court will neither invoke nor order abstention from the determination of the controversy.

The abstention doctrine provides states with the opportunity to clarify and resolve uncertain questions of state law. It promotes a harmonious relationship between the Federal and state judiciaries by avoiding any needless Federal interference in state affairs and also reduces the number of cases on already overburdened dockets of the Federal courts.

ABSTRACT ☐ A summary or an abridgment. ☐

An abstract comprises—or concentrates in itself—the essential qualities of a larger thing—or of several things—in a short, abbreviated form. It differs from a transcript, which is a verbatim copy of the thing itself and is more comprehensive. For a sample of an abstract of title, see the Appendix volume 11.

ABSTRACTION ☐ Taking from someone with an intent to injure or defraud. ☐

Wrongful abstraction is an unauthorized and illegal withdrawing of funds or an appropriation of someone else's funds for the taker's own benefit. It may be a crime under the laws of a state. It is different from EMBEZZLEMENT, which is a crime committed only if the taker had a lawful right to possession of the money when it was first taken.

ABSTRACT OF TITLE ☐ A condensed history of the ownership of a piece of land that is taken from public records or documents. ☐

An abstract of title discloses the number of times ownership or any interest in the property has been transferred from one person to another, as well as the nature of the transfer; any rights that persons other than the present owner might have in the land; and a statement of all liens—charges or liabilities to which the land may be subject—affecting the value of the property, which would be important to a prospective purchaser of it. A plat—a survey or map of the land with its boundaries noted—may also be included as part of the abstract of title.

ABUSE
☐ To reproach, disparage, revile, or malign.
☐ The wrongful or harsh treatment of a person or thing; any departure from good order or reasonable use.
☐ In civil law, the destruction of something by the use of it. ☐

ABUSED AND NEGLECTED CHILDREN
☐ Those individuals under the AGE OF MAJORITY who are suffering from serious physical or emotional injuries, whether inflicted intentionally—like some kind of bizarre punishment—or caused by neglect—like malnutrition. ☐

A state may enact special statutes that set up procedures for identifying and rescuing abused or neglected children and for punishing or rehabilitating their tormentors. See also, Child Abuse.

ABUSE OF DISCRETION ☐ A failure to take into proper consideration the facts and law relating to a particular matter; an arbitrary or unreasonable departure from precedents and settled judicial custom. ☐

Where a trial court must exercise discretion in deciding a question, it must do so in a way that is not clearly against logic and the evidence. An improvident exercise of discretion is an error of law and grounds for reversing a decision on appeal. It does not, however, necessarily amount to

The power, then, that parents have over their children arises from that duty which is incumbent on them, to take care of their offspring during the imperfect state of childhood.

JOHN LOCKE

bad faith, intentional wrong, or misconduct by the trial judge.

ABUSE OF POWER ☐ Improper use of authority by someone who has that authority because he or she holds a public office. ☐

Abuse of power is different from USURPATION of power, which is an exercise of authority that the offender does not actually have.

ABUSE OF PROCESS ☐ The use of legal PROCESS to accomplish an unlawful purpose; causing a SUMMONS, WRIT, WARRANT, MANDATE, or any other process to issue from a court in order to accomplish some purpose not intended by the law. ☐

For example, a grocer rents a small building but complains to the landlord about the inadequate heating system, leaks in the roof, and potholes in the driveway. When the landlord fails to make the required repairs, the grocer decides the property is worth less and deducts $100 a month from his rent payments. The landlord starts a lawsuit to either recover the full amount of rent due or to oust the grocer and regain possession of the premises. The law in their state is fairly clear on the question: a tenant has no right to force a landlord to make repairs by withholding a portion of the rent. The landlord knows that she has a good chance of winning her case, but she also wants to teach the grocer a lesson. On the first three occasions that the case comes up on the court calendar, the grocer closes his store and appears in court, but the landlord does not show up. On the fourth occasion, the landlord comes to court and wins her case. The grocer, in a separate action for abuse of process, claims that the landlord is using the court's power to order him to appear simply to harass him. The court agrees and awards him money damages for lost income and inconvenience.

Abuse of process is a wrong committed during the course of litigation. It is a perversion of lawfully issued process and is different from MALICIOUS PROSECUTION, a lawsuit started without any reasonable cause.

ABUSIVE ☐ Harsh or insulting. ☐

Using abusive language, even though offensive, is not criminal unless it amounts to FIGHTING WORDS that, by their very utterance, tend to incite an immediate breach of the peace.

ABUT ☐ To touch; to join at the ends. ☐

Abutting suggests a closer proximity than the term ADJACENT. When referring to real property, it means that there is no intervening land between the abutting parcels. Generally, properties that share a common boundary are abutting. A statute may require abutting owners to pay proportional shares of the cost of a street improvement project.

A/C
☐ Account.
☐ A notation much used by bookkeepers that merely identifies a transaction. ☐

When used on a check, it does not tell the bank to pay the person; it only identifies the transaction for which the check was issued.

ACADEMIC FREEDOM ☐ The right of a teacher to decide the methods he or she will use in a classroom. ☐

Academic freedom is limited by policies rightfully adopted by a school board or a board of trustees. See also, entry on Speech and Press, Freedom of; and Martin Shapiro's essay on Freedom of Speech.

ACADEMIC QUESTION ☐ An issue that does not require an answer by the court because it is not necessary for the case; a hypothetical or MOOT question. ☐

ACADEMIC YEAR ☐ That period of time necessary to complete an actual course of study during a school year. ☐

Social Security benefits may terminate at the end of an academic year, or a deferment from compulsory military service may continue only during an academic year.

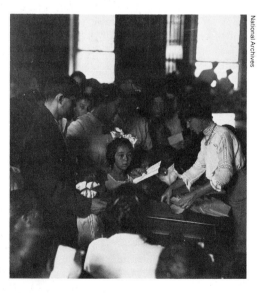

New York children registering for school in 1913

[Academic] freedom is therefore a special concern of the First Amendment, which does not tolerate laws that cast a pall of orthodoxy over the classroom . . .

WILLIAM J. BRENNAN, JR.

Where suspicion fills the air and holds scholars in line for fear of their jobs, there can be no exercise of the free intellect . . .

WILLIAM O. DOUGLAS

National Archives

ACADEMY OF CRIMINAL JUSTICE SCIENCES

The Academy of Criminal Justice Sciences (ACJS) was founded in 1963 to foster professionalism in the criminal justice system by advancing the quality of education and research programs in the field. The academy seeks to enrich education and research programs in institutions of higher learning, criminal justice agencies, and agencies in related fields by improving cooperation and communication, by serving as a clearinghouse for the collection and dissemination of information produced by the programs, and by promoting the highest ethical and personal standards in criminal justice research and education. The academy presents numerous awards for outstanding contributions by individuals in the field. The members of the academy are individual teachers, administrators, researchers, students, and practitioners.

The academy publishes the *Journal of Criminal Justice* quarterly and a directory annually. It holds annual meetings in March.

ACCEDE

□ To consent or to agree, as to accede to another's point of view.

□ To enter an office or to accept a position, as to accede to the presidency. □

ACCELERATED DEPRECIATION

□ A method of DEPRECIATION that yields larger deductions for the value of an asset during its earlier years than does the straight-line method. □

Double declining-balance and the sum of the years' digits are methods of accelerated depreciation.

ACCELERATION

□ A hastening; a shortening of the time until some event takes place. □

A person who has the right to take possession of property at some future time may have that right accelerated if the present holder loses his or her legal right to the property. If a LIFE ESTATE fails for any reason, the REMAINDER is accelerated.

The principle of acceleration can be applied when it becomes clear that one party to a contract is not going to perform his or her obligations. ANTICIPATORY REPUDIATION, or the possibility of future breach, makes it possible to move the right to remedies back to the time of repudiation rather than to wait for the time when performance would be due and an actual breach would occur.

ACCELERATION CLAUSE

□ The provision in a credit agreement, such as a MORTGAGE, NOTE, BOND, or DEED OF TRUST, that allows the lender to require immediate payment of all money due if certain conditions occur before the time that payment would otherwise be due. □

The agreement may call for acceleration whenever there is a default of any important obligation, such as nonpayment of principal or interest, or the failure to pay insurance premiums. For a sample of an acceleration clause, see the Appendix volume.

ACCEPTANCE

□ The act of a person to whom a thing is offered by another whereby he or she receives the thing with the intention of retaining it. □

When a person who is offered a GIFT by someone keeps the gift, this indicates his or her acceptance of it. In the law of SALES, which governs business dealings between merchants, a buyer demonstrates his or her acceptance of goods that are not exactly what he or she had ordered from the seller by telling the seller that he or she will keep the goods even though they are not what was ordered; by failing to reject the goods; or by doing something to the goods inconsistent with the seller's ownership of them, such as selling the goods to customers of the buyer's store.

□ The taking and receiving of anything as a tacit agreement to a preceding act. □

In the law of CONTRACTS, acceptance is one person's compliance with the terms of an OFFER made by another. Acceptance occurs in the law of INSURANCE when an insurer agrees to receive a person's application for insurance and to issue a policy protecting the person against certain risks, such as fire or theft.

□ A signed agreement by a DRAWEE stating that he or she will pay a draft when it is presented by a PAYEE. □

For example, acceptance occurs when a bank pays a check written by a customer who has a checking account with that bank.

Types of acceptance   An acceptance may be conditional, express, or implied.

Conditional acceptance   A conditional acceptance, sometimes called a qualified acceptance, occurs when a person to whom an offer has been made tells the offeror that he or she is willing to agree to the offer provided that some changes are made in its terms or that some condition or event occurs. This type of acceptance operates as a COUNTEROFFER. A counteroffer must be accepted by the original offeror before a contract can be established between the parties.

Another type of conditional acceptance occurs when a drawee promises to pay a draft upon the happening of a condition, such as a shipment of goods reaching its destination on the date specified in the contract.

Possession is very strong; rather more than nine points of the law.

LORD MANSFIELD

Express acceptance   An express acceptance occurs when a person clearly and explicitly agrees to an offer or agrees to pay a draft that is presented for payment.

Implied acceptance   An implied acceptance is one that is not directly stated but is demonstrated by any acts indicating a person's assent to the proposed bargain. An implied acceptance occurs when a shopper selects an item in a supermarket and pays for it at the cashier. The shopper's conduct indicates that he or she has agreed to the supermarket owner's offer to sell the item for the price stated on it.

ACCESS □ The freedom to approach or to communicate; the opportunity, means, or power to pass to and from, or to approach. □

Prisoners are entitled to have access to court. Prison officials cannot prevent prisoners from filing papers or appearing in court even if they honestly think that such prevention would help them maintain discipline and good order.

Owners of real property are entitled to some means of access to their property from a road or highway. They do not necessarily need to own a corridor of land from their property to the nearest road, but they may claim an EASEMENT of access.

In a PATERNITY SUIT, access means the opportunity to have had sexual relations. When there is a question about who is the father of a certain child, it is appropriate for a court to determine which man had access to the mother around the estimated time of conception. A man charged with being the father of an illegitimate child may plead the defense of multiple access—that the mother had several lovers at the time of conception.

ACCESSION
□ The commencement or inauguration of a sovereign's reign; coming into possession of a right or office.
□ Increase; augmentation; addition; the right to own whatever is added naturally to the property that a person already owns. □

For example, a person who owns property along a river also takes ownership of any addi-

The queen completes her accession to the throne when the archbishop sets the crown upon her bowed head and the people cry out "God save the queen."

UPI

tional land that builds up along the riverbank. This right may extend to additions that result from the work or skill of another person. The buyer of a car who fails to make scheduled payments cannot get back his new spark plugs after the car is repossessed because they have become a part of the whole car. The principle of accession does not necessarily apply, however, where the addition has substantially improved the value and changed the character of the property, as when by mistake someone else's grapes were made into wine or someone else's clay made into bricks. In such cases, the original owner might recover only the value of the raw material rather than take ownership of the finished product.
□ In international law, the unconditional or absolute acceptance by a nonparty nation of a treaty already concluded among other sovereigns. □

Accession may be gained in either of two ways: (1) the new member nation may be formally accepted by all the nations already parties to the treaty; or (2) the new nation may simply bind itself to the obligations already existing in the treaty. Frequently, a treaty will expressly provide that certain nations or categories of nations may

Following the death of General Francisco Franco in 1975, Spain restored its monarchy. Here the new monarch, Juan Carlos de Borbón, and Queen Sophia, *left*, pay their respects at Franco's bier.

In November 1964 Grand Duchess Charlotte of Luxemburg, *center*, abdicated in favor of her son, Prince Jean, *right*, now Grand Duke Jean.

accede. In some cases, the parties to a treaty will invite one or more nations to accede to the treaty.

ACCESSORY □ Anything that is joined or added to another thing. □

An accessory may be an ornament or an accompaniment or something necessary to complete the primary item. It may be incidental or subordinate to it.
□ In criminal law, anyone who promotes or contributes to the commission of a crime. □

An accessory is not a chief actor in the offense nor is he or she even present at its commission. An accessory aids, commands, or counsels another in the commission of the crime, either before or after the fact. A person is guilty as an accessory if he or she instigates or conceals the crime or the criminal. The penalty for being an accessory may be somewhat less severe than the penalty for the one who is convicted of committing the crime. Accessories, accomplices, and abettors all help accomplish the commission of a crime, but an ACCOMPLICE is a principal actor in the crime and an ABETTOR shares the chief actor's criminal intent. An accomplice or abettor might be present when the crime is committed, but an accessory is not.

ACCESSORY AFTER THE FACT □ One who knows that a certain person has committed a felony but nevertheless receives, comforts, or assists that person for the purpose of helping him or her escape punishment. □

An accessory after the fact may be convicted under a statute that forbids harboring a fugitive or obstructing justice.

Dr. Samuel A. Mudd set John Wilkes Booth's leg after Booth broke it leaping from President Lincoln's box in Ford's theater. Mudd was subsequently tried, convicted, and sentenced to imprisonment on the Dry Tortugas Islands off Florida as an accessory after the fact in the Lincoln assassination, but the U.S. Congress eventually pardoned him in 1979.

ACCESSORY BEFORE THE FACT

□ One who is not present when a felony is committed but who orders, counsels, encourages, or otherwise aids or abets another to commit it. □

Under the common law, an accessory before the fact was distinguished from other parties to the crime because he or she was not present when it was committed. Virtually all states have abrogated this distinction by statute and now treat accessories before the fact as principals who are subject to the same penalties as the chief actor in the crime.

ACCIDENT □ An event that under the circumstances is unusual to and unexpected by the person to whom it happens; a fortuitous occurrence; a mishap or CASUALTY. □

Accident is not always a precise legal term. It may be used generally in reference to various types of mishaps, or it may be given a technical meaning which applies when used in a certain statute or kind of case. Where it is used in a general sense, no particular significance can be attached to it. Where it is precisely defined, as in a statute, that definition strictly controls any decision about whether a certain event covered by that statute was in fact an accident.

In its most limited sense, the word *accident* is used only for events that occur without the intervention of a human being. This kind of accident also may be called an act of God. It is an event that no person caused or could have prevented—such as a tornado, a tidal wave, or an ice storm. An accident insurance policy can by its terms be limited to coverage only for this type of accident. Damage by hail to a field of wheat may be considered such an accident.

A policy of insurance, by its very nature, covers only accidents and not intentionally caused injuries. That principle explains why courts will read some exceptions into any insurance policy, whether or not they are expressly stated. For example, life insurance generally will not compensate for a suicide, and ordinary automobile insurance will not cover damages sustained when the owner is drag racing.

Accident insurance policies frequently insure not only against an act of God but also for accidents caused by a person's carelessness. An insured homeowner will expect coverage, for example, if someone drowns in his or her pool, even though the accident might have occurred because someone in the family left the gate open.

Not every unintended event is an accident for which insurance benefits can be paid; all the circumstances in a particular case must first be considered. For example, a policeman who waded into a surging crowd of forty or fifty fighting teenagers and then experienced a heart attack was found to have suffered from an accident. In another case, a man who was shot when he was found in bed with another man's wife was also found to have died in an accident because death is not the usual or expected result of adultery. However, the family of another man was not allowed to collect insurance benefits when he was shot after starting a fight with a knife. In that case, the court ruled that deadly force was a predictable response to a life-threatening attack, whether the instigator actually anticipated it or not.

Assembly line mass production brought automobiles within the price range of most consumers by the late 1920s. It also brought a steady increase in deadly accidents.

Culver Pictures

Even though river steamboats were neither exposed to violent seas nor operated far from land, many lives were lost due to accidental fires and exploding boilers.

Library of Congress

UPI

This jet engine tore loose from its wing mounts and caused an airliner accident that took 279 lives at Chicago's O'Hare airport in 1979.

[If back pay were awarded only for acts of bad faith] the remedy would become a punishment for moral turpitude, rather than a compensation for workers' injuries. . . . [A] worker's injury is no less real simply because his employer did not inflict it in 'bad faith' . . .

POTTER STEWART

Different states apply different standards when determining if an accident justifies payment of benefits under workers' compensation. Some states strictly limit benefits to events that clearly are accidents. They will permit payment when a sudden and unexpected strain causes an immediate injury during the course of work but they will not permit payment when an injury gradually results from prolonged assaults on the body. Under this approach, a worker who is asphyxiated by a lethal dose of carbon monoxide when he goes into a blast furnace to make repairs would be deemed to have suffered in an accident. However, a worker who contracts lung cancer after years of exposure to irritating dust in a factory could not claim to have been injured in an accident. Because of the remedial purpose of workers' compensation schemes, many states are liberal in allowing compensation. In one state, a woman whose existing arthritic condition was aggravated when she took a job stuffing giblets into partially frozen chickens on a conveyor belt was allowed to collect workers' compensation benefits.

Insurance policies may set limits to the amount of benefits recoverable for one accident. A certain automobile insurance policy allowed a maximum of only $200 to compensate for damaged clothing or luggage in the event of an accident. When luggage was stolen from the insured automobile, however, a court ruled that the event was not an accident and the maximum did not apply. The owner was allowed to recover the full value of the lost property.

Sometimes the duration of an accident must be determined. For example, if a drunken driver hit one car and then continued driving until he or she collided with a truck, a court might have to determine whether the two victims will share the maximum amount of money payable under the driver's liability insurance policy or whether each will collect the full maximum as a result of a separate accident.

ACCIDENTAL DEATH BENEFIT □ A provision of a life INSURANCE policy stating that if the insured—the person whose life has been insured—dies in an accident, the beneficiary of the policy—the person to whom its proceeds are payable—will receive twice the face value of the policy. □

The insurance company that is liable for the payment of such a benefit will conduct a thorough investigation into the cause of death of the insured person before paying the claim.

Another name for an accidental death benefit is a DOUBLE INDEMNITY clause.

ACCIDENTAL KILLING □ A death caused by a lawful act done under the reasonable belief that no harm was likely to result. □

Accidental killing is different from INVOLUNTARY MANSLAUGHTER, which causes death by an unlawful act or a lawful act done in an unlawful way.

ACCIDENTAL VEIN □ An imprecise term that refers generally to a continuous body of a mineral or mineralized rock filling a seam other than the principal vein that led to the discovery of the mining claim or location. □

The owner of a discovery vein, which is the basis of locating and determining the size of the claim, may or may not have rights in an accidental vein.

ACCIDENTS OF NAVIGATION □ Mishaps that are peculiar to travel by sea or to normal navigation; accidents caused at sea by the action of the elements, rather than by a failure to exercise good seamanship. Such accidents could not have been avoided by the exercise of nautical skill or prudence. □

ACCOMMODATION □ An arrangement or an agreement freely made for the benefit of another, not in exchange for consideration being received; something done to help someone else obtain credit whether in the form of a loan or COMMERCIAL PAPER. □

ACCOMMODATION ENDORSEMENT □ The act of a third person—the ACCOMMODATION PARTY—in writing his or her name on the back of a COMMERCIAL PAPER without any CONSIDERATION, but merely to benefit the person to whom the paper is payable or to enable the person who made the document—the MAKER—to obtain money or credit on it. □

An accommodation endorsement is a loan of the endorser's credit up to the face amount of the paper.

ACCOMMODATION PAPER □ A type of COMMERCIAL PAPER (such as a BILL or NOTE promising that money will be paid to someone) that is signed by another person—the ACCOMMODATION PARTY—as a favor to the promisor—the accommodated party—so that credit may be extended to him or her on the basis of the paper. □

Accommodation paper guarantees that the money lent will be repaid by the accommodation party on the date specified in the commercial paper if the accommodated party fails to repay it. A lender often uses an accommodation paper when the person who is seeking a loan is considered a poor credit risk, such as a person who has a history of being delinquent in the payment of installment loans. By having a person who is a good credit risk cosign the promissory note, the lender's financial interests are protected.

An accommodation bill and an accommodation note are two types of commercial papers. For a sample of an accommodation paper, see the Appendix volume 11.

ACCOMMODATION PARTY □ One who signs a COMMERCIAL PAPER for the purpose of lending his or her name and credit to another party to the document—the accommodated party—to help that party obtain a loan or an extension of credit. □

A person wanting to obtain a car loan, for example, may offer a finance company a promissory note for the amount of the requested loan, promising to repay the amount over a number of years. If the company does not consider the person a good credit risk (one who will be able to repay the loan), it will request that someone else sign the note to ensure that the company will be repaid. Such a person may be an ACCOMMODATION ENDORSER, because he or she endorses the note after it has been completed, or an accommodation MAKER, because he or she must sign the note with the accommodation party.

An accommodation party is liable to the person or business that extended credit to the accommodation party, but not to the accommodated party. The accommodation party is liable for the amount specified on the ACCOMMODATION PAPER. If an accommodation party repays the debt, he or she can seek reimbursement from the accommodated party.

ACCOMPANY □ To go along with; to go with or to attend as a companion or associate. □

A motor vehicle statute may require beginning drivers or drivers under a certain age to be accompanied by a licensed adult driver whenever operating an automobile. To comply with such a law, the licensed adult must supervise the beginner and be seated in such a way as to be able to render advice and assistance.

ACCOMPLICE □ One who participates in a crime committed by another. □

An accomplice may assist or encourage the principal offender with the intent to have the crime committed, the same as the chief actor. An accomplice may or may not be present when the crime is actually committed. However, without sharing the criminal INTENT, one who is merely

Bank robber Clyde Barrow and his accomplice Bonnie Parker in 1934

present when a crime occurs and stands by silently is not an accomplice, no matter how reprehensible his or her inaction.

In many states, a person may be charged as an accomplice even though that person could not be guilty of the crime itself. The crime of rape, for example, is usually defined so that only a man may be charged with committing it, but a woman who helped him could be charged as an accomplice. Other crimes are so defined that certain persons cannot be charged as accomplice even when their conduct significantly aids the chief offender. For example, a businessperson who yields to the extortion demands of a racketeer or a parent who pays ransom to a kidnapper may be unwise, but neither is a principal in the commission of the crimes. Even a victim may unwittingly create a perfect opportunity for the commission of a crime but cannot be considered an accomplice because he or she lacks a criminal intent.

If there were no bad people, there would be no good lawyers.

CHARLES
DICKENS

An accomplice may supply money, guns, or supplies. In one case, an accomplice provided his own blood to be poured on selective service files. The driver of the getaway car, a lookout, or a person who entices the victim or distracts possible witnesses is an accomplice.

An accomplice can be convicted even if the person that he or she aids or encourages is not. He or she is usually subject to the same degree of punishment as the principal offender. In the 1982 decision of *Enmund v. Florida,* 458 U.S. 782, 102 S.Ct. 3368, 73 L.Ed.2d 1140, the Supreme Court of the United States ruled that the death penalty could not be constitutionally imposed upon an accomplice to a FELONY-MURDER, a crime leading to murder, if he or she had no intention to, or did not, kill the victim. Earl Enmund drove the getaway car from a robbery that resulted in the murder of its victims, an elderly married couple. Although Enmund remained in the car during the robbery and consequent killings and the trial record did not establish that he intended to facilitate or participate in a murder, he was sentenced to death, along with the persons who actually killed the victims, upon his conviction for robbery in the first degree. The Court reasoned that to condemn such a defendant to death violated the Eighth and Fourteenth Amendments to the Constitution which prohibited CRUEL AND UNUSUAL PUNISHMENTS in state prosecutions. The death penalty was an excessive punishment in light of the "criminal culpability" of this accomplice.

ACCOMPLICE WITNESS □ A person who was connected with a crime—either as a PRINCIPAL, an ACCOMPLICE, or an ACCESSORY— and is called to testify. □

Generally, there can be no conviction solely on the basis of what is said by an accomplice witness; there must be evidence from an unrelated source to CORROBORATE the witness's testimony. The victim of a RAPE cannot be considered an accomplice witness, for example, but a woman under statutory age who willingly has sexual intercourse with a man later charged with STATUTORY RAPE may be.

ACCORD □ An agreement that settles a dispute, generally requiring a compromise or satisfaction with something less than what was originally demanded. □

ACCORD AND SATISFACTION □ A formal settlement of a dispute wherein the parties agree to give and accept something other than what was originally demanded or required. □

The *accord* is a new agreement setting terms that resolve an underlying disagreement, and *satisfaction* is the execution or performance of that new agreement. To constitute an accord and satisfaction, there must have been a genuine dispute that is settled by a meeting of the minds with an intent to compromise. Where there is an actual controversy, an accord and satisfaction may be used to settle it. The controversy may be founded on contract or tort. It can arise from a collision of motor vehicles, a failure to deliver oranges ordered and paid for, or a refusal to finish constructing an office building.

In former times, courts recognized an accord and satisfaction only when the amount of the controversy was not in dispute. Otherwise, the resolution had to be by COMPROMISE AND SETTLEMENT. The technical distinction is no longer made, however, and a compromise of amount can properly be part of an accord and satisfaction. The amount, whether disputed or not, is usually monetary, as when a pedestrian claims $10,000 in damages from the driver who struck him. The amount can be a variety of other things, however, as when a homeowner claims that she ordered a swimming pool thirty-six feet long rather than thirty-five feet or when an employee insists that he is entitled to eleven rather than ten days of vacation during the rest of the calendar year.

An accord and satisfaction can be made only by persons who have the legal capacity to enter into a contract. A settlement is not binding on an insane person, for example; and an infant may have the right to disaffirm the contract. Therefore, a person, such as a guardian, acting on behalf of a person incapable of contracting for himself or herself may make an accord and satisfaction for the person committed to his or her charge, but the law may require that the guardian's actions be supervised by a court. An executor or administrator may bind an estate; a trustee can accept an accord and satisfaction for a trust; and an officer can negotiate a settlement for a corporation.

A third person may give something in satisfaction of a party's debt. In such a case, an accord and satisfaction is effected if the creditor accepts the offer and the debtor authorizes, participates in, or later agrees to, the transaction.

For example, a widower has an automobile accident but is mentally unable to cope with a lawsuit because his wife has just died. He gratefully accepts the offer of a close family friend to talk to the other driver who has been threatening a lawsuit. The friend convinces the other driver that both drivers are at fault to some extent. The friend offers to pay the other driver $500 damages in exchange for a written statement that he will not make any claim against the widower for damages resulting from the accident. The family friend and the other driver each sign a copy of the statement for the other, and when the payment is made, the accord and satisfaction is complete. If the other driver then sues the widower for more money on account of the accident, the widower could show that he agreed to let his friend negotiate an accord and satisfaction, and the court would deny relief.

An accord and satisfaction is a contract, and all the essential elements of a contract must be present. The agreement must include a definite offer of settlement and an unconditional acceptance of the offer according to its terms. It must be final and definite, closing the matter it covers and leaving nothing unsettled or open to question. The agreement may call for full payment or some compromise and it need not be based on an earlier agreement of the parties. It does not necessarily have to be in writing unless it comes within the STATUTE OF FRAUDS.

Unless there are matters intentionally left outside the accord and satisfaction, it settles the entire controversy between the parties. It extinguishes all the obligations arising out of the underlying contract or tort. Where only one of two or more parties on one side settles, this ordinarily operates to discharge all of them. The reason for this is the rule that there should be only one satisfaction for a single injury or wrong. This rule does not apply where the satisfaction is neither given nor accepted with the intention that it settle the entire matter.

An accord without satisfaction generally means nothing. With a full satisfaction, the accord can be used to defeat any further claims by either party unless it was reached by FRAUD, DURESS, or MUTUAL MISTAKE.

An accord and satisfaction can be distinguished from other forms of resolving legal disputes. A payment or performance means that the original obligations were met. A release is a formal relinquishment of the right to enforce the original obligations and not necessarily a compromise, as in accord and satisfaction. An ARBITRATION is a settlement of the dispute by some outside person whose determination of an award is voluntarily accepted by the parties. A COMPOSITION WITH CREDITORS is very much like an accord but has elements not required for an accord and satisfaction. It is used only for disputes between a debtor and a certain number of his or her creditors, while an accord and satisfaction can be used to settle any kind of controversy—whether

arising from contract or tort—and ordinarily involves only two parties. Although distinctions have occasionally been drawn between an *accord and satisfaction* and a COMPROMISE AND SETTLEMENT, the two terms are often used interchangeably. A NOVATION is a kind of accord in which the promise alone, rather than full performance, is satisfaction, and is accepted as a binding resolution of the dispute.

ACCOUCHEMENT ☐ The act of giving birth to a child. ☐

The fact of accouchement may be proved by the direct testimony of someone who was present, such as a midwife or a physician, at the time of birth. It may be significant in proving parentage; for example, where there is some question about who is entitled to inherit property from an elderly person who died leaving only distant relatives.

ACCOUNT ☐ A written list of transactions, noting money owed and money paid; a detailed statement of mutual demands arising out of a contract or a fiduciary relationship. ☐

An account can simply list payments, losses, sales, debits, credits, and other monetary transactions, or it may go further and show a balance or the results of comparing opposite transactions, like purchases and sales. Businesspersons keep accounts; attorneys may keep *escrow accounts;* and executors must keep accounts that record transactions in administering an estate.
☐ A sum of money deposited in a bank and subject to withdrawal by the depositor. ☐

Various banks may provide for savings accounts, checking accounts, time or interest accounts, or others.
☐ A statement of conduct. ☐

A man arrested for robbing a certain office supply store on July 13 will probably want to give an account of his activities that day if he can show that he could not have been in that place at that time.
☐ A business relationship with a customer, especially one that arises from sales transactions. ☐

An auto leasing firm might consider the local telephone company its best account if the company rents its entire fleet of cars from the firm.
☐ Any right to payment for goods sold or leased or for services rendered which is not evidenced by a CHATTEL PAPER. ☐

This includes an ordinary ACCOUNT RECEIVABLE and rights arising out of a ship charter.

The law is not a series of calculating machines where definitions and answers come tumbling out when the right levers are pushed.

WILLIAM O. DOUGLAS

ACCOUNT, ACTION ON ☐ A civil lawsuit maintained under the common law to recover money owed on an account. ☐

The action on account was one of the ancient FORMS OF ACTION. Dating back to the thirteeth century, it offered a remedy for the breach of obligations owed by fiduciaries. Originally, the action allowed lords to recover money wrongfully withheld by the bailiffs of their manors, whom they appointed to collect fines and rents. Later, statutes extended the right so that lawsuits could be brought against persons who were required to act primarily for someone else's benefit, such as guardians and partners. Eventually, the action withered away because its procedure was too cumbersome, and fiduciaries came under the jurisdiction of the special court of the king, called the CHANCERY.

An action on account is different from a modern-day ACCOUNTING, which is a settling of accounts or a determination of transactions affecting two parties, often when one party asks a court to order the other party to account.

ACCOUNTANT ☐ A person who has the requisite skill and experience in establishing and maintaining accurate financial records for an individual or a business. The duties of an accountant may include designing and controlling systems of records, auditing books, and preparing financial statements. An accountant may give tax advice and prepare tax returns. ☐

A *public accountant* renders accounting or auditing services for a number of employees, each of whom pays the accountant a fee for services rendered. He or she does more than just bookkeeping but does not generally have all the qualifications of a certified public accountant.

A *certified public accountant* is one who has earned a license in his or her state that attests to a high degree of skill, training, and experience. In addition to passing an accounting examination, a candidate must have the proper business experience, education, and moral character in order to qualify for the license. The letters CPA are commonly used and generally recognized to be the abbreviation for the title Certified Public Accountant.

The practice of accounting is a highly skilled and technical profession that affects public welfare. It is entirely appropriate for the state to regulate the profession by means of a licensing system for accountants. Some states do not permit anyone to practice accounting except certified public accountants, but other states use the title to recognize the more distinguished skills of a CPA while permitting others to practice as public accountants. All states limit the use of the title and the initials to those who are licensed as certified public accountants.

All accountants are held to high standards of skill in issuing professional opinions. They can be sued for malpractice if performance of their duties falls below standards for the profession.

ACCOUNTING ☐ A system of recording or settling accounts in financial transactions; the methods of determining income and expenses for tax and other financial purposes. ☐

There are various accounting methods. The *accrual method* shows expenses incurred and income earned for a given period of time whether or not such expenses and income have been actually paid or received by that time. The CASH METHOD records income and expenses only when monies have actually been received or paid out. The *completed contract method* reports gains or losses on certain long-term contracts. Gross income and expenses are recognized under this method in the tax year the contract is completed. The *installment method* of accounting is a way regulated utilities calculate depreciation for income tax purposes.

The *cost method* of accounting records the value of assets at their actual cost, and the *fair value method* uses the present market value for the recorded value of assets. *Price level accounting* is a modern method of valuing assets in a financial statement by showing their current value in comparison to the gross national product.
☐ One of the REMEDIES available to enforce a right or to redress a wrong asserted in a lawsuit. ☐

Where a court orders an accounting, the party against whom judgment is entered must file a complete statement with the court which accounts for his or her administration of the affairs at issue in the case. An accounting is proper to show how an executor has managed the estate of a deceased person or to disclose how a partner has been handling partnership business.

An accounting was one of the ancient remedies available in courts of equity. The regular officers of the CHANCERY, who represented the king in hearing disputes that could not be taken to courts of law, were able to serve as auditors and work through complex accounts when necessary. The Chancery had the power to discover hidden assets in the hands of the defendant. Later, courts of law began to recognize and enforce regular contract claims, as actions in ASSUMPSIT,

The law embodies the story of a nation's development through many centuries, and it cannot be dealt with as if it contained only the axioms and corollaries of a book of mathematics.

OLIVER WENDELL HOLMES, JR.

and the courts of equity were justified in compelling an accounting only when the courts at law could not give relief. A plaintiff could ask for an accounting in equity when the complexity of the accounts in the case made it too difficult for a jury or when a trustee or other fiduciary was charged with violating a position of trust.

Today, courts in the United States generally have jurisdiction both AT LAW and in EQUITY. They have the power to order an accounting when necessary to determine the relative rights of the parties. An accounting may be appropriate whenever the defendant has violated an obligation to protect the plaintiff's interests. For example, an accounting may be ordered to settle disputes when a partnership is breaking up, when an heir believes that the executor of an estate has sold off assets for less than their fair market value, or when shareholders claim that directors of a corporation have appropriated for themselves a business opportunity that should have profited the corporation.

An accounting may also be an appropriate remedy against someone who has committed a wrong against the plaintiff and should not be allowed to profit from it. For example, a bank teller who embezzles money and makes "a killing" by investing it in mutual funds may be ordered to account for all the money taken and the earnings made from it. A businessperson who palms off a product as that of a more popular manufacturer might have to account for all the profit made from it. A defendant who plagiarizes another author's book can be ordered to give an account and pay over all the profits to the owner of the copyrighted material. An accounting forces the wrongdoer to trace all transactions that flowed from the legal injury, because the plaintiff is in no position to identify the profits.

ACCOUNT PAYABLE □ A debt owed by a business that arises in the normal course of its dealings, that has not been replaced by a NOTE from another debtor, and that is not necessarily due or past due. □

Bills for materials received or obligations on an OPEN ACCOUNT may be accounts payable. This kind of liability usually arises from a purchase of merchandise, materials, or supplies.

ACCOUNT RECEIVABLE □ A debt owed by a business that arises in the normal course of dealings and is not supported by a NEGOTIABLE INSTRUMENT. □

The charge accounts of a department store are accounts receivable, but income from investments usually is not. Accounts receivable generally arise from sales or service transactions. They are not necessarily due or past due. Insurance may be purchased to protect against the risk of being unable to collect on accounts receivable if records are damaged or lost.

ACCOUNT RENDERED □ A statement of transactions made out by a creditor and presented to the debtor. □

After the debtor has examined the account and accepted it, an account rendered becomes an account stated.

ACCOUNT STATED □ An amount that accurately states money due to a creditor; a debt arising out of transactions between a debtor and creditor that has been reduced to a balance due for the items of account. □

A creditor agrees to accept and a debtor agrees that a specific sum is a true and exact statement of the amount he or she owes. The debtor may agree in words to pay the amount, or it may be understood that the debtor has accepted the account stated by failing to object within a certain period of time.

ACCREDIT
□ To give official authorization or status, as to accredit a hospital so that it can serve the medical needs of the community.
□ To recognize as having sufficient academic standards to qualify graduates for higher education or for professional practice.
□ In international law, to acknowledge; to send with credentials as an envoy. □

ACCREDITED LAW SCHOOL □ A law school that has been approved by the state and the Association of American Law Schools (AALS), the American Bar Association (ABA), or both. □

In certain states—for example, California—it is acceptable for a law school to be accredited by the state and not by either the AALS or the ABA. In most states, however, only graduates of AALS or ABA accredited law schools are permitted to take the state bar exam.

ACCRETION □ The act of adding portions of soil to the soil already in possession of the owner by gradual deposition through the operation of natural causes. □

Accretion of land is of two types: (1) by *alluvion*, the washing up of sand or soil so as to form firm ground; and (2) by *dereliction*, as

The study of the law is useful in a variety of points of view. It qualifies a man to be useful to himself, to his neighbors and to the public. It is the most certain stepping-stone in a political line.

THOMAS JEFFERSON

when the sea shrinks below the usual watermark. The terms *alluvion* and *accretion* are often used interchangeably, but alluvion refers to the deposit itself while accretion denotes the act. Land uncovered by a gradual sudsidence of water is not an accretion; it is a reliction.

□ The growth of the value of a particular item given to a person as a specific BEQUEST under the provisions of a WILL between the time the will was written and the time of death of the testator—the person who wrote the will. □

ACCRUAL BASIS □ A method of AC-COUNTING that reflects expenses incurred and income earned for INCOME TAX purposes for any one year. □

Taxpayers who use the accrual method must include in their taxable income any money they have the right to receive as payment for services once it has been earned. Any expenses that they may take as deductions when computing taxable income must be due at the time the deduction is taken. For example, a surgeon performed a tonsillectomy in October, 1979, and on December 31, 1979, he received a bill for carpeting installed in the waiting room of his office. He was paid the surgical fee on January 3, 1980, the same day he paid for the carpeting. The surgical fee will be included in his taxable income for 1979, the year in which he earned it, regardless of the fact that he was not paid until the following year.

His expenses for the carpeting can be deducted from his 1979 income because once he received the bill, he was bound to pay it. The fact that he did not pay for the carpeting until the following year does not prevent him from taking the deduction.

The accrual method of accounting differs from the cash basis method, which treats income as only that which is actually received, and expense as only that which is actually paid out. If the cash method were used in the above example, the payment of the surgical fee would be included as income for the 1980 tax year, the year in which it was received by the surgeon. The surgeon could deduct the cost of the carpeting only when he actually paid for it in 1980, although it had been installed in 1979.

Unearned income, such as interest or rent, is generally taxed in the year it is received, regardless of the method of accounting used by the taxpayer.

ACCRUE □ To be added as an increase, profit, or damage. □

Taxes are what we pay for civilized society.

OLIVER WENDELL HOLMES, JR.

Interest on money that a depositor has in a bank savings account accrues, so that after a certain time the amount will be increased by the amount of interest it has earned.

□ To come into existence. □

A CAUSE OF ACTION, the facts that give a person a right to judicial relief, usually accrues on the date that the injury to the plaintiff is sustained. When the injury is not readily discoverable, the cause of action accrues when the plaintiff in fact discovers the injury. This occurs frequently in cases of FRAUD OT MALPRACTICE. A woman, for example, has an appendectomy. Three years after the surgery, she still experiences dull pain on her right side. She is examined by another physician who discovers a piece of surgical sponge near the area of the operation. Although the injury had occurred at the time of surgery three years earlier, in this case the cause of action for medical malpractice accrues on the date that the sponge is discovered by the second doctor. This distinction is important for purposes of the running of the STATUTE OF LIMITATIONS, the time set by law within which a lawsuit must be commenced after a cause of action accrues. In cases involving injuries that cannot be readily discovered, it would be unfair to bar a plaintiff from bringing a lawsuit because he or she does not start the suit within the required time from the date of injury.

ACCUMULATED EARNINGS TAX □ A levy imposed by the Federal government on CORPORATIONS that accumulate their profits rather than pay them to stockholders in the form of dividends. □

The money accumulated must be beyond the reasonable operating or expansion needs of the business. The corporation must pay the accumulated earnings tax, in addition to corporate income tax.

ACCUMULATION TRUST □ An arrangement whereby property is transferred by its owner—the SETTLOR—with the intention that it be administered by someone else—a TRUSTEE, for another person's benefit—with the direction that the trustee gather, rather than distribute, the income of the trust and any profits made from the sale of any of the property making up the trust until the time specified in the document that created the trust. □

Many states have laws governing the time over which accumulations may be made.

ACCUMULATIVE JUDGMENT □ A second or additional judgment against a person who has already been convicted and sentenced for another crime; the execution of the second judgment is postponed until the person's first sentence has been completed. □

ACCUMULATIVE SENTENCE □ A SENTENCE—a court's formal pronouncement of the legal consequences of a person's conviction of a crime—additional to others, imposed on a defendant who has been convicted upon an INDICTMENT containing several COUNTS, each charging a distinct OFFENSE, or who is under conviction at the same time for several distinct offenses; each sentence is to run consecutively, beginning at the expiration of the previous sentence. □

A person must finish one sentence before being allowed to start the next one. Another name for accumulative sentence is *cumulative* or *consecutive sentence.*

The opposite of an accumulative sentence is a *concurrent sentence*—two or more prison sentences that are to be served simultaneously, so that the prisoner is entitled to be released at the end of the longest sentence.

ACCUSATION □ A formal criminal charge against a person alleged to have committed an offense punishable by law, which is presented before a court or a magistrate having JURISDICTION to inquire into the alleged crime. □

The Sixth Amendment to the Constitution provides in part that a person accused of a crime has the right " . . . to be informed of the nature and cause of the accusation." This means that in any Federal criminal prosecution, the statute setting forth the crime in the accusation must define the offense in sufficiently clear terms so that an average person will be informed of the acts that come within its scope, and the charge must inform the accused in clear and unambiguous langauge of the offense with which he or she is being charged under the statute. An accused has the same rights when charged with violating state criminal law because the Due Process Clause of the Fourteenth Amendment has applied the guarantees of the Sixth Amendment to the states. The paper in which the accusation is set forth—such as an INDICTMENT, INFORMATION, or COMPLAINT—is called an *accusatory instrument.*

ACCUSATORY BODY □ A certain number of people chosen according to law, such as a GRAND JURY, to hear evidence so that they can decide whether or not to charge a person with a crime. □

An accusatory body differs from a petit jury, which is the ordinary jury chosen for the trial of a criminal action to determine the guilt or the innocence of the accused.

ACCUSED □ A defendant in a criminal prosecution. □

Within the meaning of the Sixth-Amendment guarantee of a speedy trial, a person becomes an "accused" only when an INDICTMENT or INFORMATION has been returned against the person or when actual restraints are imposed on the person's liberty by ARREST, whichever occurs first. See also, Craig R. Ducat's essay on Speedy Trial.

ACKNOWLEDGMENT □ The admission of an obligation or the incurring of a responsibility. □

The partial payment of a debt, for example, is considered an acknowledgment of it for purposes of tolling the statute of limitations—the time set by law for bringing a lawsuit—based on a person's failure to repay a debtor. State law usually gives a creditor six years from the date a debt is due, according to the creditor's contract with the debtor, to sue for nonpayment. If, on the last day of the fifth year, the debtor repays any part of the loan, the statute of limitations is tolled or suspended. The creditor then has another six years from the date of partial payment to sue the debtor for the balance of the loan. The debtor's partial payment indicates acceptance of responsibility to pay the loan. If the debtor had not paid anything, he or she would have escaped liability six years after the date the loan was due. □ The admission of paternity of an illegitimate child. □

An acknowledgment of paternity means recognition of parental duties—such as financial support of an illegitimate child—by written agreement, verbal declaration, or conduct of the father towards the mother and child that clearly demonstrates recognition of paternity.
□ The formal declaration made before a proper officer by a person who has completed a document stating that it is his or her genuine expression. □

The requirement for acknowledgments on certain documents—such as DEEDS transferring the ownership of real property, WILLS giving the ownership of property to a decedent's HEIRS after death, or DOCUMENTARY EVIDENCE that is to be admitted in a legal proceeding—is established by state law. If such documents do not contain acknowledgments, they are ineffective and cannot be used in any legal proceedings.

Any or all of the parties to a document may be required to acknowledge it. Only those per-

Those who make the attack ought to be very well prepared to support it.

J. ROOKE

sons specified by law, a NOTARY PUBLIC for example, may take an acknowledgment. Usually, a person making an acknowledgment does not have to explain the contents of the document to the person taking the acknowledgment. A person who ordinarily takes an acknowledgment might be disqualified from doing so if that person stands to gain some benefit from or has a financial interest in the outcome of the transaction. For example, state law requires a person making a will, a testator, to make an acknowledgment to a certain number of witnesses that the document is the genuine expression of how that person wants his or her property disposed of upon his or her death. Suppose the state requires two witnesses. If the people selected as witnesses have financial interests in the person's will, they will be disqualified for purposes of acknowledgment. This is done to deter dishonest people from fabricating a document that is beneficial to them. Such a will is legally ineffective; once the testator dies, his or her property will be transferred according to the laws of DESCENT AND DISTRIBUTION.

A certificate of acknowledgment, sometimes referred to as the acknowledgment, is evidence that the acknowledgment has been done properly. Although its contents may vary from state to state, the certificate must recite: (1) that acknowledgment before the proper officer was made by the person who completed the document; (2) the place where the acknowledgment took place; and (3) the name and authority of the officer. The certificate may be on the document itself or may be attached to it as a separate instrument.

A COELO USQUE AD CENTRUM   [*Latin, "From the heavens to the center of the earth."*]

This maxim describes the right of ownership of a landowner to the heavens above his or her property as well as to the lowest depths of the soil. In recent years this doctrine has been severely limited by the rights of commercial and private airplanes to use air corridors, and by oil and gas regulations.

A CONTRARIO SENSU   [*Latin, "In the opposite sense; on the other hand."*]

ACQUIESCENCE   □ Conduct recognizing the existence of a transaction and intended to permit the transaction to be carried into effect; a tacit agreement; consent inferred from silence. □

For example, a new beer company is concerned that the proposed label for its beer might infringe the TRADEMARK of its competitor. It submits the label to its competitor's general counsel who does not object to its use. The new company files an application to register the label as its trademark in the Patent Office and starts to use the label on the market. The competitor does not file any objection in the Patent Office. Several years later, the competitor sues the new company for infringing its trademark and demands an ACCOUNTING of the new company's profits for the years it has been using the label. A court will refuse the accounting, since by its acquiescence, the competitor tacitly approved the use of the label. The competitor, however, might be entitled to an INJUNCTION barring the new company from further use of its trademark if it is so similar to the competitor's label as to amount to an infringement.

Acquiescence is not the same as LACHES, an omission to do what the law requires to protect one's rights under circumstances misleading or prejudicing the person being sued. Acquiescence relates to inaction during the performance of an act. The failure of the competitor's general counsel to object to the use of the label and to the registration of the label as a trademark in the Patent Office is acquiescence. Failure to sue the company until after several years had elapsed from the first time the label had been used is laches.

ACQUISITION CHARGE   □ A fee imposed upon a borrower who satisfies a loan prior to the date of payment specified in the loan agreement. □

Many home MORTGAGES provide that if the persons who borrowed the money want to repay their mortgage within two years, they must pay an acquisition charge of a small percentage of the outstanding balance of the mortgage. *Prepayment penalty* is another name for acquisition charge.

ACQUISITION OF TERRITORY   See Territory, National.

ACQUIT   □ To relieve potential liability for an obligation, burden, or accusation; to legally certify the innocence of a person charged with a CRIME. □

ACQUITTAL   □ The legal and formal certification of the innocence of a person who has been charged with a crime. □

Library of Congress

A sentimental
painting by William
Henry Simmons of a
righteous man who
has been acquitted
and restored to his
family

Acquittals *in fact* take place when a jury finds a VERDICT of not guilty. Acquittals *in law* take place by operation of law such as when a person has been charged as an ACCESSORY to the crime of ROBBERY and the PRINCIPAL has been acquitted.

ACT □ Something done; usually, something done intentionally or voluntarily or with a purpose. □

The term encompasses not only physical acts—such as turning on the water or purchasing a gun—but also refers to more intangible acts—such as adopting a decree, edict, law, judgment, award, or determination. An act may be a private act, done by an individual managing his or her personal affairs, or it may be a public act, done by an official, a council, or a court. When a bill is favorably acted upon in the process of LEGISLATION, it becomes an act.

ACTIO [*Latin, "A right or cause of action."*]

In the civil law system that prevails in most of Europe and Latin America, *actio* means both the legal proceeding to enforce a right and the right itself.

ACTION
□ Conduct; behavior; something done; a series of acts.

□ A case or lawsuit; a legal and formal demand for enforcement of one's rights against another party asserted in a court of justice. □

The term *action* includes all the proceedings attendant upon a legal demand, its adjudication, and its denial or its enforcement by a court. Specifically, it is the legal proceedings, while a CAUSE OF ACTION is the underlying right that gives rise to them. In casual conversation, *action* and *cause of action* may be used interchangeably, but they are more properly distinguished. At one time, it was more correct to speak of actions AT LAW and of proceedings or suits in EQUITY. The distinction is rather technical, however, and not significant since the merger of law and equity. The term *action* is used more often for civil lawsuits than for criminal proceedings.

Parties in an action A person must have some sort of legal right before starting an action. That legal right implies a duty owed to one person by another, whether it is a duty to do something or a duty not to do something. When the other person acts wrongfully or fails to act as the law requires, such behavior is a breach, or violation, of that person's legal duty. If that breach causes harm, it is the basis for a cause of action. The injured person may seek redress by starting an action in court.

The person who starts the action is the PLAINTIFF, and the person sued is the DEFEN-

The acts of today may become the precedents of tomorrow.

FARRER HERSCHELL

DANT. They are the PARTIES in the action. Frequently, there are multiple parties on a side. The defendant may assert a DEFENSE which, if true, will defeat the plaintiff's claim. A COUNTERCLAIM may be made by the defendant against the plaintiff or a CROSS-CLAIM against another party on the same side of the lawsuit. The law may permit JOINDER of two or more claims, such as an action for property damage and an action for personal injuries, after one auto accident; or it may require CONSOLIDATION OF ACTIONS by an order of the court. Where prejudice or injustice is likely to result, the court may order a SEVERANCE of actions into different lawsuits for different parties.

Commencement of an action The time when an action may begin depends on the kind of action involved. A plaintiff cannot start a lawsuit until the cause of action has accrued. For example, a man who wants to use a parcel of land for a store where only houses are allowed must begin by applying for the VARIANCE from the local zoning board. He cannot bypass the board and start an action in court. His right to sue does not ACCRUE until the board turns down his request.

Neither can a person begin an action after the time allowed by law. Most causes of action are covered by a STATUTE OF LIMITATIONS, which specifically limits the time within which to begin the action. If the law in a particular state says that an action for libel cannot be brought more than one year after publication of a defamatory statement, then those actions must be initiated within that statutory period. Where there is no statute that limits the time to commence a particular action, a court may nevertheless dismiss the case if the claim is stale and if litigation at that point would not be fair.

A plaintiff must first select the right court, then an action can be commenced by delivery of the formal legal papers to the appropriate person. Statutes that regulate proper procedure for this must be strictly observed. A typical statute specifies that an action may be begun by delivery of a SUMMONS, or a WRIT on the defendant. At one time, common-law actions had to be pleaded according to highly technical FORMS OF ACTION, but now it is generally sufficient simply to serve papers that state facts describing a recognized cause of action. If this SERVICE OF PROCESS is done properly, the defendant has fair notice of the claim made against him or her and the court acquires jurisdiction over him or her. In some cases, the law requires delivery of the summons or writ to a specified public officer such as a U.S. marshal, who becomes responsible for serving it on the defendant.

Termination of an action After an action is commenced, it is said to be PENDING until termination. While the action is pending, neither party has the right to start another action in a different court over the same dispute or to do any act that would make the court's decision futile.

A lawsuit may be terminated because of DISMISSAL before both sides have fully argued the merits of their cases at trial. It can also be ended because of COMPROMISE AND SETTLEMENT, after which the plaintiff withdraws his or her action from the court.

Actions are terminated by the entry of final JUDGMENTS by the courts. A judgment may be based on a jury VERDICT or it may be a JUDGMENT NOTWITHSTANDING THE VERDICT. Where there has been no jury, judgment is based on the judge's DECISION. Unless one party is given leave—or permission from the court—to do something that might revive the lawsuit, such as amending an insufficient complaint, the action is at an end when judgment is formally entered on the records of the court.

ACTION ACTION's purpose is to mobilize Americans for voluntary service throughout the United States through programs that help meet basic human needs and support the self-help efforts of low-income individuals and communities.

ACTION administers and coordinates the domestic volunteer programs sponsored by the Federal government, which are linked by a commitment to a "bottoms-up" development process which fosters self-reliance and utilizes available human and economic resources to overcome conditions of poverty. Through special demonstration grants and programs, ACTION also tests new ways of bringing volunteer resources to bear on human, social, and economic problems. It identifies and develops the widest possible range of volunteer service opportunities for Americans of all ages and ethnic backgrounds.

ACTION is the principal agency in the Federal government for administering volunteer service programs. It was created as an independent agency under the provisions of Reorganization Plan No. 1 of 1971, effective July 1, 1971, and Executive Order 11603 of June 30, 1971, with legislative authority provided by the Domestic Volunteer Service Act of 1973 (87 Stat. 394; 42 U.S.C. 4951), as amended.

ACTION includes VISTA (Volunteers in Service to America), the Foster Grandparent Program, RSVP (Retired Senior Volunteer Program), the Senior Companion Program, VVLP (Vietnam Veterans Leadership Program), YVA

(Young Volunteers in ACTION), Income Consumer Counseling, and the Drug Abuse Prevention Program.

ACTION consists of a Washington, D.C., headquarters, and nine regional offices, supporting forty-nine individual state offices.

Domestic programs and activities

Foster Grandparent Program The Foster Grandparent Program was created in 1965 and offers to older men and women opportunities for close relationships with children having special or exceptional needs. It is an opportunity for older Americans to continue serving their communities and themselves in an active and meaningful capacity.

Foster grandparents are low-income persons, at least 60 years of age, who come from every kind of background. They receive both pre-service orientation and in-service instruction. Volunteers serve twenty hours per week, receive a stipend of $40 per week, as well as provisions for reimbursement of travel costs, a meal each day they serve, accident and liability insurance coverage, and a yearly physical examination.

Foster grandparents serve in schools and hospitals for retarded, disturbed, and handicapped children; in day care centers; in city hospital wards; in corrections institutions; in homes for disadvantaged, dependent, or neglected children; and in other settings within the community.

The foster grandparents' main purpose is to help provide for the emotional, mental, and physical well-being of children by affording them close, personal, and continuing relations with an adult. They furnish a fresh note of love and intimacy often missing in institutional environments. Among other responsibilities, they assist in feeding and dressing the children; they read, play games, and tell stories to them; and they aid in speech and physical therapy and other care-giving activities that tend to maximize the functional capabilities of these children.

Retired Senior Volunteer Program (RSVP) The purpose of RSVP is to create a variety of meaningful opportunities for persons of retirement age to participate, through volunteer service, more fully in the life of their communities.

RSVP projects are planned, organized, and operated at the local level, and are developed under the auspices of an established organization able to generate local financial support.

Volunteers must be at least sixty years of age and be willing and able to serve on a regular basis. There are no income or educational requirements. They perform various services according to community need and their preference

in a variety of settings—including schools; courts; and health care, rehabilitation, day care, youth, and other community centers. They also serve in outreach and advocacy roles within their community.

Senior Companion Program The Senior Companion Program provides meaningful part-time volunteer opportunities for low-income older persons to render in a mutually beneficial relationship and supportive person-to-person services to adults, especially older people with special needs in health-, education-, and welfare-related settings.

Under the sponsorship and supervision of an approved agency, the senior companion serves in and through a variety of settings: hospitals; institutions for the physically, emotionally or mentally handicapped; health care agencies; and private homes. Over 80 percent of the senior companions are serving older persons in their own homes in order to prevent or delay inappropriate institutionalization. The senior companion serves each assigned adult on a frequent and regular basis each week for as long as necessary.

National Center for Service Learning (NCSL) The National Center for Service Learning is the national resource center and information clearinghouse for service-learning. It promotes the development of service-learning nationwide by providing information and technical advice to interested schools, universities, community agencies, and national organizations. NCSL does not control local efforts, determine local needs, or place volunteers. It supports and fosters the growth of local, poverty-related service-learning efforts by:

- Producing and distributing manuals and other materials that provide information on the planning and implementation of successful programs;
- Sponsoring seminars that are designed and conducted by coordinators of exemplary service-learning programs, which cover topics such as the selection of work assignments, recruitment of students, fundraising and support activities, and program evaluation;
- Facilitating the exchange of information and expertise among service-learning educators through the publication of *Synergist* magazine, and other means;
- Collecting and distributing research data to encourage local program development; and
- Conducting demonstration projects to show new ways in which service-learning can be used to benefit communities and students.

Demonstration projects The Office of Policy and Planning has the responsibility of de-

Poverty is a great enemy to human happiness; it certainly destroys liberty, and it makes some virtues impracticable, and others extremely difficult.

SAMUEL JOHNSON

veloping special emphasis and demonstration programs which will focus on certain areas of concern where volunteers can make a special contribution in solving human and social problems. Present programs include the National Youth Community Service Demonstration, Mental Retardation, Criminal Justice, Economic Development/Income, Fixed Income Counseling, Energy, and Short-Term Volunteers. These demonstration models, if successful, and when possible, will be integrated into the agency's regular program operations and/or shared with the Office of Voluntary Citizen Participation, which will, as a technical assistance resource, distribute program models to the private voluntary organizations which have an interest and desire to replicate them.

The Urban Crime Prevention Program (UCPP) The Urban Crime Prevention Program, coadministered by ACTION and the Law Enforcement Assistance Administration, utilizes volunteers through private, nonprofit organizations in cities of 150,000 or more to develop crime prevention projects for low- and moderate-income neighborhoods. Initiated in 1980, UCPP focuses primarily on community dispute settlement, arson, property crime victimization, and victim/witness assistance, as well as locally designed crime prevention projects. Volunteers in the UCPP may be community residents who volunteer a few hours a week, full-time volunteers who receive a living allowance, or members of established volunteer organizations whose interests coincide with those of local projects.

Vietnam Veterans Leadership Program (VVLP) The Vietnam Veterans Leadership Program is a voluntary program created in July 1981 to encourage Vietnam veterans to serve as volunteers to help their fellow veterans with special needs; to ensure effective help for approximately 500,000 Vietnam veterans who still have significant lingering problems associated with their Vietnam experience, such as underemployment or unemployment; and to demonstrate the leadership capabilities of the Vietnam veteran.

The volunteers work at senior levels of the community's business and government structure to help the community build and maintain a coordinated community-wide effort to help the Vietnam veteran.

The program stimulates the flow of new, able volunteers to complement and reinforce existing government and veterans organization programs.

The program has both practical and symbolic impact. It:

- Recruits a significant number of Vietnam veterans to serve in a voluntary capacity who are not now involved in efforts to assist those Vietnam veterans with particular needs;
- Recognizes that Vietnam veterans are a leadership resource; and
- Affects national defense by affirming the integrity of military service as an honorable profession.

Volunteers in Service to America (VISTA) The creation of VISTA was authorized by Congress in 1964, to provide constructive opportunities for Americans to work on a full-time basis with locally sponsored projects designed to increase the capability of low-income people to improve the conditions of their own lives. Volunteers are assigned to local sponsors which may be Federal or state agencies or private nonprofit organizations located in the United States, Puerto Rico, the Virgin Islands, and Guam. Volunteers serve for one year and work particularly on the problems of troubled youth, low-income elderly, and the disabled or handicapped.

Volunteers live and work among the poor in urban or rural areas, or on Indian reservations. They share their skills and experience in fields such as drug abuse, education/literacy, runaway youth, refugee resettlement, community design, weatherization, and economic development. Most volunteers are recruited locally for community projects; 30 percent are low-income persons. About 15 percent are age 55 and over. A VISTA volunteer must be a resident of the United States or one of its territories. He or she must be in good health. A physical handicap does not disqualify a volunteer, providing placement can be made on a VISTA project.

Volunteers participate in orientation and training sessions conducted by ACTION and sponsor personnel at the beginning of and during VISTA service. Volunteers receive a basic living allowance which covers housing, foods, and incidentals. Health insurance is also provided. An additional $75 a month is paid as a stipend upon completion of service.

Volunteer liaison programs The programs were developed to provide a link between ACTION and the private, voluntary sector in the United States.

The state offices of the Voluntary Citizen Participation Program, established in 1974, provide grants for developing the coordination of volunteer services from the governors' offices; in 1982, nine states were involved. The staff of these offices provide leadership, contact, coordination, and cooperation with the leaders of pri-

---

Though in a state of society some must have greater luxuries and comforts than others, yet all should have the necessaries of life; and if the poor cannot exist, in vain may the rich look for happiness or prosperity. The legislature is never so well employed as when they look to the interests of those who are at a distance from them in the ranks of society. It is their duty to do so: religion calls for it; humanity calls for it; and if there are hearts who are not awake to either of those feelings, their own interests would dictate it.

LORD KENYON

vate, voluntary organizations and with public agency volunteer coordinators in the states.

The Mini-Grant program offers seed money to volunteer programs seeking independence, but which need a small amount of money to get started, or to ongoing volunteer efforts for one-time needs. These grants often, in turn, generate other fiscal resources. The program offers access by the private, voluntary sector to small grants, up to $15,000, through streamlined procedures.

The Technical Assistance program offers grants to voluntary organizations for the purpose of increasing their capacities to respond to the training and technical assistance needs of volunteers and organizations undertaking voluntary efforts. These grants average $17,000 each.

Information Support Center ACTION's Information Support Center was created to develop a communication link throughout the growing and increasingly sophisticated support structure for voluntarism. This support structure includes national resource organizations, state offices, and local volunteer centers, as well as ACTION and other Federal agencies, and serves the entire voluntary sector of this nation. Through the creation of this center, ACTION has positioned itself to serve as a resource to the existing support network and, when indicated, to the local community. This is accomplished by a referral system, which leads inquirers to specific resources, and an information and technical assistance bank, which provides services that do not exist in the present network.

The center maintains an idea bank on programs with volunteer components, collecting, processing, and disseminating information on successful and notable programs in all fields of social and human concerns which involve volunteers in substantial and meaningful roles. Programs included in the idea bank are collected from public, private, national, and local resources. In addition to the program examples, the center provides the inquirer with information on organizations within the network which can add depth, through additional examples, and/or management and training information.

The Interagency Division of the Office of Volunteer Liaison oversees the agency's agreements with other Federal agencies. In general, interagency agreements are initiated and carried out to demonstrate voluntary approaches to address local needs or problems. Three interagency agreements administrered by ACTION are: the Community Energy Project (Department of Energy); the Refugee Resettlement Program (Department of Health and Human Services); and

the Youth Employment Service (Department of Labor).

ACTION is concerned with developing volunteer program models that can be adopted locally, statewide, or regionwide through the joint efforts of the public and private sectors. In addition to coordinating the existing interagency programs, the Interagency Division engages in design and development for the creation of new agreements with other Federal agencies or departments interested in promoting local volunteer approaches to accomplish their respective legislative mandates.

The Public/Private Partnership Division has responsibility for the establishment of working relationships between the agency and the private sector. The purpose of these relationships is to educate the public and to interest the private sector in meeting social needs through the generation of voluntary activity, financial support for volunteer organizations, and the establishment of creative partnerships between the corporate sector and the ACTION agency.

Source: *The United States Government Manual 1981/ 82* and/or *1982/83.*

ACTIONABLE □ Giving sufficient legal grounds for a lawsuit; giving rise to a CAUSE OF ACTION. □

An act, event, or occurrence is said to be actionable when there are legal grounds for basing a lawsuit on it. For example, an intentional assault is an actionable TORT.

ACTIONABLE PER QUOD □ Providing a legal ground for a lawsuit only when some special damage is shown. □

Words that are not obviously slanderous in normal usage may be shown to be slanderous because of surrounding circumstances or a veiled insinuation, for example. Upon such proof, the words can amount to grounds for a lawsuit for monetary damages. They are actionable per quod.

ACTIONABLE PER SE □ Legally sufficient to support a lawsuit in itself. □

Words are actionable per se if they are obviously insulting and injurious to one's reputation. In lawsuits for libel or slander, words that impute the commission of a crime, a loathsome disease, or unchastity, or remarks that affect the plaintiff's business, trade, profession, calling, or office may be actionable per se. No special proof of actual harm done by the words is necessary to win monetary damages when words are actionable per se.

Usage, in which lies the decision, the law and the norm of speech.

HORACE

Activism

UPI

As a judicial activist, Chief Justice Earl Warren interpreted the Constitution from a "liberal" or "progressive" viewpoint in order to extend a citizen's rights and restrain government control over the individual.

Notably, in the phrase *judicial activism,* activism describes a philosophy of or a method used by judges who interpret the U.S. Constitution imaginatively so as to promote values that the Constitution is believed to represent. Sometimes identified with "liberal" as distinguished from "strict" construction of the Constitution, judicial activism is usually reflected in a greater readiness to extend individual rights and invalidate statutes and other governmental acts in order to protect such rights. Judicial activism is sometimes applied also to describe the practice of interpreting legislation "liberally" to achieve some dominant purpose or value. Judicial activism is usually contrasted with judicial self-restraint and great deference to the political branches of government.

Activism and *self-restraint* are twentieth-century terms for an older phenomenon. From the beginning the U.S. Supreme Court, in particular, has had recurrent periods of activism. Activism might be said to have begun with *Marbury v. Madison,* 5 U.S. (1 Cranch) 137, 2 L.Ed. 60 (1803), which established judicial review of congressional legislation and led to the courts becoming the final arbiter of the Constitution. A recent period of expansive constitutional and legislative interpretation was the era during which Earl Warren was chief justice of the United States. While in modern times judicial activism has been commonly associated with the "liberal–progressive" philosophy of the Warren Court, one might see judicial activism in decisions of a very different kind throughout the Court's history—for example, the decision of the Court that the section of the Missouri Compromise prohibiting slavery in the North was unconstitutional because it deprived the slave owner of property (*Dred Scott v. Sanford,* 60 U.S. [19 How.] 393, 15 L.Ed. 691 [1856]).

During much of the history of the Supreme Court, activism and self-restraint have succeeded each other as the dominant judicial mode. Judicial activism was rampant during the first decades of the twentieth century when the Court invalidated economic and social legislation by the states as well as by the United States. That judicial attitude was epitomized in *Lochner v. New York,* 198 U.S. 45, 25 S.Ct. 539, 49 L.Ed. 937 (1905), in which the Supreme Court found in the Due Process Clauses of the Constitution economic and political theories that sanctified "liberty" of contract and invalidated regulation of wages and hours and other welfare legislation. Similar activism "from the right" also imposed narrow views of Federal powers, as against that of the states, and invalidated much Federal legislation, including the early New Deal enactments (for example, *United States v. E. C. Knight Co.,* 156 U.S. 1, 15 S.Ct. 249, 39 L.Ed. 325 [1895]; *Hammer v. Dagenhart,* 247 U.S. 251, 38 S.Ct. 529, 62 L.Ed. 1101 [1918]; *Schechter Poultry Corp. v. United States,* 295 U.S. 495, 55 S.Ct. 837, 79 L.Ed. 1570 [1935]; and *Carter v. Carter Coal Co.,* 298 U.S. 238, 56 S.Ct. 855, 80 L.Ed. 1160 [1936]; compare the majority

and dissenting opinions in *United States v. Butler,* 297 U.S. 1, 56 S.Ct. 312, 80 L.Ed. 477 [1936]). Those periods of activism gave rise to a strong philosophy of judicial self-restraint first in the opinions of Justice Oliver Wendell Holmes; later, Justices Louis D. Brandeis, Benjamin Cardozo, and Harlan Fiske Stone; and thereafter, Justice Felix Frankfurter. Judicial self-restraint is often supported by selected quotations from Professor James Thayer's "The Origin and Scope of the American Doctrine of Constitutional Law," 7 *Harvard Law Review* (October 1893): 129, 143, 144; and by Judge Learned Hand, both in his opinions and in *The Bill of Rights* (1958). In the Supreme Court, Justice Stone, dissenting in *Butler,* above, summed up that attitude saying: "while unconstitutional exercise of power by the executive and legislative branches of the government is subject to judicial restraint, the only check upon our own exercise of power is our own sense of self-restraint." And "Courts are not the only agency of government that must be assumed to have capacity to govern" (297 U.S. 1, 78–79, 87, 56 S.Ct. 312, 325, 329, 80 L.Ed 477).

Conservative judicial activism, often characterized by a narrow view of the extent of state and Federal powers, was typified by the decisions of the Supreme Court in 1904–1905. Its members were, *left to right, front row,* Henry Billings Brown, John Marshall Harlan, Melville W. Fuller (chief justice), David J. Brewer, and Edward D. White, *back row,* Oliver Wendell Holmes, Rufus W. Peckham, Joseph McKenna, and William Rufus Day.

The conservative activism of the early New Deal Court precipitated the "Court-packing Plan" of President Roosevelt in 1937. With the change in the personnel of the Court that followed, the philosophy of judicial restraint prevailed and no economic–social legislation was invalidated by the Court for decades thereafter. The new philosophy was reflected in the Commerce Clause cases, *NLRB v. Jones & Laughlin Steel Corp.*, 301 U.S. 1, 57 S.Ct. 615, 81 L.Ed. 893 (1937); *United States v. Darby*, 312 U.S. 100, 618 S.Ct. 451, 85 L.Ed. 609 (1941); *Wickard v. Filburn*, 317 U.S. 111, 63 S.Ct. 82, 87 L.Ed. 122 (1942); in other cases accepting large interpretations of legislative power: *United States v. Kahriger*, 345 U.S. 22, 73 S.Ct. 510, 97 L.Ed. 754 (1953); *Steward Machine Co. v. Davis*, 301 U.S. 548, 57 S.Ct. 883, 81 L.Ed. 1279 (1937); and in due process cases like *Nebbia v. New York*, 291 U.S. 502, 54 S.Ct. 505, 78 L.Ed. 940 (1934); *West Coast Hotel v. Parrish*, 300 U.S. 379, 57 S.Ct. 578, 81 L.Ed. 703 (1937). It reached fullest expression in cases like *Williamson v. Lee Optical of Okl.*, 348 U.S. 483, 75 S.Ct. 461, 99 L.Ed. 563 (1955); *Day-Brite Lighting, Inc. v. Missouri*, 342 U.S. 421, 72 S.Ct. 405, 96 L.Ed. 469 (1952).

Judicial self-restraint in such cases, however, did not prevent the rise of activism in the interpretation and application of the Bill of Rights and other safeguards for individual rights, for example those in the Fourteenth Amendment. Justice Stone had suggested a different standard for judicial review in such cases in the famous footnote 4 to *United States v. Carolene Products Co.*, 304 U.S. 144, 58 S.Ct. 778, 82 L.Ed. 1234 (1938). This "libertarian" activism soon led to: (1) the treatment of the First-Amendment freedoms as "preferred," with infringements subject to sharper scrutiny and upheld only when serving a compelling state interest; (2) "selective incorporation" of almost all of the provisions of the Bill of Rights, making them applicable to the states; (3) the extension of the rights of those accused of crime, and of new rights to prisoners, juveniles, and school children; (4) the establishment of the right to vote; (5) limitations on involuntary loss of citizenship; (6) the new right of privacy, for example, the right to use contraceptives or to terminate pregnancy; and (7) stricter judicial scrutiny and a requirement of a compelling state interest, where classifications were suspect (for example, race), or impinged on a fundamental right or interest. See also, Martin H. Redish's essay on Marbury v. Madison; Stephen B. Presser's essay on the Dred Scott Case; Sherri A. Moreines and Stephen B. Presser's essays on Schecter Poultry Corp. v. United States; Court Packing Plan; and NLRB v. Jones & Laughlin Steel Corp.; entry on James Bradley Thayer; Harold W. Chase's essay on Judicial Self-Restraint; and Louis Lusky's essay on the Carolene Products Footnote.

Bibliography: Alexander M. Bickel, *The Supreme Court and the Idea of Progress* (1978); Wallace Mendelson, *Justices Black and Frankfurter: Conflict in the Court* (1966); J. Skelly Wright, "The Role of the Supreme Court in a Democratic Society—Judicial Activism or Restraint?" 54 *Cornell Law Review* (November 1968): 1–28.

Law must be stable, and yet it cannot stand still.

ROSCOE POUND

ACT OF BANKRUPTCY □ A designation, made under the former Federal law governing the recourse creditors had against their delinquent debtors (which no longer applies under current statute), of specific types of conduct by debtors that would allow their creditors to proceed against them under that law involuntarily—without their consent. □

Under the prior Bankruptcy Act (11 U.S.C. [1976 Ed.] § 1 et seq. [1898]), a person was considered bankrupt if he or she (1) conveyed, transferred, concealed, removed, or permitted to be concealed or removed any part of his or her property with the intent to hinder, delay, or defraud all or any of his or her creditors; (2) transferred, while insolvent, any portion of his or her property to one or more creditors with the intent to prefer such creditors over other creditors; (3) suffered or permitted, while insolvent, any creditor to obtain a lien upon any of his or her property through legal proceedings and not having vacated or discharged such a lien within thirty days from the date thereof or at least five days before the date set for any sale or other disposition of such property; (4) made a general assignment for the benefit of his or her creditors; (5) procured, permitted, or suffered voluntarily or involuntarily the appointment of a receiver or trustee to take charge of his or her property while insolvent or unable to pay debts as they matured; or (6) admitted in writing his or her inability to pay debts and his or her willingness to be adjudged a bankrupt.

The present Bankruptcy Act (11 U.S.C.A. § 101 et seq.), which took effect on October 1, 1979, has eliminated the requirement that a specific act of bankruptcy occur before creditors can seek relief pursuant to an involuntary bankruptcy proceeding. As a general rule, debtors who fail to pay their debts as they become due are subject to involuntary bankruptcy proceedings by their creditors.

ACT OF GOD □ An event that directly and exclusively results from the occurrence of natural causes that could not have been prevented by the exercise of foresight or caution; an inevitable accident. □

Courts have recognized various events as acts of God—tornados, earthquakes, death, ex-

A 1964 major earthquake displaced one side of the main street of Anchorage, Alaska, leaving it 20 feet below the other.

UPI

Library of Congress

A powerful cyclone threatens a midwestern farm.

traordinarily high tides, violent winds, and floods. INSURANCE policies for property damage will exclude from their protection damage caused by acts of God.

ACT OF SETTLEMENT □ A statute enacted by Parliament in 1701 that provided that if the marriage of King William III and Queen Anne did not produce an heir, then the succession to the Crown was limited to the Princess Sophia of Hanover, granddaughter of King James I, and the heirs of her body, but only if they were Protestants. □

The Act of Settlement was the basis for the claim of the house of Hanover to the English Crown. King George I, the son of Sophia and the first of the Hanover rulers, ascended to the throne in 1714.

Among its various provisions, the Act of Settlement also provided that persons appointed to serve on the judiciary would remain on the bench for life, conditioned upon their good behavior. This enactment gave the judiciary freedom to render decisions without fear of retribution by the Crown. It required that both houses of Parliament act jointly to remove a judge from his office and established the salaries of the members of the bench. For the complete text of the Act of Settlement, see the Appendix volume 11.

I will drive a coach and six through the Act of Settlement.

STEPHEN RICE

Library of Congress

George I and the House of Hanover based their claim to the British throne on the Act of Settlement. The Act also provided that persons appointed to the judiciary would remain for life.

Charles H. McLaughlin

Act of State Doctrine

By recognizing the independence and legal equality of national states and by promoting amicable relations among them, the courts of one state will not ordinarily sit in judgment upon or give relief from grievances caused by acts of a foreign state committed within its territory (see definitions in *Underhill v. Hernandez,* 168 U.S. 250, 252, 18 S.Ct. 83, 84, 42 L.Ed. 456 [1897]; *Banco Nacional de Cuba v. Sabbatino,* 376 U.S. 398, 425, 84 S.Ct. 923, 928, 11 L.Ed.2d 804 [1964]). Recourse of persons injured by foreign acts of state may therefore be confined to diplomatic negotiations or to international claims. An action in a foreign court to impose personal liability upon a government officer or agent who executed an act of state would be ineffective unless it could be shown he or she had violated the laws or constitution of that state; even then success would depend upon the existence of an independent judiciary able to check the executive branch. Nor would U.S. courts impose liability upon a foreign government's officer or agent for acts authorized by that government within its territory, even if he or she later came within the court's jurisdiction (*People v. McLeod,* 25 Wend. 483, 1 Hill 377, 37 Am. Dec. 328 [N.Y. Sup. 1841]; compare *Horn v. Mitchell,* 232 F. 819 [1st Cir. 1916]). British courts avoid examination of acts of a foreign state, but also use the term *act of state* with reference to the immunity British officers may claim in British courts for injuries to aliens by acts outside British territory that are authorized or ratified by the British government. Because of the doctrine that the king (that is, the state) can do no wrong, act of state cannot be pleaded in the case of a domestic injury by a British officer to a British subject or resident alien (See *Buron v. Denman,* 2 Exch. 167 [1948]; *Johnstone v. Pedlar,* 2 A.C. [H.Lds.] 262 [1921]).

In the comparable conflict of laws situation where a court must decide whether foreign law should be given effect in a private international transaction, it may refuse, when to do so would violate public policy of the forum state. A suit to give effect to a judgment or order of a foreign court is rejected if that court assumed jurisdiction improperly or failed to observe acceptable standards of due process (*Hilton v. Guyot,* 159 U.S. 113, 16 S.Ct. 139, 40 L.Ed. 95 [1895]; *Johnston v. Compagnie Gènèrale Transatlantique,* 242 N.Y. 381, 152 N.E. 121, 46 A.L.R. 435 [1925]; *Ingenohl v. Olsen & Co.,* 273 U.S. 541, 47 S.Ct. 451, 71 L.Ed. 762 [1927]). However, in a case arising under a recent prisoner exchange treaty with Mexico, a Federal court reluctantly held that a Mexican sentence of imprisonment imposed on a U.S. national, after procedures that violated minimal due process, must be carried out after exchange because of the treaty obligation, the prisoner's consent to transfer, and the danger to Americans still imprisoned in Mexico if the treaty were not executed (*Rosado v. Civiletti,* 621 F.2d 1179, 1199 [2d Cir. 1980]). These policy considerations were thought to outweigh due process objections. There is a strong disinclination to support actions or requests for execution upon foreign judgments based upon foreign criminal laws, revenue laws, or political laws (*King of Prussia v. Kuepper's Administrator,* 22 Mo. 550, 66 Am. Dec. 639 [1856]; *Queen of Holland [Married Woman] v. Drukker,* Ch. 877 [1928]). A related public law exception is the general practice of refusing to surrender political offenders under extradition treaties (*In re Castioni,* 1 Q.B. 149 [1891]; *Karadzole v. Artukovic,* 247 F.2d 198 [9th Cir. 1957], *remanded,* 355 U.S. 393, 78 S.Ct. 381, 2 L.Ed.2d 356 [1958]; *United States ex rel. Karadzole v. Artukovic,* 170 F. Supp. 383 [S.D. Cal. 1959]; *Ramos v. Diaz,* 179 F. Supp. 459 [S.D. Fla. 1959]; compare *Jimenez v. Aristeguieta,* 311 F.2d 547 [5th Cir. 1962]).

As public policy exceptions are allowed in these situations, much professional opinion favors such exceptions to application of the act of state doctrine, especially when the act violates international law. The exception of *ordre public* has in fact been recognized in civil law countries (see cases and authorities collected in footnote 21 to Justice John Marshall Harlan's majority opinion, and footnote 1 to Justice Byron R. White's dissenting opinion in *Banco Nacional de Cuba v. Sabbatino,* above). But British and U.S. courts have only recently and hesitantly moved in this direction. This may be seen in the sequence of cases on nationalization of private property held in the territory of foreign governments.

In cases brought by persons whose property has been confiscated and sold, British courts have long refused to disturb titles acquired by purchase from the confiscating government, provided only that it was recognized by the British government and passed title to property confiscated in its own territory. In *The Helena,* 4 Chr. Rob. 3 (High Ct. of Admiralty 1801), the original owner of a ship then in the port of London was not allowed to recover the ship from a respondent who had bought it in Algiers from the Dey of Algiers after Algerine corsairs had seized it piratically. The doctrine was applied to the confiscation, in Russia by the Soviet government, of plywood owned by a Russian company, which subsequently was sold to a British company. Later, recognition by Great Britain of the Soviet government was taken to validate retroactively seizure and passage of title to the plywood (*Luther v. James Sagor & Co.,* 3 K.B. 532 [Ct. of Appeal 1921]; accord, *Princess Paley Olga v. Weisz,* 1 K.B. 718 [1929]; *Lazard Bros. & Co. v. Banque Industrielle de Moscou, same v. Midland Bank Ltd.,* 1 K.B. 617 [1932], A.C. 289 [1933]). In a case in the supreme court of Aden (then a British crown colony), the court sought to limit the act of state doctrine to confiscation of property from nationals, concluding that because the government of Iran had without compensation expropriated the Abadan oil refinery and oil stocks there, owned by a British company, there was a violation of international law that rendered the taking of title by Iran and the transfer of oil to a buyer invalid (*Anglo-Iranian Oil Co. v. Jaffrate* [the *Rose Mary*], in *International Law Reports* 316 [1953]). However, the Court of Chancery, while approving the judgment on the special facts of discriminatory confiscation, rejected the Aden court's effort to limit the act of state doctrine to confiscation of the property of nationals (*In re Claim of Helbert Wagg & Co. Ltd.,* 1 Ch. 323 [1956]), holding that the courts in earlier cases had expressed it in perfectly general terms.

The earlier U.S. cases stated the doctrine with little qualification, sometimes concentrating mainly on the question of whether a recognized government was involved (*Underhill v. Hernandez,* above; *American Banana Co. v. United Fruit Co.,* 213 U.S. 347, 29 S.Ct. 511, 53 L.Ed. 826 [1909]; *Oetjen v. Central*

But the law does not consist in particular cases; but in general principles, which run through the cases, and govern the decision of them.

LORD MANSFIELD

Leather Co., 246 U.S. 297, 38 S.Ct. 309, 62 L.Ed. 726 [1918]; *Ricaud v. American Metal Co.,* 246 U.S. 304, 38 S.Ct. 312, 62 L.Ed. 733 [1918]; *Moscow Fire Ins. Co. v. Bank of New York & Trust Co.,* 280 N.Y. 286, 20 N.E.2d 758 [1939], *aff'd per cur.,* 309 U.S. 624, 60 S.Ct. 706, 84 L.Ed. 1036 [1940]; *United States v. Belmont,* 301 U.S. 324, 57 S.Ct. 758, 81 L.Ed. 1134 [1937]; *United States v. Pink,* 315 U.S. 203, 62 S.Ct. 552, 86 L.Ed. 796 [1942]). In none of these cases was the fact that an act of state constituted a breach of international law brought in issue. Another dimension was opened by the two *Bernstein* cases, which involved the seizure and sale of a ship owned by a German Jew, then still a German citizen, by the Nazi government to a purchaser with notice. In the first case his suit was dismissed on the ground of act of state (*Bernstein v. Van Heyghen Freres S.A.,* 163 F.2d 246 [2d Cir. 1947]). In the second, brought after Germany's defeat and occupation, the Department of State submitted a letter suggesting that it would be inconsistent with U.S. policy to recognize a title that depended on the validity of Nazi racist legislation. The Court allowed this exception, rejecting an act of state plea (*Bernstein v. N.V. Nederlandsche-Amerikaansche Stoomvaart-Maatschappij,* 173 F.2d 71 [2d Cir. 1949]. This opened the possibility of avoiding the doctrine by an executive statement or a legislative act advising a court that application of it would be inconsistent with U.S. policy. In a landmark case, *Banco Nacional de Cuba v. Sabbatino,* above—a claim for the proceeds from the sale of the plaintiff's property, which had been confiscated in Cuba by the Castro government—State Department officers were understood by the circuit court of appeals to believe that the confiscation violated international law because it was discriminatory, a retaliation against a U.S. embargo on Cuban sugar, and without prompt or adequate compensation; but the letters in fact declined to express a position because the case was before the court. If they favored judicial consideration of the merits, they did not assert that application of the act of state doctrine would be inconsistent with U.S. foreign policy. The district court and the court of appeals found a violation of international law and held that it invalidated the confiscation. But the majority of the Supreme Court declined to determine this question, preferring to follow precedents which they interpreted as mandating immunity for acts of state even when they violated international law. They reversed and remanded the judgment. Justice John Marshall Harlan's majority opinion based the obligation to apply the doctrine not in any international or constitutional law constraints but in the need to preserve a proper balance in the separation of powers between the judicial and political branches of government. The Court seems unreceptive to ad hoc executive statements in determining this. In *First National City Bank v. Banco Nacional de Cuba,* 406 U.S. 759, 92 S.Ct. 1808, 32 L.Ed.2d 466 (1972), three members of the majority relied on a State Department letter, following the second *Bernstein* case, but two concurring and four dissenting justices thought they should not defer to executive opinion.

     The Supreme Court might be more receptive to more formal, general policy statements not directed to particular cases. The *Sabbatino* judgment was undone by congressional legislation (the Hickenlooper amendments) that directed courts not to refuse because of the act of state doctrine to make a determination of the merits when foreign acts of state impaired titles or other rights to property in violation of international law principles, which were stated in traditional terms.

Justice John Marshall Harlan wrote the opinion in the case of *First National City Bank v. Banco Nacional de Cuba.*

On rehearing, the district and appeals courts again found a violation of international law, and the Supreme Court refused *certiorari* (*Banco Nacional de Cuba v. Farr,* 383 F.2d 166 [2nd Cir. 1967], *cert. denied,* 390 U.S. 956, 88 S.Ct. 1038, 20 L.Ed.2d 1151 [1968], *rehearing denied,* 390 U.S. 1037, 88 S.Ct. 1406, 20 L.Ed.2d 298 [1968]). The second Hickenlooper formulation, "title or other right to property," has been narrowly construed. It was held not to apply to Castro's suspension of convertibility of pesos to dollars (*French v. Banco Nacional de Cuba,* 23 N.Y.2d 46, 295 N.Y.S.2d 433, 242 N.E.2d 704 [1968]), nor to deprivation of a contractual right to explore for, extract, and sell oil, even after a working field had been developed (*Hunt v. Coastal States Gas Producing Co.,* 583 S.W.2d 322 [Tex. Sup. 1979], *cert. denied,* 444 U.S. 992, 100 S.Ct. 523, 62 L.Ed.2d 421 [1980], *rehearing denied,* 444 U.S. 1103, 100 S.Ct. 1071, 62 L.Ed.2d 790 [1980]; *Hunt v. Mobil Oil Corp.,* 550 F.2d 68 [2nd Cir. 1977], *cert. denied,* 434 U.S. 984, 98 S.Ct. 608, 54 L.Ed.2d 477 [1977]). In *Alfred Dunhill of London, Inc. v. Republic of Cuba,* 425 U.S. 682, 96 S.Ct. 1854, 48 L.Ed.2d 301 (1976), four members of the majority agreed that the act of state doctrine applied to governmental but not to commercial acts, but the fifth would not apply this distinction. Lower Federal courts in recent cases have sought to replace this commercial act exception with a balance of interests tests (*Mannington Mills, Inc. v. Congoleum Industries, Inc.,* 610 F.2d 1059 [3d Cir. 1979]; *Industrial Investment Development Corp. v. Mitsui & Co. Ltd.,* 594 F.2d 48 [5th Cir. 1979], *cert. denied,* 445 U.S. 903, 100 S. Ct. 1078, 63 L.Ed.2d 318 [1980]; compare *Rosado v. Civiletti,* above). It must be said that these suggested limitations upon the act of state doctrine await sharper definition. See also, Charles H. McLaughlin's essay on Claims, International.

Bibliography: A. B. Conant, Jr., "Act of State Doctrine and Its Exceptions," 12 *Vanderbilt Journal of Transnational Law* (Spring 1977): 259–271; Louis Henkin, "Act of State Today; Recollections in Tranquillity," 6 *Columbia Journal of Transnational Law* (Fall 1967): 175–189; Louis Henkin, *Foreign Affairs and the Constitution* (1972); W. Harrison Moore, *Act of State in English Law* (1906); Alan C. Swan, "Act of State at Bay: A Plea on Behalf of the Elusive Doctrine," 1976 *Duke Law Journal* (December 1976): 807–910.

ACTUAL AUTHORITY ☐ In the law of AGENCY, the express and implied powers given to an agent by a principal to act for him or her. ☐

When an agent faithfully exercises actual authority, it is as if the principal acts. The principal is liable for the agent's acts and is bound by them. If the owner of an apartment building names a person as an agent to collect rents and to lease apartments, those functions are express powers since they are specifically stated. In order to carry out these duties, the agent must be able to issue receipts to the building's tenants for the rents that are collected and to show apartments to prospective renters if leases are to be signed. These powers, which are necessary if the agent's express powers are to be exercised, are called implied powers. Once the rental agent has collected rents and leased apartments, it is as if the owner has done so.

Actual authority differs from APPARENT AUTHORITY, powers that the agent seems to have been given by the principal, which in fact, have not been given. For example, the owner of the building offers it for sale and tells prospective purchasers to talk to the rental agent. A buyer enters a CONTRACT with the rental agent to buy the building and makes a deposit. If the owner then enters a contract to sell the building to someone else, a court will hold the owner liable for breach of the first purchaser's contract. Because the purchaser relied upon the apparent authority of the agent, it would be unfair to penalize the agent for doing what the owner wanted her to do. The owner is responsible for acts done by the agent while exercising apparent authority.

ACTUAL CASH VALUE ☐ The fair or reasonable cash price that goods can be sold for in the marketplace during the ordinary course of business. ☐

An item offered for sale under court order, and not in the usual course of business, does not usually sell for its actual cash value. A court-ordered sale frequently results in items being sold for much less than they would be in the open market because there are no additional costs—such as the salaries of sales staff, insurance on the goods, advertising, or packaging that is usually passed along to purchasers.

Actual cash value is synonymous with FAIR MARKET VALUE and MARKET VALUE.

ACTUAL NOTICE ☐ Conveying facts to a person with the intention to apprise that person of a proceeding in which his or her interests are involved, or informing a person of some fact that he or she has a right to know and which the informer has a legal duty to communicate. ☐

When such notice has been given to someone personally, it is called *express actual notice* or *express notice*. If a tenant notifies a landlord that the elevator is broken, the landlord has express actual notice of the defect. Should the landlord fail to repair the elevator and another tenant is injured while riding it, the landlord would be liable for the tenant's injuries.

Actual notice can be presumed if an average person, having witness of the same evidence, should know that a particular fact exists. This is called implied actual notice or implied notice. If the landlord had been with the tenant when the tenant discovered the broken elevator, the landlord would be considered to have implied notice of the defect.

ACTUARY ☐ A statistician who computes INSURANCE and PENSION rates and premiums on the basis of experience of people sharing similar age and health characteristics. ☐

ADAMS, John   John Adams (*b.* October 30, 1735; *d.* July 4, 1826 in Braintree—now known as Quincy—Massachusetts) achieved prominence as a jurist, a statesman, and as the second president of the United States.

John Adams (1735–1826)—lawyer, patriot, and second president of the United States.

A graduate of Harvard College, class of 1755, Adams was admitted to the Boston bar in 1758 and established a prestigious legal practice.

During the pre-Revolutionary War years, Adams spoke against many acts enforced by the British government, such as the Townshend Acts, which unjustly taxed items such as glass and tea. He joined the Sons of Liberty—a group of lawyers, merchants, and businessmen who, in 1765, banded together to oppose the Stamp Act.

From 1774 to 1778 Adams served as the Massachusetts representative to the Continental Congress. He entered the judiciary during this period and rendered decisions as chief justice of the Superior Court of Massachusetts from 1775 to 1777. In 1776 he signed the newly created Declaration of Independence.

After the war, Adams entered the field of foreign service, acting as Commissioner to France in 1777. In 1783 Adams went to Paris with John Jay and Thomas Jefferson to successfully negotiate the Treaty of Paris with Great Britain, which officially ended the Revolutionary War and established America as an independent nation. In 1785 Adams became the first United States minister to Great Britain.

Adams returned to America in 1788 and began service to the new government with his election to the office of vice-president of the United States. He was the first person to serve in this office and was reelected for a second term in 1792.

In 1796 Adams was elected president of the United States. He was the second man to hold this position, following the retirement of the first president, George Washington. During his term of office, Adams advocated naval strength; approved the Alien and Sedition Acts of 1798 (1 Stat. 566, 570, 577, 596), which increased the restrictions concerning aliens and imposed harsh penalties on any person who attempted to obstruct the government system; averted war with France; and selected the eminent John Marshall as chief justice of the Supreme Court.

In 1800 Adams ran for the presidency for a second term but was defeated by Thomas Jefferson.

John Adams wrote several publications, including *Thoughts on Government* (1776); and *Defense of the Constitutions of the United States of America Against the Attacks of Mr. Turgot* (1787).

Adams was the father of four children, and his son, John Quincy, served as the sixth president of the United States.

ADAMS, John Quincy   John Quincy Adams (*b.* July 11, 1767 in Braintree—today known as Quincy—Massachusetts; *d.* February 23, 1848

John Quincy Adams (1767–1848) was the sixth president of the United States and a determined opponent of slavery when he served in the House of Representatives (1831–1848).

in Washington, D.C.) was the son of the second president of the United States, John Adams. He became famous for his endeavors as a diplomat, jurist, politician, and as the sixth president of the United States.

In 1787 Adams graduated from Harvard College and was admitted to the Massachusetts bar in 1790. He entered foreign service in 1794, when he was selected as minister to the Netherlands for a three-year period; he followed this with a four-year appointment as minister to Prussia.

In 1802 Adams began the political phase of his career and served in the Massachusetts Senate. He became a member of the United States Senate the following year, representing Massachusetts until his resignation in 1808.

Adams returned to foreign service in 1809 and acted as minister to Russia for the next two years. In 1814 he participated as a negotiator of the Treaty of Ghent, which ended the War of 1812 between America and Great Britain, before again serving as a foreign minister, this time to Great Britain in 1815.

In 1817 Adams joined the cabinet of President James Monroe as U.S. secretary of state for an eight-year period. During this time, he was in-

The law, in all vicissitudes of government, fluctuations of the passions, or flights of enthusiasm, will preserve a steady undeviating course; it will not bend to the uncertain wishes, imaginations and wanton tempers of men. . . . It does not enjoin that which pleases a weak, frail man, but without any regard to persons, commands that which is good and punishes evil in all, whether rich or poor, high or low— 'tis deaf, inexorable, inflexible. On the one hand it is inexorable to the cries and lamentations of the prisoners; on the other it is deaf, deaf as an adder, to the clamors of the populace.

JOHN ADAMS

strumental in the drafting of the Monroe Doctrine of 1823, which advocated a policy of isolationism for America.

Adams became the sixth president of the United States in 1825 and ran for reelection in 1829, but was defeated by Andrew Jackson.

After the presidency, Adams served in the U.S. House of Representatives as a member from Massachusetts for a seventeen-year period, beginning in 1831. He opposed slavery and the gag rule, which prohibited open discussion of an issue and was frequently applied by southern representatives in the House.

Adams wrote a twelve-volume publication titled *Memoirs,* which was released to the public posthumously between 1874 and 1877 by his son, Charles Francis Adams.

ADAPTATION ☐ The act or process of modifying an object to render it suitable for a particular or new purpose or situation. ☐

In the law of PATENTS—grants by the government to inventors for the exclusive right to manufacture, use, or market inventions for a term of years—adaptation denotes a category of patentable inventions, which entails the application of an existing product or process to a new use, accompanied by the exercise of inventive faculties. Federal law provides: "Whoever invents or discovers any new and useful process, machine, manufacture, or composition of matter, or any new and useful improvement thereof, may obtain a patent therefor, subject to the conditions and requirements of this title."

The adaptation of a device to a different field can constitute an invention if inventiveness exists in the conception of new use and with modifications necessary to render the device applicable in the new field. The progressive adaptation of well-known devices to new, but similar, uses is merely a display of an expected technical proficiency, which involves only the exercise of common reasoning abilities upon materials furnished by special knowledge ensuing from continual practice. It, therefore, does not represent a patentable invention. Ingenuity beyond the mere adaptation of teachings as could be done by a skilled mechanic is required to achieve a patentable invention; inventive talent, rather than skill in adaptation, must be manifested. To entitle a party to the benefit of the patent statute, the device must not only be new, it must be inventively new. The readaptation of old forms to new roles does not constitute invention where there is no significant alteration in the method of applying it or in the nature of the result obtained. There is no invention if the new form of the result has not previously been contemplated and,

irrespective of the remoteness of the new use from the old, if no modifications in the old device are necessary to adapt it to the new use.

Invention is generally not involved where an old process, device, or method is applied to a new subject or use that is analogous to the old, or to a new use, or the production of a new result, in the same or analogous field. If the new use is so comparable to the old that the concept of adapting the device to the new use would occur to a person proficient in the art and desirous of devising a method of effectuating the intended function, there is no invention even though significant alterations have been made. The application of an old device to a new use is normally patentable only if the new use is in a different field or involves a completely novel function. In addition, the physical modifications need not be extensive, as long as they are essential to the objective.

In the law of COPYRIGHTS—the exclusive right of the author of a literary project to reproduce, publish, and sell his or her work, which is granted by statute—adaptation refers to the creation of a derivative work, which is protected by Federal copyright laws.

A derivative work involves a recasting or translation process that incorporates preexisting material capable of protection by copyright. An adaptation is copyrighted if it meets the requirement of originality, in the sense that the author has created it by his or her own proficiency, labor, and judgment without directly copying or subtly imitating the preexisting material. Mere minor alterations will not suffice. In addition the adapter must procure the consent of the copyright owner of the underlying work if he or she wants to copy from such work. The copyright in a derivative work, however, extends only to the material contributed by the adapter and does not affect the copyright protection afforded to the preexisting material.

In the law of REAL PROPERTY, with respect to FIXTURES (articles that were personal property but became part of the realty through annexation to the premises), adaptation is the relationship between the article and the use that is made of the realty to which the article is annexed.

The prevailing view is that the adaptation or appropriation of an article affixed to real property for the purpose or use to which the premises are devoted is an important consideration in ascertaining its status as a fixture. According to this theory, if the article facilitates the realization of the purpose of the real property, the annexor presumably intends it to be a permanent accession. Numerous other cases, however, allude to the adaptation of an item to the use to which the premises are designated, as merely one of the tests or factors that should, or must, be evaluated in determining that it constitutes real property. Other cases view the character of the use of the article annexed as significant.

The special construction or fitting of an article for location and use on certain land or in a particular building, which mitigates against use in another location, indicates that is was intended to constitute a part of the land.

The adaptability of an annexed article for use in another location is sometimes viewed as demonstrating the retention of its character as personalty (personal property), but this characteristic is not conclusive. Articles not designed to comprise the realty retain their character as personalty.

AD DAMNUM   [*Latin, "To the loss."*]
☐ The clause in a COMPLAINT that sets a maximum amount of money that the plaintiff can recover under a DEFAULT JUDGMENT if the defendant fails to appear in court. ☐

It is a fundamental principle of due process that a defendant must be given fair notice of what is demanded of him or her. In a civil action, a plaintiff must include in the complaint served on a defendant a clause that states the amount of the loss or the amount of money damages claimed in the case. This clause is the *ad damnum*. It tells a defendant how much he or she stands to lose in the case.

In some states, the *ad damnum* sets an absolute limit on the amount of damages recoverable in the case, regardless of how much loss the plaintiff is able to prove at trial. The reason for this rule is that a defendant should not be exposed to greater liability than the *ad damnum* just because he or she comes into court and defends himself or herself. In states that follow this rule, a plaintiff may be given leave to increase the amount demanded by amending the complaint if later circumstances can be shown to warrant this. For example, a plaintiff who sues for $5,000 for a broken leg may find out after the action has begun that she will be permanently disabled. At that point, the court may allow the plaintiff to amend her complaint and demand damages of $50,000.

In most states and in the Federal courts, a plaintiff can collect money damages in excess of the *ad damnum* if proof can be made at trial to support the higher amount. A defendant may ask for more time to prepare the case in order not to be prejudiced at trial if it begins to look as though the plaintiff is claiming more money than the *ad damnum* demands. However, the defen-

dant cannot prevent judgment for a higher amount.

ADDICT ☐ A person who habitually uses drugs or narcotics; an individual who has developed a physiological dependence on the use of a drug. ☐

Addiction to narcotics is not a crime in itself, but that does not excuse violation of related statutes. A person charged with possession or sale of dangerous drugs cannot use the defense that his or her self-control has been lost to addiction. It may be an offense to be under the influence of an illegal drug in a public place, even though being an addict is not illegal. While such a statute is intended to protect society from the dangers of drug abuse and the antisocial conduct of drug abusers, it generally is not necessary for conviction to prove that the defendant was disturbing the peace when arrested.

ADDITIONAL EXTENDED COVERAGE
☐ A provision added to an insurance policy to extend the scope of coverage to include further risks to dwellings. ☐

The provision may cover water damage from the plumbing or heating systems, vandalism or malicious mischief, glass breakage, falling trees, damage from ice or snow storms, or additional risks not otherwise covered by the liability policy.

ADDITIONAL INSTRUCTIONS
☐ A charge given to a jury by a judge after the original INSTRUCTIONS to explain the law and guide the jury in its decision making. ☐

Additional instructions are frequently needed after the jury has begun deliberations and finds that it has a question concerning the evidence, a point of law, or some part of the original charge.

ADDITUR ☐ An order that a court may enter to increase the amount of DAMAGES awarded to a plaintiff after the jury has returned a verdict for damages of a clearly inadequate amount. ☐

Damages assessed by a jury may be set aside when the amount is shocking to the judicial conscience—so grossly inadequate that it constitutes a miscarriage of justice—or when it appears that the jury was influenced by prejudice, corruption, passion, or mistake.

For example, a sixty-one-year-old woman was mugged in a hallway of her apartment building after the landlord failed to replace a broken lock on the back service entrance. She sustained a broken shoulder, a broken arm, and numerous cuts and bruises. Her medical bills amounted to more than $2,500. She sued the landlord for his negligent maintenance of the building, and the jury returned a verdict in her favor but awarded damages of only $2,500. Her attorney immediately moved for a new trial on the ground that the verdict was shockingly inadequate. The trial judge ruled that the jury could not possibly have calculated compensation for the woman's pain and suffering, an item that should have been included under state law. The trial judge, therefore, awarded an additur of $15,000. The effect of this order was to put the defendant on notice that he must either pay the $15,000 in addition to the verdict of $2,500 or a new trial would be held. The defendant weighed the disadvantages of investing time and money in a new trial and the risk of an even higher award of monetary damages by a sympathetic jury. He consented to the additur.

An additur is not justified solely because the amount of damages is low. For example, damages of $10,000 certainly will not compensate the family of a forty-four-year-old man who had been steadily employed as a plumber until he was permanently disabled in an auto accident. In such a case, however, the jury could have found that the plaintiff's negligence contributed to the cause of the accident and reduced the damages proportionately, as is permitted in most states.

An award of additur is not permitted in every state, nor is it allowed in the Federal courts. Under the rules that govern procedure in the Federal courts, a trial judge has the power to set aside a verdict for a plaintiff on the ground that the damages awarded are clearly inadequate, but then the judge's only recourse is to grant a new trial.

ADD-ON ☐ A purchase of additional goods before payment is made for goods already purchased. ☐

An add-on may be covered by a clause in an installment payment contract that allows the seller to hold a SECURITY interest in the earlier goods until full payment is made on the later goods.

ADDUCE ☐ To present, offer, bring forward, or introduce. ☐

For example, a BILL OF PARTICULARS that lists each of the plaintiff's demands may recite that it contains all the evidence to be adduced at trial.

ADEMPTION ☐ The failure of a gift of personal property—a BEQUEST—or of real property—a DEVISE—to be distributed according to the provisions of a decedent's WILL because the property no longer belongs to the testator at the time of his or her death or because the property has been substantially changed. ☐

There are two types of ademption: by extinction and by satisfaction.

Extinction Ademption by extinction occurs when a particular item of personal property or specially designated real property is substantially changed or not part of the testator's ESTATE when he or she dies. For example, a testator makes a will giving her farm to her nephew and a diamond watch to her niece. Before she dies, she sells the farm and loses the watch. The proceeds of the sale of the farm are traced to a bank account. After the testator's death, the nephew claims the proceeds from the sale and the niece claims that the executor of the estate should pay her the value of the diamond watch. Neither claim will be upheld. Once the farm is sold, the specific devise is adeemed by extinction. The proceeds from its sale are not its equivalent for inheritance purposes. In some states, however, if all of the proceeds had not yet been paid, the nephew would be entitled to receive the unpaid balance.

Since the testator no longer owns the diamond watch when she dies, that specific bequest is also adeemed by extinction.

Satisfaction Ademption by satisfaction takes place when the testator, during his or her lifetime, gives to his or her heir all or a part of the gift he or she had intended to give by his or her will. It applies to both specific bequests and devises as well as to a general bequest or legacy payable from the general assets of the testator's estate. If the subject of the gift made while the testator is alive is the same as the subject of a provision of the will, many states presume that it is in place of the testamentary gift if there is a parent-child or grandparent-grandchild relationship. Otherwise, an ademption by satisfaction will not be found unless there is independent evidence, such as express statements or writings, that the testator intended this to occur. A father makes a will leaving his ski house to his daughter and $25,000 to his son. Before death, he gives the daughter the deed to the ski house and he gives the son $15,000 with which to complete medical school. After the father's death, the daughter will get nothing, while the son will get $10,000.

After the son received the $15,000 from his father, there was an ademption by satisfaction of the general LEGACY of $25,000 to the extent of the size of the lifetime gift, $15,000. The son is entitled to receive the remaining $10,000 of the original general legacy. Since there was a parent-child relationship, there was no need for independent proof that the $15,000 gift was intended to adeem the gift under the will.

ADEQUATE □ Sufficient; equal to what is required; suitable to the case or occasion. □

A law that requires public utilities to provide adequate service does not create a right for customers to sue the electric company whenever the meat in their freezers spoils because of a power outage in the absence of negligence. Service does not have to be perfect in order to meet a standard of adequacy.

ADEQUATE REMEDY AT LAW □ Sufficient compensation by way of monetary damages. □

Courts will not grant equitable remedies like SPECIFIC PERFORMANCE or INJUNCTIONS where monetary damages can afford complete legal relief. An equitable remedy interferes much more with the defendant's freedom of action than an order directing the defendant to pay for the harm he or she has caused, and it is much more difficult for a court to supervise and enforce judgments giving some relief other than money. Courts, therefore, will compensate an injured party whenever possible with monetary damages, called the remedy at law since the days when courts of EQUITY and courts AT LAW were different.

ADHESION CONTRACT □ A type of CONTRACT, a legally binding agreement between two parties to do a certain thing, in which one side has all the bargaining power and uses it to write the contract primarily to his or her advantage. □

An example of an adhesion contract is a standardized contract form that offers goods or services to consumers on essentially a "take it or leave it" basis without giving them realistic opportunities to negotiate terms that would benefit their interests. When this occurs, the consumer cannot obtain the desired product or service unless he or she acquiesces to the form contract.

There is nothing unenforceable or even wrong about adhesion contracts. In fact, most businesses would never conclude their volume of transactions if it were necessary to negotiate all the terms of every consumer credit contract. Insurance contracts and residential leases are other kinds of adhesion contracts. This does not mean, however, that all adhesion contracts are valid. Many adhesion contracts are UNCONSCIONABLE; they are so unfair to the weaker party that a

Now, it is of great moment that well-drawn laws should themselves define all the points they possibly can and leave as few as may be to the decision of the judges.

ARISTOTLE

court will refuse to enforce them because they shock its conscience. An example would be severe penalty provisions for failure to pay loan installments promptly which are physically hidden by small print located in the middle of an obscure paragraph of a lengthy loan agreement. In such a case a court can find that there is no meeting of the minds of the parties to the contract and that the weaker party has not accepted the terms of the contract.

AD HOC [*Latin, "For this; for this special purpose."*]

An attorney ad hoc or a GUARDIAN or curator ad hoc is one appointed for a special purpose—usually to represent a client, such as an INFANT or INCOMPETENT—in the particular action for which the appointment is made.

AD HOMINEM [*Latin, "To the person."*] □ A term used in logic to denote an argument made personally against an opponent, instead of against the opponent's argument. □

AD INTERIM [*Latin, "In the meantime."*]

An officer *ad interim* is a person appointed to fill a position that is temporarily open, or to perform the functions of a particular position during the absence or temporary incapacity of the individual who regularly fulfills those duties.

ADJACENT □ Lying near or close to; neighboring. □

Adjacent means that objects or parcels of land are not widely separated, though perhaps they are not actually touching; but adjoining implies that they are united so closely that no other object comes between them.

ADJECTIVE LAW □ All the rules of procedure that provide methods for enforcing rights or obtaining redress. □

Adjective law prescribes how the courts shall administer justice under the law. SUBSTANTIVE LAW creates and defines legal rights, the substance of the law.

ADJOINING LANDOWNERS □ Those persons, such as next-door and backyard neighbors, who own lands that share common boundaries and therefore have mutual rights, duties, and liabilities. □

The reciprocal rights and obligations of adjoining landowners existed at COMMON LAW but have been modified by various state laws and court decisions.

Rights, duties, and liabilities Landowners are expected to use their property reason-

U.S. Department of Agriculture

In situations such as the one shown here, where agricultural land joins urban development, the landowners involved have a heightened responsibility to use the land reasonably with regard to the rights of their neighbors.

ably without unduly interfering with the rights of the owners of contiguous land. Anything that a person does that appropriates adjoining land or substantially deprives an adjoining owner of the reasonable enjoyment of his or her property is an unlawful use of one's property. A man buys a house in a residentially zoned area and converts it into an office building. He paves the backyard for a parking lot, but encroaches two feet beyond his property into the lot of the adjoining landowner. His use of the property is unlawful for a number of reasons. He has appropriated his neighbor's land and substantially interfered with his neighbor's right to use it. His neighbor may sue him in a TORT action for the NUISANCE

created and if successful, will be awarded DAMAGES and an INJUNCTION to stop the unlawful use of the land. In addition, the purchaser has violated ZONING laws by using residential property for commercial purposes without seeking a VARIANCE.

Property owners have the right to grade or change the level of their land or to build foundations or embankments as long as proper precautions are taken, such as building a retaining wall to prevent soil from spilling upon adjoining land. If permitted by law, landowners may blast on their own property but will be liable for damages caused by the flying debris thrown onto adjoining land.

Lateral support An adjoining landowner has a legally enforceable right to lateral support, the right to have one's land in its natural condition held in place from the sides by the neighboring land so that it will not fall away. Land is considered in its natural condition if it has no artificial structures or buildings on it. A property owner can enforce the right to lateral support in court. A lawsuit for the removal of lateral support ACCRUES when the damage occurs, not when the excavation is done.

A landowner who excavates close to his or her boundary line has a duty to prevent injury arising from the removal of the lateral support of a neighbor's property. Because the right to lateral support is considered an absolute property right, an adjoining landowner will be liable for damages to the natural condition of the land regardless of whether or not he or she acted negligently.

When, however, an adjoining landowner has erected buildings on the land, his or her right to recover for deprivation of the lateral support is different. Since additional weight has been placed on the land, thus increasing the burden on the lateral support, the adjoining landowner can be awarded damages for injuries to the building caused by excavation only if his or her neighbor has been negligent. Sometimes local ordinances require that persons planning to excavate on their own property give notice to the adjoining landowners so that neighbors may take preventive measures to protect their property. The failure of owners who receive notice to take precautions does not necessarily absolve the excavator of liability for negligence. If, however, the excavator does not notify adjoining landowners, courts have treated this failure as negligence, and the excavator will be responsible for damages even though the excavating itself was not done negligently.

When evidence establishes that an adjoining landowner has removed the lateral support of a neighbor's land, the neighbor will recover damages in the amount of either the cost of restoring the property to its value before its support was removed or the cost of restoring the land to its former condition, whichever is less. An injunction prohibiting further excavation may be granted if it poses a clear danger to contiguous lands and if it will cause irreparable damage.

Subjacent support A landowner is entitled to subjacent support, the absolute right to have one's land supported from beneath its surface. If one person owns the surface of the land while another owns the subjacent surface, the owner of the surface is entitled to have it remain in its natural condition without subsidence caused by the subsurface owner's withdrawal of subjacent materials. An adjoining landowner who, during excavation, taps a subterranean stream causing the soil of the adjoining land to subside will be liable for any injuries that result. The surface owner's right to sue the subsurface owner for deprivation of subjacent support arises when the land actually subsides, not when the excavation is made.

The construction of buildings on the surface of the land does not lessen a person's right to subjacent support. It does, however, change the circumstances under which that person may recover for the removal of subsurface support. If such buildings are damaged, their owner must show that the removal of the support was done negligently.

Light, air, and view No landowner has an absolute right to light and air from adjoining property or to a view over adjoining lands. Zoning laws imposed by localities may, however, require that any construction undertaken by an individual not deprive an adjoining landowner of adequate air, light, and view. So too many agreements such as restrictive COVENANTS in DEEDS or EASEMENTS affect a person's duty towards his or her next-door neighbor's right to air, light, and view. In the absence of zoning laws or agreements, therefore, a person may build on his or her own property without regard to the fact that he or she is depriving the next-door neighbor of the light, air, and view that was enjoyed before the building was erected. An exception is a structure that blocks air, light, and view for the sole purpose of injuring a neighbor—such as a "spite" fence—and which is of no beneficial use or pleasure to the owner. Courts will generally not permit such structures.

Encroachments An encroachment is an intrusion upon the property of another without that person's permission. No person is legally entitled to construct buildings or other structures so that any part, regardless of size, extends beyond that person's property line and intrudes upon adjoining lands. An encroaching owner can be required to remove the eaves of a building that overhang an adjoining lot. If he or she refuses to do so, the owner of the contiguous lot may personally remove as much of the encroachment that deprives him or her of the complete enjoyment of his or her land, but if negligent, he or

Before the appropriation of land, he who gathered as much of the wild fruit, killed, caught, or tamed as many of the beasts as he could, did thereby acquire a propriety in them; but if they perished in his possession without their due use—if the fruits rotted or the venison putrefied before he could spend it, he offended against the common law of Nature, and was liable to be punished; . . .

JOHN LOCKE

she will be liable for damages. Should any expenses be incurred in the removal of the encroachment from the adjoining land, the person whose property was encroached upon can sue the owner to recover damages.

The person whose property has been encroached upon may sue the encroacher under either the theory of NUISANCE or the theory of TRESPASS to obtain monetary damages, or instead, may seek an injunction against continuation of the encroachment or to force its removal.

Trees and shrubs Landowners should not permit trees or hedges on their property to invade the rights of adjoining landowners. If an individual knows, for example, that a tree on his or her property is decayed and may fall and damage the property of another, that individual has a duty to eliminate the danger. A tree on the boundary line of contiguous land belongs to both adjoining landowners. Each owner has an interest identical with the portion standing on his or her land. Each can sever intruding tree branches or roots at the boundary line of his or her property, whether or not any injuries have been sustained by the intrusion, but reasonable care must be exercised so as not to kill the entire tree.

ADJOURNED TERM □ A continuance of a previous or regular court session that results from postponement. □

When a term is adjourned, it is actually prolonged due to a temporary putting off of the business being conducted.

ADJOURNMENT □ A putting off or postponing of proceedings; an ending or dismissal of further business by a court, legislature, or public official—either temporarily or permanently. □

If an adjournment is final, it is said to be SINE DIE, "without day" or without a time fixed to resume the work. An adjournment is different from a RECESS, which is only a short break in proceedings.

ADJUDGE □ To determine by a judge; to pass on and decide judicially. □

A person adjudged guilty is one who has been convicted in court.

ADJUDICATE □ To settle by a final judicial determination. □

Adjudicated rights, for example, are those which have been recognized and defined by a judge in court or by a hearing officer in a proceeding before an ADMINISTRATIVE AGENCY.

ADJUDICATION □ The formal pronouncement of a legal JUDGMENT in a CAUSE OF ACTION by a court or a determination of a controversy by an administrative body. □

See also, Glendon Schubert's essay on Adjudication.

ADJUDICATIVE FACTS □ Data offered to a tribunal for evaluation prior to the rendition of a judgment or decree by a court or a ruling by an administrative body. □

See also Carl A. Auerbach's essay on Adjudicative Facts.

AP/Wide World Photos

In 1916 socialist labor leader Tom Mooney was adjudged guilty of murder in connection with a San Francisco bombing. Although officials learned soon that Mooney had been convicted largely on the basis of perjured testimony, he remained in prison until 1939 when the governor of California pardoned him. Here Mooney, *left*, leaves prison after his pardon.

Glendon Schubert

Adjudication

Adjudication has evolved from a truly ancient mode of conflict resolution and policy making. Archaeology and legal anthropology jointly confirm that when the first cities arose in Mesopotamia eight thousand years ago, one of the first civil (as distinguished from theocratic or military) functions to evolve was the personal dispensation of justice to the people of a community by their recognized leader. It is, therefore, not surprising that people generally have strongly rooted conceptions concerning natural justice and due process of law, and that they identify these concepts with adjudication to a much greater extent than with legislation, administration, or political leadership.

In primitive and modern polities alike, the core function of the adjudicative process is to resolve disputes. A leading work on U.S. courts (Sheldon Goldman and Austin Sarat) distinguishes three types of disputes: private, public-initiated, and public defendant. Private disputes are between (or among) legal persons (including corporations as well as individuals or groups of natural persons) that are not recognized as constituting subdivisions of some level of government. This is the province of much of civil law. Public-initiated disputes involve some civil, but mostly criminal, law: agencies of government suing private parties, or sometimes each other. Public defendant disputes are a relatively modern development—at least their importance is (both qualitative and quantitative)—in what is almost exclusively civil law. They involve suits mostly by private parties, but sometimes by public agencies, against governmental agencies. Many public defendant suits are technically cases in administrative law, whereby citizens appeal in the regular courts for review of what are alleged to be illegal actions by public officials. Others are class actions with widespread implications, and are often symbolic. Examples range from conventional challenges to property assessments and other applications of tax laws to demands under the Federal freedom-of-information statutes for access to documentary evidence in the government's possession—which the private suitor may be able to use in some collateral proceeding involving, for instance, a legislative (rather than adjudicatory) hearing on environmental or energy policy.

The U.S. population increase has been paralleled by exponentially rising docket loads at all levels of U.S. courts. At the Supreme Court level, constitutional and political constraints on the number of justices have led to attempts to compensate bureaucratically. At other levels, appointment of more judges has been the main solution to rising case loads. However, Parkinson's Law has been confirmed, because delays in all courts—civil, criminal, trial, appellate—have increased as the judiciaries themselves have grown throughout the past half-century. In recent years this has led to widespread recourse, especially in urban slum areas, to *mediation* as a substitute for the adjudication that is not realistically available to the parties who are served by what often are called "neighborhood justice centers." At the other end of the political scale, the work of international courts conventionally *is* adjudicative. But multinational tribunals lack most of the essential attributes of domestic courts, including compulsory jurisdiction over the parties, widespread consensus on the legal norms to be applied, and the basis for getting decrees enforced (at least, in principle). Hence, realistically, the function of international courts is arbitration, occupying a position somewhere between the mediation of a neighborhood justice center and the adjudication of domestic governmental courts (national, state, or local).

In contemporary industrialized polities, the function of adjudication is the primary formal responsibility of judges—persons occupying a distinctive office characterized by unique authority and also unique restraints (Abraham). In the United States today almost all judges of the large political jurisdiction—metropolitan and state as well as Federal—are lawyers and law-school graduates, although judges without legal training continue to act in many local (especially rural) courts. Before the present century, the vast bulk of U.S. judges were not lawyers. The presumption now is that special training and experience in the practice of law are essential signs that a judge is competent to cope with the complexities of modern legal systems and law.

The U.S. Constitution itself has been interpreted to authorize a small but significant range of adjudicative functions to be performed by or in the name of the president and by members of both Houses of the Congress rather than by the judges appointed under Article III. Conversely, much time and attention has been centered, particularly during the past three decades, upon the nonadjudicative functions of U.S. courts at all levels. Typically, such nonadjudicative judicial functions are de-emphasized by their ascription (and denigration) as merely "housekeeping" tasks. In fact, they are concerned with executive, legislative, and administrative activities deemed indispensable to the relative political autonomy of the courts; they employ fiscal, statistical, and computer controls similar to those relied on elsewhere in modern government. Conversely, much of the personal authority formerly exercised by trial court judges in criminal cases, for example, now rests in the hands of a host of acolytes: psychiatrists, social workers, probation officers, parole boards, and other nonlegal specialists make the actual decisions whether and where and how persons adjudged criminal are to be rehabilitated or punished or otherwise dealt with.

Bibliography: Henry J. Abraham, *The Judicial Process*, 3d ed. (1975); Sheldon Goldman and Austin Sarat, eds., *American Court Systems* (1978).

Carl A. Auerbach

Adjudicative Facts

A case or controversy between private individuals or between private individuals and the government may involve disagreement about the facts, the law that should apply to the facts, or both. When the matter is brought before a court or administrative agency for adjudication, the tribunal must find the facts, determine the applicable law, and apply the law to the facts.

The facts that reveal what happened in the past to cause the controversy between the immediate parties are called the "adjudicative facts." They are unique to the disputing parties and usually answer the questions who did what to whom, when, how, and why. For example, in a lawsuit in which the plaintiff seeks to recover monetary damages for injuries sustained as a result of an automobile collision alleged to have been caused by the defendant's negligent driving in excess of the speed limit, certain adjudicative facts such as the speed limit and how fast the defendant was driving concern past events.

Adjudicative facts may also predict what will happen in the future. Adjudicative facts pertaining to the extent of the disability resulting from the injuries suffered by the plaintiff and the projected total loss of earnings attributable to the disability are predictions about the future.

The categorization of facts in dispute as "adjudicative" has legal consequences. The authoritative finding of adjudicative facts by a court or administrative agency will take place in the course of a "trial." By the testimony of the parties and witnesses, who will relate what they observed about the events in dispute, and by documentary and other evidence, the trial will seek to recreate what happened and lay the factual basis for predicting what will happen.

A trial by jury—or, in certain civil cases, by a judge alone—will involve principally a pretrial stage that will seek to delineate the following: the issues of fact and law in controversy; the subsequent presentation of witnesses and documentary and other evidence by the parties; cross-examination of the witnesses by the parties; right of the parties to compel, by subpoena, the testimony of witnesses and the production of other evidence; right of the parties to counsel; rules determining whether certain kinds of evidence may be presented to the tribunal or must be excluded; and, in a jury trial, the judge's instructions to the jury about the law that it should apply.

In a trial by jury, the adjudicative facts must be determined by verdict of the jury, not the judge. A trial of adjudicative facts before an administrative agency will usually be presided over by an administrative law judge. It will not have all the attributes of a trial by jury, or even a trial by a judge alone. For example, the rules of evidence governing judicial tribunals will not apply. But it will have the attributes, including cross-examination, that are essential to enable the parties to present their cases, hear the case against them, and offer rebuttals.

William Lizdas

Once the tribunal conducting the trial has found the adjudicative facts, they may not be overturned on appeal unless, in the case of a trial by jury or an administrative agency, there was no substantial evidence to support the findings, or, in the case of a trial by a judge alone, the findings were clearly erroneous.

Bibliography: K. C. Davis, *Administrative Law Treatise*, 2d ed. (1980), chapters 14–16; J. Michael and M. Adler, "The Trial of an Issue of Fact: I," 34 *Columbia Law Review* (November 1934): 1224–1306.

Because trials involve the authoritative finding of adjudicative facts,the judge and jury, *right*, listen intently to the testimony of a police officer concerning an automobile accident.

ADJUNCTION □ Attachment or affixing to another. □

Under the CIVIL LAW system which prevails in much of Europe and Latin America, adjunction is the permanent union of a thing belonging to one person to something that belongs to someone else.

□ Something attached as a dependent or auxiliary part. □

A branch agency, for example, is an adjunct of the main department or administrative agency.

ADJURATION □ A swearing; taking an oath to be truthful. □

To adjure is to command solemnly, warning that penalties may be invoked.

ADJUST □ To arrange or settle, freeing the matter from discrepancies or differences. □

Accounts are adjusted when they are settled and a balance is struck. An insurance adjustment is a determination of the amount to be paid under a policy to cover loss or damage that has been sustained.

ADJUSTED GROSS INCOME □ The term used for income tax purposes to describe gross income less certain allowable deductions such as trade and business deductions, moving expenses, alimony paid, and penalties for premature withdrawals from term savings accounts, in order to determine a person's taxable income. □

The rules for computing adjusted gross income for Federal income tax may differ from the rules in a state that imposes a state income tax.

ADJUSTER □ A person appointed or employed to settle or arrange matters that are in dispute; one who determines the amount to be paid on a claim. □

An insurance adjuster determines the extent of the insurance company's liability when a claim is submitted. A public adjuster is a self-employed person who is hired by litigants to determine or settle the amount of a claim or debt.

ADJUSTMENT SECURITIES

□ Stocks and bonds of a new corporation that are issued to stockholders during a corporate REORGANIZATION in exchange for stock held in the original corporation before it was reorganized. □

AD LITEM   [*Latin, "For the suit."*]

A GUARDIAN *ad litem* is a person appointed by a court to initiate or defend a lawsuit on behalf of another who is legally incapable of doing so, such as an INFANT or one who has been declared by a court to be an INSANE PERSON.

ADMINISTER

□ To give an oath, as to administer the oath of office to the president at the inauguration.
□ To direct the transactions of business or government. Immigration laws are administered largely by the Immigration and Naturalization Service.
□ To take care of affairs, as an executor administers the estate of a deceased person.
□ To directly cause the ingestion of medications or poisons. □

School teachers generally are not authorized to administer medicines that pupils take to school, for example.

□ To apply a court decree, enforce its provisions, or resolve disputes concerning its meaning. □

When divorced parents cannot agree on how to administer a visitation provision in a judgment granting child custody to one of them, they might have to return to court for clarification from the judge.

ADMINISTRATION

□ The performance of executive duties in an institution or business. The Small Business Administration is responsibile for administration of some disaster-relief loans.
□ In government, the practical management and direction of some department or agency in the executive branch; in general, the entire class of public officials and employees managing the executive department.
□ The management and distribution of the ESTATE of a decedent performed under the supervision of the surrogate's or probate court by a person duly qualified and legally appointed. If the decedent made a valid WILL designating someone called an executor, to handle this function, the court will issue that person LETTERS TESTAMENTARY as authority to do so. If a person dies INTESTATE or did not name an executor in his or her will, the court will appoint an administrator and grant him or her LETTERS OF ADMINISTRATION to perform the duties of administration. □

An executor or administrator must carry out the responsibilities of administration, including: collection and preservation of the decedent's assets; payment of debts and claims against the estate; payment of estate tax; and distribution of the balance of the estate to the decedent's heirs.

. . . how can institutions provide a good municipal administration if there exists such indifference to the subject that those who would administer honestly and capably cannot be induced to serve, and the duties are left to those who undertake them because they have some private interest to be promoted.

J.S. MILL

ADMINISTRATION, OFFICE OF

The Office of Administration was established within the Executive Office of the President by Reorganization Plan No. 1 of 1977 (42 FR 56101). The office was activated, effective December 4, 1977, by Executive Order 12028 of December 12, 1977 (42 FR 62895).

The Office of Administration, headed by the director, provides administrative support services to all units within the Executive Office of the President, except those services which are in direct support of the president. The services provided by the Office of Administration include information, personnel, and financial management; data processing; library services; records maintenance; and general office operations, such as nonpresidential mail, messenger, printing, procurement, and supply services.

Source: *The United States Government Manual 1981/ 82* and/or *1982/83.*

ADMINISTRATIVE ACTS

□ Whatever actions are necessary to carry out the intent of statutes; those acts required by legislative policy as it is expressed in laws enacted by the legislature. □

If a city commission votes to create the position of park superintendent, that is a LEGISLATIVE ACT that can take effect only if the commission follows all the steps required for formal LEGISLATION. When the same commission votes to rezone a parcel of real property from single-family residential to business uses, however, that is an administrative act that does not require the same formality as legislation. It is administrative because it is carrying out the zoning laws already in effect.

ADMINISTRATIVE ADJUDICATION

□ The process by which a government agency issues an order; a public agency's equivalent of a trial in court. □

Most formal proceedings before an ADMINISTRATIVE AGENCY follow the process of either RULE MAKING or adjudication. Rule making formulates policy by setting rules for the future conduct of persons governed by that agency. Adjudication applies the agency's policy to the past actions of a particular party, and it results in an order for or against that party. Both methods are strictly regulated by the law of ADMINISTRATIVE PROCEDURE.

ADMINISTRATIVE AGENCY

□ An official governmental body empowered with the authority to direct and supervise the implementation of particular legislative acts. □

An administrative agency has the power to influence the rights of private individuals, groups, and businesses. ADMINISTRATIVE LAW works to regulate agency actions and powers to ensure that individual liberties are not abused. See also, Carl A. Auerbach's essay on Administrative Agency.

The Suburban Division of the U.S. Resettlement Administration planned the construction of the entire community in Greenhills, Ohio.

Library of Congress

Carl A. Auerbach

Administrative Agency

Administrative agencies are governmental organizations created by the Constitution, Congress, state legislatures, and county and municipal law-making authorities to carry out the nation's laws and policies. These agencies vary greatly in structure, size, and purpose. The president of the United States functions as an agency. So does a local police department.

In our national government, the executive departments headed by cabinet officers consist of agencies. For example, the Food and Drug Administration (FDA) and the Social Security Administration (SSA) are agencies within the Department of Health and Human Services. In addition, agencies have been established outside these departments to implement particular laws and policies.

Some of these outside Federal agencies, like the Environmental Protection Agency (EPA), are headed by single administrators who, though appointed by the president with the advice and consent of the Senate, serve at the pleasure of the president. They may be removed by the president at any time for any reason. Other outside Federal agencies are "independent." They are usually headed by a board or commission consisting of three or more members who are appointed by the president with the advice and consent of the Senate, but may be removed by the president only for "cause" specified in the law creating the agency. The major independent Federal agencies are the Interstate Commerce Commission (ICC), Civil Aeronautics Board (CAB), Federal Power Commission (FPC), Federal Communications Commission (FCC), Securities and Exchange Commission (SEC), National Labor Relations Board (NLRB), and Federal Trade Commission (FTC).

Men register with the New York City Employment Bureau in 1914.

Library of Congress

James L. Shaffer

The Federal Aviation Administration is part of the U.S. Department of Transportation and, among other duties, operates the national system of air traffic control for civilian and military aircraft.

Agencies perform exceedingly diverse functions. They collect taxes (the Treasury Department's Internal Revenue Service), and they regulate certain industries or business activities: land, sea, and air transportation (ICC, CAB, and Federal Maritime Commission); gas and electric utilities (FPC); radio and television communications (FCC); investment markets (SEC); labor relations (NLRB); employment practices (Equal Employment Opportunity Commission); competitive trade practices (FTC); and environmental pollution (EPA).

Agencies also dispense benefits that promote social and economic well-being: for example, Social Security benefits (SSA); veterans' benefits (Veterans' Administration); unemployment insurance and worker's compensation (various state agencies); and assistance to the needy (welfare agencies). They provide services directly to people: postal service, police and fire protection, highway construction and maintenance, public education, public housing, and public hospitals. Agencies also license certain occupations and businesses: lawyers, doctors, taxicabs, morticians, barbers, racetracks, and liquor stores, for example.

It is estimated that about 15 million people are employed by the administrative agencies of the Federal, state, and local governments. About 100,000 Federal employees in eighty-three agencies are engaged in regulatory activity.

Despite traditional constitutional doctrine disapproving the combination of legislative, executive, and judicial powers, many important administrative agencies have a combination of these powers. For example, the EPA exercises legislative powers when it issues rules and regulations to minimize industrial pollution of the air. These rules and regulations have the force of laws passed by Congress. The EPA exercises executive powers when it monitors and publicizes pollution levels throughout the nation and subsidizes the construction of municipal waste treatment plants. It exercises judicial powers when it determines whether a business

Administrative agencies of government often take the lead in public service projects such as the construction of low-rent housing on the White Earth Indian Reservation in Minnesota.

firm has violated certain of its antipollution rules and regulations and then imposes penalties for the violation.

On the other hand, agencies like the Antitrust Division of the United States Department of Justice are empowered only to bring civil or criminal actions in the Federal district courts to enforce the antitrust laws.

Though administrative agencies exercise important powers, they are subject to a variety of controls. The legislature that created the agency may abolish it or curtail or modify its powers. Congress and many state legislatures have passed laws specifying the procedures that agencies must follow in exercising their powers. These administrative procedure acts give ordinary citizens and groups the opportunity to participate in the making of the agency's rules and regulations and to have their claims heard before the agency acts to affect them particularly. The actions agencies take are subject to review by the courts to assure their procedural regularity and reasonableness.

Bibliography: James O. Freedman, *Crisis and Legitimacy: The Administrative Process and American Government* (1978); James Willard Hurst, *The Growth of American Law: The Law Makers* (1950).

ADMINISTRATIVE BOARD □ A comprehensive phrase that can refer to any ADMINISTRATIVE AGENCY but usually means a public agency that holds hearings. □

An administrative board is usually obligated to represent the public interest; courts, in contrast, must remain impartial between the two parties before them. A parole board, for example, holds informal hearings where prisoners are allowed to offer evidence of their suitability for early release from prison. The strict rules observed in a courtroom do not apply to board hearings like these, and the board's decision must take into account the public's interest as well as the prisoner's rights.

ADMINISTRATIVE CONFERENCE OF THE UNITED STATES

The purpose of the Administrative Conference is to develop improvements in the procedures by which Federal agencies administer regulatory, benefit, and other government programs. As members of the conference, agency heads, other Federal officials, private lawyers, university professors, and other experts in administrative law and government are provided with a forum in which they can conduct continuing studies of selected problems involving these administrative procedures and can combine their experience and judgment in cooperative efforts toward improving the fairness and effectiveness of such procedures.

The Administrative Conference of the United States was established as a permanent independent agency by the Administrative Conference Act (5 U.S.C. 571–576) enacted in 1964. The statutory provisions prescribing the organization and activities of the conference are based in part upon the experience of two temporary conferences called by the president in 1953 and 1961, each of which operated for a period of eighteen months.

Membership The chair of the Administrative Conference of the United States is appointed by the president, with the advice and consent of the Senate, for a five-year term. The council, which is the executive board, consists of the chairman and ten other members appointed by the president for three-year terms. Federal officials named to the council may constitute no more than one-half of the total council membership. In addition to the chairman and the other members of the council, the membership of the Administrative Conference is composed of forty-four high-level officials designated from thirty-seven departments and agencies of the Federal government (or their designees) and thirty-six

private lawyers, university faculty members, and others specially informed in law and government. Members representing the private sector are appointed by the chairman, with the approval of the council, for two-year terms. The chairman is the only full-time compensated member.

The entire membership is divided into nine committees, each assigned a broad area of interest as follows: Agency Decisional Processes; Agency Organization and Personnel; Grants, Benefits, and Contracts; Informal Action; Interagency Coordination; Judicial Review; Public Access and Information; Regulation of Business; and Rulemaking. The membership meeting in plenary session is called the Assembly of the Administrative Conference, which by statute must meet at least once, and customarily meets twice, each year.

Activities Subjects for inquiry are developed by the chairman, the council, the committees, and the assembly. The committees, with staff assistance, conduct thorough studies of these subjects and develop proposed recommendations and supporting reports. The recommendations are evaluated by the council and, if ready for assembly consideration, are distributed to the membership with the supporting reports and are placed on the agenda of the next plenary session. The assembly has complete authority to approve, amend, remand, or reject recommendations presented by the committees. The deliberations of the assembly are public.

Although the Administrative Conference has the authority only to recommend changes in administrative procedures, the chairman is authorized to encourage the departments and agencies to adopt the recommendations of the conference and is required by the Administrative Conference Act to transmit to the president and to Congress an annual report and interim reports concerning the activities of the conference, including reports on the implementation of its recommendations.

Recommendations adopted by the conference may call for new legislation or for action on the part of affected agencies. A substantial number of recommendations have been implemented and others are in the process of implementation.

The chairman is authorized to make independent inquiries into procedural matters he considers important for conference consideration, including matters proposed by individuals inside or outside the government. The purpose of conducting inquiries into such individual problems is not to review the results in particular cases, but rather to determine whether the problems should be made the subject of conference study in the interests of developing fair and effective procedures for such cases.

Upon the request of the head of a department or agency, the chairman is authorized to furnish advice and assistance on matters of administrative procedure. The conference collects information and statistics from departments and agencies and publishes such reports as it considers useful for evaluating and improving administrative processes. The conference also serves as a forum for the interchange among departments and agencies of information which may be useful in improving administrative practices and procedures.

Source: *The United States Government Manual 1981/82* and/or *1982/83*.

ADMINISTRATIVE DISCRETION □ The exercise of professional expertise and judgment, as opposed to strict adherence to regulations or statutes, in making a decision or performing official acts or duties. □

A discretionary action is informal and, therefore, unprotected by the safeguards inherent in formal procedure. A public official, for example, has administrative discretion when he or she has the freedom to make a choice among potential courses of action. ABUSE OF DISCRETION is the failure to exercise reasonable judgment or discretion. It might provide a CAUSE OF ACTION for an unconstitutional invasion of rights protected by the DUE PROCESS CLAUSE of the Constitution.

ADMINISTRATIVE LAW □ That body of law which allows for the creation of public regulatory agencies and embodies all the statutes, judicial decisions, and regulations that govern them. □

The methods that governmental agencies use to do their work are regulated by the law of ADMINISTRATIVE PROCEDURE.

Agencies in the U.S. system of government An ADMINISTRATIVE AGENCY is a governmental body, other than a court or a legislature, that has authority to affect the rights of private persons, groups, and businesses. The statute that creates an agency may assign it a specific job, but often the statute defines the agency's powers in only general terms and gives it broad discretion in choosing how to do the job. Administrative law seeks to limit the powers and actions of agencies and to fix their place in our scheme of government and law. It is born of the tension created between the idea of an agency and other prevailing principles of law. Administrative law con-

trasts with traditional notions that the different branches of U.S. government must be kept separate; that they must not delegate their responsibilities to bureaucrats; and that the formalities of due process must be observed. Agencies are a streamlined part of government, but they may not ride roughshod over individual liberties.

Separation of powers The United States has a three-part system of government made up of the executive, the legislative, and the judicial branches. The Constitution sets up a system of checks and balances to keep any one branch from exercising too much power. Administrative agencies do not fit neatly into one of the three categories. They are frequently created by the legislature and sometimes are placed in the executive branch, but their functions reach into all three types of government.

For example, the Securities and Exchange Commission is a regulatory agency that formulates laws like a legislature. It does this by writing rules that spell out what disclosures must be made in a prospectus describing shares of stock offered for sale. The commission enforces its rules the way the executive branch of government does—by prosecuting violators. It can bring disciplinary actions against broker-dealers, or it can issue stop orders against corporate issuers of securities. The commission acts as judge and jury when it conducts adjudicatory hearings to determine violations or prescribe punishment. Although the commissioners who make up the membership of this agency are appointed by the president subject to the approval of the Senate, the Securities and Exchange Commission is an independent agency. It is not attached to Congress, nor is it a part of any executive department.

Combining the three functions of government allows an agency to tackle a problem and get the job done most efficiently, but the idea has not been accepted without a struggle. Legal authorities at various times have taken the position that the basic structure of the administrative law system is unconstitutional. In 1937, for example, the President's Committee on Administrative Management called governmental agencies "a headless 'fourth branch' of the Government, a haphazard deposit of irresponsible agencies and uncoordinated powers. They do violence to the basic theory of the American Constitution that there should be three major branches of the Government and only three."

Nevertheless, the Supreme Court has held that administrative agencies can exercise powers like those of a legislature or a court. Sometimes they act as agents for the other branches of government. If there is concern that such concentrations of power will allow abuses of individual freedoms, it is no solution to apply the separation-of-powers doctrine too strictly to the agencies. The answer is to supervise them through statutes that create their powers and duties within carefully drawn guidelines and provide for proper review of agency actions in the courts. The view of legal scholars today is that the danger lies in unchecked power but not in blended power.

Delegation of authority A basic rule that has contributed substantially to the development of administrative law is the delegation doctrine, sometimes called the nondelegation doctrine. This rule says that there can be no delegation of the power to legislate. Laws must be enacted by the officials elected to make them.

This rule would be completely unworkable if applied literally. The rule is often stated in absolute terms, but courts do not apply it so strictly. Congress can and does delegate responsibilities to agencies, but it must set clear standards for the administration of the duties. The Supreme Court has said that "Congress may declare its will, and after fixing a primary standard,

devolve upon administrative officers the 'power to fill up the details' by prescribing administrative rules and regulations."

Courts will invalidate a law that grants too much legislative power to a public agency. It would certainly be unconstitutional for all the U.S. senators to go to a ball game and authorize the pages at the Senate to stay behind and enact laws for them, for example, but Congress has properly designated the secretary of agriculture to set minimum quality standards for imported tea, the secretary of interior to make rules and regulations protecting public lands from fire and destruction, and the president to adjust tariff rates as much as 50 percent in order to protect domestically made goods from the competition of cheap imports. When President Franklin Roosevelt began establishing a number of agencies as part of his New Deal for economic recovery, the Supreme Court first set limits on the congressional power to delegate authority.

The National Industrial Recovery Act (48 Stat. 195 [1933]), among other things, authorized the president to prohibit interstate shipments of oil produced in violation of state board

This 1933 political cartoon idealized the cooperation between government, employers, and employees that the National Recovery Act of the New Deal was intended to facilitate.

rules that attempted to regulate crude oil production to match consumer demand. This prompted the famous Hot Oil Case (*Panama Refining Co. v. Ryan*, 293 U.S. 388, 55 S.Ct. 241, 79 L.Ed. 446 [1935]). The Panama Refining Company sued to prevent Federal officials from enforcing that prohibition, the "hot oil" law. The Supreme Court found the law unconstitutional. Congress could have passed a law prohibiting interstate shipments of hot oil, but it did not do that. It gave the president the power to do so. This has been called a case of "delegation run riot" because the law had no clear standards defining when and how the president should use the authority that the statute delegated to him.

Four months later the Supreme Court invalidated a criminal prosecution for violation of the Live Poultry Code, which was issued under another section of the National Industrial Recovery Act. This was the case of *Schechter Poultry Corp. v. United States*, 295 U.S. 495, 55 S.Ct. 837, 79 L.Ed. 1570 (1935). The problem here was not that the delegation of authority was ill-defined but that it seemed limitless. The president was to "formulate codes of fair competition" for any industry if these codes would "tend to effectuate the policy" of the law. The codes that were created were very comprehensive, establishing an elaborate regulation of prices, minimum wages, and maximum hours for all kinds of businesses. There were no procedural protections from arbitrariness or abuses by enforcement agencies. Someone charged with a violation was not given the right to notice of the charges, the right to be heard at any agency hearing, or the right to challenge the agency's determination in a lawsuit. The Court realized that the unfair procedures helped strong industrial groups use these codes to improve their commercial advantages and to hurt small producers. This law also was struck down.

Because of these two cases, no subsequent Federal law has had the "imposing generality" of the National Industrial Recovery Act. Delegations of authority to agencies now are accompanied by important provisions setting up procedures that protect against arbitrary administrative actions.

One close brush with invalidity occurred in 1958 in *Kent v. Dulles,* 357 U.S. 116, 78 S.Ct. 1113, 2 L.Ed.2d 1204. In that case the secretary of state argued that he had complete discretion to decide who might obtain a passport. The Supreme Court refused to allow the constitutional right to travel to be subjected to the total discretion of the head of a Federal department, but it did not find it necessary to invalidate the law that gave authority to the secretary. Rather, it read

the statute very narrowly, finding that the purpose of the law and the way it had been administered in the past set standards that themselves limited the right of the secretary to decide who could get a passport. In other words, the Court narrowed the amount of authority delegated to an acceptable level and then it approved it.

Due process of law   Very broad delegations of authority are upheld by Federal courts all the time. The idea of nondelegation has begun to merge with the procedural protections of due process of law. Courts now are concentrating more on requiring administrators to show a structure for their decision making and limits to their discretionary powers. This springs from the basic principle that the United States has a government of law and not of people, as guaranteed by the Due Process Clause of the Constitution.

The case of *Holmes v. New York City Housing Authority*, 398 F.2d 262 (2nd Cir. 1968), illustrates how due process principles can place limits on the exercise of agency discretion. The housing authority was receiving 90,000 applications for public housing each year, but it had units to accommodate only 10,000 families. Some preferences were allowed, but generally the applications were not processed in any reasonable or systematic manner. Each application expired after two years, and a renewed application had no better chance of success than a new application submitted on the same date. No waiting list was compiled, and no one determined whether applicants were eligible. Many applications were never even considered by the housing authority. These procedural defects aggravated the problems of favoritism and capricious decisions. When some of the applicants sued, the court held that due process requires the agency to use "ascertainable standards" for selecting eligible applicants. After these standards were established, if there were still too many equally qualified candidates, then fair procedures for selection among them had to be established. People could be given apartments by lot or in relation to the date of their application, for instance. The court did not tell the housing authority who should be allowed to live in the inexpensive public housing, but it insisted that the agency observe due process of law.

In this context, due process means that no one may be deprived of life, liberty, or property by an administrative agency unless given a reasonable opportunity, appropriate under the circumstances, to challenge the agency's action. People must be given fair warning of the limits an agency will place on their actions. It is improper, for example, for an agency to establish rate schedules for railroads without allowing reg-

[Due process is] any legal proceeding enforced by public authority, whether sanctioned by age and custom, or newly devised in the discretion of the legislative power, in furtherance of the general public good, which regards, and preserves these principles of liberty and justice.

STANLEY
MATTHEWS

ulated railroads an opportunity to show the agency or a court that the rates are not reasonable. Because the right to a jury trial and the due process requirements of criminal procedures restrict the scope of agency actions, an agency cannot be given the power to determine criminal guilt and impose criminal penalties. Agencies can, however, impose fines or issue remedial orders.

Other limits on agency action   Administrative law takes into account a variety of pressures that can be brought down on an agency whose policies fall into disfavor. An obvious control is the right of the legislature to enact more laws concerning the agency. A dissatisfied legislature can simply change the agency's job or take away the agency's authority to do certain things. The legislature also has the power of the pursestrings.

A legislature may enact a SUNSET LAW that provides for automatic termination of an agency after a stated time unless the legislature is convinced that need for the agency continues. Sometimes a sunset provision is written into the statute that creates a particular agency, but a general sunset law may terminate any agency that cannot periodically demonstrate its effectiveness. A useful agency can always be revived or retained by enactment of a new statute.

In 1964 Congress created the Administrative Conference of the United States. Its seventy-five to ninety-one members include representatives of independent regulatory commissions and executive departments, like the Department of Health and Human Services, as well as individual lawyers, scholars, and experts. The purpose of the conference is to study administrative law problems, exchange information, and develop recommendations for action by proper authorities so that private rights may be protected and regulations carried out in ways that are best for the public interest.

The president might wish to tone down an agency that has become a political liability. The most dramatic action the president can take is removal of a recalcitrant commissioner. The president also reviews agency budgets through the Office of Management and Budget; a president's disapproval of agency initiatives can block appropriations in Congress. In some instances the president may participate in agency decision making. Tariff schedules, for example, are subject to the president's approval. Governors have similar powers to restrain state agencies within their states.

During most of the years since 1932 the president has had some powers to reorganize Federal agencies under the authority of the Executive Reorganization Act (47 Stat. 413). This law recognizes that while responsibility for the organization and structure of the executive branch is vested in Congress, the president needs flexibility in order to carry out executive duties. Therefore, it gives the president the power to consolidate or transfer functions of an agency and to abolish any functions except those accomplishing law enforcement, such as civil rights protection and the collection of taxes, and those specifically required by statute, such as social security, veterans' programs, and agricultural support programs. The president submits reorganization plans to the Congress, and they become effective after sixty days unless either House of Congress adopts a resolution disapproving them. When enacted, executive reorganization laws have been effective for only two or three years at a time, and this authority to reorganize has been delegated to presidents in varying degrees. President Richard M. Nixon, for example, had no reorganization authority at all during the last two years of his administration, and no law granting the authority was enacted while Gerald R. Ford was president.

Public opinion can be a forceful weapon against unbridled agency action. A series of crises in the delivery of energy supplies, for example, focused public attention on the major regulatory commissions. It prompted some reorganization and a reallocation of financing. Much effective publicity comes from good investigative journalism or private study groups like the PUBLIC INTEREST RESEARCH GROUPS. Occasionally internal studies of an agency by itself have led to meaningful reform. A dramatic example was the "Pentagon Papers" inquiry into the escalation of the Vietnam War. Publication of this study was approved by the Supreme Court in *New York Times Co. v. United States*, 403 U.S. 713, 91 S.Ct. 2140, 29 L.Ed.2d 822 (1971). Release of these internal studies is usually at the discretion of the agency, however, and most are reluctant to publicize their shortcomings for fear of jeopardizing future programs.

A few jurisdictions in the United States have created a special public official to investigate complaints about administrative misconduct. Called ombudsmen, these officials usually have broad authority to evaluate individual complaints, to intercede on behalf of beleaguered victims of red tape, and to make reports or recommendations. See also, Harold W. Chase's essay on Separation of Powers; Sherri A. Moreines and Stephen B. Presser's essays on Schechter Poultry Corp. v. United States; and NIRA as well as Larry B. Hill's essay on Ombudsman.

ADMINISTRATIVE OFFICE OF THE UNITED STATES COURTS

The Administrative Office of the United States Courts was created by act of Congress approved August 7, 1939 (53 Stat. 1223; 28 U.S.C. 601). The office was established November 6, 1939. The director and the deputy director are appointed by the Supreme Court of the United States.

Administering the courts The director is the administrative officer of the United States courts (except the Supreme Court). Under the supervision and direction of the Judicial Conference of the United States, the director is required, among other things, to:

- Supervise all administrative matters relating to the offices of clerks and other clerical and administrative personnel of the courts;
- Examine the state of the dockets of the courts; secure information as to the courts' need of assistance; prepare and transmit quarterly to the chief judges of the circuits statistical data and reports as to the business of the courts;
- Submit to the annual meeting of the Judicial Conference of the United States, at least two weeks prior thereto, a report of the activities of the Administrative Office and the state of the business of the courts, together with the required statistical data submitted to the chief judges of the circuits, and the director's recommendations, which report, data, and recommendations shall be public documents;
- Submit to Congress and the attorney general copies of the report, data, and recommendations, as required;
- Fix the compensation of employees of the courts whose compensation is not otherwise fixed by law;
- Regulate and pay annuities to widows and surviving dependent children of judges;
- Disburse monies appropriated for the maintenance and operation of the courts;
- Examine accounts of court officers;
- Regulate travel of judicial personnel;
- Provide accommodations and supplies for the courts and their clerical and administrative personnel;
- Establish and maintain programs for the certification and utilization of court interpreters and the provision of special interpretation services in the courts;
- Perform such other duties as may be assigned to him by the Supreme Court or the Judicial Conference of the United States.

The director is also responsible for the preparation and submission of the budget of the courts, except the budget of the Supreme Court.

Probation officers The Administrative Office, through its Probation Division, exercises general supervision of the accounts and practices of the Federal probation offices, subject to the primary control by the respective district courts which they serve. The office publishes quarterly, in cooperation with the Bureau of Prisons of the Department of Justice, a magazine entitled *Federal Probation*, which is a journal "of correctional philosophy and practice."

The division also has responsibilities with respect to the ten pretrial services agencies established on a demonstration basis by the Director of the Administrative Office pursuant to the Speedy Trial Act of 1974, as amended (88 Stat. 2076; 18 U.S.C. 3161 et seq.). These agencies report to their respective courts information concerning pretrial release of persons charged with Federal offenses and supervise such persons who are released to their custody.

Bankruptcy Act The act of Congress approved November 6, 1978 (92 Stat. 2549; 11 U.S.C. 101 et seq.), substantially modified the law of bankruptcy, effective October 1, 1979, and establishes a bankruptcy court as an adjunct to the United States district court on April 1, 1984, after which bankruptcy judges are to be appointed by the president with the advice and consent of the Senate to fourteen-year terms. (The Supreme Court declared the provisions relating to judges unconstitutional in 1982.) Between October 1, 1979, and January 3, 1983, the director of the Administrative Office of the United States Courts is to conduct a survey of the number of bankruptcy judges needed throughout the country on and after April 1, 1984. The director is also required to maintain lists of qualified persons to serve as trustees in all districts, except eighteen districts specifically designated as pilot courts to test the feasibility of a United States trustee system under the Department of Justice. The director continues to maintain general supervision over the administrative matters for the bankruptcy courts.

Federal magistrates Under the Federal Magistrates Act approved October 17, 1968 (82 Stat. 1107), as amended by the Federal Magistrates Act of 1979 (93 Stat. 643; 28 U.S.C. 631), the Director of the Administrative Office, under the supervision and direction of the Judicial Conference, exercises general supervision of the administrative matters of offices of United States magistrates, and compiles and evaluates statistical and other information relating to such offices and submits reports thereon to the conference. The director reports annually to Congress on the business which has come before United States magistrates and also prepares legal and administrative manuals for the use of the magistrates. The act provides for surveys to be conducted by the Administrative Office, at such time as the Judicial Conference deems expedient, of the conditions in the judicial districts in order to make recommendations as to the number, location, and salaries of magistrates. The director exercises responsibility through the Magistrates Division of the Administrative Office.

Federal defenders The Criminal Justice Act (84 Stat. 916; 18 U.S.C. 3006A [1964]) establishes the procedure for the appointment of counsel in criminal cases for individuals who are unable to afford adequate representation. The act also provides for the establishment of Federal public defender and Federal community defender organizations by the district courts in districts where at least 200 persons annually require the appointment of counsel. Two adjacent districts may be combined to reach this total.

Each defender organization submits to the Director of the Administrative Office an annual report of its activities along with a proposed budget or, in the case of community defender organizations, a proposed grant for the coming year. The director is responsible for the submission of the proposed budgets and grants to the Judicial Conference of the United States for approval. The director also makes payments to the defender organizations out of appropriations in accordance with the approved budgets and grants.

Source: *The United States Government Manual 1981/ 82* and/or *1982/83.*

ADMINISTRATIVE PROCEDURE

☐ The methods and processes followed by AD-MINISTRATIVE AGENCIES in administering the law. ☐

Governmental agencies do not follow the CIVIL PROCEDURE set up for courts because they generally pursue their actions and decision making more informally. Agencies in general have been established to do work for the government in a simpler and more direct manner than if the legislature did the job by enacting a law and the courts applied it in various cases. The law of administrative procedure is intended to ensure that agencies do not abuse their authority even though they use simplified procedures.

Over the years, procedures have been established to govern how agencies take action informally, make rules, make judgments, and have their actions and decisions reviewed by courts.

The development of administrative procedure law Government administration by agencies has existed since the first Congress began enacting laws. Statutes, interpretations of them, and actual practices of agencies gradually

produced a body of ADMINISTRATIVE LAW. Then came the New Deal for economic recovery in the 1930s, and a host of new agencies sprang up. Antagonism toward bureaucracy was fast reaching a breaking point as existing dissatisfactions were multiplied by the number of new bureaucrats. Some critics took the view that agencies meddled too fiercely in the private rights of people and business. Many agencies, however, were administering constructive programs: the Securities and Exchange Commission was protecting investors; the National Labor Relations Board gave working people a chance to bargain; and the Social Security Administration was helping families to survive the death, retirement, or disability of a wage earner. The answer was not to abolish all the agencies but to bring them under the control of established administrative procedures.

President Franklin Roosevelt appointed a committee in 1939 to investigate the "need for procedural reform in the field of administrative law." The committee put together a comprehensive and scholarly report on all the agencies in the Federal government. While the committee was working, the Senate and the House passed a bill that could have paralyzed agency action. It was so devastating that Congress carefully exempted favored agencies. The president vetoed the bill, and World War II held up further work until 1944. Then new bills were introduced and new hearings on the problem were held. Finally, in 1946, the Administrative Procedure Act (5 U.S.C.A. § 551 et seq.) was enacted by a unanimous vote in both Houses. It made the methods used by agencies more fair so that there would be less reason to object to them, and it limited the power of the courts to review agency actions and overturn them.

In general, developments in state and local administrative procedure have been somewhat slower than those in the Federal government. In 1961 the National Conference of Commissioners on Uniform State Laws promulgated a revised Model State Administrative Procedure Act. The model act was offered as a pattern for states seeking to organize administrative procedure. Now over three-quarters of the states have general legislation governing the procedures followed by their agencies in one or more of the major ways that they take action. Many of these laws are based on the model act, and at least twenty-seven states have adopted the model statute substantially as it was proposed. Many states have also grafted on provisions from the Federal Administrative Procedure Act (5 U.S.C.A. § 551 et seq. [1966]). Provisions do vary from state to state and from agency to agency, so local law should be consulted.

Other statutes that govern the way agencies function Some Federal statutes require agencies to take into account certain factors when they are contemplating action or making decisions. The National Environmental Policy Act (42 U.S.C.A. § 4321 et seq. [1969]) directs all Federal agencies to prepare environmental impact statements that assess the environmental consequences of their proposals before action is taken. Another general statute specifies that, unless a specific law authorizes otherwise, litigation is conducted by lawyers from the Department of Justice under the direction of the attorney general of the United States whenever an agency becomes involved in a lawsuit. Another Federal law requires high-level and policy-making officials in the Federal agencies to file reports disclosing their personal financial condition so that the public has information concerning their income and its sources and the kinds of investments and debts they have. The purpose of this law is to uncover conflicts of interest that may arise in the course of an agency's work.

SUNSHINE LAWS, or open meetings provisions in laws, require agencies to do their work in public. This is sometimes called "government in the sunshine." A statute requiring open meetings usually specifies the only occasions when a meeting can be closed to the public and requires that certain procedures be followed before a meeting is closed.

FREEDOM OF INFORMATION ACTS require agencies to share with the public the information they have gathered. Exceptions are allowed, for example, in the interest of national security or to protect the PRIVACY of individuals and businesses.

Agency investigations and information Administrative agencies gather information constantly in order to do work such as regulating, protecting the environment, prosecuting frauds, collecting taxes, and issuing government grants. In many instances information comes from papers like reports, tax returns, customs declarations, or applications that are required to be filed. Necessary information may come from agency records, staff reports, public records, or information volunteered by private sources or special interest groups. Where information is not forthcoming, agency administrators may seek to compel disclosure by summoning witnesses or documents or by conducting inspections or searches.

An agency's investigation might lay the groundwork for law enforcement, as when the Department of Labor checks payroll records to see if an employer is complying with minimum wage laws. Investigations might be intended to prevent the development of situations which present dangers to the public, such as local elevator inspections or bank examinations by inspectors from the Federal Reserve Board and the Federal Deposit Insurance Corporation. Agencies might undertake investigations before approving new programs by regulated industries or proposing new legislation; for example, the Federal Trade Commission held public hearings before it recommended laws to regulate cigarette packaging and advertising.

Because it would be impossible to predict how all the agencies will need to gather information, legislatures have generally given the agencies broad authority to investigate. Almost all federal agencies are empowered:

1. to direct corporations to file annual or special reports and to answer specific questions in writing;
2. to obtain access to corporate files in order to examine or copy their contents; and
3. to subpoena the attendance of witnesses at agency hearings and the production of documents and papers.

So long as the information sought is properly identified, needed for a legitimate purpose (not, for example, to harass or intimidate someone), relevant to this purpose, and reasonable, the agency probably has a right to obtain it. Exceptions to this rule are made for information that the person targeted by the investigation is legally privileged to withhold—because, for example, it might lead to SELF-INCRIMINATION or violation of the confidentiality between ATTORNEY AND CLIENT.

While agencies are assembling vast stores of information on almost every subject imaginable, there are people who want to obtain that information for their own uses and other people who want to prevent its disclosure as much as possible. Freedom of information laws establish administrative procedures for opening up agency files to the public; privacy laws set up a structure for preventing wholesale disclosure of personal information, like an individual's tax return or Social Security records.

Informal agency action Most of the work done by agencies is accomplished with informal procedures. A person applying for a driver's license, for example, does not need or want a full trial in court in order to be found qualified. So long as the motor vehicle department follows standard fair procedures and processes the application promptly, most people are happy.

Increased government regulation to prevent accidents and to assure the quality of pro-

Law is neither formal logic nor the embodiment of inexorable scientific laws. It is a human institution, created by human agents to serve human ends.

HARLAN F. STONE

ducts and services has led to greater reliance on tests and inspections by agencies. Informal inspections determine whether cars, planes, and trains are safely equipped; whether agricultural products are sanitary; whether magazines can be mailed under second-class rates; and so on. Threats to the public health and safety demand prompt action, and informal procedures are usually adequate: for example, preventing distribution of unsafe drugs, prohibiting importation of diseased plants or animals, or suspending the license of a pilot awaiting a disciplinary hearing.

The constant surveillance of business activities by regulatory agencies is like the testing and inspecting of products by other agencies. The regulation of banks is one of the most pervasive systems of supervision. Regulatory agencies allow administrators to determine who can open a bank; whether branch banks can be opened and where; how much cash reserves have to be maintained; what auditing procedures have to be followed; what services the bank can offer; whether it can close down; and so on. An agency administrator can even take over operation of a bank without first holding a hearing if he or she decides that it is necessary in order to protect the customers. Supervision is accomplished by periodic (and often unannounced) visits by bank examiners. The value of supervision is that it permits prevention of problems rather than punishment for them later. It also makes an agency's attempts at negotiation and settlement more effective. Problems can be headed off before they become serious, and formal complaints against a company are usually not necessary.

Agencies also take informal action in approving applications or claims. The Social Security Administration passes on over five million claims for benefits, holding hearings or answering challenges to their decisions in court in only a small number of cases. Most transmitter applications before the Federal Communications Commission are approved or disapproved without any formal action. The Internal Revenue Service processes most tax returns without formal prosecution. It will also provide informal opinions to help people avoid making costly tax mistakes in their financial planning.

Anyone who objects to the informal decisions made by a government agency can invoke more formal procedures. Someone may, for example, believe that standards are unclear and should be promulgated through formal agency rule making. Or someone may feel that the decision in a particular case is unfair and demand a formal adjudicatory hearing. If one of those formal procedures does not satisfy someone, the agency's decision can be challenged in court and

a judge asked to review it. Most of the time, however, the threat of formal action prompts a person to accept the informal decision or negotiate a settlement with the agency. If the Food and Drug Administration discovers botulism in a batch of soup, for example, the manufacturer probably will destroy the cans without insisting on formal prosecution by the agency. Informal decision making accounts for most of the actions taken by agencies all over the country.

Formal agency action Most formal action taken by administrative agencies follows one of two procedures, rule making or adjudication. Rule making is the agency's formulation of policy that will apply in the future to everyone affected by the agency's activities. Adjudication is for the agency what a trial is for the courts. It applies the agency's policies to some act already done so that an order is issued for or against a party appearing for a decision. Rule making looks to the future; adjudication looks at the past. Where either of these formal procedures is used, the agency will usually give interested or affected persons notice and an opportunity to be heard before a final rule or order is issued.

Rule-making procedures General rules and regulations issued by executive branches have been a feature of our Federal and state governments for as long as they have been in existence. As government programs and regulations have grown, Congress has come to rely more and more on the agencies to formulate the rules necessary to do the work. It passes an act which creates only a skeletal framework for the resolution of a problem, leaving to an agency the job of filling out the details. The rules that agencies then promulgate are of three kinds: procedural, interpretative, and legislative.

Procedural rules identify the agency's form of organization and methods of operation. Although it is usually not required, agencies routinely seek out the advice of interested and affected persons before procedural rules are written or revised. These are housekeeping rules, usually authorized by the law that created the agency, and they must be observed by staff members. An agency action can be challenged in court on the ground that the agency did not comply with its own procedural rules.

Interpretative rules are issued by an agency to show how it intends to apply the law. They range from informal policy statements announced in a press release to authoritative rulings binding on the agency in the future and issued only after the agency has given the public an opportunity to be heard on the subject. The Administrative Procedure Act does not require a Federal agency to observe full formalities in promulgating interpretative rules, but open hearings often are held where time permits. An interpretative rule is simply the agency's opinion on the meaning of a statute or one of its terms, so it is significant but not binding on people dealing with the agency. A court is free to supply its own version of the statute if some party challenges an agency's interpretative rule in a lawsuit, but courts are likely to defer to the agency's view if it has special expertise in its field or if the subject is complicated. Courts recognize that agencies are created in order to handle government programs as experts, and certainly the legislature can rewrite the statute if it believes that the agency has misinterpreted its mandate.

Legislative rules issued by an agency are like statutes enacted by a legislature, but agencies can promulgate legislative rules only if the legislature has given them this authority. For example, the Fair Labor Standards Act (29 U.S.C.A. § 201 et seq. [1938]) gave the Administrator of the Wage and Hour Division the authority to enforce minimum wage requirements in various industries. It did not apply the minimums to certain employees canning food products for commercial sale if the cannery was close to the place where the products were grown. The reason for this was that farm workers could not demand the minimum wage at that time, and Congress was trying not to give cannery workers an advantage over them.

The statute left to the administrator the job of defining how close the canneries had to be to farms in order to avoid paying minimum wages. The administrator issued a rule defining the appropriate area and also making an exception for canneries with seven or fewer employees outside that area. Workers in some small canneries that took advantage of the exception sued to bring their pay up to the minimum wage level.

The Supreme Court held in *Addison v. Holly Hill Fruit Products,* 322 U.S. 607, 64 S.Ct. 1215, 88 L.Ed. 1488 (1944), that the workers were right. The statute gave the administrator of the program the authority to define the area within which canneries did not have to pay minimum wages, but not the power to affect employees outside those areas. The rule that exempted small canneries was invalid.

The Administrative Procedure Act sets up the procedures to be followed for administrative rule making. The procedure does not have to be followed when the agency adopts procedural or interpretative rules unless some other law requires that particular agency to do so. Otherwise an agency generally must publish advance notice in the *Federal Register,* the government's daily publication for Federal agencies, before adopting a rule. This gives persons who have an interest in, or are affected by, a proposed rule the opportunity to participate in the decision making by submitting written data or by offering views or arguments orally or in writing. Before a rule is adopted in its final form, the agency must publish it thirty days before its effective date. Formally adopted rules are published in the *Code of Federal Regulations,* a set of paperback books published by the government each year so that rules are readily available to the public.

The law allows some exceptions to this rule-making procedure. For example, an agency need not give advance notice or an opportunity to participate and it may defer the effective date of a rule when it has "good cause" for doing so. A national emergency was found to be good cause in *Nader v. Sawhill,* 514 F.2d 1064 (Em. App. 1975). In that case Ralph Nader and a group of consumers complained that the Cost of Living Council had raised the price of certain crude oil in December of 1973 without first giving the thirty-day advance notice. The court found that the council, predecessor of the Federal Energy Administration, had acted properly because the Arab oil embargo had created an urgent need for incentives to prompt increased domestic production of crude oil. The delay of thirty days would have caused intolerable problems during a period when supplies of oil were uneven.

Procedures for adjudication Agencies also take action through adjudication, or administrative hearings. Like trials, these hearings resolve disputed questions of fact, determining policy in a specific factual setting and ordering compliance with laws and regulations. Although often not as formal as courtroom trials, administrative hearings are extremely important. There are far more hearings before agencies every year than there are trials in courts, and they deal with very important subjects, such as individual claims for worker's compensation, welfare, or Social Security benefits, in addition to multimillion-dollar disputes about whether business mergers will violate antitrust rulings. These proceedings may be called hearings, adjudication, or adjudicatory proceedings. Their final disposition is an administrative order.

At first glance, many administrative proceedings appear to be just like courtroom trials. Most are open to the public and conducted in an orderly and dignified manner. Typically, a proceeding begins with a complaint filed by the agency, much as a civil trial begins with a complaint prepared by the plaintiff. After the respondent answers, there may be discovery by each side of the other's evidence and prehearing conferences. A hearing examiner presides at the hearing, giving rulings in response to applications by a party for some sort of relief. The agency presents its evidence, usually through counsel, either by a written report or in the question-and-answer style of a trial. Then the respondent offers his or her case. Witnesses may be called and cross-examined. The examiner gives a decision, usually with written findings and a written opinion, shortly after the hearing.

Unlike a trial, an administrative hearing has no jury. Rules that keep out of trials any evidence that might confuse or prejudice a jury do not apply; such evidence may be considered by hearing examiners. A hearing examiner is usually an expert in the field involved and is likely to be more concerned with overall policies than with the particular merits of one party's case. It is important to remember that agencies decide which cases will be brought to hearings, and that their hearings are not intended to be open-ended forums. The Administrative Procedure Act affords parties before Federal agencies the right to notice of the issues and proceedings, the right to counsel, and the right to confront and cross-examine witnesses. In addition, individual agencies have often adopted rules of procedure that apply specifically to their hearings. These, like other rules, are published first in the *Federal Register* and then in the *Code of Federal Regulations*.

At one time administrative orders were not self-enforcing. A respondent who did not do what the final order required had to be summoned by the agency into court, and the agency had to prove that the order was properly issued and that the respondent had not obeyed it. Meanwhile, the respondent continued to disobey the order until the court finally entered its own order and then enforced it, if necessary, by finding the respondent in contempt of court. This made the enforcement too late and too harsh. Now most orders are made final within a certain period of time after the hearing examiner issues them. After that, failure to obey incurs penalties that are spelled out in the statutes that give the agencies their authority. The orders, therefore, are self-enforcing unless the respondent challenges them by an appeal in a court.

Judicial review of agency actions

Someone who believes that he or she is the victim of administrative error or wrongdoing must first find out whether a person has the right to challenge the agency in a lawsuit. If so, the person should know what standards the court is likely to apply in testing the reasonableness of the agency's decision in the particular case and how far the court's inquiry is likely to go.

The right to have a court review an agency's decision Whether or not someone has the right to ask a court to review the action taken by an agency depends on several factors. The first question that must be answered is whether the action taken is reviewable. Overall, the law seeks to give agencies enough freedom of action to do their work while somehow ensuring that individual rights will be protected. The Administrative Procedure Act provides that courts may not second-guess agencies when they are exercising discretion that has been granted to them by statute. For example, Joseph Curran and the National Maritime Union sued Melvin Laird, the secretary of defense, when they believed that the government was shipping military cargo to Vietnam in foreign-owned vessels in violation of the Cargo Preference Act (46 U.S.C.A. § 1241 [1954]). The government responded that the law permitted use of foreign-flag vessels when U.S. ships were not available. Whether or not U.S. ships were available was a question for the administrative agency designated by the president to decide in its discretion. The court in *Curran v. Laird,* 136 U.S. App. D.C. 280, 420 F.2d 122 (1969), refused to consider the correctness of the agency's decision because it was theirs to make.

If the question at issue has been committed to agency discretion, the court may consider whether the agency has exercised its discretion. If not, the court can order the agency to look at the situation and make a decision. For example, a young man who had told his draft board that he was a conscientious objector during the Vietnam War could not have been drafted and shipped off without a hearing. A court could have ordered the board to hold a hearing and to use the discretion it was allowed in deciding the case. The court can also set aside an agency decision that is clearly wrong. The Administrative Procedure Act allows courts to overrule agency action that is found to be "arbitrary, capricious, an abuse of discretion, or otherwise not in accordance with law."

Persons angered by actions taken by an agency cannot take their cases to court unless they can show that they have standing—that is, a stake in the controversy sufficient to entitle them to review by a court. For many years courts looked at this requirement very strictly and closed the courthouse doors to many people who thought they had a complaint. People had to show more than just personal or economic harm; they had to prove violation of an existing legal right. This test of standing sent the courts in circles, asking whether a party had a case before being allowed into court to prove it.

The Administrative Procedure Act allows court review for any person "adversely affected or aggrieved by agency action within the mean-

In some respects matters of procedure constitute the very essence of ordered liberty under the Constitution.

WILEY B. RUTLEDGE

ing of a relevant statute." Finally, in 1970 the Supreme Court ruled that a person has standing to sue if "aggrieved in fact" and the interest the person seeks to protect could be said to be within the zone of those interests the statute was intended to protect. For example, a taxpayer who opposes the idea of welfare payments cannot sue to prevent the granting of benefits to a certain applicant. A person who is denied benefits, however, does have standing to seek review of the decision in court because he or she is immediately and in fact aggrieved. Furthermore, it is for such person's benefit that a statute was passed to establish the welfare department.

Review of administrative decisions is also foreclosed until the aggrieved person has exhausted all other avenues of relief and the dispute is ripe for a judicial determination. The doctrine of exhaustion and ripeness requires a person dealing with an agency to follow patiently all the steps available within the agency's procedures before resorting to court action. The rule is essential to prevent overloading the courts with questions that may not even be disputes by the time the agency determines what its final order or ruling will be. Furthermore, it allows the courts to deal efficiently with sharp issues rather than with unfocused anger or frustration with a bureaucracy.

Courts tend to balance the fitness of the question for court review with the hardship to the parties if review is denied or delayed. This principle was enunciated in *Abbott Laboratories v. Gardner,* 387 U.S. 136, 87 S.Ct. 1507, 18 L.Ed.2d 681 (1967). The Supreme Court acted promptly in that case because of the risk of overwhelming harm to thirty-seven drug manufacturers. The Commissioner of Food and Drugs had promulgated a regulation that required the manufacturers to include a drug's generic name prominently *every time* the trade name was printed. The drug companies faced exhorbitant costs, adverse public reaction, and criminal penalties if forced to test the legality of the rule by violating it. The Court, therefore, was willing to consider the validity of the regulation for all the manufacturers before any one of them was charged with a violation.

The scope of a court's review If an aggrieved person can convince a court that he or she has standing, that all available administrative remedies have been exhausted, and that the case is ripe for judicial review, the court will hear the case, but the scope of its review is limited. It is not appropriate for a court to do over again all the work of an agency just to find out whether the agency made the best decision. A court is generally limited to asking whether the agency

went outside the authority granted to it by constitutional or statutory provisions; whether it followed proper procedures in reaching its decision; and whether the decision is so clearly wrong that it must be set aside. Courts will usually accept the agency's findings of fact but are free to determine how law shall be applied to those facts in the case. The court can hold unlawful any agency action found to be arbitrary, capricious, an abuse of discretion, or otherwise not in accordance with the law. It will look at the whole record of proceedings and take into account the agency's expertise in the matter and some policies and other factors not appearing in the record. The court will not upset agency decisions for harmless errors that do not change the outcome of the case.

ADMINISTRATOR □ A person appointed by the court to manage and take charge of the assets and liabilities of a DECEDENT who has died without making a valid WILL. □

When such a person is a male, he is called an administrator, while a woman is called an administratrix. An administrator c.t.a. (*cum testamento annexo,* Latin for "with the will annexed") is appointed by the court where the testator had made an incomplete will without naming any executors or had named incapable persons, or where the executors named refuse to act. A public administrator is a public official designated by state law to perform the duties of ADMINISTRATION for persons who have died INTESTATE.

An executor differs from an administrator in that he or she is named in the decedent's will to manage the ESTATE. If an executor dies while performing these duties, a court will appoint an administrator *de bonis non cum testamento annexo* (Latin for "of the goods not (already) administered upon with the will annexed") to complete the distribution of the decedent's estate. This term is often abbreviated: administrator d.b.n.c.t.a. See also, Executors and Administrators.

ADMIRALTY □ A field of law relating to, and arising from, the practice of the admiralty courts, tribunals which exercise JURISDICTION over all CONTRACTS, TORTS, offenses, or injuries within maritime law, that regulates and settles special problems associated with sea navigation and COMMERCE. □

In admiralty, the term *vessel* refers to every type of craft capable of navigating any sea, channel, lake, or river used in commerce, even when temporarily moored, laid up, or aground. The terms *admiralty* and *maritime* are synonymous.

National Archives

The Italian passenger liner, S.S. *Andrea Doria*, heeled over and began to sink after colliding in the fog with the S.S. *Stockholm* in 1956.

National Archives

The bow of the S.S. *Stockholm* was crushed and torn when it collided with the S.S. *Andrea Doria*.

The Coast Guard rescued all 108 persons on board a Japan Air Lines DC8 from Tokyo that crash-landed in the sea near San Francisco International Airport in 1969. Any litigation resulting from this crash would fall under admiralty jurisdiction.

Jurisdiction   A merchant ship on the high seas belongs to the country under whose flag it sails; therefore, the jurisdiction of a nation extends to a vessel throughout its voyages. The laws and tribunals of the flag nation determine all legal issues concerning owners, officers, crew, passengers, and cargo shippers. Relations among vessels and various nations are still governed by INTERNATIONAL LAW as expressed in TREATIES and CUSTOMS.

The Constitution assigns to Congress the power to legislate with respect to maritime law and vests exclusive admiralty jurisdiction in the Federal courts. The rules of FEDERAL CIVIL PROCEDURE and the Supplemental Rules for Certain Admiralty and Maritime Claims govern admiralty actions, and Federal law controls whenever U.S. law applies. Federal admiralty jurisdiction encompasses voyages on navigable waters of the United States, even if the voyage is intrastate in nature.

Admiralty jurisdiction is not limited to the high seas and tidewaters, but extends to all waters that comprise the stream of interstate or foreign commerce, such as the Great Lakes. All privately owned and operated vessels, including pleasure craft, that navigate United States waters are subject to the jurisdiction of a Federal court of admiralty.

Vessels in drydock are normally regarded as within admiralty jurisdiction, but nonmaritime property is beyond its scope. A dispute concerning a contract to construct a vessel would not be determined by an admiralty court.

Personal injuries   Admiralty jurisdiction extends to personal injuries sustained aboard a ship upon navigable waters as well as to injuries ensuing from the crash of an airplane into such waters. In addition, injuries suffered by airplane passengers traversing airspace over navigable waters are within admiralty jurisdiction, even though there is no impact with the water. A personal injury sustained on a dock, wharf, pier, or bridge, however, is not ordinarily within the jurisdiction of an admiralty court.

Seizure of a vessel   A ship is brought into the jursidction of an admiralty court when a Federal MARSHAL assumes CUSTODY or control of it. If a ship's cargo is perishable, the court may order any portion of it sold pending a hearing. The sale proceeds may be distributed to those persons possessing a claim on the property; but if the owner fails to claim a portion, the court may distribute it among CREDITORS. See also, Joseph C. Sweeney's essay on Maritime Law.

ADMIRALTY AND MARITIME JURISDICTION   See Maritime Law.

ADMISSIBLE □ A term used to describe information that is relevant to a determination of issues in any judicial proceeding so that such information can be properly considered by a judge or jury in making a decision. □

EVIDENCE is admissible if it is of such a character that the court is bound to accept it during the trial so that it may be evaluated by the judge or jury. Admissible evidence is the foundation of the deliberation process by which a court or jury decides upon a judgment or verdict.

The Federal Rules of Evidence regulate the admissibility of evidence in Federal courts. State rules of evidence determine evidence that is admissible in state court proceedings.

ADMISSION ☐ A voluntary acknowledgment made by a party to a lawsuit or in a criminal prosecution that certain facts which are inconsistent with the party's claims in the controversy are true. ☐

In a lawsuit over whether a defendant negligently drove a car into the plaintiff pedestrian, the defendant's apology to the plaintiff and payment of the plaintiff's medical bills are admissions that may be introduced as EVIDENCE against the defendant.

An admission may be express, such as a written or verbal statement by a person concerning the truth, or it may be implied by a person's conduct. If someone fails to deny certain assertions which, if false, would be denied by any reasonable person, such failure indicates that the person has accepted the truth of the ALLEGATIONS.

An admission is not the same as a confession. A confession is an acknowledgment of guilt in a criminal case. Admissions usually apply to civil matters; in criminal cases they apply only to matters of fact which do not involve criminal intent.

Purposes Admissions are used primarily as a method of DISCOVERY, as a pleading device, and as evidence in a trial.

Discovery tool Once a COMPLAINT is filed to commence a lawsuit, the parties can obtain facts and information about the case from each other to assist their preparation for the trial through the use of discovery devices. One type of discovery tool is a request for admission: a written statement submitted to an opposing party before the trial begins asking that the truth of certain facts or the genuineness of particular documents concerning the case be acknowledged or denied. When the facts or documents are admitted as being true, the court will accept them as such so that they need not be proven at trial. If they are denied, the statements or documents become an issue to be argued during the trial. Should a party refuse to answer the request, the other party can ask the court for an order of preclusion that prohibits denial of these facts and allows them to be treated as if they had been admitted.

By eliminating undisputed facts as issues in a case, requests for admissions expedite trials. Matters that are admitted are binding only for the pending case and not for any other lawsuit.

Pleading device Judicial admissions—made in court by a party or his attorney as formal acknowledgments of the truth of some matter, or as STIPULATIONS—are not considered evidence that may be rebutted but are a type of pleading device. Averments in a pleading to which a responsive pleading is required are admitted if they are not denied in the responsive pleading. If a party has made an admission in a pleading that has subsequently been amended, the pleading containing the admission will be admissible as evidence in the case. In civil actions any offers to settle the case cannot be admitted into evidence.

A plea of guilty in a criminal case may usually be shown as an admission in a later civil or criminal proceeding, but it is not conclusive. The defendant may explain the circumstances that brought it about, such as a PLEA BARGAINING deal. Any admissions or offers to plead guilty during the plea-bargaining process are inadmissible as evidence. Many courts refuse to admit a guilty plea to a traffic offense as evidence since many people plead guilty to avoid wasting their time and money by appearing in traffic court. A guilty plea that has subsequently been withdrawn and followed by a plea of not guilty cannot be used as an admission in either a criminal or civil case. It is considered an unreliable admission that has a potentially prejudicial effect on the opportunity of the defendant to get a fair trial.

Evidence Admissions are used as a type of evidence in a trial to bolster the case of one party at the expense of the other, who is compelled to admit the truth of certain facts. They may be made directly by a party to a lawsuit, either in or out of court; or implicitly, by the conduct of a party or the actions of someone else which bind the party to a lawsuit. When an admission is made out of court, it is HEARSAY because it was not made under oath and not subject to cross-examination. Although hearsay cannot be used as evidence in a trial because of its unreliable nature, admissions can be introduced as evidence because they are considered trustworthy. An admission by a party can be used only to prove the existence of the fact admitted and to impeach the credibility of the party. An admission by a witness can be introduced as evidence only to discredit the witness's testimony.

ADMISSIONS AGAINST INTEREST An admission against interest is a statement made by a party to a lawsuit, usually before the suit, that contradicts what he or she is now alleging in the case. Because the statements tend to establish or disprove a material fact in the case, they are considered admissions against interest. The truth of such statements is presumed because people do not make detrimental statements about themselves unless they are true.

Such an admission is considered an exception to the hearsay rule and, therefore, can be used as evidence in a lawsuit.

The law has prescribed a particular method, and we cannot alter the law, nor prevent the inconveniences.

C. J. HOLT

John F. Dobbyn

Admission to Law School

Incredible as it seems now, until the 1960s the admissions process at most law schools was an eager attempt on the part of the administration to scare up enough live applicants to fill the available seats without dipping to a level of talent that would be embarrassing to its standards. Since the mid-1960s, however, when the national craving for a legal education grew from an outbreak to an epidemic, the role of admissions people has changed from that of holding the door open in the hopes of attracting a crowd to that of guarding the door like Cerberus against the onslaught. While they share the common goal of sifting and culling through an abundance of increasingly qualified applicants to pluck out "the best" for admission, there is radical disagreement among the law schools on the question of how to define "the best." Through the years the debate has come to focus on the question of the relative weight to be given to each of the following four criteria.

College grade point average. While it makes eminent good sense in judging an applicant's chances for success in an academic program to give great weight to his or her track record in a similar setting, this indicator has become increasingly "soft" and difficult to evaluate. Over the past twenty years colleges generally have been in a neck-and-neck race to outdo each other in the inflation of their course grades, with the result that law school admissions people have found themselves measuring with a rubber yardstick. In an attempt to work their way down to solid ground, it has become necessary to temper the raw grade point average by placing

The Harvard Law School as it appeared in about 1860

Larry Kramer, Time, Inc.

it in the context of the overall grading pattern of the applicant's particular college. Frequently admissions people are less impressed by an astronomical grade point average than by the more telling statistic of the applicant's relative rank in his or her class. Even this figure needs to be backstopped by a close consideration of the courses taken by the applicant. Many admissions people prefer to bypass the third-ranking graduate whose transcript of courses looks like a noninterference pact between the student and the college and dip down to number thirty with a solid major in classics or chemistry.

One other consideration that can catch the eye of an attentive admissions person, and even help to obscure a "playful" freshman year, is a strongly improving grade point average through the later years of college.

Law school aptitude test. Every accredited law school in the country now requires its applicants (with the exception of some handicapped applicants) to submit to the Law School Aptitude Test (LSAT). Despite the limited purpose of the

Students concentrate on the Law School Aptitude Test.

Photo Hirschl & Adler Galleries, Inc. by permission of Owner

A painting of jurist George
Sharswood lecturing to
informally attentive students
at the University of
Pennsylvania Law School

test and the repeated sincere warnings of the test's progenitor, the Law School Admission Council, not to strain the test's usefulness beyond its intended purpose, most law schools rank LSAT scores close to (in some cases above) parity with the four-year grade point average in choosing applicants. The avowed purpose of the test is solely to predict success in the *first* year of law school. While it has statistical validity for evaluation of an entire class, admissions people are coming to an increasing awareness that for *individuals* the test can be skewed by a natural inability to perform in that type of standardized test. (The best indicator of this situation is an applicant who scored dismally on the precollege SAT and then burned up the track in his or her college performance.) In spite of these caveats, this ready-made ranking of applicants has a seductive simplicity that has led some law schools to admit and reject solely on the basis of an "index number" that is a combination of grade point average and LSAT score. Fortunately most law schools take this index number with the two grains of salt discussed below.

Recommendations. Some law schools require them; others do not. But nearly every law school will read them if the applicant cares to submit them. Among that majority of law schools that take the time to sift through the crop of applicants for people who have shown some spark of character to indicate that they might serve the profession admirably as attorneys as well as pepper their law school transcripts with high grades, the right recommendation could be the touchstone to acceptance. Because of the limited background of many applicants, the most fertile source of recommendations is an applicant's college professors—at least, those who have personal knowledge of the applicant's qualities of intellect, maturity, and responsibility. Some faculty members will, on request, grind out for any one of the 200 students in their survey course a recommendation that makes no distinction between a superior student and an also-ran. Other excellent sources of recommendations are employers (law-related, if possible)—and practically anyone who can attest that the applicant is a person who can be entrusted with clients' lives, property, and liberty.

Wild card. This criterion is undefinable. It is any experience or accomplishment in the applicant's background—from military service, graduate school, business or political experience, to community service and points beyond—that tells the admissions people that they are dealing with an applicant of more proven depth than the multitude who have simply slid down the prescribed pipeline from kindergarten through college. In the rare case, a wild card has even been a criminal background—or, rather, the overcoming of a criminal background—with the result that the applicant had come to the door of the law school by a far more torturous and demanding path than followed by the average competition.

The actual procedure of admissions varies somewhat from law school to law school. Generally, though, the process fits into one of two categories. Many law schools deal with applications as they come in, basing their comparisons on an objective standard derived from the experience of previous years. Others prefer to fix a deadline (such as January 31) for the filing of all applications, so that immediately after that date they can begin to set up relative rankings among the year's crop. They will then send out a wave of acceptances and wait for the responses of the applicants. If the class is not filled on the first wave, a second wave of acceptances is sent out, and so on until a sufficient number of deposits are received to ensure a full entering class. This numbers game of how many applicants to accept in any given wave is complicated by the fact that most applicants apply to a number of law schools (frequently up to ten). The admissions committee therefore has little basis other than past experience for predicting how many of the applicants they accept will simply delay response and wait for an acceptance at a law school higher on their list. For this reason it is frequently well into August before the final wave of acceptances produces the final deposit to complete the class. See also, Robert B. McKay's essay on Law Schools.

Bibliography: John F. Dobbyn, *So You Want to Go to Law School*, a pre-law handbook prepared by the Association of American Law Schools, the Law School Admission Council, and Educational Testing Service (1976).

The only road to the highest stations in this country is that of the law.

SIR WILLIAM JONES

ADMISSION TO THE BAR ☐ The procedure that governs the authorization of attorneys to practice law before the state and Federal courts. ☐

Statutes, rules, and regulations governing admission to practice law have been enacted to protect the public interest, in terms of preventing the victimization of clients by incompetent practitioners. The courts have inherent power to promulgate reasonable rules and regulations for admission to the bar. Although this authority is vested exclusively in the courts, the legislature can, subject to constitutional limitations, issue reasonable rules and regulations governing bar admission provided they do not conflict with judicial pronouncements.

The highest state court administers the admission of applicants to the state bar, usually requiring successful completion of a bar examination and evidence of good moral character. With respect to admission to the Federal bar, Federal district courts are empowered to issue requirements for admission separately from those of the state courts. If, however, a district court, pursuant to a rule, derivatively admits to its bar those admitted to the state bar, it cannot arbitrarily deny admission to an applicant who is a member in good standing of the state bar. In most instances, the Federal district courts have considerable latitude in establishing requirements for admission to practice before them, but their rules must not contravene Federal law.

In terms of the Federal bar, an attorney is also eligible for admission to the bar of a court of appeals, if he or she has been admitted to practice before the Supreme Court, or the highest court of a state, or another Federal court, and if the lawyer is of good moral and professional character. The attorney must comply with the procedural requirements and take and subscribe to the following oath: "I, [name] , do solemnly swear (or affirm) that I will demean myself as an attorney and counselor of this court, uprightly and according to law; and that I will support the Constitution of the United States."

In order to gain admission to the bar of the Supreme Court, an attorney must have practiced for three years in the highest court of a state, territory, district, commonwealth, or possession. The person must be of good character in terms of both his or her private and professional lives, and complete the specified procedures, including taking or subscribing the following oath: "I, [name] , do solemnly swear (or affirm) that as an attorney and as a counsellor of this court I will conduct myself uprightly, and according to law, and that I will support the Constitution of the United States."

In some instances, a particular board is empowered to promulgate rules pertaining to applicants seeking to practice before it as attorneys. For example, the Securities and Exchange Commission has implied authority under its general statutory power to determine qualifications for attorneys practicing before it. Under Federal law, the Commissioner of Patents and Trademarks, subject to the approval of the secretary of commerce, can promulgate regulations governing the recognition and conduct of attorneys appearing before the Patent and Trademark Office.

Qualifications for admission to the bar must be rationally related to the applicant's fitness to practice law; therefore, a state cannot prevent a person from practicing law for racial, political, or religious reasons. Good moral character is a prerequisite to the right to admission to practice law and, at a minimum, consists of honesty. Lack of good moral character is demonstrated by an immutable dishonest and corrupt nature and not in radical political beliefs or membership in lawful but controversial political parties.

In regard to the effect of criminal conduct upon the evaluation of an applicant's character, a conviction for the commission of a FELONY is not, per se, sufficient to demonstrate a lack of good moral character. It will be incumbent, however, upon the applicant to prove complete rehabilitation. Although a conditional pardon is insufficient to remove objections to bar admission, a felony conviction will not prevent an applicant from practicing law if he or she has received a full pardon and is otherwise qualified.

Misdemeanor convictions do not necessarily result in a finding of lack of good moral character, but mere conduct that does not culminate in a conviction might present an insurmountable obstacle to admission if it indicates a lack of moral fitness. In some cases, an applicant has been rejected for want of good moral character because he or she has made false statements or concealed material facts in the application for admission or in other legal documents. In other cases, the withholding or falsification on the application of minor matters has been viewed as of no effect on an evaluation of character; the same principle applies to unintentional concealment of information.

Admission to the bar cannot be denied because the applicant is not a United States citizen, but the states can impose reasonable residency requirements upon all applicants prior to, or during, the time a license is sought. This requirement enables the state examining authority to investigate the character of the applicant, but it must be rationally related to the attainment of this objective. While a majority of states have some form of residency requirement for admission to the bar, the emerging trend is to nullify durational residency requirements, which mandate that an attorney live in a state for a prescribed period as a prerequisite to certification to practice law. See also, Residency Laws.

Applicants for admission to practice law must take a bar examination, unless they are exempted from this requirement by statute or court rule. Attorneys from other states can be admitted to practice in the state without examination upon providing the required proof of practice in another state that has reciprocity provisions, pursuant to which an attorney licensed in one state can be admitted to the bar of another state, if the first state grants reciprocal rights to attorneys admitted to practice in the other state. Under the device of PRO HAC VICE, an attorney can be admitted to practice in a jurisdiction without having to take the bar examination, but only on a limited basis and only for a particular case. Such an attorney must be a member of a bar in good standing of other states or countries.

In order to practice law, an attorney must obtain a certificate or license, which is a privilege rather than a property right. Attorneys must also comply with the court rules or statutes governing the registration system, which is used to maintain a current list of all attorneys authorized to practice law in the state. Generally, admission by court order constitutes sufficient registration, but in some states, attorneys sign the roll or file a certificate with the clerk of the court to establish that they have been duly admitted to practice.

An applicant for admission to the bar is entitled to notice of, and a hearing on, the grounds for rejection either before the committee on character and fitness or the court. The courts can review the decision of bar examiners denying an applicant admission to the bar and ascertain whether the examiners acted after a fair investigation and hearing, exercised their discretion impartially and reasonably, and conducted their proceedings in compliance with the requirements of procedural due process.

ADMONITION
- Any formal verbal statement made during a trial by a judge to advise and caution the jury on their duty as jurors, on the admissibility or nonadmissibility of evidence, or on the purpose for which any evidence admitted may be considered by them.
- A reprimand directed by the court to an attorney appearing before it cautioning the attorney about the unacceptability of his or her conduct before the court. If the attorney continues to act in the same way, ignoring the admonition, the judge will find him or her in CONTEMPT of court, punishable by a fine, imprisonment, or both.
- In criminal prosecution, before the court receives and records the plea of the accused, a statement made by a judge informing the ACCUSED on the effect and consequences of a plea of guilty to criminal charges. □

ADOPT
- To accept, appropriate, choose, or select, as to adopt a child. See also, Adoption.
- To consent to and put into effect, as to adopt a constitution or a law. □

ADOPTION □ A two-step judicial process in conformance to state statutory provisions in which the legal obligations and rights of a child toward the biological parents are terminated and new rights and obligations are created in the acquired parents. □

Adoption involves the creation of the relation of parent and child between individuals who are not naturally so related. The adopted child is given the rights, privileges, and duties of a child and HEIR by the adoptive family.

Since adoption was not recognized at COMMON LAW, all adoption procedures in the United States are regulated by statute. Adoption statutes prescribe the conditions, manner, means, and consequences of adoption. In addition, they specify the rights and responsibilities of all parties involved.

De facto adoption is a voidable agreement to adopt a child, based on a statutory proceeding in a particular state, which becomes lawful when the petition to adopt is properly presented.

EQUITABLE ADOPTION, sometimes referred to as *virtual adoption,* is treated by the law as final for certain purposes in spite of the fact that it has not been formally executed. When adoption appears to comply with standards of fairness and justice, some states will grant a child the rights of one who has been adopted even though the adoption procedure is incomplete. An equitable adoption might be enforced by the court for the benefit of a child in order to determine inheritance rights, for example. Similarly, adoption by estoppel is the equitable adoption of a child by promises and acts that prevent the adoptive parents and their ESTATES from denying the child adoptive status.

Who may adopt To be entitled to adopt a child, an individual must meet the qualifications under the laws of his or her state, since the state has sole power to determine who may be-

UPI

Roy Rogers and Dale Evans, known as King of the Cowboys and Queen of the West because of their careers in movies and show business, are the adoptive parents of four children. Here they have gathered with six of their living children and thirteen of their grandchildren.

come an adoptive parent. Unless otherwise provided by state statute, United States citizenship is not a prerequisite for adoption.

A child may be jointly adopted by a husband and wife. If not contrary to statutory provision, either may adopt without being joined by the other. Unmarried people may adopt unless prohibited by law.

A growing area of controversy by the courts is whether or not adoption by a child's grandparents is a viable alternative. Such adoption might be considered in the child's best interests if the natural parents die or if the custodial parent is found unfit. A legal guardian may adopt a child but is not ordinarily given preference in the court proceedings.

The best interests of the child are of paramount importance in policy considerations toward adoption. Although legislative policy prefers such conditions as adoption by people of the same religion as the prospective adoptee, interfaith adoptions are allowed when it does not adversely affect the welfare of the child.

Elements in determining who will be suitable adoptive parents include race, religion, economic status, home environment, age, and health. Most of these criteria are taken into consideration in placements by agencies or in private placements where state law requires that adoptive parents be investigated.

Who may be adopted Since the status of an adopted person is regulated by state statutes that authorize the adoption, state law determines whether an individual is a proper candidate for adoption. In addition, to be subject to adoption in a particular state, the individual must be living within that state.

Children may be adopted in situations where their natural parents are living, dead, or unknown, or where they have been abandoned. An adoption will not be prevented by the fact that a child has a legal guardian.

Some statutes expressly limit adoption to minors, and others expressly provide for adoption of adults. The adoption of adults is regarded by statutes and the courts in a manner similar to the adoption of children. Practically, however, the adoption of adults differs greatly since it serves different purposes and creates few of the difficulties arising out of the adoption of children. In most cases, the purpose of adult adoption is to facilitate a device for inheritance. One may designate an heir by adopting an adult. Generally, the adoptee would not otherwise be entitled to inherit but for the adoption. In a state that allowed adult adoptions, an adult man was permitted to adopt his adult wife so that she would be entitled to inherit under a trust created by his mother. The adoption was not regarded as an incestuous relationship.

Social considerations In the past, adoption was viewed primarily as a means for a childless married couple to "normalize" their relationship. The focus has switched, however; now adoption is ordinarily seen as an institution that exists to help place children into improved environments.

A number of states have, in recent years, enacted statutes that permit subsidization of adoptions. The adoption procedure thereby became a social instrument for the improvement of the lives of underprivileged children. Subsidized adoption tends to encourage adoption of children by suitable individuals who would otherwise be unable to afford it. This type of adoption has a significant effect upon placement of children labeled "hard-to-place." Such children, who are frequently either physically or mentally handicapped or nonwhite, might have no other alternative except protracted institutionalization.

State law may require that the adopting parent have custody of a child for a certain period before obtaining an adoption decree. This requirement is designed to prevent premature action and to establish whether or not the best interests of the child will be furthered by the adoption.

Consent Virtually all statutes make parental consent to adoption an indispensable condition. Most statutes set forth detailed requirements for the form and procedure of such consent. Ordinarily statutes dispense with the parental consent requirement only when a parent has reached a serious level of unfitness that would be so significant as to terminate parental rights, or when such rights have already been judicially terminated.

In addition to parental consent, most states require a child to consent to the adoption if the child has reached a certain age, generally between ten and fourteen years.

The increasing number of divorces has resulted in de-emphasis of the necessity of consent to adoption by noncustodial parents, the purpose being to ease integration of children of a former marriage into the family created by a subsequent marriage. Some statutes allow adoption without the consent of the noncustodial parent if that parent has been unable to or has failed to contribute to the support of a child for a certain period of time. Grounds for termination of noncustodial parental rights are generally more easily provable than those governing normal severance of such rights. Courts are more inclined to find ABANDONMENT—a common ground for termination of parental rights—in cases involving noncustodial divorced parents.

Unmarried father's consent Historically, if a child was illegitimate, most JURISDICTIONS required only the consent of the child's natural mother to the adoption of the child. The right to grant or withhold such consent was not extended to the fathers of illegitimate offspring, since they were not considered to have sufficient interest in the benefits and obligations of raising a child to determine whether the child should be released for adoption.

In 1979 this trend was reversed in *Caban v. Mohammed,* 441 U.S. 380, 99 S.Ct. 1760, 60 L.Ed.2d 297 (1979). The key issue was whether the consent of an unwed biological father need be obtained before an adoption could be finalized.

In *Caban,* a mother of illegitimate children and her husband filed a petition for adoption. The children's natural father filed a cross petition to adopt. The New York Surrogate's Court granted the mother's petition, and an appeal was brought by the natural father. The decision was affirmed by the Supreme Court, Appellate Division, and subsequently affirmed by the New York Court of Appeals.

On appeal, the United States Supreme Court ruled that a law depriving all unwed fathers of the right to decide against adoption, whether or not they actually took care of the children in question, was unconstitutional and a form of sex discrimination. The unwed father in *Caban* had lived with the mother of the children for five years prior to the birth of the children. The Court held that he had the right to block their adoption by a man who subsequently married the mother.

Consents that are signed by the parents either immediately before or after the birth of the child may be particularly subject to challenge by the natural mother. Due to the mother's weakened physical and mental condition, findings of involuntary consent have frequently been handed down in such cases.

A parent can forfeit the right to give or deny consent for the adoption of his or her child in certain instances. Abandonment, the nonperformance of the natural obligations of caring for the child, including support, is one such case. The parent and child will ordinarily be kept together by the courts when the parent exhibits a continuing interest in the child's welfare.

A finding of abandonment may terminate a parent's rights and free the child for adoption with or without parental consent. A parent's rights may also be severed in cases of serious CHILD ABUSE or neglect. Some statutes provide that a noncustodial parent cannot veto an adoption; however, that parent is generally entitled to be heard when a court considers the case. This is particularly true when the parent has established some kind of family tie with the child, either by having been married to, or having lived with, the custodial parent or by taking the child into his or her home.

State law may require that if a child has been placed in the custody of an agency, the agency's consent is a prerequisite for an adoption. Similarly, consent of a guardian having custody of a child is necessary. The consent of the natural mother's parents may also be required if she is under eighteen years of age and unwed.

Methods of adoption   There are several types of adoption placement procedures. Agency placement and independent placement are governed by statute, as is adoption by contract or by DEED. Some people adopt through illegal purchase of a child or arrange to have a child by a surrogate mother.

Agency placement   In agency placement of a child, the arrangements are made by a licensed public or private agency. Such agencies exist solely for the placement of children, and part of their responsibility involves a thorough investigation of the suitability of the potential adoptive parents. Such an investigation is ordinarily quite detailed and takes into consideration the background of both child and prospective parents.

Statutes generally provide for agencies that are operated or licensed by the government to act in an intermediary role between natural and adoptive parents. The method by which a child is transferred to an adoption or placement agency is by the execution of a formal surrender agreement which the natural parents sign. By surrendering a child to an agency, the parent relinquishes all rights to the child. The agency is then given complete authority to arrange for adoption. In arranging for an adoption, agencies must take into consideration such factors as whether a particular child is a proper subject for adoption, whether the proposed home is a suitable one, and whether the adoption is in the child's best interests.

Agency placement has advantages as well as disadvantages. There are three basic advantages. (1) It minimizes such risks as the adoption of nonhealthy children, the discovery of the adoptive parents' identity by the natural mother, as well as the natural mother changing her mind about the adoption. (2) The suitability of adoptive parents is determined by a stringent investigation, which minimizes the risk that a child will be adopted by unfit parents. (3) Adoption through an agency minimizes fees incidental to the adoption.

The two essential disadvantages of agency placement are that it involves a long, detailed process. The adoptive parents might be forced to wait an interminable amount of time for the child while they are being investigated as to their suitability. This, in turn, results in a limited number of children being available for adoption through agencies.

Independent placement   In independent placement, or private adoption, a child is directly transferred from the natural mother, or her representative, to the parents seeking to adopt. This type of placement is ordinarily arranged by the natural mother's family or doctor. Generally neither the natural nor the adoptive parents are thoroughly investigated. The adoptive parents often arrange to pay all medical bills incidental to the pregnancy and birth in addition to legal expenses. Private adoptions are lawful in a majority of states.

Like agency placement, there are both advantages and disadvantages to independent placement. Private placement facilitates the adoption of a child by parents who might otherwise be forced to endure an extended waiting period or who might be unable to find a child through agency channels because of stringent requirements or mere nonavailability of adoptable children. On the other hand, there is an inherent risk that the natural mother might change her mind and never complete the adoption procedure.

While private adoption gives the natural mother anonymity, there is an increased likelihood that the natural mother will discover the identity of the adoptive parents and attempt to reclaim her child.

Independent placement aids mothers who do not have financial resources by arranging for the payment of medical expenses by the adoptive parents. Such a procedure can, however, lead to a black market if not carefully monitored.

Other disadvantages of private placements are the risks of adoption of an unhealthy child or of nonsuitability of the adoptive parents.

Black-market babies   The *black market* in babies provides childless people with the opportunity to adopt a child. It has arisen from dissatisfaction with the prolonged delays and complicated procedures required by adoption agencies and the courts, and from the unavailability of adoptable children. Since there is no investigation, the black market makes the adoption procedure faster and affords the natural mother secrecy.

Black-market adoption, unlike private placement, is illegal due to the size of the payment of money by the adoptive parents and because of a lack of safeguards for the well-being of the child. Although the natural mother may legally be reimbursed for medical expenses, it is illegal for her to take money for the infant itself, since buying and selling children is unlawful. The main requirement for adoption of a baby in the black market is that the adoptive parents be able to afford the fees—which in 1980 went as high as $20,000 demanded by the black-market operator.

The main dangers inherent in black-market adoption are that children may be placed in unsafe or inadequate homes and that women in financial trouble will arrange to have babies strictly for the purpose of collecting large fees.

Surrogate motherhood performed for a fee is also growing in popularity. In the surrogate process, a woman agrees to bear a child by artificial insemination from the husband of a woman who is unable to bear a child. This process violates the PUBLIC POLICY against the buying and selling of children and is illegal in all states.

Some states prohibit lawyers from obtaining babies for adoption by clients under any circumstances. Attorneys, however, are ordinarily permitted to accept fees for handling the legal aspects of adoption.

Adoption by contract or agreement
Generally an adoptive relationship cannot be formed by private contract, either express or implied. Although adoption contracts are not usually considered to be injurious to public welfare, they are discouraged in some states on the basis of the principle that a parent should not be permitted to trade away his or her child.

A court may, however, choose to treat a contract of adoption as an agreement to be enforced, with the outcome being equivalent to a formal adoption. The courts have upheld contracts between parents and institutions. In addi-

tion, in a number of states an adoption contract between a natural parent and an institution that provides that the parent is not to be informed of the child's location is enforceable.

Since courts are not eager to deprive natural parents of the right to care for a child, adoption contracts are not enforced whenever they are in conflict with the welfare of the child. Some states provide that a contract made by one parent alone, absent a showing of clear consent by the other, is not valid. The procedure for adoption by a written declaration or deed is permitted in some states. Ordinarily it must be properly recorded before the adoption will be valid.

REVOCATION   A court will allow an agreement for the adoption of a child to be broken by a natural parent if the circumstances warrant it, such as when a parent was forced into an adoption agreement.

The court has discretion over whether or not to permit revocation of an adoption agreement. In such cases the court will scrutinize the circumstances under which the parent gave consent as well as the parent's reasons to revoke the contract.

Consequences of adoption   Adoption ordinarily terminates the rights and responsibilities of a child and the natural parents to one another. A child's relationship to the natural parents is not changed when an adoptive parent dies. The relationship that exists between a child and natural relatives aside from parents, however, is not severed by the new status.

Adoption creates the same rights and responsibilities between a child and adoptive parents as existed between natural parent and child. An adopted child is entitled to the same rights as a natural child. When an adult is adopted, however, the adoptive parent does not assume the usual duty of support.

State law governs whether or not the name of a child will be affected by adoption. When a minor child is adopted, his or her legal RESIDENCE is changed from that of the natural to that of the adoptive parent.

Inheritance   A state legislature has the authority to impart or remove inheritance rights of adopted children or adoptive parents. Statutes usually provide that adopted children can inherit from adoptive parents in the same capacity as natural children and, conversely, adoptive parents can inherit the property of an adopted child who predeceases them.

Revocation of adoption   If an adoption decree is acquired by fraud, it may be revoked. In addition, in the absence of the requisite consent of all concerned parties, an order of adop-

. . . little power does the bare act of begetting give a man over his issue, if all his care ends there, and this be all the title he hath to the name and authority of a father.

JOHN LOCKE

tion is void. After a decree is revoked, a child assumes the status he or she had prior to the adoption proceedings.

Summary of adoption procedure   The formal steps in adoption of a child are generally uniform in all states.

Notice   Notice of adoption proceedings is given to all parties who have a legal interest in the case except the child itself. In the case of illegitimacy, both natural parents should be given notice.

Some statutes provide that a parent who has failed to support a child is not entitled to notice. Ordinarily a parent who has lost custody of a child in a divorce or separation case is, however, entitled to notice. Similarly, an adoption agency that has custody of the child is entitled to notice.

Petition   The parents seeking to adopt must file a PETITION in court that supplies information about their situation as well as the situation of the child. The filing of a proper petition is ordinarily a prerequisite to the court's jurisdiction.

The petition indicates the names of the adoptive parents, the child, and the natural parents, if known. In addition, the child's gender and age are stated, and some states mandate that a medical report on the child must also accompany the petition. An example of such a petition is found on page 103.

Consent   Written consent of the adoption agency or the child's natural parents accompanies the petition for adoption. Consent of the natural parents is not required if a child has been removed from their custody due to neglect.

Hearing   A hearing is held so that the court may examine the qualifications of the prospective parents and either grant or deny the petition. There must be an opportunity for the parties to present testimony and to examine witnesses at such a hearing.

Adoption proceedings are confidential, so the hearing is conducted in a closed courtroom.

Ordinarily the records of an adoption hearing are available for inspection only by court order. Confidentiality is thought to promote a sense of security by the child with his or her new family.

Probation   A majority of states require a period of probation in adoption proceedings. During this period the child lives with the adoptive parents, and the appropriate state agency monitors the development of the relationship. The agency's prime concern is the ability of the adoptive parents to properly care for the child. If the relationship is working well for all concerned parties, the state agency will request that the court issue a permanent decree of adoption.

If the relationship is unsatisfactory, the child is either returned to his or her previous home or is taken care of by the state.

Decree   An adoption decree is a JUDGMENT of the court and is given the same force and effect as any other judgment.

Birth certificate   Following the adoption proceedings, a certificate of adoption is issued for the adopted child to replace the birth certificate. It lists the new family name, the date and place of the child's birth, and the ages of the adoptive parents at the time the child was born.

Generally the certificate of adoption does not indicate the names of the child's natural parents or the date and place of adoption. A child may never know that he or she was adopted unless the adoptive parents reveal the information, since the old birth certificate is sealed away and may be opened only by court order.

Right to information on natural parents   Ordinarily all information concerning an adopted child's origins is sealed, in compliance with the court adoption proceedings, to facilitate development of a relationship between the adoptive parents and child free from the natural parents' influence.

Most state statutes deny adoptees access to records that disclose information about the natural parents. Often the natural parents make their consent to the adoption contingent upon the condition that no information about them should ever be revealed.

In recent times, because of the growing public interest in tracing ethnic and family backgrounds, many adoptees, as adults, have been calling for the right to obtain access to sealed adoption records.

The adult adoptees are cognizant of the fact that a disclosure of this kind of information could be traumatic to minor adoptees, but they contend that lack of access could cause serious psychological trauma to them as adults. In addition, they cite medical problems or misdiagnoses that could be caused by absence of genetic history, lack of religious identity, and fear of unwitting incest.

Adult adoptees contend that most adoption statutes do not make a distinction between adoptees as minors and later as adults, which causes the adults to be deprived of the right to trace their background. In addition, the adults allege that they have been denied EQUAL PROTECTION OF

FAMILY COURT OF THE STATE OF _____
         COUNTY OF _____

In the Matter of the
Adoption by

      of   Index No.

a minor having the first
    name of

                                 PETITION
whose last name is contained   (Agency)
in the Schedule annexed to
the Petition herein.

TO THE FAMILY COURT:

1. (a) The name and place of residence of the petitioning adoptive mother is:

      Name:

      Address: (include county)

She is (of full age) (a minor), born on

She is (unmarried) (married to
and they are living together as husband and wife).

Her religious faith is

Her occupation is

and her approximate annual income is $

    (b) The name and place of residence of the petitioning adoptive father is:

      Name:

      Address: (include county)

He is (of full age) (a minor), born on

He is (unmarried) (married to
and they are living together as husband and wife).

His religious faith is

His occupation is

and his approximate annual income is $

2. As nearly as the same can be ascertained, the full name, date and place of birth of the (male) (female) adoptive child are set forth in the Schedule annexed to this Petition and verified by a duly constituted official of an authorized agency.

3. (a) As nearly as the same can be ascertained, the religious faith of the adoptive child is

    (b) As nearly as the same can be ascertained, the religious faith of the natural parents of the adoptive child is

4. The manner in which the adoptive parents obtained the adoptive child is as follows:

5. The adoptive child has resided continuously with the adoptive parents since

6. The name by which the adoptive child is to be known is

7. The consent of the above-mentioned authorized agency has been duly executed and is filed herewith. The consent of the natural parents of the adoptive child is not required because

8. No previous application has been made to any court or judge for the relief sought herein, except

9. The adoptive child has not been previously adopted, except

10. To the best of petitioners' information and belief, there are no persons other than those hereinbefore mentioned interested in this proceeding except

11. WHEREFORE, your Petitioners pray for an order approving the adoption of the aforesaid adoptive child by the above named adoptive parents and directing that the said adoptive child shall be regarded and treated in all respects as the child of the said adoptive parents and directing that the name of the said adoptive child be changed as specified in paragraph 6 above and the henceforth (s)he shall be known by that name.

LAW because their status precludes them from receiving medical information readily available to nonadoptees.

Various approaches are being used to resolve this problem. One approach involves the enactment of a legislative requirement that public and private adoption agencies be required to open their records upon request to adults who were adopted as children, with certain limitations. For example, if the child had been placed by the natural parents prior to the effective date of the legislation, the natural parents could prevent the adoptee from seeing the records.

The issue of right to access to adoption records by adoptees when they reach adulthood also encompasses the legal consideration of the natural parents' right to PRIVACY, which could potentially be violated if free access to sealed court records were given to adult adoptees. There must be a balance between the adult adoptees' right to know and their natural parents' right to privacy. The way to achieve such a balance, however, has never been clearly determined. See also, Craig R. Ducat's essay on Privacy, Right of.

ADULT □ A person who by virtue of attaining a certain age, generally eighteen, is regarded in the eyes of the law as being able to manage his or her own affairs. □

The age specified by law, called the legal age of majority, indicates that a person acquires full legal CAPACITY to be bound by various documents, such as CONTRACTS and DEEDS, that he or she makes with others and to commit other legal acts such as voting in ELECTIONS and entering MARRIAGE. The age at which a person becomes an adult varies from state to state and often varies within a state, depending upon the nature of the action taken by the person. Thus, a person wishing to obtain a license to operate a MOTOR VEHICLE may be considered an adult at age sixteen, but may not reach adulthood until age eighteen for purposes of marriage, or age twenty-one for purposes of purchasing INTOXICATING LIQUORS.

Anyone who has not reached the age of adulthood is legally considered an INFANT.

ADULTERATION □ Mixing something impure with something genuine, or an inferior article with a superior one of the same kind. □

Adulteration usually refers to mixing other matter of an inferior and sometimes harmful quality with food or drink intended to be sold. As a result of adulteration, food or drink becomes impure and unfit for human consumption. The Federal Food and Drug Administration prohibits transportation of adulterated foods, drugs, and cosmetics in interstate com-

To safeguard the consumer against adulteration, these dressed hogs are inspected before the board of health stamp is applied.

merce, as provided under the Food, Drug and Cosmetic Act (21 U.S.C.A. § 301 et seq. [1938]). State and local agencies, acting under the authority of local laws, do the same to ban the use of such impure goods within their borders.

ADULTERY □ Voluntary sexual relations between an individual who is married and someone who is not the spouse. □

Adultery is viewed by the law as an OFFENSE injurious to public morals and a mistreatment of the MARRIAGE relationship.

Statutes attempt to inhibit adultery by making such behavior punishable as a CRIME and by allowing a blameless party to obtain a DIVORCE against an adulterous spouse.

Although adultery has ordinarily been regarded as a legal wrong, it has not always been considered a crime. Historically it was punishable solely in courts created by the church to impose good morals. In the ECCLESIASTICAL COURTS, adultery was any act of sexual intercourse by a married person with someone not his or her spouse. The act was considered wrongful regardless of whether or not the other person was married. At common law, adultery was wrongful intercourse between a married woman and any man other than her husband.

Criminal laws Several state legislatures have statutorily defined adultery as a crime. The PUBLIC POLICY reason for this classification is to further peace and order in society by preservation of the sanctity of family relationships and to proscribe conduct that undermines such relationships.

Under some statutes, both parties to an adulterous relationship are guilty of a crime if either of them is married to someone else. Other statutes provide that the act is criminal only if the woman is married.

Under the law of some states, one act of adultery constitutes a crime, whereas in others, there must be an ongoing and notorious relationship. The punishment set by statute may be greater for an individual who engages in repeated acts of adultery than for one who commits an isolated act.

Defenses An individual who has been charged with committing adultery may have a valid legal defense, such as the failure or physical incapacity to consummate the sex act.

A woman is not guilty of adultery if the sex act resulted from rape. Some states recognize ignorance of the accused regarding the marital status of his or her lover as a defense. In some states, only the married party can be prosecuted for adultery. If the other party to the relationship is not married, he or she may be prosecuted for fornication instead of adultery.

Initiation of criminal proceedings Under some statutes, a prosecution for adultery can be brought only by the spouse of the accused person although technically the action is initiated in the name of the state. Other states provide that a husband or wife is precluded from commencing prosecution for adultery since those states have laws that prohibit a husband or wife from testifying against his or her spouse. In such states, a complaint can be filed by a husband or wife against the adulterous spouse's lover.

Evidence Customary rules prescribe the types of EVIDENCE which can be offered to prove guilt or innocence. There must be a showing by the prosecutor that the accused party and another named party had sexual relations. Depending on state statutes, the prosecutor must show that either one or both parties to the adultery were wed to someone else at the time of their relationship.

Evidence of a chance to have sexual relations coupled with a desire, or *opportunity* and *inclination,* might be sufficient to prove guilt. Photographs, or the testimony of a witness who observed the couple having sexual intercourse, is not necessary. The fact that a married woman accused of adultery became pregnant during a time when her husband was absent might be ADMISSIBLE to demonstrate that someone, other than her spouse, had access to her for the opportunity of engaging in illicit sex. In addition, evidence that an accused woman gave birth to an illegitimate child might also be admissible.

Letters in which the accused parties have written about their amorous feelings or clandestine encounters may be introduced in court to support the assertion that the parties had the inclination to engage in sexual relations. CHARACTER EVIDENCE indicating the good or bad reputation of each party may be brought before the jury. Although evidence of a woman's sexual relationships with men other than the party to the adultery cannot be used, if her reputation as a prostitute can be demonstrated, it may be offered as evidence.

Suspicious activities and incriminating circumstances may be offered as CIRCUMSTANTIAL EVIDENCE.

Enforcement of statutes Although adultery is a crime in many states, the prosecution of offenders is rare. The legal system of the United States is currently reevaluating crimes such as adultery in light of the question of whether or not it is expedient to use jail time and fines to punish consenting adults for their sexual activities, even when family stability is threatened.

As a defense Occasionally, adultery has been successfully asserted as a defense to the crime of MURDER by an individual charged with killing his or her spouse's lover. Courts are loath, however, to excuse the heinous crime of murder on the ground that the accused party was agitated about a spouse's adulterous activities, unless the spouse acted in HEAT OF PASSION.

Divorce Based on the state's interest in the marital status of its residents, all legislatures had traditionally assigned statutes enumerating the grounds on which a divorce would be granted. These grounds, listed separately in the laws of each JURISDICTION, generally included DESERTION, NONSUPPORT, and adultery.

The basis of adultery as a ground for divorce has been discussed in various cases. There is an overriding public policy in favor of preserving the sanctity of marital relationships and family unity, and a fear that adultery will serve to undermine these societal objectives.

Recent changes in divorce laws, primarily the enactment of NO-FAULT divorce statutes in many states, have made it easier for couples seeking divorce to end their marriages without

Law can discover sin, but not remove, Save by those shadowy expiations weak.

JOHN MILTON

having to prove adultery or any other ground. In the past many unhappy couples resorted to trickery to attempt to obtain a divorce through staging the discovery of allegedly adulterous conduct. See also, Collusion.

AD VALOREM ☐ According to value. ☐

The term *ad valorem* is derived from the Latin *ad valentiam,* meaning "to the value." It is commonly applied to a tax imposed on the value of property. Real property taxes that are imposed by the states, counties, and cities are the most common type of *ad valorem* taxes. *Ad valorem* taxes can, however, be imposed upon personal property. For example, a motor vehicle tax may be imposed upon personal property such as an automobile. See also, Property Tax.

An article of COMMERCE may be subjected to an *ad valorem* tax in proportion to its value, which is determined by ASSESSMENT or APPRAISAL.

DUTIES, taxes on goods imported or brought into this country from a foreign country, are either *ad valorem* or specific. An *ad valorem* duty is one in the form of a percentage on the value of the property, unlike a specific duty that is a fixed sum imposed on each article of a class, such as all Swiss wristwatches, regardless of their individual values.

ADVANCE ☐ To pay money or give something of value before the date designated to do so; to provide CAPITAL to help a planned enterprise, expecting a return from it; to give someone an item before payment has been made for it. ☐

ADVANCEMENT ☐ A gift of money or property made by a person while alive to his or her child or other legally recognized HEIR, the value of which the person intends to be deducted from the child's or heir's eventual share in the estate after the giver's death. ☐

An advancement is not the same as a GIFT or a loan because the person intends that the "advance" of the heir's share of the estate be applied against what the heir would normally inherit. Although sometimes used to describe situations involving both people who have died intestate (without leaving a valid will) and people who have left a will, the term advancement should be used only when there is no valid will. The laws of DESCENT and DISTRIBUTION regulate the distribution of an intestate's property. The term ADEMPTION applies to lifetime gifts that reduce a beneficiary's share under a will.

ADVANCE SHEETS ☐ Pamphlets containing recently decided opinions of Federal courts or state courts of a particular region. ☐

Cases appearing in advance sheets are subsequently published in bound volumes containing several past pamphlets, usually with the same volume and page numbers as appeared in the advance sheets. Sometimes a court will publish an individual opinion soon after it has been rendered by the court. This is called a SLIP OPINION, which later may appear in an advance sheet.

Advance sheets in the National Reporter System The National Reporter System, published by West Publishing Company, St. Paul, Minnesota, is the most comprehensive collection of the decisions of the appellate courts of the states and of the United States. There are sixteen reporters in the National Reporter System. Six of the units cover Federal courts and ten units cover the fifty states and the District of Columbia.

Advance sheets are published fifty times each year (weekly, except for the last week of September and the first week of October) for the regional units reporting state cases. Three units report Federal cases fifty-two times per year. Of the remaining units, one publishes advance sheets biweekly, one monthly, and one semimonthly, during the term of the United States Supreme Court.

All decisions, opinions, and memoranda of the United States Supreme Court are published in the *Supreme Court Reporter* (cited as S.Ct.). The advance sheets are issued semimonthly during the term of the Court. At the end of the term, two or three hardbound volumes are published, depending on the number of cases decided.

The *Federal Reporter, Second Series* (F., F.2d) contains the reported cases of the United States Courts of Appeal, Court of Claims, Court of Customs and Patent Appeals, and Temporary Emergency Court of Appeals. The *Federal Supplement* (F.Supp.) reports decisions of the United States District Courts, the United States Court of International Trade, and the Judicial Panel on Multistate Litigation. *Federal Rules Decisions* (F.R.D.) contains District Court opinions construing the Federal Rules of Civil Procedure. *Military Justice Reporter* (M.J.) carries the cases of the Court of Military Appeals and Courts of Military Review. *Bankruptcy Reporter* (Bankr.) reports decisions of the United States Bankruptcy Courts and bankruptcy decisions of other Federal courts.

The regional units of the National Reporter System report the opinions of the highest courts of all fifty states and the District of Columbia. In addition, these reporters contain opinions of state intermediate appellate courts that are selected by the courts for publication. Many of the states have designated the unit of the National

1034 Ind. 442 NORTH EASTERN REPORTER, 2d SERIES

Dirk WEBSTER, Appellant,

v.

STATE of Indiana, Appellee.

No. 1281S350.

Supreme Court of Indiana.

Dec. 14, 1982.

Following reversal of defendant's original conviction and remand, 413 N.E.2d 898, defendant was again convicted before the Lake Superior Court, James E. Clement, J., of murder, and he appealed. The Supreme Court, DeBruler, J., held that: (1) double jeopardy did not bar defendant's retrial, even though defendant's original conviction had been reversed on the basis of insufficiency of evidence, since the case, as presented at original trial, would have been sufficient to support guilty verdict except for limitation on use of witness' prior testimony, and (2) evidence sustained conviction.

Affirmed.

Prentice, J., dissented.

1. Criminal Law ⟜193

Double jeopardy did not bar defendant's retrial, even though defendant's original conviction had been reversed on the basis of insufficiency of evidence, since the case, as presented at original trial, would have been sufficient to support guilty verdict except for limitation on use of witness' prior testimony. U.S.C.A. Const.Amend. 5.

2. Criminal Law ⟜1144.13(6), 1159.2(7, 9), 1159.4(1)

In reviewing a claim of insufficiency of evidence, Supreme Court does not weigh the evidence or resolve questions of credibility, but only looks to the evidence and reasonable inferences therefrom which support the verdict; if from that viewpoint there was evidence of probative value from which reasonable trier of fact could conclude that defendant was guilty beyond reasonable doubt, conviction will be affirmed.

3. Homicide ⟜250

Evidence in prosecution for murder sustained conviction.

Terry C. Gray, Gary, for appellant.

Linley E. Pearson, Atty. Gen., Palmer K. Ward, Deputy Atty. Gen., Indianapolis, for appellee.

DeBRULER, Justice.

Defendant-appellant, Dirk Webster, was originally charged with and convicted of two counts of murder, Ind.Code § 35–42–1–1(1) (Burns 1979 Repl.), and was sentenced to serve two consecutive forty-five year terms of imprisonment. Following an appeal to this Court, defendant's conviction was reversed, and a new trial was ordered. *Webster v. State*, (1980) Ind., 413 N.E.2d 898 (Prentice, J., dissenting). Defendant was again convicted upon retrial, and the same sentence was imposed. In this appeal, defendant contends that the retrial was barred by the double jeopardy clause of the Fifth Amendment to the United States Constitution and of Article 1, § 14 of the Indiana Constitution. He also urges that there was not sufficient credible evidence to support the verdict rendered here.

[1] The question of whether defendant's retrial was prohibited by the double jeopardy clause has already been considered, discussed and decided adversely to defendant's claim in this case on its initial appeal. We said there that while in the usual case a reversal for evidentiary insufficiency precludes a retrial because of double jeopardy considerations, *Burks v. United States*, (1978) 437 U.S. 1, 98 S.Ct. 2141, 57 L.Ed.2d 1, the *Burks* rationale does not apply in this case. *Webster, supra*, 413 N.E.2d at 902. Although the State may not appeal from an acquittal of a defendant by the trier of fact, no matter how erroneous the foundation for that acquittal, *Fong Foo v. United States*, (1962) 369 U.S. 141, 82 S.Ct. 671, 7 L.Ed.2d 629, here, a judgment of conviction was rendered by the jury in defendant's first trial. The question of whether the State had "one fair opportunity to offer whatever

---

IN RE CUSTODY OF HELWIG Ind. **1035**
Cite as, Ind., 442 N.E.2d 1035

proof it could assemble", *Burks, supra*, 437 U.S. at 16, 98 S.Ct. at 2150, 57 L.Ed.2d at 12, may be considered when a judgment of conviction has been returned and defendant appeals, alleging evidentiary insufficiency, and attempts to avoid retrial.

Prior to defendant's retrial, he filed a motion to dismiss based on the double jeopardy claim. At a hearing on that motion, the trial judge denied such relief, determining that he should conduct the retrial we had ordered. The denial of the motion was not error.

Defendant also claims that the State did not present credible witnesses whose testimony could be believed beyond a reasonable doubt, and therefore there was insufficient evidence to support the jury's verdict. He argues that Aurelius James Allen, an accomplice who testified and described defendant's participation in the murders, impeached his own credibility and was not a believable witness. The determination of a witness's credibility, however, is for the jury. *Taylor v. State*, (1981) Ind., 425 N.E.2d 141.

[2, 3] In reviewing a claim of insufficient evidence, this Court does not weigh the evidence or resolve questions of credibility, but only looks to the evidence and reasonable inferences therefrom which support the verdict. *Smith v. State*, (1970) 254 Ind. 401, 260 N.E.2d 558. If from that viewpoint there was evidence of probative value from which a reasonable trier of fact could conclude that a defendant was guilty beyond a reasonable doubt, we will affirm the conviction. *Taylor v. State*, (1973) 260 Ind. 64, 291 N.E.2d 890; *Glover v. State*, (1970) 253 Ind. 536, 255 N.E.2d 657. Allen testified directly about the defendant's participation in the murders of Betty DeBowles and Robin Thomas and detailed the events surrounding these crimes. The jurors could have concluded beyond a reasonable doubt from this and other evidence that the defendant was guilty.

The conviction is affirmed.

GIVAN, C.J., and HUNTER and PIVARNIK, JJ., concur.

PRENTICE, J., dissents.

In re the CUSTODY OF Lisa HELWIG and Elaine Helwig, Minors.

William D. HELWIG, Respondent-Appellant,

v.

The Honorable Robert E. KINNEY, Circuit Judge, Circuit Court, Oneida County, Wisconsin, Matilda G. Anderson, Enforcement Requestors-Appellees.

Nos. 1282S483, 2–1180A360.

Supreme Court of Indiana.

Dec. 15, 1982.

Father appealed from order of the Superior Court, Delaware County, Robert L. Barnet, J., directing father to deliver children to Wisconsin for custody proceedings in such state. The Court of Appeals, Shields, J., 433 N.E.2d 398, dismissed the appeal. On petition to transfer, the Supreme Court, Pivarnik, J., held that: (1) such order was not an interlocutory order, but, rather, was a "final judgment" from which appeal could be taken; (2) Superior Court had no authority to act in such case where a circuit court in Indiana had granted custody to father and had not relinquished its jurisdiction; and (3) mother could not prevail on theory that father waived question of jurisdiction and submitted to jurisdiction of Wisconsin court when he and Wisconsin attorney signed stipulation agreeing to submit custody matter to judge of such court.

Transfer granted; opinion of the Court of Appeals, vacated; and cause remanded.

DeBruler, J., dissented and filed opinion.

1. Judgment ⟜217

"Final judgment" determines rights of the parties in suit, or a distinct and definite

---

Reporter System in which their cases appear as their official reports.

The regional units of this system are the *Atlantic Reporter, Second Series* (A., A.2d); *North Western Reporter, Second Series* (N.W., N.W.2d); *Pacific Reporter, Second Series* (P., P.2d); *South Eastern Reporter, Second Series* (S.E., S.E.2d); *Southern Reporter, Second Series* (So., So.2d); and *South Western Reporter, Second Series* (S.W., S.W.2d). Because of the large volume of reported cases, three states have their own reporter units. They are the *California Reporter* (Cal. Rptr.); *Illinois Decisions* (Ill. Dec.); and *New York Supplement* and *New York Supplement, Second Series* (N.Y.S., N.Y.S.2d).

ADVERSARY PROCEEDING □ Any action, hearing, investigation, inquest, or inquiry brought by one party against another in which the party seeking relief has given legal notice to and provided the other party with an opportunity to contest the claims that have been made against him or her. □

A court trial is a typical example of an adversary hearing.

ADVERSARY SYSTEM □ The scheme of American jurisprudence wherein a judge renders a decision in a controversy between parties who assert contradictory positions during a judicial examination such as a trial or hearing. □

The opposing parties who argue against one another for a result or decision favorable to themselves can be individuals, specific classes of people, PARTNERSHIPS, ASSOCIATIONS, CORPORATIONS, and the government. See also, Stephen A. Saltzburg's essay on Adversary System.

This advance sheet from the *North Eastern Reporter* gives the court's opinion in the case of *Webster v. Indiana*.

Stephen A. Saltzburg

Adversary System

Legal adversaries Clarence Darrow, *left*, and William Jennings Bryan relax during a recess in the Scopes Monkey Trial in Dayton, Tennessee, in 1925.

The initiation of judicial criminal proceedings is far from a mere formalism. It is the starting point of our whole system of adversary criminal justice . . .

POTTER STEWART

An adversary system is a judicial system that places on competing litigants, rather than on court officials, principal responsibility for gathering evidence, formulating legal theories, and presenting evidence and theories at trial to a judge or jury. Such a system assumes that the litigants have the appropriate incentive and the capability to discover and to bring before a tribunal everything that might possibly help their respective causes. It also assumes that accurate and fair decisions are likely to be made when the parties bring forward everything they can to assist the decision maker. The decision maker—judge or jury—is expected to be neutral and to approach the case with an open mind. Generally the decision maker will not make an independent effort to investigate the case or to gather evidence but will resolve the dispute largely on the basis of what the litigants present.

Judges are aware, and juries are told, that they must be careful not to judge the merits of a case prematurely. In an adversary proceeding one side usually will present all its evidence before the other side begins to present its evidence. Thus a complete picture of a case will not develop until all evidence has been presented.

Litigants who wish to dispute legal matters—statutory or case-law points, procedural issues, or evidence questions—usually must raise their legal claims on their own and support them with appropriate authority. Since laypersons are unlikely to know enough law to do this successfully, it is common in an adversary system to find that litigants are represented by counsel who speak for them. Counsel not only argue about legal matters, they also supervise the gathering of evidence before trial and its introduction at trial.

In most places the pure adversary model, in which the decision maker does nothing but listen to the parties, does not exist. Whether a case is tried to a judge or to a jury, the judge may ask questions to clarify or to complete the testimony of witnesses called by the litigants. In many courts jurors also are permitted to ask questions. Less often the judge may call witnesses that the parties have chosen not to call. When there is, or is likely to be, a difference of opinion between expert witnesses, the judge may appoint a "court's expert" to give additional assistance in the case.

One important modern influence on the adversary system has been the development of discovery rules that permit one litigant to find out some of the information another litigant has gathered in preparation for trial. Although discovery is more prominent in civil cases than in criminal cases in which the defendant has a privilege not to incriminate himself or herself, it affects all proceedings. Discovery rules reflect a belief that litigants should gather their own evidence and present it themselves, but they should not be able to unfairly surprise an opponent at trial.

Bibliography: John Thibaut and Laurens Walker, "A Theory of Procedure," 66 *California Law Review* (May 1978): 541–566.

ADVERSE INTEREST □ The legal right or liability of a person called to testify as a witness in a lawsuit that might be lost or impaired if the party who called him or her to testify wins the case. □

This interest against the interest of the party calling a witness to the stand makes him or her an adverse or hostile witness. Although usually the party calling a witness to testify cannot impeach that person's credibility, if the person has an adverse interest, the testimony may be discredited by the party who called that witness to the stand.

ADVERSE POSSESSION □ A method of gaining legal title to real property by the actual, open, hostile, and continuous possession of it to the exclusion of its true owner for the period prescribed by state law. Personal property may also be acquired by adverse possession. □

Adverse possession is similar to PRESCRIPTION, another way to acquire title to real property by occupying it for a period of time. Prescription is not the same, however, because title acquired under it is presumed to have resulted from a lost grant, as opposed to the expiration of the statutory time limit in adverse possession.

Real property Title to land is acquired by adverse possession as a result of the lapse of the statute of limitations for EJECTMENT, which bars the commencement of a lawsuit by the true owner to recover possession of the land. Adverse possession depends upon the intent of the occupant to claim and hold real property in opposition to all the world and the demonstration of this intention by visible and hostile possession of the land so that the owner is or should be aware that adverse claims are being made.

The legal theory underlying the vesting of title to land by adverse possession is that title to land must be certain. Since the owner has, by his or her own fault and neglect, failed to protect the land against the hostile actions of the adverse possessor, an adverse possessor who has treated the land as his or her own for a significant period of time is recognized as its owner.

Title by adverse possession may be acquired against any person or corporation not excepted by statute. Property held by the Federal government, a state, or a municipal corporation cannot be taken by adverse possession. As long as the property has a public use, as a highway or school property, its ownership cannot be lost through adverse possession.

Anyone, including corporations, the Federal government, states, and municipal corporations, can be an adverse possessor.

Elements In order that adverse possession ripen into legal title, nonpermissive use by the adverse claimant that is actual, open and notorious, exclusive, hostile, and continuous for the statutory period must be established. All of these elements must coexist if title is to be acquired by adverse possession. The character, location, present state of the land, and the uses to which it is put are evaluated in each case. The adverse claimant has the burden of proving each element by a PREPONDERANCE OF THE EVIDENCE.

ACTUAL Adverse possession consists of actual occupation of the land with the intent to keep it solely for oneself. Merely claiming the land or paying taxes on it, without actually possessing it, is insufficient. Entry on the land, whether legal or not, is essential. A trespass may commence adverse possession, but there must be more than temporary use of the property by a trespasser for adverse possession to be established. Physical acts must show that the possessor is exercising the dominion over the land that an average owner of similar property would exercise. Ordinary use of the property—for example, planting and harvesting crops or cutting and selling timber—indicates actual possession. In some states acts that constitute actual possession are found in statute.

OPEN AND NOTORIOUS An adverse possessor must possess land openly for all the world to see, as a true owner would. Secretly occupying another's land does not give the occupant any legal rights. Clearing, fencing, cultivating, or improving the land demonstrates open and notorious possession, while actual residence on the land is the most open and notorious possession of all. The owner must have actual knowledge of the adverse use, or the claimant's possession must be so notorious that it is generally known by the public or the people in the neighborhood. The notoriety of the possession puts the owner on notice that the land will be lost unless he or she seeks to recover possession of it within a certain time.

EXCLUSIVE Adverse possession will not ripen into title unless the claimant has had exclusive possession of the land. Exclusive possession means sole physical occupancy. The claimant must hold the property as his or her own, in opposition to the claims of all others. Physical improvement of the land, as by the construction of fences or houses, is evidence of exclusive possession.

An adverse claimant cannot possess the property jointly with the owner. Two people may, however, claim title by adverse possession as joint tenants if they share occupancy of the land. When others or the general public have reg-

. . . the right of property is the most sacred of all the rights of citizenship, and even more important in some respects than liberty itself; either because it more nearly affects the preservation of life, or because, property being more easily usurped and more difficult to defend than life, the law ought to pay a greater attention to what is most easily taken away; or finally, because property is the true foundation of civil society.

JEAN JACQUES ROUSSEAU

ularly used or occupied the land with the adverse claimant, the requirement of exclusive possession is not satisfied. Casual use of the property by others is not, however, inconsistent with exclusive possession. Generally, EASEMENTS do not affect the exclusive possession by an adverse possessor. In some jurisdictions easements exercised by the public or railroad rights of way will destroy exclusive possession.

HOSTILE Possession must be hostile, sometimes called adverse, if title is to mature from adverse possession. Hostile possession means that the claimant must occupy the land in opposition to the true owner's rights. There need not be a dispute or fighting over title as long as the claimant intends to claim the land and hold it against the interests of the owner and all the world. Possession must be hostile from its commencement and must continue throughout the statutory period.

One type of hostile possession occurs when the claimant enters and remains on land under COLOR OF TITLE. Color of title is the appearance of title as a result of a DEED that seems by its language to give the claimant valid title but, in fact, does not because some aspect of it is defective. If a person, for example, was suffering from a legal disability at the time he or she executed a deed, the grantee-claimant does not receive actual title. But the grantee-claimant does have color of title because it would appear to anyone reading the deed that good title had been conveyed. If a claimant possesses the land in the manner required by law for the full statutory period, his or her color of title will become actual title as a result of adverse possession.

CONTINUOUS Adverse possession must be continuous for the full statutory period if title is to vest. Continuity means regular, uninterrupted occupancy of the land. Mere occasional or sporadic use is not enough. Continuity is sometimes explained as the daily control of the land by the adverse claimant for the length of the statutory period. If a person has continuously occupied only a part of all the land claimed under adverse possession, he or she will acquire title only to the occupied portion.

While continuous possession is required for the acquisition of title by adverse possession, it is not necessary that only one person hold the land continuously for the statutory period. The time periods that successive adverse occupants have possessed the land may be added together to meet the continuity requirement if PRIVITY exists between the parties. The addition of these different periods is called *tacking*. Privity refers to the giving of possession of the land from one owner to ʰe next so that it is continuously occupied by a possessor. Privity exists between different per-

sons whose interests are related to each other by a sale or inheritance of the land or by operation of law, as possession by a trustee in bankruptcy.

Tacking is permitted only when the possession by the prior occupant had been adverse or under color of title. If any time lapses between the end of one owner's possession and the start of another's occupation, there is no continuity, so tacking will not be allowed.

Interruption of continuous possession deprives the adverse possessor of the legal effect of his or her prior occupancy. The statute of limitations will begin to run again from the time he or she starts actual, open, hostile, notorious, and exclusive possession. The length of the interruption is insignificant as long as it disturbs continuous possession. At that time the law restores constructive possession of the land to the true owner.

The commencement of a lawsuit by the owner against the occupant over the right of ownership and possession of the land is one way to interrupt continuous possession. It may be an action to quiet title, for trespass, for an injunction involving possessive rights, or to file a petition for registration of title. Such lawsuits will destroy the continuity of possession only if successfully pursued to final judgments. If the owner chooses to abandon or settle a suit, or if a court dismisses it, the continuity of possession is not breached.

The entry of the owner upon the land with the intent to repossess it is a clear exercise of ownership that disturbs possession. A survey of the land made at the request of the true owner does not interrupt possession unless the purpose is to help the true owner take possession. The owner's actions must be notorious and open so there can be no doubt as to what is intended. An accidental, casual, secret, or permissive entry is ineffective. While the entry must be notorious, it must also be peaceable to prevent violence and warfare, which might otherwise result.

The payment of real estate taxes by the owner, while demonstrating that he or she has not abandoned land, is not considered to have any impact on continuous possession.

The adverse claimant may destroy his or her continuous possession by abandoning the land or giving it to someone else, even the owner, before the time at which title to it would vest. It does not matter how long or brief the abandonment is as long as it was intentional. A temporary absence from the land is not the same as an abandonment and has no effect on the occupancy, provided it is for a reasonable period of time.

STATUTORY PERIOD The time period of the statute of limitations that must expire before title can be acquired by adverse possession varies from state to state. No statute will begin to run until the adverse claimant actually possesses the property in question under color of title or claim of right, where necessary. As of that time, the landowner is entitled to bring a lawsuit against the possessor to recover the property.

The possessor must occupy the property for the full statutory period. In jurisdictions that also require color of title, it must coexist with possession for the complete period.

If the statute of limitations has been suspended—for example, because there is a lawsuit pending between the owner and the claimant or the owner is insane, an infant, or serving in the armed services—that amount of time will not be counted toward the time necessary for the acquisition of title.

Acquired title Once adverse possession is completed, the claimant has full legal title of the property. The expiration of the statutory period eliminates any cause of action or liability for ejectment or trespass regarding the new owner's prior unlawful possession of the property. Once the time period is satisfied, the adverse possessor is considered the original owner of the land. He or she may use the land any way he or she sees fit provided it is lawful.

Personal property Ownership of personal property may be acquired by adverse possession if the same requisites are met. The claimant must possess the property actually, openly, notoriously, exclusively, hostilely, under claim of right, and uninterrupted for the statutory period.

ADVISE □ To give an opinion or recommend a plan or course of action; to give notice; to encourage, inform, or acquaint. □

Advise does not mean the same as instruct or persuade. If a statute authorized a trial court to acquit, the court has no power to instruct the jury to acquit. The court can only counsel, and the jury is not bound by the advice.

ADVISEMENT □ Deliberation; consultation. □

A court takes a case "under advisement" after it has heard the arguments made by the counsel of opposing sides in the lawsuit but before it renders its decision.

ADVISORY JURY □ A body of persons selected according to law to give a verdict in a lawsuit even though their decision is not binding on the court. □

An advisory jury determines facts, and it functions the same as a petit jury in any other trial except that its decisions are merely persuasive to, but not binding upon, the court. In cases where there is no right to demand a jury trial, a party may by MOTION ask the judge to call in an advisory jury, or the judge may decide to do so on his or her own initiative. The jury may be asked to determine one or more issues in the case, but the judge may enter judgment contrary to its decision at his or her own DISCRETION.

ADVISORY OPINION □ A statement issued by a court in response to the request of the government or an interested party which indicates how it would decide a matter if a lawsuit were commenced. □

An advisory opinion is a judicial interpretation of the law without having any binding effect on the parties or precedential value under the principle of *stare decisis*. It is not the same as a DECLARATORY JUDGMENT, a determination of a justiciable controversy between the parties which clearly delineates their respective legal rights.

Not all courts render advisory opinions. While the INTERNATIONAL COURT OF JUSTICE and some state courts will issue advisory opinions, FEDERAL COURTS do not since their jurisdiction is limited to CASES OR CONTROVERSIES.

Regardless of the scope of their jurisdiction, many courts refuse to issue advisory opinions for policy reasons. Some courts regard situations in which advisory opinions are sought as lacking concrete facts which are integral to a careful and thoughtful analysis of the legal principles most likely governing the situation. The significance and reliability of the opinion rendered by a court might be materially affected by the subsequent disclosure of new facts. Also, a proceeding for an advisory opinion might not include all the interested parties and, therefore, all the relevant facts might not be presented for consideration of the court.

The staggering workload composed of cases that are RIPE for decision by the courts is another reason for the refusing to entertain suits seeking advisory opinions. The additional time and administrative expenses that would be spent in rendering the opinions would diminish the valuable time available to the court to determine actual controversies. Such opinions might eventually lead to litigation, thereby creating an increased burden on the court's limited resources and time, in addition to the time already spent in issuing the advisory opinion.

Finally, the rendering of advisory opinions often places a court in situations where there is the likelihood of a conflict with other government departments, unless the parties are actually engaged in a real controversy.

See also, Robert J. Harris's essay on Advisory Opinions.

Advisory Opinions

Justice William R. Day wrote the Court's opinion in the *Muskrat* case of 1911.

An advisory opinion is one given in response to the request of a member of the executive branch or the legislature for advice pertaining to legal issues which are not presented in the regular course of adjudication. Advisory opinions were once common in England, where the monarch was regarded as the fountain of justice, but after the judicial functions of the House of Lords were transferred to the law lords, the advice of the justices has seldom been invoked.

In the United States the framers of the Constitution rejected James Madison's proposal to authorize advisory opinions and another proposal for a Council of Revision. These proposals would have involved the courts in collaboration with the political departments of government on issues of constitutionality. In 1793 when Secretary of State Thomas Jefferson, acting on behalf of President George Washington, sought to obtain answers to many questions pertaining to neutrality during the wars arising out of the French Revolution, the justices of the Supreme Court, with polite reluctance tinged with the pride of independence, refused to comply. The justices asserted that the giving of advice was no part of the judicial power, which under the Constitution extended only to cases and controversies. Thus the rule against advisory opinions seems to be a mandate of the Constitution and the separation of powers.

Among all the rules emanating from that elusive concept "justiciability," the Supreme Court has been most consistent in applying that against advisory opinions. It has extended the rule to include acts of Congress authorizing suits to test the legality of action where any decision would be merely advisory or a mere recommendation. Thus the Court invalidated an act of Congress authorizing certain Indians to sue the United States to challenge the validity of an allotment respecting the claims of individual or groups of Indians because the act "would require the Court" to give opinions in the nature of advice concerning legislative action (*Muskrat v. United States*, 219 U.S. 346, 362, 31 S.Ct. 250, 256, 55 L.Ed. 246 [1911]). Many years later the Court refused to review a proceeding of the Civil Aeronautics Board which required presidential approval to become effective. The attempt to interpose judicial review between the board and the president was called "an advisory opinion in its most obnoxious form. . ." (*Chicago & Southern Airlines, Inc. v. Waterman S. S. Corporation*, 333 U.S. 103, 113, 68 S.Ct 431, 437, 92 L.Ed. 568 [1948]; see also, *United Public Workers of America v. Mitchell*, 330 U.S. 75, 89, 67 S.Ct. 556, 564, 91 L.Ed 754 [1947]).

In contrast to Federal practice, a few state constitutions authorize advisory opinions, most notably that of Massachusetts. But there, and in other states, the highest courts may refuse to respond to unreasonable requests. Such opinions are not *res judicata* and are not precedents. The Massachusetts Supreme Court of

Judicial Errors will not give advice on existing statutes or pass upon the facts at issue.

The Canadian courts may render advisory opinions; the Australians may not. See also, William F. Swindler's essay on Framers of the Constitution; and Harold W. Chase's essay on Separation of Powers.

Bibliography: Edward S. Corwin, ed., *The Constitution of the United States: Analysis and Interpretation* (1953); Felix Frankfurter, "Advisory Opinions," *Encyclopedia of the Social Sciences*; Gerald Gunther, *Cases and Materials on Constitutional Law*, 9th ed. (1975) and references there cited.

ADVOCACY ☐ The act of pleading or arguing a case or a position; forceful persuasion. ☐

ADVOCATE

☐ To support or defend by argument; to recommend publicly.

☐ An individual who presents or argues another's case; one who gives legal advice and pleads the cause of another before a court or tribunal; a COUNSELOR.

☐ A person admitted to the practice of law who advises clients of their legal rights and argues their cases in court. ☐

AERIAL WARFARE, LAWS OF   See Warfare, International Regulation of.

AERONAUTICS ☐ The science and art of flight, encompassing the functioning and ownership of aircraft vehicles from balloons to those that travel into space. ☐

Aviation is travel by means of an aircraft that is heavier than air. *Aerospace* is a term used in reference to the atmosphere and the area beyond, such as the *aerospace industry*, which is involved with the planning and building of vehicles operating in both air and space.

Airspace is the region which extends above REAL PROPERTY. *Air transportation*, as set forth by Federal statute, refers to interstate and distant conveyance of people, cargo, and mail by United States and foreign aircraft vehicles.

Airspace rights The Federal government has jurisdiction over airspace within its domain, and each state has authority over the space above the grounds within its borders except in places within the domain of Federal regulation. An aircraft is subject to the authority of the Federal government and to the authority of a particular state while traveling over it, but such power does not deprive landowners of their lawful rights in surface sail. Landowners have AIR RIGHTS that extend upward beyond their property, the boundaries of which are delineated by local ZONING ordinances. These air rights ordinarily may be used to the extent that they are connected to the enjoyment of the property.

Since the general public has a right to freedom of travel in the navigable airspace of the United States, an aircraft may have legal access to airspace above private property. A landowner might have a civil cause of action for TRESPASS or NUISANCE, however, where an aircraft enters his or her airspace in such manner as to constitute an infringement on the landowner's right to the use and possession of the property. In some instances the landowner is entitled to an INJUNCTION to prohibit unlawful intrusion of his or her airspace.

The Wright Brothers made the first successful powered airplane flight on December 17, 1903, at Kitty Hawk, N.C. This historic photo shows the first of four flights that day with Orville at the controls and Wilbur running alongside the take-off track.

1   The earth seen from 22,000 miles in space.   2 The *Skylab* space station in earth orbit, *above right,* with its solar panels extended.

Space and the Law

The launching of the Soviet satellite Sputnik in 1957 demonstrated irrefutably that the space age was upon us. Subsequent space activities increased the accuracy of our geographic knowledge of the earth, sharpened our weather predictions, and vastly extended our communications networks. The space expeditions of the late 1960s and early 1970s placed astronauts on the moon and demonstrated the feasibility of sustained human activity outside the earth's atmosphere.

Space technology has also shown a potentially dangerous side that makes a compelling argument for the development of space law. Spy and killer satellites, possible orbiting weapons systems, and the likelihood of falling space satellites or radioactive space debris have raised questions about the scope of space law by the general public.

Over the last twenty-five years, the United Nations General Assembly has passed a series of resolutions that outline the development of space law. The essential thrust of these resolutions is that all space activities shall be peaceful, that all nations shall have the same freedom to explore outer space, that no nation shall own any part of outer space or a celestial body, and that any nation engaging in space exploration will be liable for any damages it may cause. Whether these resolutions will have any significant impact on current space research and exploration remains to be seen.

3   Launched on July 16, 1969, the first men to land on the moon were Neil A. Armstrong and Edwin E. Aldrin, Jr. Here, Aldrin explores the landing site on the Sea of Tranquility.

4   The moon, seen from *Gemini VII,* rises above the vapor-filled atmosphere of the earth.

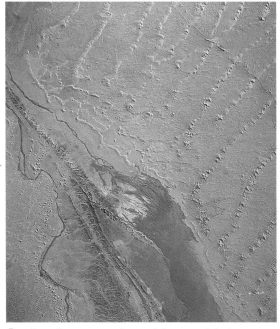

5   Seen from space, the sand dunes and drainage systems produced by wind and water in an Algerian desert are more easily comprehended.

6   NASA has designed "personal rescue enclosures" containing compact life support and communications systems that enable an astronaut to transfer from a disabled space vehicle to a rescue ship without becoming depressurized.

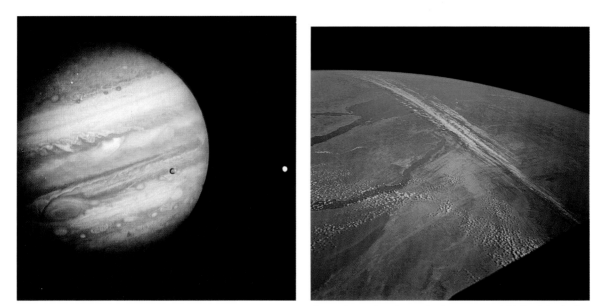

7   The moons of Jupiter appear dwarfed by the giant planet as they revolve above its turbid and inhospitable atmosphere.

8   Cirrus clouds mark the course of high-altitude jet stream winds over the Red Sea and the Nile River valley.

9   Measuring 375 miles in diameter and 78,000 feet high, Mount Olympus on Mars is the greatest known mountain in the solar system. The orbiter *Viking I* photographed it on July 31, 1976, surrounded by Martian cloud systems resembling those of earth.

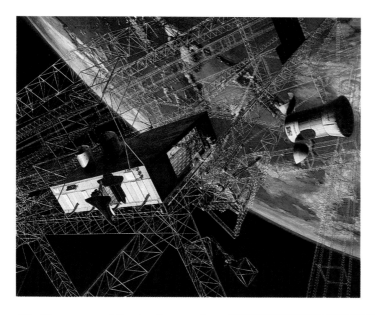

10 Once building materials are in earth orbit, the assembly of large space structures will be relatively easy because there is no gravity, wind, or moisture to contend with. In this artist's conception, space engineers assemble an extensive framework to support solar energy collectors.

11 The prerequisite to large-scale space construction is a shuttlecraft capable of transporting equipment and people back and forth between the surface of the earth and outer space. Here, the shuttlecraft *Columbia* makes a landing approach after a mission in space.

12 The interior of a space colony of the future will simulate the ecological and social conditions of the earth complete with lakes, forests, and neighboring communities. A transparent wheel one mile in diameter revolving at one revolution per minute will contain an earthlike atmosphere and provide the gravity needed to hold the environment in place.

Air transportation regulation Initially Congress granted the Federal Civil Aeronautics Board (CAB) sole power over the financial management of the entire air transportation industry. Included in this responsibility was the authority to give licenses to airlines, to accept or reject proposed rates and fares, to aid and promote air travel in small communities, and to endorse or disapprove proposed MERGERS and CONSOLIDATIONS of airline companies. The abolition of the CAB is a certainty, however, since congressional legislation of the late 1970s was designed to bring about the deregulation of the airline industry.

The Federal Aviation Administration (FAA) is the agency with the authority to govern air commerce. The intent of such regulation is to advance the growth and safety of air travel while simultaneously satisfying national defense needs. The director of the FAA has the power to engage in, or monitor, work and testing that will bring about the production of advanced aircraft; to set forth prescribed rules and regulations for the planning and servicing of airplanes; and to administer stringent sanctions if the regulations are not observed. The FAA is also responsible for air traffic control at airports. The National Transportation Safety Board (NTSB) is charged with the responsibility of investigating the circumstances surrounding, and the causes of, accidents involving aircraft.

Certificate requirements An airplane must have a valid airworthiness certificate in order for it to be lawfully operated. The airworthiness of a plane is determined by an inspector authorized by the FAA. The inspector may neither delegate this duty to inspect the aircraft nor depart from procedures for inspection which have been prescribed by the administrator of the FAA.

The FAA administrator is empowered to create minimum standards for the inspection, maintenance, and repair of air carrier equipment as well as for safe operation of the vehicle. Another important function of the administrator is to issue certificates to eligible aeronautical personnel: that includes people who inspect, maintain, overhaul, and repair aircraft as well as pilots and navigators. The administrator specifies the particular function which each of these individuals is qualified to perform.

Certain prerequisites exist for an airline pilot rating, including a great degree of technical skill, medical fitness, care, judgment, and emotional stability. If public safety is endangered, the FAA administrator will either revoke or suspend a pilot's license. An airman is entitled to NOTICE and a fair hearing before the revocation or suspension of his or her certification, absent an emergency that warrants such immediate action. The airman may appeal the order of suspension or revocation to the NTSB, and subsequent appeals may be brought to the usual appellate channels of FEDERAL COURTS.

Regulation on the state and local level A state or municipality has the authority to regulate the air traffic that affects it. This power, however, is limited by the condition that the regulation must not interfere or conflict with either interstate commerce or Federal restraints. State or municipal regulations on noise precipitated by aircraft engines may not, for example, conflict with Federal rules governing noise pollution.

Airport operation The state can give a local legislature the power to regulate airports and their connected facilities. States may join together to form a regional airport authority to operate an airport. An airport may also be built and maintained by a private party or a CORPORATION, subject to the requirement that use and enjoyment of neighboring landowners' property is not unreasonably disrupted.

Airports that are not properly constructed and operated might amount to nuisances. A private homeowner can sue for damages in the event that an improperly run airport constitutes a nuisance, and can attempt to have the court suspend its operation pursuant to the provisions of an injunction. Notice must be given to the municipality before such a cause of action may be commenced against it. In considering the need for intervention concerning the building and operation of airports, courts examine the interests of the concerned parties in light of prevailing PUBLIC POLICY in favor of encouraging quiet use and enjoyment of one's land compared to the interests of society at large in accessible and convenient air travel.

The creation and maintenance of airports are subject to zoning regulations. In certain jurisdictions a public agency is empowered by the state to adopt zoning laws which limit the use of adjacent property. Such ordinances are designed to reduce interference with the operation of the airport.

The owner of a public airport may arrange leases for its use, and a municipality that owns an airport may charge reasonable fees for the right to do business there. A public airport owner has the power to govern its ground transportation, to give exclusive privileges to transport passengers to and from the airport to qualified individuals and companies, and to run an automobile rental company on airport grounds.

Use and ownership of aircraft vehicles The legality of the SALE or conveyance of an aircraft is regulated by the statute of the jurisdiction where the document of conveyance or sale is transferred.

Federal law mandates the registration of aircraft and the proper recording of any paper that affects its TITLE, such as a MORTGAGE. Such recording must take place at the administration and records branch of the FAA. In addition, documents creating SECURITY interests in the aircraft must be recorded to provide notice to prospective purchasers of prior claims to the vehicle.

General principles of contract law govern aircraft rental and parties to the agreement are ordinarily bound by its terms. The renter of a defective vehicle might, however, have the right to terminate the contract since the individual offering the aircraft for rent is obligated to provide a vehicle in satisfactory operating condition.

Duties in aircraft operation   An individual who is injured as a result of the operation of an aircraft usually has a legally enforceable right to DAMAGES for any injuries or losses sustained.

Manufacturers   A manufacturer is under a duty to exercise reasonable care and profi-

ciency in the design, production, and assembly of an aircraft vehicle. Liability for a departure from this duty may be extended to the manufacturer regardless of whether that company was directly involved in the manufacture of the parts. The law will imply a WARRANTY of proper design and manufacture of an aircraft. A manufacturer of parts will also be held responsible for damage caused by the product and must use a high degree of care in their production, although they need not be made accident-proof. A manufacturer is not relieved of a continuing obligation to improve the component parts of an air vehicle when there is continuing risk to safe travel.

Pilots   The pilot of a private aircraft is subject to ordinary NEGLIGENCE standards in the absence of a special law. The pilot is required to exercise ordinary, but not extreme, care and caution regarding its operation. Negligence rules, however, impose a greater standard of care when applied to aviation, because of the severity and magnitude of potential harm posed by improper operation of an aircraft.

Owners   Generally ownership of an aircraft vehicle is insufficient to render an owner

Newspapers announced the success of Charles Lindbergh's transatlantic flight with great acclaim, demonstrating how high public esteem was for individual achievement and technological innovation in aeronautics in the 1920s.

Chicago Sunday Tribune

liable for damage resulting from its unreasonable operation by another. In certain jurisdictions, however, an owner who lends a plane to an individual he or she knows to be reckless or incompetent will be held responsible. Similarly, the Federal or state government cannot evade liability for damage arising out of the improper operation of its aircraft by government employees.

Passengers Passengers in a private aircraft have the obligation to exercise reasonable care for their own well-being. They must subscribe to the REASONABLE PERSON standard and refrain from going on a particular flight that would be an obvious danger, such as a flight during a hurricane.

Passengers on airlines and other air common carriers must observe safety precautions by obeying instructions of flight attendants, such as by fastening their seatbelts.

Operators of airplanes An airport operator has the duty to exercise ordinary care in protecting aircraft on its premises and the people who use airport facilities. Neglecting to maintain the airport premises in a reasonably safe condition results in TORT liability for resulting injuries to persons present.

Air traffic control The Federal government has total responsibility for air traffic control. Air traffic controllers have a duty to keep aircraft from colliding with each other by guiding their paths. Liability can be extended to the Federal government for the negligence of its air traffic controllers. CONTRIBUTORY NEGLIGENCE by the individual harmed might, however, block recovery against the United States for damage caused only partially by the negligence of controllers.

Airlines An airline has the duty to employ the greatest degree of care possible to protect its passengers. Liability might be imposed for harm to a passenger resulting from wrongful behavior of its employees. It must also take steps to guard passengers against misconduct of fellow passengers.

Companies that accept goods for air transport must exercise a high degree of care to properly handle and deliver such goods. Liability for loss or damage may be restricted to a prearranged amount, which must be listed on the passenger's ticket in the case of baggage or on the BILL OF LADING regarding the goods shipped.

Flying schools A flying school that maintains facilities that interfere with the customary use and enjoyment of property by neighboring landowners can be liable for nuisance or trespass. A student pilot flying with a flight instructor is considered legally as a passenger, and,

Fastest, and most controversial of all commercial jetliners, the original Anglo-French-built supersonic Concorde undergoes flight tests.

therefore, the school owes the same duty of care to the student as a commercial airline owes to its passenger. A trainee, however, assumes certain risks while being taught to fly and the school can sucessfully assert the defense of assumption of the risk in tort cases. A member of a flight CLUB, as an owner of an airplane that belongs to the club, may be held personally liable for accidents that might occur while he or she is piloting the craft. Statutes which govern the liability of a flight club member should be consulted.

Air piracy Aircraft piracy or an attempt to hijack an airplane is a Federal offense, punishable by either death or imprisonment. Airlines can deny an individual passage on an airplane if a magnetometer (an instrument used to measure magnetic intensity) indicates the presence of a metal object, such as a weapon, on that person by registering a positive reading and the person refuses to surrender to the appropriate officials any metal object that might have energized the instrument.

Aerospace The National Aeronautics and Space Administration (NASA) was established by Congress to organize, direct, and carry

Aviation pioneer, Amelia Earhart, first woman to fly the Atlantic, disappeared mysteriously during a trans-Pacific flight in 1937.

Astronaut Alan B. Shepard, Jr., commander of the Apollo 14 mission in 1971, stands beside the U.S. flag deployed on the moon.

One of the newest and most technically advanced passenger planes, the Boeing 767, was designed for fuel economy and medium-range service.

The reusable space shuttle *Columbia* touches down gracefully after a successful 54½ hour mission in space.

out research into difficulties attached to flight within and beyond the atmosphere of the earth and to facilitate the development and functioning of aeronautical vehicles.

AFFIDAVIT ☐ A written statement of facts voluntarily made by an affiant under an OATH or AFFIRMATION administered by a person authorized to do so by law. ☐

Distinctions An affidavit is voluntarily made without any cross-examination of the affiant and, therefore, is not the same as a DEPOSITION, a record of an examination of a witness or a party made either voluntarily or pursuant to a SUBPOENA, as if the party were testifying in court under cross-examination. A PLEADING—a request to a court to exercise its judicial power in favor of a party that contains allegations or conclusions of facts that are not necessarily verified—differs from an affidavit, which states facts under oath.

Basis An affidavit is based upon either the personal knowledge of the affiant or his or her information and belief. Personal knowledge is the recognition of particular facts by either direct observation or experience. Information and belief is what the affiant feels he or she can state as true, although not based on firsthand knowledge.

The affiant Any person having the intellectual capacity to take an oath or make an affirmation and who has knowledge of the facts that are in dispute may make an affidavit. There is no age requirement for an affiant. As long as a person is old enough to understand the facts and the significance of the oath or affirmation he or she makes, the affidavit is valid. A criminal conviction does not make a person incapable of making an affidavit, but an adjudication of incompetency does.

Someone familiar with the matters in question may make an affidavit on behalf of another, but that person's authority to do so must be clear. A guardian may make an affidavit for a minor or insane person incapable of doing so. An attorney may make an affidavit for a client if it is impossible for the client to do so. When necessary to the performance of duties, a personal representative, agent, or corporate officer or partner may execute an affidavit that indicates the capacity in which the affiant acts.

A court cannot force a person to make an affidavit, since, by definition, an affidavit is a voluntary statement.

The taker of the affidavit Any public officer authorized by law to administer oaths and affirmations—such as city recorders, court clerks, notaries, county clerks, commissioners of deeds, and court commissioners—may take affidavits. Justices of the peace and magistrates are sometimes authorized to take affidavits. Unless restricted by state law, judges may take affidavits involving controversies before them.

An officer cannot take affidavits outside of the particular jurisdiction in which he or she exercises authority. The source of this authority must appear at the bottom of the affidavit. A notary, for example, would indicate the county in which he or she is commissioned and the expiration date of the commission.

An official SEAL is not essential to the validity of the affidavit but may be placed on it by the proper official.

The oath or affirmation Unless otherwise provided by statute, an oath is essential to an affidavit. The statement of the affiant does not become an affidavit unless the proper official administers the oath.

When religious convictions prevent the affiant from taking an oath, he or she may affirm that the statements in the affidavit are true.

Contents There is no standard form or language to be used in an affidavit as long as the facts contained within it are stated clearly and definitely. Unnecessary language or legal arguments should not appear. Clerical and grammatical errors, while to be avoided, are inconsequential.

The affidavit usually must contain the address of the affiant and the date that the statement was made, in addition to the affiant's signature or mark. Where the affidavit has been made is also noted. When an affidavit is based on the affiant's information and belief, it must state the source of the affiant's information and the grounds for the affiant's belief in the accuracy of such information. This permits the court to draw its own conclusions about the information in the affidavit.

An affiant is strictly responsible for the truth and accuracy of the contents of the affidavit. If false statements are made, the affiant can be prosecuted for PERJURY.

Functions Affidavits are used in business and in judicial and administrative proceedings.

Business Generally affidavits are used in business whenever an official statement which others might rely upon is needed. Statements of the financial stability of a corporation, the pedigree of animals, and the financial conditions of a person applying for CREDIT are examples of affidavits used in the commercial world.

AFFIDAVIT

A sample affidavit

UNITED STATES DISTRICT COURT
EASTERN DISTRICT OF NEW YORK

-----------------------------------x

IN THE MATTER OF THE APPLICATION OF
          JOHN DOE   SPONSORING AFFIDAVIT

TO BE ADMITTED AS AN ATTORNEY, PROCTOR,
COUNSELLOR, SOLICITOR AND ADVOCATE

-----------------------------------x

STATE OF NEW YORK   )   ss:
COUNTY OF NASSAU   )

   FREDERICK ROE, being duly sworn, deposes and says:

   FIRST: I reside at 200 Valentines Road, Westbury, New York, and maintain offices and official address for the general practice of law at 44 Court Street, County of Nassau, State of New York.

   SECOND: I am an attorney at law having been admitted to practice in the Supreme Court, Appellate Division of the Second Department of New York during the May, 1953 Term, and the United States District Court for the Eastern District of New York, July 14, 1955. That I am now a member of the New York State Bar in good standing.

   THIRD: I have known the petitioner since January 14, 1970, and have visited with him on numerous occasions.

   FOURTH: I know that the petitioner has practiced law in all of its branches in the various courts of the State of New York for more than five years; that petitioner is a man of good moral character and fully qualified to be admitted to practice in this court.

   FIFTH: I know that the petitioner has been attorney in actions on contracts and breach of contract, commercial actions and proceedings, matrimonial, negligence, Surrogate's and injunction proceedings. He has also drafted certificates of incorporation, copartnership agreements and various contracts and has been engaged in the general practice of law.

   SIXTH: In my opinion petitioner believes in the fundamental principles of the Constitution of the United States and will make an honorable and capable member of the bar of this Court.

                                       FREDERICK ROE

                                          ————————————————

                                              (signed)

SIGNED TO BEFORE ME THIS

———————— day of ——————— 19————

Judicial proceedings Affidavits serve as EVIDENCE in civil actions and criminal prosecutions in certain instances. They are considered a very weak type of evidence because they are not taken in court, and the affiant is not subject to cross-examination. Their use is usually restricted to times when no better evidence can be offered. If a witness who has made an affidavit is not available to testify at a trial, his affidavit may be admitted as evidence. If the witness is present, his affidavit is inadmissible except when used to impeach the witness's testimony, or to help the witness with past recollection of facts.

Affidavits are also used as evidence in EX PARTE proceedings such as a hearing for the issuance of a temporary restraining order or an order to show cause. The expeditious nature of such proceedings is considered to substantially outweigh the weak probative value of the affidavits. In addition, there is normally a subsequent opportunity in the course of litigation for the opposing party to refute the affidavits or cross-examine the affiants.

An affidavit based on the knowledge of the affiant is accorded more weight than one based on information and belief. When admissible, affidavits are not conclusive evidence of the facts stated therein.

Administrative proceedings Affidavits are frequently used in administrative and quasi-judicial proceedings as evidence when no objection is made to their admission and there is an opportunity for cross-examination.

For a sample of an affidavit that must be filed by an attorney sponsoring another attorney for admission to the Federal bar, see page 120.

AFFILIATION PROCEEDING ☐ A court hearing to determine whether a man against whom the action is brought is the father of an illegitimate child and thus legally bound to provide financial support for the child. ☐

See also, Illegitimacy.

AFFINITY ☐ The relationship that a person has to the blood relatives of a spouse by virtue of the marriage. ☐

The doctrine of affinity developed from a maxim of CANON LAW that a husband and wife were made one by their marriage. There are three types of affinity. *Direct affinity* exists between the husband and his wife's relations by blood, or between the wife and the husband's relations by blood. *Secondary affinity* is between a spouse and the other spouse's relatives by marriage. *Collateral affinity* exits between a spouse and the relatives of the other spouse's relatives. The de-termination of affinity is important in various legal matters, such as deciding whether to prosecute a person for INCEST or whether to disqualify a JUROR for BIAS.

AFFIRM
☐ To ratify, establish, or reassert.
☐ To make a solemn and formal declaration, as a substitute for an oath, that the statements contained in an AFFIDAVIT are true or that a WITNESS will tell the truth.
☐ In the practice of appellate courts, to declare a judgment, decree, or order valid and to concur in its correctness so that it must stand as rendered in the lower court. ☐

A judgment, decree, or order that is not affirmed is either remanded (sent back to the lower court with instructions to correct the irregularities noted in the appellate opinion) or reversed (changed by the appellate court so that the decision of the lower court is overturned).
☐ As a matter of PLEADING, to allege or aver a matter of fact. ☐

AFFIRMANCE ☐ A delaration by an appellate court that a judgment, order, or decree of a lower court that has been brought before it for review is valid and will be upheld. ☐

AFFIRMATION ☐ A solemn and formal declaration of the truth of a statement, such as an AFFIDAVIT or the actual or prospective testimony of a witness or a party that is in place of an OATH. ☐

An affirmation is used when a person cannot take an oath because of religious convictions.

AFFIRMATIVE ACTION ☐ A concerted effort by an employer, educational institution, or organization to rectify past prejudicial practices against specific classes of individuals, such as blacks or women, by affording them temporary preferential treatment until such time as true equal opportunity is achieved. ☐

Affirmative action might, for example, be taken voluntarily by private industry or as a result of a court order or legislative provision. It is designed to protect the CIVIL RIGHTS of certain groups. Employers and unions have, in the past, argued that programs of this nature have caused discrimination against those who were already employed. Affirmative action programs in education have also been attacked as reverse discrimination. See also, Arthur Larson's essay on Affirmative Action; entries on Bakke and on Weber, as well as J. Harvie Wilkinson III's essays on the Bakke Case; and on the Weber Case.

. . . not to use the laws is as bad as to have no laws at all.

ARISTOTLE

Arthur Larson

Affirmative Action

Hired in 1969 as a temporary assistant professor of chemistry at the University of Minnesota, Dr. Shyamala Rajender sued the university in 1973 over tenure. The U.S. District Court certified her complaint as a class action suit in 1977. The court decided the case in 1980 finding that the university had engaged in discrimination against Dr. Rajender. Although the university does not admit that it discriminated, the settlement covers all non-student female academic employees, applicants, and potential applicants for the years from 1972 to 1989 as well as an award of $100,000 to Dr. Rajender.

Courtesy of St. Paul Pioneer Press

Affirmative action in discrimination law means taking measures that go beyond merely ceasing or avoiding discrimination; it means taking measures that attempt to undo or compensate for the effects of past discrimination.

The principle is encountered in several major categories of discrimination—most notably employment and education, but also such areas as housing and government contracting.

The concept is a relatively recent one in U.S. law. The nearest thing to it, for many years, was an occasional concession to American Indians, such as the Minnesota statute granting them the exclusive right to gather wild rice within reservations. The first major application of the principle was in public school desegregation. After *Brown v. Board of Education of Topeka, Kansas,* 347 U.S. 483, 74 S.Ct. 686, 98 L.Ed. 873 (1954) established the substantive constitutional right to a nonsegregated education, there ensued a decade or more in which it became apparent that, if the law said no more than "stop your past illegal segregating," almost no visible change occurred in the actual racial composition of classrooms. Finally, in 1964 the Supreme Court decreed in *Green v. County School Board,* 391 U.S. 430, 88 S.Ct. 1689, 20 L.Ed.2d 716 (1968), that the only thing that counted was measurable results. There followed the enforced adoption of an array of devices such as redistricting, majority to minority transfers, school pairings, "magnet schools," new school constructions, abandonment of all-black schools, and, of course, busing. The full weight of the Supreme Court was thrown behind a massive busing plan in *Swann v. Charlotte-Mecklenburg Board,* 402 U.S. 1, 91 S.Ct. 1267, 28 L.Ed.2d 554 (1971).

In employment, two basic categories of affirmative action can be identified: (1) coercive and (2) voluntary. Coercive plans, in turn, fall into two groups: (a) plans imposed as a condition of government contracts or grants under Executive Order 11246 (42 U.S.C.A. § 2000e note [1965]) and to benefit the handicapped under the Rehabilitation Act of 1973 (29 U.S.C.A. § 701 et seq.); and (b) court-imposed remedies under Title VII of the Civil Rights Act of 1964 (42 U.S.C.A. § 2000e et seq.). Voluntary plans are those adopted by an employer, university, or the like, when under no direct legal compulsion to do so.

The earliest affirmative action plans were concerned with race, but plans now frequently extend to sex, national origin, and religion.

The first major legal setback to voluntary affirmative action was *Regents of University of California v. Bakke,* 438 U.S. 265, 98 S.Ct. 2733, 57 L.Ed.2d 750 (1978). By a closely split vote, the Supreme Court struck down a university admissions plan that set aside a specific number of places for minority applicants. The key opinion, that of Justice Lewis Powell, recognized that affirmative action might sometimes be appropriate to undo past wrongs but held that it had to be based upon proved constitutional or statutory violations found by an authorized body—a condition not satisfied here. The next landmark case, *United Steelworkers v. Weber,* 443 U.S. 193, 99 S.Ct. 2721, 61 L.Ed.2d 480 (1979), was expected by many to extend this same reasoning to the area of employment but did not. Kaiser Aluminum Company had voluntarily adopted a plan under which blacks were given preference over more-senior whites in a special training program. For various reasons, including the absence of Justices Powell and John Paul Stevens from the case, the Court upheld the plan. The third landmark case was *Fullilove v. Klutznick,* 448 U.S. 448, 100 S.Ct. 2758, 65 L.Ed.2d 902 (1980), in which the Court, in

A picket outside the Detroit Federal Building protests against Bakke's reverse-discrimination contention.

Affirmative action programs at the Federal and local levels have sometimes brought out negative reactions. When Allan Bakke sued the Regents of the University of California because he was denied admission to the university's medical school due to its affirmative action program, the case prompted serious discussion of the possibility of "reverse discrimination" resulting from the type of plan the university employed. A year after the Supreme Court decided the *Bakke* case in his favor, the Court rejected a suit brought by Brian Weber against the Kaiser Aluminum Company and the United Steelworkers of America that claimed he had suffered reverse discrimination in a company job-training program.

an opinion by Chief Justice Warren E. Burger, upheld a congressionally enacted 10 percent set-aside for minority business enterprise. Significantly, however, six of the justices agreed that in affirmative action cases there must be a finding by a competent body of past constitutional or statutory violations.

Legal issues surrounding affirmative action can be reduced to three main questions. If the past injustice has given rise to a debt that should be paid:

Who decides?
Who pays?
Who receives?

In the school desegregation cases, the answers were satisfactory: the courts decided; the offending school district itself paid; and the very students who had been deprived received. But in *Bakke* the answers were all unsatisfactory: the university had no authority to decide; the students who were favored might or might not have suffered from past discrimination; and, as to "who pays?" why should Bakke shoulder society's debt by perhaps losing the benefit of a medical education? In *Weber* the same difficulties appeared, but the court sidestepped them and relied on broad considerations of obtaining a desirable result. Finally, in *Fullilove* the "who decides?" was easier, since it was Congress, and the "who pays?" and "who receives?" answers were not so disturbing.

The future of affirmative action is uncertain. The Reagan transition team report favored, in effect, abolishing affirmative action, especially quotas. Senator Orrin G. Hatch sponsored a constitutional amendment forbidding Federal and state governments to require racial quotas. Since the only employment affirmative action embedded in a statute is that for the handicapped, the executive has it in its power to abolish or drastically curtail the elaborate system of affirmative action plans based on its own executive order.

Opposition to complex university employment quota plans has been intense and increasing. The Berkeley plan, for example, was a book four inches thick in which each of seventy-five academic departments was analyzed as to race and sex of its faculty. For example, 178 positions held by white males in a total staff of 1,489 were to be taken over during a thirty-year period by 97 women, 20 blacks, 42 Asians, 10 Chicanos, and 9 other persons—but no native American males.

Critics of affirmative action in employment can also point to the disappointing results of the original "Philadelphia Plan" and other city plans designed particularly to increase the proportion of blacks in the building trades. In Washington in 1981, after ten years of such a plan, with a population 70 percent black, only 10 percent of building trades journeymen were black.

In view of the inherent vulnerability of the legal underpinnings of affirmative action, as well as the strength of opposition to affirmative action among those in a position to change it, the best prediction is that affirmative action will be a diminishing factor in American law for some years to come. See also, Louis H. Pollak's essay on Brown v. Board of Education of Topeka, Kansas; J. Harvie Wilkinson III's essays on the Bakke Case and on the Weber Case.

Bibliography: Arthur Larson, *The Law of Employment Discrimination,* vol. 2 (1981), § 57.

National Archives

Affirmative action programs have made it possible for women to obtain jobs that were previously held exclusively by men. Here, a female laboratory technician analyzes water from a ship's ballast tanks, as a precaution against pollution before it is discharged into an Alaskan harbor.

AFFIRMATIVE DEFENSE □ A new fact or set of facts that operates to defeat a claim even if the facts supporting that claim are true. □

A plaintiff sets forth a claim in a civil action by making statements in the document called the COMPLAINT. These statements must be sufficient to warrant relief from the court. The defendant responds to the plaintiff's claims by preparing an ANSWER in which the defendant may deny the truth of the plaintiff's allegations or assert that there are additional facts which constitute a defense to the plaintiff's action. For example, a plaintiff may demand compensation for damage done to his or her vehicle in an automobile accident. Without denying responsibility for the accident, the defendant may claim to have an affirmative defense, such as the plaintiff's CONTRIBUTORY NEGLIGENCE or expiration of the STATUTE OF LIMITATIONS.

An affirmative defense is also allowed under rules of CRIMINAL PROCEDURE. For example, a defendant accused of assault may claim to have been intoxicated or insane, to have struck out in self-defense, or to have had an ALIBI for the night in question. Any one of these affirmative defenses must be asserted by showing that there are facts in addition to the ones in the INDICTMENT or INFORMATION charging the defendant and that those additional facts are legally sufficient to excuse the defendant.

The rules that govern PLEADING in most courts require a defendant to raise all affirmative defenses when first responding to the civil claim or criminal charges against him or her. Failure to do so may preclude assertion of that kind of defense later in the trial. See also, Andre A. Moenssen's essay on Self-Defense.

AFFRAY □ A criminal offense generally defined as the fighting of two or more persons in a public place that disturbs others. □

The offense originated under the COMMON LAW and in some jurisdictions has become a statutory crime. Although an agreement to fight is not an element of the crime under the common-law definition, some statutes provide that an affray can occur only when two or more persons agree to fight in a public place.

An affray is a type of DISORDERLY CONDUCT and a BREACH OF THE PEACE since it is conduct that disturbs the peace of the community. It is punishable by a fine, imprisonment, or both.

AFORESAID □ Before, already said, referred to, or recited. □

This term is used frequently in DEEDS, LEASES, and CONTRACTS of sale of REAL PROPERTY to refer to the property without describing it in detail each time it is mentioned; for example, "the aforesaid premises."

AFORETHOUGHT □ In criminal law, intentional, deliberate, planned, or premeditated. □

MURDER in the first degree, for example, requires MALICE aforethought; that is, the murder must have been planned for a period of time, regardless how short, before it was committed.

A FORTIORI [*Latin, "With stronger reason."*]

This phrase is used in logic to denote an argument to the effect that because one ascertained fact exists, therefore another which is included in it or analogous to it and is less improbable, unusual, or surprising must also exist.

AFRICAN LAW ASSOCIATION IN AMERICA   The African Law Association in America was founded in 1965 to promote the study of African law. Members of the association write for and edit *African Law Studies*. The membership includes lawyers, law professors, government officials, university libraries, and other individuals and institutions. The association holds annual meetings in conjunction with the meeting of the American Association of Law Schools.

AFROYIM v. RUSK □ A 1967 decision by the Supreme Court, 387 U.S. 253, 87 S.Ct. 1660, 18 L.Ed.2d 757, that held that a person could not be deprived of U.S. citizenship for voting in a political election in a foreign country. □

Beys Afroyim was a naturalized citizen who went to Israel in 1950 and in 1951 voted in an election for the Israeli Knesset, the legislative body. He applied to the Department of State for renewal of his U.S. passport in 1960, but his application was refused. The department based its decision on a section of the Nationality Act of 1940 (8 U.S.C.A. § 1101 et seq.) that required loss of United States citizenship for someone voting "in a political election in a foreign state."

Afroyim brought an action in Federal district court against Secretary of State Dean Rusk, to have the statutory provision declared unconstitutional as a violation of the DUE PROCESS CLAUSE of the Fifth Amendment and Section 1, Clause 1 of the Fourteenth Amendment, which

Nobody desires that laws should interfere with the whole detail of private life; yet every one allows that in all daily conduct a person may and does show himself to be either just or unjust.

J.S. MILL

grants citizenship to all persons native born or naturalized. He argued that nowhere in the Constitution was Congress given the power to strip a person of citizenship, and, therefore, citizenship could be lost only by voluntary renunciation. The government made a motion for SUMMARY JUDGMENT in its favor, claiming that it had merely done what it was empowered by the statute to do. The district court and, on appeal, the court of appeals granted and affirmed summary judgment for the government.

Afroyim obtained CERTIORARI and his case went before the Supreme Court. The issue of the case was whether, in light of the Fourteenth Amendment grant of citizenship to native-born and naturalized persons, Congress could enact a law that deprived a person of citizenship which the person never voluntarily renounced. In the past the Court had ruled that Congress had the power to strip anyone of citizenship by virtue of its implied power to regulate foreign affairs and the NECESSARY AND PROPER CLAUSE, Article I, Section 8, Clause 18, that empowers Congress to use whatever means necessary and proper to carry out all powers vested in it. The Court had reasoned that the Fourteenth Amendment imposed no restriction on the power of Congress to withdraw citizenship.

After reevaluating its earlier position, the Court overruled its prior decisions and agreed with Afroyim that he was unconstitutionally deprived of his citizenship. Congress had only the powers specifically granted to it and those necessary and proper to carry out its express ones. The Fourteenth Amendment did not give the Federal government power to strip away citizenship at will. It could, however, be reasonably interpreted as bestowing citizenship that could be lost only if given up voluntarily. The original intent of its citizenship provision at the time of enactment in 1868 was to give freed slaves permanent and secure citizenship. Its LEGISLATIVE HISTORY revealed the feeling in Congress that no one could lose citizenship unless it was voluntarily renounced or abandoned. If the Court were to affirm that Congress had power to strip a person of citizenship because the person voted in a foreign election, the Fourteenth Amendment would be violated.

AFTER-ACQUIRED PROPERTY

☐ Goods or land obtained by a mortgagor after the date of the execution of a loan and a MORTGAGE that automatically becomes additional COLLATERAL for the mortgage if there is a specific clause in the mortgage to this effect.

☐ Goods or land that a TESTATOR received subsequent to the making of a WILL and which,

upon the testator's death, will be distributed according to the terms of the will. If the provisions of the will make it impossible to do so, the after-acquired property will be distributed according to the laws of DESCENT AND DISTRIBUTION.

☐ Goods that a debtor obtains after perfection of a SECURED TRANSACTION which provides that such goods will serve as additional collateral for the loan. ☐

An after-acquired property provision in a security agreement would state that "any or all obligations covered by the security agreement are to be secured by all inventory now or hereafter acquired by the debtor." After-acquired property is commonly found as collateral in secured transactions by which creditors lend money to debtors with businesses in which inventory or accounts "turn over" in the normal course of business. The increase of existing collateral is one type of after-acquired property. A security agreement covering the cattle of a debtor, for example, also covers the increase if one of the cattle gives birth to a calf. The finished products that result from the conversion of raw materials that serve as collateral to a security agreement are also after-acquired property. Consumer goods are rarely considered after-acquired property.

When after-acquired property is collateral for a secured transaction, the creditor is said to have a FLOATING LIEN.

AFTER-ACQUIRED PROPERTY CLAUSE

☐ A phrase in a MORTGAGE (an interest in land that furnishes security for payment of a debt or performance of an obligation) that provides that any holdings obtained by the borrower subsequent to the date of the loan and mortgage will automatically constitute additional security for the loan. ☐

For a sample of an after-acquired property clause, see the Appendix volume 11.

AFTER-ACQUIRED TITLE
☐ A legal doctrine under which, if a GRANTOR conveys what is mistakenly believed to be good TITLE to land that he or she did not own, and the grantor later acquires that title, it vests automatically in the GRANTEE. ☐

AFTER-BORN CHILD
☐ A child born after a WILL has been executed by either parent or after the time in which a class gift made according to a TRUST arrangement expires. ☐

The existence of an after-born child has significant legal ramifications upon gifts made under wills and trusts. Under the law of wills, the birth of an after-born child after the parent

Where . . . there is no superiority of jurisdiction of one over another, what any may do in prosecution of that law, every one must needs have a right to do.

JOHN LOCKE

makes a will does not revoke it but has the effect of modifying its provisions. Generally, the after-born child must be given the share of the parent's ESTATE that the child would have been entitled to if the parent had died without leaving a will, according to the law of DESCENT AND DISTRIBUTION. The beneficiaries of the will must contribute a proportionate share of what they inherited to make up the after-born child's share.

Under the law of trusts, a gift to a class is one in which the creator of the trust, the settlor, directs that the principal of the trust should be distributed to a specifically designated group of persons, such as to grandchildren, who are alive at a certain time, such as at the settlor's death. Any child born after this time would not be entitled to a proportionate share of the trust principal unless conceived before the settlor died. An after-born child born eleven months after the settlor's death, therefore, would not share in the principal, since the class had closed nine months after the settlor's death.

AGENCY □ A legal relationship entered with the mutual consent of two parties in which one person, the AGENT, is authorized to act on behalf of the other, the PRINCIPAL, to effectuate certain transactions with third parties according to the direction and subject to the control of the principal. □

The traditional legal maxim that one who acts through another acts for himself is the foundation of agency law. A voluntary, GOOD FAITH relationship of trust, called a FIDUCIARY relationship, exists between a principal and the agent for the benefit of the principal. An agent has a duty of loyalty to the principal and must exercise reasonable care in serving and protecting the interests of the principal. An agent who acts in his or her own self-interest violates the fiduciary duty and will be financially liable to the principal for any loss incurred. A principal may select a person to act as agent with knowledge of their conflicting interests as long as any third parties engaging in transactions with the agent are notified of the conflict.

An agent may be authorized to perform a variety of tasks or may be restricted to a specific function. The agent represents the principal and is subject to his or her control. As a result, a principal is liable for injurious consequences of acts which he or she has directed the agent to perform. The majority of commercial transactions—for example, the purchase and sale of real estate, securities, or insurance—are conducted by means of an agency relationship.

Creation An agency relationship is a consensual relationship, since both parties must consent to it. No one can unwittingly become an agent for another. It is sometimes called a contractual relationship, although, unlike a CONTRACT, the exchange of consideration is not essential for its creation. No particular method is necessary for an agency relationship to be created as long as it is clear that the principal and the agent intend to be bound by an agency agreement. The intent of the parties, whether expressed in words or implied by conduct, determines whether such a relationship exists. A written contract disclosing (1) the intention of the principal to be bound by an agent and (2) the identity of the agent and his or her functions is the usual way in which an agency relationship is created.

Control One of the most important aspects of the agency relationship is the control that the principal possesses over the agent. The principal does not need to exercise this control over the agent's conduct; it is sufficient that he or she has the power to do so. The existence of control is what distinguishes an agent from an independent contractor. An independent contractor is subject to the control of an employer only to the extent that the final work product is what was contracted for by the employer. The independent contractor can use whatever reasonable means he or she wants to achieve that end. In contrast, an agent is subject to the principal's control from the time of becoming an agent until the purpose of the agency is completed.

Categories of principals and agents In the typical situation, a principal wants an agent to disclose this identity to the third party with whom he or she is entering an agreement in order to induce the third party to deal with the agent—for example, because of the principal's reputation or creditworthiness. The agent will usually sign any correspondence or contracts with his or her name followed by "as agent for _____." naming the principal. A principal whose identity is revealed is called a *disclosed principal*.

A *partially disclosed principal* is one whose agent reveals that he or she is acting in the capacity of agent but does not reveal the name of the principal.

An agent acting for an *undisclosed principal* does not notify anyone that he or she is acting in the capacity of agent. Although there is no mention of the principal, he or she is liable for any action taken by the agent within the scope of the agent's authority.

A *universal agent* is one who is authorized by a principal to do all acts that are legally delegable. This type of agency is extremely rare and

I will never, if I can help it, put myself into the hands of a man who may determine as to my head; where my life and honour shall more depend upon the skill and diligence of my attorney than on my own innocence . . .

MICHEL DE MONTAIGNE

can be created only by express, specific language, as in a written contract. A *general agent* is one employed to conduct all business of a particular kind or to do all acts connected with a particular trade or employment that involves a continuity of action. Such an agent typically has express and implied powers which arise from whatever is customary in the regular course of business.

In contrast, a *special agent* is empowered to represent the principal in a single transaction or a series of isolated, independent transactions. The special agent has limited powers which can be used only for a particular purpose.

An *actual agent* is one who is expressly authorized to perform certain functions. There must be no doubt that the agent is acting pursuant to directions of the principal.

An *apparent or ostensible agent* is one who the principal has, by words or conduct, intentionally or unintentionally, led third persons to believe is his or her duly authorized representative although no such authority has been granted.

Responsibilities of the relationship

The terms of the agency determine the responsibilities of the principal and the agent.

Unless instructed to the contrary, an agent should exercise reasonable care and observe the customary practices of the principal's particular business. An agent must obey all instructions of the principal unless they are illegal. An agent who fails to do so may lose any right he or she has to compensation and be sued by the principal for any losses incurred by the failure to follow instructions.

A principal is deemed to have knowledge of any material facts learned by an agent acting within the scope of his or her authority during the course of the agent's employment, even if the agent has not disclosed such information to the principal. The principal is bound by the agent's knowledge.

Contractual liability

An agent is not personally liable to a third party for a contract he or she has entered as a representative of the principal so long as the agent acted within the scope of his or her authority and signed the contract as an agent for a named principal. An agent exceeding his or her authority by entering a particular contract is financially responsible to the principal for violating the fiduciary duty to the principal and may also be sued by the third party for FRAUD.

A principal is not bound by the unauthorized acts of an agent in the execution of a contract unless similar contracts had been customarily entered into by the agent pursuant to the principal's direction. In this situation, the principal would be liable to the third party unless the principal gave notice that the agent was no longer representing the principal in such transactions. To otherwise relieve the principal of liability would punish third parties who had been led by the principal to rely on the authority of the agent.

A principal may decide to accept the obligations imposed by a contract made by an agent who exceeded his or her authority. A principal who does so is said to ratify or affirm the contract. RATIFICATION is demonstrated by a statement or conduct by the principal that establishes the intention to be bound by the contract—such as retaining the benefits acquired under it.

Tort liability

A principal is responsible for any TORT (a civil wrong that injures property or persons) committed by an agent while acting within his or her authority during the course of the agent's employment. This principle is embodied in the doctrine of RESPONDEAT SUPERIOR—Latin for "let the master answer," which traditionally applied in master-servant cases, but which has expanded under the theory of VICARIOUS LIABILITY to include all agency relationships.

An agent also is personally liable to the injured party. Practically speaking, however, the principal is usually better able to satisfy any monetary judgment rendered against him or her, making it more likely that the principal rather than the agent will be sued. If the agent commits a tort while on his or her own business, or while acting in a manner that adversely affects the principal, the agent alone will be personally liable for any losses incurred.

When a judgment awarded against a principal because of some fault on the agent's part is paid, the principal may seek INDEMNITY from the agent.

Criminal liability

Although an agency relationship cannot be created for an illegal purpose, a principal is responsible for any criminal acts done by an authorized agent or to which the principal has consented. The principal will usually be prosecuted as an ACCESSORY to the crime since he or she has directed its commission. Under statute, a corporation may be held criminally liable for the acts of its agents committed in the transaction of specific corporate business since it can only act through its officers. Only the agent can be prosecuted for the crime, regardless of whether the act was committed within the scope of his or her employment, if the corporation itself could not be convicted of the offense. It must be established BEYOND A REASONABLE DOUBT that the acts were done, directed, or approved by the corporate agent or officer.

Termination A principal has the absolute power to revoke an agent's authority at any time but may be liable for damages if doing so violates a provision of an agency contract. If an agency is created for a particular purpose, achievement of the purpose will end the power of the agent to act.

An agency may be ended by OPERATION OF LAW—such as by the death, insanity, or bankruptcy of the principal, or where performance of the objective of the agency becomes illegal.

AGENT □ One who agrees and is authorized to act on behalf of another, a PRINCIPAL, to legally bind an individual in particular business transactions with third parties pursuant to an AGENCY relationship. □

AGE OF CONSENT
□ The age at which a person may marry without parental approval.
□ The age at which a female is legally capable of agreeing to sexual intercourse, so that a male who engages in sex with her cannot be prosecuted for STATUTORY RAPE. □

A person below the age of consent is sometimes called an INFANT or MINOR.

AGE OF MAJORITY □ The age at which a person, formerly a MINOR or an INFANT, is recognized by law to be an ADULT, capable of managing his or her own affairs and responsible for any legal obligations created by his or her actions. □

A person who has reached the age of majority is bound by any CONTRACTS, DEEDS, or legal relationships, such as MARRIAGE, which he or she undertakes. In most states the age of majority is eighteen, but it may vary depending upon the nature of the activity in which the person is engaged. In the same state the age of majority for driving may be sixteen while that for drinking alcoholic beverages is nineteen.

Another name for the age of majority is LEGAL AGE.

AGE OF REASON □ The age at which a child is considered capable of acting responsibly. □

Under COMMON LAW, seven was the age of reason. Children under the age of seven were conclusively presumed incapable of committing a crime because they did not possess the reasoning ability to understand that their conduct violated the standards of acceptable community behavior. Those between the ages of seven and fourteen were presumed incapable of committing a crime, but this PRESUMPTION could be overcome by evidence, such as the child having possession of the gun immediately after the shooting. The rebuttable presumption for this age group was based on the assumption that, as the child grew older, he or she learned to differentiate between right and wrong. A child over the age of fourteen was considered to be fully responsible for his or her actions. Many states have modified the age of criminal responsibility by statute.

All states have enacted legislation creating juvenile courts to handle the adjudication of young persons, usually under eighteen, for criminal conduct rather than have them face criminal prosecution as an adult. However, a child of thirteen who commits a violent crime may be tried as an adult in many jurisdictions.

Caril Ann Fugate, 14, leaves jail in the company of law enforcement officials to be tried in 1958 on charges of assisting Charles Starkweather, 19, in killing ten people in Nebraska and Wyoming. Despite her youth, Fugate had reached the age of reason and was subsequently convicted of first degree murder and sentenced to life in prison.

Charles H. Backstrom

Age Requirement
for Holding Office

Framers of constitutions typically set a minimum age below which a person is not eligible for elective office. The effect of this is to restrict the voters' power to evaluate candidates for public office on whatever criteria they choose.

Only three U.S. states (Massachusetts, New York, and Vermont) have no age qualification for a state representative in their constitution or statutes. An obvious minimum age for holding office—voting age, or legal age—is specified in nine states. An additional four states mention age eighteen specifically. Just over half of the states (twenty-six) require a minimum age of twenty-one for service in their lower house, but only eight allow persons of this age in their state senates (in addition to the thirteen states that make no mention of age or allow eighteen-year-olds in their upper house). The highest age requirement is twenty-five for representative (four states) and thirty for senator (six states).

For governor, most states (thirty-four) require a minimum age of thirty; one (Oklahoma) has a minimum of thirty-one. Four states have no age qualification for governor; five allow age eighteen; and six specify twenty-five.

Court challenges to these age qualifications have failed. The holding is that the 1971 Twenty-sixth Amendment to the United States Constitution forbidding a state to deny the vote to persons eighteen years old because of age alone did only that; it did not cancel higher age requirements for holding office. Argument that equal protection was denied to persons under the specified age has been similarly dismissed on the grounds that holding office is not a fundamental right that states cannot restrict; that age is a reasonable basis of discrimination in the attempt to ensure maturity, experience, and competence in office. An underage write-in candidate was not allowed to take office on similar grounds—that age is the only way to ensure fitness to hold office.

We think the strongest logic is that of experience.

BENJAMIN GRAHAM

Of three states that adopted new constitutions since the ratification of the Twenty-sixth Amendment, Louisiana and Montana now authorize eighteen-year-olds to serve in the legislature, but Georgia maintained twenty-one and twenty-five, respectively, as ages for state house and senate.

Apparently the reasons advanced during the drafting of the United States Constitution are still widely held. James Madison defended a minimum age of thirty for the United States Senate, relying on "the nature of the Senatorial trust; which, requiring greater extent of information and stability of character, requires, at the same time, that the Senator should have reached a period of life most likely to supply these advantages." For the House of Representatives, George Mason of Virginia, suggesting the minimum age of twenty-five that prevailed, argued that

the political opinions of twenty-one-year-olds were "too crude and erroneous to merit an influence on public measures." James Wilson of Pennsylvania ineffectively countered that the proposal would "damp the effects of genius and of laudable ambition," and said there was "no more reason for incapacitating youth than age."

To be president of the United States, one must be at least thirty-five—the highest age qualification for any office in the United States.

Apparently nowhere in the United States is there an upper age limit as a qualification for office.

When John F. Kennedy, *right,* became president of the United States at the age of 43, he was the youngest man elected to that office. President Ronald W. Reagan, *left,* has the distinction of being the oldest man to assume the office. He was just short of his seventieth birthday when he was sworn in.

Bibliography: Council of State Governments, *The Book of the States, 1980–1981;* Alexander Hamilton, James Madison, and John Jay, *The Federalist Papers*; *Meyers v. Roberts,* 310 Minn. 358, 246 N.W.2d 186 (1976); Arthur T. Prescott, ed., *Drafting the Federal Constitution* (1941; 1968); *Wurtzel v. Falcey,* 69 N.J. 401, 354 A.2d 617 (1976).

AGGRAVATED ASSAULT ☐ The CRIME of deliberately attempting or threatening to physically injure a person, causing the victim to fear immediate bodily harm, done with the intent to commit a more serious crime, or taking place under circumstances that increase the injurious results. ☐

An aggravated assault can be committed without actually touching, striking, or doing physical harm to another, if the perpetrator has the requisite intent, if the assault is carried out with a deadly weapon, or if the victim has a special status, such as a police or fire officer performing their duties. In some states aggravated assault occurs only if there has been a combination of these factors.

At common law, aggravated assault was considered a MISDEMEANOR. Today, in all states, criminal statutes punish aggravated assault such as assault with intent to rape, assault with a deadly weapon, or assault of a police officer more severely than "simple" assaults, treating them as FELONIES.

AGGRAVATION ☐ Any circumstances surrounding the commission of a CRIME that increase its seriousness or add to its injurious consequences. ☐

Such circumstances are not essential elements of the crime but go above and beyond them. The aggravation of a crime is usually a result of intentional actions of the perpetrator. Such crimes are punished more severely than the crime itself. One of the most common crimes that is caused by aggravation is AGGRAVATED ASSAULT.

AGGRESSION ☐ Unjustified planned, threatened, or carried out use of force by one nation against another. ☐

The key word in the definition of aggression is "unjustified"—that is, in violation of international law, treaties, or agreements. It was the basic charge leveled against Nazi Germany at the Nuremberg Trials in 1946.

AGGRESSIVE COLLECTION ☐ Various legal methods used by a creditor to force a debtor to repay an outstanding obligation. ☐

ATTACHMENT of the debtor's property and GARNISHMENT of his or her salary are common kinds of aggressive collection.

AGGRIEVED PARTY ☐ An individual who is entitled to commence a lawsuit against another because his or her legal rights have been violated. ☐

A person whose financial interest is directly affected by a decree, judgment, or statute is also considered an aggrieved party entitled to bring an ACTION challenging the legality of the decree, judgment, or statute.

AGREATION   See Diplomatic Agents.

AGREEMENT ☐ A meeting of minds with the understanding and acceptance of reciprocal legal rights and duties as to particular actions or obligations which the PARTIES intend to exchange; a mutual assent to do or refrain from doing something; a CONTRACT. ☐

Statesmen, *from left to right,* Anthony Eden, Konrad Adenauer, Dean Acheson, and Robert Schuman give the appearance of being in general agreement at a conference in 1952.

An agreement is not always synonymous with a contract because it might lack an essential element of a contract, such as CONSIDERATION, for example.
☐ The writing or document that records the meeting of the minds of the parties. An oral COMPACT between two parties who join together for a common purpose intending to change their rights and duties. ☐

AGRICULTURAL ADJUSTMENT ACTS
☐ A series of Federal statutes, adopted and amended over a period of years, providing aid to farmers. ☐

The Agricultural Adjustment Acts are comprised of the original Agricultural Adjustment Act, which was enacted in 1933 and which appears to have been partially invalidated, the Agricultural Marketing Agreement Act of 1937 and the Agricultural Adjustment Act of 1938 (7 U.S.C.A. § 601 et seq.). The last two acts are coordinate parts of a unitary plan for raising farm

The object of the [Agricultural Adjustment] Act [of 1938] and the Regulation was to prevent an over-production of cotton. It was not a crime to produce cotton in excess of the allotment, but if there was such over-production the penalty was imposed, not as a punishment for a crime but, to prevent over-production of the commodity. The grower was at liberty to produce all the cotton he wished to produce provided this penalty was complied with.

ELLIOTT NORTHCOTT

prices to parity levels. The Agricultural Marketing Agreement Act of 1937 authorizes the secretary of agriculture to issue orders regulating the interstate marketing of agricultural products whenever there is reason to believe the issuance of an order will tend to effectuate the expressed policy of the legislation.

Congress adopted agricultural adjustment legislation in recognition of the national public interest inherent in the orderly exchange of commodities in interstate commerce. Disruption of this process was deemed to impair the purchasing power of farmers and destroy the value of agricultural assets bolstering the national credit structure.

The primary purpose of the legislation was to extend aid to farmers so that they might obtain a parity price for commodities they produced. Parity prices maintain, to the extent possible, a particular level between production and necessary outlays equivalent to the purchasing power possessed by agricultural commodities in previous years. By promoting an orderly flow of commodities to the market during the regular marketing season, the legislation inhibits unreasonable fluctuations in supplies and prices, thereby benefiting both farmers and consumers.

The objective of the legislation is to regain for farmers the favorable fiscal conditions that they enjoyed, without economic or marketing control, during the base period, which is accomplished by raising prices. National and individual farm production and marketing are restricted to prescribed quotas so that prices will increase.

The general scheme of the Agricultural Adjustment Act of 1938, in terms of specific crops, is to control the volume of crops moving in interstate and foreign commerce in order to avoid surpluses and shortages and the resulting abnormally high or low prices and obstructions to commerce. It also continues the policies and procedures outlined by other Federal statutes with respect to the conservation of national resources.

The Agricultural Adjustment Act of 1938, as amended, does not discourage the production of food sufficient to maintain normal domestic human consumption but directs the secretary of agriculture to give appropriate consideration to the maintenance of a continuous and stable supply of agricultural commodities from domestic production adequate to meet consumer demand at prices fair to both consumers and producers.

AGRICULTURE ☐ The cultivation of various crops and the raising and management of livestock to provide a food supply for human and animal consumption. ☐

Government regulation The promotion and regulation of agriculture is an area of vital economic importance to the nation and is subject to the supervision of the Federal government and the state government.

Federal law Congress is empowered by virtue of the COMMERCE CLAUSE to enact laws to aid farmers and to create regulatory agencies to offer assistance and guidance to the agricultural industry. The secretary of agriculture, appointed by the president and approved by the Senate, is responsible for the administration and coordination of various Federal farming programs to be implemented by the Department of Agriculture. The Agricultural Adjustment Acts (7 U.S.C.A. § 601 et seq. [1933]) establish and maintain fair

Library of Congress

This photograph from the early 1900s juxtaposes the old animal-powered agriculture with the new tractor-powered cultivation.

prices for crops by preventing extreme fluctuations in the availability of products. Regulation of the production and price of agricultural commodities is accomplished by a system of allotment of national acreage to be used for the cultivation of a particular crop. The secretary decides how much land should be planted with a crop, and that amount of acreage is apportioned among those states capable of producing it. State agricultural committees are notified of the state's allotment and divide it among various counties, which subsequently apportion it among local farms. In this way the Federal government prevents overabundance of one crop and scarcity of another, preserving economic stability by circumventing extreme fluctuations in the prices of crops. The Commodity Credit Corporation affects prices offered for farm products to be sold on the open market in accordance with the program of price support administered by the secretary of agriculture. The Federal Crop Insurance Corporation, an agency of the Department of Agriculture, sponsors a system of CROP INSURANCE to provide indemnity to farmers whose crops have been lost through destructive natural forces.

The Farm Credit Administration, established by Congress as an agency in the executive branch of government, assists farmers who are unable to purchase feed for livestock or seed for

U.S. Department of Agriculture

A U.S. Department of Agriculture conservationist checks soil moisture in a drought-stunted cornfield in North Dakota in 1980.

In 1980 a lack of moisture destroyed a cotton crop in Texas, and left the fields vulnerable to wind erosion.

U.S. Department of Agriculture

crops by providing funds for loans for the purchase of such items. This assistance promotes the participation of debtor-farmers in the management, control, and ultimate ownership of a system of agricultural credit made available through lending institutions subject to the supervision of the Farm Credit Administration.

The livestock aspect of agriculture is also within the purview of Federal legislation and of the secretary of agriculture. The Packers and Stockyards Act (7 U.S.C.A. § 181 et seq. [1921]) enacted by Congress regulates the livestock marketing and meat packing industries, thereby assuring the farmers of fair business practices in their transactions. The secretary of agriculture, acting pursuant to the Soil Conservation and Domestic Allotment Act (16 U.S.C.A. § 590a et seq. [1935]), aids farmers and ranchers in implementing practices geared toward preserving the quality of the soil. The Federal food stamp program was initiated in 1964 to promote the general welfare by providing low-income households with economic assistance to purchase nutritionally adequate food. The secretary of agriculture administers this program which increases the domestic consumption of agricultural commodities by encouraging and subsidizing their use among low-income groups.

State law States acting pursuant to their POLICE POWER may enact legislation dealing with the production and marketing of agricultural products, provided such laws do not infringe upon Federal statutes and regulations. State laws often involve the granting of assistance, whether in the form of loans or emergency aid. The inspection, grading, sale, and storage of grain, fertilizers, and plant seed are a few of the areas subject to state supervision.

Some states have enacted laws creating agricultural LIENS—a claim upon a crop for unpaid debts resulting from the purchase of supplies or agricultural services, or for a loan made to the farmer in cultivating and harvesting crops.

Agricultural organizations Various organizations have been formed to promote agricultural interests. An agricultural society or club, such as the 4-H club, functions as an educational institution, providing information on the latest technological advances in farming in order to encourage greater productivity.

An agricultural cooperative is an association of local farmers who join together for their mutual benefit to cultivate, harvest, and market farm products and to purchase farm supplies at reasonable prices. The cooperative is an influential source in determining the agricultural practices to be observed in a region.

AGRICULTURE DEPARTMENT The Department of Agriculture (USDA) serves all Americans daily. It works to improve and maintain farm income and to develop and expand markets abroad for agricultural products. The department helps to curb and to cure poverty, hunger, and malnutrition. It works to enhance the environment and to maintain our production capacity by helping landowners protect the soil, water, forests, and other natural resources. Rural development, credit, and conservation programs are key resources for carrying out national growth policies. USDA research findings directly or indirectly benefit all Americans. The department, through inspection and grading services, safeguards and assures standards of quality in the daily food supply.

The act of Congress, approved May 15, 1862, created the Department of Agriculture, which was administered by a commissioner of agriculture until 1889 (12 Stat. 387; 5 U.S.C. 511, 514, 516). By act of February 9, 1889 (21 U.S.C. 119), the powers and duties of the department were enlarged. The department was made the eighth executive department in the Federal government, and the commissioner became the secretary of agriculture.

Staff offices

Administration The assistant secretary for administration serves as the principal adviser to the secretary on all administrative management and related matters. Five departmental staff offices report to the assistant secretary and assist in providing staff support to top policy officials and program agencies to ensure the effi-

Lack of moisture forced this Kansas farmer to plow under his corn crop because the drought prevented his plants from pollinating.

U.S. Department of Agriculture

cient and effective management and operation of the department. These are the Office of Personnel, the Office of Equal Opportunity, the Office of Safety and Health Management, the Office of Small and Disadvantaged Business Utilization, and the Office of Operations and Finance. These offices coordinate the department's personnel management program; equal opportunity and civil rights activities; safety and health activities; management improvement programs; accounting, fiscal, and financial activities; automated data processing administration; procurement and contracts; and management of real and personal property.

In addition, two quasi-judicial agencies, the Office of Administrative Law Judges and the Board of Contract Appeals, report to the assistant secretary. Both organizations operate autonomously when adjudicating cases and deciding contract disputes.

The assistant secretary for administration serves as the department's director of Equal Employment Opportunity and oversees all equal opportunity and civil rights programs within USDA.

General counsel   The general counsel is the principal legal adviser to the secretary and the chief law officer of the department.

Inspector general   The Office of Inspector General, established by the Inspector General Act of 1978 (92 Stat. 1101; 5 U.S.C. App. 1), conducts and supervises all audits and investigations relating to the programs and operations of the department. The office also is responsible for coordinating, conducting, or supervising all other activities carried out by the department for the purpose of promoting program economy and efficiency and preventing and detecting fraud. The investigation of employee complaints, physical security of the secretary, review of legislation and regulations for their impact on program efficiency and susceptibility to abuse, and relations with governmental and nongovernmental units concerning program efficiency and prevention of fraud also are responsibilities of the office. The office is headed by an inspector general who is appointed by the president and confirmed by the Senate.

Office of Governmental and Public Affairs   The Office of Governmental and Public Affairs (GPA) provides policy direction, review, and coordination of all information programs of the department. The office is assigned responsibility for maintaining the flow of information and providing liaison between the Department of Agriculture and the Congress, the mass communication media, state and local governments, and the public.

Judicial officer   The judicial officer serves as the final deciding officer, in the place of the secretary, in regulatory proceedings and appeals of a quasi-judicial nature where a hearing is statutorily required.

SMALL COMMUNITY AND RURAL DEVELOPMENT

Farmers Home Administration   The Farmers Home Administration (FmHA), an agency within the Department of Agriculture, provides credit for those in rural America who are unable to get credit from other sources at reasonable rates and terms.

The agency operates principally under the Consolidated Farm and Rural Development Act (7 U.S.C. 1921 et seq. [1972]) and Title V of the Housing Act of 1949 (42 U.S.C. 1471).

Applications for loans are made at the agency's 2,200 local county and district offices, generally located in county seats. A county or area committee of three individuals, at least two of whom are farmers, certifies or recommends as to eligibility of individual farm loan applicants and reviews borrowers' progress.

The Farmers Home Administration makes loans from three revolving funds (Agricultural Credit Insurance Fund, Rural Housing Insurance Fund, Rural Development Insurance Fund) and with funds derived from sales to the Federal Financing Bank of Certificates of Beneficial Ownership, which represent actual loans made by the agency.

FmHA provides financial and management assistance through the following types of loans.

Operating loans   Operating loans enable operators of not larger than family farms, who cannot get the credit they need from conventional sources, to acquire needed resources, to make improved use of their land and labor resources, and make adjustments necessary for successful farming, recreation, and nonfarm enterprises. Funds may be advanced to pay for equipment, livestock, feed, seed, fertilizer, other farm and home operating needs; refinance chattel debts; provide operating credit to fish farmers; carry out forestry purposes; and develop income-producing recreation and other nonfarm enterprises.

For loans made directly by FmHA, the interest rate is set periodically, based on the Federal government's cost of borrowing. For loans made by other lenders and guaranteed by FmHA, the interest rate is negotiated between the lender and the borrower. The limit on farm operating loans made by FmHA is $100,000, and on guaranteed loans the limit is $200,000. Loans may be repaid over one to seven years. Other reliable agricultural credit sources are encouraged to furnish as much as possible of the essential needs of loan applicants with the balance being supplied with operating loan funds from the Farmers Home Administration. Operating loan borrowers are expected to refinance their operating loans and return to conventional credit when able to do so.

Youth project loans Farmers Home Administration makes loans to individual rural residents between ten and twenty-one years of age to establish and operate income-producing enterprises of modest size, either on the farm or in other locations. The interest rate is determined by formula each year. Repayment terms depend upon the type of project for which the loan is made.

Emergency loans FmHA emergency loans are made to eligible farmers, ranchers, and aquaculture operators for losses, major adjustments, operating expenses, and other essential needs arising from natural disasters so that they may continue their operations and return to local sources of credit as soon as possible.

Each loan is scheduled for repayment as rapidly as feasible, in annual installments, consistent with the borrower's reasonable ability to pay. The schedule varies according to the purpose of the loan.

The interest rate for emergency loans offsetting actual losses is 5 percent. Interest rates for other farm real estate purposes and for operating purposes will be those prevailing in the private market for comparable long-term and intermediate credit, based on a determination by the secretary of agriculture.

Farm ownership loans Farm ownership loans enable farmers and ranchers to buy farms, and owners of inadequate or underimproved farms to enlarge or develop farms. Loans are limited to farms which are not larger than family-size farms. Loans may include funds to construct or repair farm homes and service buildings and facilities; improve land; develop water, forestry, and fish farming resources; establish recreation and other nonfarm enterprises to supplement farm income; and refinance debts.

Repayment is scheduled according to the borrower's ability to repay, but the maximum term is forty years. The interest rate is set periodically, based on the cost of government borrowing. The maximum for insured loans is $200,000 and for guaranteed loans, $300,000. The loan may not exceed the market value of the farm or other security.

Loans to limited-resource farmers FmHA makes loans to help low-income farmers and ranchers improve their farming and earn a better living. These loans are made on easier terms than ordinary farm loans and are intended to give the limited-resource farmer a chance to become more successful in farming.

Limited-resource farmers are owners or tenants of small farms that yield low production and low income due to factors such as lack of land, equipment, or opportunity to get necessary financing, or limited education in farming or management.

Loans to limited-resource farmers may be made for farm purchases or operating. Loans for purchases of farm real estate start with an interest rate of 5 percent. The interest rate on production loans starts at 7 percent. The loans are evaluated every two years, and the borrower pays whatever interest rate he or she can afford as long as it is not less than 7 percent or more than the full rate ordinarily charged for FmHA farm loans. Repayment terms vary according to purposes of the loan. While the needs of limited-resource farmers are usually well below FmHA's limits, the agency can make a real estate loan of up to $200,000 and a production loan of up to $100,000 under this program.

Soil and water conservation loans Loans are made to owners or operators of farms and ranches including farming partnerships and domestic corporations to assist them in developing, conserving, and making proper use of their land and other resources. Loans are repayable in not more than forty years. Loans may be made by FmHA or by other lenders with a FmHA guarantee.

Recreation loans Recreation loans enable farmers and ranchers to convert all or a portion of the farms or ranches owned or leased by them to outdoor income-producing recreational enterprises. Loan terms are the same as for soil and water conservation loans.

Loans to Indian tribes Loans to Indian tribes and tribal corporations are made for the acquisition of land, including interest therein within the reservation or community. Loans are made for up to forty years. The interest rate is set periodically, based on the cost of government borrowing.

Loans to associations Loans may be made to eligible groups of farmers and ranchers to develop irrigation systems, drain farmland, and carry out soil conservation measures. Loans may be made for the development of recreational facilities and for shifts in land use to develop grazing areas and forest lands.

Rural housing loans Loans are made to families of low and moderate income for housing located in open country and small rural communities with populations of not more than 10,000 and in rural towns of 10,000 to 20,000 where there is a lack of housing mortgage credit. Loans are made to build, buy, and repair needed homes and to buy and improve building sites.

The maximum term is thirty-three years. The basic interest rate is determined periodically. Cosigners on promissory notes are permitted in the case of applicants who are deficient in repayment ability.

Loans from private lenders to families of above-moderate income also may be guaranteed by the agency.

Builders may obtain from the agency "conditional commitments" which are assurances to a builder or seller that if their houses meet FmHA lending, design, and construction requirements, then the agency will make loans to qualified borrowers to buy them.

An owner-occupant who cannot qualify for a regular rural housing loan may obtain a loan or, in the case of senior citizens, a grant of up to $5,000 to make home repairs and improvements to remove hazards to the health and safety of the family. These loans, available only to very low-income families, are made at 1 percent interest.

Loans are made to private nonprofit corporations, consumer cooperatives, state or local public agencies, and individuals or organizations operating on a profit or limited profit basis, to provide rental or cooperative housing in rural areas for persons of low and moderate income. Maximum term is fifty years. Rental assistance may be given to help defray rent paid by low-income families.

The agency is authorized to pay expenses incurred by nonprofit organizations to assist in developing or administering technical and supervisory assistance for low-income persons and families who are helping to build their own homes.

Loans and grants are authorized for housing for farm laborers.

Loans repayable in two years are authorized to nonprofit organizations to purchase and develop land for resale as homesites for persons of low-to-moderate income.

Watershed-protection and flood-prevention loans   These loans enable local organizations approved by the Soil Conservation Service to finance projects that protect and develop land and water resources in small watersheds.

Loans may be repaid over fifty years at an interest rate based on the average rate paid by the U.S. Treasury on obligations of similar maturity. Total loans outstanding on any one watershed project may not exceed $5 million. Authority for these loans is contained in section 8 of the Watershed Protection and Flood Prevention Act of 1954 (16 U.S.C. 1006a).

Resource conservation and development loans   These loans enable sponsors of projects approved for operation by the Soil Conservation Service to finance projects for natural resource conservation and development in designated areas. Such loans may be made for periods up to thirty years with repayment of principal and interest deferred up to five years, if necessary. Authority for these loans is contained in section 32(e) of the Bankhead-Jones Farm Tenant Act (7 U.S.C. 1011[e] [1937]), and subtitle A of the Consolidated Farm and Rural Development Act (7 U.S.C. 192 et seq. [1972]).

Community facility loans   Loans are authorized to public and quasi-public bodies and nonprofit associations and to certain Indian tribes for essential community facilities, such as water and waste disposal systems and other facilities useful to the entire community. Necessary related equipment may also be purchased.

The interest rate cannot exceed 5 percent. Water and waste disposal projects may serve residents of open country and rural towns of not more than 10,000 population. Community facility loans may be made in towns of up to 20,000.

Grants may be made for up to 75 percent of the cost for such projects when necessary to bring user costs to a reasonable level.

Business and industry loans   The agency is authorized to make or guarantee loans to public, private, or cooperative associations organized for profit or nonprofit, to certain Indian tribes or tribal groups, or to individuals for the purpose of improving, developing, or financing business, industry, and employment and improving the economic and environmental climate in rural communities. Grants also may be made for projects to improve water, waste disposal, and industrial site facilities.

The purpose is to develop business enterprises in rural areas and cities of up to 50,000 population, with priority to applications for projects in open country, rural communities and towns of 25,000 and smaller.

Private lenders initiate, process, close, service, and supervise guaranteed loans; the Farmers Home Administration guarantees a lender against loss on up to 90 percent of principal and interest. Interest rates are determined between borrower and lender.

Biomass energy and alcohol fuels   Under the authority of Title II of the Energy Security Act of 1980 (94 Stat. 683; 42 U.S.C. 8801 et seq.), the agency makes insured and guaranteed loans for small- and intermediate-scale biomass fuel projects with a capacity of up to 15 million gallons per year.

There are no geographical limits for these projects. Equity, at least 10 percent for insured loans, 20 percent for guaranteed loans, is required.

Area development assistance Grants are authorized to states, sub-state districts, local units of government, and certain community-based organizations to encourage and help meet the cost of comprehensive planning in rural areas.

Grants are also authorized by section 601 of the Powerplant and Industrial Fuel Use Act of 1978 (92 Stat. 3323; 42 U.S.C. 8401) to provide local governments in areas severely affected by sudden growth because of coal or uranium production assistance in planned and orderly growth management.

Rural development planning and coordination The planning of rural development program goals and coordination of supportive programs administered by various agencies is managed in FmHA by its Policy Coordination Staff. This unit previously functioned as the Rural Development Service (RDS), a separate agency of USDA established by secretarial order in 1973. RDS was merged with FmHA by secretarial order in 1978. The work of planning and coordination is mandated in section 603 of the Consolidated Farm and Rural Development Act of 1972 (7 U.S.C. 2201).

Rural Electrification Administration

The Rural Electrification Administration (REA) finances electric and telephone facilities in rural areas of the United States and its territories. About 1,000 rural electric and 900 rural telephone utility systems in forty-seven states have received loans from REA. REA does not own or operate rural electric or telephone facilities. Its function is to provide, through self-liquidating loans and technical assistance, adequate and dependable electric and telephone service to rural people under rates and conditions that permit full and productive use of these utility services.

The agency was established on May 11, 1935, by Executive Order No. 7037 as an emergency relief program. Statutory authority was provided by the Rural Electrification Act of 1936 (7 U.S.C. 901–950b). The act established REA as a lending agency with responsibility for developing a program for rural electrification. An October 28, 1949, amendment to the Rural Electrification Act authorized REA to make loans to improve and extend telephone service in rural areas. On May 11, 1973, authority to guarantee loans, made by non-REA lenders was authorized by an amendment to the act. The REA administrator is appointed by the president, subject to Senate confirmation.

REA loans REA loans are made from the Rural Electrification and Telephone Revolving Fund in the U.S. Treasury. These funds are generally loaned at 5 percent interest. Borrowers meeting specified criteria, however, may obtain loans at 2 percent interest. The fund is replenished through collections on outstanding and future REA loans, through borrowings from the secretary of the treasury, and through sales of beneficial ownership interests in borrowers' notes held in trust by REA.

REA loan guarantees REA also guarantees loans to facilitate the obtaining of financing for large-scale electric and telephone facilities from non-REA sources. Guarantees are considered if such loans could have been made by REA under the act, and may be made concurrently with an REA loan. Guaranteed loans may be obtained from any legally organized lending agency qualified to make, hold, and service the loan. All policies and procedures of REA are applicable to a guaranteed loan. In 1974 REA entered into an agreement with the Federal Financing Bank (FFB), whereby FFB agreed to purchase obligations guaranteed by the REA administrator. REA acts as the agent for the FFB and all borrowers' dealings are with REA.

Supplemental financing Borrowers who meet specified criteria are required to obtain part of their financing from non-REA sources. The National Rural Utilities Cooperative Finance Corporation, Banks for Cooperatives, and other financial institutions provide a substantial portion of the borrowers' capital needs.

Electric program In the field of rural electrification, REA is empowered by Congress through the Rural Electrification Act of 1936, as amended, to make loans to qualified borrowers, with preference to nonprofit and cooperative associations and to public bodies. The loans finance the construction and operation of generating plants and transmissions and distribution lines to provide initial and continued adequate electric service to persons in rural areas.

Telephone program In authorizing the telephone loan program in 1949, Congress directed that it be conducted to "assure the availability of adequate telephone service to the widest practicable number of rural users of such service." About two-thirds of the telephone systems financed by REA are commercial companies, and about one-third are subscriber-owned cooperatives.

Rural Telephone Bank The Rural Telephone Bank, an agency of the United States, was established in 1971. Bank loans are made, in preference to REA loans, to telephone systems able to meet its requirements. The bank's man-

It is not debatable that it is part of the public policy of this state [of Iowa], evidenced by our constitution and numerous statutes, to encourage agriculture. It seems equally plain the encouragement of our basic industry serves the public interest.

THEODORE G. GARFIELD

Both courts and administrative bodies are law-enforcing agencies, utilized by Congress as such. In construing the enforcement provisions of legislation like the [Agricultural] Marketing Act, it is important to remember that courts and administrative agencies are collaborative "instrumentalities of justice", and not business rivals.

FELIX FRANKFURTER

agement is vested in a governor (the REA administrator) and a board of directors, including six who are elected by the bank's stockholders. Bank loans are being made for the same purposes as loans made by REA but bear interest at a rate consistent with the bank's cost of money. In addition, loans may be made to purchase stock in the bank required as a condition of obtaining a loan. The bank uses the facilities and services of REA and other Department of Agriculture agencies.

MARKETING AND INSPECTION SERVICES

Agricultural Cooperative Service The Agricultural Cooperative Service helps farmers to help themselves through the use of cooperative organizations. Studies are conducted to support cooperatives that market farm products, purchase production supplies, and perform related business services. These studies concentrate on the financial, organizational, legal, social, and economic aspects of cooperative activity in U.S. agriculture. The service provides technical assistance and research to improve cooperative performance in organizing new cooperatives, the merits of merging cooperatives, the changing business structure, and developing strategies for growth. Applied research is conducted to give farmers relevant and expert assistance pertaining to their cooperatives.

The service also collects and publishes basic statistics regarding the role and scope of cooperative activity in U.S. agriculture. Its monthly magazine, *Farmer Cooperatives,* reports current developments and research for cooperative management.

Agricultural Marketing Service The Agricultural Marketing Service (AMS) administers standardization, grading, inspection, market news, marketing orders, regulatory, and related programs.

Market news This service provides current, unbiased information to producers, processors, distributors, and others to assist them in the orderly marketing and distribution of farm commodities. Information is collected and disseminated on supplies, demand, prices, movement, location, quality, condition, and other market data on farm products in specific markets and marketing areas.

Standardization, inspection, grading, classing, and testing Classing and testing services are provided to buyers and sellers of cotton and cotton products. Grading, inspection, and standardization also are provided for buyers and sellers of tobacco. Standards are developed with the benefit of views from those in the industries directly affected and others interested. Standardization and grading of live cattle, swine, sheep, wool, and mohair are also carried out by AMS, as well as certification of turpentine and other naval stores products and standardization and testing of seed.

Regulatory programs AMS administers several regulatory programs designed collectively to protect producers, handlers, and consumers of agricultural commodities from financial loss or personal injury resulting from careless, deceptive, or fraudulent marketing practices.

Administrattion of the Packers and Stockyards Act of 1921 (7 U.S.C. 181–229), as amended, encourages free, open competition in the marketing of livestock, meat, and poultry, as well as meat and poultry products. It sets out rules for fair business practices that stockyards, meatpackers, livestock commission firms, and poultry dealers and processors must follow. It specifically prohibits certain practices which inhibit competition.

Other AMS regulatory programs encourage fair trading practices in the marketing of fruits and vegetables (Perishable Agricultural Commodities Act, 46 Stat. 531; 7 U.S.C. 499a–499s [1930]); require truth in seed labeling and advertising (Federal Seed Act, 53 Stat. 1275; 7 U.S.C. 1551–1611 [1939]), cover the licensing, bonding, and examination of warehouses operating under provisions of the U.S. Warehouse Act (7 U.S.C. 241–273 [1916]) and the examination of warehouses operating under storage agreements or contracts with the Commodity Credit Corporation; and protect farmers' rights to organize cooperatives (Agricultural Fair Practices Act, 82 Stat. 93; 7 U.S.C. 2301–2306 [1967]).

Marketing agreements and orders These programs, under authority of the Agricultural Marketing Agreement Act of 1937 (7 U.S.C. 601 et seq.), help to establish and maintain orderly marketing conditions for certain commodities. Milk marketing orders establish minimum prices that handlers or distributors are required to pay producers. Programs for fruits, vegetables, and related speciality crops like nuts and hops help stabilize supplies and market prices. In some cases, they also authorize research and market development activities, including advertising supported by assessments that handlers pay. Through orderly marketing, adjusting the supply to demand, and avoiding unreasonable fluctuations during the marketing season, the income of producers is increased by normal market forces, and consumer interests are protected through quality and quantity control.

Plant variety protection program
Under authority of the Plant Variety Protection Act (7 U.S.C. 2321 et seq. [1970]), AMS administers a program which provides for the issuance of "certificates of plant variety protection." These certificates afford developers of novel varieties of sexually reproduced plants exclusive rights to sell, reproduce, import, or export such varieties, or use them in the production of hybrids or different varieties for a period of eighteen years.

Research and promotion programs
AMS monitors certain industry-sponsored research, promotion, and information programs authorized by Federal laws. These programs provide farmers with a means to finance and operate various research, promotion, and information activities for cotton, potatoes, eggs, wheat, wool, lamb, and mohair.

Other marketing services   Other marketing service activities of AMS include financial grants to states for marketing improvement projects. AMS also has responsibility for the conduct of studies of the facilities and methods used in the physical distribution of food and other farm products; for research designed to improve the handling of all agricultural products as they move from farm to consumers; and for increasing marketing efficiency by developing improved operating methods, facilities, and equipment for processing, handling, and distributing dairy, poultry, and meat products. In addition, AMS provides promotional assistance for foods that are temporarily in burdensome supply on the market.

Field organization   AMS programs and activities in the field are carried out through a variety of different types of organizations reporting to their respective Washington components. Depending upon the program or activity, they range from small individual local offices to relatively large regional offices.

Animal and Plant Health Inspection Service   The Animal and Plant Health Inspection Service (APHIS) was reestablished by the secretary of agriculture March 14, 1977, pursuant to authority contained in 5 U.S.C. 301 and Reorganization Plan 2 of 1953.

APHIS was established to conduct regulatory and control programs to protect and improve animal and plant health for the benefit of man and his environment. In cooperation with state governments, the service administers Federal laws and regulations pertaining to animal and plant health and quarantine, humane treatment of animals, and the control and eradication of pests and diseases.

Plant protection and quarantine programs   Plant protection officials are responsible for programs to control or eradicate plant pests and diseases. These programs are carried out in cooperation with the states involved, other Federal agencies, farmers, and private organizations. Programs are carried out in cooperation with Canada and Mexico when the pest is a joint problem or presents a threat to this country. Pest control programs use a single tool or a combination of pest control techniques, both chemical and nonchemical, that are both effective and safe.

Agricultural quarantine inspection officials administer Federal regulations that prohibit or restrict the entry of foreign pests and plants, plant products, animal products and by-products, and other materials that may harbor pests. Inspection service is maintained at all major ocean, air, border, and interior ports of entry in the continental United States and in Hawaii, Alaska, Puerto Rico, American Virgin Islands, Bahamas, and Bermuda. Services are also provided on a regular or on-call basis at some 500 outlying ports and military installations throughout the country. In addition, inspectors work in several foreign countries. Another responsibility is the inspection and certification of domestic commodities for export.

Veterinary services programs   Veterinary services officials are responsibile for determining the existence and extent of outbreaks of communicable diseases and pests affecting livestock and poultry. They organize and conduct control and eradication programs in cooperation with state officials, and cooperate with animal health officials in other countries in planning and conducting disease control efforts in those countries. Veterinary services officials maintain inspection and quarantine service at designated ports of entry for imported animals. They are responsible for the health certification of livestock and poultry exported to other countries. Veterinary services also administers Federal laws concerned with the humane handling of livestock and poultry in interstate commerce and governing the transportation, sale, and handling of dogs, cats, circus and zoo animals, and other animals intended to be used in laboratory research or for exhibition. Veterinary services is responsible for enforcement of the Horse Protection Act of 1970 (84 Stat. 1404; 15 U.S.C. 1821 et seq.), a Federal law which prohibits "soring" of horses shipped interstate to be shown or sold.

Veterinary services officials are also responsible for administering a Federal law intended to assure that all biological products shipped or sold in interstate commerce for use in the diagnosis, prevention, and treatment of animal diseases are pure, safe, potent, and effective. This responsibility is met through a program regulating biologics manufacturers that produce products subject to the act. This includes licensing the manufacturing establishment and its products; inspecting production facilities and production methods; and testing surveillance by veterinary services.

Federal Grain Inspection Service   The Federal Grain Inspection Service (FGIS) was established in the U.S. Department of Agriculture on November 20, 1976. The primary task of the agency is to carry out the provisions of the U.S. Grain Standards Act (7 U.S.C. 71 et seq.), to assure integrity in the inspection, weighing, and handling of American grain. An administrator, appointed by the president and subject to Senate confirmation, heads the agency.

FGIS is responsible for establishing official U.S. standards for grain and other assigned commodities and administration of a nationwide system of official inspection and weighing. In addition to FGIS, private firms and state agencies may, upon application, be authorized to operate in the official inspection system, under criteria contained in the act.

FGIS is headquartered in Washington, D.C., with most employees working in field offices around the nation.

Inspection   The U.S. Grain Standards Act requires that, with some exceptions, all U.S. export grain be officially inspected as it is loaded on board the vessel that will carry it overseas. The inspection is performed by FGIS or by state agencies that have been delegated export inspection authority by the administrator.

For domestic grain, marketed at inland locations, the administrator designates private firms and state agencies to provide official inspection services on request. To ensure that the official U.S. grain standards are applied uniformly nationwide, FGIS field offices supervise the inspection work of all licensees employed by non-Federal agencies, both at export and inland inspection points.

Buyers and sellers dissatisfied with inspection results can request appeal inspections, first from a FGIS field office and then, if desired, from the Board of Appeals and Review. In addition to performing appeal inspections, the Board provides technical supervision over the FGIS field offices, making sure that all field offices apply uniformly the U.S. standards for grain.

Weighing   At export facilities, official weighing and certification of weight, is performed by FGIS or by state agencies that have been delegated export weighing authority by the administrator. Only those states eligible to apply for export inspection authority can apply for export weighing authority. As with export inspection, FGIS field offices closely supervise the weighing of export grain by states.

In the interior, official weighing of domestic grain will ordinarily be provided on a request basis by designated private agencies under FGIS supervision.

Standardization   Official U.S. standards exist for corn, wheat, rye, oats, barley, flaxseed, sorghum, soybeans, triticale, and mixed grains. Establishing standards and revising them, when needed, is the responsibility of standardization officials. To develop improved grain standards, FGIS has been given authority to perform applied research leading toward standardization of methods and procedures. Standards, when drafted, are proposed in the *Federal Register* for review by users before they are implemented.

When the secretary of agriculture established FGIS, he assigned the agency standardization and inspection responsibilities for rice, dry beans, peas, lentils, hay, straw, and hops under the Agricultural Marketing Act of 1946 (7 U.S.C. 1621 et seq.)

Office of Transportation   The Office of Transportation (OT) is responsible for development of USDA transportation policies for agriculture and rural development, including coordination of USDA programs in education, information, loans, grants, and research to meet policy goals, and representation of agricultural and rural transportation interests before regulatory bodies.

Regulatory representation   OT is delegated the authority under section 201 of the Agricultural Adjustment Act of 1938 (7 U.S.C. 1291) and section 203(j) of the Agricultural Marketing Act of 1946 (7 U.S.C. 1622[j]) to assist in obtaining equitable transportation facilities for agricultural products and farm supplies by making complaint or petition to the Interstate Commerce Commission, the Federal Maritime Commission, the Civil Aeronautics Board, or other Federal or state transportation regulatory bodies with respect to rates, charges, tariffs, practices and services, or by working directly with individual carriers or groups of carriers.

Facilities research and development   OT conducts research to improve the physical distribution of agricultural products between farms and consumers, to maintain quality and prevent spoilage of products in marketing channels, to reduce costs, and improve transportation services for agricultural commodities moving to markets. This research includes evaluation and improvement of facilities, equipment, procedures, and operations of shippers, carriers, and receivers.

Economic analysis OT conducts economic and market analysis to help develop new transportation and physical distribution systems and to improve existing systems for farmer cooperatives. The office also provides technical assistance to improve cooperative performance.

Foreign market development OT identifies transportation problems in areas of export and foreign trade and initiates remedial actions. It conducts seminars involving shippers and carriers to focus on transportation problems associated with exports.

Rural development The office advises local communities of Federal programs available for improvement or continued operation of local transportation services and provides liaison and coordination between Farmers Home Administration and the Department of Transportation (DOT) concerning financial assistance for local rail service facilities.

FOOD AND CONSUMER SERVICES

Food and Nutrition Service The Food and Nutrition Service (FNS) is the agency of the department that administers the programs to make food assistance available to people who need it. These programs are operated in cooperation with states and with local government.

FNS was established on August 8, 1969, by the secretary of agriculture, under authority of 5 U.S.C. 301 and Reorganization Plan 2 of 1953.

Family nutrition program Principal of these food assistance activities is the food stamp program which, under an approved state plan of operation and through state and local welfare agencies, provides food coupons to needy persons to increase their food purchasing power so they may feed their families properly. The coupons are used by program participants to buy food in any retail store which has been approved by FNS to accept and redeem the food coupons.

Special nutrition programs FNS administers several programs designed to improve the nutrition of children, and particularly those who come from low-income families.

Principal of these is the National School Lunch Program which provides financial assis-

Children take part in the USDA school lunch program.

tance to public and nonprofit private schools of high school grade and under, in operating nonprofit school lunch programs.

The School Breakfast Program provides cash assistance to state educational agencies to help schools in operating nonprofit breakfast programs meeting established nutritional standards. It is especially important in improving the diets of needy children who may receive breakfast free or at reduced prices.

The Summer Food Service Program for Children helps to get nutritious meals to needy preschool and school-aged children in recreation centers, summer camps, or during vacations in areas operating under a continuous school calendar. Through grants-in-aid and other means, states can initiate, maintain, and expand nonprofit food service programs for children through cooperating service institutions.

Any nonresidential public or private nonprofit institution or residential public or private nonprofit summer camp is eligible if it develops a summer food program for children from low-income areas. All meals are served free.

The Child Care Food Program is a companion activity that helps to get nutritious meals to preschool and school-aged children in child-care facilities. Through grants-in-aid states can initiate, maintain, or expand nonprofit food service programs for children in institutions providing child care.

Any licensed public or private nonprofit institution providing nonresidential day-care services may be eligible. Such institutions include day-care centers, settlement houses, recreation centers, family day-care programs, Head Start centers, and institutions providing day-care services for handicapped children.

The Special Milk Program for Children is designed to help child nutrition by paying a share of the cost of increased servings of fluid milk made to children.

Food distribution The Food Distribution Program makes foods available, in kind, to eligible recipients. Foods purchased by the department are made available principally to children in school lunch and breakfast programs, in summer camps, and child-care centers, and to the nutrition program for the elderly.

Supplemental food programs The Special Supplemental Food Program for Women, Infants, and Children—the WIC Program—provides specified nutritious food supplements to pregnant and nursing women up to six months postpartum, and to children up to five years of age. Participants are determined by competent professionals (physicians, nutritionists, nurses, and other health officials) to be health risks because of inadequate nutrition and low income.

Cash grants are made available to participating state health departments or comparable state agencies, or recognized Indian tribes, bands, or groups. The state agencies distribute funds to the local agencies, and the funds are used to provide foods for WIC recipients and to pay specified administrative and clinical costs.

Commodity Supplemental Food Program The Commodity Supplemental Food Program provides supplemental foods to infants and children and to pregnant, postpartum, and breast-feeding women with low incomes who are vulnerable to malnutrition and reside in approved project areas. The department purchases the foods for distribution through state agencies. The program is currently operating in twenty-one project areas in eleven states and the District of Columbia.

Nutrition education and training Under this program funds are granted to the states for the dissemination of nutrition information to children and for in-service training of food service and teaching personnel. The program is for all children in public and private schools and child-care institutions.

No person may be discriminated against—in the operation of any of the programs administered by the Food and Nutrition Service—because of race, color, sex, creed, or national origin.

Food Safety and Quality Service The Food Safety and Quality Service (FSQS) was established by the secretary of agriculture March 14, 1977, pursuant to authority contained in 5 U.S.C. 301 and Reorganization Plan 2 of 1953. It was created to provide assurance to the consumer that foods are safe, wholesome, and nutritious, that they are of good quality, and that they are informatively and honestly labeled; and to provide assistance to the marketing system through purchase of surplus food commodities and those needed in the National Food Assistance Programs.

Meat and poultry inspection Federal inspection is provided for all meat, poultry, and related products processed by plants shipping in interstate and foreign commerce as mandatorily required by law. The work includes inspection of poultry and animals at the time of slaughter and of processed products during various stages of production and handling to assure wholesomeness of products and truthfulness in labeling. Plant facilities and equipment are checked for adherence to Federal sanitation standards. Federal inspectors also conduct surveillance of foreign inspection systems and establishments producing meat and poultry products for export to the United States (21 U.S.C. 451–470 and 601–691).

Other activities include:
- Monitoring livestock slaughter activities to ensure that humane slaughter techniques are effectively applied under the Humane Slaughter Act (7 U.S.C. 1901–1906 [1958]);
- Providing voluntary meat and poultry inspection and certification service relating to wholesomeness of edible products not subject to Federal meat inspection laws and certification of meat and poultry products for use as food for dogs, cats, and other carnivores (7 U.S.C. 1622, 1624); and
- Cooperating with state agencies in the performance of meat and poultry inspection in federally inspected establishments (7 U.S.C. 450).

Egg products inspection Under the Egg Products Inspection Act, the service provides mandatory inspection in all plants processing liquid, dried, or frozen egg products, and also controls the disposition of restricted shell eggs (eggs that might contain harmful bacteria which cause food illlness) (84 Stat. 1620; 21 U.S.C. 1031 et seq. [1970]).

Standardization, inspection, and grading—meat and poultry, dairy products, fresh and processed fruit and vegetables United States grade standards for food and farm products are developed to help buyers and sellers trade on agreed-to specifications. United States grade standards have been established for more than 300 major agricultural products. Grading and inspection are provided to certify the grade and quality of products. These services are mainly voluntary, provided on request and for a fee.

Food quality assurance Under a government-wide quality assurance program, the service is responsible for the development and revision of Federal specifications used in food procurement by Federal agencies. It also coordinates and approves certification programs designed to ensure conformity of products purchased with the specification requirements.

Section 32 programs Under section 32 of the act of August 24, 1935, as amended (7 U.S.C. 612c), 30 percent of customs receipts collected during each calendar year are automatically appropriated for expanding outlets for nonbasic commodities. Portions of these funds are transferred to other agencies in the Department of Agriculture and in the Department of Commerce. Those funds remaining in FSQS are used to purchase commodities for the National School Lunch Program, for other feeding programs, and for diversion to other outlets.

INTERNATIONAL AFFAIRS AND COMMODITY PROGRAMS

Agricultural Stabilization and Conservation Service The Agricultural Stabilization and Conservation Service (ASCS) was established June 5, 1961, by the secretary of agriculture under authority of revised statutes (5 U.S.C. 301), and Reorganization Plan 2 of 1953, as well as all other statutes and prior reorganization plans vesting authority in the secretary of agriculture.

ASCS is the agency of the Department of Agriculture that administers specified commodity and related land-use programs designed for voluntary production adjustment, resource protection, and price, market, and farm income stabilization.

In each state, operations are supervised by a state committee of three to five members appointed by the secretary of agriculture. A state executive director, appointed by the secretary, and staff carry on day-to-day operations of the state office. The state director of the Agricultural Extension Service is an ex officio member of the state committee.

In each of approximately 3,050 agricultural counties, a county committee of three farmer members is responsible for local administration. While two are held over, one is elected yearly by farmer-elected delegates to a county convention. The county agricultural extension agent is a nonvoting ex officio member or secretary of the county committee. A county executive director, with other necessary staff, is employed to carry on day-to-day operations of the county office, usually located in the county seat. There are 2,740 county offices.

Commodity programs ASCS administers commodity stabilization programs for wheat, corn, cotton (upland and extra long staple), soybeans, crude pine gum, peanuts, rice, tobacco, milk, wool, mohair, barley, oats, sugar beets, sugarcane, sorghum, rye, and honey.

Commodity stabilization is achieved, singly or in combination, through loans, purchases, and payments, all at announced levels. Present legislation is designed to make some export commodities more competitive in world markets. At the same time, growers' incomes are protected by deficiency payments for wheat, certain feed grains, rice, and upland cotton when required. Deficiency payments are made whenever the average market price received by farmers during the first five months of the marketing year (calendar year in which the crop is planted, in the case of cotton) falls below established or "target" prices.

For most commodities, loans are made directly to producers on the unprocessed commodity through ASCS county offices. Smaller quantities of some commodities are also purchased from producers. The price of milk is stabilized through purchases of processed dairy products. Price stabilization programs for tobacco, peanuts, and naval stores are carried out through loans to producer associations that, in turn, make program benefits available to producers. Price support loans can also be made available through cooperative marketing associations for cotton, wheat, feed grains, soybeans, rice, and honey. Stabilization of sugar beet and sugarcane prices is carried out through loans to sugar processors, who in turn make program benefits available to producers.

Loans to producers are ordinarily "nonrecourse." If market prices rise above loan levels, producers or their agents can pay off their loans and market their commodity. If market prices fail to rise above loan levels, producers or their agents can forfeit or deliver the commodity to the Commodity Credit Corporation (CCC) and discharge their obligations in full.

Commodity stabilization for wool and mohair is accomplished through payments which in combination with producer marketing returns bring their total return up to the announced level.

Eligibility for commodity loans, purchases, and payments is in most cases conditioned on participation in set-aside (if announced) allotment, or quota programs in effect for the particular crop.

Courts are not the only agency of government that must be assumed to have capacity to govern.

HARLAN F. STONE

Production adjustment Cropland set-aside, acreage allotments, normal crop acreage, and marketing quotas, when applicable, are used singly or in combination in an effort to keep the production of commodities designated by law in line with demand. Normal crop acreage applies when there is a set-aside for wheat, certain feed grains, upland cotton, or rice. Allotments apply also to extra-long-staple cotton, rice, peanuts, and most kinds of tobacco.

When supplies of certain commodities, such as peanuts, tobacco, or long-staple cotton, become excessive, marketing quotas are used in conjunction with acreage allotments if at least two-thirds of the producers voting in a referendum approve the quotas. When quotas are in effect, any excess production of the crop—that is, in general, the production from acreage in excess of the farm acreage allotment—is subject to penalties.

There is an acreage-poundage program in effect for flue-cured tobacco and peanuts and a poundage program in effect for burley tobacco.

Diversion and deficiency payments made under the Food and Agriculture Act of 1977 (7 U.S.C. 1281 et seq.) were limited to an annual ceiling of $40,000 per person on the total payments of upland cotton, wheat, and feed grain programs for the 1978 crop and $45,000 for the 1979 crop. Effective for the 1978 rice crop the payment limitation was $52,250 and $50,000 for the 1979 crop. A $50,000 limitation applied to all the listed crops in 1980 and 1981. This limitation does not include loans or purchases or any payment which is determined to represent resource adjustment or compensation for disaster loss.

Resource conservation programs The Agriculture Conservation Program (ACP) provides cost-sharing up to 75 percent with farmers to carry out needed conservation and environmental measures under annual and long-term agreements. The emphasis of the program is to meet some of the more pressing farm-related conservation and environmental problems; to practice long-range preservation of the environment, which will provide substantial benefits to the public at the least possible cost; and to increase forest production.

The Forestry Incentives Program (FIP), authorized in 1973, provides for the cost-sharing of tree planting and timber stand improvement with private landowners. The Federal share of these costs ranges from up to 75 percent, depending on the cost-share rate set in a particular state and county by the Agricultural Stabilization and Conservation Committee. The aims of the program are to increase the production of timber and improve the environment. The program is

available in counties designated on the basis of a Forest Service (USDA) survey of total eligible private timber acreage and acreage potentially suitable for production of timber products. The maximum cost-share that a person can earn annually for forestry practices under the program is $10,000.

The Water Bank Program, authorized in 1970, provides that persons having eligible wetlands in important migratory waterfowl nesting and breeding areas could enter into ten-year agreements and receive annual payments for the purpose of preventing the serious loss of wetlands and of preserving, restoring, and improving inland fresh water and designated adjacent areas.

The Experimental Rural Clean Water Program (RCWP), authorized in the Agricultural Appropriations Act for 1979 (92 Stat. 1073), provides cost-sharing and technical assistance for the installation of measures to control non-point source pollution from agricultural lands to improve water quality in rural America. The RCWP funding is available in approved project areas designated by the secretary of agriculture, with concurrence by the Environmental Protection Agency, in the Best Management Practices (BMP) to be carried out by the farmers. The Federal cost-share level for project areas is not to exceed 75 percent unless waived. The participants enter into long-term (three to ten years) contracts with the government.

The program is administered by the Agricultural Stabilization and Conservation state and county committees, assisted by other USDA agencies, EPA, and state and local conservation and water quality agencies. The activities of these agencies and organizations are coordinated through national, state, and local coordinating committees.

Incentive program The Wool Incentive Payment Program is designed to promote a sound and profitable domestic wool industry by making payments to producers to bring the national average of prices received by all wool growers up to a predetermined support level.

Indemnity program The Dairy Indemnity Payment Program provides indemnity payments to dairy farmers whose milk has been removed from the commercial market because it contained residues of chemicals or toxic substances, including nuclear radiation or fallout.

Emergency assistance Emergency assistance programs offered farmers in emergency-designated areas may include any or all of the following:
• Providing assistance to livestock owners of up to 50 percent of the cost (not to exceed $.02 per

pound) of purchasing feed to replace that which normally is produced on the farm but which was not because of a natural disaster;

• Furnishing CCC-owned feed grains to eligible livestock producers when available at reduced prices, and, in some instances, by donation; and

• Cost-sharing with farmers who carry out emergency conservation practices to rehabilitate farmland damaged by natural disaster.

ASCS administers disaster payments for farmers participating in the wheat, feed grain, and cotton programs. Farmers may be considered for two types of payments: for prevented planting or abnormally low yield if the cause can be attributed to natural forces and coordinates the dissemination of information to farmers on the National Flood Insurance Program (NFIP) for the Federal Emergency Management Agency (FEMA).

ASCS also administers programs prescribed by FEMA as a result of a presidential declaration of disaster or emergency and coordinates the dissemination of information to farmers on the NFIP for FEMA.

ASCS is responsible for defense preparedness plans and programs relating to farmer production, conservation, and stabilization; food processing, storage, and wholesale distribution; controlled distribution of farm machinery and equipment, spare parts, distribution of fertilizer, feed, and seed; and the handling, storage, and distribution of all grains before export or processing.

ASCS also provides certain USDA-wide defense coordinating services including consolidating services for nonfood requisites and manpower necessary to support food and agricultural operations and other programs for which USDA is responsible; activities relating to expansion of productive capacity, materials, and facilities under the Defense Production Act of 1950 (64 Stat. 798; 50 U.S.C. App. 2061 et seq.), as amended; plans for management, control, and allocation of water to be used for agricultural production and food processing; and guarantees payments or makes loans, as needed, for the continuation of food and agriculture activities in a national defense emergency.

ASCS provides the accounting and budget support for the general sales manager of the Foreign Agricultural Service in administering CCC export credit sales and guarantee programs and Public Law 480 (Food for Peace) programs.

Commodity Credit Corporation The Commodity Credit Corporation (CCC) was organized October 17, 1933, pursuant to Executive Order 6340 of October 16, 1933, under the laws of the state of Delaware, as an agency of the United States. From October 17, 1933, to July 1, 1939, the CCC was managed and operated in close affiliation with the Reconstruction Finance Corporation. On July 1, 1939, the CCC was transferred to the Department of Agriculture by the President's Reorganization Plan 1 of 1939. Approval of the Commodity Credit Corporation Charter Act on June 29, 1948 (62 Stat. 1070; 15 U.S.C. 714 et seq.), subsequently amended, established the CCC, effective July 1, 1948, as an agency and instrumentality of the United States under a permanent Federal charter.

The purpose of CCC is to stabilize and protect farm income and prices, to assist in maintaining balanced and adequate supplies of agricultural commodities and their products, and to facilitate the orderly distribution of commodities.

The CCC is managed by a board of directors, subject to the general supervision and direction of the secretary of agriculture, who is an ex officio director and chairman of the board. The board consists of seven members (in addition to the secretary of agriculture), who are appointed by the president of the United States by and with the advice and consent of the Senate.

The CCC is capitalized at $100 million. CCC also has authority to borrow not to exceed $20 billion for use in carrying out its programs.

In carrying out its principal operations, the CCC utilizes the personnel and facilities of the Agricultural Stabilization and Conservation Service and, in certain foreign trade operations, the Foreign Agricultural Service.

A commodity office in Kansas City, Mo., has specific responsibilities concerned with the acquisition, handling, storage, and disposal of designated commodities and products held by the Commodity Credit Corporation.

Commodity stabilization Loan, purchase, and/or payment programs are administered by CCC for wheat, corn, cotton, peanuts, rice, tobacco, milk, wool, mohair, honey, barley, oats, grain sorghums, rye, soybeans, sugar beets, sugarcane, and crude pine gum.

The Food and Agriculture Act of 1977 authorized target prices for wheat, feed grains, rice, and upland cotton; set minimum loan rates for wheat and feed grains; and established loan levels for upland cotton and peanuts which may be adjusted according to changes in world and domestic market conditions. Government payments for the four commodities are required when the established prices for those commodities exceed the national average market prices received by farmers during the first five months of the marketing year (calendar year in which the crop is planted, in the case of cotton) or the loan rate, whichever is higher. Target prices for all crops covered will be adjusted annually beyond 1978 to reflect changes in cost of production. In addition, the act provides for making disaster payments to producers who are prevented from planting feed grains, wheat, or upland cotton because of a natural disaster or conditions beyond the control of the producers or who, because of such a disaster or condition, harvest less than a specified quantity.

Commodities acquired under the stabilization program are disposed of through domestic and export sales, transfers to other government agencies, and donations for domestic and foreign welfare use. The CCC is also authorized to exchange surplus agricultural commodities acquired by the CCC for strategic and other materials and services produced abroad.

Farm Facility Loan Program   Under the Farm Facility Loan Program, the CCC offers financial assistance through loans to producers needing on-farm storage and drying facilities for various agricultural commodities. The program is designed to encourage farmers to have adequate on-farm storage and drying facilities, which enables them to have greater crop handling and marketing flexibility. The program is administered by the Agricultural Stabilization and Conservation Service.

Grain Reserve Program   The Agricultural Stabilization and Conservation Service has implemented a producer storage program for farmer-owned barley, corn, oats, rice, sorghum, and wheat which are under CCC loan and purchase agreement as provided for under the 1977 act. The program is designed to isolate excess supplies of grain from the market for up to three years or until the national average market price reaches a specified percentage of the then current national average loan rate for the respective grain, when the producer may redeem the reserve loan without penalty. When the national average market price reaches specified percentages of the then current national average loan rate for the respective grain, the reserve loans will be called.

Foreign assistance   Under Public Law 480, the Agricultural Trade Development and Assistance Act of 1954, as amended (7 U.S.C. 1691 et seq.), CCC carries out assigned activities. Major emphasis is also being directed toward meeting the needs of developing nations under the Food for Peace Act of 1966 which further amends the Agricultural Trade Development and Assistance Act of 1954. Under these authorities, agricultural commodities are procured and exported to combat hunger and malnutrition and to encourage economic development in the developing countries.

In 1976 a heavy yield of winter wheat was temporarily stored in the street of Fairfield, Washington.

U.S. Department of Agriculture

Federal Crop Insurance Corporation

The corporation was created within the Department of Agriculture under Title V of the Agricultural Adjustment Act of 1938, cited as the Federal Crop Insurance Act, approved February 16, 1938 (52 Stat. 72; 7 U.S.C. 1501 et seq.). The scope of the corporation's functions has been modified from time to time by amendatory legislation.

The basic purpose of the Federal Crop Insurance Corporation is to promote the general welfare by providing crop insurance against loss from unavoidable causes, such as weather, insects, and disease. Thus, the financial position of the farmers and the community is strengthened.

All capital stock of the Federal Crop Insurance Corporation is owned by the United States.

The management of the Federal Crop Insurance Corporation is vested in the board of directors, subject to the general supervision of the secretary of agriculture.

Functions and activities The Federal Crop Insurance Act, as amended, authorizes the corporation to insure crops against unavoidable losses and to develop the most practical plan, terms, and conditions of insurance for agricultural commodities. The immediate objective is to continue the development of a sound system of crop insurance, and the ultimate objective is to make this protection generally available to farmers on the major part of their annual crop investments.

It does not insure profit for the farmer nor cover avoidable losses such as those due to neglect or poor farming practices. Legislation limits the maximum level of coverage to 75 percent of the average yield but not more than the cost of producing the crop in the area. Crop insurance may be offered each year in not more than 150 counties in addition to the number of counties in which such insurance was offered the preceding year. Insurance may be offered each year on not more than three agricultural commodities in addition to those previously insured. The number of counties in which crop insurance on one or more crops is offered has been gradually expanded since 1948 to more than half of the nation's agricultural counties. The corporation insures wheat, cotton, tobacco, corn, flax, dry beans, soybeans, barley, grain sorghum, oats, rice, citrus fruit, peaches, peanuts, peas, raisins, apples, tomatoes, sugar beets, sugarcane, grapes, forage, potatoes, sunflowers, and sweet corn, as well as the investment in several crops under a combined crop protection plan.

The corporation is directed to develop this insurance so that the premiums paid by the farmers will cover indemnities paid and build a reasonable premium reserve. Administrative costs are financed by annual appropriations and by authorized use of specified amounts of premium income. Legislation limits the appropriation for administration to $12 million. The legislation does not permit including administrative costs in the premium rates. Premium rates are varied throughout the nation and even within counties to reflect differences in productivity and risk of loss. As insurance experience is obtained, it is incorporated into the rate structure. Over $2 billion of crop investments were protected for the 1979 crop year.

Foreign Agricultural Service

The Foreign Agricultural Service (FAS) is the export promotion and service agency for the U.S. Department of Agriculture. It was created in 1953 to stimulate overseas markets for U.S. agricultural products. In fiscal year 1981, shipments of U.S. farm products abroad are expected to reach about $47 billion.

FAS fulfills its role as the promotional agency for the world's largest agricultural export business through its network of agricultural counselors, attachés, and trade officers stationed overseas and its backup team of analysts, marketing specialists, negotiators, and related specialists.

The work of FAS covers several broad areas:

FAS maintains a worldwide agricultural intelligence and reporting system through its attaché service. This service consists of a team of about 100 U.S. professional agriculturalists, posted at approximately seventy American embassies around the world. Their areas of responsibility encompass more than 110 countries. They represent the secretary of agriculture and handle all matters of trade, information needs, food aid, technical programs, and other agricultural endeavors.

The Agricultural Trade Act of 1978 (92 Stat. 1685; 7 U.S.C. 1761 et seq.) established the diplomatic title of counselor for agricultural representatives abroad. Thirty such counselors are now in place.

Attaché reporting includes information and data on foreign government agricultural policies, analysis of supply and demand conditions, commercial trade relationships, and market opportunities. Attachés report not only on more than 200 farm commodities but also on weather, economic factors, and related subjects affecting agriculture.

In FAS/Washington, commodity experts and economists analyze these reports. This analysis is supplemented by accumulated background information and by the Crop Condition

In fact, the whole philosophy of the Agricultural Adjustment Act is based on the theory that the public will be benefited, not damaged, if farmers produce and market within these quotas, thereby avoiding the payment of penalties.

HUGO L. BLACK

Assessment (CCA) system, which analyzes Landsat satellite, weather, and other data. The CCA facility is located at the Johnson Space Center in Houston, Tex., with a small liaison group in Washington, DC.

FAS also has a continuing market development program to develop, service, and expand commercial export markets for U.S. agricultural products. FAS marketing activities involve work with nonprofit commodity groups, called cooperators, trade associations, state agriculture departments and their regional associations, and promotional and trade-servicing operations, such as trade fairs and sales teams.

By virtue of the Agricultural Trade Act of 1978, FAS received authority to open at least six and not more than twenty-five agricultural trade offices to develop, maintain, and expand international markets for U.S. agricultural commodities. These offices are located in such key markets as West Germany, Singapore, and England.

To improve access for U.S. farm products abroad, FAS international trade policy specialists coordinate and direct USDA's responsibilities in international trade agreement programs and negotiations. They maintain an ongoing effort to reduce foreign trade barriers and practices that discourage the export of U.S. farm products.

To maintain watch on foreign governmental actions that affect the market for U.S. agricultural commodities, FAS relies on its agricultural counselors and attachés. Special offices are maintained to work with the headquarters of the European Community in Brussels, Belgium; the Organization for Economic Cooperation and Development in Paris, France; the International Negotiations Center in Geneva, Switzerland; and the Food and Agriculture Organization of the United Nations (FAO) in Rome, Italy.

In Washington, a staff of international trade specialists analyzes the activities of international trade conducted under regional economic organizations and bilateral agreements. During international negotiations, FAS provides the staff and support work for U.S. agricultural representation.

FAS also manages the Public Law 480 Program, Titles I, II, III (Food for Peace Program), and the Commodity Credit Corporation (CCC) Export Credit Guarantee Program. Public Law 480 is aimed at long-range improvement in the economies of developing countries. The credit program provides exporter-risk insurance for financing the agricultural products purchased by some countries.

Title I, the concessional sales section of Public Law 480, provides for low interest, long-term credit to recipients of U.S. farm commodities. Payment is made in dollars, and proceeds from sales into commercial channels are used by the recipient country for agricultural self-help measures and general economic development.

Title II of Public Law 480 provides for direct donations of U.S. farm products in cases of natural disaster or other crises and through voluntary relief agencies and the World Food Program.

New provisions under Title III permit multiyear programming and forgiveness of dollar payments, provided the recipient country undertakes specific agricultural and economic development projects for commodities delivered under Title I agreements.

The CCC Export Credit Guarantee Program (GSM-102) encourages the development or expansion of overseas markets for U.S. agricultural commodities by providing guarantees on private financing of U.S. exports to foreign buyers purchasing on credit terms.

The foreign buyer contracts for the purchase of U.S. commodities on a deferred payment basis of three years or less, and the foreign buyer's bank issues a letter of credit to guarantee payment to the U.S. exporter or an assignee U.S. bank. To receive the payment guarantee, the exporter registers the sale with the CCC and pays a guarantee fee. The payment guarantee is implemented only if the foreign bank fails to pay the exporter or the assignee bank.

The CCC will consider coverage on sales of any agricultural commodities which have the potential of expanding U.S. export markets. A U.S. exporter, private foreign buyer, or foreign government may submit requests for coverage.

Office of International Cooperation and Development   The Office of International Cooperation and Development (OICD) coordinates, plans, and directs the department's efforts in international development and technical cooperation in food and agriculture, including international cooperative research. OICD also coordinates international organization affairs and scientific exchange programs for the department.

The objective of OICD is to provide liaison and coordination for the Department of Agriculture and, to a limited extent, the land-grant university system in planning agricultural development policy, formulating international technical assistance and training programs, reviewing and evaluating agricultural assistance efforts, and providing greater departmental emphasis on scientific exchanges and international research with other countries and the international research centers.

In carrying out its responsibilities, OICD works closely with other U.S. and international organizations to assist them in utilizing the scientific and institutional resources of American agriculture in carrying out development assistance programs, and develops and maintains effective relationships with international and U.S. organizations in planning and coordinating departmental activities designed to support U.S. programs to reduce world hunger and malnutrition.

SCIENCE AND EDUCATION

Science and Education Administration The Science and Education Administration (SEA) was established by the secretary of agriculture on January 24, 1978 (43 FR 3254).

The basic mission of SEA is to improve the nationwide effectiveness of research, extension, and teaching in the food and agricultural sciences. Its basic functions are to:

• Provide support for and coordination and planning of food and agricultural research, extension, and teaching efforts responsive to local, state, regional, and national goals;

• Promote and support the identification of high priority national objectives in the food and agricultural sciences and initiate special projects to meet those objectives;

• Support programs and activities responsive to world food and agricultural needs;

• Develop and provide information and expertise needed by policy, regulatory, and action agencies of the Department of Agriculture and other Federal agencies;

• Build on present partnership and cooperative arrangements and develop with all performers and supporters of food and agricultural research, extension, and teaching activities, whatever their source of funding, improved cooperation and coordination in the planning and execution of these programs and activities;

• Conduct Federal research programs in the food and agricultural sciences;

• Ensure that the results of agricultural research are effectively communicated and demonstrated to farmers, processors, handlers, consumers, and other users; and

• Support and promote information systems and libraries in the food and agricultural sciences and encourage their effective use in coordinating, planning, and implementing research, extension, and teaching programs.

The scope of SEA activities includes the social, economic, and political considerations of agriculture, including soil and water conservation and use, the use of organic waste materials to improve soil tilth and fertility, plant and animal production and protection, and plant and animal health; the processing, distributing, marketing, and utilization of food and agricultural products; forestry, including range management, production of forest and range products, multiple use of forest and range lands, and urban forestry; aquaculture; home economics, human nutrition, and family life; and rural and community development.

Agricultural Research The Agricultural Research staff administers a basic, applied, and developmental research program in animal and plant production; the use and improvement of soil, water, and air; the processing, storage, and distribution of farm products; and food safety and consumer services. The research applies to a wide range of goals, commodities, natural resources, fields of science, and geographic, climatic, and environmental conditions.

Research activities are carried out at 140 separate field locations in cooperation with the state agricultural experiment stations, other Federal agencies, and private organizations. The field activities are managed on a geographical basis through four regional offices, seventeen area offices, and seven major research centers.

Human Nutrition The Human Nutrition staff administers and directs a Federal research program on human nutrition and provides leadership for the collaborative efforts in human nutrition research, extension, and teaching, both nationally and internationally, among all Federal and non-Federal cooperators. The human nutrition program includes but is not limited to human nutritional requirements; nutrient composition of foods and the effects of agricultural practices, handling, food processing, and cooking on the nutrients they contain; surveillance of the nutritional benefits provided to participants in the food programs administered by the Department of Agriculture; factors affecting food preference and habits; development of techniques and equipment to assist consumers in the home or institutions in selecting food that supplies a nutritionally adequate diet.

The headquarters staff is located in the Washington, D.C. area, and the research is conducted at six laboratory locations in the United States.

Cooperative Research The Cooperative Research staff administers Federal grant funds for research in agriculture, agricultural marketing, rural development, and forestry. Funds are made available to the state agricultural experiment stations, the 1,890 land-grant universities, and other designated state institutions in the fifty states, Puerto Rico, Guam, the Virgin Islands, and the District of Columbia. Cooperative Research also administers a specific grant program for research on special problems in agriculture.

The scientific staff reviews research proposals received from the institutions and individuals, conducts on-site reviews of research in progress, gives leadership in planning and coordinating research, and encourages cooperation by and between the stations.

Extension   The Extension staff serves as partners with state governments, through their land-grant universities and county governments, to form the Cooperative Extension Service. These levels of government share in financing and conducting educational programs to help the public learn about and apply to everyday activities the latest technology and management knowledge developed through research by the land-grant universities, the Department of Agriculture, and other sources. Major areas of assistance are agricultural production, marketing, natural resources, home economics, food and nutrition, 4-H youth development, community and rural development, and related subjects.

Extension is a small staff of professional specialists and national program leaders. The state land-grant universities' Cooperative Extension Services have a similar staff of specialists, plus area and county agents working directly with individuals, families, and groups to help them apply the newest proven technology and management techniques to the everyday problems and opportunities of living and making a living.

There are programs for:

• Farmers and ranchers to show how to apply new and improved production and marketing technology to their operations;
• Agri-business, involving processing and marketing farm products and those selling supplies to producers;
• Producer cooperatives and groups considering formation and operation of cooperatives;
• Families to assist in improving their quality of living in nutrition, resource management, energy conservation, clothing, and health safety;
• 4-H Club youth to develop leadership skills, explore careers, and other development activities;
• Homeowners, including lawn and garden care, use of pesticides and herbicides, ornamental horticulture, and family living;
• Community groups and local officials to assist in analyzing needs and resources needed for community development and organizing to secure facilities and services for economic and human development.

Special programs are conducted for low-income people. Low-income families and youth are given individual assistance through paid aides and volunteers. Major attention in low-income and minority programs is devoted to helping families improve their nutritional level. This Expanded Food and Nutrition Education Program (EFNEP) is now operating in the fifty states, Puerto Rico, and the Virgin Islands. Extension in many instances has an established referral system with other groups or organizations concerned with helping low-income people.

Higher Education   The Higher Education staff administers a program of Federal grants and other funds to support the futherance of education in the food and agricultural sciences in all colleges and universities and the establishment of schools of veterinary medicine. The staff also administers a program of predoctoral and postdoctoral fellowships in the food and agricultural sciences.

Technical Information Systems   The Technical Information Systems staff provides leadership to the continuing development and coordination of comprehensive technical information and library systems for the food and agricultural sciences and related USDA needs. The systems and services include the following:

The 4-H Club provides young people with access to the latest agricultural technology, and encourages them to use it in competition with each other.

Minnesota Historical Society

LIBRARY SERVICES Identifies, acquires, catalogs, and maintains a permanent worldwide collection of books and journals; collects catalogs, and maintains a complete inventory of USDA-authored publications; provides library services, including bibliographic references, loans, and reprints to USDA personnel, other libraries, domestic and foreign research and extension professionals, and the general public, as appropriate; and promotes cooperation among USDA agencies, land-grant institutions, colleges, and universities in the provision of library services, including the development of library networks.

FOOD AND NUTRITION INFORMATION Assembles and collects food and nutrition education materials, including the results of nutrition research, training methods, procedures, and related materials; maintains such information and materials in a library; and provides for the dissemination of such information.

INFORMATION SYSTEMS Promotes the effective dissemination of information concerning research, extension, and teaching efforts and results to scientific and professional personnel and other users by developing, maintaining, coordinating, and promoting the effective utilization of information systems, such as indexes of citations for current food and agricultural science and education publications (AGRICOLA); indexes of citations from all USDA-authored publications; a continuing inventory of ongoing and completed research projects (CRIS); a compilation of solar energy research projects related to agriculture which are being carried out by Federal, state, private, and nonprofit institutions and, where available, the results of such projects; a system for documenting and reporting the level of effort devoted to a variety of extension efforts by Federal and state extension professionals (EMIS); a system for documenting and reporting the Federal research resources being utilized for specific problems, commodities, and disciplines in different geographic areas (PARIS); citations of current scientific publications in specific food, agriculture, and related scientific disciplines to aid scientists in maintaining an awareness of new knowledge in their disciplines (Current Awareness Literature Service); and specialized bibliographic files to meet the needs of research, extension, and teaching professionals and organizations.

NATURAL RESOURCES AND ENVIRONMENT

Forest Service The Forest Service was created by the act of February 1, 1905 (33 Stat. 628; 16 U.S.C. 472), which transferred the Federal forest reserves, and the responsibility for their management, from the Department of the Interior to the Department of Agriculture. The forest reserves were established by the president from the public domain under authority of the creative act of March 3, 1891 (26 Stat. 1103; 16 U.S.C. 471). The protection and development of the reserves (which became the national forests in 1907) are governed by the organic act of June 4, 1897 (30 Stat. 34–36; 16 U.S.C. 473–478), as amended, and the Multiple Use-Sustained Yield Act of June 12, 1960 (74 Stat. 215; 16 U.S.C. 528–531), the Forest and Rangeland Renewable Resources Planning Act of 1974 (88 Stat. 476; 16 U.S.C. 1601–1610), and the National Forest Management Act of 1976 (90 Stat. 2947). The Weeks law of March 1, 1911 (36 Stat. 961–963; 16 U.S.C. 480), as amended, allowed the government to purchase and exchange land for national forests.

Objectives The Forest Service has the Federal responsibility for national leadership in forestry. To do this it has adopted the following objectives and policies:

• Promotion and achievement of a pattern of natural resource uses that will best meet the needs of people now and in the future;
• Protection and improvement of the quality of air, water, soil, and natural beauty;
• Protection and improvement of the quality of the open space environment in urban and community areas;
• Generation of forestry opportunities to accelerate rural community growth;
• Encouragement of the growth and development of forestry-based enterprises that readily respond to consumers' changing needs;
• Encouragement of optimum forest landownership patterns;
• Improvement of the welfare of underprivileged members of society;
• Involvement of the public in forestry policy and program formulation;
• Encouragement of the development of forestry throughout the world;
• Expansion of public understanding of environmental conservation; and
• Development and availabilty of a firm scientific base for the advancement of society.

National forest system The Forest Service manages 154 national forests and nineteen national grasslands comprising 188 million acres in forty-one states and Puerto Rico, under the principles of multiple use and sustained yield. The nation's tremendous need for wood and paper products is balanced with the other vital renewable resources or benefits which the national forests and grasslands provide: recreation and natural beauty, wildlife habitat, livestock forage, and water supplies. The guiding principle is the greatest good to the greatest number in the long run.

These lands are protected as much as possible from wildfire, epidemics of disease and insect pests, erosion, floods, and water and air pollution. Burned areas get emergency seeding treatment to prevent massive erosion and stream siltation. Roads and trails are built where needed to allow for closely regulated timber harvesting and to give the public access to outdoor recreation areas and provide scenic drives and hikes. Picnic, camping, water-sport, skiing, and other areas are provided with facilities for public convenience and enjoyment. Timber harvesting methods are used which will protect the land and streams, assure rapid renewal of the forest, provide food and cover for wildlife and fish, and have minimum impact on scenic and recreation values. Local communities benefit from the logging and milling activities. Rangelands are improved for millions of livestock and game animals. The national forests provide a refuge for many species of endangered birds, animals, and fish. Some 12.6 million acres are set aside as wilderness and 3.1 as primitive areas where timber will not be harvested.

Cooperation with the states The Forest Service provides national leadership and financial and technical assistance to non-Federal forest landowners, operators, processors of forest products, and urban forestry interests. Through its cooperative state and private forestry programs, the Forest Service protects and improves the quality of air, water, soil, and open space and encourages uses of natural resources on non-Federal lands which best meet the needs of the nation, while protecting the environment.

Cooperative programs are carried out through the state foresters or equivalent state officials, who receive grant funding under the Cooperative Forestry Assistance Act of 1978 (92 Stat. 365; 16 U.S.C. 2101 et seq.). Cooperators at the state and local level provide the delivery system for most state and private forestry programs.

Grant funds and technical assistance are available for rural forestry assistance, forestry incentives, insect and disease control, urban forestry assistance, rural fire prevention and control, organization management assistance, state forest resource planning, and technology implementation.

The Forest Service also cooperates with the Soil Conservation Service, the Agricultural Stabilization and Conservation Service, and other USDA agencies in providing leadership and technical assistance for the forestry aspects of conservation programs.

State and private forestry also is responsible for ensuring that the Forest Service and its cooperators keep abreast of the best knowledge and technology in carrying out Forest Service programs, and helping to develop technology-transfer plans for implementing research results for a broad range of potential users.

Forest research The Forest Service carries on basic research throughout the country, often in cooperation with state agricultural colleges, under the authority of the McSweeney-McNary Act of May 22, 1928 (45 Stat. 699; 16 U.S.C. 581–581i), as amended and supplemented. Research is carried on in all the fields previously mentioned in addition to many others including genetics, nutrition, improved methods of harvesting, prevention, detection, and mapping of lightning fires, better processing methods for forest products, and environmental improvement.

Human resource programs The Forest Service participates with other Federal agencies in several human resource programs that involve the nation's citizens, both young and old, in forestry-related activities. Included in these programs are the Youth Conservation Corps, Job Corps, Volunteers, Senior Community Service Employment Program, and the new Young Adult Conservation Corps. These programs annually accomplish millions of dollars worth of conservation work, while providing participants with such benefits as training, paid employment, and meaningful outdoor experiences.

Soil Conservation Service The Soil Conservation Service (SCS) was established under authority of the Soil Conservation Act of 1935 (49 Stat. 163; 16 U.S.C. 590a–590f). It has responsibility for developing and carrying out a national soil and water conservation program in cooperation with landowners and operators and other land users and developers, with community planning agencies and regional resource groups, and with other Federal, state, and local government agencies. The SCS also assists in agricultural pollution control, environmental improvement, and rural community development.

The soil and water conservation program is carried on through technical help to locally organized and operated conservation districts; local sponsors of watershed protection projects and resource conservation and development projects; and consultive assistance to other individuals and groups. About 2,950 conservation districts cover more than 2 billion acres in all the states, Puerto Rico, and the Virgin Islands.

Conservation operations SCS provides technical assistance through conservation districts to landowners and operators in carrying out locally adapted soil and water conservation programs.

Technical assistance is given to district co-operators and other landowners in the development of conservation plans and application of conservation treatment. Assistance to district co-operators (individuals and communities) includes: providing a soil map and other resource data; providing information about practical alternatives for treating and using the land; developing a plan for installing the treatment measures and making the land use changes needed; and helping to apply parts of the plan that require special skills or knowledge.

Soil surveys are made to determine soil use potentials and conservation treatment needs, and publication of soil surveys with interpretations useful to cooperators, other Federal agencies, state and local organizations. One important basis for conservation planning is the National Cooperative Soil Survey for which the SCS has the Federal part of the responsibility. The work is carried out in cooperation with state agricultural experiment stations and other state and Federal agencies.

Plant materials centers are operated to assemble, test, and encourage increased use of promising plant species in conservation programs; and snow surveys in the western states are made to develop stream-flow forecasts.

Unchecked erosion carves up 60 acres of upper midwest farmland.

Contour plowing is practiced on a midwestern farm as a soil conservation measure.

Under the Soil and Water Resources Conservation Act of 1977 (91 Stat. 1407; 16 U.S.C. 2001 et seq.), the service is responsible for appraising the status and condition of soil, water, and related resources and trends in their use; designing long-range conservation programs with the aid of local soil conservation districts and the public; and evaluating progress in meeting conservation needs. SCS inventory and monitoring data are used at all governmental levels for conservation, use and development of land, and for protecting environmental quality. The service also publishes maps showing the location of important farmlands, usually on a county basis.

River basin surveys and investigations   The service, along with the Economics, Statistics, and Cooperatives Service, Forest Service, and Science and Education Administration, cooperates with other Federal, state, and local agencies in studying the watersheds of rivers and other waterways. These studies include cooperative river basin surveys that serve as a basis for developing coordinated water resource programs; floodplain management studies that furnish technical data, assistance, and information for state and local governments to use in floodplain management programs; joint investigations and reports with the Department of the Army under Public Law 87-639 (16 U.S.C. 1009); special studies in the Colorado River Basin to identify opportunities for reducing salt load to the river from agricultural activities; and interagency coordination under the aegis of the Water Resources Council.

Watershed planning   The service has general responsibility for administration of activities consisting of investigations and surveys of proposed small watershed projects in response to requests made by sponsoring local organizations, and for assisting sponsors in the development of watershed plans.

Watershed and flood prevention operations   The service has general responsibility for administration of activities which include cooperation with local sponsors, state, and other public agencies in the installation of planned works of improvement to reduce erosion, floodwater, and sediment damage; conserve, develop, utilize, and dispose of water; plan and install works of improvement for flood prevention including the development of recreational facilities and the improvement of fish and wildlife habitat; and provide loans to local organizations to help finance the local share of the cost of carrying out planned watershed and flood prevention works of improvement. The Farmers Home Administration administers the loan program.

The SCS also has responsibility for carrying out emergency watershed protection under section 216 of the Flood Control Act of 1950 (64 Stat. 170; 33 U.S.C. 701b–1) and section 403 of the Agricultural Credit Act of 1978 (92 Stat. 420; 16 U.S.C. 2203).

Great Plains Conservation Program   The service has general responsibility for administration of the program designed to promote conservation and greater agricultural stability in the Great Plains area. Activities include cost-sharing of conservation practices under three- to ten-year contracts with farmers and ranchers in designated counties of the ten Great Plains states, and technical services to help make needed land use adjustments and install conservation measures specified in conservation plans in accordance with contract schedules.

Resource Conservation and Development Program   The service has general responsibility for assisting local units of government accelerate planning and development of land and water resources in multiple county areas. Projects include work for such things as erosion control, flood prevention, farm irrigation, water-based recreation, fish and wildlife facilities, agriculture-related pollutant control, and water quality. Efforts also are directed toward improving recreation facilities, including historic and scenic attractions; encouraging new industries to locate in the area and to process products of the area; improving markets for crop and livestock products; upgrading and protecting the quality of the environment; and long-range planning to coordinate public efforts in the area.

Activities include investigations and surveys to help develop programs and plans of land conservation and utilization, technical services and financial assistance to sponsors, local groups, and individuals, and making loans for resource improvements and developments in approved projects. The Farmers Home Administration administers the loans.

Rural Abandoned Mine Program   The service has USDA leadership for administration of the program to assist land users in reclaiming abandoned or inadequately reclaimed coal-mined lands and water, provided there is no continuing reclamation responsibility on the part of the mine operator, permit holder, or agent. The program provides cost-sharing aid ranging from 25–100 percent, as well as technical assistance to land users, under contracts of five to ten years. The goal is to reclaim, conserve, and develop unreclaimed coal lands that are adversely affecting people or their environment.

Under the Surface Mining Control and Reclamation Act of 1977 (91 Stat. 445; 30 U.S.C. 1201 et seq.), the service also has responsibilities in helping identify areas of prime farmland within areas that may be surface mined in the future, providing technical assistance to mine operators for reclaiming coal-mined lands, reviewing and commenting on permits for surface mining which involve prime farmland, and reviewing and commenting on state reclamation plans.

Other programs SCS gives technical help to the Farmers Home Administration in making soil and water conservation loans to landowners and operators. SCS assists landowners and operators in developing recreation areas and facilities on private land.

SCS gives technical assistance to participants in the Agricultural Conservation Program (ACP), Rural Clean Water Program (RCWP), and the Waterbank Program (WBP). Under ACP, RCWP, and WBP, SCS provides technical assistance in developing conservation plans that are the basis of long-term agreements between the department and landowners and operators. SCS assists in the design, layout, and certification of some conservation practices installed under these programs.

ECONOMICS

Economic Research Service The Economics and Statistics Service formulates, develops and administers a program of economic, statistical, and other social science research, analysis, and information related to food, agriculture, and rural resources and communities; a program to collect and publish statistics related to food, agriculture and rural resources and communities. The results of these activities are made available to users through research and statistical reports and through outlook and situation reports on major commodities, rural areas, and the national and international economies.

Research Specifically, the service carries out a national program of research relating to the production and marketing of farm commodities. It includes evaluations of the organization and performance of major commodity subsectors; costs and returns to farmers and marketers; situation and outlook; commodity projections; price spreads; and analysis of U.S. farm commodity programs. The service deals with the entire agriculture sector on issues related to consumer demand; agricultural finance; farm inputs; pricing policies and programs; structure and adjustments in the agriculture sector; long-run projections; and overall performance measures in agriculture such as farm income, the marketing bill, and others. It focuses on world-wide supply and demand conditions; the impact of U.S. and foreign policies on world farm trade; and publishes information that traders, government officials, and trade negotiators need to tap world markets.

The service also conducts research on the use, conservation, development, and control of natural resources and their contribution to local, regional, and national economic growth. Analysis of environmental issues is an important element of this responsibility. In addition, the service maintains current information on the principal social and economic factors affecting life in nonmetropolitan areas and identifies and evaluates alternative public and private actions which impact on these areas.

Statistics The service provides data and estimates on a wide range of production, supply, price, and other items necessary to the orderly operation of the United States agricultural economy. The reports include statistics on field crops, fruits and vegetables, cattle, hogs, poultry, and related products. Other estimates concern prices received by farmers for products sold and prices paid for commodities and services, indexes of prices received and paid, parity prices, farm employment, and farm wage rates. These estimates are prepared through a complex system of sample surveys of producers, processors, buyers, and others associated with agriculture, who are contacted by mail, telephone, personal interview, and field visits.

The forty-four state-Federal offices, serving all states, and the national office prepare monthly, annual, and other periodic reports for distribution to the news media and the general public. Data on about 150 crops and livestock products appear in some 500 reports issued each year. Cooperative agreements with state agencies permit preparation and publication of estimates of individual crops and livestock not only for states and the nation but also by counties in most cases.

World Food and Agricultural Outlook Board The World Food and Agricultural Outlook Board coordinates and reviews all commodity and aggregate agricultural and food data and analyses used to develop outlook and situation material prepared within the Department of Agriculture.

The aim is to improve the consistency, objectivity, and reliability of the material being disseminated to the public. The board also coordinates the weather and climate information and monitoring activities within USDA, and is the focal point for weather and climatic information and impact assessment. In carrying out its responsibilities, the board oversees and clears for consistency of analytical assumptions and results all estimates and analyses which significantly relate to international and domestic commodity supply and demand.

Office of Budget, Planning and Evaluation The Office of Budget, Planning and Evaluation coordinates the preparation of departmental budget estimates and legislative reports; administers systems for the management and control of funds; provides policy, program, and budgetary analysis of USDA proposals; and provides staff assistance to USDA agencies in meeting their responsibilities for public participation in the development of regulations, as required by Executive Order 12044 of March 23, 1978.

Source: *The United States Government Manual 1981/82* and/or *1982/83.*

AGRICULTURE DEPARTMENT—GRADUATE SCHOOL
The Graduate School, U.S. Department of Agriculture, is a nonprofit school for adults. It is self-supporting and does not receive direct appropriated funds from Congress or the Department of Agriculture. Fees charged individuals and government agencies are nominal. Courses are planned with the help of government professionals and specialists.

The faculty is mostly part-time and is drawn from throughout government and the community at large. They are selected because of their professional and specialized knowledge and experience and thus bring a practicality and currency to their classrooms. Faculty members are paid an honorarium and take annual leave or leave without pay when they teach during normal working hours. The school does not grant degrees but does provide planned sequences of courses leading to certificates of accomplishment in a number of occupational fields important to government. It offers occasional free public lectures on current affairs of special interest to government employees and supports a press which publishes some of those lectures, films, videotapes, and other manuscripts.

The graduate school's objective is to help improve government services by providing needed continuing education and training opportunities for government employees and agencies. The graduate school, administered by a director and governed by a general administration board appointed by the secretary of agriculture, was established by the secretary of agriculture on September 2, 1921, pursuant to the act of May 15, 1862 (R.S. 520; 7 U.S.C. 2201), the Joint Resolu-

tion of April 12, 1892 (27 Stat. 395), and the Deficiency Appropriation Act of March 3, 1901 (31 Stat. 1039; 20 U.S.C. 91).

Source: *The United States Government Manual 1981/82* and/or *1982/83.*

AID AND ABET □ To assist another in the commission of a crime by words or conduct. □

The person who aids and abets participates in the commission of a crime by performing some overt act or by giving advice or encouragement. He or she must share the criminal intent of the person who actually commits the crime, but it is not necessary for the aider and abettor to be physically present at the scene of the crime.

An aider and abettor is a party to a crime and may be criminally liable as a PRINCIPAL, an ACCESSORY BEFORE THE FACT, or an ACCESSORY AFTER THE FACT.

AID AND COMFORT □ To render assistance or counsel. □

Article 3, Section 3, Clause 1 of the Constitution specifies that the giving of aid and comfort to the enemy is an element in the crime of TREASON.

Aid and comfort may consist of substantial assistance or merely attempting to provide some support. Actual help or the success of the enterprise is not necessary. Any act that deliberately strengthens or tends to strengthen enemies of the United States or that weakens or tends to weaken the power of the United States to resist and attack such enemies is aid and comfort.

AIDER BY VERDICT
□ The correction of a technical defect in a PLEADING or in an INDICTMENT or INFORMATION that might have been objected to before the judgment or verdict by the rendering of the decision. For purposes of curing defective pleadings, a finding or judgment by the court without a jury has the same effect as a verdict.
□ The presumption made by a court after it has rendered a judgment in a civil action or a verdict in a criminal prosecution that an error in the pleading or indictment that should have been amended during the trial has been made by virtue of its decision. □

Civil actions Aider by verdict, recognized as a rule of COMMON LAW and of statute, applies to all types of pleadings, such as COMPLAINTS, ANSWERS, COUNTERCLAIMS, and pleas of SETOFF. A pleading is usually sufficient if it contains allegations for which every fact necessary to maintain an action or establish a defense can be reasonably inferred and without which a jury could not have reached a verdict. When, for example, a complaint alleges facts that establish a cause of action, all other defects to which no objection has been made are cured by the verdict. After the verdict has been made, the existence of a defective statement or omission of a material fact in a pleading does not necessitate a reversal of the verdict and a new trial if proof of such a fact had been admitted without objection and the matter had been fully litigated. If, however, the pleading is not supported by the evidence, aider by verdict cannot occur.

Different errors such as a mistake in the form of action or the theory upon which it is based can be cured by aider by verdict. At every stage of the lawsuit, the court will disregard defects in pleading as long as they do not substantially affect the rights of the party against whom the pleadings will be used. This rule does not apply where the pleadings fail to state a cause of action or defense. In such cases, the court cannot presume that the omitted allegations have been duly proven at trial.

Although aider by verdict cures errors in pleading, a party may seek to amend a pleading after the verdict, to "aid" the trial record by conforming pleading to the evidence. Such amendment is permitted under state codes of CIVIL PROCEDURE and the rules of FEDERAL CIVIL PROCEDURE. In practice, courts rarely concern themselves with the validity of pleadings after a judgment has been made. When aider by verdict is used, every amendment that should have been made is deemed to have been made after the verdict.

Criminal prosecutions Aider by verdict may correct technical defects in an INDICTMENT or INFORMATION as long as such errors did not impair a defendant's constitutional rights to be tried upon the indictment of the GRAND JURY or other ACCUSATORY BODY. The rules of Federal CRIMINAL PROCEDURE as well as state codes of criminal procedure permit aider by verdict only when the errors in the indictment are immaterial, such as grammatical errors or SURPLUSAGE.

AIDING THE ENEMY ACTS

The outbreak of war normally ends all forms of normal relations between belligerent states. In support of the war effort municipal laws may be implemented to prevent citizens and other persons within a belligerent state's jurisdiction from assisting an enemy state through trade or other forms of contact. In the United States, for example, the Trading with the Enemy Act (40 Stat. 411 as amended [1917]) suspends all forms of trade or communication with persons in enemy territory. The statutory or executive restrictions imposed under the Trading with the Enemy Act are limited to formal periods of war, although other authority exists permitting the president to impose restrictions on trade or communications with a country without a declaration of war.

AIRCRAFT, JURISDICTION OVER

See Jurisdiction of States under International Law; National Character of Aircraft and Ships.

AIR FORCE DEPARTMENT

The Department of the Air Force is responsible for providing an air force that is capable, in conjunction with the other armed forces, of preserving the peace and security of the United States.

The Department was established as part of the National Military Establishment by the National Security Act of 1947 and came into being on September 18, 1947 (61 Stat. 495). The National Security Act Amendments of 1949 redesignated the National Military Establishment as the Department of Defense, established it as an executive department, and made the Department of the Air Force a military department within the Department of Defense (63 Stat. 578).

The Department of the Air Force is separately organized under the Secretary of the Air Force. It operates under the authority, direction, and control of the Secretary of Defense (10 U.S.C. 8010). The Department consists of the Office of the Secretary of the Air Force, the Air Staff, and the field organization.

Office of the Secretary

The Office of the Secretary includes the Under Secretary, three Assistant Secretaries, the Administrative Assistant, the General Counsel, and the Directors of Legislative Liaison, Information, Space Systems, Small and Disadvantaged Business Utilization, and Auditor General. The heads of these offices are staff advisers to the Secretary for functions he assigns to them.

The Department of the Air Force is administered by the Secretary of the Air Force who is responsible for and has the authority to conduct all affairs of the Department. The Secretary is specifically responsible for overall direction, guidance, and supervision of the space programs and space activities of the Air Force. The principal assistant is the Under Secretary who acts with full authority of the Secretary on all affairs of the Department.

Assistant secretaries The three Assistant Secretaries are authorized to act for and with the authority of the Secretary on any matters within their respective areas of research, development and logistics, manpower, reserve affairs and installations, and financial management.

The safety of the State is the highest law.

JUSTINIAN

Supporting offices   The Administrative Assistant serves as principal adviser to the Secretary of the Air Force and other statutory appointees on all phases of internal administration and management policies and assures administrative continuity in the Office of the Secretary during changes of top officials.

The General Counsel is the final legal authority on all matters arising within or referred to the Department of the Air Force, except those relating to the administration of military justice and such other matters as may be assigned to the Judge Advocate General.

The Director of Legislative Liaison advises and assists the Secretary and all other principal civilian and military officials of the Department concerning Air Force legislative affairs and congressional relations.

The Director of Public Affairs supervises USAF information activities to include informing the public of Air Force activities, developing and monitoring Air Force internal information programs, and directing Air Force community relations efforts.

The Director of Space Systems is primarily responsible for assisting the Secretary in discharging his responsibility for the direction, supervision, policy, security, and control of space systems.

The Director of Small and Disadvantaged Business Utilization is responsible for the implementation and execution of the Air Force's program to aid, counsel, and assist small and disadvantaged firms in obtaining a fair proportion of Air Force prime contracts and subcontracts. The Director is also responsible for the Air Force's Labor Surplus Area Contracting Program and for assisting women-owned business firms in obtaining contracts.

Air Staff

Mission   The mission of the Air Staff is to furnish professional assistance to the Secretary, the Under Secretary, the Assistant Secretaries of the Air Force, and the Chief of Staff.

Structure   The Air Staff is a management headquarters functional organization under the Chief of Staff, United States Air Force. Titles throughout all organizational levels reflect the functions involved. In addition, there is a board structure, a Chief Master Sergeant of the Air Force, a foreign liaison office, and an administrative management function. The Air Staff is commonly referred to as "Headquarters, USAF."

Functions and activities   Air Staff functions are specialized into well-defined areas to effect the management principles of functionality, integration, flexibility, simplicity and decentralization. The Air Staff retains those management functions that legally cannot be delegated or decentralized, are needed by the Secretary and Chief of Staff, are essential to respond promptly to the Secretary of Defense, or are required to determine the design and structure of the Air Force in the future.

Chief of Staff   The Chief of Staff is directly responsible to the Secretary of the Air Force for the efficiency and operational readiness of the Air Force. He is a member of the Joint Chiefs of Staff (JCS) of the Department of Defense. He is assisted in all responsibilities, except for JCS, by the Vice Chief of Staff. The Assistant Vice Chief of Staff assists the Chief and Vice Chief in the discharge of their duties.

Special Staff   The Special Staff is an adjunct to the Chief of Staff, independent of the basic staff structure, and provides advisory and support services to both the Chief of Staff and the Air Staff. The Special Staff consists of a chaplain and inspector, legal, medical, intelligence, studies and analyses, chief scientist, Reserve and Air National Guard functions.

Deputy Chiefs of Staff   The Deputy Chiefs of Staff (DCS's) function primarily as a coordinating level on policy matters and represent the corporate structure. Substantive functions are organized under the DCS's in homogeneous groups, which are called Directorates. Under the directorates, functions are further broken down into descriptive groups, divisions, and branches.

Comptroller of the Air Force   The Comptroller of the Air Force functions in the same manner as the DCS's except that he is directly responsible to the Assistant Secretary of the Air Force for Financial Management with concurrent responsibility to the Chief of Staff.

Board structure   The board structure in the Air Staff consists of the Air Force Council and below it the Air Staff Board. The Air Force Council presents the recommendations of the DCS's on an agenda item to the Chief of Staff. The Air Staff Board presents the recommendations of the directors on an agenda item to the staff responsible or sponsors the recommendations before the Air Force Council. Membership on the Council is at DCS, Comptroller, Special Staff level while membership on the Board is at Directorate level.

Administration   Administrative and logistical support is provided to the headquarters by the 1947th Administrative Support Group.

Field organization

The major commands, separate operating agencies, and direct reporting units together represent the field organization of the United States Air Force. These commands are organized primarily on a functional basis in the United States and on an area basis overseas. Commands are given the responsibility for accomplishing certain phases of the worldwide activities of the USAF. They are responsible for organizing, administering, equipping, and training their subordinate elements for the accomplishment of assigned missions.

Air Force Logistics Command The Air Force Logistics Command provides worldwide logistical support to the Air Force. This includes procurement, storage, and distribution of supplies and the performance of or arrangement for the performance of depot level maintenance on materiel.

Air Force Systems Command The responsibility of the Air Force Systems Command is to advance aerospace technology, adapt it into operational aerospace systems, and acquire qualitatively superior aerospace systems and material needed to accomplish the United States Air Force mission.

Air Training Command The Air Training Command is responsible for Air Force recruiting, individual training for Air Force officers and airmen, and higher education of Air Force officers. Training includes basic training and indoctrination for recruits; flying training; and technical, field, and special training. Education activities include the Air War College, Air Command and Staff College, Air Force Institute of Technology, Extension Course Institute, Leadership and Management Development Center, and Air Force ROTC.

Military Airlift Command The Military Airlift Command (MAC) is a major command of the United States Air Force and a Joint Chiefs of Staff specified command. Its primary mission is to provide air transportation for personnel and cargo for all the military services on a worldwide basis. In addition, MAC furnishes weather, rescue, and audiovisual services for the Air Force.

Strategic Air Command The Strategic Air Command is a major command of the United States Air Force and a Joint Chiefs of Staff specified command. Its primary mission is to organize, train, equip, administer, and prepare strategic air forces for combat, including bombardment, missile, special mission, and strategic reconnaissance units and to conduct strategic air operations. The Command also performs the space surveillance and strategic warning mission for the U.S. Air Force.

Tactical Air Command The Tactical Air Command's mission is to organize, train, and equip forces to participate in tactical air operations. This includes tactical fighter, tactical air reconnaissance, special operations, close combat air support, and joint amphibious and airborne operations. It is the Air Force component of U.S. Readiness Command and U.S. Atlantic Command. It participates with other services in developing doctrine, procedures, tactics, techniques, training, and equipment for joint operations. It provides combat ready air elements to the Readiness Command.

Electronic Security Command The Electronic Security Command monitors Air Force communications in all parts of the world to ensure compliance with established communication security practices and procedures. Additionally, Electronic Security Command units occasionally conduct research in communication phenomena in support of various elements of the U.S. government.

Air Force Communications Command The Air Force Communications Command provides base and point-to-point communications, flight facilities, air traffic control, and automated data processing (ADP) services, primarily to the Air Force, but also to other agencies, governmental and civil, national and foreign.

United States Air Forces in Europe The United States Air Forces in Europe is a major command of the United States Air Force and is the Air Force component of the U.S. European Command. Its primary mission is to organize, train, equip, administer, and prepare assigned forces for combat, including tactical fighter, tactical air reconnaissance, tactical air control, close air support, and defense suppression units to conduct defensive and offensive air operations. It provides combat ready air elements to the U.S. European Command and participates in joint and combined air operations.

Pacific Air Forces The Pacific Air Forces is a major command of the United States Air Force and is the Air Force component of the U.S. Pacific Command. Its primary mission is to organize, train, equip, administer, and prepare assigned forces for combat, including tactical fighter, tactical air reconnaissance, tactical air control, close air support, and defense suppression units to conduct defensive and offensive air operations. It provides combat ready air elements to the U.S. Pacific Command and participates in joint and combined air operations.

We, like the eagles, were born to be free. Yet we are obliged, in order to live at all, to make a cage of laws for ourselves and to stand on the perch.

WILLIAM BOLITHO

Alaskan Air Command Alaskan Air Command is a major command of the United States Air Force. Its primary mission is to conduct aerospace defense operations according to tasks assigned by the Commander in Chief, North American Air Defense Command (CINCNORAD). The Command plans, conducts, controls, and coordinates offensive and defensive air operations, and is the coordinating authority for all joint military administrative and logistical matters in Alaska, and is the military point of contact for the state of Alaska.

Separate operating agencies The Air Force Accounting and Finance Center provides technical supervision, advice, and guidance to Air Force accounting and finance field activities and finance operation.

The Air Force Audit Agency provides independent internal audit and appraisal of financial, operational, management, and support activities as a service to all levels of management.

The Air Force Inspection and Safety Center directs the Air Force inspection and safety programs, evaluating operational readiness, accident prevention, and management systems.

The Air Force Office of Special Investigations provides criminal, counterintelligence, personnel security, and special investigative services to Air Force activities; collects, analyzes, and reports significant information about these matters.

The Air Force Manpower and Personnel Center executes personnel plans and programs and supervises procedures applicable to the worldwide management and administration of Air Force military personnel and performs certain civilian personnel operating activities. It also develops and maintains Air Force manpower standards for the purpose of improving manpower utilization; implements the Air Force Management Engineering Program; and exercises direct supervision over assigned Management Engineering Teams engaged in developing specialized and functional manpower standards and related data.

The Air Force Intelligence Service provides specialized intelligence service in support of USAF operations through the conduct of comprehensive research, direction of collection activities, processing and dissemination of intelligence information and intelligence, and the exercise of management and control of intelligence systems and special security systems.

The Air Force Test and Evaluation Center manages the Air Force Operational Test and Evaluation (OT&E) program; assesses the operational utility of all major and selected nonmajor Air Force systems using, implementing, and supporting commands as required; and is responsible for recommending policy, and for planning, directing, evaluating, and reporting on the Air Force OT&E program.

The Air Force Engineering and Services Center provides specialized engineering and services, technical assistance, and operating support to Air Force bases and organizations. This includes food, laundry, dry cleaning, and linen exchange services; regional civil engineering; and the highly specialized, interdisciplinary civil engineering functions.

The Air Force Commissary Service provides subsistence support to appropriated and nonappropriated fund food activities and to authorized individual patrons. It also operates a resale store system to provide service and facilities for the sale of Department of Defense authorized merchandise at the lowest practical price to authorized patrons.

The Air Force Legal Services Center provides Air Force-wide legal services in the functional areas of military justice, patents, claims and tort litigation, general litigation, labor law, preventive law, and legal aid. It also administers the Federal Legal Information Through Electronics (FLITE) Program for the Air Force as Executive Agent for the Department of Defense.

The Air Force Service Information and News Center plans and executes the USAF internal information program for all military and civilian personnel. It develops, produces, and distributes materials in support of information, orientation, motivation, and unit morale goals and provides information about Air Force people and missions to hometown news media and national commercial magazines.

The Air Force Medical Service Center assists and supports the Air Force Surgeon General in developing and implementing practices for health care in peacetime and wartime environments; and performs studies and research on how Air Force medical policies and programs are executed and recommends appropriate modifications to the Air Force Surgeon General.

The Air Force Office of Security Police develops operational policies and practices in peacetime and wartime environments to carry out programs for the security of Air Force resources and information and the delivery of law enforcement services. The Office implements plans, policies, and programs for base defense, management of security police personnel, training, systems and equipment programs, and the physical security of Air Force resources; the information, personnel and industrial security programs and the wartime information security program; maintenance of law and order; prisoner rehabilitation and corrections programs; vehicle traffic management; and the military working-dog program.

The Air Force Audit Agency provides independent internal audit and appraisal of financial, operational, management, and support activities as a service to all levels of management.

Direct reporting units The United States Air Force Academy provides a four-year educational curriculum for cadets that includes a baccalaureate level education in airmanship, related sciences, and the humanities. Besides a classical education, each cadet is trained to appreciate the role of airpower, its capabilities and limitations, high ideals of individual integrity, patriotism, loyalty, honor, physical fitness, sense of responsibility, and a dedication of selfless and honorable service.

The Air Force Reserve performs the USAF Chief of Staff field responsibilities for command of the Air Force Reserve; is responsible for participation in the formulation of plans for the management, administration, and execution of programs affecting Air Force Reserve (AFRes) units; and provides for personnel administration

of the Air Reserve Forces and mobilization of these reserves when needed.

The Aerospace Defense Center is the administrative and resource management organization for organizing, training, and equipping Air Force personnel supporting the North American Air Defense Command and Aerospace Defense Command (the Joint Chiefs of Staff specified command) functions.

The Air Force Technical Applications Center operates and maintains the United States Atomic Energy Detection System (AEDS) to monitor compliance of signatories to nuclear test ban treaties. The AEDS consists of a worldwide network of sensors and collection equipment, analysis laboratories, a depot to support the AEDS, and a headquarters staff to perform operational management functions.

Source: *The United States Government Manual 1981/82* and/or *1982/83.*

AIR POLLUTION REGULATION ☐ The area of ENVIRONMENTAL LAW that centers upon legislation created to protect human health from the hazards of unclear atmospheric conditions. ☐

U.S. Department of Agriculture

Tires burning at the Bozeman, Montana, city dump darkened the sky in 1969.

This photo is part of a U.S. Department of Agriculture study of the effects of nitrogen dioxide or sulfur dioxide (acid rain) on the leaf of the white birch.

At COMMON LAW, air pollution control was attempted largely through the application of a NUISANCE doctrine. The possessor of land was regarded as being under the duty to make a reasonable use of his or her property that caused no harm to other individuals in the area. An individual who filled the air with poisonous fumes would be liable for a breach of this obligation.

The first significant legislation concerning air pollution was the Air Pollution Control Act, enacted in 1955, which gave the secretary of health, education, and welfare the power to undertake and recommend research programs for air pollution control. This act, known as the Clean Air Act, was largely amended, with the most significant alterations occurring in 1977 (42 U.S.C.A. § 7401 et seq.).

The 1977 amendments indicated that the central responsibility for air pollution control and prevention was at the state and local governmental level. They provided Federal economic aid and guidance to facilitate the development of programs of cooperation on all governmental levels. One component of the 1977 amendments commands the Environmental Protection Agency (EPA) to aid Federal, state, and local agencies in their formulation of programs designed to inspect and control motor vehicle emissions, regulate parking on the streets, deter automobile use in crowded areas, limit the idling of motor vehicles, arrange for bicycle lanes, and encourage car pooling sponsored by employers. In addition, the EPA has prescribed standards of air quality for different regions throughout the country and set forth legal constraints for certain pollutants.

The EPA possesses the power to stringently enforce its prescribed standards for control of air pollution. The EPA regulates sulfur dioxide, particulates, carbon monoxide, hydrocarbons, nitrogen dioxide, and photochemical oxidants. In locations where the levels of the most harmful pollutants exceed EPA standards, such levels must be brought within the requisite limitations before any further industrial expansion will be permitted. Many pollutants have been regulated to further the enactment of laws relating to auto-exhaust emissions. Such laws require automobiles to be tested regularly for auto-emission problems.

Another important provision in the Clean Air Act permits citizens to bring suit against any individual who fails to comply with the law, thereby precipitating pollution. Citizens may also sue the government, and, if the EPA is not strict enough in its control of pollution, it may also be sued through the citizen suit provision. See also, Joseph L. Sax's essay on Environmental Law.

AIR RIGHTS ☐ The power and authority of a landowner or a LESSOR to use all or a segment of the airspace extending above his or her land. ☐

Airspace rights are ordinarily vested by a grant such as a FEE SIMPLE, absolute ownership, or a LEASE.

Commercial airlines have the right to reasonably interfere with an individual's air rights by flying over his or her land. If the flight paths adversely affect the owner's right to quiet use and enjoyment of the property, however, he or she is generally entitled to recover the extent of DAMAGES suffered. See also, Aeronautics.

THE FUTURE OF TRINITY CHURCH.

The magazine *Puck* published this cartoon in 1907 satirizing the capacity of skyscrapers to interfere with the access of other buildings to light and air.

UPI

The Los Angeles Unified School District sued the city for $95.8 million on the grounds that jet plane noise disrupted the education of thousands of students daily.

AIRSPACE Traditional international law provides that each nation has complete and exclusive jurisdiction over its airspace, that area to which a nation and its territorial waters is subjacent. Some nations have attempted to extend the horizontal base of this jurisdiction through the establishment of Air Defense Identification Zones, by which other nations must notify or gain approval from establishing nations prior to entering airspace above waters neighboring territorial seas. While the vertical jurisdiction traditionally extends *usque ad coelum* (Latin for "to the heavens"), modern events have necessitated a distinction between airspace and outerspace. Certainly such a demarcation is difficult, but inevitably must lie somewhere between the maximum altitude for conventional airflights and the minimum altitude for orbit.

ALDERMAN ☐ A public officer of a town or city council or a local legislative body who is elected to the position by the persons he or she represents. ☐

ALEATORY CONTRACT ☐ A mutual agreement between two parties in which the performance of the contractual obligations of one or both parties depends upon a fortuitous event. ☐

The most common type of aleatory CONTRACT is an INSURANCE policy in which an insured pays a premium in exchange for an insurance company's promise to pay damages up to the face amount of the policy in the event that one's house is destroyed by fire. The insurance company must perform its obligation only after the fortuitous event, the fire, occurs.

ALEXANDER, James James Alexander (*b.* 1691, in Scotland; *d.* April 2, 1756, in Albany, New York) was an eminent lawyer who became famous for his support of freedom of the press.

In 1715, Alexander emigrated to America, and began a career of public service to New York and New Jersey. He performed the duties of surveyor general for the Province of New Jersey in 1715, and three years later served as recorder of Perth Amboy.

Alexander participated in the Council of New York from 1721 to 1732 but continued to be active in New Jersey. He was admitted to the New Jersey Provincial bar in 1723, and joined the Council of New Jersey in that same year, serving until 1735. From 1723 to 1727 Alexander performed the duties of New Jersey attorney general.

In 1735, journalist John Peter Zenger was on trial, accused of libelous attacks on the administration of New York Governor William Cosby. Alexander served as codefense lawyer at this trial, and Alexander Hamilton pleaded the case. Zenger was acquitted, and the success of this defense was a triumph for the principles of a free press. See also, Stephen B. Presser's essay on Zenger's Trial.

ALIA [*Latin, "Other things."*] See also, *Inter alia*.

ALI-ABA COMMITTEE ON CONTINUING PROFESSIONAL EDUCATION
Formed in 1947, the ALI-ABA Committee serves to design, organize, and administer programs for the education of practicing attorneys. Programs range in length from one-day institutes to courses of a week or longer for advanced and specialized training. The members are representatives of the American Law Institute and the American Bar Association.

The committee publishes the following: *Review* (a weekly); *Preview of U.S. Supreme Court Decisions* (weekly, Sept.–Apr.); *Register* (monthly); *Practical Lawyer* (eight times a year); *Course Materials Journal* (bimonthly). It also publishes material on business and commercial transactions, criminal law, family law, Federal legislation, investments, labor laws, law office management, trial techniques, and Uniform Commercial Code.

ALIAS [*Latin, "Otherwise called."*]
□ A term used to indicate that a person is known by more than one name. □

Alias is a short and more popular phrase for *alias dictus*. The abbreviation, a.k.a., also known as, is frequently used in connection with the description of a person sought by law enforcement officers to disclose the names that the person has been known to use. A fictitious name assumed by a person is popularly termed an alias.

ALIAS WRIT □ A second writ, or court order, issued in the same case after an earlier writ of that kind has been issued but has not been effective. □

Oh Sammy, Sammy, vy won't there a alleybi?

CHARLES DICKENS

ALIBI □ A defense used in a criminal prosecution that at the time that a crime was committed, the defendant was in a place other than the scene of the crime so that it would have been impossible for him or her to be the guilty party. □

In prosecutions for federal crimes, a defendant's attorney must notify the government's attorney of intended use of the defense of alibi. State laws governing criminal procedure may require the same in state prosecutions.

ALIEN □ A foreign born person who has not been naturalized to become a U.S. citizen under Federal law and the Constitution. □

The Federal immigration laws determine whether or not a person is an alien. Generally, a person born in a foreign country is an alien, but a child born in a foreign nation to parents who are U.S. citizens is a U.S. citizen. The term *alien* also refers to a native-born American who has relinquished citizenship by moving to, and becoming a citizen of, a foreign country.

Classification Statutes frequently distinguish between resident and nonresident aliens, such as those that concern an alien's right to inherit property. Aliens are also categorized as friends and enemies of the United States. An alien friend is a citizen of an amicable nation that is at peace with the United States, whereas an enemy alien is a citizen of a hostile country. The term *alien*, employed by itself, generally refers to alien friends.

Status under the law Aliens do not have an absolute right to be in the United States. They are permitted to enter and remain in the country provided they comply with the law.

Aliens within the United States are protected by the Constitution, but not all of its provisions are applicable to them. Aliens do not receive the protection of the PRIVILEGES AND IMMUNITIES Clauses of either Article IV or Fourteenth Amendment, since those clauses apply only to citizens. The term *person* in the Self-incrimination Clause of the Fifth Amendment does, however, protect aliens within the United States from compulsory self-incrimination. Aliens are also regarded as persons for the purposes of the DUE PROCESS Clauses of the Fifth and Fourteenth Amendments, and the EQUAL PROTECTION Clause of the Fourteenth Amendment. In 1982, the Supreme Court ruled in the case of *Plyler v. Doe,* 457 U.S. 202, 102 S.Ct. 2382, 72 L.Ed.2d 786, that illegal aliens, those who do not enter the United States in accordance with immigration laws, were protected by the Equal Protection Clause of the Fourteenth Amendment. The Fourth Amendment guarantee of the right of the people to be free from unreasonable searches and seizures is also applicable to aliens.

Aliens are normally subject to prosecution and punishment for crimes committed in violation of state and Federal laws, in the same manner as citizens are. In addition, certain criminal statutes pertain to aliens in particular, such as the law that requires aliens to register annually with the Immigration and Naturalization Service. Statutes may also proscribe the ownership or possession of firearms by aliens. It is a Federal offense for aliens to misrepresent themselves as U.S. citizens to persons who have a right to inquire into their status.

General rights, duties, and disabilities The power to control the rights, duties, and legal obligations of aliens rests exclusively with Congress and encompasses the right to determine whether aliens may reside in the United States or in any of the individual states. Federal, rather than state, law governs the conditions of residence.

Aliens who lawfully reside within the United States have guaranteed rights regarding their physical safety. Since their duties and responsibilities are similar to those of citizens, aliens might be required to serve in the ARMED FORCES for national defense in time of war.

The states also may grant rights to aliens, but a state cannot discriminate against them in violation of Federal law or the Constitution. The

Federal government may confer rights to aliens by treaty, without hindrance from a state, because a treaty predominates when a state law conflicts with a treaty provision. For example, a state cannot deny a right to employment granted by treaty, but if no such right is conferred, state laws may proscribe such employment.

Personal and political rights and privileges Resident aliens are generally entitled to the same rights as citizens, and Federal laws protect them from state laws that afford disparate treatment solely because of their noncitizen status. Their right to travel temporarily outside of the United States may, however, be restricted in a manner that is inapplicable to citizens but each resident alien must first have an opportunity for a hearing on this issue before the restriction can be enforced.

Aliens cannot participate in political activities, such as ELECTIONS, and are regarded as possessing no right to lobby for the amendment of the Constitution.

Property rights and disabilities An alien ordinarily may own personal property in the same manner as a citizen. A state has the power to decide whether an alien may own real property within its boundaries, and the extent and conditions of such ownership, but the power of the state is subject to Federal law, the Constitution, and treaties of the United States.

An alien may obtain real property by purchasing it or by receiving it as a GIFT. Only the state can challenge the person's right to ownership and if the state does not do so, he or she is entitled to the ownership of the property. States exercise judiciously the right to question alien ownership of realty, but they always retain the power to invoke it.

If the state disputes an alien's right to own the property, it institutes legal proceedings to ascertain whether he or she is an alien. If the court finds that the owner is an alien, the state is entitled to assume the ownership and possession of the property. In some cases, the court will permit a person who has contracted to sell real property to an alien to retain ownership, provided that the CONTRACT has not been completely performed and all persons have acted in GOOD FAITH.

Normally, aliens who become citizens subsequent to ownership of real property and prior to the initiation of legal proceedings against them by the state cannot be divested of title pursuant to state action. Statutes may require the completion of certain procedures such as filing a statement of intention to become a citizen before

an alien has a legally enforceable right to own real estate.

Aliens may be prohibited by the state from acquiring land under a LEASE when they have not declared their intention to become citizens or are ineligible to attain this status. Only the state, not a private citizen, may sue to cancel a lease proscribed by law. The Federal government may grant aliens the right to lease real property pursuant to a treaty provision which controls in the event of a conflict with state law.

An alien may obtain a MORTGAGE on real property when no state law or constitutional provision prohibits the person from doing so.

As an incident to any right to own real property conferred by statute, an alien may serve as a TRUSTEE of property, or a TRUST may be established for his or her benefit. When an alien is the beneficiary of a trust, the legal title to the land is reserved by the trustee, but any rental proceeds and other profits belong to the alien, and he or she may also reside on the property if the terms of the trust so permit.

Personal property may be bequeathed by a WILL to an alien. When a person dies INTESTATE, without a will or a validly executed will, and alien relatives and citizen relatives survive, the personal property of the DECEDENT is generally distributed to both according to the statutory scheme.

A will may devise real property to an alien with the condition that if he or she is prohibited by law from owning it, the property will be transferred to another person, in order to prevent an ESCHEAT of title to the state, thereby giving it ownership.

Some states have enacted statutes that grant to aliens the right to receive real property under a will. In states where it is prohibited, the validity of the gift may be challenged by those who would have inherited the gift had it not been devised to the alien.

Some states require a nonresident alien who is to receive real property by will or inheritance to appear and claim it within a specified period of time. Any act that informs the person in control of the property of the existence of the claim of an alien is usually sufficient, such as an appearance made by the alien's attorney on his or her behalf. If the alien fails to appear and claim the property, it is distributed to the person who is next in line to inherit it.

Some states prescribe a definite period during which an alien must become a citizen and take possession of the land, or sell it. In this instance, the alien becomes the owner of the real property when the previous owner dies, but his

[A]lthough we extend to aliens the right to education and public welfare, along with the ability to earn a livelihood and engage in licensed professions, the right to govern is reserved to citizens.

WARREN E. BURGER

or her ownership is contingent upon attaining citizenship or selling the property within the specified time.

Some state laws grant nonresident aliens the right to receive real or personal property under a will or by inheritance only when a U.S. citizen has the reciprocal right in the alien's country which is enforceable without qualification in the courts of the alien's nation. If the right is merely discretionary with the foreign government, its counterpart cannot exist in the United States.

Aliens have the right to execute a will pursuant to legislation and treaties.

Aliens as legal parties   An alien has access to institute legal proceedings in the courts on the basis of the COMITY of nations, the acknowledgment that one nation extends within its territory to the executive, legislative, or judicial acts of another country. As a general rule, an alien is permitted to commence personal ACTIONS, such as the institution of a suit to recover money due under a contract, or a proceeding in TORT to recover for personal injuries. Unless explicitly proscribed by statute, an alien may be able to enforce a right granted by a statute, such as the WORKER'S COMPENSATION law.

An alien is entitled to bring an action against another alien whether the action involves contracts entered into in foreign countries, or torts committed in a foreign nation or on the high seas, if the court has JURISDICTION over the parties. An alien who is entitled to own real property under a state statute may commence litigation to enforce his or her rights and similarly an action may be initiated against an alien in a court that has jurisdiction over his or her property or person. Any legal DEFENSE to the action that is available to a defendant who is a citizen may be asserted by an alien.

Immigration   The Immigration and Nationality Act (8 U.S.C.A. § 1101 et seq.), a Federal law, controls immigration—which encompasses the admission, exclusion, detention, deportation, and expulsion of aliens. An *immigrant* is a person who comes to this country in order to obtain permanent residence. An *alien immigrant* is a foreigner who has departed from the United States but intends to return.

Federal regulation   The Federal government has the exclusive power to control immigration, and the individual states may not impinge upon that power. The attorney general of the United States, the commissioner of immigration and naturalization, and the Immigration and Naturalization Service are responsible for the administration and enforcement of immigration laws. Immigration officers possess broad powers, including, in some instances, the right to ARREST or search for aliens without a WARRANT provided the circumstances justify such drastic action. The promulgation of rules and regulations by immigration authorities have the force and effect of law and must be obeyed.

Admission, entry, and exclusion   An alien who enters the United States from a foreign port, country, or outlying possession must do so in accordance with the immigration laws. If not lawfully admitted, he or she has no constitutional right to enter or to remain, and usually cannot establish a DOMICILE, or a permanent residence in this country.

A resident alien who voluntarily visits a foreign country is considered an entering alien when returning to the United States, and is thereby subject to the exclusion provisions of the immigration laws. If, however, the sojourn was brief, and the person did not intend to leave his or her permanent U.S. residence, then his or her visit does not qualify as an entry.

To seek readmission, an alien must have either a current immigration visa or a reentry permit. The attorney general issues the reentry permit if he determines that the alien has been lawfully admitted for permanent residence and wants to recommence residency.

Visas   A VISA is a document of entry that must be submitted by all aliens who desire to enter the United States. Visas constitute a method of screening prospective immigrants, to ascertain whether or not individual aliens should be granted entry to the United States. American consular officers stationed in foreign countries are empowered to issue visas in accordance with the quota and preference provisions of the immigration laws. A visa procured by FRAUD or by misrepresenting a salient fact, such as the commission of a crime, is not valid and the applicant may be subject to criminal prosecution.

Federal law provides that various categories of aliens are ineligible to receive visas and may be excluded from this country. Among them are: persons afflicted with mental retardation, insanity, psychopathic personality, which the Supreme Court has interpreted to encompass homosexuality, any dangerous contagious disease, mental or physical disease or defect; drug addicts, chronic alcoholics, paupers, sexual deviates, anarchists, members of the Communist party, and those who participated in persecution through affiliation with the Nazi government in Germany; aliens likely to become public charges;

History should not require retelling. But old and established freedoms vanish when history is forgotten.

WILEY RUTLEDGE

those seeking employment as skilled or unskilled workers, unless the secretary of labor certifies that there is a shortage of such workers and that the employment of aliens will not adversely affect U.S. workers; and criminals convicted of a crime involving moral turpitude, such as BIGAMY, BRIBERY, BURGLARY, EMBEZZLEMENT, LARCENY, PERJURY, ROBBERY, and various sex offenses, such as sexual assault and RAPE.

ADMISSION PROCEDURES At the various points of entry into the United States, immigration officers question an arriving alien about his or her right to enter, medical officers of the United States Public Health Service administer a physical and mental examination, and the alien is fingerprinted and registered with the Immigration and Naturalization Service. Those aliens who are not registered upon entry must do so within thirty days after their fourteenth birthday.

If an alien is qualified for admission, but for the presence of physical defects, diseases, or disabilities that will prevent him or her from working, he or she may enter the United States after furnishing a BOND to the Federal and state governments. The bond operates as security against his or her procurement of public welfare benefits. When an alien leaves the United States, becomes a citizen, or dies, any money retained under the bond must be returned to the person who provided it or to the alien's estate if he or she posted the bond prior to death. A nonimmigrant alien, temporarily visiting, may be required to provide a bond to ensure timely departure but this is rarely, if ever, done.

An alien might be required to file an AFFIDAVIT of support provided by a citizen who acts as a sponsor and who is responsible for the alien if he or she is unable to be self-supporting. The sponsor cannot, however, be compelled to support the alien or repay the government for any support it furnishes thereby minimizing the value of the affidavit as a type of financial protection. The affidavit remains a device to screen prospective applicants for entry.

Qualifications for immigration A selection system restricted to an annual quota determines the admission of immigrants into the United States. Race, sex, nationality, place of birth, or place of residence are impermissible considerations. The previous quota system, which admitted immigrants on the basis of their country of origin, has been abrogated.

Immediate relatives of citizens such as children, spouse, and parents, and particular categories of special immigrants, such as ones who were formerly citizens and eligible to regain citizenship are considered for entry independently of the quota system.

Within the quota system, others, such as the alien brothers and sisters of citizens, receive preferential treatment. So, too, do professionals—such as engineers and physicians—who will advance the economic, cultural, and social development of the United States, and refugees from Communist nations—compelled to flee because of their race, religion, or political beliefs.

Certain nonimmigrants are admitted to promote harmonious international relations. Alien aircraft or ship crew members qualify as nonimmigrants, whose transient presence exempts them from immigration requirements. Visitors on business or pleasure trips and qualified students who wish to enter the United States solely to study at a school approved by the attorney general are also exempt.

EXCLUSION PROCEEDINGS Exclusion proceedings conducted by a special inquiry officer, also known as an immigration judge, are held to ascertain if aliens may enter the United States. Normally, an alien who has a visa but is denied admission is entitled to a hearing by the immigration judge. Such a proceeding determines whether valid reasons exist for exclusion and whether a claim of citizenship is valid.

An exclusionary order is reviewable by the Board of Immigration Appeals. The board's decision is subject to review by the attorney general. In some instances, a judicial review of a final order of exclusion may be obtained, but it is generally restricted to a determination of whether the hearings were fair and in compliance with the law.

Naturalization Naturalization is the process by which an alien becomes a citizen subsequent to satisfaction of the requisite legal qualifications.

An alien must have been lawfully admitted for permanent residence and must have resided within the United States for five years. During that period, he or she must have been physically present for at least half the time; a continuous absence for one year interrupts the period of residence and starts the residency requirement anew. Residency for six months in the state where the naturalization petition is filed is also required. The residency requirement provides the alien with an opportunity to learn the principles of U.S. government and enables immigration authorities to investigate the applicant.

The applicant must accept the political system and institutions of the United States, and obey the laws ensuing from them. This requirement ensures that only those who are in general accord with fundamental American principles become citizens, but this requirement must not deprive an applicant of his or her freedom of conscience.

The alien must acquire knowledge of U.S. history and government, and demonstrate his or her ability to read, write, and speak ordinary conversational English.

Throughout the mandatory period of residence, the alien must evince good moral character, comparable to that of the average citizen in the community where he or she resides.

Proceedings   Naturalization proceedings are judicial in nature and are generally conducted in Federal court. The applicant must file a written sworn and signed petition for naturalization with the clerk of the Federal district court which states all the salient facts concerning the applicant's naturalization, including the dates of lawful entry and formal admission in accordance with the immigration rules, intent to remain in the United States permanently, good moral character, and residence for the required period.

The applicant has the BURDEN OF PROOF concerning his or her eligibility for citizenship at the naturalization proceeding. The testimony of two witnesses who are citizens and cognizant of the applicant's residence is required to establish the applicant's continuous five-year residency. Any relevant evidence regarding the applicant's good moral character must also be presented before the court.

Upon the favorable conclusion of the naturalization proceeding, the court issues an order admitting the alien to citizenship, which is a final JUDGMENT.

Oath of allegiance   An applicant must take an oath, or an affirmation if his or her religion forbids taking an oath, by which he or she renounces loyalty to his or her nation of origin, swears allegiance to the United States, and pledges to uphold and defend the Constitution and laws of the United States. The duties, rights, and privileges of citizenship accrue upon the taking of the oath.

The naturalized person receives a certificate of naturalization as evidence of his citizenship, but its absence does not deprive a person of his or her United States citizenship.

Deportation or expulsion   Deportation is the compulsory return of an alien to the country from which he or she emigrated. Provisions for deportation apply to all aliens and to those naturalized citizens whose naturalization has been rescinded.

Congress establishes the grounds for deportation, and may authorize the deportation of aliens on grounds developed subsequent to the date of their entry. Numerous grounds for deportation exist: illegal entry or presence, fraud or misrepresentation in securing entry, entry without a required passport or visa, entry in violation of a quota provision of the immigration law, entry without inspection, breach of a condition of entry, overstaying the transitory period for which the alien was permitted to enter, becoming a public charge, affliction with a physical or mental illness at the time of entry, and membership in a subversive organization.

If an alien who is presently residing in the United States has been convicted of a crime involving moral turpitude prior to entry into the United States, or if he or she admits its commission, the alien may be subject to deportation. Conviction of any two Federal or state crimes for which the cumulative prison sentence is five or more years makes the alien subject to deportation.

Deportation proceedings, which are civil not criminal in nature, are governed by the Immigration and Nationality Act and administrative regulations. Diligence must be exercised to ensure that the proceedings are conducted impartially, since the rules used in a court of law are inapplicable.

An alien must have notice of the charges against him or her and is entitled to a hearing on those charges. A special officer presides over the hearing, and the alien has the right to counsel of his or her choice, to testify, to call witnesses, and to present evidence in his or her own behalf. The deportation decision must be based on the charges lodged against the alien and must be supported by the evidence presented at the hearing.

The Board of Immigration Appeals has the power to review a deportation decision rendered by a hearing officer and issue a new decision but exercises this power sparingly. A deportation order is ordinarily subject to judicial review, and the court, like the Board of Immigration Appeals, must reach its decision by examining the administrative record upon which the deportation order was based. See also, Charles Gordon's essay on Alien.

ALIENABLE □ The character of property that makes it capable of sale or transfer. □

ALIEN AMI □ An international law term for alien friend, a citizen or subject of the government of a nation that is at peace with the United States. □

Charles Gordon

Alien

In its popular connotation the term *alien* denotes an outsider, one who is not a member of the group. This also is the legal conception, for the alien is a person who is not a member of the national society. Thus, section 101(a)(3) of the Immigration and Nationality Act (8 U.S.C.A. § 1101[a][3] [1952]) defines an alien as a person who is not a citizen or national of the United States.

As a nation of immigrants, the United States has welcomed millions of aliens, a phenomenon that has persevered until the present time. In our open society, the alien has enjoyed benefits that are far superior to benefits accorded to aliens in any other country. At the same time, the alien's inferior political status has subjected him or her to important disadvantages, so long as he or she remains an alien. Most obvious of these is the inability to vote or hold public office. In addition, an alien may be barred from entering the United States on any ground specified by Congress. If the individual leaves the United States, no assurance of return is guaranteed. An alien permitted to enter the United States temporarily must abide by the conditions of the temporary stay. An alien living in the United States, even if granted entry as an immigrant, remains perpetually subject to deportation, so long as the status of alien remains, for impropriety in original entry, or for specified infractions (Section 241, Immigration and Nationality Act [8 U.S.C.A. § 1251]); and every alien in the United States is subject to a requirement of reporting his or her current address each January (Section 265, Immigration and Nationality Act [8 U.S.C.A. § 1305]).

At the same time the alien enjoys many significant rights and benefits. Thus, the mandates of the Fifth and Fourteenth Amendments assuring due process of law to all "persons" in the United States shelter aliens as well as citizens. Consequently a state cannot arbitrarily deprive a resident alien of the opportunity to earn a livelihood (*Yick Wo v. Hopkins*, 118 U.S. 356, 6 S.Ct. 1064, 30 L.Ed. 220 [1886]), or of welfare benefits available to citizens (*Graham v. Richardson*, 403 U.S. 365, 91 S.Ct. 1848, 29 L.Ed.2d. 534 [1971]). The exclusion of aliens from municipal employment (*Sugarman v. Dougall*, 413 U.S. 634, 93 S.Ct. 2842, 37 L.Ed.2d 853 [1973]) and from admission to the bar (*In re Griffiths*, 413 U.S. 717, 93 S.Ct. 2851, 37 L.Ed.2d 910 [1973]) also have been declared invalid. But later decisions recognized a compelling state interest in barring aliens from employment as policemen (*Foley v. Connelie*, 435 U.S. 291, 98 S.Ct. 1067, 55 L.Ed.2d 287 [1978]) and as teachers (*Ambach v. Norwick*, 441 U.S. 68, 99 S.Ct. 1589, 60 L.Ed.2d 49 [1979]).

The Fifth Amendments's due process mandate has been read somewhat differently in regard to the Federal government, in the light of the paramount power to control immigration. A major limitation of Federal power is that no alien can be expelled from the United States unless he or she has been accorded a fair hear-

Physicians examine a group of
Jewish immigrants in 1907.

ing (*The Japanese Immigrant Case*, 189 U.S. 86, 23 S.Ct. 611, 47 L.Ed. 721
[1903]). But, unlike the states, the Federal government thus far has been immune
to challenges for alleged discriminations in granting immigration benefits (*Fiallo v.
Bell*, 430 U.S. 787, 97 S.Ct. 1473, 52 L.Ed.2d 50 [1977]), excluding aliens from
Federal civil service employment (*Hampton v. Mow Sun Wong*, 426 U.S. 88, 96
S.Ct. 1895, 48 L.Ed.2d 495 [1976]) and barring Medicare benefits for resident
aliens who have not been in the United States for at least five years (*Mathews v.
Diaz*, 426 U.S. 67, 96 S.Ct. 1883, 48 L.Ed.2d 478 [1976]). See also, Richard G.
Singer's essay on Due Process of Law; and Harold W. Chase's essay on Japanese-
American Evacuation Cases.

Bibliography: Charles Gordon and Harry N. Rosenfield, *Immigration Law and Procedure*,
rev. ed., 6 vols. (1979–1981).

Stephen B. Presser

Alien and Sedition Acts

The "Alien and Sedition Acts" was the popular name given to several legislative measures passed in 1798 that inaugurated what Thomas Jefferson referred to as the Federalist's "reign of witches." These statutes were thought by the Federalists to be a necessary response to what they perceived as an outrageous campaign of mendacity on the part of opponents of the John Adams administration, and what they believed to be a serious threat of French Jacobin infiltration into America.

By the first of these acts, the Act of June 18, 1798 (1 Stat. 566), the period of residence in the United States required for United States citizenship was lengthened from five to fourteen years, and aliens from nations with which the United States might be at war were forbidden to be admitted to citizenship. A system of registration of aliens was also established by that act, with fines for failure to register, and a requirement of sureties "of the peace and good behaviour" during an

Library of Congress

Differences between the Federalists and Republicans, which led to the passing of the Alien and Sedition Acts, were so intense that Roger Griswold, a Federalist from Connecticut, attacked Matthew Lyon, a Republican from Vermont, with a cane.

173

alien's residence. In the second of these measures, the Act of June 25, 1798 (1 Stat. 570), the president was authorized to order deported any aliens whom he "shall judge dangerous to the peace and safety of the United States, or shall have reasonable grounds to suspect are concerned in any treasonable or secret machinations against the government." Failure to comply with such a deportation order was to be punished by three years imprisonment and permanent ineligibility for U.S. citizenship. By this act also, masters or commanders of ships were required to report the identity, occupation, description, and nationality of any aliens they brought into the country. This act was to continue in force only for two years. The third act, the Act of July 6, 1798 (1 Stat. 577), provided that if war were to be declared between the United States and any other nation, or whenever "any invasion or predatory incursion shall be perpetrated, attempted, or threatened against the territory of the United States" by any foreign nation, all male aliens from that hostile nation over the age of fourteen residing within the United States were made "liable to be apprehended, restrained, secured and removed, as alien enemies." The president was given the authority to determine how and in what degree to institute proceedings against any aliens liable under the statute. Perhaps the most noteworthy of the four measures was the last, the Act of July 14, 1798 (1 Stat. 596). This statute mandated stiff fines and imprisonment for any persons conspiring to "oppose any measure or measures of the government of the United States" or conspiring to commit a variety of other means of obstructing the Federal government, whether or not their efforts were successful. Of particular importance, however, was a section of this fourth act, which made the publishing of "any false, scandalous and malicious writing . . . against the government of the United States, or either house of the Congress . . . , or the President . . . , with intent to defame [them], . . . , or to excite against them . . . the hatred of the good people of the United States, or to stir up sedition within the United States, or to excite any unlawful combinations therein, for opposing or resisting any law of the United States," or other governmental acts, a Federal crime, also punishable by heavy fines. While the act established, in effect, a Federal statutory law of seditious libel, the act also clearly provided that the truth of any allegedly seditious writing could be given in evidence in defense, and also that the jury "shall have a right to determine the law and the fact, under the direction of the court, as in other cases." These last provisions were intended, apparently, to blunt criticism of the new seditious libel law, by declaring an intention not to punish true assertions against the government, and by making clear that the jury was to be the ultimate judge of criminality, thus avoiding the taint of suppression visited on the prosecutors of the Seven Bishops and John Peter Zenger. The Act of July 14, 1798, was to expire, by its own terms, on March 3, 1801.

The four acts immediately excited the opposition of the Republican Press, and in the Virginia and Kentucky Resolves the leaders of the Republican opposition to the Federalists, James Madison and Thomas Jefferson, argued that there was no constitutional authority to support the passage of the acts. No other states supported the opposition of Virginia and Kentucky against these acts, however, and as they were passed at a time when Francophobia was high, following the XYZ affair and extraordinarily aggressive behavior on the part of the French in

Europe and on the high seas, public opinion initially appears to have been supportive of the acts. In the course of several prosecutions under the new seditious libel
law, however, particularly in the months before the presidential election of 1800,
the acts' Federalist sponsors appear to have lost the support of the public.

    Some of the trials under the act were conducted in a manner that ostensi-
bly gave the accused the benefit of doubts, and of the usual presumption of innocence in criminal cases, although in all of the seventeen cases of seditious libel for
which indictments were returned, save one, the defendants appear to have been
convicted and fined or imprisoned (Smith, below at 185). Still, this appears to be a
relatively small number of prosecutions. No one was capitally punished, and thus
it is difficult really to compare these Federalist excesses with the Contemporary
French Reign of Terror, as some Republicans sought to do. Nevertheless, there
were some Federalist actions, particularly those of Samuel Chase, in connection
with the enforcement of the seditious libel law, which did provide a basis for Republican criticism.

    For example, in *United States v. Cooper*, 25 F.Cas. No. 14, 865 (C.C.D.
Pa. 1800), a trial in the Pennsylvania Federal circuit court over which Justice
Chase presided, he put the burden of proving the truth "beyond a marrow" of all
matters for which the defendant had been charged with seditious libel on the defendant himself. Since the defendant had made statements that were really matters of
belief as to the appropriate interpretation to be placed on political acts, and not
matters easily subject to factual proof, the defendant found it impossible to meet
the standard required for acquittal, and could not escape conviction. Chase's interpretation of the seditious libel law not only went against the usual Anglo-
American notions that there ought to be a presumption of innocence and that the
government ought to have the burden of proving the guilt of the defendant, but his
interpretation, if widely shared, would have had the effect of shutting off all critical debate over political issues that did not lend itself to easy verification.

    In *United States v. Callender*, 25 F.Cas. No. 14, 709 (C.C.D. Va. 1800), a
case in which Chase presided in the Virginia Federal circuit court, he appeared determined to teach the obstreperous Virginia Republicans—whose leaders, Jefferson and Madison, had done so much to discredit the Federalists—a lesson in submission to the lawful government. The three counsel for the defendant (a
somewhat scurrilous Republican publicist who later turned violently on Jefferson
after some perceived personal slight) were prominent young Republicans, who
were just as determined to teach Chase a lesson, and to expose what they believed
to be the tyrannical nature of the Federalist prosecution. Chase appears to have
treated many of the arguments of these counsel with derision, and in several instances this may have been the appropriate, although the unjudicial, manner of
treating them. In what was the most important such argument, Callender's counsel
sought to argue that the Virginia jury should have the right, as the ultimate judges
of law, according to the sedition act itself, to pass on the constitutionality of the
act. Chase maintained, according to the argument of no less an authority than
Alexander Hamilton in the *Federalist Papers*, that the job of passing on the constitutionality of a statute was solely for the judge, and not for the jury. Chase's opinion on this point was heard by John Marshall who was sitting in the audience at the

[T]he judicature of the country is of the greatest consequence to the liberties and existence of a nation. If your Constitution was destroyed, so long as the judiciary department remained free and uncontrolled, the liberties of the people would not be endangered. Suffer your courts of judicature to be destroyed: there is an end to your liberties.

SAMUEL CHASE

Callender trial, and who was soon to write the classic opinion on the court's power of judicial review in *Marbury v. Madison*, 5 U.S. (1 Cranch) 137, 2 L.Ed. 60 (1803). In any event, though Chase may have been correct on his interpretation of the question of the jury's role in questions of constitutionality, his rather flippant attitude toward Callender's counsel, and his ruling on some procedural and evidentiary technicalities in a manner adverse to the defendant, resulted in vitriolic attacks on him in the Republican press, and the Republican charges were later to appear as counts against him in his trial for impeachment some years later.

While there may not have been a great number of Federal trials for seditious libel, one of them was so mean and so ludicrous that it provided the Republican press with an incredible opportunity for ridiculing and condemning of the Federalists. This was the infamous trial of Luther Baldwin. Baldwin, a citizen of Newark, while in a somewhat tipsy state, heard the sound of gunfire and proceeded to ask some of his tavern cronies what had caused it. He was told that President Adams had just passed through town, and his exit was being ceremoniously followed with a twenty-one gun salute. Baldwin, apparently a critic of the incumbent administration, remarked that it was his wish that those administering the salute might aim their pieces at the posterior of the president, and that some of their shot might lodge. He was swiftly and successfully prosecuted for seditious libel, and fined a modest amount of money.

The Republican criticism of the Federalists's efforts at seditious libel prosecutions and the Federalists's extreme (even if understandable) reaction to the threat posed by external and internal enemies, coupled with extraordinary ineptness on the part of John Adams in managing to alienate some of his most important natural supporters by an unsuccessful search for popularity, resulted in the victory of the Republicans in the presidential election of 1800. What Jefferson and Madison were unable to achieve in 1798 and 1799 by their Virginia and Kentucky Resolves, was thus accomplished for these Republicans by the Federalists themselves. The governmental philosophy inherent in the Federalists's Alien and Sedition Acts, which seems to have been popular in the time of quasi-war with France, became totally unacceptable once the threat of a French invasion vanished. From that time to this, similar efforts at the repression of dissent—from the congressional "gag rule" on proposals for the abolition of slavery, to attempts to punish syndicalists and anarchists in the late nineteenth and early twentieth centuries, through the difficulties of the McCarthy Era in the early fifties and the antics of the "plumbers" during the Watergate Affair—have been tried, and all, inexorably, have met the ultimate fate of the Alien and Sedition Acts, and have resulted in disgrace and usually displacement for their proponents. See also, Stephen B. Presser's essays on the Seven Bishop's Trial; the Zenger's Trial; the Virginia and Kentucky Resolves; and the Watergate Affair; Morton J. Frisch's essay on the Federalist Papers; and Martin H. Redish's essay on Marbury v. Madison.

Bibliography: J. Goebel, Jr., *A History of the Supreme Court: Antecedents and Beginnings to 1801* (1971); J. Miller, *Crisis in Freedom: The Alien and Sedition Acts* (1951); Stephen B. Presser, "A Tale of Two Judges: Richard Peters, Samuel Chase and the Broken Promise of Federalist Jurisprudence," 73 *Northwestern University Law Review* (March–April 1978): 26–111; J. Smith, *Freedom's Fetters: The Alien and Sedition Laws and American Civil Liberties* (1956).

Although Americans of Japanese ancestry, such as this young girl, were legally citizens of the United States, the War Relocation Authority treated them as enemy aliens.

National Archives

ALIENATE ☐ To voluntarily convey or transfer title to real property either by GIFT, disposition by WILL or the laws of DESCENT AND DISTRIBUTION, or by sale. ☐

ALIENATION   See Nationality.

ALIENATION CLAUSE ☐ A provision in a document permitting or forbidding a person from transferring property that is the subject of the document. ☐

In a fire INSURANCE policy, an alienation clause prohibits the alienation of the insured premises while the policy is in effect. If the insured violates this provision, the policy is void.

ALIENATION OF AFFECTION ☐ The removal of love, companionship, or aid of another individual's spouse. ☐

Historically, alienation of affection furnished grounds for an action against the individual who interloped in a marital relationship. The harm caused was viewed as a deprivation of an individual's rights of CONSORTIUM.

The elements of the action generally included wrongful conduct by the interfering party with the complainant's spouse, the loss of affection or consortium, and a nexus between the conduct of the defendant and the impairment or loss of consortium, which included a deprivation of such rights as services, assistance, and sexual relations.

Today, the action has fallen into disuse and no longer constitutes a ground for a lawsuit in most states.

ALIEN ENEMY ☐ In international law, a foreign born citizen or subject of a nation or power that is hostile to the United States. ☐

An alien enemy is an individual who, due to permanent or temporary allegiance to a hostile power, is regarded as an enemy in wartime. The term is used to describe any and all subjects of a foreign nation that is at war with the United States.

ALIEN PROPERTY IN WARTIME   Traditional international law accepted the authority of a warring nation to confiscate all public and private alien enemy property, and cancel any debts due the enemy or its nationals. Treaties providing for the withdrawal of alien subjects and their property at the end of wartime began to modify this rule of customary international law, at least with respect to most private alien property. Treatment of such property has been significantly affected by treaties establishing national agencies to act as guardians of the property, with responsibilities for its eventual return, as well as agreements at the conclusion of hostilities providing either for the removal of the property or limiting the confiscation thereof to an amount equal that owed the nation by the other belligerent. Public alien enemy property, like private alien enemy property potentially useful in a belligerent's military operations, still remains subject to the dictates of a nation. Belligerent property in neutral states usually cannot be legally confiscated by the other belligerent.

Charles Gordon

Alien Registration Act

The Alien Registration Act (54 Stat. 670) was enacted in 1940 and was conceived as a measure to safeguard the national security. It has remained a permanent feature of our laws since then. The Immigration and Nationality Act of 1952 (8 U.S.C.A. § 1101 et seq.) codified the registration requirements as a permanent feature of our immigration laws.

The basic requirement of the present statute precludes the issuance of a visa to any alien wishing to enter the United States unless the person has been registered and fingerprinted as required by law (Section 261, Immigration and Nationality Act [8 U.S.C.A. § 1301]). Every immigrant is required to be registered and fingerprinted at the time of application for an immigrant visa (Section 221[b], Immigration and Nationality Act [8 U.S.C.A. § 1201(b)]). The fingerprinting requirement for nonimmigrants (temporary entrants) is waived on a basis of reciprocity. In addition, every alien in the United States who is fourteen years of age or older, who remains in the United States thirty days or longer, and has not previously registered, must apply for registration and fingerprinting (Section 262, Immigration and Nationality Act [8 U.S.C.A. § 1302]).

An alien who has been registered receives an alien registration receipt card. If the person is eighteen years of age or older, he or she is required to have this document in possession at all times and may be guilty of a misdemeanor for failure to do so (Section 264[d] and [e], Immigration and Nationality Act [8 U.S.C.A. § 1304(d) and (e)]).

Another familiar feature of the Alien Registration Act is its requirement that every alien who is within the United States on January 1 of each year must report his or her current address and furnish other required information during the month of January. Generally overlooked are the additional requirements that every alien must report changes of address and every alien in lawful temporary status must report his or her address every three months (Section 265, Immigration and Nationality Act [8 U.S.C.A. § 1305]).

Willful failure to comply with the registration or reporting requirements incurs criminal penalties. In addition, willful failure to comply with the reporting requirements may subject the alien to deportation.

Bibliography: Charles Gordon and Harry N. Rosenfield, *Immigration Law and Procedure*, rev. ed., 6 vols. (1979–1981).

Charles Gordon

Aliens, Admission and Exclusion

For the first 100 years of its existence, the United States had no restrictions on immigration. The frontier was open and all who wished to come were welcomed.

A number of states sought to impose restrictions on the entry of aliens, but these were declared unconstitutional by the Supreme Court as an infringement of the exclusive power of the Federal government to regulate foreign commerce.

Limited controls, aimed at convicts and prostitutes, were enacted by the Federal government in 1875, and were followed in 1882 by more general restrictions. Thereafter, successive statutory codifications and expansions of the immigration restrictions culminated in the Immigration and Nationality Act of 1952, known as the McCarran-Walter Act (8 U.S.C.A. § 1101 et seq.). The power of Congress to enact the immigration statutes has been upheld by the Supreme Court, as an incident of national sovereignty, in a series of decisions commencing with *The Chinese Exclusion Case*, 130 U.S. 581, 9 S.Ct. 623, 32 L.Ed. 1068 (1889).

These Japanese immigrants received vaccinations while still aboard ship en route to Hawaii in 1904.

The original restrictions dealt only with the quality of the immigrant and related to health, economic status, criminal record, subversive activities, etc. Numerical restrictions were imposed for the first time in 1921, and were established on a permanent basis in 1924, under a discriminatory national origin formula. The National Origins Quota System was replaced in 1965 by unified quotas of 170,000 for the Eastern Hemisphere and 120,000 for the Western Hemisphere. The separate hemisphere quotas were merged in 1978 into a single worldwide quota of 290,000. Allocations within that quota are made, without discrimination, on the basis of preferences, four of which are geared to family relationship and two to family need. The annual quota was reduced to 270,000 by the Refugee Act of 1980 (8 U.S.C.A. § 1101 et seq.), which authorized additional allocations for refugees, in numbers determined by the president, after consultation with Congress. Certain groups are exempt from the numerical limitations. These are chiefly immediate relatives of U.S. citizens, who are defined as spouses, children, and parents (of children over twenty-one years of age) of U.S. citizens.

An alien who wishes to come to the United States must first apply to an American consul abroad for a visa. If one seeks to come as an immigrant, he or she applies for an immigrant visa, and the consul determines his or her admissibility under the qualitative and numeric restrictions. If an alien wishes to come temporarily, he or she can be issued a nonimmigrant visa only if the individual satisfies the qualitative restrictions on entry. There are no numerical limitations on the number of qualified nonimmigrants who can come.

The consul's denial of a visa is not subject to review, except that the consul will consider additional evidence that may cause him to change his decision. If

Americanization classes, such as the one shown in which students represented nine different nationalities, were often conducted by a local board of education in cooperation with the Naturalization Bureau.

the consul approves the application, he issues a visa which enables the applicant to travel to the United States. An immigrant visa must be used within four months. A nonimmigrant visa must be used within the time fixed by the consul.

The issuance of the visa does not guarantee entry into the United States. Upon arrival, the holder of the visa must satisfy the immigration officer at the port of entry that he or she is qualified for admission. Ordinarily this is not a difficult process, since the applicant has already satisfied the American consul. However, if the immigration officer doubts the applicant's admissibility he refers the applicant for a hearing by an immigration judge. With limited exceptions in security cases, the hearing is full and fair, and the applicant can testify, call witnesses and present evidence, and be represented by counsel.

If the immigration judge rules in his or her favor, the applicant is admitted to the United States. If the decision is adverse he or she has a right to appeal to the Board of Immigration Appeals, an appellate body established by the attorney general, and eventually to the courts. The entry applicant who succeeds in reaching the United States thus is ordinarily assured fair consideration.

Bibliography: David Carliner, *The Rights of Aliens* (1977); Charles Gordon and Harry N. Rosenfield, *Immigration Law and Procedure*, rev. ed., 6 vols. (1979–1981).

Charles Gordon

Aliens, Deportation

In many respects, the alien in the United States enjoys a protected status. In other respects, that status may be insecure. A major aspect of such insecurity is the possible amenability to deportation.

There is no specific mandate in the Constitution that gives Congress the power to prescribe for the deportation of aliens. Such power doubtless could be implied from the constitutional grants of authority to regulate foreign commerce and to provide for the common defense. However, in *Fong Yue Ting v. United States*, 149 U.S. 698, 13 S.Ct. 1016, 37 L.Ed. 905 (1893), the Supreme Court held that the power of Congress to provide for the deportation of aliens, like the power to provide for their exclusion, is not dependent on any specific constitutional provision but is inherent in national sovereignty.

Having found that the power to prescribe for deportation is a sovereign attribute and not derived from the Constitution, the Supreme Court repeatedly has rejected efforts to limit that power. The power of Congress often has been described as plenary and unlimited. While it is conceivable that modern courts may not tolerate extreme expressions of that power, no case thus far has recognized any such limitations.

Moreover, the courts have rejected efforts to characterize deportation as a criminal proceeding. They have declared that, regardless of its harsh consequences, deportation is a civil proceeding. Therefore, the constitutional safeguards regarding the imposition of criminal punishment—such as the Ex post facto Clause, the prohibition of cruel and unusual punishment, and the assurances of indictment, bail, and jury trial—have been found inapplicable. At the same time, the courts have recognized, since *Ng Fung Ho v. White*, 259 U.S. 276, 42 S.Ct. 492, 66 L.Ed. 938 (1922), that deportation is a penalty, which deprives the deportee "of all that makes life worth living." Therefore, in *Fong Haw Tan v. Phelan*, 33 U.S. 6, 68 S.Ct. 374, 92 L.Ed. 433 (1948), the Supreme Court expounded a rule of strict construction, under which deportation statutes are narrowly construed.

Section 241(a) of the Immigration and Nationality Act (8 U.S.C.A. § 1251[a] [1952]) sets forth seventeen categories of deportable aliens. Of particular interest are the grounds for expulsion of any aliens who entered in violation of law or without undergoing immigration inspection; any aliens who became public charges within five years after entry; any aliens who were convicted of a crime involving moral turpitude committed within five years after entry or two crimes involving moral turpitude at any time after entry; any aliens who have been members or affiliates of the Communist party or various other subversive groups; any alien admitted temporarily as a nonimmigrant who has remained beyond an authorized stay or otherwise violated the conditions of nonimmigrant status; any alien who is addicted to narcotics or has been convicted of a narcotic offense; any alien who has engaged in prostitution or activities related to prostitution.

. . . classifications based on alienage, like those based on nationality or race, are inherently suspect and subject to close judicial scrutiny.

HARRY A. BLACKMUN

No statute of limitations is prescribed, and the alien remains liable to deportation at any time after entry, upon any of the grounds listed in the statute.

It should be noted, however, that the statute permits relief from deportation in some situations. Thus, the deportation grounds relating to conviction for crimes involving moral turpitude are specifically made inapplicable if the crime was political or if the alien was the beneficiary of a pardon or a timely recommendation against deportation by the convicting court. Deportation is prohibited if the deportee would be subject to deportation on the ground of race, religion, nationality, membership in a particular social group, or political opinion. Moreover, an otherwise deportable alien can achieve permanent residence status if he or she is currently qualified for that status. And virtually any ground for deportation can be expunged for long-time residents through a process known as suspension of deportation, which entails discretionary approval by the attorney general and endorsement by Congress.

Although the power to prescribe grounds for deportation is vast, the procedures for accomplishing expulsion must conform to the assurance of the Fifth Amendment and its due process of law. This dichotomy between substantive due process and procedural due process has been recognized since *The Japanese Immigrant Case*, 189 U.S. 86, 23 S.Ct. 611, 47 L.Ed. 721 (1903).

The enforcement of the immigration laws is entrusted to administrative officers who are given extensive powers to interrogate, to arrest, to detain, and to deport. But since immigration officers must conform to the constitutional mandate of due process, they cannot expel any alien until he or she is accorded a fair hearing, which conforms to current concepts of due process. This means that the alien must receive reasonable notice of the charges, an opportunity to oppose those charges at a public hearing before an impartial tribunal, the privilege of being represented by counsel, an opportunity to testify and to present evidence and to cross-examine opposing witnesses, and a decision based on substantial evidence in the record.

The statute specifically provides for the hearing in deportation cases to be conducted by a special-inquiry officer, now known as an immigration judge. It also spells out some of the elements of a fair hearing. The regulations permit an appeal from the decision of the immigration judge to the Board of Immigration Appeals, a body established by the attorney general to rule on appeals in immigration cases. And a final order of deportation may be challenged by an appeal to the Federal courts.

Bibliography: Charles Gordon and Harry N. Rosenfield, *Immigration Law and Procedure*, rev. ed., 6 vols. (1979–1981).

. . . it is precisely in . . . clashes between what is absolutely right and what arbitrariness makes pass as right that there lies the need for studying the fundamentals of right.

GEORG WILHELM FRIEDRICH HEGEL

Charles Gordon

Aliens, Discrimination Against

By definition, citizens are full members of a society. Conversely, aliens do not share all of the society's benefits and protections until they become citizens.

To some extent, this concept applies in the United States, but it has been modified by several factors unique to the United States. In the first place, we are a nation of immigrants and we have welcomed over 50 million alien settlers.

Secondly, most of our constitutional safeguards shelter all persons in the United States. Thus, the Fifth and Fourteenth Amendments assure due process of law and equal protection to "persons" and thus encompass both citizens and aliens.

This reading has been reaffirmed by the Supreme Court on numerous occasions. Since *Yick Wo v. Hopkins*, 118 U.S. 356, 6 S.Ct. 1064, 30 L.Ed. 220 (1886), the Fourteenth Amendment's Equal Protection Clause has safeguarded resident aliens against various discriminations by the states. For many years, however, the Supreme Court endorsed a variety of state measures excluding aliens from specific occupations on the ground that the state was justified in limiting such occupations to citizens. This line of decision was repudiated by the Supreme Court in *Graham v. Richardson*, 403 U.S. 365, 91 S.Ct. 1848, 29 L.Ed.2d 534 (1971), which ruled that the exclusion of aliens from welfare benefits available to citizens was unconstitutional. This decision was soon followed by *Sugarman v. Dougall*, 413 U.S. 634, 93 S.Ct. 2842, 37 L.Ed.2d 853 (1973), which held that states and mu-

AND WE OPEN OUR ARMS TO THEM!

In 1883 *Life* published a cartoon depicting immigrants as disagreeable refuse that the aristocracy of Europe swept up and dumped in the United States.

Library of Congress

183

This political cartoon of 1889 illustrated President Benjamin Harrison's opinion, as stated in his inaugural address, that immigrants who would be "a burden upon our public revenues, or a threat to social order" should be excluded from the United States.

nicipalities could not bar resident aliens from normal civil service employment, and *In re Griffiths*, 413 U.S. 717, 93 S.Ct. 2851, 37 L.Ed.2d 910 (1973), which held that states could not exclude resident aliens from qualifying as lawyers. However, later decisions recognized a compelling state interest in barring aliens from employment as police officers (*Foley v. Connelie*, 435 U.S. 291, 98 S.Ct. 1067, 55 L.Ed.2d 287 [1978]) and as teachers (*Ambach v. Norwick*, 441 U.S. 68, 99 S.Ct. 1589, 60 L.Ed.2d 49 [1979]).

Different considerations apply to discriminations against aliens imposed by the Federal government because of its paramount authority over aliens, inherent in national sovereignty. Federal discriminatory measures to restrict immigration have been upheld since *The Chinese Exclusion Case*, 130 U.S. 581, 9 S.Ct. 623, 32 L.Ed. 1068 (1889). On the other hand, aliens have been entitled to the procedural protections of the Fifth Amendment's Due Process Clause since *The Japanese Immigrant Case*, 189 U.S. 86, 23 S.Ct. 611, 47 L.Ed. 721 (1903).

Thus, in regard to discriminatory measures imposed by the Federal government, the Supreme Court has established a distinction between substantive and procedural due process. This distinction recently has been invoked to uphold Federal measures limiting immigration benefits for children born out-of-wedlock (*Fiallo v. Bell*, 430 U.S. 787, 97 S.Ct. 1473, 52 L.Ed.2d 50 [1977]), excluding aliens from civil service employment (*Hampton v. Mow Sun Wong*, 420 U.S. 88, 96 S.Ct. 1895, 48 L.Ed.2d 495 [1976]), and barring Medicare benefits for resident aliens who have not been in the United States for at least five years (*Mathews v. Diaz*, 426 U.S. 67, 96 S.Ct. 1883, 48 L.Ed.2d 478 [1976]).

Bibliography: David Carliner, *The Rights of Aliens* (1977); Charles Gordon and Harry N. Rosenfield, *Immigration Law and Procedure*, rev. ed., 6 vols. (1979–1981).

Charles Gordon

Aliens, Registration

While requirements for the registration of aliens have long been a familiar phenomenon in many other countries, they were first adopted in the United States in 1940. The Alien Registration Act of 1940 (54 Stat. 670) was enacted as a security measure, on the eve of the United States involvement in World War II. The registration requirements were codified as a permanent feature of our immigration laws in the Immigration and Nationality Act of 1952 (8 U.S.C.A. § 1101 et seq.).

The present statute requires registration and fingerprinting of every alien to whom a visa for entry to the United States is issued. The fingerprinting requirement may be waived, on the basis of reciprocity, for aliens seeking to enter the United States as nonimmigrants (temporarily). In addition, every alien in the United States who is fourteen years of age or older, who remains in the United States for thirty days or longer, and has not previously registered, is required to apply for registration and fingerprinting before the expiration of such thirty days. The parent or legal guardian of an alien under fourteen is required to register on his or her behalf. And when an alien attains his or her fourteenth birthday in the United States, the teenager is required to apply in person for registration and fingerprinting within thirty days thereafter.

An alien in the United States who has been registered and fingerprinted in compliance with the above requirements receives a certificate or alien registration receipt card. If the person is eighteen years of age or older, he or she is required to have this document in personal possession at all times, and may be guilty of a misdemeanor for failure to do so.

In addition, the law requires every alien subject to the registration requirements who is within the United States on January 1 of each year to report his or her current address and to furnish any additionally required information during the month of January. If the individual is temporarily absent from the United States at that time, he or she is required to report his or her address within ten days after returning. Additional requirements that are generally overlooked are that every alien must report any change of address and any alien in lawful temporary status must report his or her address every three months.

Willful failure to comply with the registration or reporting requirements incurs criminal penalties. In addition, willful failure to comply with the reporting requirements may subject the alien to deportation.

Bibliography: Charles Gordon and Harry N. Rosenfield, *Immigration Law and Procedure*, rev. ed., 6 vols. (1979–1981).

. . . [I]t is unquestionably reasonable for Congress to make an alien's eligibility [for supplementary medical benefits] depend on both the character and the duration of his residence.

JOHN PAUL STEVENS

ALIMONY AND CHILD SUPPORT

☐ Remuneration made as a result of a court order by a person to a spouse or former spouse for his or her support and the support of any children of the marriage upon SEPARATION OR DIVORCE. ☐

Temporary alimony is money paid as an allowance for a spouse while a divorce action is pending. Included in this payment may be fees for the preparation of the suit in addition to money for support. *Permanent alimony*, also known as maintenance, is the order for support of the spouse set forth in the final divorce judgment.

Historical background of alimony Alimony in the United States has its origin in English law, where it was used as financial support for women who were separated from their husbands, but, nevertheless, still remained married to them. Alimony can be traced back to the period during which the only remedies for broken marriages were limited to divorce A MENSA ET THORO (Latin for "from bed and board"), whereby a couple were authorized to live apart from one another but were not freed from the marriage bond, and to ANNULMENT. Limited divorce did not terminate the marriage, since the parties were not permitted to remarry. Alimony, therefore, was no more than a continuation of the husband's marital support obligation. The traditional idea was that a woman was supported by her father until marriage, at which time her husband acquired the obligation to support her for life. If a husband died, a wife was generally permitted to use one-third of his property for the duration of her life under the principle of DOWER.

Subsequently, a full divorce became possible and the concept of alimony was adopted from limited divorce. There has been a marked lack of accord among the courts concerning the theoretical basis for alimony when a marriage is completely terminated. Some judges opine that alimony is a mere continuation of the support that the wife was entitled to obtain during the existence of the marriage. Other courts view alimony as payment of DAMAGES for the wrongful breach of the marriage contract by the husband. Alimony is also viewed as a penalty imposed on a guilty husband by some courts. In divorce actions in some states, if a woman is found to be at fault for breaking up the marriage, then she will be denied alimony.

Factors to consider In determining whether or not to award alimony or maintenance as well as the amount to be awarded, courts ordinarily take into consideration all circumstances relating to the financial status of both parties.

Many states use the Uniform Marriage and Divorce Act as a guideline when constructing their own laws. Factors that this act suggests that a court consider are:
1. the financial condition of the party requesting support payments;
2. the time required either to acquire education or be trained for employment;
3. the standard of living adhered to during the marriage;
4. the length of the marriage;
5. the age, physical condition, and emotional state of the party seeking support; and
6. the ability of the party who is being sued for alimony to provide for personal support and still contribute funds to the spouse seeking support.

The recommendation set forth by this model statute is that support should only be ordered where the one requesting it has inadequate PROPERTY to meet his or her own needs and is unable to earn satisfactory income or has custody of a child that precludes him or her from working outside the home.

Fault In some states, alimony is regarded as something that is awarded or withheld on the basis of fault. Some states strictly prohibit alimony to the party against whom the divorce judgment is rendered and others bar alimony in an action where an individual has been divorced on ADULTERY grounds. EVIDENCE of marital misconduct will be taken into consideration by some states in setting the amount of alimony.

The Uniform Marriage and Divorce Act specifically provides that support should be ordered where appropriate without consideration of misconduct during the marriage. States with NO-FAULT divorce statutes are now faced with the decision of whether alimony should be allowed, regardless of fault. Some states take the modern position that the court should take the financial positions of both spouses into account when deciding whether to award alimony.

When the amount changes or terminates As a general rule, alimony payments continue until their modification by the court, the death of either spouse, or the remarriage of the recipient.

Modification in alimony can be made by the same court at a future time if warranted by significant changes in circumstances, such as a greatly reduced income for one party or a higher salary for one. In some states, alimony may be increased to keep in step with inflation provided the individual who is paying can afford it.

The law of each individual state determines whether or not alimony can be awarded later if not ordered in the original judgment of divorce.

As manners make laws, manners likewise repeal them.

SAMUEL JOHNSON

The wording of the initial decree is often used to answer that question. A judgment expressly prohibiting alimony will not be altered later to provide for an award regardless of whether or not circumstances have changed.

Some cases have ordered alimony for a wife until the time of her death or remarriage. Other courts consider alimony to create a right for the wife to acquire funds from a deceased ex-husband's ESTATE to furnish her support for life. Ordinarily, a divorced wife has no legal right to share in the estate of her ex-husband and courts are reluctant to extend alimony beyond the termination of a husband's life. In some instances, an estranged husband is obligated to maintain a life INSURANCE policy for the benefit of an ex-wife whose support and maintenance depends solely on alimony. This type of provision is generally made when a woman is past an employable age in order to give her financial security upon the death of her former spouse.

An automatic termination of alimony upon the remarriage of its recipient is permitted in many states. A few states require that the spouse providing remuneration apply to the court for termination of alimony, pleading the recipient's remarriage as a change in circumstances. One state recognized that the changing sexual preference of a wife could serve as a reason for the termination of alimony, when a man's ex-wife became a lesbian. This ruling was based upon a material change in circumstances, but does not constitute legal PRECEDENT.

Cohabitation as a factor Problems arise in cases where a divorced woman cohabits with a man without being legally married to him. See also, Marriage.

Historically, there was a strong PUBLIC POLICY against relationships without the benefit of clergy, which was reflected in the law. The basis of this was to preserve the sanctity of marriage and of the family, and to promote the stability of society. Many laws initially provided that alimony payments could be severed if the cohabitating couple acted as though they were married. A man should not be required to support a former wife who holds herself out to the world as being another man's spouse, even though a formal marriage ceremony has not been performed.

With social disapproval of informal relationships decreasing, a woman who has neither remarried nor led the world to believe that she is married to another man, is still entitled to receive alimony payments in some jurisdictions.

Some courts have lowered the amount of alimony, however, to assure that none of the money is used for the support of the ex-wife's new partner.

Constitutional problems are inherent if a court attempts to regulate an ex-wife's sex life too extensively. Although a former husband should not be compelled to support another man who moves into the former marital abode, a court cannot require the recipient of alimony to totally abstain from sexual relationships when the sexual privacy and freedom of the person paying alimony is not regulated.

Following an annulment A number of cases have involved a subsequent marriage by an ex-wife that is either void or voidable. A problem arises if a woman believes she is marrying and the marriage is afterwards declared invalid in an ANNULMENT proceeding. The issue is whether or not the original ex-husband must commence alimony payments again.

Most states will reestablish the support order following the annulment of a void marriage on the premise that there is no way that it could ever have been valid. A marriage that was merely voidable at the wife's option will not ordinarily result in reinstatement of alimony payments by the original former husband.

Support for children Where there are children of the marriage, a divorce decree provides for CUSTODY of minor children, ordinarily to one of the parents.

Frequently, an order governing child support payments from the noncustodial to the custodial parent will be a component of the settlement of economic relations between the parties to a divorce. In some instances, a parent will be commanded to recompense the child directly or will be ordered to pay a GUARDIAN, who manages the property of a child. The court might order payments to be made directly into a fund to be held for the child to use at some future date, such as a TRUST.

Payments to support children In spite of the fact that a number of states have lowered the AGE OF MAJORITY for most purposes to the age of eighteen, states retain the right to mandate support of a child by a parent beyond that age. A child support provision in a divorce decree therefore might order payments to the age of twenty-one or until such time as the child no longer attends school on a full-time basis. Some states provide that support payments may be terminated prior to age eighteen if the child marries, obtains full-time employment, or exhibits a willful refusal to accept a parent's discipline or guidance.

Support payments generally end when the child or parent dies. A child's maintenance might be provided for by a supporting parent by the purchase of a life insurance policy for the child's benefit. A supporting parent might also leave

Alimony is not awarded as a reward to the receiving spouse or as punishment of the spouse against whom it is charged. It is an effort, insofar as is reasonably possible, to rectify the frequent economic imbalance in the earning power and standard of living of the divorced husband and wife. Its continuation is not dependent on the good conduct of either spouse.

JOHN D. ELDRIDGE

property to the child in a WILL. A court will sometimes order a supporting parent to maintain a life insurance policy, naming either the child or the custodial parent as beneficiary.

Unless the custodial parent can adequately provide for himself or herself, it is considered to be a better practice to name the custodial parent rather than the child on the insurance policy unless the custodial parent is completely untrustworthy or irresponsible. The reason for this is that money can be tied up in court after the death of the supporting parent until an adult is named to accept payment for the child and the child might not have ready access to it.

Amount of payments In arranging the amount of child support all factors that affect the child's maintenance are balanced by the courts.

A reasonable list of factors to be considered is set forth by the Uniform Parentage Act, a model statute that states use as a guideline.

The considerations suggested are:
1. the child's necessities;
2. the parent's standard of living and circumstances;
3. the financial status of the parents;
4. the earning capacity of each individual parent;
5. the future educational plans of the child;
6. the child's age;
7. the earning ability and fiscal resources of the child;
8. the duty of each parent to support other people; and
9. the value of care given by the custodial parent.

Parents may make allowance for a certain level of child support in a separation agreement, but it does not preclude judicial review. The well-established rule is that neither parent may bargain away the rights of the child.

Altering the amount An award for child support can be changed when necessary. Courts, however, consistently insist that a significant change of circumstances should be exhibited before the court will allow for a modification of the amount of a child support order.

A frequent argument set forth by fathers is that their remarriage constitutes a significant change in circumstances. In the past, courts uniformly ruled against such pleas. The rationale was that the child should not be burdened by the father's undertaking of added responsibilities. Courts have begun to recognize the needs of the father's current family.

A man's decision to change careers has also been a source of recurrent litigation. Support payments are sometimes reduced to encourage

an individual to embark on a new career that pays lower wages at first but offers a better financial future. Courts have usually exhibited respect for an individual's choice of work. The only issue that usually arises is whether or not the father is being fair to the child.

Property settlements Upon the end of a marriage, the property must be divided between the husband and wife. Three basic systems currently set forth rules for property settlements. These rules govern the transactions between the parties entering a separation agreement and delineate the approach to be taken by a judge if he or she must resolve the controversy.

Separate property A large number of states view all property and assets in marriage as separate property. Each party retains ownership of everything held by him or her prior to the marriage, in addition to anything obtained during the marriage by way of GIFT, INHERITANCE, or INCOME acquired from earnings or investments. One spouse can only receive an interest in property owned by the other spouse where it is conveyed as a gift from one party to the other, where allowed, through a business undertaking.

The *title rule,* in a few states, apportions property according to the name on the title, and preserves the property owned by each party before the marriage.

Separate property jurisdictions increasingly view marriage as a PARTNERSHIP and few adhere to the rule of separate property.

Equitable distribution A number of states have recently discarded separate property rules in favor of marital property. Judges must distribute property in divorce settlements based on the needs and contributions of each party to the marriage. The rationale behind the law is that modern marriage should be viewed as a partnership of equal parties, and that assets should, therefore, be divided according to each party's contributions to them. See also, Equitable Distribution.

Community property A small number of states regard the property accumulated during marriage to be COMMUNITY PROPERTY, to which each spouse has an equal claim.

Essentially, this system reverts to each partner whatever he or she owned before the marriage and splits the remainder equally upon divorce based upon the economic value of the contributions made by a non-wage-earning spouse to the marriage. The courts ordinarily reserve the power to determine what is an equal division of the property, and examine financial factors aside from which property belonged to which party and the amount that was gained dur-

For a judge rarely performs his functions adequately unless the case before him is adequately presented.

LOUIS D. BRANDEIS

ing the marriage. This method of settling assets is not, however, entirely predictable.

Differences among settlements In a majority of jurisdictions, there are variations among alimony, child support, and property settlements. Alimony and child support may be judicially enforced through wage GARNISHMENT and imprisonment for CONTEMPT, while property settlements are enforced by civil actions. The individual paying alimony deducts it from the amount of his income for income tax purposes, while the recipient adds it to her income; however, child support payments are not deductible from the income of a person paying them, nor are they income to the receiving parent. Alimony and child support amounts can be modified upon a substantial alteration of circumstances whereas property settlements cannot. The divorcing parties can generally reach an agreement between themselves concerning alimony and property settlements as part of their negotiations, but child support agreements are always supervised by the court. Alimony terminates upon the remarriage of the receiving party; and child support continues, in most cases, until the child reaches the age of majority. The death of either the person paying, or the person receiving, also terminates alimony and child support. Installments in a property settlement continue until the total amount is paid and can be enforced either by or against the estate of an individual who has died. Alimony and child support duties continue despite BANKRUPTCY, but a property settlement is dischargeable.

Economic considerations Other factors must be considered regarding monetary settlements. In some instances, a dependent wife might wish to postpone a divorce upon discovering that she is eligible to collect SOCIAL SECURITY on her husband's account, though estranged, if the marriage lasts at least ten years. Both parties should be apprised as to their PENSION rights, whether in their individual right, with provisions for their spouse, or obtained through the spouse.

Tax consequences Tax considerations should be weighed for diversified options. An individual who believes that he cannot afford to pay child support because his salary is too low might discover that labeling a portion of such payments alimony will alter his tax liability to an extent sufficient to give the effect of a higher income. Another possibility is that an individual can retain title to the marital home while his former wife and children reside there, make mortgage payments, and use the amount that is interest on the mortgage to reduce his taxable income. In addition, the parties can decide who will take

the children as dependents for tax exemption purposes.

Depending upon whether the divorce is in a separate property, equitable distribution, or community property state, it is essential that responsibility for capital gains taxes be considered in connection with property settlements.

Property suits over unmarried relationships The growing prevalence of cohabitation of couples without marriage has created new problems concerning whether or not such couples may sue each other for alimony or property settlements upon termination of the relationship.

Alimony paid out for nonmarital unions is colloquially known as *palimony.* In 1976, the California State Supreme Court ruled in *Marvin v. Marvin,* 18 Cal.3d 660, 134 Cal. Rptr. 815, 557 P.2d 106 that, although public policy is to encourage and foster the institution of marriage, an equitable distribution of property accumulated during a nonmarital relationship is not precluded. In this case, a woman who had cohabited with a man for seven years without a formal marriage brought an action to enforce an alleged oral contractual agreement under which she was entitled to half the property accumulated during the seven-year period, as well as support payments. The Los Angeles County Superior Court granted judgment on the pleadings for the defendant, and the plaintiff appealed.

The state supreme court held that the court may employ the doctrine of QUANTUM MERUIT, or the equitable awarding of what a person deserves, when warranted by the facts of the case. The court stated that the mere fact that two people have not participated in a valid marriage ceremony does not serve as a basis for inference by the court that the couple had the intention to keep their earnings and property separate. The intention of the parties must be ascertained by a deeper inquiry into the nature of their relationship.

The state supreme court permitted a promise made while an unmarried couple cohabited to form the basis of a marital type of recovery. Although in the *Marvin* case the plaintiff was unsuccessful in recovering DAMAGES on a breach of contract basis, she was awarded on remand money for purposes of aiding her in her attempt to regain financial independence, but that award was reversed on appeal.

The *Marvin* case resulted in the initiation of similar lawsuits throughout the country. Legislatures in various states are currently considering requirements that support promises made during cohabitation be in writing to be enforceable. In addition, to guard against liability, couples who

Words in themselves may be harmless, while accent and manner may make them deadly.

MARMADUKE H. DENT

live together are frequently using *prenuptial agreements* or *cohabitation contracts* to spell out their expectations and intentions.

ALIUNDE   [*Latin, "From another source"; "from outside."*]

Evidence *aliunde* explains a document, the provisions of which are unclear and can be interpreted in various ways. Such evidence is obtained from sources beyond the language of the document itself; for example, the testimony of witnesses present when admissions were made by the parties. PAROL EVIDENCE used to clarify the ambiguous terms of a contract is evidence *aliunde*.

ALLEGATION   □ The assertion, claim, declaration, or statement by a party made in a PLEADING that sets out his or her position in a civil action. □

If the allegations in a plaintiff's COMPLAINT are insufficient to establish that the person's legal rights have been violated, the defendant can make a motion to the court to dismiss the complaint for failure to state a CAUSE OF ACTION. If the allegations in the defendant's ANSWER do not contradict the allegations in the complaint, the plaintiff can make a motion for SUMMARY JUDGMENT.

□ A charge in an INDICTMENT that an accused has violated the law that will result in criminal prosecution □

ALLEGE   □ To state, recite, assert, or charge the existence of particular facts in a PLEADING or an INDICTMENT; to make an ALLEGATION. □

ALLEGIANCE   □ In English law, the duty of loyalty and obedience owed by all persons born within the king's realm that attaches immediately

In 1913 thirty-two Indian chiefs signed a document called a "Declaration of Allegiance to the United States Government by the North American Indian." It was the first time that these Indians declared themselves to be part of the United States.

Benedict Arnold's oath of allegiance to the United States of America, sworn in 1778 at Valley Forge.

I Benedict Arnold Major General do acknowledge the UNITED STATES of AMERICA to be Free, Independent and Sovereign States, and declare that the people thereof owe no allegiance or obedience to George the Third, King of Great-Britain; and I renounce, refuse and abjure any allegiance or obedience to him; and I do *Swear* that I will, to the utmost of my power, support, maintain and defend the said United States against the said King George the Third, his heirs and successors, and his or their abettors, assistants and adherents, and will serve the said United States in the office of *Major General* which I now hold, with fidelity, according to the best of my skill and understanding.

Sworn before me this 30th May 1778 at the Artillery Park Valley Forge

B Arnold

Henry B Gist

upon their birth and that they cannot be relieved of by their own actions. ☐

In U.S. law, the obligation of fidelity and obedience that is owed by native born and naturalized American citizens to the United States that cannot be relinquished without the consent of the government expressed by a statutory enactment.

ALLEN CHARGE ☐ An instruction given by a judge in a criminal prosecution to the jurors advising them to have respect for each other's views and to listen to each other's arguments with a temperament towards being convinced because the case must be decided. ☐

The *Allen* charge recommends that dissenting jurors consider whether their doubts are reasonable in light of the majority's opinion. If the majority is for acquittal, the *Allen* charge instructs the minority members to consider whether their judgment is correct. The name of the instruction is taken from the case of *Allen v. United States*, 164 U.S. 492, 17 S.Ct. 154, 41 L.Ed. 528 (1896), wherein the instruction was approved.

The *Allen* charge has been called the dynamite charge because its original purpose was to blast loose a jury that was deadlocked in reaching a verdict. Originally, its use was confined to cases in which absolute certainty could not be expected and in which the jury had unsuccessfully deliberated for many hours. Soon judges were giving jurors the *Allen* charge in cases where the jury had only begun to deliberate or had not even entered the jury room. In a few cases, the charge was given because the judge and jury were eager to go home because it was the last case to be heard in a particular court for a particular term.

Many states prohibit the use of the *Allen* charge because it is an unwarranted intrusion by a judge into the exclusive sphere of fact-finding by the jury. It has been viewed as limiting full and free discussion in the jury room, falsely enhancing the validity and force of the majority opinion, and depriving an accused of a hung jury and a mistrial by silencing the dissenting voices of the minority jurors. One of the values of the jury system is that the jurors deliberate conscientiously and patiently before reaching a verdict. An *Allen* charge undermines this value because the judge, in effect, pressures a minority of jurors to abandon their consciences in order to bring in a verdict.

The *Allen* charge is known, in some jurisdictions, as the shotgun or third-degree instruction.

ALL FOURS ☐ Identical; similar. ☐

All fours specifically refers to two cases or decisions that have similar fact patterns and raise identical legal issues. Since the circumstances leading to their individual determinations are virtually the same, the decision rendered by the court in each case will be similar. Such cases or decisions are said to be on *all fours* with each other.

ALLOCATION ☐ The apportionment or designation of an item for a specific purpose or to a particular place. ☐

In the law of TRUSTS, the allocation of cash dividends earned by a stock that makes up the principal of a trust for a beneficiary usually means that the dividends will be treated as income to be paid to the beneficiary. The allocation of stock dividends generally means that such dividends will be added to the shares of stock held as prinicpal, thereby increasing its size.

ALLOCUTION ☐ The formal inquiry by a judge of an accused person, convicted of a crime, as to whether the person has any legal cause to show why JUDGMENT should not be pronounced against him or her or as to whether the person has anything to say to the court before being sentenced. ☐

ALLODIAL
☐ Free; not subject to the rights of any lord or superior; owned without obligation of vassalage or fealty; the opposite of feudal.
☐ A description given to the outright ownership of land that did not impose upon its owner the performance of feudal duties. ☐

ALLOGRAPH ☐ A writing or signature made by one person for another. ☐

When a PRINCIPAL gives his or her AGENT the power to pay creditors, the checks written by the agent are allographs for the principal.

An autograph is the opposite of an allograph.

ALLONGE ☐ Additional paper firmly attached to COMMERCIAL PAPER, such as a promissory note, to provide room to write ENDORSEMENTS. ☐

An allonge is necessary when there is insufficient space on the document itself for the endorsements. It is considered part of the commercial paper as long as the allonge remains affixed thereto.

Men are more often bribed by their loyalties and ambitions than by money.

ROBERT H. JACKSON

ALLOTMENT
☐ A portion, share, or division.
☐ The proportionate distribution of shares of stock in a CORPORATION.
☐ The PARTITION and distribution of land. ☐

ALLUVION   See Territory, National.

ALTERATION   ☐ Modification; changing a thing without obliterating it. ☐

An alteration is a variation made in the language or terms of a legal document that affects the rights and obligations of the parties to it. When this occurs, the alteration is MATERIAL and the party who did not consent to the change can be released from his or her duties under the document by a court.

When an essential part of a writing has been cut, torn, burned, or erased, the alteration is also known as a MUTILATION.

The alteration of a document by someone other than a party to it is called a SPOLIATION.

ALTERATION OF INSTRUMENTS   ☐ A change in the meaning or language of a legal document, such as a CONTRACT, DEED, LEASE, or COMMERCIAL PAPER, that is made by one party to the document without the consent of the other after it has been signed or completed. ☐

If such a change is made by a third party without the consent of either party to the instrument, it is called a SPOLIATION or MUTILATION.

Method   The face of an instrument is changed by its alteration. A difference in handwriting, a change in words or figures, an erasure, and the striking out of particular words are some methods used to alter an instrument. Since there must be a change in the meaning or language of a document, retracing an original writing—as when a figure written in pencil is retraced in ink—is not an alteration.

Material changes   The alteration of an instrument materially changes it. The document no longer reflects the terms that the parties originally intended to serve as the basis of their legal obligation to each other. To be material, the change must affect an important part of the instrument and the rights of the parties to it. Any material alteration relieves the nonconsenting party of any obligation to perform according to the terms of the instrument. If the altered instrument is a contract, then the original contract is void. The nonconsenting party cannot be legally obligated by the new contract since he or she never agreed to it. A document that has been materi-

ally altered does not regain its original validity if it is restored to its original form by erasing or deleting unauthorized words.

Particular changes   The date of an instrument is often considered a material provision when it establishes the time within which the parties to a document must perform their obligations under it. An unauthorized change of date that shortens the time of payment or extends the time of performance so that more interest will become due is a material alteration.

An alteration of a signature that changes the legal effect of an instrument is material. Erasing words that show that the signer is acting as an agent, for example, changes the signer's liability under the instrument and, therefore, is a material alteration. However, when a signature that was improperly placed on a document is erased, there is no material alteration since the legal meaning of the document is not changed.

Any change in the terms of the instrument that affects the obligations of the parties is material. In a contract to sell land on commission, a change in the rate of commission is material. A change in a description in a deed so that it transfers a smaller piece of land, a change in the name of a purchaser in a sales contract, or an alteration in the terms of financing set forth in a MORTGAGE are also material.

Time of alteration   A modification in a document before its completion is not an alteration. The parties are bound to review the document and to have agreed upon its terms before executing it. In order for an alteration to nullify the legal effect of an instrument, the change must be made after its completion.

Intention   A material change must be intentionally made. The motive behind the alteration is unimportant. If a mistake or accident causes a change, this is not considered a material alteration, but the document may be reformed or rescinded. See also, Reformation; Rescission.

The person making the change   The change to the instrument must be made by a party or someone authorized by him or her to do so. No change made by a third person without the consent of either party to the document will invalidate it if its original terms can be learned. When a material alteration is made by a party to commercial paper, such as a check or promissory note, the paper will be enforced as originally written against the party who made the changes.

Consensual alteration   A change in an instrument made with the consent of the parties is binding upon them. Such consensual alteration is usually evidenced by the signing by each party of his or her initials and the date that the agreement to the changes to the instrument was reached.

ALTER EGO ☐ A doctrine used by the courts to ignore the corporate status of a group of stockholders, officers, and directors of a CORPORATION in reference to their limited liability in order to hold them personally liable for their actions when they have acted fraudulently or unjustly, or when to refuse to do so will deprive an innocent victim of redress for an injury caused by them. ☐

A corporation is considered the alter ego of its stockholders, directors, or officers when it is used merely for the transaction of their personal business for which they want immunity from individual liability. A parent corporation is the alter ego of a subsidiary corporation if it controls and directs its activities so that it will have limited liability for its wrongful acts.

The alter ego doctrine is also known as the INSTRUMENTALITY RULE because the corporation becomes an instrument for the personal advantage of its parent corporation, stockholders, directors, or officers. When a court applies it, the court is said to PIERCE THE CORPORATE VEIL.

ALTERNATIVE PLEADING ☐ An assertion by a party of two or more claims or defenses in a lawsuit in such a way that the court may recognize or accept one statement or another. ☐

Under the system of COMMON-LAW PLEADING that prevailed in England and the United States at least through the middle of the nineteenth century, a party was not permitted to plead in the alternative. He or she had to make one claim or one defense to the other party's claim, and the case was won or lost on that single theory. Over the years, this rule of pleading was more and more criticized because it closed off discussion rather than opening it up to the truth. Today, courts operate under rules of CODE PLEADING or pleading as established by the rules of FEDERAL CIVIL PROCEDURE, and these rules specifically allow alternative pleading. This permits both parties to plead in an either-or fashion and leaves it to the court to decide what actually happened.

ALTERNATIVE RELIEF

☐ REMEDIES sought in a lawsuit in various forms or in the alternative, such as a demand for SPECIFIC PERFORMANCE of a contract or monetary damages to compensate for the failure to perform the obligation, or both. ☐

Modern rules governing PLEADING in courts now specifically permit a party to demand relief in the alternative. This eliminates the harsh consequences of the rule of COMMON-LAW PLEADING that required a party to make one demand for one type of relief and to lose the case if a different remedy were more appropriate. Today, a party can ask for alternative forms of relief and recover what is later proved to be most appropriate at trial.

ALTERNATIVE WRIT ☐ An order, issued originally by the king in England but more recently by a court, commanding a person to do a specific thing or to appear and explain why he or she should not be compelled to do it. ☐

Under the common law, the writs of PROHIBITION and MANDAMUS were alternative writs. In modern systems of court procedure, an order to SHOW CAUSE serves the same purpose. It commands a person to do something or come into court and show cause why he or she should not be made to do it.

AMBASSADOR   See Diplomatic Agents.

AMBASSADORS AND CONSULS

☐ An *ambassador* is the foreign diplomatic representative of a nation who is authorized to handle political negotiations between his or her country and the country where the ambassador has been assigned. A *consul* is the commercial AGENT of a nation, who is empowered only to engage in business transactions, and not political matters in the country where he or she is stationed. ☐

The president with the consent of the Senate appoints ambassadors and consuls whereas the secretary of state appoints staff officers and other subordinate employees.

Powers and duties   The powers of an ambassador are specified in his or her credentials, or documents of introduction, which the ambassador submits to the foreign government. In addition to responsibility for political negotiations, an American ambassador may initiate legal proceedings on behalf of the United States and defend suits instituted against it. A foreign ambassador in the United States has similar duties regarding his or her government.

In general, a consul is authorized to safeguard the legal rights and property interests of the citizens of his or her country and to appear in court to ascertain that the laws of the nation where he or she is assigned are administered impartially to all of the ambassador's compatriots. A U.S. citizen who has legal difficulties in a foreign country should consult the United States consul.

Consuls are also empowered and obligated to protect the estates of their countrymen and women who die within their consular districts. This duty terminates when the decedent's HEIRS are represented by an ATTORNEY.

Diplomatic immunity The development of harmonious international relations and protection against ARREST, harassment, or other unjustified actions taken against diplomatic representatives constitutes the objectives of diplomatic immunity. The Vienna Convention on Diplomatic Relations, which became effective as part of the Federal law in 1972, governs diplomatic immunity by granting various degrees of immunity from civil and criminal liability to the members of diplomatic missions.

Diplomatic agents The supervisor of a mission, such as an ambassador, and members of the mission staff who possess diplomatic rank are diplomatic agents. Such an agent is immune from criminal liability in the nation in which he or she serves, but the commission of a crime may result in a recall request to the ambassador's country. His or her expulsion may ensue upon the refusal of any such request.

In addition, a diplomatic agent is immune from civil lawsuits, except for actions involving estates, when he or she is the EXECUTOR, ADMINISTRATOR, or BENEFICIARY; actions concerning real property held by the diplomatic agent for personal, not official functions; and actions relating to professional or business activities that are beyond the scope of diplomatic duties. A diplomatic agent is not required to testify as a witness; and the family members living in the agent's household enjoy the same immunities.

Due to the hardship imposed on the victims of motor vehicle accidents in the United States caused by foreign diplomats who have diplomatic immunity, Federal law mandates that mission members and their families insure their personal motor vehicles, boats, and airplanes. If the mission has similar vehicles registered in its name, it also must purchase liability insurance. An action for damages for property loss, personal injuries, or WRONGFUL DEATH can be maintained directly against the diplomat's insurance company and is tried by the court, presiding without a jury.

Staff members The administrative and technical staffs and families and household members of the mission are completely immune from criminal liability, but are immune from civil liability only for official acts. Similar rules apply to members of the service staff employed as domestics, but their families and private servants employed by staff members are not so protected against liability.

Consuls Consuls are not diplomatic agents and, therefore, they are usually amenable to civil lawsuits and criminal prosecution in the country where they are assigned. Federal law, however, extends immunity to consuls from all suits and proceedings in state courts. This prevents any embarrassment to foreign nations that might ensue from such proceedings.

Other exemptions Diplomatic agents in the United States and the members of their households are generally exempt from Federal, state, and municipal taxes. They are responsible, however, for indirect taxes that are part of the price of goods, taxes on property inherited from a citizen, taxes on any real property they own privately, or capital gains TAXES on profits from personal investments. Diplomatic agents have no obligation to serve in the U.S. armed forces. These exemptions also apply to the administrative and technical staffs of the mission and their families. The service staff and private servants are exempt from taxes on wages received from their employment with the mission or its members.

AMBIGUITY ☐ Uncertainty or doubtfulness of the meaning of language. ☐

When language is capable of being understood in more than one way by a reasonable person, ambiguity exists. It is not the use of peculiar words or of common words used in a peculiar sense. Words are ambiguous when their significance is unclear to persons with competent knowledge and skill to understand them.

There are two categories of ambiguity: *latent* and *patent*. Latent ambiguity exists when the language used is clear and intelligible so that it suggests one meaning but some extrinsic fact or evidence creates a need for interpretation or a choice among two or more possible meanings. In a classic case, *Raffles v. Wichelhaus*, 159 Eng. Rep. 375 (Ex. 1864), a CONTRACT was made to sell 125 bales of cotton that were to arrive on a ship called Peerless that sailed from Bombay, India. Unknown to the parties to the contract, two ships of the same name were to arrive from the same port during different months of the same year. This extraneous fact necessitated the interpretation of an otherwise clear and definite term of the contract. In such cases, extrinsic or PAROL EVIDENCE may be admitted to explain what was

One-half the doubts in life arise from the defects of language . . .

WILLIAM JOHNSON

meant or to identify the property referred to in the writing.

A patent ambiguity is one that appears on the face of a document or writing because uncertain or obscure language has been used.

In the law of contracts, ambiguity means more than that the language has more than one meaning upon which reasonable persons could differ. It means that after a court has applied rules of interpretation, such as the PLAIN MEANING, COURSE OF DEALING, COURSE OF PERFORMANCE, or TRADE USAGE rules to the unclear terms, the court still cannot say with certainty what meaning was intended by the parties to the contract. When this occurs, the court will admit as evidence extraneous proof of prior or contemporaneous agreements to determine the meaning of the ambiguous language. Parol evidence may be used to explain the meaning of a writing as long as its use does not vary the terms of the writing. If there is no such evidence, the court may hear evidence of the subjective intention or understanding of the parties to clarify the ambiguity.

Sometimes, courts decide the meaning of ambiguous language on the basis of who was responsible or at fault for the ambiguity. When only one party knew or should have known of the ambiguity, the unsuspecting party's subjective knowledge of the meaning will control. If both parties knew or should have known of the uncertainty, the court will look to the subjective understanding of both. The ambiguity no longer exists if the parties agree upon its meaning. If the parties disagree and the ambiguous provisions are material, no contract is formed because of lack of mutual assent.

Courts frequently interpret an ambiguous contract term against the interests of the party who prepared the contract and created the ambiguity. This is common in cases of adhesion and INSURANCE contracts. A drafter of a document should not benefit at the expense of an innocent party because he or she was careless in drafting the agreement.

In CONSTITUTIONAL LAW, statutes that contain ambiguous language are void for vagueness. The language of such laws is considered so obscure and uncertain that a reasonable person cannot determine from a reading what the law purports to command or prohibit. This statutory ambiguity deprives a person of the notice requirement of DUE PROCESS OF LAW, and, therefore, renders the statute unconstitutional. See also, Martin Shapiro's essay on "Void for Vagueness" Doctrine.

AMBIT
□ A boundary line that indicates ownership of a parcel of land as opposed to other parcels; an exterior or enclosing line.
□ The limits of a power or JURISDICTION.
□ The delineation of the scope of a particular subject matter. □

AMBULANCE CHASER □ A colloquial phrase that is used derisively for a person who is hired by an attorney to seek out NEGLIGENCE cases at the scenes of accidents or in hospitals where injured parties are treated, in exchange for a percentage of the damages that will be recovered in the case. □

An ambulance chaser also describes the practice of some attorneys who, upon learning of a personal injury that might have been caused by the negligence or the wrongful act of another, immediately contact the victim for consent to represent him or her in a lawsuit in exchange for a CONTINGENT FEE, a percentage of the judgment recovered.

AMBULATORY □ Movable; revocable; subject to change; capable of alteration. □

An ambulatory court was the former name of the Court of King's Bench in England. It would convene wherever the king who presided over it could be found, moving its location as the king moved.

An ambulatory disposition is a JUDGMENT, decree, or sentence that is subject to change, amendment, or revocation.

A WILL is considered ambulatory because as long as the person who made it lives, it can always be changed or revoked.

AMENDMENT □ The modification of materials by the addition of supplemental information; the deletion of unnecessary, undesirable, or outdated information; or the correction of errors existing in the text. □

In practice, a change in the PLEADINGS—statements of the allegations of the parties in a lawsuit—may be achieved if the parties agree to the amendment or if the court in which the proceeding is pending grants a motion for the amendment made by one party. A JUDGMENT may be altered by an amendment if a motion to do so is made within a certain time after its entry and granted by the court. The amendment of pleadings and judgments is regulated by state codes of CIVIL PROCEDURE and the rules of FEDERAL CIVIL PROCEDURE.

Why may not that be the skull of a lawyer? Where be his quiddities now, his quillets, his cases, his tenures, and his tricks?

SHAKESPEARE

ALCOHOL---The Great Enemy

The fly, through its germ-spreading proclivities, is said by government experts to cost the nation more than $150,000,000 a year, besides the cost in loss of human life. But we've a greater enemy. In the years 1900-08, 33,000 men, from twenty-five to sixty-five years of age, were reported to have died in the United States, in the "registration area" alone, from alcoholism and from hardened liver due to alcoholism,—11,000 more than died from typhoid fever.

' Thirty-Six States Can Stop It By Constitutional Amendment

Series G. No. 16.

THE AMERICAN ISSUE PUBLISHING CO., WESTERVILLE, OHIO.

This cartoon promoted a prohibition amendment to the Constitution by pointing out that more lives were lost due to alcohol than to typhoid fever.

A CONSTITUTION or a STATUTE may be changed by an amendment.

A WILL, TRUST, corporate CHARTER, and other legal documents are subject to amendment.

A MENSA ET THORO   [*Latin, "From table and bed,"*] but more commonly translated as "from bed and board."

This phrase designates a divorce which is really akin to a separation granted by a court whereby a husband and wife are not legally obligated to live together, but their marriage has not been dissolved. Neither spouse has the right to remarry where there is a divorce *a mensa et thoro*; only parties who have been awarded a divorce *a vinculo matrimonii*, the more common type of divorce, can do so.

AMERICAN ACADEMY FOR PROFESSIONAL LAW ENFORCEMENT   Founded in 1974, the American Academy for Professional Law Enforcement is an organization dedicated to further professionalization of law enforcement and to achieving the highest levels of standards and ethical practices in the field.

The academy functions as a voice for professional law enforcement and for professionals within law enforcement regardless of their rank. It encourages, supports, generates, and carries out research on matters that have potential for improving law enforcement; provides support for professional law enforcement personnel of all ranks who are interested in improving standards and practices; and constitutes a forum for discussing and publicizing the major problems affecting law enforcement.

The academy carries out broad programs and specific projects to further professionalize law enforcement and improve standards and practices. Programs include national symposia on issues of importance to the law enforcement community, which provide both information on new developments and opportunities to express opinions. The focus of local action projects is to encourage implementation of improved policies, procedures, and practices in law enforcement agencies. Academy members are encouraged to participate and are supported by the national office.

The academy publishes *Police Studies* (quarterly); *Annual Proceedings*; *Workshop Proceedings* (annually); *Rape: The Violent Crime*; *Corruption and Its Management*; and a newsletter. It holds annual meetings in May. The membership is composed of academicians and police practitioners with college degrees.

AMERICAN ACADEMY OF FORENSIC SCIENCES   Founded in 1948, the American Academy of Forensic Sciences (AAFS) seeks to plan, organize, and execute meetings, reports, and other projects for the stimulation and advancement of the forensic sciences. The academy seeks to promote study and raise standards in the field and to encourage the standardization of scientific techniques, tests, and criteria. Activities include the presentation of various awards, the sponsorship of seminars, the operation of the Forensic Sciences Placement Service, and the administration of selected government research. The academy maintains a 2,000-volume library. The membership includes anthropologists, biologists, criminologists, engineers, examiners of questioned documents, members of the bench and bar, odontologists, pathologists, psychiatrists, and toxicologists.

The academy is organized into the following sections: Criminalistics; General Jurisprudence; Odontology; Pathology and Biology; Physical Anthropology; Psychiatry; Questioned Documents; and Toxicology. The academy publishes the *Journal of Forensic Studies* (quarterly), a *Newsletter* (quarterly), and a *Membership*

The law is but words and paper without the hands and swords of men.

JAMES HARRINGTON

Directory (annually). It holds annual meetings in February.

AMERICAN ACADEMY OF MATRIMONIAL LAWYERS

The American Academy of Matrimonial Lawyers was founded in 1962 by a group of leading matrimonial lawyers. Their goal is to assist in the creation of improved coordinated programs to ameliorate legislative and judicial attitudes in the administration of justice for those enduring a breakdown of marriage and the family unit. They stated that their purpose in forming this national academy was to "encourage the study, improve the practice, elevate the standards, and advance the cause of matrimonial law, to the end that the welfare of the family and society be preserved."

The academy has stressed education in matrimonial law for its members, the allied professions, law schools, and the public by sponsoring continuing legal education for practicing attorneys and judges. The academy's Annual Institute of Matrimonial Law has pioneered in-depth study of the taxation and estate consequences of divorce and marital settlement. In addition, the institute initiated the study of the most effective process to be used in adjusting and resolving custody, support, and enforcement procedures. At the same time, the institute has recognized the emotional, psychological, and psychiatric factors underlying divorce.

The academy chapters conduct local and statewide seminars and symposia designed to emphasize and contribute to the development and better understanding of family and matrimonial practice, both on a national and local basis. Many of its distinguished members continue to provide expert practical knowledge in this vital area of law to civic, legislative, educational, and social groups, as well as the media. Its membership consists of certified attorneys specializing in the field of matrimonial and family law.

The academy publishes *Proceedings* (semiannually), *List of Certified Fellows* (annually), and newsletters. It holds its meetings semiannually.

AMERICAN ACADEMY OF PSYCHIATRY AND THE LAW

The American Academy of Psychiatry and the Law (AAPL) is an organization of psychiatrists who are concerned about the practice and teaching of legal psychiatry, the training of young forensic psychiatrists, and the development of research in the relationship of psychiatry and the law. The academy was developed by a number of distinguished psychiatrists in Miami in 1969, and it was formally founded in Baltimore, Maryland, in November of 1969. The academy is an organization of psychiatrists, and only practicing psychiatrists or those in recognized psychiatric training programs are eligible for membership. This is so that they may share with each other contemporary issues and problems that arise in socio-legal psychiatry as they know them. The goals of the academy include the advancement of teaching of forensic psychiatry; the promotion of continued research in problems of law and psychiatry; the publication of appropriate material and information in learned journals, including their own *Bulletin of the American Academy of Psychiatry and the Law*; and the development of standards of practice in forensic psychiatry, including sponsorship in the American Board of Forensic Psychiatry.

To further these goals, the academy meets during the third week of October. In addition to presenting many quality papers, each annual meeting features an intensive teaching session. Such educational procedures enable the academy to explore that wide area for participation and contribution in psychiatric and legal matters going beyond traditional roles in criminal procedures (i.e., competency, criminal responsibility, and correction). It thereby encourages young psychiatrists to take formal training in forensic and socio-legal psychiatry and to elevate the practice of legal psychiatry to even higher standards.

Another aim of the academy is to serve as an organized voice for forensic psychiatry in advising professional and governmental bodies on contemporary legal and legislative issues and problems. Its aim is to clarify confusing problems that have arisen by contributing to the legislative procedure in areas that pertain to its special body of knowledge. Although it is not officially affiliated with the American Psychiatric Association, a requirement for membership in AAPL is membership in the APA or, in the case of non-United States members, membership in the national body that certifies or recognizes qualified psychiatrists. Increasingly, it is becoming international in scope as it has Canadian, Australian, and European members. Many of its members serve on relevant committees of the APA or other national bodies, and it is through this active participation that contributions continue to grow.

AMERICAN ARBITRATION ASSOCIATION

The American Arbitration Association (AAA) was founded in 1926 as a nonprofit, public service organization dedicated to the resolution of disputes through arbitration, mediation, democratic election, and other voluntary methods. Activities include the provision of arbitration administrative services, standard arbitration rules of procedure adaptable under arbitration law, and education training programs in all forms of voluntary dispute settlement. The AAA does not decide cases but supplies lists from which parties mutually select impartial arbitrators. Arbitration is conducted by specific rules and procedures, and the awards by the arbitrators are legally binding and enforceable. Cases covered include automobile accident claims and commercial, community, labor, and international disputes. Over 45,000 cases were handled in 1980.

The AAA also administers fact-finding, conciliation, and mediation procedures, either separately or in conjunction with arbitration. These techniques can be used to resolve a wide variety of disputes: labor, commercial, community, and interpersonal. The association sponsors research in community dispute resolution, international arbitration, and labor arbitration and maintains a 16,000-volume library covering all forms of arbitration.

The membership of the association includes panel members and contributing members. It has the following committees: International, Law, National Construction Industry Arbitration, and Practice. The association operates a research institute and the general arbitration council of the textile industry as a division. The organization publishes: *Summary of Labor Arbitration Awards*, *Arbitration in the Schools*, *Labor Arbitration in Government*, *The Arbitration Journal* (quarterly), *Lawyer's Arbitration Letter* (quarterly), *Digest of Court Opinions* (quarterly), *News and Views* (quarterly), and *Study Time* (quarterly). It also publishes pamphlets, manuals, and outlines for teaching labor-management arbitration and arbitration law courses. The association holds an annual meeting each April.

AMERICAN ASSOCIATION FOR THE COMPARATIVE STUDY OF LAW   The American Association for the Comparative Study of Law (AACSL) was founded in 1951 to enhance the comparative study of law and to improve the understanding of foreign legal systems. Its activities feature the nonprofit publication of books, papers, and pamphlets relating to comparative, foreign, or private international law. The membership is comprised of forty law schools.

The association publishes the *American Journal of Comparative Law* (quarterly) and a reader of comparative law.

AMERICAN ASSOCIATION FOR THE INTERNATIONAL COMMISSION OF JURISTS   The American Association for the International Commission of Jurists (AAICJ) was formed in 1967 to help encourage the protection of the Rule of Law and human rights by operating alone and in conjunction with other agencies, principally the International Commission of Jurists. (The members are primarily lawyers.) AAICJ sponsors conferences and intergovernmental briefings on human rights and foreign policy. It maintains a documentation service and an internship program as well as a library of United Nations documents on human rights. The library also contains related newsletters, journals, and clippings files.

The association publishes a *Newsletter* (quarterly), *The Centre for the Independence of Judges and Lawyers Bulletin* (semiannually), and *The International Commission of Jurists Review* (semiannually). It also publishes special studies, reports of its observers at trials, and reports of its international congress and regional conferences. See also, International Commission of Jurists.

AMERICAN ASSOCIATION OF ATTORNEY-CERTIFIED PUBLIC ACCOUNTANTS   The American Association of Attorney-Certified Public Accountants (AAA-CPA) was formed in 1964. The association attempts to encourage high ethical and professional standards and to secure and protect the legal and professional rights of persons qualified both as attorneys and CPAs. The association compiles a list of American attorney-CPAs, administers a biennial economic and practice survey, and maintains channels of communication with bar associations and accounting groups. Other activities include the maintenance of a collection of fifty articles on the subject of dual licensing and dual practice, together with continuing research on these subjects. Extensive self-education programs are run by state groups. There are nineteen such groups. The membership is comprised of individuals licensed in both fields.

The association committees include Continuing Education, Cooperation with Bar and Accounting Groups, Ethics and Opinions, and Relations with Government Groups. It publishes

There is no magic in parchment or in wax.

WILLIAM HENRY ASHURST

The Attorney-CPA (quarterly) and a membership list. The association holds semiannual meetings.

AMERICAN ASSOCIATION OF CORRECTIONAL PSYCHOLOGISTS

he American Association of Correctional Psychologists (AACP) was founded in 1953. Its members are psychologists involved in correctional rehabilitation throughout the criminal justice systems, particularly in prisons, reformatories, juvenile institutions, and probation and parole agencies.

The association publishes the *Journal of Criminal Justice and Behavior* (quarterly) and a *Newsletter* (quarterly). It holds an annual meeting in August in conjunction with the American Correctional Association.

AMERICAN ASSOCIATION OF LAW
LIBRARIES The American Association of Law Libraries (AALL), founded in 1906, is an educational and scientific organization that serves to promote the science of law librarianship, to develop and increase the usefulness of law libraries, and to foster a spirit of cooperation among the members of the profession. The association conducts institutes during the week before the annual meeting and presents scholarship awards. Other activities include the management of the procedure of exchange of duplicate materials among libraries and a certification program for law librarians. The membership is comprised of librarians who serve the legal profession in the courts, law schools, bar associations, private law firms, government, and business. Book dealers and others involved in publication and related fields may become associate members.

The association has twenty-three standing committees, five special committees, eleven special interest sections, and fifteen local groups. Among the committees are Audio-Visual; Cataloging and Classification; Conference of Newer Law Librarians; Copyright; Education; Foreign, Comparative, and International Law; Indexing of Periodical Literature; Legislation and Legal Developments; and Scholarships.

The association publishes the *Law Library Journal* (quarterly), the *Index to Foreign Legal Periodicals* (quarterly), and the *Directory of Law Libraries* (biennial). It also publishes a *Biographical Directory of Law Libraries* and the AALL Publication Series of manuals and institute proceedings dealing with law library administration and techniques. The association holds an annual meeting in June.

AMERICAN ASSOCIATION OF
MEDICO-LEGAL CONSULTANTS The American Association of Medico-Legal Consultants (AAMC) was founded in 1972 to serve as a national screening panel for medical malpractice. An officer of the association described its objectives this way: "the defined objectives of the AAMC are: alleviation of the malpractice litigation, improvement in legal management of malpractice claims, and early settlement where justified. It also hopes to hasten the demise of the 'gun-for-hire' medical witness who is a hazard to physicians and lawyers alike, not to mention the integrity of the judicial process."

The members of the association are physicians and physician-attorneys. Activities include seminars for physicians and attorneys concerned with medical-legal problems and the maintenance of a library.

AMERICAN BAR ASSOCIATION
Section of Legal Education and Admissions to the Bar
Consultant on Legal Education The Section of Legal Education and Admissions to the Bar is the section of the American Bar Association (ABA) that has been assigned the task of establishing and monitoring compliance with the ABA Standards for Approval of Law School. The Consultant on Legal Education to the ABA is charged with the responsibility of advising ABA-approved law schools and potential candidates for approval of their compliance with the standards.

History In 1878 the American Bar Association (ABA) was founded. One of the seven committees originally created by the ABA constitution was the Committee on Legal Education and Admissions to the Bar. In 1893, fifteen years after the ABA was founded, the association's first section was established; it was the Section of Legal Education.

In 1921 the American Bar Association adopted its statement of minimum standards of legal education and provided for the publication of a list of schools that complied with those standards. The most recent comprehensive revision of these standards occurred in 1973. The Section of Legal Education and Admissions to the Bar was assigned the administration of this program.

The highest courts of several states in the East became concerned about the competency of the persons admitted to the practice of law within their states and in the early 1920s began to look to the accreditation standards of the Ameri-

The perfect lawyer, like the perfect orator, must accomplish himself for his duties by familiarity with every study.

JOSEPH P. STORY

can Bar Association to determine bar admission criteria. By 1930 all but eight states adopted rules requiring graduation from an ABA-accredited law school to be admitted to practice within the state.

The United States Department of Education to furnish the statutory basis for approval of Federal funds for educational purposes, officially recognized the ABA as the "nationally recognized accrediting agency" for professional schools of law.

Governance The section is headed by a chair: the other officers are the chairperson-elect, vice-chair, secretary, section delegate to the House of Delegates, and the last retiring chair. These officers plus twelve persons elected for staggered four-year terms constitute the council, which is charged with carrying out the work of the section. The officers and council members are elected by those section members present at the annual meeting. The council meets four times a year, two of the meetings take place at the annual and midyear meeting of the ABA.

Staff The Consultant on Legal Education to the ABA serves as the chief advisor to the council, its Accreditation Committee, the section, and ABA leadership on matters relating to the accreditation process. In addition, the consultant is available to law schools and universities for advice concerning legal education matters. The consultant collects and disseminates annual statistical data and processes student and faculty complaints against approved law schools.

Presently the office of the consultant is additionally staffed by four administrative secretaries and a part-time research assistant. An associate consultant position is planned for the future.

The Section of Legal Education and Admissions to the Bar is also served at the American Bar Center in Chicago by a staff director, assistant staff director, and an administrative assistant. The responsibilities of the staff director include all matters relating to bar admissions, the planning of meetings and the educational programs for the section, and assisting the various committees of the section. This office is also responsible for the section's publications, including an annual Review of Legal Education, a quarterly newsletter, an Approval of Law Schools-Standards and Rules of Procedure pamphlet, and proceedings of conferences and workshops.

Finances The majority of the funds for operating the section come from the general funds of the ABA and for the office of the consultant from the American Bar Association's

Fund for Public Education, which in turn receives grants from the American Bar Endowment. Applicants for provisional approval pay an initial inspection fee and schools subject to reinspection pay a fee. Approved schools wishing to receive statistical memoranda pay an annual service fee.

Committee section and other divisions Committees are established by the council action and their membership is appointed by the section chairperson.

One of the most active section committees is the Accreditation Committee. The Accreditation Committee was created by the council of the Section of Legal Education and Admissions to the Bar at its annual meeting in St. Louis in August, 1970. The committee was charged with the responsibility of reviewing all inspection reports, whether on approved or unapproved schools. An institution adversely affected by an Accreditation Committee action may petition the Accreditation Committee for a review of its action. The institution may appeal to the council as a matter of right only (a) any determination adverse to the institution relating to the granting of provisional or full approval; (b) determinations of hearing commissioners recommending removal of approval. This fourteen-member committee has two nonlawyer public members. Other committees include the Bar Admissions Committee, Clinical Legal Education Committee, Educational Policy Committee, Legal Education Opportunity Committee, and the Standards Review Committee. The section also has two special task forces: the Task Force on Lawyer Competency—the Law School Role; and the Task Force for Improvement of Legal Education and Professional Opportunity for the Disadvantaged.

Organizational affiliation The Section of Legal Education and Admissions to the Bar is a member of the council on Postsecondary Accreditation and a founding member of the Cooperative Council on Legal Education. The ABA is a founding member of the Council on Legal Education Opportunity.

Annual meeting The ABA has an annual meeting each August and a midyear meeting each February. The Section of Legal Education has its annual meeting in conjunction with the ABA annual meeting in August. The section also sponsors a Dean's Workshop for all deans of ABA-approved law schools at the midyear meeting.

Publications Various publications are published.

Review of legal education in the United States The annual review contains information concerning all approved law schools and some that are unapproved. In addition, a summary is presented of the bar admission requirements of the several jurisdictions. This information is collected through cooperation of the law school deans, the National Conference of Bar Examiners, and the state bar admission agencies.

American Bar Association Standards and Rules of Procedure This booklet is revised yearly and contains the latest standards and rules of procedure used in ABA process of accrediting law schools. Interpretations of the standards are published periodically.

Research The Office of the Consultant, on a regular basis, researches problems related to legal education and law school administration, such as minority admissions to approved schools, library holdings and faculty salaries, and the decrease in faculty purchasing power. See also, the entry on American Bar Association as well as Bernard G. Segal's essay on the American Bar Association.

AMERICAN BAR ASSOCIATION The
American Bar Association (ABA), is a nationwide organization to which qualified attorneys voluntarily belong.

The American Bar Association was founded in 1878 to improve legal education, to set requirements to be satisfied to gain admittance to the bar, and to facilitate the exchange of ideas and information among its members. Over the years, the ABA has been responsibile for the further development of American jurisprudence, the establishment of formal education requirements for persons seeking to become attorneys, the formulation of ethical principles that govern the practice of law, and the creation of the American Law Institute and the Conference of Commissioners on Uniform State Laws, which advance the fair administration of justice through encouraging uniformity of statutes and judicial decisions whenever practicable. In recent years, the ABA has been prominently involved in the recommendation and selection of candidates for the Federal judiciary, the accreditation of law schools, and the refinement of rules of legal and judicial ethics.

An applicant for membership in the ABA must meet certain criteria. One must be a member in good standing of the bar of a state, territory, or possession of the United States. One must have good moral character and pay the designated dues. Law students qualify to be members of the Law Student Division of the ABA if they attend an ABA-approved law school and pay the specified dues.

The ABA provides various forums through which attorneys continue their legal education during their careers. Its national institutes are held frequently in areas of law that have become topical or have undergone sweeping reform. In conjunction with the American Law Institute (ALI), the ABA holds seminars in order to continue the professional education of interested members.

Within the ABA, members may participate in the activities of numerous sections, which are organized according to specialized areas of law. Various committees exist that deal with such topics as judicial selection, professional responsibility and discipline, lawyer referral services, and the unauthorized practice of law. Other committees are concerned with topical areas, such as prepaid legal services, malpractice, legal problems of the elderly, and public-interest law.

The ABA holds annual conventions and midyear meetings to discuss designated legal topics and ABA matters. It publishes the monthly *American Bar Association Journal,* an annual directory, and various journals and newsletters reporting the work of its sections and committees. The ABA also supports the activities of affiliated organizations—such as the American Bar Endowment, which provides group insurance for ABA members—and the American Bar Foundation, which sponsors research activities in law.

The ABA also provides a social outlet for its members through which members meet to freely exchange ideas and experiences that add to the human dimension in the practice of law. See also, Bernard G. Segal's essay on the American Bar Association.

It is a matter of common knowledge that the American Bar Association is a representative body composed of members of the bar from every part of the Union; an organization national in scope, whose purpose is to uphold and maintain the highest traditions of the legal profession.

CHRISTOPHER L. AVERY

The American Bar Association meeting at one of its annual conventions

Bernard G. Segal

American Bar Association

Founder Simeon E. Baldwin

Although some two-thirds of this country's founders who gathered in Philadelphia in 1787 to draft the Constitution of the United States were lawyers, a century later the lawyers of the nation still had not formed a national professional organization.

In 1878, at a meeting of the Connecticut Bar Association Simeon E. Baldwin, a practicing lawyer and professor at Yale—later to become chief justice of the Connecticut supreme court of errors, and after that governor of the state—made a motion that a committee be appointed to consider organizing a national association of American lawyers. The motion was approved, and 607 lawyers in the nation's forty-one states, at that time, and territories and the District of Columbia were sent invitations to attend an informal meeting in Saratoga, New York on August 21, 1878. Seventy-five lawyers from twenty-one states and the District of Columbia attended the meeting, and the American Bar Association was formed there with a membership of 289 from twenty-nine states.

The objects of the new association were "to advance the science of jurisprudence, promote the administration of justice, and uniformity of legislation throughout the Union to uphold the honor of the profession of law and encourage social intercourse among the members of the American Bar." The objects have remained essentially the same throughout the years, with the following additions: to uphold and defend the Constitution of the United States and maintain representative government; to apply the knowledge and experience of the profession to the promotion of the public good; and to correlate and promote the actions of the bar organizations in the nation with these purposes and in the interest of the profession and of the public.

The ABA grew slowly during its early years, certainly due in part to the selective basis on which membership was solicited and granted. By 1900, after twenty-two years, the ABA still had only 1,540 members, or 1.3 percent of the country's lawyers. By 1930, although the membership had increased to 27,000, that was still only about 18 percent of the nation's lawyers.

In 1912, the ABA had begun a new phase of membership policy. While it continued to be selective, it did campaign to enlarge the membership. Nevertheless, the general membership at its annual meeting on August 27 that year, although approving the "inadvertent" election by the executive committee of the first three "colored attorneys" ever to become members of the ABA, declared that "it has never been contemplated that colored men were to be members of this Association." In 1914, the ABA adopted a resolution that all applications for membership must state the race and sex of the applicant. Not until thirty years later, at the annual meeting in 1943, did the ABA adopt a resolution that "membership in the American Bar Association is not dependent upon race, creed or color." Today black lawyers participate actively and occupy key posts in the ABA.

During the first half-century of the ABA its principal activities were sponsoring reforms in legal education and standards of admission to the bar and preparing and recommending uniform laws for adoption by the states. The ABA took the lead in forming and securing financing for the National Conference of Commissioners on Uniform State Laws, which over the years has been responsible for formulation of the large number of uniform laws adopted by the states. The ABA has actively participated in promoting and lobbying for passage of uniform laws.

Up to 1936 the ABA had operated entirely autonomously, having little relationship with state and local bar associations and other professional organizations. In that year it adopted a new constitution, which provided that its governing body, the House of Delegates, would consist of delegates from state and local bar associations and various other professional groups and official bodies. This was a highly effective step toward federation of the ABA with other bar associations and professional groups throughout the country.

Between 1936 and 1950, the ABA became increasingly active in movements to improve the administration of justice. In 1939, it put its support behind the American Judicature Society plan for merit selection of judges, enlisting the aid of state and local bar associations. This combination of components of the organized bar has operated so effectively that, despite the opposition of powerful political leaders, today more than forty states have merit-selection procedures for judges in some of their courts, and many states have merit selection in all their courts. At the same time, the ABA also became active in recommending and helping to secure improvements in our judicial system that would make court structure, procedures, quality, and service more effective.

In recent years there has been enormous growth in membership, and concurrently the scope and influence of the ABA have grown. While intensified recruiting has undoubtedly helped produce this result, other factors have also been significant. One has been the much greater scope of ABA programs. Another contributing factor has been the fact that the media gives national coverage when the ABA president or the chairpersons of sections, commissions, and committees or other ABA representatives appear before congressional and state legislative committees or otherwise make public statements—and also when statements are made by distinguished jurists, legislators, and others who attend the ABA meetings. The major factor, however, is the enormous increase in the number of lawyers currently practicing in the United States contrasted with only little over a decade ago. The number of attorneys in private practice today—constituting 70 percent of the bar of this country—has increased 55 percent since 1970.

The ABA is now the largest professional organization in the world. As of February 1982 it had more than 292,000 regular members plus approximately 40,000 law-student members, comprising approximately 55 percent of the lawyers in the country. Almost 50 percent of the regular members of the ABA are in the Young Lawyers Division—that is, they are under thirty-six years of age.

The operating revenue of the ABA for fiscal year 1980–81 was $31,500,000. In addition, during that year its Fund for Public Education received approximately $7.5 million for ABA education and public service projects. The ABA staff of 600 is divided between its headquarters in Chicago and its offices in Washington, D.C.

And do as adversaries do in law,
Strive mightily, but eat and drink
as friends.

SHAKESPEARE

The policymaking body of the ABA is its House of Delegates, with 385 members, who are delegates primarily from state and local bar associations and the bar associations of the District of Columbia and Puerto Rico. Other professional organizations represented by delegates include: the American Judicature Society, American Law Institute, Association of American Law Schools, Conference of Chief Justices, Judge Advocates Association, National Association of Attorneys General, National Association of Women Lawyers, National Bar Association, National Conference of Bar Examiners, National Conference of Commissioners on Uniform State Laws, National District Attorneys Association, National Legal Aid and Defender Association, and organizations of lawyers practicing in specialized fields. In addition, the membership includes the attorney general of the United States and the director of the administrative office of the U.S. courts. The general ABA membership has opportunities to vote for delegates, both for a representative from their own state, known as a state delegate, and for one from several states comprising a district, known as an assembly delegate.

The House of Delegates elects the officers of the association and the members of the board of governors—in both instances upon nomination by the state delegates, although nominations may also be made by nominating petitions by varying numbers of ABA members. Such petitions are rare. The house meets twice a year to conduct the business of the ABA. The debates are often intense and controversial. Between meetings of the house, the board of governors manages the affairs of the ABA, exercising considerable authority, since the house meets only biennially.

Much of the work of the ABA is done through its sections and divisions, comprised of ABA members who join them voluntarily, and of standing and special committees and commissions, whose members are appointed by the ABA president-elect, with terms to begin when the president-elect becomes ABA president. Today there are twenty-five sections and three divisions, each with its own substructure of committees appointed by the chairperson. The respective memberships range from 2,091 in the Section on Public Contract Law to 45,000 in the Section on Corporation, Banking, and Business Law. Sections cover most of the areas of substantive law—for example, antitrust law, criminal justice, and taxation; and also more general subjects—for example, economics of law practice, and legal education and admission to the bar. The divisions are: the Judicial Administration Division, subdivided into conferences, each representing a different group of judges; the Young Lawyers Division; and the Law Student Division. The commissions were created to permit appointment of nonlawyers to serve on them; their subjects are broad, ranging for example, from the Commission on Public Understanding about the Law to the Commission on Evaluation of Professional Standards. The ABA standing and special committees normally have seven to nine members each, although they sometimes have greater numbers. The functions of the committees cover the full range of activities of the ABA.

The ABA is one of the largest law publishers in the United States in terms of the number of different publications it produces and their frequency. In addition to the *ABA Journal*, its flagship monthly publication, the ABA publishes magazines, newsletters, scholarly journals, books, booklets, and brochures on behalf of the various constituent entities. The ABA staff of 600 has been referred to,

We rate the judge who is only a lawyer, higher than the judge who is only a philosopher.

CUTHBERT W. POUND

The monthly *American Bar Association Journal* is only one of numerous publications of the American Bar Association.

but most of the work for the association is accomplished by member volunteers who contribute an untold number of hours.

The general membership constitutes the assembly at the annual meeting, which considers amendments to the ABA constitution and resolutions submitted by ABA members. The amendments or resolutions proposed to the assembly are referred to the House of Delegates. If the assembly and the house ultimately disagree—which does not occur often—a mail referendum of all ABA members is held.

At the annual meeting most of the sections, divisions, committees, and commissions hold sessions in addition to the large number of special meetings, lectures, programs, and social events for lawyers and their families. Attendance at a recent annual meeting was 7,953 members, with a total number, including family and guests, of 13,315. On the other hand, the midyear meeting consists primarily of meetings of the House of Delegates and business sessions of the sections, divisions, committees, and commissions. Accordingly, at the last midyear meeting only 1,554 members were present, and total attendance was 2,593.

Three affiliates of the association are necessary for its daily operations and attainment of its goals: the American Bar Endowment, the American Bar Foundation, and the Fund for Public Education.

The profession of the law is the only aristocratic element which can be amalgamated without violence with the natural elements of democracy . . . I cannot believe that a republic could subsist if the influence of lawyers in public business did not increase in proportion to the power of the people.

DE TOCQUEVILLE

The American Bar Endowment was created in 1942 as a not-for-profit organization. Its affairs are managed by an independent ten-member board of directors elected by the ABA members at their annual meeting.

Every member of the ABA is automatically a member of the endowment, and as such may purchase life or disability insurance in any one or more of the five group-insurance programs the endowment administers for this purpose. The member names the beneficiary but agrees to donate to the endowment all dividends and experience credits under the policy. Revenues from these policies are the source of the endowment's funds.

The endowment provides the primary funding for the American Bar Foundation and a large amount of funding for the law-related public service projects administered through the ABA's Fund for Public Education. The endowment also makes grants to other tax-exempt legal organizations, such as the National Legal Aid and Defender Association, and on occasion to nonlegal groups for law-related activities, a typical one having been the Boy Scouts of America. The foundation's funds come primarily from the dividends and experience credits of 70,000 ABA members insured in from one to three of the five group-insurance programs the endowment administers for this purpose.

The American Bar Foundation is the legal research affiliate of the ABA. Its purpose is to conduct research that will enlarge the understanding of law and legal institutions and improve their functioning. The foundation's staff of lawyers, social scientists, and technologists and the annual visiting law professors are skilled in empirical research as well as traditional legal scholarship. Their numerous publications circulated throughout the bar cover a tremendous diversity of subjects. Besides the funding by the American Bar Endowment already mentioned, the foundation also receives other funding through the ABA: dues from the 2,980 fellows of the foundation (additional fellows are elected by the board each year) and grants for particular research projects from private foundations and government agencies. The board of governors of the ABA constitutes the membership of the foundation—which, however, operates with an independent board of directors, having as ex officio members the three principal officers of the ABA and the president of the endowment.

The Fund for Public Education was created by the ABA in 1961 as the instrumentality through which the ABA solicits and receives tax-deductible grants and gifts in support of law-related public service activities. Of the $7.5 million received by the fund in a recent fiscal year, $2.5 million came from the American Bar Endowment and the rest from foundations, government grants, corporate donations, and similar sources. The ABA officers, other than the chairman of the House of Delegates and the members of the board of governors, serve in the same capacities for the Fund for Public Education.

The ABA functions in three major areas. The first is to work for improvement and education of the legal profession, a function of the ABA since its inception. The second is to work for improvement of the instrumentalities of justice and, thereby, the U.S. legal system. This aspect has received increasing emphasis over the years and now is a major share of ABA activities. The third is to play a leadership role in the pursuit of a just and ordered society. The last area—which some writers consider the "higher calling of the bar"—and which the ABA became substantially involved in less than fifteen years ago, merits some elaboration.

        Individual lawyers have always played key roles in efforts to solve great
issues facing our nation. It has already been noted that two-thirds of the members
of the Constitutional Convention in 1787 were lawyers. Twenty-three of the nation's thirty-nine presidents have been lawyers. Lawyers typically have comprised
well over a majority of the U.S. Senate and about half of the House of Representatives. Nevertheless, during most of its history, the ABA has tended to stay aloof
from the major social issues of the time, despite the importunings of distinguished
leaders of the bar over the years.

        In 1963, forty-six lawyers—including past and current leaders of the
ABA and other professional legal organizations—triggered the action of President
John F. Kennedy in convening a White House conference of lawyers on the subject of civil rights, out of which grew the Lawyers' Committee for Civil Rights Under Law. One of the first actions of the committee was to open, in the state of Mississippi, with the cooperation of the officials of the Mississippi state bar even in
that day, a pioneering law office to advise and represent, without charge, both
black and white citizens who were denied their civil rights. The committee was
broadly based and operated on many fronts. It was a powerful lobby for the Civil
Rights Act of 1964 (42 U.S.C.A. § 2000a et seq.). Promptly after the appointment
of the lawyers' committee the ABA created a special committee on civil rights and
racial unrest to cooperate with the lawyers' committee—a significant development.

        Another significant milestone in ABA activity took place in 1965 when
the ABA assumed the lead in vigorously supporting the creation of a new and comprehensive federally supported program of legal services for the poor; this was an
enormous expansion of its long-time activities in the legal aid field.

        Beginning in the late 1960s, presidents of the ABA have often devoted a
major portion of their programs to the overriding social issues of our time. Accordingly, today ABA projects cover not only virtually every area of professional
performance and many of the problems confronting our system of justice, they
also increasingly address the pressing issues of our society. Limitations of space
will permit review of only a small proportion of them.

Improvements in the system of justice

        One of the ABA's pioneering and most successful efforts has been its pro-
gram to improve the quality of the Federal judiciary. In 1953, the ABA became actively involved in the merit selection of Federal judges at the nomination level.
With President Dwight D. Eisenhower's approval, Attorney General Herbert
Brownell and Deputy Attorney General William P. Rogers agreed to ask the ABA
standing committee on Federal judiciary to investigate and report on the competence, integrity, and judicial temperament of every person under consideration for
nomination as a Federal judge. Since then every president and every attorney general has followed this procedure, with vacillations only with respect to nominations for the Supreme Court—and this phase too now appears to be satisfactorily
resolved. In the past quarter-century rarely has a president nominated a person
whom the committee has reported as "not qualified." Indeed, every president, attorney general, and deputy attorney general has been gratified when a prospective
nominee has been rated "well qualified" or "exceptionally well qualified." There

*The wise know that foolish
legislation is a rope of sand
which perishes in the
twisting. . . . The law is only a
memorandum. . . . Our statute
is a currency which we stamp
with our own portrait.*

RALPH WALDO EMERSON

can be no doubt that this cooperative effort has contributed materially to enhancing the quality of the judges in the U.S. courts.

Starting in 1953 the organized bar began to work for much needed salary increases for Federal judges, so the salaries would be large enough to attract first-rate lawyers to the bench and keep them there. In the first year of the effort, Congress was persuaded to increase the very low salaries of all Federal justices and judges by 40–50 percent. Progress has been made, but in recent years the cost of living has outstripped the increases in judicial salaries, resulting in an inordinate number of resignations and difficulty in attracting successful lawyers from private practice to the bench.

In 1964, the ABA sponsored formation of a National Judicial College of Judges to educate trial judges at all levels. The ABA also has a continuing project dealing with continuing appellate education.

In 1970, in the first recorded briefing for the press ever held in the Supreme Court conference room, with Chief Justice Warren E. Burger in attendance, the ABA president announced that the association, joined by the American Judicature Society and the Institute for Judicial Administration, was creating the Institute for Court Management as the nation's first training facility to produce a corps of skilled court managers. The chief justice had said that unavailability of adequately trained court administrators and other officials was one of the greatest handicaps of both the Federal and the state judicial systems. The institute has broadened its functioning to conduct advanced and continuing education programs for court personnel. It also publishes *The Justice System Journal: A Management Review* and conducts a variety of other activities to aid court officials and employees. The institute now has 360 graduates of the court executive development program: seven are circuit executives in U.S. circuits, fifteen are administrators of state judicial systems, and the rest are administrators or clerks of various courts. Seventy-eight hundred certificates have been issued to those completing education programs.

Also in 1970, with the urging and the vigorous support of Chief Justice Warren E. Burger, the ABA established the Commission on Correctional Facilities and Services. To mount a national effort to improve the abysmal correctional and rehabilitative procedures in the nation's prisons and to enlist citizens' support for such reform. The members of the commission were national leaders in a variety of disciplines.

Some of the ABA's most important activities in recent years have involved formulation and promotion of comprehensive standards. The ABA's criminal justice standards, representing more than a decade of effort, have been characterized by Chief Justice Warren E. Burger as "the single most comprehensive and probably the most monumental undertaking in the field of justice ever attempted by the legal profession." Similar comprehensive standards of juvenile justice were sponsored and completed by the Institute of Judicial Administration and the ABA. They constitute a landmark contribution toward improving the juvenile justice system in the United States.

At the 1906 ABA annual meeting Dean Roscoe Pound of the Harvard Law School delivered his now celebrated address, "The Causes of Popular Dissatisfaction With the Administration of Justice." It received a chilly reception at the

Chief Justice Warren E. Burger

Reformer Roscoe Pound

time. Seventy years later, in 1976, at the instigation of Chief Justice Burger, the ABA, the Conference of Chief Justices, and the Judicial Conference of the United States jointly sponsored "The Pound Conference" to deal with "the causes of popular dissatisfaction with the administration of justice." With national leaders from all branches of the legal profession attending, the conference probed the problems and urged reforms in our judicial and legal systems. A follow-up task force summarized a long list of critical recommendations for the years ahead.

More recently the ABA, particularly through its Action Commission to Reduce Court Costs, has been making major efforts to improve the judicial system by addressing the pressing problems of delay, court costs, and the need for alternative forms of dispute resolution.

Equal access to justice

A major concern of the association today is to ensure equal access to justice by improving the delivery of legal services to all in need of them. Legal services have long been unavailable to the poor. As late as 1964, only $5 million per year was being spent by government and privately for legal aid for some thirty million people in poverty circumstances throughout the nation. In 1974 the association was influential in persuading Congress to establish the Legal Services Corporation, an independent agency created to provide legal services to the poor. In 1981, the corporation received an appropriation of $321 million, and the program financed the employment of more than 7,000 lawyers representing the poor in every state—an amazing achievement for only fifteen years.

When the Reagan administration announced soon after assuming office an intention to discontinue the Legal Services Corporation, the ABA led an effective campaign in opposition, which resulted in defeating this objective in Congress. Unfortunately, however, the appropriation was reduced by 25 percent to $241 million, requiring a drastic reduction in legal services for the poor; and the danger that the corporation will be discontinued remains acute. The situation calls for the greatest vigilance and effort of the ABA and other segments of the organized bar.

Recently the ABA initiated a pro bono activities project to stimulate state and local bar organizations to persuade their members to supply free legal services to the poor on a regional basis.

Although today every ninth American is elderly, relatively few have had access to legal services. In 1978, the ABA established a commission of nationally known experts in the field of aging to identify priority needs for action and to work with state and local bar committees to encourage and develop a wide variety of services for the elderly.

In 1973, the ABA established a commission on the mentally disabled, which now publishes *The Mentally Disabled Reporter*, the only publication reporting comprehensive legal developments in this field. The commission has also furnished start-up costs and technical aid for a variety of lawyer-sponsored programs to assist the mentally disabled, including those in need of immediate after-care facilities.

Through its Young Lawyers Division, the ABA has launched a National Legal Resource Center to improve the quality of legal representation for children

The first element of good government, therefore, being the virtue and intelligence of the human beings composing the community, the most important point of excellence which any form of government can possess is to promote the virtue and intelligence of the people themselves.

J.S. MILL

and to foster interdisciplinary cooperation for treatment and protection of abused and neglected children. The center also provides support for many state and local bar associations in their own recently initiated programs to alleviate child abuse and neglect.

Another project in this area is the ABA's victim/witness assistance project, which is seeking to work out a comprehensive strategy for dealing with the diverse problems of the victim and the witness in court proceedings.

As the cost of legal services has risen greatly with inflation, many other people, in the middle as well as lower income levels, have been inadequately served. In response the ABA greatly increased its efforts to improve the lawyer referral services operated principally by local bar associations. These services refer persons in the low- and middle-income groups to a cooperating lawyer competent and willing to handle the particular problem involved at especially moderate fees. The ABA has also paid increased attention to development of plans for prepaid legal services programs that would provide ongoing legal services at low cost for members of large groups, such as unions and other organizations.

Assuring the highest standards of ethical conduct and professional competence

Early in its existence the ABA recognized that the bar would be permitted to continue to regulate itself only as long as it did so responsibly. Accordingly, the establishment and maintenance of high standards of professional conduct have been a central mission of the ABA throughout its history. In 1908, it adopted the Canons of Professional Ethics, a comprehensive set of rules to guide and control the professional conduct of lawyers. Enforcement of the canons necessarily rested with state and local bar associations, subject to a right of appeal to the courts by a lawyer who had been disciplined.

In 1969, the ABA adopted the Code of Professional Responsibility to replace the Canons of Professional Ethics, which by then had been found to be inadequate and outdated.

Necessarily, such review and revision must be continuing. Accordingly, the ABA has proposed a comprehensive revision of the code, called Model Rules of Professional Conduct, which have been vigorously debated at the ABA and at state and local bar association levels throughout the country. The House of Delegates has already voted that the new rules should take the form of the Restatements of the American Law Institute.

While enforcement is by state and local bar associations (with courts in some states having assumed closer direction of the process in recent years), the ABA through its National Center for Professional Responsibility, continues to serve as a nationwide resource center for information on professional responsibility, ethics, unauthorized practice, and clients' securities standards. It maintains a national discipline data bank of information on all lawyers who have been publicly disciplined. The data bank also develops criteria for evaluating disciplinary enforcement standards.

The ABA is certified by the U.S. Department of Health and Human Services as the sole national accrediting agency for law schools. In most states only graduates of an ABA-approved law school are permitted to take the bar examination; 170 law schools have this accreditation today.

In recent years the ABA has been increasingly active with respect to law student training and the role of law schools in developing lawyer competency.

Since 1947 the ABA has also expressed a strong commitment to continuing legal education for lawyers, primarily, although not exclusively, in conjunction with the American Law Institute. The ABA National Institute-Seminar also conducts programs on current topics in conjunction with the relevant ABA sections.

The ABA policy during the first sixty-five years of its existence against the admission of black lawyers as members has changed entirely in recent years. The National Bar Association, comprised of black lawyers, is now affiliated with the ABA and has a delegate in the House of Delegates, which also has other black members. Shortly after the Lawyers' Committee for Civil Rights Under Law commenced its activities, a group of ABA members succeeded in having the House of Delegates create the Section of Individual Rights and Responsibilities for the primary purpose of dealing with problems created by discrimination against minorities and women. A black lawyer was elected chairman of the section, and black lawyers have other key assignments throughout the ABA.

In 1968, less than one percent of the lawyers in the country were black, and most blacks desiring to become lawyers were unable to secure a legal education. To help remedy the underrepresentation of disadvantaged groups in the legal profession by expanding their opportunities to enter law school and become members of the bar, in 1968 the Council on Legal Education Opportunity (CLEO) was formed under the sponsorship of the ABA, the Association of American Law Schools, the National Bar Association, and the Law School Admissions Test Council. CLEO's first project was to increase black enrollment in law schools substantially. It provided intensive pre-law-school training to help make up the educational deficiencies that often handicapped minority students and to provide motivation for them to go to law school. CLEO then assisted these students to obtain scholarships or loan funds and also provided $1,500 a year for each student's living expenses while at law school—with funds originally coming from foundation grants and later from the Federal government. CLEO continues to provide assistance to black students and students of other racial minorities as well as to economically disadvantaged students who are white.

Increasing understanding of the law

The ABA has been deeply involved in efforts to promote public understanding of our legal system. In 1958 the ABA launched a national program to have a special day, May 1, each year to foster understanding of the role that law plays in the life of every citizen and to demonstrate the importance of equal justice under law. To give the event national emphasis, the ABA secured an official proclamation by President Eisenhower calling for observance throughout the nation. Later the day was proclaimed Law Day U.S.A. by a continuing joint resolution of the Congress, and each year since then it has been marked by a presidential proclamation. Each year the president of the ABA makes at least one major address on that day, and throughout the nation as many as 40,000 Law Day programs take place in schools, churches, and courthouses with ceremonies organized by business, professional, civic, communal, and other groups.

At the opening session of the 1970 annual meeting the ABA president announced that he had, with the approval of the board of governors, requested the chief justice of the U.S. Supreme Court to deliver a state of the judiciary address, to be an annual event thereafter, by analogy to the annual state of the union address of the president of the United States. The chief justice's message, carried by all three major television and radio networks, provided an unprecedented opportunity to express the major problems and needs of our judicial system to the public.

In announcing this innovation, the ABA president stated that he was suggesting to the chief justice or other presiding official of the highest court of each state that a comparable annual state of the judiciary address be instituted there, with delivery to the state legislature if this could be arranged. Such addresses have now been delivered in forty-three states and Guam, twenty-seven of them to the respective legislatures.

Recently the ABA created the Commission on Public Understanding about the Law, charged with initiating programs in four areas: identifying personal legal problems; learning where and how lawyers can assist in resolving these problems; understanding individual rights and responsibilities under the law; and obtaining a better grasp of the law in our society.

To help educators develop programs which cultivate an understanding of the law in America, the ABA created the Special Committee on Youth Education for Citizenship. Educators can now choose from over 2,000 classroom guides and films addressed to students at every grade level concerning a wide variety of law-related issues.

Providing leadership in the improvement of the law

The ABA has addressed numerous other current issues of vital concern to the American public, such as energy, environment, and housing, which have far-reaching legal ramifications. The ABA Special Commission on Energy Law, the Standing Committee on Environmental Law, and the Special Committee on Housing and Urban Development Law are actively analyzing and reporting on conditions and problems in their respective fields in relation to the complex issues of law involved.

The ABA also has been involved in streamlining Federal procedures to help make government more responsive to citizens' needs. For example, after the ABA's Commission on Law and Economy issued a comprehensive report on the way branches and agencies of the government approach and make economic decisions, many of the commission's recommendations were incorporated into legislative proposals. Formulating model legislative provisions is an ongoing task of ABA sections, committees, and commissions.

Serving as the national representative
of the legal profession

The ABA is a coordinating arm for a large variety of state, local, and specialized organizations of lawyers with which it maintains liaison. ABA representatives testify frequently before congressional committees on issues of important national concern. Its officers speak at national forums, conduct press conferences, and appear on national TV and radio to express their views on matters involving national and international issues. The president of the ABA travels continually throughout the nation, speaking to bar associations and other groups both in and out of the legal profession. The president-elect and the chairman of the House of Delegates perform similar functions.

There are two sorts of contests amongst men, the one managed by law, the other by force; and these are of that nature that where the one ends, the other always begins.

JOHN LOCKE

AMERICAN BAR CENTER The American Bar Center (ABC) is the building housing the headquarters of the American Bar Association, the American Bar Foundation, and the American Bar Endowment.

For descriptions of these organizations, see also, American Bar Association and American Bar Foundation.

AMERICAN BAR FOUNDATION The American Bar Foundation (ABF) was founded in 1952 to promote legal research for the purpose of improving and facilitating the administration of justice. The foundation also seeks to upgrade the legal profession through research and the improvement of legal education. Research on the delivery of legal services, professional ethics, the administration of criminal justice, business law, insurance law, the courts and judicial administration, legal education, and other such topics is conducted by the foundation staff, with the help of advisory committees of practicing lawyers, law faculty members, and nonlegal specialists

for major projects. Additional activities include the maintenance of the Cromwell Library, which houses proceedings and documents of the organized bar reports and special collections related to particular projects.

The foundation publishes the *Research Journal* (quarterly), reports treatises, and prints occasional papers on legal subjects. It holds an annual meeting in August in conjunction with the American Bar Association convention.

AMERICAN BATTLE MONUMENTS COMMISSION

The American Battle Monuments Commission is responsible for the design, construction, and permanent maintenance of military cemeteries and memorials on foreign soil, as well as for certain memorials on American soil. The commission controls the design and provides regulations for the erection of monuments, markers, and memorials in foreign countries by other U.S. citizens and organizations, public or private.

Created by act of March 4, 1923 (42 Stat. 1509), as amended, and its authority expanded

Good counsellors lack no clients.

SHAKESPEARE

The U.S. flag flies over the military cemetery at Suresnes, France, where U.S. soldiers who died in France during World War II are buried. The American Battle Monuments Commission maintains the cemetery.

American Battle Monuments Commission, Washington, D.C., 20314

by subsequent legislation, the American Battle Monuments Commission is administered by the secretary under the guidance of the commissioners, who serve without pay (42 Stat. 1509; 36 U.S.C. 121-138b; 24 U.S.C. 279a).

The commission provides, upon request, to the general public the exact location and other information concerning place of interment or memorialization of the dead; best routes and modes of travel in-country to the cemeteries and memorials; and arranges for the placement of floral decorations at gravesites or the Tablets of the Missing. For next of kin and members of the immediate family, the commission also provides letters authorizing "nonfee" passports; escort service within the cemetery; color lithographs of cemeteries together with photographs of the appropriate gravesite or section of the Tablets of the Missing.

Source: *The United States Government Manual 1981/82* and/or *1982/83*.

The Law is what it is—a majestic edifice, sheltering all of us, each stone of which rests on another.

JOHN GALSWORTHY

AMERICAN BLIND LAWYERS ASSOCIATION

The American Blind Lawyers Association (ABLA) is a national, nonprofit membership organization established in 1969. Its purposes are to provide a forum for discussion of the special problems encountered by blind persons licensed to practice law and of blind students in training for the legal profession; to protect the interests of blind members of the legal profession; to acquire, preserve, and maintain law libraries and periodicals of special interest to blind lawyers and blind law students; to promote the production and dissemination of information concerning legal materials in braille or recorded forms suitable for use by blind lawyers and blind law students; and to do all lawful things necessary or desirable for the advancement of the legal profession. Any licensed blind attorney is eligible for active membership; and any blind law student or prospective blind law student is eligible for student membership. Anyone else who is interested in supporting the purposes of the organization is eligible for associate membership.

Each year (usually in July), the ABLA sponsors a national membership conference in a different major city. These conferences feature individual presentations, panel and group discussions, appropriate exhibits and demonstrations, and an open business meeting. Recent presentations by blind lawyers have related to the blind attorney as a tax specialist, as an elected judge, as a professor of a prestigious law school,

as a state prosecutor, as Federal departmental counsel, as a city attorney, and as a private practitioner. Other presentations of great interest to blind attorneys and law students have related to such topics as the taking of law school admission tests and bar examinations, the establishment of a private law practice, obtaining employment as other than a private practitioner, the compiling of a central legal index of all braille and recorded legal materials, actions to be taken by the ABLA in expansion of employment opportunities, and the provision of important recorded material to all members on a continuing and regular basis. All of the presentations, discussions, and business meetings during the recent national conferences have been recorded on tape and are available to members.

Each month, the ABLA publishes and distributes to its members a cassette-record publication entitled, "Cases on Cassette," which contains "Supreme Court Report" and "What's New in the Law," from the *Journal of the American Bar Association*, as well as selected short articles of general interest on a wide variety of subjects. Another major project operated under the auspices of ABLA is the Gerritt Smith Van Valkenburgh Legal Index, administered by the Tulsa County Bar Auxiliary. This index is not a library, but rather a central source of information concerning what legal materials are available in braille or on tape and where such material can be obtained.

AMERICAN BUSINESS LAW ASSOCIATION

The American Business Law Association (ABLA) was founded in 1923 to promote and encourage scholarship and superior teaching of business law and other legal studies in colleges and universities outside of law school. The association encourages friendly and cooperative relations among teachers and scholars in the area of legal studies, fosters understanding between university administrators and those who teach and research in the field, and supports high ethical standards in all aspects of business. The association represents the interests of its members in the academic community, maintains liaison with related associations and operates a placement service for business law teachers. Meetings feature formal presentations, panels, workshops, and opportunities for informal exchange of information. Its members are teachers in business law and related fields. The association embraces eleven regional associations, holds annual meetings, and publishes *American Business Law Journal* (quarterly) and a newsletter.

Norman Dorsen

American Civil Liberties Union

The American Civil Liberties Union (ACLU) is an important organization in the United States dedicated to the protection of individual liberty. It was founded in 1920 by a distinguished group that included Jane Addams, Roger Baldwin, Felix Frankfurter, Helen Keller, and Norman Thomas. The principles that the ACLU defends are expressed in the Bill of Rights:

- The right to free expression—above all, the freedom to dissent from the official view and majority opinion.

Jane Addams

Roger Baldwin

Norman Thomas

Felix Frankfurter

Helen Keller

215

- The right to equal treatment regardless of race, sex, religion, national origin, or physical handicap.
- The right to due process in encounters with government institutions—courts, schools, police, bureaucracy—and with the repositories of great private power.
- The right to be let alone—to be secure from spying, from the unwarranted collection of personal information, and from interference in private lives.

These principles have led the ACLU to participation in numerous controversial cases. It represented John Scopes when he was fired for teaching evolution; it fought for the rights of Nicola Sacco and Bartolomeo Vanzetti; it defended the Scottsboro Boys, who were denied a fair trial for alleged rape; it fought the Customs Bureau when it banned James Joyce's *Ulysses*; and it opposed the censorship of the Pentagon Papers.

The ACLU has supported religious and racial minorities and the right of labor to organize, and it has opposed the arbitrary treatment of persons in closed institutions—such as mental patients, prisoners, military personnel, and students.

The ACLU has participated in the civil rights and women's rights movements, the protests against the undeclared Vietnam War, and the proposed impeachment of President Nixon for violations of civil liberty.

The ACLU represented these individuals and groups not because it is always sympathetic to their cause, but because it defends the constitutional rights of all, especially the weak, the unpopular, and the despised. A recent example was its defense of the right of American Nazis to demonstrate peacefully in Skokie, Illinois. Although the courts ultimately upheld free expression, the controversy temporarily cost the ACLU members and financial support.

The ACLU has more than 200,000 members organized in affiliates and chapters in all fifty states. These units are affiliated with the national organization through revenue sharing, participation in national policy decisions, and united action on national goals. Each affiliate is autonomous in electing its board of directors and hiring its staff. A cardinal precept of the ACLU and all its units is nonpartisanship; the organization does not endorse or oppose candidates for office.

The national headquarters of the ACLU is in New York City, and it maintains a legislative office in Washington, D.C., and regional offices in Atlanta and Denver. It also sponsors special projects, including those on women's rights, reproductive freedom, children's rights, capital punishment, prisoners' rights, national security, and civil liberties. The ACLU participates in about 6,000 cases annually, plus thousands of administrative actions and negotiations. This work is performed by about 300 full-time staff members and thousands of volunteers.

In 1970 Chief Justice Earl Warren extolled the role of the ACLU in defending individual liberty:

The ACLU has stood foursquare against the recurring tides of hysteria that from time to time threaten freedom everywhere. . . Indeed, it is difficult to appreciate how far our freedoms might have eroded had it not been for the Union's valiant representation in the courts of the constitutional rights of people of all persuasion.

Bibliography: *ACLU Annual Reports*, 7 vols. (January 1920–December 1969); D. Johnson, *The Challenge to American Freedoms: World War I and the Rise of the American Civil Liberties Union* (1963); C. L. Markmann, *The Noblest Cry: A History of the American Civil Liberties Union* (1965).

The best use of good laws is to teach men to trample bad laws under their feet.

WENDELL PHILLIPS

Not what has been done under a statute, but what may reasonably be done under it is the test of its validity.

BENJAMIN N. CARDOZO

AMERICAN COLLEGE OF LEGAL MEDICINE

Founded in 1955, the American College of Legal Medicine describes itself as the oldest and most prestigious organization in the United States devoted to problems at the interface of law and medicine. Its membership—made up of professionals in law, medicine, osteopathy, and some of the other allied sciences—is concerned with medical jurisprudence and forensic medicine. Medical jurisprudence deals with the impact of laws and legal processes upon the practice of medicine. Forensic medicine, on the other hand, is concerned with the introduction of medical science into courts of law to resolve legal disputes.

The college has organized and implemented a number of programs for the development and dissemination, to its members and to the medical and legal professions in general, of information of a medical-legal nature. These programs include: the annual convocation, which is open to members and nonmembers and held each May in a resort-type area to afford relaxation and camaraderie as well as education and dissemination of information; a midwinter scientific meeting, which covers topics of current medical-legal interest (held at a motel near a centrally located airport and open to members and nonmembers); and the Letourneau and Schwartz awards, which are given annually to the best papers by law and medical students, respectively, to encourage scholarly activity in the medical-legal area. Various committees of the college have engaged in the development, drafting, and publication of other materials, including a recommended medical-legal curriculum and a textbook to accompany its use in graduate medical and legal education.

The college publishes the *Journal of Legal Medicine*, which is a scholarly law review and scientifically-oriented journal that is published quarterly for the membership and available to nonmembers by subscription; *Legal Aspects of Medical Practice*, which is a monthly journal consisting of short articles and other materials of current medical-legal interest that is sent to the membership and under controlled subscription to over 100,000 American physicians and is also available to others by subscription; *Newsletter of the College*, which is issued periodically for members of the college and contains meeting notices, reports of meetings and from various committees, book reviews, and occasional brief articles; and *Membership Directory*, which is issued annually and includes brief biographical listings of members and geographic and specialty listings.

AMERICAN COLLEGE OF PROBATE COUNSEL

Founded in 1948, the American College of Probate Counsel (ACPL) is an association of attorneys who specialize in probate law.

The college publishes *Newsletter* (quarterly), *Membership Roster* (annually), plus studies, charts, and other materials of interest to members. It holds a yearly spring meeting as well as annual meetings in August.

AMERICAN COLLEGE OF TRIAL LAWYERS

Founded in 1950, the American College of Trial Lawyers (ACTL) is an honorary society for practicing and former trial lawyers.

A variety of trial advocacy programs are carried out by the college, which has fifty-one state groups. In addition to practicing trial lawyers, the membership includes former trial lawyers not holding elective and appointive posts and judges in courts of record. The group holds annual meetings.

AMERICAN CONVENTION ON HUMAN RIGHTS, 1969

See Human Rights.

AMERICAN CORRECTIONAL ASSOCIATION

The American Correctional Association (ACA) was founded in 1870 to exert a positive influence on the shaping of national and international correctional policy, and to promote the professional development of persons working within all aspects of corrections. The association seeks to upgrade standards in the selection of correctional personnel; the provision of adequate facilities; and the care, education, training, supervision, and employment of inmates. The association also supports the study of the causes and prevention of crime and juvenile delinquency. Research programs, the compilation of correctional statistics, the presentation of awards as well as the operation of a placement service are among association activities. The membership includes correctional administrators, wardens, superintendents, members of prison and parole boards, probation officers, psychologists, sociologists, and other individuals and institutions in correctional fields.

The association includes state chapters. It publishes *Corrections Today* (bimonthly), a bimonthly newsletter, an annual directory, *Proceedings* (annual), as well as a number of books on correctional topics. It holds meetings twice annually.

AMERICAN CRIMINAL JUSTICE ASSOCIATION—LAMBDA ALPHA EPSILON

The American Criminal Justice Association—Lambda Alpha Epsilon (ACJA-LAE) was formed in 1937 to promote the assistance and understanding of the goals and problems of criminal justice agencies and to upgrade professional standards in the field. The association sponsors seminars and workshops, compiles statistics, presents key awards for scholastic achievement, and conducts a scholastic research paper competition. The membership includes persons employed in or honorably retired from, a career in a field related to criminal justice, students enrolled in college or university programs in the field, and persons involved in volunteer work who are approved by the Executive Board of Grand Chapter.

The association holds annual meetings each spring. It publishes the *Journal* (quarterly) and the *Newsletter* (quarterly).

AMERICAN DIGEST SYSTEM®

A multivolume set of books that arranges by topic summaries of decisions, originally reported chronologically in the various units of the National Reporter System. □

All written opinions on a similar point of law can be found under a specific subject classification. The system contains over 400 topics, each of which corresponds to a legal concept (CONTRACTS, for example). Cases decided during the period from 1658 to 1896 are reported in the CENTURY DIGEST. Eight DECENNIAL DIGESTS classify cases reported during the periods 1897 to 1905, and in ten-year periods thereafter. Until the next ten-year period is completed in 1986, summaries of reported cases from 1976 to date are found in the annual volumes of the GENERAL DIGEST, 5th Series. The American Digest System functions as a master index to all reported case law.

AMERICAN ENTERPRISE INSTITUTE FOR PUBLIC POLICY RESEARCH

Founded in 1943, the American Enterprise Institute for Public Policy Research (AEI) is a nonpartisan research and educational organization that is dedicated to the assistance of policy makers, scholars, businesspersons, the press, and the public through the provision of research relating

These pages from the *Eighth Decennial Digest* illustrate how the digests provide a convenient subject-classification system for legal cases.

to national and international issues. In the interest of promoting the competition of ideas, the institute (which is supported by foundation grants and contributions from individuals and corporations) does not take official positions on policy issues. Areas studied include government regulation, economics, energy, health, foreign policy, defense, politics, social processes, and law and legislation. A Council of Academic Advisors, a program-priorities advisory committee and panels of distinguished scholars monitor the programs and studies of the organization.

The institute publishes *Public Opinion* (bimonthly), *Regulation* (bimonthly), *Economist* (monthly), and the *Foreign Policy and Defense Review*. It also publishes books and monographs and produces a monthly television series. The board of trustees meets annually.

AMERICAN FOREIGN LAW ASSOCIATION
The American Foreign Law Association was formed in 1925 to promote the study and practice of international law. The association sponsors research and education programs, monthly luncheon discussions, and an International Law Weekend. The association serves as a consultant to the United Nations Economic and Social Council. The membership is composed of educators and practicing attorneys in the field of private and public international law.

The association has branch offices in Chicago and Philadelphia. It publishes the *American Journal of Comparative Law* (quarterly) and a triennial newsletter. It holds annual meetings.

AMERICAN INDIAN LAW CENTER
The American Indian Law Center (AILC) was founded in 1970 to provide assistance of a broad legal nature, primarily in the areas of research and training to Indian tribes and public and private agencies. The center assists tribes in making legal decisions, in ensuring that tribal justice comports with the Indian Civil Rights Act (25 U.S.C.A. § 1301 et seq. [1968]) by serving as a consultant to the National Indian Court Judges Association, and by planning and conducting national training programs for tribal judges and prosecutors. The center provides admissions advice, financial assistance, tutorial aids, and placement services to students through the Special Scholarship Program in Law for American Indians; it also conducts a summer prelaw session for American Indians who are interested in attending law school. The center conducts research in basic Indian law, sponsors conferences and seminars, and supports a library. The center, which has a staff of Indian Law School gradu-

ates and attorneys, is a branch of the University of New Mexico Law School.

The center publishes the *American Indian Law Newsletter* (monthly) and manuals for tribal prosecutors and judges on Indian criminal court procedures and other legal subjects.

AMERICAN JUDGES ASSOCIATION
According to the constitution of the American Judges Association, membership "shall be open to all present and former Judges, by whatever title known, provided that such a traditional judicial function. . . . The objective and purpose of this Association shall be to promote and improve the effective administration of justice, to maintain the status of and the independence of the judiciary and to provide a forum for the continuing education of its members and the interchange of ideas of a judicial nature among all Judges."

Formed in 1960 the activities of the association include support of the American Academy of Judicial Education, the presentation of an annual Award of Merit, the sponsorship of workshops, and the maintenance of a library. The association has the following committees: Civil Court Operations; Clinical Treatment of Misdemeanants; Court Administration, Rules, and Procedures; Counsel for Indigent Misdemeanants; Driver Improvement School; Ethics and Grievances; Independence of the Judiciary; Insurance and Retirement; Judicial Bibliography; Judicial Training; Jurisdiction; Law Day; Night Courts; Parents and Juvenile Offenders; Presiding Judges; Probation; Selection, Tenure and Compensation; Sentencing Procedures; Survey of Courts; and Traffic Offenses.

The association publishes *Benchers Briefs* (monthly) and *Court Review* (quarterly). It holds an annual and midyear meeting.

AMERICAN JUDICATURE SOCIETY
The American Judicature Society (AJS) was founded in 1913 to promote the effective administration of justice. The society conducts empirical research, holds citizen conferences and seminars, maintains an information and consultation service, and operates a library of 2,000 volumes on judicial administration. The society works to combat congestion and delay in the court system and helps coordinate state efforts to police the judiciary through the Center for Judicial Conduct Organizations. Awards are presented for contributions at the state and national levels. The members include lawyers, judges, law teachers, and governmental officials.

The society publishes *Judicature*, *Update* (bimonthly), and *Judicial Conduct Reporter* (quarterly).

Robert C. Berring

American Law Book Publishing

Law book publishing in the United States began late and developed slowly. The nature of legal materials, with a vast body of primary source materials and the dominance of the serial format, has created a quite specialized set of publishers and publications. Several law publishers have enhanced the special nature of law publishing by marketing their publications directly rather than through the national book trade. Legal publishers represent only a small percentage of American book publishing in dollar figures, but they have an importance that runs beyond total sales. Some argue that the patterns of legal publishing have affected the development of the substance of the law.

Although there have been some scholarly disputes over the number of American law books published in treatise form before the year 1800, even those who point to a wide range of titles admit that the material actually published was of small circulation. Such treatises frequently were reprints of English law books, or, if originals, often were compendiums of forms. There were no "legal publishers" as such, most being done by the printer/publishers of the day, for example, Matthew Carey and Robert Bell.

From the beginning, legal publishing wrestled with several problems. There is a need to constantly update materials. Law is always changing. Publishers have used supplementary volumes, pocket parts, pamphlet supplements, and now a looseleaf format to meet this need. Another problem is the multiplicity of jurisdictions in the United States. Any text runs the risk of being either too general or too specific.

It has been frequently remarked, with great propriety, that a voluminous code of laws is one of the inconveniences necessarily connected with the advantages of a free government.

ALEXANDER HAMILTON

Systematic legal publication began with the reporting of cases. The first volume of cases was published in 1785 by Ephraim Kirby of Connecticut. Kirby was a prototype of the early case reporters who were individual practitioners of the law, frequently men of some reputation, who felt it important to record the decisions of domestic courts. Prior to this time, the decisions of English courts had been used and referred to; and English treatises like that of William Blackstone, published in 1765, carried enormous influence. Out of patriotic ideals, U.S. reporters attempted to create a body of American case authority at a time of public distrust of judges and lawyers. They were followed by "official" reporters, people paid by the state to publish court decisions. The "official" subsidized volumes obviated the need for the private reporter.

Throughout the nineteenth century, the growth of the number of practicing lawyers spawned a number of legal publishers. Some of them, through a number of transformations, continue today. The most signal event of the nineteenth century was the development of the West Publishing Company and its comprehensive publication scheme. This came about in the 1880s. John West was a Minnesota publisher who began by publishing a weekly newspaper that covered the decisions of the Minnesota Supreme Court. His success led him to extend his coverage to other states in his region, and eventually Mr. West divided the country into seven

THE SYLLABI.

VOL. I.   SATURDAY, OCT. 21, 1876.   No. I.

The syllabi of the decisions of the Supreme Court of Minnesota have heretofore appeared in the daily papers only as it happened to suit the convenience of a reporter, or when a scarcity of news made them useful in filling up space, sometimes being in one paper, and sometimes in another.

It has been a matter of much annoyance to the attorneys of our State that these decisions have not been published regularly in some one paper, immediately after being filed, and well knowing the importance of such a publication to the profession, we purpose issuing the "Syllabi."

It will contain the syllabus, (prepared by the Judge, writing the opinion,) of each decision of the Supreme Court of Minnesota, as soon after the same is filed as may be practicable, accompanied, when desirable to a proper understanding of the points decided, with an abstract of the case itself, and when the decision is one of general interest and importance, with the full opinion of the Court.

It will also contain abstracts of, and opinions in the more important decisions in the United States Courts of Minnesota, as well as those of particular interest decided in the several District Courts of the State. The general design being to furnish the legal profession of the State, with prompt and reliable intelligence as to the various questions adjudicated by our own Courts, and at a date long prior to the publication of the regular reports.

It is not our purpose to confine our attention exclusively to reports from our own State, but while making those first in importance, also to furnish digests or opinions in cases decided in other States, which may have a special importance here or be of more than general interest.

New law books will be noticed as they appear.

We shall endeavor to make the Syllabi indispensible to Minnesota Attorneys, by making it prompt, interesting, full, and at all times *thoroughly reliable*, and the better to enable us to do so we respectfully request the cordial support of the members of the Bar.

JOHN B. WEST & Co.

Publishers.

Four early leaders of West
Publishing Company were, *left
to right,* John B. West,
Charles W. Ames, Peyton
Boyle, and Horatio D. West.

regions, publishing the decisions from the appellate courts in each. In 1896, West began a digest, which was based on a unique "key number" system, to provide subject access to the case reporters. Today, West Publishing Company continues to supply appellate decisions from states across the country and throughout the Federal system. Official government printers continued to publish judicial decisions throughout the country in sets paralleling West's reporters. Recently, however, several states have discontinued the duplication.

West and a number of other publishers have also developed annotated sets of legislative codes, usually unofficial, but useful for their indexes, annotations, and other editorial features. West and several other publishers also produce a variety of treatises and research aids in law. However, through its reporter system, digests, and other publications, West is the major publisher in the field of law.

Several other companies founded in the nineteenth century continue today. Two of the originals, the Lawyers Cooperative Publishing Company (neither run by lawyers nor a cooperative enterprise) and the Bancroft-Whitney Company merged and still continue under their former names. This company specializes in publication of secondary aids and annotated case reports. Little, Brown and Company, a company of venerable lineage, still is in the business of publishing text and research aids. Matthew Bender, one of the survivors by descent of the old Banks and Gould, is an active publisher of monographs and practice aids.

The Shepards Company has played a unique role in American legal publishing. This company developed a comprehensive system of compiling citations to

Editor Francis Rawle of Philadelphia stands next to his manuscript for the third revision of *Bouvier's Law Dictionary,* published by West in 1914.

cases and statutes. Recently, periodical citations have been added to Shepards's systems. Shepards's citators allow the researcher to update and verify the validity of citations. Material published by Shepards covers all American jurisdictions. As with many law book publishers, Shepards prints other material as well, but it is the Shepards's citator that is best known.

American law publishing has been affected by three facts. One is the common-law tradition of case law reporting, which has combined with the litigious nature of U.S. society to produce an inundation of case law, related citators, and finding tools. The second is the increasing role of legislatures and, through legislative delegation, of regulatory agencies, or lawmaking. The vast secondary literature is designed to ease the rigors of research, but its very size makes the task seem more complicated. The third factor has been the influential role of scholarly publications, especially legal periodicals. While commercial periodicals played an important role in the early nineteenth century, the end of the nineteenth century saw the rise of academic law reviews. These law reviews, which are published by student-managed boards, contain the cutting edge of U.S. legal thinking. In recent years, the proliferation of these reviews has made available several hundred academic law reviews containing the best of legal thought. The law school law reviews are the prestige vehicles for legal publication. Thus, the role for commercial publishers of serials has been severely circumscribed.

One form of commercially produced serial that has flourished has been the looseleaf service. These periodically updated binders allow the publisher to

Minnesota Historical Society

The home office and printing plant of West Publishing Company situated on the bluff above the Mississippi river at St. Paul, Minnesota, in the late 1920s.

Sewing machine operators stitch the individual signatures together into book form in about 1927.

Typesetters stationed at their job cases in the composing room at West in 1885.

keep the subscriber abreast of all new developments in specific topics. Looseleaf publication is especially popular in taxation and specialties subject to administrative regulation that have proliferated since the New Deal. Some such services are updated *daily*. Although three companies—Commerce Clearing House, Prentice-Hall, and the Bureau of National Affairs—are the largest in this field, even some monographs are currently issued in looseleaf format by other publishers.

Recent years have seen the development of a number of commercially-produced serial publications designed to serve the general practicing bar. Although bar association journals have long served as vehicles for communication in the practicing profession, recently national legal newspapers have arisen to provide news of legal developments, excerpts of primary sources, and gossip.

The last several decades have also seen the expansion of "law-for-the-layperson" books, an increasing number of "how-to" manuals, and publications from bar-sponsored continuing education programs. The pervasive effect of law on the lives of citizens has created an intense awareness of law and its implications everywhere.

The next step will be the computerization of legal literature. Already large proportions of case law and federal administrative materials are accessible through either LEXIS or WESTLAW. The speed of computer-aided retrieval soon may branch into secondary source materials as well.

Bibliography: Jenni Parrish, "Law Books and Legal Publishing in America, 1760–1840," 72 *Law Library Journal* (Summer 1979): 355–452 and sources cited there; Erwin C. Surrency, "Law Reports in the United States," 25 *American Journal of Legal History* (January 1981): 48–66; Charles Warren, *A History of the American Bar* (1980), chapter 13.

WESTLAW is a computer-assisted legal research system. It is designed to enable a researcher who has identified a legal problem to use the speed and capacity of a computer to retrieve relevant legal materials. By utilizing a video display terminal, keyboard, and printer, the researcher has access through a phone line to a vast storage of case law and other legal material in the West computer in St. Paul, Minnesota. Once the researcher has located the information desired, a copy of the retrieved document can be obtained via the printer attached to the video terminal.

AMERICAN LAW ENFORCEMENT OFFICERS ASSOCIATION

The American Law Enforcement Officers Association was formed in 1976 as a fraternal organization for public and private enforcement officials to offer services to members and to inspire cooperation to help unify law enforcement personnel who have been split by forces of dissension and strife. The association opposes unions. Association services include training programs and a professional accreditation program for a Certificate in Law Enforcement Science. The association also supports research through a library and the National Law Enforcement Academy.

The association has members in fifty state branches that are grouped into eight regions. Publications include *Police Times* (monthly), *Who's Who in American Law Enforcement*, and training manuals. The association holds annual meetings.

AMERICAN LAW INSTITUTE

The American Law Institute (ALI), is a group of legal scholars who formulate the RESTATEMENTS in various areas of law and who, with the National Conference of Commissioners on Uniform State Laws, draft some UNIFORM ACTS, such as the UNIFORM COMMERCIAL CODE.

The ALI, which was founded in 1923, is composed of judges, law educators, and attorneys. Its objective is to encourage the fair administration of justice throughout the nation by advancing the uniformity of law, whenever practicable. This goal is accomplished by the work of the ALI in proposing MODEL ACTS, statutory provisions that state legislatures may enact in whole, in part, or not at all.

The ALI acts in conjunction with the American Bar Association (ABA), in sponsoring a program of continuing legal education for attorneys. It publishes an annual report of its proceedings as well as preliminary and official drafts of its work. The ALI holds annual meetings at its headquarters in Philadelphia. See also, Bernard G. Segal's essay on the American Law Institute.

Brown Brothers

Among the founding members and influential contributors to the American Law Institute were Elihu Root, *opposite*, Charles Evans Hughes, *below right*, and William Howard Taft.

Library of Congress

Library of Congress

Bernard G. Segal

American Law Institute

The American Law Institute was founded in 1923 as the result of a recommendation of The Committee on the Establishment of a Permanent Organization for the Improvement of the Law, which consisted of some of the nation's leading judges, lawyers, and law teachers. The institute's incorporators, who included former Chief Justices William Howard Taft and Charles Evans Hughes and former Secretary of State Elihu Root, stated its purposes to be "to promote the clarification and simplification of the law and its better adaptation to social needs, to secure the better administration of justice and to encourage and carry on scholarly and scientific legal work."

In proposing the establishment of the institute, the committee listed as two primary defects in U.S. law "its uncertainty and its complexity," defects that cause needless litigation, often make it impossible to advise persons of their rights, and create useless delay and expense for litigants. The committee urged that the initial undertaking of the institute be a restatement of the law, which its first director, Dr. William Draper Lewis, happily referred to as "the desire of the legal profession for an orderly statement of our Common Law."

When one realizes that a very large portion of the law (sometimes referred to as judge-made law—law that does not rest for its authority upon a statute and has its earliest origins in the common law of England), the importance of this objective becomes apparent. The foresight of this wise group of leaders of the legal profession almost six decades ago, seeking a procedure to have the common law applied more uniformly by judges throughout the country, is apparent when a person recognizes that in our country today there are almost 27,000 state and local court judges and more than 2,200 Federal judges producing decisions, a vast number of which are intended to declare the common law.

Completion of the first restatement project, comprising separate restatements of eight common-law subjects—agency, conflict of laws, contracts, judgments, property, restitution, torts, and trusts—consumed more than twenty years (1923 to 1944), resulting in twenty-four volumes totaling more than 17,000 pages.

The form of the restatement was designed to set forth the basic principles of the law on a given subject by means of a coherent series of "black-letter" principles, drafted with the precision of a well-drawn statute, consistent with the best traditions of the common law, rooted in precedent, yet flexible enough to accommodate future developments and needs. Each black-letter principle is explained and supported by commentary and concrete examples of its application. While every effort is made to adhere to the common law in resolving inconsistency among court decisions, when genuine conflicts exist, the institute's approach in the restatement is to adopt what it regards as the best-reasoned rule, the one most responsive to contemporary needs and sound public policy.

There is hardly any kind of intellectual work which so much needs to be done, not only by experienced and exercised minds, but by minds trained to the task through long and laborious study, as the business of making laws.

J.S. MILL

George F. Wickersham was the
first president of the American
Law Institute.

*Law is nothing but a correct
principle drawn from the
inspiration of the gods,
commanding what is honest,
and forbidding the contrary.*

CICERO

From the beginning, courts welcomed references by counsel to the restatement and to its commentaries and examples. Citation by courts to restatement black-letter and to the commentary in its support are legion. Again and again in states all over the country, a court has expressly adopted a section of the restatement although the court's common-law precedent differed from the restatement's black-letter principle or where the court had no precedent in its common law.

The formulation of the first restatement, therefore, proved highly influential and useful in the development of the common law in our courts—Federal, state, and local. However, by the time of the completion of the restatement, it had become apparent that revision was needed to reflect subsequent major developments in both law and society. Accordingly, in 1953, the institute began work on *Restatement, Second*, again a monumental project; and now twenty-nine years later, it is still in progress. *Restatement, Second* is far more than a simple updating of its predecessor; it constitutes a thorough rethinking, and reformulation where indicated, of propositions contained in every one of the major subjects of the law treated in the first restatement. It serves to keep the common law current and to continue to resolve inconsistencies that inevitably arise among court decisions across the nation.

The authority of the institute's work can be attributed in large measure not only to the high level of the participants in its formulation—leading judges, law professors, and lawyers—but also to its working methods, which have remained essentially the same since the beginning of the institute. The institute's director, subject to the approval of its governing body, the council, designates a reporter for each project to be undertaken. This individual is a recognized leading national expert on the subjects to be studied; he or she is usually a professor of law, who becomes responsible for organizing the project and for the basic research and drafting. Also appointed is a group of advisers—primarily judges, lawyers, and teachers with special knowledge of the field—who meet with the reporter and thoroughly review the draft he or she has prepared.

When the director deems that a draft is ready, it is submitted to the council for detailed consideration with the reporter. If approved by the council, it is published as a tentative draft and submitted to the membership at the annual meeting. The council meets two or three times a year, with each session that is devoted to reviewing drafts consuming three to four days; and the membership meets annually for four days, for discussion, debate, and voting. At each stage of review, a draft may be referred back to the reporter for revision. The process is slow and painstaking—for example, *Torts Restatement, Second* (dealing with the law of private wrongs and injuries) involved twenty-two preliminary drafts, forty-one council drafts, and twenty-three tentative drafts produced over a period of twenty-two years: but the result has always been a product of genuine group scholarship, drawing upon both specialized knowledge and practical experience and reflecting the considered views of a broad spectrum of the legal community, so as to constitute a synthesis of the best available thought on the subject.

Today, the institute has an elected membership of approximately 1,800 carefully selected judges, lawyers, and teachers of law, and an ex-officio membership consisting of the chief justice and the associate justices of the Supreme Court of the United States, the chief judge of each United States Court of Appeals, the attorney general and the solicitor general of the United States, the chief justice or chief judge of the highest court of each state, deans of law schools, and prominent incumbent bar association officials.

Election to membership in the institute is the responsibility of the council, on recommendation of its membership committee. The process is initiated with a proposal by a member of the institute. The proposal form must contain certain relevant factual information, be signed by the person proposed, and be accompanied by personal letters from the proposer and from two seconding members. Since the number of elected members is limited to 1,800, there is from time to time a waiting list until vacancies in membership occur.

Painstakingly deliberate at each stage, the institute's processes are inevitably costly. Overhead expenses are met from dues and contributions of elected members. However, no project is undertaken without separate funding. Projects have been funded by foundations, business and banking corporations, the organized bar, and in a few instances the Federal government. Grants from these sources have exceeded a total of $10 million.

Great as has been the institute's contribution through its restatements, the restatements today constitute but one of the very significant contributions of the institute to the development of the law in the United States. The restatements, as has been said, address themselves to aspects of judge-made law not superseded by statute. The founding committee made clear in its report that led to the creation of the institute that the institute's initial focus should be on restating the principles in legislation, the law-making function of the legislatures of the country. Nevertheless, as early as 1930, the institute had also directed some effort toward statutory reform by the promulgation of a Code of Criminal Procedure and in the early 1940s with other significant legislative projects. However, the real impetus for proposals of codification of statutory law by the institute came with the Uniform Commercial Code, which the institute undertook with the cooperation of the National Conference of Commissioners on Uniform State Laws—a body consisting of representatives from each state. In due course, significant institute statutory projects were completed on a variety of important Federal and state legislative subjects.

The substantial influence that the institute has had on statutory law in the United States, where its impact must be on legislatures rather than on courts, is best evidenced by the fact that the Commercial Code has been adopted in forty-nine states, partially in Louisiana, and also in the District of Columbia and in the Virgin Islands. The institute's Model Penal Code has been the touchstone for penal law revision throughout the nation. The institute's codification efforts have likewise been influential in various other areas, if not through statutory enactments then by adoption by administrative agencies. Its array of code projects include the Model Land Development Code; the Code of Criminal Procedure previously mentioned; the Model Code of Evidence; the Federal Securities Code; and various Federal tax projects in income, estate, and gift taxation. Its procedures for evolving a statutory proposal are, with minor deviations, virtually the same as those described above with respect to the restatements.

In 1959, Chief Justice Earl Warren, addressing the annual meeting of the American Law Institute, urged that the institute undertake a special study of the

The remoter and more general aspects of the law are those which give it universal interest. It is through them that you not only become a great master in your calling, but connect your subject with the universe and catch an echo of the infinite, a glimpse of its unfathomable process, a hint of the universal law.

OLIVER WENDELL HOLMES, JR.

Dr. William Draper Lewis was the first director of the American Law Institute.

appropriate division of jurisdiction between state and Federal courts. Noting that another study of the institute had been recognized as "a major contribution to the development of judicial administration in the United States," the chief justice commended the institute's members by observing that they have "consistently demonstrated a vision and a will toward the administration of justice in our country that is a wellspring of inspiration." It is customary for each chief justice to address the opening session at the annual meeting, either bringing to its attention events in the law during the preceding year or recommending that the institute undertake a specific project as Chief Justice Warren did in 1959. Annual meetings in recent years are also regularly addressed by the attorney general of the United States.

In 1947, the institute started a postadmission legal education program through the Committee on Continuing Legal Education of the American Law Institute in collaboration with the American Bar Association. Originally created in response to the needs of servicemen returning to the practice of law at the end of World War II, the committee undertook an extensive program of courses of instruction and publications for lawyers, and at the same time embarked on a program to stimulate continuing legal education by groups of various kinds throughout the United States.

Today the committee, with much greater participation by the American Bar Association than for some years after 1947 and known as the Committee of the American Law Institute and the American Bar Association on Continuing Professional Education (ALI-ABA), conducts approximately seventy programs of oral instructions a year (some presented by satellite in sixty cities at a time), publishes five periodicals of which *The Practical Lawyer* is the best known, produces audio and video tapes, and offers the profession a list of more than 100 books.

Much of the institute's success in conceiving and sustaining its projects over the length of time needed to bring them to fruition is due to its remarkable continuity of leadership and direction. Since 1923 it has had only six presidents—George W. Wickersham (1923–36), George Wharton Pepper (1936–47), Harrison Tweed (1947–61), Norris Darrell (1961–76), R. Ammi Cutter (1976–80), and Roswell B. Perkins (1980–), and three directors—William Draper Lewis (1923–47), Herbert F. Goodrich (1947–62), and Herbert Wechsler (1962–).

The institute has thus continued to maintain what Chief Justice Warren E. Burger has called the "quality of studied and restrained response, of careful innovation and progress, progress without haste or hysteria" that makes it "one of the great resources . . . for the improvement of our legal institutions."

Bibliography: "Analysis of the ALI's Approach to the State-Federal Jurisdictional Dilemma," 21 *American University Law Review* (April 1972): 287–327; N. M. Crystal, "Codification and the Rise of the Restatement Movement," 54 *Washington Law Review* (March 1979): 239–273; N. Darrello and P. A. Wolkin, "American Law Institute," 52 *New York State Bar Journal* (Fall 1980): 99–101.

AMERICAN LAW REPORTS □ A series of volumes containing annotated reports of selected state and Federal cases that are organized according to the point of law with which they deal. □

American Law Reports (ALR) are unofficial reports of cases that have been chosen by a law book publisher from the extensive mass of decisions as those that have the widest legal significance. Statements or annotations have been added to the selected cases that list and analyze other cases that deal with a particular point of law.

AMERICAN LEGISLATIVE EXCHANGE COUNCIL Formed in 1973, the American Legislative Exchange Council (ALEC) is a nonpartisan research and public affairs association that promotes basic American values and institutions, such as individual liberties, property rights, productive free enterprise, and limited government. The council provides factual analyses, research information, and model legislation; it sponsors legislative conferences that bring together elected representatives and experts in fields of national interest. Proposals emphasize lowering taxes, reducing the bureaucracy, encouraging fiscal responsibility, safeguarding of liberties, and promoting grass-roots government as an alternative to centralized Federal government.

The membership includes state and national legislators, business organizations, and concerned citizens. The council publishes *First Reading* (monthly newsletter) and *Source Book of American State Legislation* (biennial). It holds annual meetings.

AMERICAN LEGISLATORS ASSOCIATION See Council of State Governments.

AMERICAN PATENT LAW ASSOCIATION Founded in 1897, the American Patent Law Association (APLA) is dedicated to continuous improvement in the administration and practice of intellectual property law in all its facets, including particularly patents, trade secrets, trademarks, copyrights, and unfair competition. The association seeks to protect and advance the incentives to invent and invest inherent in our system of protection for intellectual property. In pursuit of these goals, APLA lobbies for appropriate legislation, useful international agreements, and, in particular, sound interpretation of the law by the courts and government agencies, such as the Copyright Office and the Patent

and Trademark Office. The association works closely with these agencies and other groups to improve practices and procedures in the area of patent law. Other activities include efforts to promote public understanding of the importance of these protections for national developments and programs designed to maintain the highest ethical standards in the profession.

The members are lawyers interested in intellectual property law. It has thirty-four committees, each of which is assigned a specific segment of the association's interests, such as Antitrust Law, Amicus, Federal Practice and Procedure, Government Patent Policy, Inventor Assistance, and Patent Law.

The association publishes a *Quarterly Journal* and a *Bulletin*. It holds spring and winter meetings as well as an annual fall meeting.

AMERICAN PRINTING HOUSE FOR THE BLIND The American Printing House for the Blind was incorporated by the Kentucky Legislature in 1858 to assist in the education of the blind by distributing braille books, talking books, and educational aids without cost to educational institutions educating blind children pursuant to the act "To Promote the Education of the Blind," adopted by Congress in 1879 (20 Stat. 467, as amended). Today, the American Printing House for the Blind is supported in part by Federal funds appropriated in the budget of the Department of Education.

Source: *The United States Government Manual 1981/82* and/or *1982/83*.

AMERICAN PSYCHOLOGY-LAW SOCIETY The American Psychology-Law Society (AP-LS) was formed in 1968 for the mutual enchancement of the fields of law and psychology. The goals of the society, as stated in its literature, are as follows:

To promote exchanges between the disciplines of psychology and law in areas of mutual interest, such as teaching, research, administration of justice, jurisprudence, as well as other matters at the psychology-law interface.

To promote research relevant to legal problems using psychological knowledge and methods and to promote psychological research using the legal setting and related legal research techniques.

To promote the education of lawyers and psychologists with respect to each other's professional field.

To promote legislation and social policies consistent with current states of psychological knowledge.

To promote the effective use of psychologists in the processes and settings of the law.

The society publishes *Journal of Law and Human Behavior* and a newsletter, both quarterly. It holds biennial meetings.

AMERICANS FOR EFFECTIVE LAW ENFORCEMENT

The Americans for Effective Law Enforcement (AELE) was founded in 1966 for the express purpose "of establishing an 'organized voice' for the law-abiding citizens regarding this country's crime problem, and to lend support to professional law enforcement." Toward that end the organization seeks to raise public awareness of the need for the effective enforcement of criminal law in order to meet the nation's crime problems; and to enhance the effective and fair administration of criminal law by providing assistance to police, prosecutors, and the courts, while rejecting any support from advocates of racial bias and other unconstitutional ideas. AELE endeavors to represent the law-abiding public through amicus curiae briefs in Supreme Court and other court cases that deal with issues relating to effective law enforcement. AELE is also active in litigation on the behalf of crime victims through the Law Enforcement Legal Defense Center and in support of the police in civil suits alleging police misconduct. Other activities include compiling statistics, maintaining a library, and drafting model legislation and constitutional amendments designed to help enforcement officials protect the public.

AELE publishes *Jail Administration Law Bulletin* (monthly), *Law Enforcement Legal Liability Reporter* (monthly), *Police Plaintiff* (quarterly), and *Law Enforcement Legal Defense Manual* (quarterly); it also publishes court briefs.

AMERICAN SOCIETY FOR LEGAL HISTORY

Founded in 1956, the American Society for Legal History (ASLH) is dedicated to fostering study, teaching, and publishing in the history of the law and institutions of all legal systems, both Anglo-American and foreign. The society is concerned with the preservation of legal and legislative records, the discovery of historical items, and the use of legal history in the formulation of legal policy. Its members are primarily judges; lawyers; legal educators; professors of political science, history, and economics; and students. It has committees on Aids in Teaching Legal History, Legal History, Foundations, Legal Research, and Preservation of Legal Records.

The society publishes the *American Journal of Legal History* (quarterly) and a newsletter (published in April and October). It holds annual meetings, usually in October.

AMERICAN SOCIETY FOR PHARMACY LAW

The American Society for Pharmacy Law (ASPL) was formed in 1974 to communicate accurate legal information to attorneys and pharmacists; to foster knowledge and education pertaining to the rights and duties of pharmacists; to distribute information of interest to the membership via a newsletter and other appropriate publications; and to provide a forum for exchange of information pertaining to pharmacy law.

The society publishes *RX Ipsa Loquitur* (monthly) and holds annual meetings. Its members are pharmacists, lawyers, and students.

AMERICAN SOCIETY FOR POLITICAL AND LEGAL PHILOSOPHY

The American Society for Political and Legal Philosophy (ASPLP) was founded in 1955 to encourage interdisciplinary exploration, treatment, and discussion of those issues of political and legal philosophy that are of common interest to those in the social sciences, law, and philosophy. The society has explored such topics as authority, community, coercion, equality, justice, liberty, participation, political and legal obligation, public interest, rational decision, representation, revolution, and voluntary association.

The members are teachers, scholars, and others who have made contributions to the fields of political or legal philosophy. It publishes *Nomos* annually and holds annual meetings.

AMERICAN SOCIETY OF HOSPITAL ATTORNEYS

The American Society of Hospital Attorneys was formed in 1968 to make available information on health care law and legislation and to inform members of court decisions in the health care field. The society maintains a collection of leading health law decisions, provides model forms for agreements, and holds legal seminars and institutes.

The membership is comprised of attorneys who represent hospitals and other health organizations. The society includes eight state groups and publishes a monthly newsletter and an annual membership roster. It holds an annual meeting in June.

AMERICAN SOCIETY OF INTERNATIONAL LAW

Founded in 1906, the American Society of International Law is a professional association with over 5,000 members in some 100 countries that is devoted to fostering the study of international law and promoting international relations based on law and justice. The society serves as (1) a forum for exchange of views on current legal topics arising from both public and private international activities; (2) a center for research in both the traditional subjects of international law and new issues of international law and policy; and (3) a sponsor of student activities in international law.

The society brings together lawyers, political scientists, economists, and people from other disciplines, as well as government officials and students, to focus attention on such issues as (1) the ratification of human rights treaties; (2) the reform of international trade institutions; (3) the clarification of legal aspects of relations with China; (4) the resolution of ocean boundary disputes; (5) the evaluation of UN programs; (6) the protection of the environment in the oceans, in Antarctica, and in the management of river basins; (7) the promotion of codes of conduct for transnational corporations; and many others.

The society's program is designed to keep its membership informed of ongoing developments in international law and policy and to explore specific areas in detail through publications, research, study, annual and regional meetings, a library, the work of committees, the Association of Student International Law Societies, and the various awards presented for distinguished contributions to the field of international law. Its members are lawyers, educators, government officials, and others interested in international law.

The society publishes *International Legal Materials* (bimonthly), *American Journal of International Law* (quarterly), a quarterly newsletter, *Proceedings* (annually), and *Studies in International Legal Policy.* It holds an annual meeting each April.

AMERICAN SOCIETY OF LAW AND MEDICINE

Formed in 1972, the objective of the American Society of Law and Medicine is to promote an interdisciplinary approach to problems involving law, medicine, and health care. To initiate a clearer understanding of complex medicolegal issues, the society seeks to act as a catalyst of communication among various professions. The society has several vehicles for communication: three publications, a speakers' bureau, a newsletter, educational conferences, and a medicolegal library. Areas covered by these services include: hospital law, medical malpractice, patients' rights, health care legislation and regulation, bioethics, worker's compensation, and forensic medicine.

Every year, the society sponsors a number of conferences on a variety of medicolegal topics. The meetings, which are held nationwide, are designed to educate health care professionals and attorneys about medicolegal issues. Often cosponsored by national or state organizations interested in the conference topic, the programs provide continuing education credit and a unique opportunity to explore issues from an interdisciplinary perspective. Other activities include the annual presentation of an Honorary Life Membership for outstanding contributions in the field of medicolegal education and an annual student essay competition.

The members of the society are physicians, attorneys, health care management professionals, nurses, insurance personnel, and others interested in health law and medicolegal relations. The society publishes *Nursing, Law and Ethics* (monthly), *Medicolegal News* (biannually), and *American Journal of Law and Medicine* (quarterly).

AMERICAN SOCIETY OF QUESTIONED DOCUMENT EXAMINERS

The American Society of Questioned Document Examiners (ASQDE) was founded in 1942 to enhance the administration of justice by improving techniques for discovering and proving facts related to various problems concerning documents, including handwriting, typewriting, ink, and paper. The purposes of the society as set forth in its bylaws:

The purposes of the society and of its members are to foster education, sponsor scientific research, establish standards, exchange experience, and provide instruction in the field of questioned document examination; and to promote justice in matters that involve questions about documents.

To accomplish these purposes the society and its members subscribe to the following objectives:

1. To establish and maintain high professional standards for ethics, for education and training, and for excellence in work performance.

2. To engage upon and to encourage scientific research and development in document examination and related matters and to disseminate the results by presentation at annual meetings and by publication.

3. To prepare, maintain, and administer a comprehensive course of training in document examination; to record, preserve, and correlate significant experience in solving questioned document problems.

4. To improve knowledge and understanding of the work of document examination by the public, the bar, the judiciary, and among the forensic sciences.

In law, it is good policy to never plead what you need not, lest you oblige yourself to prove what you cannot.

ABRAHAM LINCOLN

5. To discover prospective document examiners of good character and good potential for development and to assist in their training.

The society, which is composed of members who are public and private professional document examiners, has committees on Education, Ethics, and Research. It holds annual meetings.

AMERICAN SOCIETY OF WRITERS ON LEGAL SUBJECTS   See Scribes.

AMERICANS UNITED FOR LIFE— LEGAL DEFENSE FUND
Founded in 1971, Americans United for Life (AUL) is an association expressly dedicated "to the protection of all human life born and unborn." AUL describes itself as "a multi-faceted organization, combining an internationally-respected educational program with the prolife movement's foremost legal resource, the AUL Legal Defense Fund." The organization is especially concerned with issues surrounding abortion, fetal experimentation, and euthanasia.

The association operates a library and a Legal Resource Center, containing information related to these areas of concern. Americans United for Life publishes *Lex Vitae* (quarterly) and *Studies in Law and Medicine.*

AMERICAN TRIAL LAWYERS ASSOCIATION   See Association of Trial Lawyers of America.

AMES, James Barr
James Barr Ames (*b.* June 22, 1846, in Boston; *d.* January 8, 1910, in Wilton, New Hampshire) achieved prominence as an educator and concentrated his career efforts at Harvard University.

A graduate of Harvard College in 1868, Ames earned a master of arts degree in 1871 and attended Harvard Law School in 1872. He received several doctor of laws degrees from various universities, including the University of Pennsylvania in 1899, Northwestern University in 1903, and Harvard in 1904.

In 1868, Ames began his teaching career as an instructor for a private school in Boston. Three years later he began his professional association with Harvard, acting as a tutor in French and German until 1872 and continuing as an instructor in medieval history for the next year. From 1873 to 1877 he was an associate professor of law; in 1877, he became a professor of law. From 1895 to 1910 he performed the duties of

James Barr Ames .

dean of the law school. In 1897, he participated in the establishment of the *Harvard Law Review.*

Ames distinguished himself as a teacher of law by utilizing the case method introduced by legal educator and former Harvard Dean Christopher Columbus Langdell. Langdell's approach presented principles of law in relation to actual cases to which they were applied. By studying the cases, a student of law was given an accurate example of the law at work.

Ames extended his talents to the field of literature. He is the author of *Lectures on Legal History*, which was published in 1913.

AMES, Samuel
Samuel Ames (*b.* September 6, 1806; *d.* December 20, 1865, in Providence, Rhode Island) graduated from Brown University in 1823 and was admitted to the Rhode Island bar in 1826.

From 1841 to 1851 Ames represented Providence in the Rhode Island general assembly. During his tenure, he was a prominent supporter of state authority in the "Dorr Rebellion." This insurrection occurred in 1842 as a protest against the limited voting rights that existed in Rhode Island. The protest resulted in a more liberal interpretation of the right to suffrage.

Beginning in 1856 Ames served as chief justice of the Rhode Island Supreme Court. In 1861, he was the representative from Rhode Island during a series of unsuccessful negotiations

Law, grown a forest, where perplex The mazes, and the brambles vex.

MATTHEW GREEN

Samuel Ames

come of the action nor does the person or organization have a right to present views to the court. The filing of an amicus curiae brief is a matter decided by the court in the exercise of its discretion. It is commonly filed in APPEALS of cases affecting social issues, such as CIVIL RIGHTS. The rules governing state and Federal appellate procedure must be observed by a person or organization seeking designation as an amicus curiae. For example, in cases of appeals to the Federal court of appeals, an amicus curiae brief can be filed only upon the written consent of all the parties; by leave which is permission of the court obtained upon the motion of one of the parties; or by request of the court. If, however, the brief is presented by the United States, its officer or agency, consent or leave of the court is not necessary. An amicus curiae brief that is sought to be filed in the SUPREME COURT must adhere to the revised rules governing practice before the Supreme Court.

Once an appellate court has permitted an amicus curiae brief to be filed, it has discretion in deciding whether to heed or ignore the arguments advanced in it.

In some jurisdictions, an amicus curiae can advance arguments by an APPEARANCE or by an AFFIDAVIT. See also, Erwin N. Griswold's essay on Amicus Curiae.

He who knows only his own side of the case, knows little of that.

J.S. MILL

to effect a peace between the North and South during the Civil War. See also, Jamil S. Zainaldin's essay on the Dorr Rebellion.

AMICABLE ACTION □ An action, commenced and maintained by the mutual consent and arrangement of the parties, to obtain a judgment of a court on a doubtful question of law that is based upon facts that both parties accept as being correct and complete. □

The action is considered amicable because there is no dispute as to the facts but only as to the conclusions of law that a judge can reach from consideration of the facts. An amicable action is considered a JUSTICIABLE controversy because there is a real and substantive disagreement between the parties as to the appropriate relief to be granted by the court.

Other names for an amicable action are a CASE AGREED ON, a CASE STATED, or a FRIENDLY SUIT.

AMICUS CURIAE [*Latin, "A friend of the court."*]
□ The designation given to a BRIEF (a written document filed in a lawsuit stating arguments why a court should act a certain way) which is filed with an appellate court, allegedly on behalf of one of the parties, by an individual or organization not a party to the action but who has a substantial interest in the action. □

The amicus curiae, the person filing the brief, cannot have a personal stake in the out-

When the Supreme Court heard oral arguments in the 1983 capital punishment case of *Thomas A. Barefoot v. W. J. Estelle, Jr.,* Jack Greenberg, Director-Counsel of the NAACP Legal Defense and Educational Fund, presented an amicus curiae brief on behalf of Barefoot.

Amicus Curiae

Amicus curiae means literally, "friend of the court." Its plural is amici curiae. An amicus curiae is any person or organization, other than a party or a party's counsel, who seeks to bring facts or legal materials to the attention of a court. Such action may be taken in any court. For example, in a trial court, an amicus curiae may suggest to the court that a party has died, or, in the case of a corporation, that steps were not taken so that a corporate defendant was properly served with process. Ordinarily, the amicus is a lawyer, but he or she need not be. In all cases the amicus can appear only with the consent of the court, although this consent is ordinarily given if the amicus obtains the consent of all parties to the case.

Appearance by an amicus curiae is most frequently made in an appellate court, and is usually by a formal brief filed by counsel. Because of the rule of *stare decisis*, or precedent, which is followed in U.S. courts, a decision in a case may be of direct concern to persons who are not actually parties to the case before the court. In such a situation, an affected person (or corporation) may seek to present views to the court through the medium of a brief filed on his or her behalf as an amicus curiae. In rare instances, the amicus curiae may also be allowed to present oral argument before the court.

The amicus brief is most effective when it presents substantial professional argument backed by appropriate authorities. This may be material not known to the parties of the case, or it may involve analysis of the facts and issues, or theories with respect to the law, which the amicus feels that he or she can present more effectively than has been done by the party whose side he or she supports.

In recent years, amicus curiae briefs are most frequently filed in civil liberties or "public interest" cases. Thus, in cases involving school desegregation or discrimination in employment, amicus briefs may be filed by the National Association for the Advancement of Colored People or by the Lawyers' Committee for Civil Rights Under Law. In cases involving the environment, amicus briefs may be filed by such organizations as the Sierra Club or The Friends of the Earth. The United States, through the solicitor general, frequently files briefs as an amicus in the U.S. Supreme Court, often at the invitation of the Court. This was done, for example; in the case of *Brown v. Board of Education of Topeka, Kansas*, 344 U.S. 141, 73 S.Ct. 124, 97 L.Ed. 152, the original school desegregation case, decided in 1952 and again in 1954.

Carefully prepared amicus briefs can be of assistance to the courts by aiding in the full presentation of important matters, and by giving the court opportunity to consider every point of view. Sometimes this is overdone. In the case of *Regents of University of California v. Bakke*, 438 U.S. 265, 98 S.Ct. 2733, 57

Society between equals can only exist on the understanding that the interests of all are to be regarded equally.

J.S. MILL

L.Ed.2d 750 (1978), involving the validity of "affirmative action" in admission to a medical school, more than fifty amicus briefs were filed. The court, of course, is under no obligation to read the briefs. In such a situation, presumably, it picks and chooses, examining the briefs as far as it finds them helpful. See also, Louis H. Pollak's essay on Brown v. Board of Education of Topeka, Kansas; and J. Harvie Wilkinson III's essay on the Bakke Case.

Bibliography: ; Samuel Krislov, "Amicus Curiae Brief: From Friendship to Advocacy," 72 *Yale Law Journal* (March 1963): 694–721; Robert L. Stern and Eugene Gressman, *Supreme Court Practice*, 5th ed. (1978), pp.495–499, 723–729.

A friend in court is worth a penny in a man's purse.

JOHN RAY

AMNESTY □ The action of a government by which all persons or certain groups of persons who have committed a criminal offense—usually of a political nature that threatens the sovereignty of the government (such as SEDITION or TREASON)—are granted immunity from prosecution. □

Amnesty is an act of oblivion that in effect officially ignores or forgets the offense before the accused is prosecuted on the charges. Unlike other situations in which the government grants immunity from criminal prosecution in exchange for information to be used to convict others of the same crime, amnesty is usually conditioned only upon the person's return to civil obedience and responsibility within a designated period of time.

The power to grant amnesty lies with the chief executive of the jurisdiction. If the offense involves a violation of Federal law, only the president has the authority to grant amnesty to its violators. When the criminal conduct infringes upon state or local law, the governor of the state or the chief executive of the locality who is empowered to enforce the local law can grant amnesty.

Amnesty differs from a PARDON in that it is a deliberate neglect to prosecute a person accused of a crime, while a pardon is an act of forgiveness granted by the chief executive subsequent to the trial and conviction of a person who has committed a Federal or state crime.

The word *pardon* has occasionally been used when, in fact, amnesty has been granted to an individual. Legally the terms are not synonymous, although some legal authorities view amnesty as a general pardon of individuals who have committed serious political offenses. See also, Joseph L. Sax's essay on Amnesty.

President Andrew Johnson favored a lenient reconstruction policy toward the South after the Civil War, and granted amnesty to the rebels.

Harper's Weekly, October 14, 1865

Joseph L. Sax

Amnesty

Amnesty is an act of the legal sovereign that overlooks or officially forgets a crime committed against the state. Ordinarily, amnesty is granted to a specified group following a war, and it relieves those to whom it is granted from liability to prosecution or punishment from political offenses, such as treason, rebellion, desertion from the military or refusal to serve in the armed forces. There is no legal right to amnesty; it is a purely discretionary act of sovereign grace. It may be granted for compassionate reasons, but most often it is a politically advantageous act of reconciliation.

The best known amnesties in U.S. history occurred during and after the Civil War. These were intended to encourage "some persons heretofore engaged in [the] rebellion to resume their allegiance to the United States and to reinaugurate loyal State governments." Amnesties have also been commonly employed in situations of widespread military desertion to induce deserting soldiers to return to their posts.

Amnesties have a long history dating back to the fifth century B.C. in Greece. They were also a feature of Roman law and are well-accepted elements of law in many countries, including France, England, Norway, Germany, Belgium, Japan, and the Netherlands. In many countries amnesties are granted legislatively; in the United States they are more often granted by and in the name of the president. They have been a familiar feature of U.S. law throughout the nation's history. In 1795, George Washington pardoned participants in the so-called Whisky Rebellion (an insurrection arising out of attempts to collect an excessive tax on distilled spirits), if these persons gave assurances of future submission to the laws of the United States. The most recent amnesty was President Gerald Ford's 1974 proclamation relieving Vietnam War draft evaders of prosecution and punishment if they acknowledged allegiance to the United States and agreed to perform a period of alternative nonmilitary national service.

Amnesty is nowhere mentioned in express terms in the U.S. Constitution and there is some ambiguity about its legal status. The U.S. Supreme Court has said that it is in practical effect indistinguishable from a pardon. Article II, Section 2 of the Constitution grants the president authority "to Grant Reprieves and Pardons for Offenses against the United States, except in Cases of Impeachment."

Ordinarily, pardons are thought of as applying to individuals, for ordinary crimes, and are granted following conviction. Amnesties usually cover whole classes of people, deal with political offenses, and are granted prior to conviction, or even prosecution. There are no fixed rules or explicit legal constraints, however. What are called amnesties—such as Washington's relief from prosecution of participants in the Whisky Rebellion—are usually proclaimed by presidents as pardons under Article II, Section 2 of the Constitution. And while a pardon usually follows conviction, President Ford's pardon of former President Richard M. Nixon preceded any act of prosecution.

A strict observance of the written laws is doubtless one of the high virtues of a good citizen, but it is not the highest. The laws of necessity, of self-preservation, of saving our country when in danger, are of higher obligation.

THOMAS JEFFERSON

239

In 1974 President Ford signed an order of conditional amnesty for thousands of draft evaders who had avoided serving in the military during the Vietnam War.

A president may pardon (or grant amnesty), and Congress cannot infringe that power. At the time of the Civil War, Congress sought to control the pardoning or amnestying of former Confederates, and to bend the president to its will; but—except for Section 3 of the Fourteenth Amendment—it is clear that the president, by use of the pardoning power, may achieve independently, the result of an amnesty without the consent or even the acquiescence of Congress. There is some controversy, however, over whether the Congress also has independent power to pardon and amnesty. The Supreme Court has opined that it does, though it has never expressly so held. It has been suggested by some writers that amnesty is different from pardon, and that *only* the legislature can grant an amnesty. The claim is that whereas amnesty overlooks the offense, a pardon merely remits punishment. This seems to be a slender distinction.

An amnesty may be general or particular; that is, it may cover all offenses during a given time period or only a single crime. It may be absolute and unlimited, or it may be heavily conditioned—as by requiring an oath of allegiance or a return to military service—as long as the conditions imposed are not themselves independently unconstitutional. The one clear constraint is that an amnesty may not be granted for future crimes not yet committed; it may not serve as a license to violate the law in the future.

While the practical effect of an amnesty is usually clear—it relieves the offender of prosecution and punishment—there is a continuing debate about its philosophical status.

The word *amnesty* is taken from the Greek, meaning oblivion or forgetfulness. Strictly speaking, an amnesty is neither more nor less than a voluntary extinction from memory of a crime. In the earliest known amnesty, Thrasybulus, in 404 B.C., declared as his goal "to erase civil strife by the imposition of legal oblivion." An amnesty is not necessarily an act of forgiveness, or of condonation, and certainly it is not tantamount to a declaration that no crime has been committed. It is an act of political reconciliation.

In addition to the uncertain distinction between amnesty and pardon, there are a number of other related concepts easily confused with amnesty. Clemency is what is granted by a pardon; so that a pardon is simply the order that grants clemency. A reprieve is a lesser act than either pardon or amnesty. It only suspends a punishment, often for a particular period of time, whereas pardon and amnesty relieve from punishment permanently. Commutation is the substitution of a lighter for a heavier punishment, and parole is the early release from a punishment already imposed and is usually accompanied by conditions the violation of which will reinstate the punishment.

The best men are but men, and are sometimes transported with passion.

SIR ROBERT ATKYNS

Bibliography: "Amnesty," *Encyclopedia of the Social Sciences* (1937): 36–39; John C. Etridge, "Amnesty: A Brief Historical Overview" *Multilith No. 72–35F.* Library of Congress Congressional Research Service (Feb. 28, 1972); Louis Lusky, "Congressional Amnesty for War Resisters: Policy Considerations and Constitutional Problems," 25 *Vanderbilt Law Review* (April 1972): 525–555.

AMNESTY INTERNATIONAL, U.S.A. AFFILIATE

Formed in 1966, Amnesty International, U.S.A. Affiliate (AIUSA) works impartially for the release of men and women detained for their conscientiously held beliefs, color, ethnic origin, sex, religion, or language, and other prisoners of conscience, provided they have never used or advocated violence. Amnesty International, which was awarded the Nobel Prize for Peace in 1977, advocates prompt and fair trials for all political prisoners. The group is opposed to torture and the death penalty. The organization serves as a consultant to the United Nations and the Council of Europe, maintains cooperative relations with the Inter-American Commission on Human Rights of the Organization of American States, and has observer status with the Organization of African Unity.

The international headquarters of Amnesty International is in London. Amnesty International currently has thirty-five national sections. The AIUSA publishes *Amnesty Action, Matchbox, Annual Report,* and *Chronical of Current Events;* it also prints country briefing papers, mission reports, and other special reports.

AMORTIZATION

☐ The reduction of a debt incurred, for example, in the purchase of stocks or bonds, by regular payments consisting of interest and part of the principal made over a specified time period upon the expiration of which the entire debt is repaid. A MORTGAGE is amortized when it is repaid with periodic payments over a particular term. After a certain portion of each payment is applied to the interest on the debt, any balance reduces the principal.

☐ The allocation of the cost of an INTANGIBLE asset, for example, a PATENT or COPYRIGHT, over its estimated useful life that is considered an expense of doing business and is used to offset the earnings of the asset by its declining value. If an intangible asset has an indefinite life, such as GOODWILL, it cannot be amortized. ☐

Amortization is not the same as DEPRECIATION, which is the allocation of the original cost of a TANGIBLE asset computed over its anticipated useful life, based on its physical wear and tear and the passage of time. Amortization of intangible assets and depreciation of tangible assets are used for tax purposes to reduce the yearly income generated by the assets by their decreasing values so that the tax imposed upon the earnings of assets is less. Amortization differs from depletion, which is a reduction in the BOOK VALUE of a natural resource, such as a mineral, resulting from its conversion into a marketable product. Depletion is used for a similar tax purpose as amortization and depreciation—to reduce the yearly income generated by the asset by the expenses involved in its sale so that less tax will be due.

AMOTION

☐ Putting out; removal; taking away; dispossession of lands. ☐

Amotion essentially means the deprivation of possession. The term has been used to describe a wrongful seizure of personal chattels.

The most common legal use of the word is in CORPORATION law. In that context, amotion is the ousting of an officer from his or her post in the corporation prior to the end of the term for which the officer was appointed or elected, without taking away the person's right to be a member of the corporation. It can be distinguished from DISFRANCHISEMENT, which is the total expulsion of a corporation's officer or official representative.

AMOUNT IN CONTROVERSY

☐ The value of the relief demanded or the amount of monetary damages claimed in a lawsuit. ☐

Some courts have jurisdiction, or the power to hear cases, only if the amount in controversy is more or less than an amount specified by law. For example, Federal district courts can hear lawsuits concerning questions of Federal law and controversies between citizens of different states, but they can do this only if the amounts in controversy are more than $10,000. Some lower-level state courts, such as those that hear SMALL CLAIMS, have no authority to hear controversies involving more than certain maximum amounts.

When the amount in controversy determines the court's authority to hear a particular case, it may also be called the jurisdictional amount.

ANALOGY

☐ The inference that two or more things that are similar to each other in some respects are also similar in other respects. ☐

An analogy denotes that similarity exists in some characteristics of things that are otherwise not alike.

In a legal argument, an analogy may be used when there is no precedent (prior case law close in facts and legal principles) in point. Reasoning by analogy involves referring to a case that concerns unrelated subject matter but is governed by the same general principles and applying those principles to the case at hand.

Edgar Bodenheimer

Analytical Jurisprudence

According to John Chipman Gray, a prominent nineteenth-century professor of law at Harvard, the task of the analytic student of the law is the task of classification and, included in this, of definition. He suggested that a scholar who could perfectly classify the law would have a perfect knowledge of the law.

The English jurist John Austin (*b.* 1790; *d.* 1859) became the founder of the analytical school of law, although some of his basic ideas had been foreshadowed by others, especially Jeremy Bentham. The function of jurisprudence, in the opinion of Austin, is the exposition of the principles, notions, and distinctions that are common to developed systems of law. This task involves the definition and elucidation of the fundamental terms of the law, such as *right, obligation, injury, sanction, punishment,* and *redress*. It also entails, among other things, the categorization of rights, the classification of obligations, the elaboration of distinctions between law and other modes of social control, and a treatment of the sources of law (for example, precedents, legislation, custom). Other analytical jurists have pointed out that a comparative analysis of developed systems of law is not an essential ingredient of analytical jurisprudence; this discipline properly limits its attention to the exposition of the leading conceptions of a single legal system.

The ideas of Jeremy Bentham anticipated some of the ideas found in Austin's principals of analytical jurisprudence.

Characteristic of Austinian analytical jurisprudence is its restriction of the scope of its investigations to the positive law enforced by the state, considered without reference to whether it is good or bad. Inquiries concerning the existence of a natural law or law of God, as well as speculations regarding the fundamental requirements of justice, are deemed to be beyond the competence of the analytical jurist. His or her task is viewed as a descriptive one, excluding criticism and evaluation of the legal order. Austin was convinced that the positive law, itself, was the standard of human justice. According to this position, a law enacted by the state in conformity with established procedures is a valid law regardless of its content; disregard of it can never be legally justified, although it may in some instances be excusable from a purely moral point of view.

A neoanalytic school of law arose in England and the United States in the second half of the twentieth century. The representatives of this movement abandoned the exclusivity with which earlier analytical jurists sought to confine the province of law to an exegesis of basic legal notions and conceptions. They were ready to admit the legitimacy of other ways to deal with the phenomenon of law, such as sociological interpretations and inquiries concerning the existence of natural law.

The new analytical jurists have made extensive use of the modern sharpened tools of logic, such as symbolic logic and computer science. They have also utilized the findings of contemporary linguistic research. These findings have con-

243

vinced them that the meaning of basic legal terms is not as stable as the earlier analytical jurists assumed. Although a legal concept may have a core meaning that is generally accepted, it may become indeterminate at its fringes, and its applicability or nonapplicability in a given situation may depend on the factual context or the special character of the legal problem presented. See also, Thomas M. Feldstein and Stephen B. Presser's essay on John Austin; and Stephen B. Presser's essay on Jeremy Bentham.

Bibliography: John Austin, *The Province of Jurisprudence Determined* (H. L. A. Hart, ed.) (1954), pp. 365–372; Robert S. Summers, "The New Analytical Jurists," 41 *New York University Law Review* (November 1966):861–896.

ANARCHY ☐ A society in which there is no structured government or law or in which there is violent resistance to all current forms of government, causing political disorder and lawlessness. ☐

Criminal anarchy is based upon the principle that organized government should be destroyed by unlawful methods and violence. Federal law, which has preempted the area of SEDITION, makes the advocacy of criminal anarchy against the Federal government a FELONY, punishable by a fine of not more than $20,000, imprisonment, or both, and the ineligibility for employment in the Federal government for five years subsequent to conviction. See also, Mulford Q. Sibley's essay on Anarchy.

Library of Congress

"Red Emma," as Emma Goldman came to be known, was born in Russia in 1869. Imprisoned in the United States in 1916 for advocating birth control and again in 1917 for obstructing the draft, Goldman was subsequently deported to her homeland.

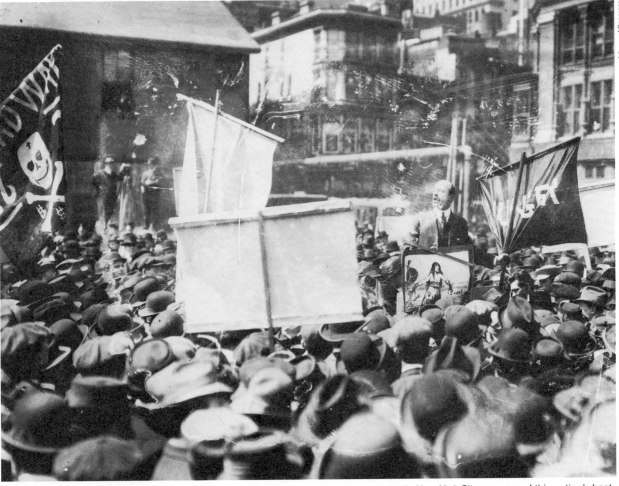

Library of Congress

Along with Emma Goldman, Alexander Berkman, seen here addressing a mass meeting in New York City, was one of this nation's best known anarchists in the early 1900s.

Anarchy

Anarchy means without rule (*an-archos*) or rulerless. Hence an anarchy is a society without rules or rulers.

Those who support the goal of anarchy are called anarchists and believe that an anarchy, contrary to its critics, is the only form of community that can be free and orderly.

In general, all anarchists see the principle of political authority as the foundation for much of what is wrong with the world. The existence of rule means that the many must subordinate themselves to the few—a form of slavery. The state, anarchists argue, is essentially based on force, and law is an expression of violence against human personality. Like the Marxists, many anarchists see law as an instrument of the ruling class for promoting its own interests. Human freedom cannot be achieved, they maintain, in a society characterized by state-imposed rigidities, bureaucracy, class-tainted "justice," and centralization of power.

Anarchist attitudes go far back into human history. Lao-tze, the ancient Chinese philosopher (sixth century, B.C.), might be regarded by many as an anarchist. The early Hebrew writers who seemed to praise the premonarchial state of society were apparently suspicious of all political rulership. Some of the early Christians also appeared to have had an anarchist outlook, which possibly provoked St. Paul to write the thirteenth chapter of Romans in which Christians are admonished to obey "the powers that be." There were also anarchist sectarians during the Middle Ages.

Modern anarchism may be said to have begun with William Godwin (1756–1836) who in his *Enquiry Concerning Political Justice* (1793) argued that through enlightenment and nonviolent resistance human beings could be freed from what he regarded as the enslaving factors of promises, law, and the state. The poet Percy B. Shelley (1792–1822) was a follower of Godwin and helped popularize his views.

But modern anarchists have not been united on what they regard as the implications of anarchism. Some, like Max Stirner (1806–1856), have taken extreme individualist positions. But others, like the French thinker Pierre Joseph Proudhon (1809–1865), have emphasized family life and small communities bound together by agreements. Yet others, of whom Peter Kropotkin (1842–1921) is perhaps the best example, are known as communist anarchists because they stress the great possibilities of voluntary mutual aid and accept communist distributive principles. While a few anarchists have advocated violence as a political strategy—Mikhail Bakunin (1814–1876), for example, and the so-called "anarchists of the deed"—perhaps most would think of violence as a defensive "last resort" technique (in this resembling democrats and liberals). Not a few anarchists, such as Leo Tolstoy (1828–1910), have been pacifists, rejecting violence for any purpose.

"Whatever is, is not," is the maxim of the anarchist, as often as anything comes across him in the shape of a law which he happens not to like.

RICHARD BENTLEY

TIME TO DRAW AND STRIKE.

In this allegorical political cartoon, military law is a weapon the government will use to subdue the snake of anarchy.

Two early contributors to the development of anarchist thought in the United States were Josiah Warren, *left*, and Henry David Thoreau.

The ultimate goal of Marxist theory is anarchistic. But Marxists, unlike anarchists, believe that the state must be used to liquidate the old class-dominated system of capitalism and to prepare the way for communist anarchy.

Anarchists have been divided in their attitudes to industrialism. Kropotkin believed that a considerable degree of industrial and technological development was compatible with the highly decentralized social order favored by anarchists. Others, however, most notably Tolstoy, have taken the contrary position, seeing complex technology, the state, and industrialism as utterly incompatible with the ideal of anarchy.

Anarchists have generally been severe critics of both American-style capitalism and of such authoritarian systems as that of the Soviet Union.

The first American anarchist philosopher was Josiah Warren (1798–1874). Anarchism in the United States has in some measure been inspired by certain strains in transcendentalism, particularly those stemming from Henry D. Thoreau (1817–1862). In the twentieth century, two prominent U.S. communist anarchists have been Emma Goldman (1869–1940) and Alexander Berkman (1870–1936). Akin to anarchism has been anarcho-syndicalism, which stresses the industrial union as the basis for a reorganization of society and which has been reflected in twentieth-century U.S. life by the Industrial Workers of the World (IWW).

American public opinion has often associated anarchist philosophy with advocacy and commission of violence and this image was a factor in leading Congress to forbid the naturalization of professed anarchists.

As a worldwide political movement, anarchism reached its height early in the twentieth century and began to decline after World War I. But it remained, and continues to remain, relatively strong in Spain.

Bibliography: George Woodcock, *Anarchism: A History of Libertarian Ideas and Movements* (1962).

ANCIENT LIGHTS ☐ A doctrine of English COMMON LAW that gives a landowner an EASEMENT or right by PRESCRIPTION to the unobstructed passage of light and air from adjoining land if the landowner has had uninterrupted use of the lights for twenty years. ☐

Once a person gains the right to ancient lights, the owner of the adjoining land cannot obscure them, such as by erecting a building. If the neighbor does so, he or she can be sued under a theory of NUISANCE, and DAMAGES could be awarded.

The doctrine of ancient lights has not been adopted in the United States since it would greatly hinder commercial and residential growth and the expansion of towns and cities.

ANCIENT WRITING ☐ An original document affecting the transfer of real property, which can be admitted as EVIDENCE in a lawsuit because its aged condition and its location upon discovery sufficiently establish its authenticity. ☐

Under COMMON LAW, an ancient writing, sometimes called an ancient document, could be offered as evidence only if certain conditions were met. The document had to be at least thirty years old, the equivalent of a generation. It had to appear genuine and free from suspicion. For example, if the date of the document or the signatures of the parties to it appeared to have been altered, it was not considered genuine. When found, the document must have been in a likely location or in the possession of a person who would logically have had access to it, such as a deed found in the office of the county clerk or in the custody of the attorney for one of the parties to the writing. An ancient writing must also have related to the transfer of real property, for example, a will, a deed, or a mortgage. When all these requirements were met, an ancient writing was presumed to be genuine upon its presentation for admission as evidence without any additional proof.

Today various state rules of evidence and the Federal Rules of Evidence have expanded the admissibility of ancient writings. An ancient writing can now be offered as evidence if its condition does not suggest doubt as to its authenticity, if it is found in a likely place, and if it is at least twenty years old at the time it is presented for admission into evidence.

Some states still adhere to the requirement that a document be at least thirty years old before it comes within the ancient writing exception to the HEARSAY rule. A few states recognize

In designing the buildings and skyscrapers that surround the Old State House in Boston, the architects must have had the doctrine of ancient lights in mind.

ancient documents only if, in addition to these basic requirements, the person seeking the admission of the ancient writing has taken possession of the property in question.

An ancient writing is admissible in a trial as an exception to the rule that prohibits hearsay from being used as evidence in a trial. In a case where no other evidence exists, the legitimacy of the writing must be considered if the case is to be determined on its merits. The probability that such a document is trustworthy is determined by its condition and location upon discovery. These factors permit a court and a jury to presume the authenticity of an ancient writing.

ANCILLARY

☐ Subordinate; aiding.

☐ A legal proceeding that is not the primary dispute but which aids the judgment rendered in or the outcome of the main action. ☐

For example, a plaintiff wins a judgment for a specified sum of money against a defendant in a NEGLIGENCE action. The defendant refuses to pay the judgment. The plaintiff begins another proceeding for a WRIT OF ATTACHMENT so that the judgment will be satisfied by the sale of the defendant's property seized under the writ. The attachment proceeding is ancillary, or subordinate, to the negligence suit. An ancillary proceeding is sometimes called an ancillary suit or bill. See also, Ancillary Administration.

☐ A descriptive term that denotes a legal claim, the existence of which is dependent upon or reasonably linked to a main claim. ☐

A claim for ALIMONY is an ancillary claim dependent upon the primary claim that there are sufficient legal grounds for a court to grant a DIVORCE.

ANCILLARY ADMINISTRATION ☐ The

settlement and distribution of a decedent's property in the state where it is located and which is other than the state in which the decedent was domiciled. ☐

Ancillary administration occurs in a state to enable an EXECUTOR or ADMINISTRATOR to collect assets or to commence litigation on behalf of the estate in that jurisdiction.

ANCILLARY JURISDICTION

☐ The authority of a court to hear and resolve matters that are incidental to the exercise of its primary power to act in a particular case and that it otherwise would not be authorized to hear.

☐ The doctrine by which a Federal district court obtains JURISDICTION of a CASE OR CONTROVERSY as an entirety, so that it can decide other matters raised by the case—matters which if independently presented are not normally handled in Federal court due to lack of DIVERSITY OF CITIZENSHIP, the requisite AMOUNT IN CONTROVERSY, or any other basis of Federal jurisdiction. ☐

The concept of ancillary jurisdiction was developed by the Supreme Court as a matter of necessity. Its purpose is to make an action taken in Federal court effective in cases involving Federal claims that include certain aspects that are not ordinarily cognizable in a Federal court. To illustrate, in one case brought in Federal court on the basis of diversity of citizenship, a United States marshal seized several railroad cars pursuant to writs of attachment. The mortgage holders of the railroad cars sued the marshal in state court for REPLEVIN, the recovery of goods wrongfully seized, and won. The Supreme Court reviewed the state court decision and decided that, since the railroad cars were under the control of a Federal court, the state court was powerless to interfere. This decision recognized that the Federal court had ancillary jurisdiction to determine the disposition of the railroad cars, although such a controversy by itself would not normally be determined in Federal court. To decide otherwise would result in a conflict between state and Federal courts, thereby undermining the effectiveness of Federal courts.

The Supreme Court later expanded the concept of ancillary jurisdiction to include the disposition of issues that are procedurally convenient to the ultimate disposition of the case if they arise from the same transaction as the complaint. The Court also decided that a non-Federal counterclaim asserted in response to a COMPLAINT based on Federal law, and which arose from the same transaction, could be adjudicated in Federal court, even though the complaint was dismissed. The Supreme Court reasoned that the relationship between the complaint and counterclaim was so close that the dismissal of the complaint established the basis for granting relief on the courterclaim.

Ancillary jurisdiction exists in cases involving compulsory counterclaims, CROSS-CLAIMS, IMPLEADER, INTERPLEADER, and INTERVENTION as of right, as governed by the FEDERAL RULES OF CIVIL PROCEDURE. Permissive counterclaims, which do not arise from the same transaction as the complaint, and permissive intervention are allowed in Federal courts only if an independent basis for Federal jurisdiction exists.

ANGARY, RIGHT OF ☐ The authority of a

belligerent to appropriate property belonging to a neutral country, which has been temporarily placed in the belligerent's own territory or in that of another belligerent, either for use or destruction in case of necessity, provided the appropriation is for military purposes. ☐

The term *angary* formerly applied to the right asserted by a belligerent to seize merchant vessels located in its harbors and force them, on payment of freight, to transport troops and supplies to a specific port.

Anthony D'Amato & Stephen B. Presser

Anglo-Saxon Law

Anglo-Saxon law is the name generally used to refer to the legal system that prevailed in Britian for approximately the five centuries before the Norman Conquest in 1066. It was the law of the Germanic tribes that ruled the nation following their victory over the Danes. It had much in common with the jurisprudence of related peoples on the Continent, and many customs of Anglo-Saxon law evolved into a form that survives in English and American common law. Still the system was appropriate for a rural, essentially tribal, society in which magic and ritual played much more of a role than reason and science. In what courts there were, usually bodies convened by the local temporal or spiritual noble, the primary mode of proof was by oath, and an oath that went not to the truth of a specific fact but to the justice of the claim or defense as a whole. If the oath was performed properly, with the right number of oath helpers, who were also required to perform flawlessly, the oath was conclusive. If the oath was inconclusive, however, the court resorted to other ancient forms of proof, such as the ordeal. In two of the most popular ordeals, the hot water and the hot iron ordeals, the offender would be made to plunge his or her hand into boiling water or to grasp a red hot iron, and the manner in which the wound healed demonstrated guilt or innocence. In this way, divine providence was asked to indicate the manner in which cases would be decided.

There were few official sanctions for failure to comply with judicial procedures, although the device of "outlawry" was sometimes used. An "outlaw" put himself out of the protection of the laws and could normally be killed by anyone, without fear of official or unofficial retribution. All of an outlaw's goods would also be forfeit to the king. Criminal offenses at Anglo-Saxon law included murder, theft, wounding, treason, and the "contumelous outrage of binding a free man, or shaving his head in derision, or shaving off his beard." Imprisonment was rarely used as a means of punishment. Instead, those guilty of the worst crimes suffered capital punishment or were placed into slavery.

For all but the very worst crimes, however, defendants or their kinsmen could offer restitution by paying specified sums to the injured parties. Restitution even extended to many cases of murder, with the payment for that offense called by the Anglo-Saxon name *wergeld*. A person's *wer*, or worth, varied with his or her station—a member of the nobility, a free person, or a slave. A person's *wer* also determined the amount of fine levied if he or she failed to perform a public duty or committed an offense against public order. There was no jury discretion in matters of damages, with compensation specified in particular cases by preexisting ordinance, custom, or statute. As the concept of *wer* indicates, the Anglo-Saxon legal system was based on a very stratified society with status often depending on individuals' relationships to the land or to their lord. Slavery was very common, and slave traders operated from English ports, bringing slaves to and from Britain.

Too many there be to whom a dead enemy smells well, and who find musk and amber in revenge.

SIR THOMAS BROWNE

Manumission was also practiced and seems to have resulted in the integration of freed slaves into the general community. Laws of contract were virtually nonexistent, and the law of property depended principally upon possession.

To an American law student, Anglo-Saxon law might have antiquarian interest only, except for a vital link between that law and current United States law. When the American colonies were established, the rules that governed decisions in cases that were heard in the various colonial courts were the precedents established by the "common law" of England, which included many rules derived from Anglo-Saxon law. Even after the United States of America was proclaimed an independent nation, the rules of decision in the courts continued to be built upon the old English precedents.

Not only did Anglo-Saxon law, through the later English common law, give us a wealth of precedent for the new nation, but it also bequeathed to us two separate judicial systems that looked at "law" in different ways. The "common-law courts," the more ancient of the two, comprised all cases (with few exceptions) where monetary damages were awarded. Since the earliest times these cases were presided over by judges specially trained in the legal doctrines. If a plaintiff's injury could be expressed in monetary terms, and if a monetary judgment would satisfy or vindicate the plaintiff's rights, then the common-law system heard the case. On the other hand, if the plaintiff requested that the defendant be ordered to do (or refrain from doing) something, other than payment of monetary damages, or sought relief not available through the rigidly conducted common-law courts, then the plaintiff had to bring a suit in the "equity" courts. The equity courts arose in England in response to the fact that the common-law courts could not provide for all judicial redress required under all circumstances.

At first equity was dispensed by the king himself, for example, under Anglo-Saxon law, to compel redress against defendants protected by a powerful noble. Eventually the duty passed to the king's chancellor, and, finally, in the fourteenth and fifteenth centuries, there had grown up another specialized judicial system, the equity courts, or Courts of Chancery. These courts provided a simple remedy addressed to the defendant—either do what the court says, or go to jail. Once in jail, the defendant had the "keys in his pocket" to leave; he or she could leave providing he or she carried out the court's order. The order of the court could be to convey a unique piece of land to the plaintiff (sometimes money cannot be the equivalent of land because of its uniqueness), or to pay alimony to the plaintiff (even today, a spouse who refuses to pay alimony can be put in jail by the equity court), or to refrain from violating the plaintiff's rights in some specific way. Today, for example, U.S. equity courts often have the responsibility to see to it that schools are desegregated (the busing of schoolchildren is a direct function of the orders of U.S. equity courts upon school officials and administrators).

The Anglo-Saxon system of Germanic laws was often remarkably different from the contemporary laws of other parts of continental Europe. The latter were more closely influenced by Roman law, whereas English laws, like the Scandinavian, were the expression of Teutonic legal thought. Thomas Jefferson, among other early Americans, venerated this legal system, believing that the Teutonic influence emphasized popular participation and liberty more than the authoritarian beliefs of the Normans. Jefferson's views on the "purity" of the Anglo-Saxon common law may have been extraordinarily incorrect, however, given the Anglo-

All laws are useless, for good men do not need them and bad men are made no better by them.

PLUTARCH

The first printed collection of Anglo-Saxon laws was *Apxaionomia*. Translated and edited by William Lambarde, the book was published in London by John Day in 1568. It gave the Anglo-Saxon text with a parallel translation in Latin. The first English translation of these laws was published in 1840.

Saxon system's tolerance of slavery, its preoccupation with status, and its lack of any really "popular" institutions.

Like sources of law today, the Anglo-Saxon laws could be found in statutes, in authoritative statements of custom, and in various compilations of legal rules and enactments. Many royal proclamations or provisions of treaties made up the first category. In the second category, a prominent example of a compilation of local customs was the Domesday Book, a collection of Anglo-Saxon "dooms" or laws ordered by the Normans. In the third, there were many manuals on various practices, such as the formalities of betrothal, the duties of judges, collections of oaths, and so on. The various provisions of the criminal law, including lists of fines, punishments, outlawry, confiscation, and rules of procedure, far exceeded in number and detail the provisions of the civil law. It is some measure of the change in the legal order that while Anglo-Saxon law had no real conception of contract, and almost no sophistication in the law of property, modern common-law jurisprudence relegates criminal matters to a position of minor importance and is preoccupied with the rules of commerce, manufacture, trade, and administration. Finally, while the foundation of the old laws was the spiritual power of the church, and the legal system made little or no attempt to separate religious from secular rights and duties, modern Anglo-American jurisprudence takes as a central tenet the separation of church and state.

*For such law as man giveth
  other wight,
He should him-selven usen it by
  right.*

CHAUCER

Bibliography: Frederick Pollock and Frederic W. Maitland, *The History of English Law*, 2d ed., vol. 1 (1968), pp. 25–63; T. F. T. Plucknett, *A Concise History of the Common Law*, 5th ed. (1956), pp. 6–10 and sources cited there.

ANIMALS ☐ Any living beings, other than humans, that are capable of voluntary movement. ☐

Domestic animals encompass those tamed through lengthy human contact and training, such as cats and dogs, and those deliberately tamed, such as horses, cows, and chickens. *Wild animals* are those that cannot be totally domesticated, since force or skill is constantly required to maintain control over them, such as alligators, minks, lions, rats, snakes, and bees.

Legal status All domestic animals constitute personal property and entail the same ownership rights as other types of personal property. The owner's rights regarding his or her animals are, however, subject to the state's POLICE POWER—the right of the state to legislate laws that provide for the health, safety, welfare, and morals of its citizens. The vaccination and licensing of animals are regulations which illustrate the exercise of a state's police power.

The owner of domestic animals has permanent property rights. When an animal strays and is discovered by another person, the finder does not gain its ownership unless the old owner cannot be found. In general, the person who owns the mother also owns the offspring, and when an animal dies, the carcass remains the owner's property.

All wild animals within its boundaries are owned by the state which acts as a trustee for the benefit and use of its residents. The state has authority to proscribe and regulate all matters relating to wild animals found within its boundaries and to determine what property rights a person might acquire in such animals. Wild animals in their natural habitat are not the property of private citizens. A person becomes the owner of a wild animal when he or she captures or kills it and removes it from its natural environment, but if the acquisition is illegal, the state retains ownership of the animal.

Landowners have limited property interests in wild animals living on their land, which become unqualified when a wild animal is captured or killed. The exclusive right of landowners to hunt animals on their land is subject only to state regulation, as in the case of a specified hunting season. A person who locates wild animals on another person's property has no legal rights toward them, unless the landowner grants permission to enter and seize them.

Ownership of wild animals is ordinarily irretrievable when they escape and return to nature, but if a wild animal escapes temporarily and is promptly pursued and captured by the original captor or his agents, ownership is not lost.

Brands and marks A brand is an emblem burned on an animal by a hot iron, most commonly used to identify cattle, mules, and horses. A mark is a change made in some part of the animal by a knife or other method, usually employed to identify cattle and hogs.

The right to use a livestock brand or mark is a valuable property right since it identifies the

This unusual photograph from 1907 shows that at the Bide-A-Wee Home for Animals, sun hats were as useful for horses as for humans.

ownership of the animal. Several states have enacted legislation regulating branding and marking in order to protect the owner and prevent the theft of livestock by furnishing a clear identification method. Some statutes require brand and mark inspection of livestock in shipment, with the inspector empowered to seize unbranded or unmarked animals thought to be stolen.

Brands and marks may be sold or transferred. Some state laws make the alteration of a brand or mark on another person's animal without consent and with the intent to defraud a crime.

Employment The employment of an animal creates a BAILMENT, a delivery of personal property from one person to another in trust for the attainment of a particular objective with respect to the property. The owner of the animal, the BAILOR, must furnish an animal that is sound, appropriate, and safe for the designated purposes. The bailor has a duty to inform the bailee, the person who hires the animal, of any violent or dangerous tendencies that the animal might possess. A bailor is not obligated, however, to advise the bailee of habits not ordinarily perilous to persons or property.

A bailee must exercise ordinary care with respect to the animal, but he or she is not an insurer and is thereby not liable for an injury to the animal or for its death, unless it is due to his or her negligence.

Cruelty The majority of states have enacted legislation proscribing cruelty to animals. Some statutes protect all animals, whereas others are restricted to domestic animals.

Cruelty encompasses any unreasonable act or omission inducing pain, suffering, or death, such as overworking, underfeeding, or not furnishing the animal with sufficient protection. It is determined by whether the act in question is reasonable under the circumstances, since the slaughter of a diseased or injured animal is considered by society an act of mercy, not cruelty. The infliction of pain in branding an animal does not constitute cruelty since its purpose is reasonable.

Methods of slaughter that inflict unnecessary pain are proscribed, as is nonessential killing, such as in bullfights. Some statutes provide that poisoning an animal is an act of cruelty. The applicable statutes and circumstances determine whether killing, injuring, or abusing animals for sport constitutes cruelty in violation of the law.

Licenses States frequently enact legislation imposing the payment of a license fee, or a tax upon the owner of the dog for the privilege of possessing it. A dog license is required by the state where the dog is kept and not where the owner resides, if the two locations are different. In accordance with the law, an application for a dog license must be made in a timely manner. A late application is not grounds to refuse to issue a license, but it might result in the imposition of a PENALTY. Failure to license a dog when required by law is punishable by a fine. Some licensing laws mandate a description of the dog, which the owner must provide with accuracy for identification purposes to ensure that the owner has licensed all the dogs he or she owns and to enable public officials to locate the owner of a dog which poses a danger to the public health or safety.

Running at large Owners of domestic animals may legally permit them to roam at large unless there are regulations to the contrary. They must, however, exercise ordinary care to prevent the animals from straying onto heavily traveled roadways or endangering public safety. A state that prohibits animals from running at large may require that they be retained within fenced areas by their owners. The capture and sale of those animals discovered running at large may also be required under statute.

Trespassing animals A landowner can use only reasonably necessary force to drive off a trespassing animal from his or her property. A landowner can kill an animal only when essential to personal safety or the protection of property, but must balance the value of the animal in relation to the extent of the potential property damage before doing so.

Liability of dog owners A dog owner who is aware that his or her pet has a vicious inclination or condition that threatens a person or property has a duty to control or confine it. Failure to do so will render the owner liable for injuries caused by his or her pet as a result of these tendencies. The retention of a savage animal as a pet is also considered to constitute a NUISANCE, interference with another person's use and enjoyment of his or her property, and liability will ensue under this theory for any injuries caused by the animal. An owner of a rabid dog which inflicts rabies on a person or another animal is not liable for damages unless the owner knows or has reason to believe that the dog is dangerous. The law imposes liability for injuries directly arising from an owner's negligence in maintaining or controlling his or her dog, irrespective of his or her knowledge of its vicious tendencies.

A person is usually entitled to keep a ferocious dog for the protection of life and property. He is usually not liable for injuries to a person who enters the premises during the night, even if the person is present for a lawful purpose. Some courts have ruled, however, that if an owner allows a dog to roam at will on the premises and, consequently, a person is injured by it during the daytime, the owner is liable even to a trespasser, one who has intentionally and without authority or permission entered the property of another.

A number of courts have held that the owner of a vicious dog retained to guard the owner's premises has no duty to issue or to post notice of the dog's vicious nature. Other courts, however, have decided to the contrary. As a general rule, an owner is deemed to have acted reasonably by posting signs and chaining his or her dog to keep it within the property line.

A person who invites social guests to his or her premises has to act with ordinary care while they are present. Unless the owner knows of a vicious predilection, he or she is not negligent in allowing a dog free rein within the house. If both the owner and the guest are aware that a dog is on the premises, the owner is not liable for negligence if the guest is injured because of his collision with the dog.

Some statutes prescribe liability for dog bites even though the owner has no knowledge of the dog's inclination to bite. These "dog bite" laws, however, do not impose STRICT LIABILITY upon an owner for all injuries caused by the dog.

An individual who keeps a dog to protect his or her business must use reasonable care to safeguard visitors against injury caused by the dog. Such steps as posting signs that warn of the dog's presence and ascertaining that the dog is securely confined are normally enough. If a business visitor is bitten by a dog known to be vicious, the visitor may sue the owner in TORT under the theory of strict liability regardless of whether the owner was negligent.

In some jurisdictions, the distinctions among the duties owed various categories of visitors have been abolished. The emerging view is that landowners and occupiers must exercise reasonable care in regard to all persons who enter their land, even trespassers.

Injuries to persons   Owners of any domestic animal are liable for injuries caused by it only when the owners have been negligent or when the injuries are the consequence of the animal's known savage inclination.

The most common theory of recovery for an injury by an animal, which has no known vicious tendencies, is negligence. The owner's negligent act must have been the direct or PROXIMATE CAUSE of the injury, and the injury must have been one the owner could have reasonably anticipated or foreseen.

A vicious tendency is a propensity to perform an act that endangers another person or that person's property. It has no bearing on the issue of liability that the act was caused by friski-

ness or mischief, instead of savagery. If the animal has a recognized predilection to act threateningly, the owner is liable for ensuing injuries to others. If, however, the injury is caused by a fierce tendency that is not natural or common in that type of animal, and the owner has no knowledge of it, the owner will not be subject to liability.

An owner might have actual or implied knowledge of the vicious tendencies of his animal. Personal knowledge is not required because if an agent or employee responsible for the animal is aware of its vicious tendencies, that knowledge is assumed to be imputed, or transferred, to the owner.

The need to establish that an owner knew that the animal was dangerous is contingent upon whether the animal was in its rightful place at the time of the injury. If the animal was there, proof of the owner's knowledge of its propensities must be presented, but if the animal was elsewhere when the injury occurred, there is no need to establish the owner's knowledge.

Property damage   An owner is strictly liable for property damage if the animal belongs to the category of animals that are known to wander, escape, or trespass and thereby injure neighboring property, such as cattle, horses, hogs, fowl, and wild boars.

In the case of a domestic animal, such as a dog or cat, a majority of courts impose absolute liability upon an owner for DAMAGES caused by the trespassing animal only if the owner knew, or should have known, of the pet's trait which caused the damages.

These general principles might be modified by statute or by judicial decisions, and, therefore, the applicable state law must be consulted.

Injury or death of an animal   When someone intentionally or negligently injures or kills a domestic animal, the owner is ordinarily entitled to damages, limited to the market value of the animal. There is no compensation for the owner's emotional suffering caused by the animal's death.

The injury or death of an animal resulting from motor vehicle accidents, vehicle noises, and airplanes flying at low altitudes are common cases entitling an owner to the recovery of damages. Liability might also ensue from the negligent use or disposal of pollutants, poisons, or waste products which harm or kill animals.

ANIMUS   [*Latin, "Mind, soul, or intention."*]
□ A tendency or an inclination toward a definite, sometimes unavoidable, goal; an aim, objective, or purpose. □

The welfare of the people is the chief law.

CICERO

When *animus* is used in conjunction with other words of Latin origin, its most common meaning is "the intention of." For example, *animus revocandi* is the intention of revoking; *animus possidendi* is the intention of possessing.

Animo, meaning "with intent," may be employed in a manner similar to *animus.* For example, *animo felonico* means with felonious intent.

ANIMUS REVERTENDI □ The intention of returning. □

To establish DESERTION as a ground for DIVORCE, the injured person must prove that his or her spouse unjustifiably abandoned him or her for a specific period of time and did not possess any *animus revertendi.*

ANNEXATION □ The act of attaching, uniting, or joining together in a physical sense; consolidating. □

The term is generally used to signify the connection of a smaller or subordinate unit to a larger or principal unit. For example, a smaller piece of land may be annexed to a larger one. Similarly, a smaller document may be annexed to a larger one, such as a CODICIL to a WILL.

Although physical joining is implied, actual contact is not always necessary. For example, an annexation occurs when a country acquires new territory even though the new territory is not immediately adjacent to the existing country.

In the law of REAL PROPERTY, annexation is used to describe the manner in which a CHATTEL is joined to property. See also, Fixtures.

ANNOTATED STATUTES □ A multivolume set of books containing the text of laws enacted by a legislature, citations of law review articles, attorney general opinions, and legislative histories that explain the law, and ANNOTATIONS, or brief statements of similar points of law discussed in reported cases. □

The UNITED STATES CODE ANNOTATED, popularly known as U.S.C.A., is a set of annotated Federal statutes. The laws of all fifty states, the District of Columbia, Puerto Rico, and the Virgin Islands are available in the form of annotated statutes.

ANNOTATION □ A note, summary, or commentary on some section of a book or a statute that is intended to explain or illustrate its meaning. □

An annotation serves as a brief summary of the law and the facts of a case and demonstrates how a particular law enacted by Congress or a state legislature is interpreted and applied. Annotations usually follow the text of the statute they interpret in ANNOTATED STATUTES.

ANNUAL PERCENTAGE RATE □ The actual cost of borrowing money, expressed in the form of a yearly measure to allow consumers to compare the cost of borrowing money among several lenders. □

The Federal TRUTH-IN-LENDING ACT (15 U.S.C.A. § 1601 et seq. [1968]) mandates the complete disclosure of this rate in addition to other CREDIT terms.

ANNUAL REPORT □ A yearly account prepared by a CORPORATION for stockholders and other interested parties. An annual report encompasses an income statement; a BALANCE SHEET, which shows alterations in its financial worth; a reconciliation of changes in owner's EQUITY accounts; the auditor's report; an analysis from management concerning the year's transactions and prospects for the following year; and other explanatory material. □

By law, any public corporation that conducts a yearly stockholders' meeting is required to provide an annual report.

ANNUITY □ A right to receive periodic payments, usually fixed in size, for life or a term of years that is created by a contract or other legal document. □

The most common form of an annuity is akin to a savings account. The annuitant, the person who creates an annuity for his or her own benefit, deposits a sum of money, the principal, with an individual, business, or insurance company to be invested so that the principal will earn income at a certain percentage, usually specified by the terms of the annuity. This income is used by the company to pay the annuitant. Each payment received by the annuitant, sometimes called the primary beneficiary, represents a partial return of the principal and a portion of the income generated by its investment. Such annuities are employed frequently to provide a source of income to persons upon their retirement. A group annuity contract supplies periodic payments to a retired individual member of a group of employees covered by their employer's master contract. A retirement annuity is a policy paid to the annuitant after retirement. If the annuitant dies prior to the expiration of the annuity or wants to surrender the policy, an amount specified in the terms of the annuity is returned to the annuitant's estate or designated beneficiary.

Classification Annuities are classified according to the nature of the payment and the duration of time for payment. A *fixed annuity* requires payment in a specified amount to be made for the term of the annuity regardless of economic changes due to inflation or the fluctuation of the ventures in which the principal is invested. A *variable annuity* provides for payments that fluctuate in size contingent upon the success of the investment of the principal. Such variation offsets the effect of inflation upon the annuitant. If, however, the investment has fared poorly, the size of the payments decreases.

A *straight annuity* is a contract by an insurance company to make variable payments at monthly or yearly intervals. A *life* or *straight life annuity* is payable to an annuitant only during the annuitant's lifetime and ceases upon his or her death. The size of the periodic payment is usually fixed based upon actuarial charts that project the expected life span of a person based upon age and physical condition. This type of annuity often contains provisions that promise payment to be made to a secondary beneficiary, named by the annuitant to receive benefits in case of the annuitant's death, or to the annuitant's HEIRS for a period of time even if the annuitant has died before the expiration of the designated period. A *deferred annuity* is one in which payments start at a stipulated future date only if the annuitant is alive at that time. Payment of the INCOME TAX due on the income generated is delayed until payments start. A deferred annuity is used primarily by a person who does not want to receive payments until he or she is in a lower tax bracket, such as upon retirement.

A *refund annuity,* sometimes called a *cash refund annuity,* is a policy that promises to pay a set amount annually during the annuitant's life. In case the annuitant dies before receiving payments for the full amount of the annuity, his or her estate will receive a sum that is the difference between the purchase price and the sum paid during the annuitant's lifetime.

A *joint annuity* is one that is payable to two named persons but upon the death of one, the annuity terminates. A *joint and survivorship annuity* is a policy payable to the named annuitants during their lives and continues for the benefit of the surviving annuitant upon the death of the other.

Tax aspects   When an annuity is paid to an annuitant, he or she receives a portion of the principal and part of the return it has earned. For Federal and state income tax purposes, only the amount attributable to the income generated by the principal, not the principal itself, is considered taxable income. The INTERNAL REVENUE CODE provides an exclusion ratio to determine the amount of taxable income paid to the annuitant. Special tax rules apply to annuities that are qualified employee retirement plans. See also, Pensions.

The annuity payments made to the estate of a decedent might be subject to ESTATE TAX as an asset of the decedent's gross estate. Federal and state laws governing estate tax must be consulted to determine the liability for such taxes.

ANNULMENT □ A judgment by a court that retroactively invalidates a MARRIAGE to the date of its origin. □

An annulment differs from a DIVORCE, a court order that terminates a marriage, since it is a judicial statement that there was never a marriage. A divorce, which can only take place where there has been a valid marriage, means that the two parties are no longer husband and wife once the decree is issued. An annulment means that the individuals were never united in marriage as husband and wife.

Various religions have different methods for obtaining a church divorce, or annulment, but these procedures have no legal force or effect upon a marriage that complied with the requirements of law. Such a marriage must be legally annulled.

History   English COMMON LAW did not provide for annulment. Prior to the mid-nineteenth century, the only courts in England with the power to annul an invalid marriage, when fairness mandated it, were the ECCLESIASTICAL COURTS. There was no statute that provided relief of this kind.

Northeastern American colonies passed laws enabling courts or legislatures to grant annulments, while other colonies adhered more closely to English traditions. The American tradition of keeping church and state separate precluded the establishment of ecclesiastical courts in the United States. Following the American Revolution, the civil courts in a majority of states never assumed that they had the authority to hear annulment cases.

A number of states eventually enacted laws authorizing annulment in recognition of the belief that it is unfair to require people to fulfill marital duties when a marriage is invalid.

Currently, most states have annulment statutes. In states that do not, courts declare that no marriage exists if the laws regulating marriage have not been observed.

Types of marriage   An annulment declares that a marriage, which appears to be valid, is actually invalid. Two kinds of invalid marriages exist: *void marriages* and *voidable marriages.*

A void marriage is one that was invalid from its very beginning and, therefore, could never lawfully exist in any way.

Katharine of Aragon (1485–1536) refused to accept the annulment of her marriage to Henry VIII on his authority rather than that of the Roman Catholic church.

Henry VIII (1491–1547), king of England, claimed that he had the authority to annul his own marriage to Katharine of Aragon after she failed to produce a male heir and Henry had become infatuated with Anne Boleyn.

State law determines what makes a marriage void. A void marriage exists when an individual commits BIGAMY, the crime of marrying while still wed to someone else. In addition, when one individual is entirely incapable of giving consent and marrying voluntarily, such as a person under the legal age to marry, marriage of that person to another is void unless certain legal prerequisites are satisfied.

A marriage is void for INCEST if the couple is related in any way prohibited by state law for purposes of marriage. Ordinarily, the prohibition applies to relation by blood, such as a parent and child or brother and sister. It is sometimes also extended to cousins and second cousins and people related through only one parent. States sometimes recognize the validity of a marriage between relatives if such a marriage was legal in the state where it was performed.

A voidable marriage is one that can be declared illegal but that continues as valid until an annulment is sought. The annulment takes effect only from the time a court renders its decision. A void marriage is never legal, regardless of whether either party ever seeks an annulment.

Grounds The major grounds for a void marriage are incest, bigamy, and lack of consent. Once these grounds are established, the court will grant a decree of annulment.

State law governs the grounds for annulling a voidable marriage. Couples should not be obligated by the serious duties incident to marriage if no genuine intention to be married ever existed.

Fraud FRAUD is the most prevalent ground for annulment. In most states, the innocent party is required to establish that he or she was misled or lied to by the guilty party, no marriage would have occurred if he or she was apprised of the truth, and that a reasonable person would have been similarly defrauded under the circumstances. The misrepresentation, whether by lies or concealment of the truth, must encompass something directly pertinent to the marriage, such as religion, children, or sex, which society considers the foundation of a marital relationship.

Actual false statements or the failure to speak when a fundamental aspect of the marriage is involved constitutes fraud. If one individual has no intention to have children, that party has a duty to state this prior to the marriage. Although courts are reluctant to enforce an agreement not to have children, an annulment is not ordinarily available when an individual changes his or her mind about wanting to have children after the couple is married.

An annulment action for fraud can be successfully brought based upon the concealment of various sexual problems. Since sexual relations are regarded as a fundamental aspect of marriage, any known condition hampering a normal sex life must be disclosed prior to the marriage. Fraud occurs if either individual knowingly chooses not to disclose an inability to have children or to engage in sexual relations. In addition, annulments have been granted where there is a marked discrepancy in sexual predilections. Homosexuality has almost always been legally recognized as grounds for annulment.

Physical and emotional conditions
The law protects the rights of an individual to have sexual relations and procreate in marriage. A marriage can be declared invalid even in the absence of fraud if a physical or emotional condition prevents procreation from the outset of the marriage.

If a couple were aware of one partner's inability to have children from the beginning of the marriage, they cannot later assert this as a basis for an annulment. Such would be the case where two elderly people enter what is sometimes labeled a *companionate marriage,* which is one entered into for the comfort of an interpersonal relationship. Since neither party had any real expectation to have children, the court does not accept the allegation that an essential aspect of marriage has been thwarted.

The law of many jurisdictions allows annulment for an inability to engage in normal sex, or procreate, despite an absence of proof of fraud. The right to bear children is protected in such states even though the physically incapacitated party was unaware of his or her problem before marriage.

Other health conditions providing grounds for annulment include alcoholism, incurable INSANITY, and epilepsy. The mere existence of one of these conditions is a sufficient ground for

an annulment in some states, whereas in others, an annulment may be obtained for fraud if such a condition was concealed.

Lack of consent Courts grant annulments on lack of consent grounds only when it is believed that a couple never had any intention to be married. For example, courts have permitted annulments when the parties enter into a marriage only to legitimize a child. Other courts, however, have refused to grant annulments in such circumstances, based on the tenet that making children legitimate is an essential purpose of marriage.

An individual who suffers from mental illness or senility cannot be deemed to have given voluntary consent to a marriage.

Mistake A mistake involving some essential aspect of marriage might be a sufficient ground for an annulment, such as an erroneous belief that impotence or insanity has been cured. Since mistake means that one party has entered the marriage not fully cognizant, an annulment may be granted if the man or woman was so inebriated as not to comprehend that a marriage ceremony was taking place. In such cases, evidence must clearly establish that at least one party was totally incapable of making a rational decision.

Duress Many states allow annulment if one party has been forced to marry by DURESS, which deprives a party of voluntary freedom of choice in deciding to enter into a marital relationship.

Consummation and cohabitation
Courts take into account the act of consummating a marriage by sexual relations and cohabiting by sharing an abode and sex. A marriage that has not been consummated is more likely to be annulled by a court than one where the parties have acted as husband and wife toward each other. In most cases, the ground for annulment based on lack of consummation must stem from an inability that existed at the time of the marriage. Absence of cohabitation increases the likelihood that the court will view the ground serious enough to nullify the marriage.

Annulment for a condition subsequent to marriage A few exceptions exist in some jurisdictions to the general principle that an annulment may be granted solely for a condition occurring at the time of the marriage. Two such grounds are the insanity of an individual for at least five years that is apparently incurable and the unexplainable absence of one partner for a period of time and under circumstances that seriously suggest, but cannot conclusively establish,

Human laws, made to direct the will, ought to give precepts, and not counsels; religion, made to influence the heart should give many counsels, and few precepts.

CHARLES DE MONTESQUIEU

that the marriage partner has died. The dissolution of a marriage in the latter case may not be labeled an annulment or divorce but simply a court order, which has similar legal ramifications.

Opposition to annulment One marriage partner might assert defenses to prevent an annulment for various reasons. An individual might wish to remain married or prefer to obtain a divorce for the financial advantages of ALIMONY AND CHILD SUPPORT, which some states do not provide following an annulment.

Defenses A party might contest a spouse's attempt to have a marriage annulled through one of several defenses.

STATUTE OF LIMITATIONS is the defense most readily established. If the legal action is not commenced by the individual seeking annulment within the statutory time limit specified for the particular ground he or she is asserting, the court will dismiss the case. His or her alternative then is to remain married or bring an action for divorce if there are sufficient grounds.

Antenuptial knowledge may be a defense if the annulment action is based on fraud. Evidence exhibiting knowledge of the facts prior to the wedding indicates an absence of fraud or deception and acceptance of those facts by the party alleging them as grounds for an annulment.

The clean hands doctrine requires that an individual must come to court free from fault in the situation at issue or else the defendant can assert the plaintiff's fault to defeat the action. For instance, a man seeks an annulment on the basis that his wife tricked him into marrying her by claiming that he was the father of her illegitimate child. The wife's claim—that he had reason to believe he was the father of her illegitimate child and therefore could not be considered an innocent victim of fraud—would be accepted under the clean hands doctrine.

RATIFICATION is another key annulment defense. If a condition that might make a marriage invalid is accepted by one party, which is evidenced by cohabitation with his or her spouse for a length of time, such behavior indicates confirmation or acceptance of the condition and, therefore, defeats his or her action for annulment.

Standing to seek an annulment The aggrieved party has STANDING to initiate an action for annulment. If fraud is the basis of the lawsuit, the individual who was deceived may seek an annulment, but the guilty party may not. Similarly, an individual below the age of consent can request an annulment, but his or her partner cannot.

Ordinarily, either party to a void marriage can obtain a declaration that the marriage is invalid.

Under certain circumstances, an individual other than either party to the marriage can ask the court to annul a marriage. If, for example, a partner was under the legal age to marry, his or her parents might have standing to have the marriage annulled.

Consequences State law governs the consequences of an annulment. Customarily, an annulment was a court declaration that no marriage had ever existed, but this created various problems. If a marriage was dissolved by divorce, the children of the marriage were legitimate and the parent awarded custody could be awarded alimony. No such provisions, however, were made in an annulment. A majority of states have rectified this situation by statutory provisions. In most states, children of voidable, and sometimes void, marriages are legitimate. In addition, some states provide for alimony and property settlements upon the granting of an annulment. Several other jurisdictions allow their courts to devise a fair allocation of property where necessary and equitable.

For a sample annulment decree, see the Appendix volume 11.

ANON. ☐ An abbreviation for anonymous, nameless, or name unknown. ☐

ANSWER
☐ To assume the liability of another person, as to answer for the debts of one's spouse.
☐ The pleading by which a defendant resists the claims set out by a plaintiff in a COMPLAINT; a formal written statement in which a defendant denies the statements made by the plaintiff in a complaint or acknowledges them and asserts additional reasons why the plaintiff should not be given relief in the lawsuit. ☐

A defendant has several options when responding to the demands made in the plaintiff's complaint, whether the defendant's answer is governed by CODE PLEADING or by rules, such as those set forth in the FEDERAL RULES of CIVIL PROCEDURE. The defendant can deny everything, introduce an AFFIRMATIVE DEFENSE, demand relief from the plaintiff, or combine these options in some way. Different assertions in an answer can be inconsistent or set up alternatives.

There are different kinds of denials, and in each type the issue being denied becomes the point of contention. Any kind of denial must be truthful and cannot mislead. A general denial denies the truth of every fact in the complaint

ANSWER

A representative answer in which Richard Roe, the defendant, denies John Doe's claim for a debt of money and demands relief with a counterclaim against Doe.

UNITED STATES DISTRICT COURT FOR THE SOUTHERN
DISTRICT OF NEW YORK

Civil Action, File Number 000000

John Doe, Plaintiff	)	
	)	
v.	)	ANSWER
	)	
Richard Roe Co., Inc., Defendant	)	

First Defense

The complaint fails to state a claim against defendant upon which relief can be granted.

Second Defense

If defendant is indebted to plaintiff for the goods mentioned in the complaint as having been sold and delivered by plaintiff to defendant, defendant owes plaintiff less than $10,000 (ten thousand dollars).

Third Defense

Defendant admits that it is a corporation incorporated under the laws of the State of New York; alleges that it is without knowledge or information sufficient to form a belief as to the truth of the allegation concerning the place of plaintiff's citizenship; and denies each and every other allegation contained in the complaint.

Fourth Defense

The right of action set forth in the complaint did not accrue within six years prior to the commencement of this action.

Counterclaim

After March 19, 1977, and continuously since that time, the plaintiff has been inducing suppliers not to sell ready-to-wear women's dresses to defendant and has otherwise been engaging in unfair trade practices and unfair competition against plaintiff to defendant's irreparable damage and has diverted business worth at least $100,000 away from defendant.

WHEREFORE, defendant demands judgment against plaintiff for the sum of $100,000 (one hundred thousand dollars), interest, and costs.

Signed: _____
Attorney for Defendant

Address: _____

and, therefore, is seldom used since it is unlikely that *every* fact presented is false. A specific denial is based on certain paragraphs in the complaint with which the defendant disagrees. Paragraphs not specifically denied are assumed to be admitted as true. Similarly, a qualified denial may point to certain statements within a given paragraph that the defendant claims are untrue. These are the assertions most commonly made in an answer.

Most jurisdictions permit a defendant to enter a denial on the ground that he or she has insufficient knowledge to form a belief concerning the veracity or falsity of a certain allegation in the complaint. This is allowable only when it can be determined that the fact is outside the defendant's knowledge and that the denial concerns a point that the defendant could not easily have discovered. It is called a denial on information and belief. It is often used by a corporation that is being sued because of an action by one of its employees.

In addition to pleading some form of denial, a defendant's answer may include an affirmative defense to the plaintiff's cause of action. This is a statement that introduces new facts that defeat the plaintiff's claim, even if the facts in the complaint are true. A defendant may also demand relief in the form of a COUNTERCLAIM against an opposing party or, under some rules of pleading, a CROSS-CLAIM against another defendant. When the defendant affirmatively asserts a counterclaim or cross-claim, he or she is bound by the rules that apply to a complaint.

An example of a typical answer form is shown on page 262.

ANTARCTICA □ The polar land adjacent to the South Pole. □

According to the Antarctic Treaty of 1959, Antarctica is considered "international" territory, like that of the high seas; it is not under the jurisdiction of any nation. Its legal status, therefore, is governed by international law. For the complete text of the Antarctic Treaty of 1959, see the Appendix volume.

ANTE [*Latin, "Before."*]
□ A reference to a previous portion of a report or textbook. □

Ante is synonymous with SUPRA.

ANTECEDENT DEBT □ A legally enforceable obligation that has been in existence prior to the time in question to reimburse another with money or property. □

Principles of CONTRACT law vary from jurisdiction to jurisdiction regarding whether an antecedent debt constitutes good CONSIDERATION since the debtor does not incur any new detriment at the time that he enters a contract with another party. COMMERCIAL PAPER that has been given in exchange for an antecedent debt is deemed by the UNIFORM COMMERCIAL CODE to be supported by adequate consideration.

Under statutes governing BANKRUPTCY, a transfer of property made by a debtor because of an antecedent debt might be considered a voidable preference, depending upon the length of time between the creation of the debt and the filing of the petition for bankruptcy. A bankruptcy court may set aside a voidable preference since it gives one creditor a better right to payment than other creditors who are similarly situated.

ANTENUPTIAL □ Made or done prior to an impending marriage. □

An antenuptial agreement is a CONTRACT made between the prospective spouses in contemplation of their marriage. Such agreements are designed to resolve issues of support, distribution of wealth, and division of property in the event that the intended marriage is ended by SEPARATION, DIVORCE, or death. To be enforceable, antenuptial agreements must usually be in writing and the parties must know and understand their legal rights and duties under such a document. Another name for an antenuptial agreement is an antenuptial settlement. See also, Marriage.

ANTENUPTIAL AGREEMENT □ A CONTRACT made by two individuals prior to, and in contemplation of, marriage. □

The function of an antenuptial agreement is to clearly delineate the PROPERTY rights of the HUSBAND AND WIFE, as well as to resolve issues of support and distribution of wealth in the event that the marriage is terminated by DIVORCE, SEPARATION, or death.

Antenuptial agreements are subject to the STATUTE OF FRAUDS and must be in writing. In order for such an agreement to be valid, there must be full disclosure, equitable and reasonable support provisions, and binding CONSIDERATION. In determining whether or not an antenuptial agreement is both fair and reasonable, various factors are considered by the court. Elements to be considered include the relative financial situation of the prospective husband and wife, their ages, properties, family ties, and needs.

E. Adamson Hoebel

Anthropological Jurisprudence

Anthropology is the study of humanity around the world, in all times—prehistoric, ancient, and modern. It is concerned with the biological nature and evolution of the human species *and* with the variable forms and workings of all kinds of human societies—primitive and civilized. The anthropological study of law focuses on the ways in which different societies handle internal disputes or *trouble cases*. It also emphasizes how the forms and functions of particular law systems relate to the basic values and total cultures of specific types of societies.

The first significant work in anthropological jurisprudence was Sir Henry Maine's *Ancient Law*, published in 1861. Maine painstakingly contrasted early Roman law and its later development with nineteenth-century English law.

Early in the twentieth century, German and Dutch jurisprudents undertook extensive surveys of the indigenous and tribal legal systems of their respective countries' colonial empires. Their results were purely descriptive, drawing no theoretical conclusions and leaving little impression on either legal or anthropological thought.

In 1926 when Bronislaw Malinowski published a challenging study of law in the Trobriand Islands, a southwestern Pacific society, life was breathed into the then moribund field of anthropological jurisprudence. Malinowski dealt with law not in terms of formal rules but rather as a system of balanced obligations and rights between individuals. He particularly stimulated such legal realists as Jerome Frank, Thurmond Arnold, and Karl Llewellyn.

In 1941, lawyer Karl N. Llewellyn and anthropologist E. Adamson Hoebel wrote *The Cheyenne Way: Conflict and Case Law in Primitive Jurisprudence*, which opened a new era in the anthropology of law. Their field study of the Cheyenne Indians of the Great Plains of North America bypassed the usual method of simply gathering rules of law. Instead they concentrated on gathering oral accounts from the Cheyennes of cases of grievance, dispute, and conflict. Their inquiries sought to determine what the troubles were and what was done about them. This approach to the anthropology of law focused on actual patterns of dispute settlement and inductive formulation of how legal systems work in their total sociocultural settings.

The 1950s and 1960s saw the production of a number of detailed, high-quality research studies into systems of African tribal law by such English anthropologists as Max Gluckman, I. Shapera, and Philip Gulliver, as well as the Americans Paul Bohannon and Lloyd Fallers, all using the so-called *trouble-case* method. Other excellent works on Pacific tribal law systems were carried through to completion in New Guinea by Leo Pospisil and Klaus-Frederick Klaus and in the Philippines by the Americans Stuart Schlegel and Edward Dozier.

In *Ancient Law* (1861), Sir Henry Maine first focused attention on the relationship between the basic culture of a society and its legal system.

Broad-ranging comparative syntheses of primitive law systems, all empirically based, have been produced by Hoebel (*The Law of Primitive Man* [1954]), Gluckman (*The Ideas in Barotse Jurisprudence* [1965]), and Pospisil (*Anthropology of Law* [1971]).

Work in the field of anthropological jurisprudence continues in Mexico, Africa, India, Indonesia, and, in particular, the Middle East, with the emphasis tending to shift away from the functions of law in the maintenance of societal institutions to the strategies used by individuals and groups in gratifying their individual self-interests through manipulations of dispute management processes. See also, Sue Sheridan Walker's essay on Sir Henry James Sumner Maine; and Anthony D'Amato's essay on Karl Llewellyn.

Every law which the state enacts indicates a fact in human nature.

RALPH WALDO EMERSON

Bibliography: Max Gluckman, *Politics, Law and Ritual in Tribal Societies* (1977); E. Adamson Hoebel, *The Law of Primitive Man: A Study in Comparative Legal Dynamics* (1954); Leopold J. Pospisil, *Anthropology of Law* (1971); and *The Ethnology of Law* (1972).

ANTIBALLISTIC MISSILE SYSTEMS TREATY ON THE LIMITATIONS OF 1972

A treaty signed on May 26, 1972, entitled the Limitation on Antiballistic Missile Systems (commonly referrred to as SALT I) restricts the Soviet Union and the United States to two antiballistic missile system sites each: one for the defense of each nation's capital and the other for the protection of an intercontinental ballistic missile installation. For the purpose of limiting the nuclear arms race and consequently reducing the possibilities of nuclear war, the treaty also prohibits the development, testing, or deployment of sea-based, air-based, space-based, or mobile land-based antiballistic missile systems, as well as the transfer or deployment of antiballistic missile systems to or in other nations. The treaty is of unlimited duration, but each nation may withdraw from the treaty on six months' notice if extraordinary events have jeopardized that country's interests. For the complete text of the 1972 Treaty on the Limitation of Antiballistic Missile Systems (SALT I), see the Appendix volume 11.

ANTICIPATION

☐ The performance of an act or obligation before it is legally due. ☐

In the law of NEGLIGENCE, anticipation refers to the knowledge that there is a reasonable probability that the consequences of particular conduct of one individual will result in injury to others.

☐ In PATENT law, the publication of the existence of an invention that has already been patented or has a patent pending, which are grounds for denying a patent to an invention that has substantially the same structure and function as the earlier invention. ☐

The anticipation of an invention also occurs if the later invention is merely an adaptation of an earlier patent, which would be obvious to a skilled person who need only exercise some mechanical skill to develop the same adaptation.

ANTICIPATORY REPUDIATION

☐ The unjustifiable denial by a party to a CONTRACT of any intention to perform contractual duties, which occurs prior to the time performance is due. ☐

This form of breach, also known as anticipatory breach of contract, occurs when one party positively states that he or she will not substantially perform a contract. The mere assertion that the party is encountering difficulties in preparing to perform, is dissatisfied with the bargain, or is otherwise uncertain whether performance will be rendered when due is insufficient to constitute a repudiation. Another type of anticipatory breach consists of any voluntary act by a party that destroys, or seriously impairs, that party's ability to perform the contract.

The remedies available to the nonrepudiating party upon an anticipatory repudiation entail certain obligations. If the nonrepudiating party chooses to ignore the repudiation and proceeds with his or her performance, the duty to mitigate DAMAGES—which imposes on the injured party an obligation to exercise reasonable effort to minimize losses—mandates that the nonrepudiating party not perform if the consequence of performance would be to increase the damages. In addition, this duty requires, where applicable, the procurement of a substitute performance.

If the nonrepudiating party implores or insists that the other party perform, this demand, in and of itself, does not divest the nonrepudiating party's right to damages. The presence or absence of a breach of contract depends solely upon the repudiating party's actions. The prevailing view is that the nonrepudiating party may pursue any remedy for breach of contract, even though he or she has informed the repudiating party that he would await the latter's performance.

The nonrepudiating party also possesses the option to do nothing and to commence an action for breach after the time for performance. Under the majority view, such an action can be instituted without tendering the nonrepudiating party's performance or even alleging or proving that the party was ready, willing, and able to perform. The nonrepudiating party must demonstrate, however, that he or she would have been ready, willing, and able to perform but for the repudiation.

In regard to the law of SALES, the UNIFORM COMMERCIAL CODE (UCC), a body of law governing commercial transactions by the states, provides that anticipatory repudiation entails the right of one party to a contract to sue for breach before the performance date when the other party communicates the intention not to perform. The repudiation can, however, be retracted before the performance date if the nonrepudiating party has not acted on the basis of the repudiation. Some jurisdictions direct the injured party to await the performance date before instituting an action.

ANTIHIJACKING ACT OF 1974

See Hijacking of Aircraft.

ANTILAW MOVEMENT

Throughout early U.S. history, legal practitioners were the subject of ambivalence on the part of the general public. The attitude against lawyers reached its peak after the Revolutionary War and remained

A wood engraving from an 1884 *Harper's Monthly* shows Daniel Shays and his comrades occupying a courthouse to prevent the court from directing legal action at debt-ridden farmers in 1786.

New York Historical Society

hostile until the beginning of the nineteenth century.

During the early days of the colonies, the system for the administration of justice was based on arbitration and religious principles, and lawyers specially educated and skilled in the law were presumably not needed and were often restricted or prohibited from practicing. Judges were ordinary men who used unpolished methods of questioning to determine the facts of each case; defendants were their own lawyers. This system remained successful as long as the population of each community remained small and manageable, and the people were clear about their rights and obligations to their neighbors and the community.

By the end of the seventeenth century, the colonies experienced a period of growth, and the original judicial system became unsatisfactory. Formal pleading and skilled lawyers began to replace the primitive methods of earlier colonial times.

After the Revolutionary War, Americans sought a new form of jurisprudence to interact with their newly gained freedoms. Laws were less confining, due to the belief that moral fiber was more important to satisfactory conduct than legislation.

During this period, the antilawyer movement gained momentum. Historians speculate that it evolved as a result of former prejudices and conflicts toward the legal profession. Although lawyers in the past had not been viewed favorably, they achieved prominence and esteem as strong proponents of freedom from England during the Revolutionary War. After the war,

When some citizens of Massachusetts challenged the authority of the law in their state, Governor James Bowdoin issued a proclamation in 1786 that called for all authorities to suppress and prevent citizens from interfering with the functioning of the courts.

Commonwealth of Maſſachuſetts.

By His EXCELLENCY

JAMES BOWDOIN, Eſquire,

Governour of the Commonwealth of Maſſachuſetts.

A Proclamation.

WHEREAS information has been given to the Supreme Executive of this Commonwealth, that on Tueſday laſt, the 29th of Auguſt, being the day appointed by law for the ſitting of the Court of Common Pleas and Court of General Seſſions of the Peace, at Northampton, in the county of Hampſhire, within this Commonwealth, a large concourſe of people, from ſeveral parts of that county, aſſembled at the Court-Houſe in Northampton, many of whom were armed with guns, ſwords and other deadly weapons, and with drums beating and fifes playing, in contempt and open defiance of the authority of this Government, did, by their threats of violence and keeping poſſeſſion of the Court-Houſe until twelve o'clock on the night of the ſame day, prevent the ſitting of the Court, and the orderly adminiſtration of juſtice in that county :

AND WHEREAS this high-handed offence is fraught with the moſt fatal and pernicious conſequences, muſt tend to ſubvert all law and government ; to diſſolve our excellent Conſtitution, and introduce univerſal riot, anarchy and confuſion, which would probably terminate in abſolute deſpotiſm, and conſequently deſtroy the faireſt proſpects of political happineſs, that any people was ever favoured with :

I HAVE therefore thought fit, by and with the advice of the Council, to iſſue this Proclamation, calling upon all Judges, Juſtices, Sheriffs, Conſtables, and other officers, civil and military, within this Commonwealth, to prevent and ſuppreſs all ſuch violent and riotous proceedings, if they ſhould be attempted in their ſeveral counties.

AND I DO hereby, purſuant to the indiſpenſible duty I owe to the good people of this Commonwealth, moſt ſolemnly call upon them, as they value the bleſſings of freedom and independence, which at the expence of ſo much blood and treaſure they have purchaſed—as they regard their faith, which in the ſight of GOD and the world, they pledged to one another, and to the people of the United States, when they adopted the preſent Conſtitution of Government—as they would not diſappoint the hopes, and thereby become contemptible in the eyes of other nations, in the view of whom they have riſen to glory and empire—as they would not deprive themſelves of the ſecurity derived from well-regulated Society, to their lives, liberties and property ; and as they would not devolve upon their children, inſtead of peace, freedom and ſafety, a ſtate of anarchy, confuſion and ſlavery,—I do moſt earneſtly and moſt ſolemnly call upon them to aid and aſſiſt with their utmoſt efforts the aforeſaid officers, and to unite in preventing and ſuppreſſing all ſuch treaſonable proceedings, and every meaſure that has a tendency to encourage them.

GIVEN at the COUNCIL-CHAMBER, in BOSTON, this ſecond day of September, in the year of our LORD, one thouſand ſeven hundred and eighty-ſix, and in the eleventh year of the Independence of the United States of AMERICA.

JAMES BOWDOIN.

By his Excellency's command.

JOHN AVERY, jun. Secretary.

BOSTON : Printed by ADAMS and NOURSE, Printers to the GENERAL COURT.

lawyers were once again an important part of the legal system but were used primarily by the wealthy. As a result, they were often in conflict with those who were poor and could not pay their debts, which led to a resurrection of the old negative attitudes against them.

Lawyers were regarded with suspicion. They were accused of initiating unnecessary lawsuits, impeding the justice system, and prolonging trials to secure additional fees from unsuspecting clients. They were also criticized for the use of legal jargon, causing simple matters to seem complicated.

Despite these attacks, lawyers managed to attain political power. They were regarded as conspirators, however, for people could not accept the idea that lawyers who served as politicians made the laws by which they secured a living as legal practitioners. It was also feared that lawyers, judges, and legislators would band together to control society, depriving the common people of some of their hard-won freedoms. Although the fears were exaggerated, they were true to some degree, for lawyers did earn a living from the ramifications that legislation had upon the general public.

Two remedies were recommended to reconcile the proponents of the antilawyer sentiment and lawyers. The first suggestion was an updated version of the early colonial justice system, which prohibited laywers to practice. A judge representing the interests of the community presided over the court and instructed the jury. Judges were educated aristocrats that could be impeached if their conduct so warranted. If a legal representative was deemed necessary, a friend of the defendant was allowed to participate in the arbitration.

The second suggestion provided for a small group of professional lawyers to practice as public servants. Their salaries and actions were controlled by the state, and their chief function was to clarify legal principles of each case for the jury.

The conflicting feelings towards lawyers culminated in several incidents, the most noteworthy of which was known as Shays's Rebellion. The rebellion began in 1786 when Massachusetts voters elected a majority of nonlawyers to the General Court. This action led to a riot, and hostile agrarian mobs overran the courthouses, closing them down. The governor dispatched the state army, which successfully quelled the agitators.

Shays's Rebellion did not stop the people of Massachusetts from electing lawyers to political positions. The very tactics they feared in the courtroom were highly desirable in politics to control government officials; in spite of their conflicting feelings, voters were still attracted to legal skills.

The new methods of justice proved to be inefficient. Arbitration was fruitless, and laymen were fallible as lawyers. By 1790, most cases were again tried by lawyers, and the antilawyer movement began to wane. See also, Jamil S. Zainaldin's essay on Shays's Rebellion.

ANTINOMY ☐ An expression in law and logic to indicate that two authorities, laws, or propositions are inconsistent with each other. ☐

ANTI-SMUGGLING ACT OF 1935 See Contiguous Zones.

ANTITRUST ACTS ☐ Legislation enacted by the Federal and various state governments to regulate trade and commerce by preventing unlawful restraints, price fixing, and MONOPOLIES, to promote competition, and to encourage the

Assistant Attorney General Thurman Arnold appears before a Senate committee in 1942 to ask for amendments to the antitrust laws.

A.Y. Owen, *Life Magazine* © 1960, Time Inc.

A group of 112 lawyers was employed to defend 29 oil companies in a single antitrust suit in 1957.

Brown Brothers

John D. Rockefeller *(center)* on his way to court to participate in an antitrust case.

production of quality goods and services at the lowest prices. ☐

Many states have modeled their statutes upon Federal antitrust laws, such as the SHERMAN ACT (15 U.S.C.A. § 1 et seq. [1890]), the CLAYTON ACT (15 U.S.C.A. § 12 et seq. [1914]), and the ROBINSON-PATMAN ACT (15 U.S.C.A. § 13 et seq. [1936]). The primary goal of such laws is to safeguard public welfare by ensuring that consumer demands will be met by the manufacture and sale of goods at reasonable prices.

ANTITRUST LAWS, APPLICATION OUT-SIDE OF UNITED STATES See Jurisdiction of States under International Law.

A POSTERIORI [*Latin, "From the effect to the cause."*]

A posteriori describes a method of reasoning from given, express observations or experiments to reach and formulate general principles from them. This is also called inductive reasoning.

APPALACHIAN REGIONAL COMMISSION The Appalachian Regional Commission is a Federal-state governmental agency concerned with the economic, physical, and social development of the thirteen-state Appalachian region, which includes parts of Alabama, Georgia, Kentucky, Maryland, Mississippi, New York, North Carolina, Ohio, Pennsylvania, South Carolina, Tennessee, Virginia, and all of West Virginia. The comprehensive goals of the commission are to provide the people of Appalachia with the health and skills they need to compete for opportunities and to develop a self-sustaining economy and environment capable of supporting a population with rising incomes and standards of living and increasing employment opportunities. To accomplish this task, the commission has concentrated on areas of development in which there remain great needs throughout the region: community development and housing, education, the environment, health and child development, industrial development and management, tourism, and transportation.

The Appalachian Regional Commission was created to develop plans and programs authorized under the Appalachian Regional Development Act of 1965 (79 Stat. 5; 40 U.S.C. App. 1). The commission consists of the governors (or their alternates) of the thirteen Appalachian states, and a permanent Federal cochairperson appointed by the president with the advice and consent of the Senate. The state members elect an Appalachian governor to serve as states' cochairperson. This position rotates every year.

Functions   Each state is required to file an Appalachian Development Plan every year. The commission staff in Washington reviews and provides technical assistance in specific projects submitted under those general plans by the states. It is the staff's responsibility to see that certain guidelines are met before projects can be approved for funding. When a project is determined to be consistent with the commission's general plan for regional development, the project is passed on to the basic Federal agency involved in that type of program—transportation, health, education, etc.—for evaluation and actual execution.

Under the act, project proposals must originate in the states and be presented to the commission; no project can be approved unless it is first approved by the State concerned.

All recommendations of the commission must be approved by a majority of the governors and by the Federal cochairperson.

Because of the state-Federal nature of the commission, its staff members are not Federal employees. Commission expenses are shared equally by the Federal government and the Appalachian states.

Activities   The act authorizes a broad spectrum of economic development programs that will contribute to the growth of the 397-county region. These programs include: construction of a development highway system, construction of access roads, construction and operation of multicounty health projects, construction of vocational education facilities, technical assistance and planning loans for low- and moderate-income housing construction, application of land treatment and erosion control measures, reclamation of land damaged by past mining practices, support of timber development organizations, research grants, operation of a comprehensive water resources survey, construction of sewage treatment facilities, and the supplementation of a number of existing grant-in-aid programs providing for the acquisition of land and the construction and equipment of public facilities.

In 1981 Congress asked the Commission for a plan to complete the Appalachian Regional Development Highway System and complete the ARC area development program in 3 to 5 years. The proposed plan would:
- Limit ARC highway assistance to construction of only the highest priority 550 miles of the 1,303 unimproved miles in the planned Appalachian Development Highway System;
- Focus major Commission area development activities on a 5-year jobs and private investment program;
- Complete in 3 years the Commission's health program by bringing basic health care to those counties not yet reached and reducing infant mortality in counties with rates of more than 150 percent of the national average;
- Assist, by means of a 5-year program, approximately 60 of the most distressed and underdeveloped counties in the region to meet their most critical needs, especially for safe drinking water and waste disposal; and
- Seek help from the private sector, through a development foundation, so that a regional effort can continue after the termination of the Commission.

Source: *The United States Government Manual 1981/82* and/or *1982/83*.

APPARENT □ That which is clear, plain, and evident. □

In the law of AGENCY, an agent has *apparent authority* to represent the person, or principal, for whom he or she acts, when the principal acts in such a manner toward the agent that a reasonable person would plainly assume that the agent was acting for the principal.

APPEAL □ Timely resort by an unsuccessful party in a lawsuit or administrative proceeding to an appropriate superior court empowered to review a final decision on the ground that it was based upon an erroneous application of law. □

A person who initiates an appeal—the APPELLANT, sometimes called the plaintiff in error—must file a notice of appeal, along with the necessary documents, to commence appellate review. The person against whom the appeal is brought, the APPELLEE, then files a brief in response to the appellant's allegations.

There are usually two stages of review in the FEDERAL COURT and in many state COURT systems: an appeal from a trial court to an intermediate appellate court and thereafter to the highest appellate court in the JURISDICTION. Within the appellate rules of ADMINISTRATIVE PROCE-

The history of liberty has largely been the history of observance of procedural safeguards.

FELIX FRANKFURTER

DURE, there might be several levels of appeals from a determination made by an administrative agency. For example, an appeal of the decision of an administrative law judge may be heard by a reviewing body within the agency and from that body the appeal may go to a trial court, such as a Federal district court. Thereafter, the appeal might travel the same route as an appeal taken from a judicial decision, going from an intermediate to a superior appellate court, or it might go directly to a superior appellate court for review, by-passing the intermediate stage. The rules of appellate procedure applicable to a particular court governs its review of cases.

Right to appeal   There is no absolute right of appeal for all decisions rendered by a lower court or administrative agency. Federal and state constitutions and statutory provisions create appellate courts and prescribe the types of cases that are within their jurisdiction. An appeal may be granted as a matter of right, such as from a trial court to an intermediate appellate court, or only at the discretion of a superior appellate court, for example, by a grant of CERTIORARI by the SUPREME COURT. If the decision presented does not meet the statutory requirements for review, the appellate court is powerless to hear the appeal and review is denied.

The right to appeal a decision is limited to those parties to the proceeding who are aggrieved by the decision because it has a direct and adverse effect upon their persons or property. In addition, an actual CASE OR CONTROVERSY must exist at the time of review. Issues that have become MOOT while the appeal is pending and cases that have been settled during that time are not reviewable.

Final decision   A final judgment or order must have been reached by the trial court in order for a case to be appealable. A judgment is considered final for purposes of appeal when it ends the action in the court in which it was brought and nothing more is to be decided. This rule is intended to prevent the piecemeal litigation of a lawsuit, to avoid delay resulting from INTERLOCUTORY appeals, and to give the trial court the opportunity to render a decision in the case to the satisfaction of both parties, thereby obviating the need for appeal. The consideration of incidental matters, such as the computation of interest, attorneys' fees, or court costs, does not prevent a judgment or order from being appealed.

Grounds   Error is the basis for review of a final decision rendered by a court or administrative agency. Error is called to the attention of a court through the use of objections, protests made during the course of a proceeding that an action taken by the opposing side in a controversy is unfair or illegal. Decisions rendered in favor of one party at trial level are presumed by an appellate court to be correct unless objections have been made to the issues in question during the trial. Failure to do so will preclude their review on appeal. An objection must be made as promptly and specifically as possible for each act to which it is directed so that the court may make an intelligent decision regarding its merits. The trial judge rules on the objection, and the decision is included in the trial record. If the attorney for either party disagrees with the ruling, he or she may take an exception, an objection taken to a decision of a court on a matter of law, which is noted in the trial record to be preserved for purposes of appeal. Appellate jurisdiction is limited only to a review of actions taken by an inferior court. No new objections can be raised before an appellate court for its consideration unless exceptional circumstances exist to justify the appellate court raising the issues SUA SPONTE, on its own motion. Exceptional circumstances mean the presence at trial of PLAIN ERROR, a mistake in the proceedings that substantially affects the rights of the party against whom the decision has been made and undermines the fairness and integrity of the judicial system, causing a MISCARRIAGE OF JUSTICE.

Time of appeal   Appeals must be made within the time prescribed by statute or by the governing rules of the appellate court. Such statutes begin to run only after a final decision has been made. The timely filing of the notice of appeal with the clerk of the appellate court and the appellee completes, or perfects, the procedure. If the appeal is not taken and perfected within the time set by statute, the right to appeal is foreclosed. Extensions of time for the filing of an appeal may be granted, however, if extenuating circumstances exist, such as if either party is adjudicated incompetent or dies.

Notice of appeal   A notice of appeal—a written document filed by the appellant with the court and a copy of which is sent to the appellee—is the initial step in the appeals process. It informs the court and the party in whose favor a judgment or order has been made that the unsuccessful party seeks a review of the case. Failure to file a notice of appeal according to the statutory requirements will preclude appeal.

Bonds   An appeal BOND, a promise to pay a sum of money, must often be posted by an appellant to secure the appellee against the costs of the appeal, if the appellee is successful and the appellant fails to pay. Its amount is determined by the court itself or by statute. The imposition of such a bond discourages frivolous appeals. If successive appeals are taken from an intermediate appellate court to a superior one, a new bond is usually required.

Record on appeal The function of the appellate court is limited to a review of the trial record sent up from the lower court and the BRIEFS filed by the appellant and appellee. AMICUS CURIAE briefs, if permitted by the appellate court, also become part of the record on appeal. The trial record, sometimes called the record proper, must show the PLEADINGS that initiated the case, the complete transcript (in cases of jury trial) of lower court proceedings, the VERDICT, and the entry of the final judgment or order. The appellant must clearly demonstrate that the grounds for review had been raised and unsuccessfully decided upon at the trial level and, therefore, prejudicial error exists to warrant the reversal of the decision of the lower court.

In some jurisdictions, a BILL OF EXCEPTIONS—a written statement of the objections made by a party to the ruling, decision, charge, or opinion of the trial judge—must be submitted to the appellate court to provide a history of the trial proceedings. It should not include matters that belong in the record proper but, instead, state those points concerning questions of law raised by the exceptions taken during the trial. The appellant's attorney prepares the bill and presents it to the trial judge for settlement, an agreement between the trial judge and the appellant that the bill contains a truthful account of the events of the trial. If there is disagreement, the judge returns the bill to the appellant with an explanation. The appellee must be given notice of the time and place of the settlement of the bill of exceptions in order to object to or approve its contents. The settled bill of exceptions becomes part of the trial transcript, which is part of the record on appeal. The appellant must submit a complete unabridged transcript of the trial that is prepared by the clerk of the trial court.

The entire trial record is printed and filed with the appellate court, and a copy is also sent to the appellee.

Assignment of errors A statement by the appellant of the errors alleged to have been committed in the lower court is an assignment of errors, a type of appellate pleading used to point out to the appellate court the grounds for review. It controls the scope of an appeal because if a ground for review is not contained in it, it will not ordinarily be considered by the court. The assignment of errors is usually part of the notice of appeal, the bill of exceptions, the transcript of

the record, or the brief, although in some jurisdictions, it is a separate document.

Appellate brief The appellant and appellee must file individual briefs to aid the appellate court in its consideration of the issues presented. Failure to do so results in a dismissal of the appeal. The facts of the case, the grounds for review, and the arguments relating to those questions must be concisely stated. Any statements referring to the trial record must be supported by an appropriate reference to it.

The appellant's brief must specifically discuss the alleged errors that entitle the appellant to a reversal and discuss why each ruling of the lower court was wrong, citing authority, such as a case in which a similar point of law has been decided or a statute that applies to the particular point in issue. Disrespectful or abusive language directed against the lower court, the appellate court, the parties, witnesses, or opposing counsel cannot be used. If it is, it will be stricken from the brief, and the costs of the brief that might have been awarded are disallowed.

Review Appellate courts have jurisdiction to decide only issues actually before them on appeal and nothing else. They cannot render opinions on controversies or declare principles of law that have no practical effect in settling the rights of the litigants.

Only conclusions of law, not findings of fact made by a lower court, are reviewable.

Harmless error The appellate court must decide whether the errors alleged to have been made by the trial court are harmless or prejudicial. If the error substantially injures the rights of one party, it is called a prejudicial or reversible error and warrants the reversal of the final judgment or order. However, when the error is technical or minimally affects the rights of the parties or the outcome of the lawsuit, it is considered a harmless error, insufficient to require a reversal or modification of the decision of the lower court.

Hearing The clerk of the appellate court schedules on the court CALENDAR the date of the hearing on which each side may present an oral argument. Oral arguments, usually ten to fifteen minutes for each side, help the court understand the issues argued in the brief and persuade the court to rule in favor of the arguing party. During the arguments of appellant and appellee, it is not unusual for the appellate judge to interrupt with questions on particular issues or points of law.

The appellant's argument briefly discusses the facts on which the cause of action is based and traces the history of the case through the

Lawyers' gowns are lined with the wilfulness of their clients.

H.G. BOHN

lower courts. It includes the legal issues raised by the exceptions taken to the allegedly erroneous rulings of the trial judge. Thereafter, the appellee's counsel presents arguments in favor of affirming the original decision.

Determination An appellate court has broad powers over the scope of its decision and the relief to be granted. After reviewing the controlling issues in an action, it may affirm the decision of the inferior tribunal, modify it, reverse it, or remand the case for a new trial in the lower court pursuant to its order.

When a decision is affirmed, the appellate court accepts the decision of the lower court and rejects the appellant's contention that it was erroneously made. The modification of a decision by an appellate court means that, while it accepts part of the trial court's decision, the appellant was correct that the decision was partly erroneous. The trial court's decision is then modified accordingly.

A reversal of a decision means that the appellate court agrees with the appellant that the decision was erroneously made. The party who lost the case at the trial level becomes the winning party in appellate court.

In some cases, a decision might be reversed but the lawsuit is still unresolved. The appellate court then orders the reversal with the direction that the case be remanded to a lower court for the determination of the issues that remain unsettled.

If a judgment or order is reversed in an intermediate appellate court, the losing party may file an appeal with a superior appellate court for relief and the appellate process begins again. The decision rendered by a superior appellate court cannot ordinarily be reviewed. In state cases involving issues based on Federal statutes or the Constitution, however, an appeal may be brought in the Federal court system on those questions that are within its jurisdiction.

APPEAR ☐ To come before a court as a party or a witness in a lawsuit. ☐

APPEARANCE

☐ An initial court proceeding governed by state and Federal rules of CRIMINAL PROCEDURE, during which the judge advises a defendant charged with a FELONY of the charges and his or her rights, considers BAIL or other conditions of release, and schedules a PRELIMINARY HEARING.

☐ The name given to a DOCKET, a listing kept by the clerk of the court for the purpose of entering the names of those parties who have sub-

mitted to the JURISDICTION of the court and recording a brief abstract of all the proceedings.

☐ The conduct of an attorney in maintaining a lawsuit on behalf of a client.

☐ A document filed with a court that states that the attorney who composed it is representing a client in a lawsuit.

☐ A document submitted by a defendant to a plaintiff and the clerk of the court stating that the defendant will come before the court in person or through an attorney.

☐ A formal act by which the defendant in a civil suit, personally or through an attorney, comes before the court to submit to, or challenge, the court's jurisdiction. ☐

Any party can appear in person or through an attorney or a duly authorized representative. The physical presence of the party or an attorney before the court is not necessary for an appearance. An appearance can be made by filing a notice of appearance with the clerk of the court and the plaintiff, which states that the defendant will submit to the authority of the court or will challenge its jurisdiction. A plaintiff or the plaintiff's attorney cannot appear for a defendant, even if authorized to do so. In a lawsuit involving multiple defendants, an appearance by one is not an appearance for the other codefendants. Valid SERVICE OF PROCESS is not essential for an appearance to be made.

At COMMON LAW, appearances were classified as voluntary or compulsory. If the defendant willingly came before the court in person or by filing a document without being compelled to do so by the service of process, the appearance was voluntary. An appearance made in response to a SUMMONS was a compulsory one. Statutes generally categorize appearances as general and specific.

General appearance A general appearance is an unqualified submission to the personal jurisdiction of a court by which the defendant agrees that the court has power to bind him or her by its actions. The defendant waives the right to raise any jurisdictional defects, for example, claiming that the service of process was improper. Any action by which the defendant recognizes the jurisdiction of the court to act is a general appearance. Attacking the sufficiency of the complaint, demanding a BILL OF PARTICULARS, or demanding a jury trial is considered a general appearance.

A general appearance is treated as the equivalent of valid service of process. Although it precludes the defendant from alleging defects in PERSONAL JURISDICTION, it does not waive any substantive rights or defenses, such as the court's lack of jurisdiction over the subject matter of the case or the expiration of the statute of limitations. A general appearance waives the objection that a case is brought in the wrong VENUE.

Special appearance A special appearance is one made for the limited purpose of challenging the sufficiency of the service of process or the personal jurisdiction of the court to determine whether the defendant can be bound by the action of the court. It prevents a DEFAULT JUDGMENT from being rendered against a defendant for failing to file a pleading until the court decides whether it has jurisdiction.

The right to make a special appearance is almost universally recognized, except where abolished by statute. As a rule, LEAVE of court must first be obtained, but this is not always the case. A special appearance must be made before a general appearance, which waives all objections to the jurisdiction of the court.

When a defendant makes a special appearance, no other issues can be raised without such appearance becoming a general appearance. A REMOVAL proceeding, which determines whether a case should be moved from state court to Federal court, is regarded as a special appearance.

If the court decides that it does not have jurisdiction over the defendant, it will dismiss the action. When, however, the court finds against the defendant, a direct appeal is necessary for review of the court's decision. The question may be raised only on a direct appeal from the final judgment in some states, while in others, an INTERLOCUTORY appeal may be taken immediately following the ruling and prior to defending the action on its merits, thereby precluding consideration on an appeal from the final judgment. The defendant will be denied relief if he or she defaults in the action and tries to collaterally attack the judgment on the grounds that the court lacked personal jurisdiction.

Federal rules Federal courts and states that have adopted the FEDERAL RULES OF CIVIL PROCEDURE have eliminated the distinction between general and special appearances. A defendant can object to the lack of personal jurisdiction by use of a pretrial motion to dismiss the cause of action or by an answer when no pretrial motion to dismiss has been made. Nonjurisdiction may be asserted at this time. Failure to raise objections to personal jurisdiction will result in their waiver. Once such objections have been raised, however, they may be asserted on direct appeal but not as a COLLATERAL ATTACK.

Delay or failure to appear If a defendant delays in making an appearance before the time prescribed by statute or court rules, he or she may lose certain rights. However, a court may extend the time of appearance if the circumstances warrant it.

A defendant who fails to appear in court pursuant to the service of process might have a default judgment entered against him or her and be held in CONTEMPT. Such failure does not, however, result in a waiver of objections to the jurisdiction of the court to bind the defendant.

Withdrawal A defendant who has appeared has no power to deprive the court of its jurisdiction by withdrawing the appearance. The discretion of the court may permit a withdrawal of the appearance if it serves the interests of justice, such as withdrawing an appearance that has been entered through fraud or mistake or after the plaintiff's complaint has been materially amended. A proper withdrawal is treated as if no appearance at all had been entered in the case, depriving the court of its jurisdiction. A defendant who has withdrawn a general appearance may ask the court for leave to file a special appearance to challenge its authority.

If someone makes an unauthorized appearance, it may be stricken or set aside by a motion of any party with an interest in the proceeding.

Limited appearance In a number of states, a defendant in a lawsuit based on QUASI IN REM JURISDICTION may make a limited appearance to defend himself or herself. This is a special category of appearance since it involves the *quasi in rem* jurisdiction of a court. A court with such jurisdiction is empowered to bind a defendant only to the extent of the monetary value of property that is located within the geographical boundaries of the court's authority, as opposed to the amount of alleged damages. The presence of the property is the basis of the court's jurisdiction. The court does not have personal jurisdiction over the defendant.

A limited appearance enables a defendant to defend an action on the merits, but, should the defendant be unsuccessful, he or she will be held liable only up to the value of the property, not for all the damages. Where there is no provision for a limited appearance, a defendant is considered to submit to the personal jurisdiction of the court, thereby facing full liability. However, a defendant who makes a limited appearance and is successful can be sued by a plaintiff in another court that does have personal jurisdiction over the defendant.

In states where a limited appearance is not provided, a defendant can avoid being subject to the personal jurisdiction of the state if he or she refuses to appear, thereby causing a default and

Moreover, although the law is a highly learned profession, we are well aware that it is an intensely practical one.

FRED M. VINSON

a consequent forfeiture of the property or the defendant can come before the court to defend the case on its merits, thereby submitting to the personal jurisdiction of the court. The defendant must decide which course of action is best after an evaluation of the value of the seized property in contrast to the damages being sought by the plaintiff.

The Federal Rules of Civil Procedure do not establish the availability of limited appearances in Federal court proceedings but, instead, defer to state law as the controlling law on that issue. A slightly greater number of courts permit limited appearances than those that do not. The law of the jurisdiction in which the action is brought must be consulted to determine whether limited appearances are permissible.

APPELLANT ☐ A person who, dissatisfied with the judgment rendered in a lawsuit decided in a lower court or the findings from a proceeding before an administrative agency, asks a superior court to review the decision. ☐

An appellant, sometimes called the petitioner, must demonstrate sufficient grounds for appeal, which are usually specified by statute, in order to challenge the judgment or findings. See also, Appeal.

Whether a party was a plaintiff or defendant in the lower court has no bearing on his or her status as an appellant.

APPELLATE ☐ Relating to appeals; reviews by superior courts of decisions of inferior courts or administrative agencies and other proceedings. ☐

APPELLATE COURT ☐ A Federal or state tribunal empowered by law to accept a case for review that has already been decided by a lower court, but which is challenged by the party against whom the judgment was rendered on the grounds of error or impropriety. ☐

There are different levels of appellate courts. An intermediate appellate court hears an appeal from a court of the first instance—that is, a court where the action was first brought. The Federal COURT OF APPEALS is an intermediate appellate court because it hears appeals from the Federal district court. An appellate court that entertains an appeal from a case reviewed by an intermediate appellate court is a superior or supreme appellate court, such as the SUPREME COURT of the United States.

Cases reach appellate courts for review by APPEAL, CERTIORARI, or ERROR.

APPELLEE ☐ A PARTY who has won a judgment in a lawsuit or favorable findings in an ad-

ministrative proceeding, which judgment or findings the losing party, the appellant, seeks to have a higher court reverse or set aside. ☐

The designation as appellee is not related to a person's status as plaintiff or defendant in the lower court.

Another name for appellee is RESPONDENT.

APPLETON, John John Appleton (b. February 11, 1815, in Beverly, Massachusettes; d. August 22, 1864, in Portland, Maine) achieved prominence in the fields of law, journalism, and politics. He was a graduate of Bowdoin College in 1834 and was admitted to the Cumberland County, Maine, bar in 1837.

From 1839 to 1844 Appleton was the editor of the *Eastern Argus*. In 1845 he served as chief clerk in the Navy Department, a position he held until 1848, when he began service in the State Department. In that same year he was appointed envoy to Bolivia, an assignment that lasted until 1849.

Politically, Appleton was affiliated with the Democratic party and represented Maine in the House of Representatives from 1851 to 1853. From 1855 to 1856 he served under the ambassador to England, James Buchanan, who became president of the United States in 1857.

During the years 1857 to 1860 Appleton was the United States assistant secretary of state. He acted as a United States diplomat to Russia under President Buchanan from 1860 to 1861.

Library of Congress

John Appleton

APPOINT ☐ To designate, select, or assign authority to a position or an office. ☐

Although sometimes used interchangeably, elect and appoint do not have the same meaning. *Election* refers to the selection of a public officer by the qualified voters of the community, and *appointment* refers to the selection of a public officer by one authorized by law to do so.

Robert B. McKay

Apportionment

Legislative apportionment is the system by which representation in a legislative body is allocated.

The principle and practice of legislative apportionment is by no means new. In primitive assemblies and in ancient Athens, tribal leaders, warriors, and nonslave citizens were directly represented in their respective assemblies. In the courts and councils of kings and emperors in later centuries, several classes of estates, such as the nobility, guilds, and universities, were represented. With the rise of democracy, the extension of the right to vote, and the development of political parties, legislative apportionment took on new meaning and became more complex. Unlike the earlier notions of apportionment, the objective of modern apportionment is—or at least should be—to allocate the right of representation to reflect as accurately as possible the will of the electorate.

The prevailing systems of legislative apportionment can be divided into six principal categories:

1. Geographical apportionment, in which each legislative district has specified boundaries that enclose a defined number of votes. This is the most common form of apportionment. The proper objective is to draw the lines so that the number of persons in each district is as nearly equal as possible to that of other districts represented in the same legislative body.
2. Apportionment among units of government, such as towns, counties, cities, and states, each of which is represented by one or more persons in the regional or national legislative body. Thus, for example, two Senators represent each state in the United States Senate, regardless of population.
3. Apportionment on the basis of occupational, ethnic, social, or business classification.
4. Apportionment on the basis of party representation. Known as proportional representation, the objective is to achieve representation of as many types of voter opinion as possible. In proportional representation the group or party is regarded as the constituency.
5. Apportionment on the basis of wealth. For example, some of the states in early United States history imposed property requirements upon the right of franchise.
6. Apportionment among official bodies that serve as a constituency. For example, state legislatures directly elected United States Senators until the adoption of the Seventeenth Amendment in 1913.

. . . the basic principle of representative government remains, and must remain, unchanged—the weight of a citizen's vote cannot be made to depend on where he lives.

EARL WARREN

Apportionment should be the handmaiden of representative democracy. But when abused, as it often has been, it becomes the tool of political partisans and other special interest groups. Outstanding examples of abuse were once found in the "rotten boroughs" in Britain, in which representation had nothing to do with voter constituency, and in the serious malapportionment common to most American states before the mid-1960s. Both abuses have been largely corrected, by legislation in Britain and by judicial decision in the United States that led to legislative reform to correct unconstitutional apportionment.

In the United States, state legislative malapportionment developed out of the common practice of providing representation to subunits of state government regardless of population. With the general movement to urban areas, the imbalance became as great as several hundred to one in the ratio of population to elected representative. In other states that did not apportion on the basis of county or township lines, dominant political leaders often skewed the lines to their political advantage in what is known as gerrymandering. These violations of democratic theory principles and of equality continued for many decades because the Supreme Court of the United States long held that apportionment was a political issue that was not justiciable. But in *Baker v. Carr*, 369 U.S. 186, 82 S.Ct. 691, 7 L.Ed.2d 663 (1962), the Supreme Court at last held the issue justiciable; and within two years the Court held that legislative districts must be as nearly equal as possible in terms of population. See *Wesberry v. Sanders*, 376 U.S. 1, 84 S.Ct. 526, 11 L.Ed.2d 481 (1964); *Reynolds v. Sims*, 377 U.S. 533, 84 S.Ct. 1362, 12 L.Ed.2d 506 (1964). From this came the not quite accurate slogan "one man, one vote," which was conceptually easier than the more precise "substantial population equality." See also, Martin H. Redish's essay on Baker v. Carr.

Bibliography: Robert Dixon, *Democratic Representation* (1968); Robert B. McKay, *Reapportionment: The Law and Politics of Equal Representation* (1965).

APPRAISAL ☐ A valuation or an approximation of value by impartial, properly qualified persons; the process of determining the value of an ASSET or LIABILITY which entails expert opinion rather than express commercial transactions. ☐

APPRAISER ☐ A person selected or appointed by a competent authority or an interested PARTY to evaluate the financial worth of property. ☐

Appraisers are frequently appointed in PROBATE and CONDEMNATION proceedings and are also used by banks and real estate concerns to determine the market value of real property.

APPRECIATION

☐ The fair and reasonable estimation of the value of an item.
☐ The increase in the financial worth of an asset as compared to its value at a particular earlier date as a result of inflation or greater market demand. ☐

APPREHENSION

☐ The seizure and arrest of a person who is suspected of having committed a crime.
☐ A reasonable belief of the possibility of imminent injury or death at the hands of another that justifies a person acting in self-defense against the potential attack. ☐

An apprehension of attack is an element of the defense of self-defense that can be used in a criminal prosecution for ASSAULT AND BATTERY, MANSLAUGHTER, or MURDER. An individual who acts under apprehension of attack does not have to fear injury. It is sufficient that there is a likelihood of actual injury to justify the person's taking steps to protect himself or herself.

APPRENTICE ☐ A person who agrees to work for a specified time in order to learn a trade, craft, or profession in which the employer, traditionally called the master, assents to instruct him or her. ☐

Parties to apprenticeships Both MINORS and adults can be legally obligated under the terms of an apprenticeship CONTRACT, and any person who has the capacity to manage his or her own affairs may engage an apprentice. In some states, a minor may VOID a contract of apprenticeship, but in cases where the contract is beneficial to the minor, other jurisdictions do not permit the minor to void it. There must be strict compliance with statutes that govern a minor's actions concerning an apprenticeship.

The contract An apprenticeship must arise from an agreement, sometimes labeled an INDENTURE, which possesses all the requisites of a valid contract. If the contract cannot be performed within a year, it must be in writing, in order to satisfy the STATUTE OF FRAUDS, an old English law adopted in the United States, which requires certain agreements to be in writing. The apprentice, the employer, and, if the apprentice is a minor, his or her parents or GUARDIANS must sign the apprenticeship agreement. Some jurisdictions require explicit consensual language in addition to the signature or signatures of one or both parents, depending upon the applicable statute. The contract must include the provisions required by law and drafted for the benefit of the minor such as those relating to his or her education and training. A breach of apprenticeship contract might justify an award of DAMAGES, and, unless authorized by statute, there can be no ASSIGNMENT, or transfer, of the contract of apprenticeship to another that would bind the apprentice to a new service.

A person who lures an apprentice from his or her employer may be sued by the employer, but the employer cannot recover unless the defendant knew of the apprentice relationship.

Termination of apprenticeship The apprenticeship may be concluded by either PARTY for good cause, where no definite term of service is specified, by mutual consent, or by a dismissal of the apprentice. Automatic termination ensues from the expiration of the term of service, involuntary removal of the apprentice from the jurisdiction where he or she was bound, or service in the armed forces even though voluntary and without the consent of the employer. The death of either party terminates the relationship, as does the attainment of the AGE OF MAJORITY by the apprentice, in most instances. Courts may terminate such contracts when they violate statutes. The master's cruelty, immorality, interference with the apprentice's religious beliefs or duties, or other misconduct and the misbehavior of the apprentice also constitute grounds for termination.

Certificate of Completion of Apprenticeship
United States Department of Labor
Bureau of Apprenticeship and Training

Before an individual can qualify for journeyman status or a skilled labor grade, he or she must complete an apprenticeship program and receive a certificate such as the one shown here.

Charles R. McKirdy

Apprenticeship

Prior to 1900 the dominant form of legal education in the United States was the apprentice, or clerkship, system. This system evolved in the colonial period to fill the need for trained lawyers, which the rudimentary colonial colleges and distant Inns of Court in England could not meet. Although time wrought some alterations in the apprenticeship system, it basically remained unchanged for approximately 250 years.

The legal clerkship was modeled after the apprenticeship system common in the trades in both England and America. It was based upon a contract, written or oral, between student and lawyer. The student exchanged a fee and services as a law clerk in return for instruction in the law and, perhaps, room and board.

Ideally, this system placed the student in a situation where education was a total experience balanced between the theoretical and practical aspects of the law. The student would learn by copying documents, transcribing contracts, and performing the other mundane but necessary duties of a law office. The student would learn by listening to fellow students, the teacher, and other members of the bar. The student would learn by attending court and paying careful attention to all that transpired there. He would learn by reading the law books available to him and by taking copious notes. In all aspects of his training, the student would be guided by his mentor, a lawyer versed in the law and concerned with the education of his charges.

Unfortunately, the ideal of the legal apprenticeship system and its everyday reality often were worlds apart. This stemmed in part, from the very nature of the apprenticeship concept, which places primary emphasis on practical application rather than theoretical knowledge. In the skilled trades, such a technique works well because theory plays a relatively small part, but in the law, as in all professions, theory is at least as important as practice. Another problem was inherent in the dual nature of the law clerk's position. In an era before typewriters, duplicating machines, and large law firms, the clerk's duties as copyist and stenographer often left little time for study.

Reading provided the chief theoretical input into a law clerk's education under the apprenticeship system, but the extent of this input depended on the amount of time the student could spend in his teacher's library and the number and nature of books found there. The difficulties of studying in a busy law office are obvious. Furthermore, many lawyers, especially in colonial America, on the frontier or in rural areas, had very limited libraries. Often a clerk's reading was limited to one or two works, such as *Coke on Littleton* in the eighteenth century and Sir William Blackstone's *Commentaries* in the first half of the nineteenth century. Although the situation improved significantly in the latter decades of the nineteenth

American Philosophical Society

This document outlines the terms and responsibilities between Benjamin Franklin and his apprentice in 1740.

I oft have heard him say how he admir'd
Men of your large profession, that could speak
To every cause, and things mere contraries,
Till they were hoarse again, yet all be law.

BEN JONSON

century, most of the law books available to the legal apprentice were not intended as textbooks, were borne down with technicalities, and were written in a style that defied comprehension. Finally, the legal clerk's studies were hindered by the fact that often he had to pursue them alone. Many lawyers simply could not afford to take time away from their practices in order to assist their struggling charges.

Of course, there were practitioners who were excellent teachers. In fact, some became famous for their teaching and all but abandoned the practice of law for the teaching of it. Nevertheless, by 1900, university-affiliated law schools had replaced legal apprenticeship as the primary mode of legal education. Today only California, Virginia, and Washington still permit admission to the bar on the basis of law office study and examination.

The primary weakness of the apprenticeship system was that its quality was as varied as the students and teachers involved in it. Still, names such as John Adams, John Marshall, and Daniel Webster testify to the fact that the apprenticeship system was capable of producing first-rate lawyers.

Bibliography: Charles R. McKirdy, "The Lawyer as Apprentice: Legal Education in Eighteenth Century Massachusetts," 28 *Journal of Legal Education* (1976): 124–136; A. Z. Reed, *Training for the Public Profession of Law* (1921).

APPROPRIATION

☐ The designation by the government or an individual of the use to which a fund of money is to be applied. ☐

An *appropriation bill* is a proposal placed before the legislative branch of the government by one or a group of its members to earmark a particular portion of general revenue or treasury funds for use for a governmental objective. Federal appropriation bills can originate only in the HOUSE OF REPRESENTATIVES as mandated by Article I, Section 7 of the Constitution. Once an appropriation law is enacted, a definite amount of money is set aside so that public officials can pay incurred or anticipated expenditures. When a law authorizes funds to be used for a particular purpose, it is known as a *specific appropriation*.

The appropriation of money by an individual occurs within the context of a debtor-creditor relationship. If a creditor is owed two separate debts by the same debtor who makes a payment without specifying the debt to which it is to be applied, the creditor can appropriate the payment to either debt.

☐ The selection and setting apart of privately-owned land by the government for public use, such as a military reservation or public building. ☐

When used in this sense, appropriation refers to the physical taking and occupation of property by the government or its actual, substantial interference with the owner's right to use the land according to personal wishes by virtue of its power of EMINENT DOMAIN.

☐ The diversion of water flowing on PUBLIC DOMAIN from its natural course by means of a canal or ditch for a private beneficial use of the appropriator. ☐

This right of an individual to use water that belongs to the public is embodied in the *prior appropriation doctrine* applied in arid western states where water supplies are not available in sufficient quantity to all who might need them. An individual landowner who first diverts water for personal benefit is entitled to its continued use as long as there is a reasonable need and the water is actually used. See also, Water.

APPROPRIATION THEORY (Water Law)
See International Waterways.

APPROVAL

☐ The present confirmation, ratification, or assent to some action or thing done by another, which is submitted to an individual, group, or governmental body for judgment.

☐ The acceptance by a judge of a BOND, security, or other document that is required by law to meet with the judge's satisfaction before it becomes legally effective. ☐

APPURTENANCE

☐ An accessory or adjunct that is attached and incidental to something that has greater importance or value.

☐ As applied to real property, an object attached to or a right to be used with land as an incidental benefit but which is necessary to the complete use and enjoyment of the property. ☐

When a landowner has been given an EASEMENT for the passage of light and air over an adjoining lot, the easement is an appurtenance to the land. Other common appurtenances to land include barns, outhouses, fences, drainage and irrigation ditches, and rights of way.

A PRIORI   [*Latin, "From the cause to the effect."*]

This phrase refers to a type of reasoning that examines given general principles to discover what particular facts or real-life observations can be derived from them. Another name for this method is deductive reasoning.

AQUINAS, Thomas

Thomas Aquinas (*b.* circa 1225, in Roccasecca, Italy; *d.* March 7, 1274, in Fossanuova, Italy) achieved prominence as a philosopher and theologian. He was educated at Monte Cassino and Naples and became a member of the Dominican order circa 1244. From 1245 to 1248 he was a student of Albertus Magnus, an eminent philosopher. In 1248 he went to Cologne, where he began his teaching career.

In 1252 Aquinas relocated to Paris for a four-year period and established a reputation as a teacher of theology. He settled in Italy in 1259 and performed the duties of teacher at the Pontifical Curia and served as an advisor to the papal court.

Aquinas returned to Paris in 1268 and became involved in a controversy with a group known as the Averroists concerning the meaning of the principles of Aristotle. The Averroists followed the teachings of the Spanish-Arabian philosopher Averroës, who interpreted the teachings of Aristotle in a way contrary to the beliefs of Aquinas and the Catholic church. Aquinas particularly attacked the theory that philosophic truth is elicited solely from reason and that faith has no part in the formation of truth. The leader of the Averroists at this time was Siger de Brabant, a French theologian who advocated the teachings of Averroës and also advanced the theory that what was true in philosophy could be untrue when applied to religious belief. Aquinas argued that truth and faith complement one another. He emerged the victor and his philosophies became more widely accepted as a result.

James L. Shaffer

Thomas Aquinas

In 1272 Aquinas accepted a teaching position in Naples. Two years later, Pope Gregory X requested that he attend the General Council of Lyons for the purpose of uniting the Latin and Greek churches. Aquinas died en route to the Council. In 1323 he was declared a saint by Pope John XXII, and the principles of Aquinas were declared to be the basis of Catholic philosophy in 1879 by Pope Leo XIII.

The works of Aquinas are many; his most important works are the *Summa Contra Gentiles* (1258–1260) and the *Summa Theologica* (1267–1273). In the former, he expounded on his theories of the concordant relationship between faith and reason. *Summa Theologica* attempted to represent all knowledge, which Aquinas believed was separated into three parts: Part I discusses the essence of philosophy and the existence of God; Part II explores ethics, morality, and human beings and is primarily based on the teachings of Aristotle; and Part III is a treatment of the work of Christ and the sacraments.

ARBITER [*Latin, "One who attends something to view it as a spectator or witness."*]
☐ Any person who is given an absolute power to judge and rule on a matter in dispute. ☐

An arbiter is usually chosen or appointed by parties or by a court on their behalf. The decision of an arbiter is made according to the rules

of law and equity. The arbiter is distinguished from the arbitrator, who proceeds at his or her own discretion, so that the decision is made according to the judgment of a reasonable person.

An arbiter may perform the same function as an umpire, a person who decides a controversy when arbitrators cannot agree.

ARBITRAGE ☐ A specialized type of trading in which securities or commodities are bought in one market and sold in another with the objective of making a profit on the price variations in the different markets. ☐

To secure the obligation to perform on an arbitrage agreement, a person may post an arbitrage bond.

ARBITRARY ☐ Irrational; capricious. ☐

The term *arbitrary* describes a course of action or a decision that is not based on reason or judgment but on personal will or discretion without regard to rules or standards.

An arbitrary decision is one made without regard for the facts and circumstances presented, and it connotes a disregard of the evidence.

In many instances, the term implies an element of BAD FAITH, and it may be used synonymously with tyrannical or despotic.

ARBITRATION ☐ The submission of a dispute to an unbiased third person designated by the parties to the controversy, who agree in advance to comply with the AWARD—a decision to be issued after a hearing at which both parties have an opportunity to be heard. ☐

Arbitration is employed to avoid the formalities, delay, expense, and inconvenience of ordinary litigation in the courts. Most jurisdictions allow specific differences to be referred to arbitration, but divergence exists with respect to the validity of a contract to arbitrate all disputes that might arise from it. As a general rule, courts favor arbitration as a method of removing disputes from the realm of litigation.

Types of arbitration *Compulsory arbitration* occurs when the CONSENT of one of the parties is enforced by statute, as in the case of a state statute providing for compulsory arbitration of labor disputes involving public employees. *Voluntary arbitration* occurs by the mutual and free consent of the parties.

Interest arbitration entails the settlement of terms of a CONTRACT between the parties, as distinguished from *grievance arbitration*, which concerns the interpretation or violation of an existing contract.

Agreement and submission Agreements may provide for arbitration of either existing or future controversies. Unless there is a binding submission—an agreement to refer the dispute to arbitration and to abide by the decision—arbitration cannot occur. These agreements are also subject to the laws governing contracts.

Parties As a general rule, all persons or CORPORATIONS with the CAPACITY to contract may submit controversies arising out of their contracts to arbitration. If one party breaches the agreement to arbitrate, the nonrepudiating party may insist on the arbitration or abandon the agreement. Diverse views exist as to whether all parties must join in a submission to arbitration, although persons who are not parties may agree to submit if they are interested in the subject matter.

Subject matter Unless there is a statutory restriction, nearly every type of dispute can be referred to arbitration, but a legal cause of action is not required. An honest difference of opinion is enough to warrant arbitration, but it is essential that a matter must be in dispute. Legal and factual issues are arbitrable.

Requisites An arbitration agreement or submission need not exist in any particular form or be in writing unless a statute provides to the contrary. It may even be implied from the conduct of the parties which indicates the intent to arbitrate. If the agreement results from FRAUD or DURESS, the victimized party cannot be compelled to arbitrate. A submission must designate the parties to it, the time and place of the proceeding, and the subject matter of the arbitration with reasonable certainty. When mandated by statute, the submission must also specify the court to which the award is to be returned for enforcement, if necessary.

Operation and effect A submission, which has been executed, that is, brought to an award, constitutes a WAIVER, an intentional relinquishment of a known right, of all claims within its scope. While arbitration usually remedies the breach of a contract containing an arbitration clause, the parties may retain the right to institute an action should their arbitration efforts fail. If an action is pending, and the parties decide to arbitrate, this usually results in a DISCONTINUANCE of the suit. A party to a contract that provides for arbitration is usually entitled to a STAY, or a suspension, of an action initiated on a disputed, arbitrable contract issue until arbitration is commenced in accordance with the agreement.

Waiver of right to arbitration No fixed rule defines what conduct constitutes a waiver of the right to arbitrate, since the question depends on the facts of the particular case. Such a right might be surrendered by disavowing the contract that provides for arbitration, by an unjustified refusal to arbitrate, by withdrawing from the arbitration proceedings, or by engaging in conduct that did not acknowledge the existence of the arbitration provision, such as by commencing an action on the matter subject to arbitration.

Amendment, modification, and revocation At any time prior to the making of the award or even after the original award is delivered, the parties may modify or amend the terms of the submission. The modified submission operates in lieu of the original submission. An agreement in a submission that it shall be irrevocable does not destroy its revocability, since a party has the power, although not the right, to revoke. In the event of a revocation, the party who had a right to arbitration can seek redress by an action for DAMAGES. Some event or conduct that necessarily terminates the proceedings, such as the death or insanity of a party, the death or refusal of the arbitrator to act, and the initiation of a suit concerning the same subject matter as that submitted to arbitration constitute revocation.

Arbitrators and umpires An arbitrator is a person selected by the parties to an arbitration agreement or submission to determine the matters in question. An UMPIRE is a person who acts alone in deciding the controversy if the original arbitrators cannot agree. Although the umpire is usually chosen by the arbitrators, he or she acts independently and is VESTED with the sole authority to make a final decision on the issues that have been presented.

Arbitrators must be fair and unbiased, and are legally obligated to reveal any information that might disqualify them or any transactions that might convey an impression of possible prejudice. The parties may waive objections to the arbitrator's qualifications. Whether an arbitrator must take an oath is a statutory matter. As a general rule, arbitrators have no power to delegate to others the whole, or any substantial portion, of the authority granted to them. They are not precluded, however, from seeking the advice of experts or legal counsel to enable them to perform their duties or attain greater comprehension of the matters presented to them. They have authority to act until an award, a revocation of a submission, or the expiration of the time in which the award must be made. In general, arbi-

It is just as important that there should be a place to end as that there should be a place to begin litigation.

STANLEY REED

trators are not personally liable to either party for their failure to exercise skill or CARE, but they might be criminally liable if they agree in advance to render a particular award.

Proceedings Arbitration does not require the formality of a judicial proceeding, and the technical rules used in court proceedings do not apply. The arbitration proceedings must be equitable and unbiased and in compliance with the provisions of the arbitration agreement or submission and any controlling statutes. As a general rule, unless there is a specific statutory provision or an agreement of the parties to the contrary, participants in arbitration are entitled to a full hearing with the opportunity to be heard and present evidence. The right to a hearing, however, does not encompass oral argument, unless the parties request it.

All of the arbitrators must receive notice of the meeting, and unless the submission prescribes an alternative, or a waiver of the necessity for the presence of the parties is expressed or implied, all arbitrators must attend and participate in the hearings, especially meetings at which evidence is heard. They are generally entitled to be present at the hearing of the evidence or the examination of WITNESSES. Unless explicitly restrained by the terms of the arbitration agreement or submission, arbitrators are not required to observe the strict legal rules of evidence, and they may apply their own knowledge and information. The arbitrators determine the weight and sufficiency of the evidence, and, in the absence of an express limitation, arbitrators have the power to determine whether evidence is ADMISSIBLE and COMPETENT. They may admit evidence that is not legally competent or admissible, but, as a general rule, they have no authority to refuse to hear competent evidence submitted on behalf of one of the parties. Arbitrators may issue SUBPOENAS—documents commanding a person to appear at a designated time and place to testify with respect to a particular matter—only where statutes confer this authority. As a general rule, when a matter other than one of public concern is submitted, the decision of the arbitrators must be unanimous, unless controlling statutes expressly permit a decision by a majority.

Defects or irregularities in arbitration proceedings, such as those concerning notice, presence, and oaths, generally must be raised through proper and timely OBJECTIONS by the party claiming prejudice, in accordance with the prescribed procedure. However, waiver of such defects or irregularities may be expressed or implied.

Award An arbitration award is a decision of a TRIBUNAL, which the parties themselves have created. The parties have mutually agreed to abide by the judgment of the tribunal. An arbitration award is not restricted to a precise form; it is sufficient that the language manifests an intention to render an award and that the matters submitted have been evaluated and decided by the arbitrators.

An arbitration agreement or a statute may prescribe a time within which an award is to be made, but if no mandatory time limit exists, an award may be made within a reasonable time. The time within which an award is required to be made may be extended by a subsequent agreement of the parties, unless a statute prescribes the manner of extending the time.

An award may be made either in writing or orally unless a written award is required by the STATUTE OF FRAUDS (an old English law adopted in America that prescribes that certain contracts must be in writing), by the terms of the submission, or by statute. The failure to satisfy this requirement can invalidate the award.

Ratification or acceptance by the parties may validate an award, which is VOIDABLE because it has some defect that does not pertain to the jurisdiction of the arbitrators, and is not essential to the effectiveness of a valid award. However, an award that is VOID cannot be rendered operative by ratification. The ratification of a voidable award may be either expressed or implied. No new CONSIDERATION—the inducement to enter into a contract—is necessary, but there must usually be knowledge of the irregularities in the award at the time of the ratification.

Although an award may be abrogated by the mutual consent of the parties, an attempt to do so by only one of the parties does not affect an award that is otherwise valid. The abandonment of the award restores the parties to their original rights, and neither party can enforce the award or rely on it as a bar to an action predicated on the original dispute.

In order to attain the objective of eliminating litigation, an award must be final as to all matters submitted so that the rights and obligations of the parties are definitely determined. An award may provide alternatives to the parties and still be final, but all awards must be so unequivocal that no doubt remains in regard to the intention of the arbitrators. An award that has been completed cannot be altered, modified, or augmented by the arbitrators, but ambiguities may be elucidated and mistakes discernible on the face of an award may be corrected. Unless required by the submission or statutory provisions, the award need not be confirmed or accepted by a court to establish its validity. Once it is confirmed, however, the award becomes a judgment of the court. Although an award must be fundamentally rational, every reasonable interpretation to support it must be made. An award is ordinarily ineffective to establish the rights and obligations of those who are not parties to the submission.

Statutes generally govern the enforcement of awards. The courts permit an arbitration award to be impeached or vacated only when it is illegal or when there has been fraud, misconduct, or gross MISTAKE or error. If the arbitrators are biased, this constitutes misconduct that may warrant the setting aside of the award. Newly discovered evidence is an insufficient basis for vacating an award. An arbitration award may be set aside when the arbitrators exceed their powers and the award cannot be corrected without affecting the merits of the decision upon the dispute submitted.

As a general rule, when an award is successfully impeached or vacated, the entire matter is reopened, the issues remain undetermined, the parties are relegated to their previous rights, and an action may be instituted on the original demand. Under some statutes, however, after setting aside an award the court may resubmit the controversy to arbitration, and it has been held that impeachment or vacation of an award invariably results in a new arbitration.

The court to which an award is returned normally has the power to recommit it to the arbitrators only when so authorized by the parties or by statute. The exercise of such power when conferred is predominantly within the discretion of the court. An award may properly be recommitted on any of the grounds specified by statute, but such grounds are not necessarily exclusive, especially when the power to recommit is not derived from the statute.

Ordinarily, the prevailing party is entitled to neither the expenses incurred in the arbitration nor those of a pending suit that has been submitted unless such costs have been specifically awarded or agreed upon or included in the judgment on the award. Arbitrators have authority to award the costs and expenses of the arbitration when such power has been granted to them by the submission or the terms of the statutes under which the arbitration is commenced. The costs of arbitration cannot be allowed by a court enforcing an award unless authorized by statute or by the arbitration agreement. Howev-er, court costs which accompany the enforcement of an award may be permitted to the prevailing party under statutes or court rules unless that right is waived.

Security for submission Although a performance BOND is not essential to a valid arbitration, such a bond is frequently employed to avoid the necessity of an action to enforce the award. See also, Charles H. McLaughlin's essay on Arbitration, International.

ARBITRATION ACTS ☐ Federal and state statutes that provide for the referral of controversies, such as labor grievances and disputes involving public employees, to an impartial third person selected by the PARTIES to the dispute, who concur in advance to comply with the AWARD, a decision to be issued subsequent to a hearing at which both parties have an opportunity to be heard. ☐

Such acts are designed to legalize arbitration agreements, render the arbitration process effective, provide necessary safeguards, and furnish an efficient procedure when judicial assistance is required.

ARBITRATION AND AWARD ☐ Under the rules of FEDERAL CIVIL PROCEDURE, an AFFIRMATIVE DEFENSE—new matter offered to diminish plaintiff's cause of action or to defeat recovery—which establishes that the subject matter of the action has been settled by a previous arrangement, in which an impartial third party, selected by the parties to the dispute, has decided the matter, and the parties have agreed to abide by that decision. ☐

ARBITRATION BOARD ☐ A panel of mediators appointed to hear and determine a controversy between parties who have agreed to comply with the decision rendered in the dispute. ☐

Such services are offered by the American Arbitration Association, a private, nonprofit organization committed to the improvement and expansion of the arbitration process.

ARBITRATION CLAUSE ☐ A phrase inserted in a CONTRACT that provides for compulsory mediation in the event of a controversy, such as a dispute arising under a union COLLECTIVE-BARGAINING AGREEMENT or an altercation between a consumer and a manufacturer concerning rights or liabilities under contract. ☐

For a sample arbitration clause, see the Appendix volume 11.

Charles H. McLaughlin

Arbitration, International

Arbitration is used in international law to resolve a variety of disputes according to law by means of a tribunal appointed by the disputants. The tribunal may be appointed by the disputants ad hoc or it may be a previously constituted tribunal. There are three classes of arbitration: public international arbitration, international claims, and international commercial arbitration.

Public international arbitration

Public disputes between governments of two or more states or between international organizations and their member states have long been submitted to arbitration. In the ancient and medieval eras, the process of arbitration had not become wholly differentiated from that of conciliation, except in those instances where there was prior agreement that the award should be binding on the disputants. Although seeking law common to the disputants in such universal systems as Roman civil law, the law of nations (*ius gentium*), and natural law, medieval European arbitrators were likely to be as much influenced by equity as by strict law. Arbitration fell into disuse during the wars of religion and struggle for colonial empire from the sixteenth through the eighteenth century. It was revived by the Jay Treaty of 1794, in which Great Britain and the United States agreed to arbitrate issues left unsettled by the peace treaty of 1783. In the era that followed, international law reached a degree of maturity that provided a legal standard for arbitration, increasingly distinguishing it from various forms of diplomatic settlement. Although equity can be used to supplement law when the parties so stipulate, arbitration became a genuine process of adjudication in the nineteenth century. As there were then no international courts, the parties chose the judges ad hoc. Procedure was less formal than that of regularly organized courts, and the obligation to submit to the jurisdiction of the tribunal and to accept its award rested wholly in the consent of the parties by the arbitral agreement.

The Jay Treaty gave impetus to the use of arbitration by successfully settling part of the northeast boundary, making 553 awards to Americans for ship seizures and 12 awards to British creditors for defaulted debts. By the middle of the century arbitral clauses were often included in bilateral commercial treaties. The Treaty of Guadalupe Hidalgo (1848) authorized arbitration not only of differences over interpretation of the treaty but also future political and commercial disputes, but this model was not much followed until after 1871. Even then agreements to submit unknown future issues to compulsory arbitration were restricted to those "it may not have been possible to settle by diplomacy" and invariably excluded "questions affecting the vital interests, the independence and the honor" of the signatories. If, when a dispute arose, signatories of such treaties did honor the obligation to arbitrate, it became necessary to conclude a supplementary agreement called a *compromis*, in which the signatories defined the particular issues and pro-

ULTIMATUM ON THE OREGON QUESTION.

vided for the formation of the tribunal, its jurisdiction, and procedure. Although limited in scope, arbitration flourished. Of 238 formal arbitrations between 1794 and 1900, more than 100 (42 involving the United States) occurred before 1871; there were also 250 informal arbitrations by boards or commissions.

The Alabama Claims Award under the Treaty of Washington (1871) was seen as a landmark in the progress of arbitration because it settled a sharp political issue between major powers. However, it should be noted that the principle of neutral liability for construction and release of the Confederate cruisers by Great Britain, then a doubtful point in international law, was actually settled by the treaty, leaving the arbitrators to determine only the amount of the award. Still, the result encouraged hope that arbitration might become important in pacific settlement of political disputes. It greatly stimulated bilateral treaties for submission of all future disputes to arbitration. By the end of the century, the first Hague Peace Conference was trying to move to institutionalized arbitration, with the establishment of the Permanent Court of Arbitration by the Hague Convention for the Pacific Settlement of International Disputes in 1899. This was slightly modified by the 1907 Convention; seventy-three states are now parties to one or both. The conven-

This 1846 political cartoon depicts the Oregon boundary dispute between Queen Victoria *(left)* of Great Britain and President James Polk *(right)*. Although Polk and his party had campaigned in 1844 on the slogan "Fifty-four forty or fight," negotiations between the two nations eventually led to a settlement of the boundary questions at the forty-ninth parallel.

tions also outlined basic principles and procedures of arbitration. However, the Permanent Court of Arbitration is not a true court but a large panel of legal experts from which disputant states may select arbitrators for a particular case, which they submit in accordance with a *compromis*. Adherence to the conventions does not in itself obligate signatories to use these facilities. In the Anglo-French Treaty of 1903 and the Anglo-American Treaty of 1908, the parties agreed in advance to submit all legal disputes or questions of treaty interpretation to Hague tribunals, but with the usual "vital interests" exception. Efforts by eight states at the 1907 conference to obtain a multipartite agreement to submit nonpolitical disputes without reservations failed, as did an Anglo-American draft treaty in 1911 for submission of all international disputes that were "justiciable in their nature by reason of being susceptible of decision by the application of the principles of law or equity." Whether the concept of justiciability in this sense can be workable continues to be a matter of controversy. Hague arbitration tribunals did enjoy moderate success until the 1920s, making awards in twenty-one cases, which included the politically sensitive *Venezuelan Preferential Claims Case* (Germany-Great Britain-Italy, 1904) and the *North Atlantic Coast Fisheries Case* (Great Britain-United States, 1910) as well as other cases that contributed to the development of international law (for example, *Orinoco Steamship Company Case* [United States-Venezuela, 1910]; *Savarkar Case* [France-Great Britain 1911]; *Canevaro Case* [Italy-Peru, 1912]; *Russian Indemnity Case* [Russia-Turkey, 1912]; *Island of Palmas Case* [United States-Netherlands, 1928]). For these cases see Scott, *Hague Court Reports*, I (1916): 55, 141, 226, 275, 284, 297; II (1932): 83.

In the period since World War I, international courts have become available—the Permanent Court of International Justice, succeeded by the International Court of Justice, and more recently regional courts of the European Community and the Organization of American States. These have preempted some business that otherwise might have gone to arbitral tribunals, since compulsory court jurisdiction exists under various treaties or by acceptance of the optional clause in the statute of the World Court. Arbitration lost some of its prewar appeal with the evaporation of the optimism that it could provide an effective alternative to war. Nevertheless there continued to be much activity in concluding bilateral arbitration treaties, and some significant multilateral agreements, notably the Locarno Treaties (1925), the General Treaty of Inter-American Arbitration (1929), and the Buenos Aires treaties of 1936. The Kellogg-Briand Pact (1928) also stimulated the League of Nations to try to draw together in the General Act for Pacific Settlement of International Disputes (1928) a multilateral obligation not to resort to war without first exhausting the progressive steps and agencies of pacific settlement available in good offices, mediation, conciliation, arbitration, and judicial settlement. This would have assigned legal disputes to the Permanent Court of International Justice, leaving to arbitration the nonlegal disputes, to be decided *ex aequo et bono* (Latin for "in justice and fairness"), if the sources of law stated in article 38 of the Permanent Court's statute provided no norm. If the hopes embodied in these efforts are not realized, there yet remains a very substantial network of treaty commitments to use arbitration and standing facilities available for that purpose.

The arbitral process may be summarized as follows: (a) arbitral jurisdiction is always defined and limited by the terms of the basic arbitral treaty and the

Unlimited power is apt to corrupt the minds of those who possess it; and this I know, my lords, that where laws end, tyranny begins.

WILLIAM PITT

compromis, which covers the particular submission—usually the tribunal is free to interpret these instruments; (b) the composition of the tribunal is determined by the parties, including the number and qualifications of the arbitrators (usually an equal number chosen by each party), along with the decision to include an umpire and the umpire's role; (c) evidence, which may include oral testimony but usually is documentary, is presented by agents for the respective parties with few restrictions upon admissibility—the parties rely upon the tribunal to assign proper weight to evidence in terms of credibility, probability, and relevance; (d) customary international law and relevant treaties are regularly applied—special rules and equity may be used if specified in the agreement (for an example of the use of equity see The Cayuga Indians, United States-Great Britain Claims Arbitration [1926]; Nielsen's Rept. 307); and (e) the *compromis* determines the majority required for an award—if this is not specified, a simple majority prevails and an umpire has a casting vote.

     Awards have come to be given in written form with an exposition of the tribunal's reasons and citation of legal authority. In accordance with their prior consent, the award is binding upon the parties and not subject to appeal. However, it may be pronounced null or be revised by the tribunal on a showing by either party of additional evidence previously unknown to it and the tribunal, or of corruption of an arbitrator, or a finding of "essential error" by reason of mistake of fact or gross error in the application of law by the tribunal (*United States* [*LeHigh Valley Ry. Co.*] *v. Germany*, United States-Germany Mixed Claims Comm., 1933, Report of Amer. Comr., 63; 8 *UN Repts. Intl. Arb. Awards* 226 [1958]). However, nullity of awards is the subject of much disagreement. There remains also the possibility, of which examples are few, that one party will conclude the award has ex-

The Kellogg Treaty, outlawing war, was signed in Paris by fifteen nations on August 27, 1928. It encouraged the use of arbitration for the settlement of international disputes.

ceeded the jurisdiction assigned the tribunal by the *compromis* and therefore will refuse to accept it. There is then no obvious manner of enforcement or of considering whether jurisdiction was exceeded. This situation could be turned over to a second arbitration; there is an example of this in the *Orinoco Steamship Case* (1910). The refusal of the United States to carry out the award in the Chamizal Arbitration of the Rio Grande boundary between El Paso and Juarez created a diplomatic impasse for a half century and was finally settled by a new boundary treaty in 1963. Model Rules on Arbitral Procedure drafted in 1958 by the United Nations International Law Commission (ILC Yrbk. 1958, II, 83–86) suggested submission of disputes over arbitrability, fulfilment of the obligation to appoint arbitrators, or interpretation of the validity of the award to the International Court of Justice, but many states consider this inconsistent with the consensual nature of the process.

International claims

Claims of private persons or companies for injuries suffered in the territory of a foreign state by crime, tort, or breach of contract may become public international claims. Such claims are brought by the government of the state of which the injured party is a national against the government of the state in which the party is injured if (a) officers or agents of the latter government have deliberately or negligently failed in their duty to protect the party or (b) the respondent government has failed, after exhaustion of the legal remedies, to provide just redress for injuries inflicted by private persons. Such claims proceed as arbitrations under agreements between the two states. Their special features are discussed in Charles H. McLaughlin's essay on Claims, International. See also the preceding section on Public International Arbitration.

International commercial arbitration

Disputes arising from private contracts and transactions (largely commercial) between individuals or companies of different nationalities, or sometimes between individuals or companies and a foreign state, are often governed by contractual agreements that submit them to binding arbitration. Such commercial arbitration agreements commonly resolve conflict of law issues by specifying the national forum and law governing the transaction and seek, at least in the first instance, to avoid resorting to regular courts, thereby designating arbitrators whose award they agree to accept. They may do this in the expectation that the arbitrators they select will assure a cheaper, less formal, more expeditious procedure, or neutral attitudes, or expert comprehension of the business involved, or greater privacy. Not infrequently, such agreements incorporate by reference detailed arbitral procedures developed by a national or regional agency that provides arbitral services; for example, the rules of the International Chamber of Commerce (1955), the United Naitons Economic Commission for Asia and the Far East (1966), the United Nations Economic Commission for Europe (1966), the Inter-American Commercial Arbitration Commission (1969), the International Law Association (Copenhagen Rules, 1950); for these and others see United Nations Commission on International Trade Law (UNCITRAL), *Register of Texts of Conventions and Other Instruments concerning International Trade Law*, II (1973), Ch. I. Arbitral rules were also drafted by UNCITRAL in 1976 (text in 15 *International Legal Materials* [1976]: 701–717). Substantive rules approved by appropriate trade associations are also sometimes incorporated into commercial contracts and may be given effect in so far as they consist with the law of the forum. In order to encourage the movement of private investment capital into foreign countries that need it by creating "an atmosphere of mutual confidence," the International Bank for Reconstruction and Development framed in 1965 a Convention on the Settlement of Investment Disputes between States and Nationals of Other States, to which sixty-six states, including the United States, were parties on January 1, 1981. It provides conciliation and arbitration services in such disputes in an International Centre for Settlement of Investment Disputes at the principal office of the bank. Within the framework of any such arrangements, the basic arbitral process is pursued: receiving evidence in a somewhat informal but orderly way, finding facts according to the evidence, and applying the law to the facts.

The special problems arising in this context concern enforcement of the agreement to arbitrate and enforcement of the award. These matters are not widely controlled by the United Nations Convention on Recognition and Enforcement of Foreign Arbitral Awards (1958; United States accession in 1970; over fifty-nine countries are parties; 21 UST 2517, 330 UNTS 3) and national legislation implementing it, in this country the United States Arbitration Act as amended in 1970 (9 U.S.C.A. § 201 et seq.), which applies to maritime and international commercial transactions. If in violation of contract one party refuses to participate in an arbitration, the other party may petition any court that would have had jurisdiction of the dispute in the absence of the arbitral agreement and obtain an order to compel arbitration according to the agreement (*Victory Transport Inc. v. Comisaria General*, 336 F.2d 354 [2d Cir. 1964], *cert. denied*, 381 U.S. 934, 85 S.Ct. 1763, 14 L.Ed.2d 698 [1965]; *Petition of Petrol Shipping Corp.*, 360 F.2d 103 [2d Cir. 1966]). If one party brings suit in a court in a cause of action that should have been submitted to arbitration, and the other party pleads the arbitral agreement in bar of the action, the courts will sustain the plea (*Scherk v. Alberto-Culver*, 417 U.S. 506, 94 S.Ct. 2449, 41 L.Ed.2d 270 [1973], *rehearing denied*, 419 U.S. 885, 95 S.Ct. 157, 42 L.Ed.2d 129 [1974]; *Sam Reisfeld & Son Import Co. v. S. A. Eteco*, 530 F.2d 679, [5th Cir. 1976]; *Hanes Corp. v. Millard,* 174 U.S. App. D.C. 253, 531 F.2d 585 [1976]). If the judicial action is begun after the arbitration is already in progress, the court will stay proceedings until completion of the arbitration (*In re Fotochrome, Inc.,* 377 F.Supp. 26 [E.D.N.Y. 1974]; *Siderius, Inc. v. Compania de Acero del Pacifico*, 453 F.Supp. 22 [S.D.N.Y. 1978]). When an award has been made under a binding arbitration agreement by an arbitral tribunal in another country and judgment entered on the award by a court there, United States courts (and presumably courts of other countries parties to the United Nations Convention) will enforce the terms of the award (*In re Fotochrome, Inc.,* above; *Splosna Plovba of Piran v. Agrelak Steamship Corp.*, 381 F.Supp. 1368 [S.D.N.Y. 1974]; *Parsons & Whittemore Overseas Co., Inc. v. Societé Générale de L'Industrie du Papier*, 508 F.2d 969 [2d Cir. 1974]; *Imperial Ethiopian Government v. Baruch-Foster Corp.,* 535 F.2d 334 [5th Cir. 1976]; *Audi NSU Auto Union Aktiengesellschaft v. Overseas Motors*, 418 F.Supp. 982 [D.C. Mich. 1976]). Exceptions may be made if the arbitral agreement is tainted by fraud or coercion, perhaps if the tribunal is improperly composed (compare *Imperial Ethiopian Government v. Baruch-Forster Corp.,* above; *Sam Reisfeld & Son Import Co. v. S.A. Eteco,* above) or if

The Washington Naval Disarmament Conference of 1921 shown in this photo successfully negotiated the famous 5:5:3 ratio for capital ships of the United States, Great Britain, and Japan.

some questions are brought before the tribunal that are not open to arbitration, such as the validity of patents under federal law, the salvage of public ships, or antitrust claims (*Hanes Corp. v. Millard*, above; *B.V. Bureau Wijsmuller v. United States*, 487 F.Supp. 156 [S.D.N.Y. 1979]; *American Journal on International Law* 411 (1978); *Sam Reisfeld & Son Import Co. v. S.A. Eteco*, above). Public policy exceptions to confirmation and enforcement of foreign arbitral awards are allowable but closely scrutinized (*Libyan American Oil Co. v. Socialist People's Libyan Arab Jamahirya*, 482 F.Supp. 1175 [D.C.D.C. 1980]; *Parsons & Whittemore Overseas Co., Inc. v. Societé Générale de L'Industrie du Papier*, above).

Bibliography: Martin Domke, ed., *International Trade Arbitration* (1933); John Bassett Moore, *International Adjudications,* Modern Series, vol. 1 (1929), pp. xv-xci; John Bassett Moore, *International Law and Some Current Illusions* (1924), chapter 3; Jackson H. Ralston, *International Arbitration from Athens to Lacarno* (1929); Jackson H. Ralston, *The Law and Procedure of International Tribunals* (1926), *supplement* (1932); Julius Stone, *Legal Controls of International Conflict* (1954), chapter 4; J. Gillis Wetter, *The International Arbitral Process: Public and Private,* 5 vols. (1979); for reports, see John Bassett Moore, *History and Digest of the International Arbitrations to Which the United States Has Been a Party,* 6 vols. (1898); W. Michael Reisman, *Nullity and Revision* (1971); James Brown Scott, *Hague Court Reports,* 2 vols. (1916, 1932); A. M. Stuyt, *Survey of International Arbitrations: 1794–1938* (1939); United Nations, *Reports of International Arbitral Awards,* 16 vols. (1948–1969).

ARBITRATOR ☐ A private, neutral person, who is designated by the PARTIES to a dispute to hear their agruments and issue an AWARD, or decision, concerning the matters submitted. ☐

Types Arbitrators can be temporary or permanent and may be appointed singly or as part of a panel. The three most common combinations are the single permanent arbitrator, the permanent tripartite board, and the temporary arbitrator, who may sit alone or as the impartial member of a panel.

The single permanent arbitrator system Sometimes called the "impartial chairman" or "umpire" system, the single permanent arbitrator system has a number of important advantages. The permanent arbitrator, who is only "permanent" for a specified period or as long as both parties desire his or her services, possesses greater familiarity with the parties, their CONTRACT, and their expectations concerning the role of the arbitrator. This familiarity results in more expeditious hearings and decisions and increased confidence in those decisions. However, some disadvantages exist within this system. The parties might select an arbitrator and then discover that the arbitrator does not fulfill their expectations, which renders dismissal awkward or problematic. The availability and minimum fee of a permanent arbitrator frequently encourage the parties to take their grievance procedure less seriously and submit to the arbitrator cases that should be resolved between the parties themselves. It can be difficult to engage an experienced arbitrator with the expertise and temperament necessary to successfully manage the continuous relationship created by this system. There is also a risk that the arbitrator will attempt to determine what is beneficial to the parties instead of what the contract requires.

The permanent tripartite board Parties select the tripartite format rather than the single arbitrator to ensure that their actual positions, which might differ from their public positions, are emphatically presented to the neutral member of the panel. This is possible because each side usually selects one member of the panel, the third member is selected by agreement, and the member chosen by one party is likely to be an advocate of that party's position. In addition, the majority vote requirement of the panel form lends greater weight to arbitration awards. However, a dissenting opinion by the dissatisfied party undercuts the authority of the award and provides a basis for future grievances on the same issue.

The temporary arbitrator system As a general rule, AD HOC, or temporary, arbitrators are designated in a COLLECTIVE-BARGAINING AGREEMENT, an accord between an employer and a labor union that governs the terms and conditions of employment. This system allows the parties to search for particular qualifications necessary to address specialized questions and to change arbitrators easily if experience creates dissatisfaction. The temporary system does not preclude frequent or exclusive reselection of an arbitrator who satisfies both parties, but it does eliminate some of the advantages of permanent systems.

The disadvantages of the temporary system are nearly the exact opposite of the advantages of the permanent system. Ad hoc arbitrators lack familiarity with the parties, are not as consistent as a single arbitrator—although most give some deference to prior decisions on the same issue—and lack the necessary experience to deal with certain cases. Given these possibilities, it is probable that a losing party will seek to relitigate a similar issue before a new arbitrator to attain a more favorable outcome, which is not conducive to stable labor relations.

Methods of selection There are numerous methods of selecting an arbitrator. Some companies and UNIONS appoint permanent mediators to hear all arbitrations, either for a specified period of time or at the continued will of the parties. Some large companies and industries appoint panels of arbitrators and call upon panel members in rotation. Others select new arbitrators for each case by consensus, a method that has a serious disadvantage in that it does not resolve deadlocks over the choice of an individual.

Most contracts under temporary arbitrator systems provide that an arbitrator be chosen from a list of names submitted by an arbitration agency. The American Arbitration Association, a private, nonprofit organization dedicated to the enhancement and expansion of the arbitration process, and the Federal Mediation and Conciliation Service (FMCS), an agency of the Federal government, and several state agencies maintain files of persons qualified by education and experience to serve as arbitrators. Upon request, an agency will supply the parties with a panel of names drawn from this list. The parties select one person from the panel and then ascertain whether the chosen arbitrator is available for appointment.

The two most common methods for choosing one name from the panel are alternate striking and ranking. In the former case, the parties

Discourage litigation. Persuade your neighbors to compromise whenever you can . . . As a peacemaker the lawyer has a superior opportunity of being a good man. There will still be business enough.

ABRAHAM LINCOLN

agree upon which party is to strike a name from the list first and then each party alternately eliminates the least desirable name until only one remains. Both strategic and pragmatic reasons demand that some consideration be given to the striking process at the time the ARBITRATION CLAUSE is negotiated. The prevailing view is that the final stike is the most significant one, for it is nearly identical to possessing the sole strike in a panel of two names. The party who strikes first controls the even strikes so that the last strike belongs to the adversary party. During negotiations attorneys frequently attempt to ensure that the arbitration clause gives the first strike to the other party. Striking provisions must be carefully drafted, because if the contract is silent or ambiguous, an impasse can ensue in regard to which party is to make the initial strike.

The second method of selection eliminates some of these difficulties. Each party strikes any arbitrator deemed completely unacceptable from the list and ranks the remainder in descending order from one to whatever the number of names remaining on the list is. The rankings of those arbitrators not eliminated by either party are then added, and the person with the lowest total is selected. If no person is left after the eliminations, another list can be procured; this problem can be prevented by restricting the number of strikes each party is permitted to make.

This method, however, can also present some difficulties. Problems arise if two persons are tied for the lowest total ranking—for example, when a company ranks one arbitrator first and another arbitrator second, and a union selects the same arbitrators but reverses their order. The most expedient manner of preventing such difficulties is to incorporate, by reference, the rules of the American Arbitration Association or the FMCS, both of which provide for an appointment by the agency if for any reason the parties cannot concur upon a choice.

Appointment When using an arbitration agency, the parties notify the agency of their selection and the agency makes the formal appointment. Unlike the FMCS, the American Arbitration Association requires that the chosen arbitrator execute a form that avers impartiality. Many parties designate arbitrators by mutual agreement without the assistance of arbitration agencies. In such cases, one party contacts the selected arbitrator to schedule a convenient hearing date.

Authority of arbitrators As a general rule, the power and authority of arbitrators is derived from the provisions of the arbitration agreement or submission under which they have been appointed. Unless a court order directs arbitration, the arbitrators derive JURISDICTION from the agreement of the parties and not from statutes and constitutional provisions. The parties to an arbitration can vest the arbitrators with such powers as they deem appropriate, provided they do not violate any law.

The functions of arbitrators are quasi-judicial. In fact, arbitrators have been regarded as judges or as exercising judicial functions or power. However, strictly speaking, they are neither judges nor officers of the court.

Scope Unless arbitration ensues from a court order (in which case the extent of authority of arbitrators is ascertained by the provisions of the order), the scope of authority of arbitrators generally depends on the intention of the parties to an arbitration and is determined by the agreement of submission. Such agreement or submission serves not only to define but also to restrict the authority of arbitrators.

Arbitrators must act within the scope of authority granted to them in deciding all issues submitted. They cannot exceed their authority or determine matters not submitted. Arbitrators cannot exercise powers they do not possess, such as rewriting agreements between the parties or determining the rights and obligations of persons who are not parties to the agreement or the proceedings. Arbitrators cannot deviate from their instructions or decide issues that the agreement does not give them power to decide, although the parties may confer on them the authority to decide questions not originally comtemplated.

The absence of a valid, binding agreement restricts the arbitrator's authority. When the agreement expires, is obtained by FRAUD, or is not properly ratified, the courts hold that an arbitrator lacks authority to apply the terms of the document or that there can be no arbitration if the agreement itself is contained only in the challenged document.

The broadest power of arbitrators is to issue a binding decision on all the matters submitted to them by the arbitration agreement or submission. They have wide and nearly unrestricted powers when acting on matters properly under submission. Controversy has arisen, however, with respect to whether arbitrators may, should, or must rule on questions of law relating to contractual grievances.

As a general rule, arbitrators can properly examine the law to assist in the interpretation of a contract where contractual and legal provisions overlap but are not necessarily in conflict. In cases where the contract term is susceptible to two interpretations, one of which is consistent with the contract, arbitrators can reasonably assume that the parties intended the lawful interpretation.

There are divergent views concerning the role of arbitrators in cases where a definite conflict exists between the law and the contract. The traditional position is that the arbitrator's sole function is to interpret the contract. When such a conflict exists, the arbitrator should respect the agreement and not attempt to resolve the legal questions. To do so would be to act beyond the scope of the submission agreement and the limits of the claim to expertise in arbitration. There is no problem if the parties ask the arbitrator for an opinion on the law. If the parties have incorporated legal standards in their agreement, the arbitrator might then be required to interpret the law.

The opposite viewpoint maintains that if the arbitrator ignores legal issues, he or she does the parties a disservice by requiring them to engage in additional litigation. Also, some arbitrators believe that the parties intend that all of their agreement be legal and feel that it is the arbitrator's duty to reform the agreement to achieve that objective.

A compromise position recommends that arbitrators examine the law only to avoid issuing a decision that would require a party to violate it.

If the arbitrator does rule on a legal question in the course of interpreting a contract, different views exist as to whether the interpretation is binding. One viewpoint maintains that because such issues are extraneous to the arbitrator's authority and expertise, a ruling on the legal issue should be regarded as advisory only, subject to a DE NOVO, or second review, if the parties seek enforcement or vacation of the award in court. Another position maintains that if the parties intended the arbitrator to resolve legal issues, the interpretation should be binding between the parties. If the arbitrator interprets a Federal law in an appropriate case, such as imposing a stricter obligation on an employer than the reviewing court would find the law to require, the arbitrator's opinion should govern.

Termination Arbitrators can only render binding awards during the time they have jurisdiction, which can be terminated through various means.

Time limitations established in the collective-bargaining agreement, the submission agreement, or in a separate accord are valid, so that the arbitrator's authority expires automatically if those limits are ignored.

Under the doctrine of *functus officio* (Latin for "a task performed"), an arbitrator's power ceases when the task for which he or she was selected is completed, that is, when a final award is issued. Many arbitrators, however, routinely retain jurisdiction for thirty to sixty days after a decision is returned in the event the parties have difficulty applying the award.

State statutes occasionally provide for a few automatic terminations. The most evident of these is the death or DISABILITY of the arbitrator. The death or disability of one of the parties is less apparent and perhaps irrelevant in most cases today because of the continuing nature of corporate and labor organizations.

ARCHIPELAGO, ARCHIPELAGIC STATE
☐ A country or body of land or series of islands surrounded by water. ☐

In international law, an archipelagic state, by virtue of its geography, has certain rights and duties. A certain degree of international cooperation is required from such nations.

ARCHITECT ☐ A person who prepares the plan and design of a building or other structure and sometimes supervises its construction. ☐

A landscape architect is responsible for the arrangement of scenery over a tract of land for natural or aesthetic purposes in order to enhance or preserve the property.

Regulation The practice of planning and designing a building requires the application

Dictionary of American Portraits

The seminal American architect Louis H. Sullivan believed that the external form of a building should express the internal use of the structure so that "form follows function." He also wrote that architecture should embody the efficiency of industrial engineering, the beauty of intricate surface design, and the individuality of the architect.

Frank Lloyd Wright worked under Louis H. Sullivan and developed his own philosophy of functionalism which he called "organic" architecture. He went on to build homes from natural wood and stone that were skillfully and harmoniously integrated into the natural environment of the individual home site. His style evolved continuously and became highly expressive of his own personality and much less closely related to the requirements of function and site. Wright's later buildings became the immediate forerunners of those contemporary banks, office buildings, and hotels whose aura is one of expressive fantasy rather than function.

of specialized skill and knowledge. Because the product of an architect's work is used by members of the general public, the legislature of a state may regulate the practice of those engaged in the profession. Regulatory statutes designed to protect public health and safety are created under the inherent authority of a state to protect the welfare of its citizens. As a general rule, regulatory statutes are valid, provided they are not unreasonable.

Statutes requiring that architects must be registered and licensed are based on public policy aimed at protecting citizens from unqualified practitioners. In many states, statutes call for the revocation of a license for such conduct as fraud, dishonesty, recklessness, incompetence, or misrepresentation when an architect acts in his or her professional capacity.

The power to revoke a license is commonly given by the legislature to a state board of architects who must act in a manner prescribed by statute. Generally, an architect is entitled to notice and a hearing when the board seeks to revoke his or her license. The architect can appeal a revocation.

Qualifications   Statutes setting forth the requirements for obtaining a license or registration generally require that the applicants are of legal age, of good moral character, have completed a certain course of study, and that they have a certain amount of practical experience. Many states have an additional requirement that applicants must pass an examination. A legislature may provide that certain persons who have practiced architecture for a period of time prior to legislation requiring an examination may register as an architect without an examination. Such a statutory provision is called a GRANDFATHER CLAUSE.

Persons who present themselves to the public as architects must comply with the statutory registration and licensing requirements. The failure to do so is unlawful. In most states, persons who falsely hold themselves out as licensed architects are guilty of a MISDEMEANOR, and contracts rendered by them with others are void and unenforceable.

Employment   The terms and conditions of an architect's employment are designated in a contract and are governed by general rules of contract law. Ordinarily, the person who employs the architect becomes the owner of the plans, unless the employment contract states otherwise. Customarily, the architect retains the plans after they have been paid for and the builder may possess and use them while constructing the building.

Authority and powers   The power and authority of architects is determined by general rules of AGENCY law. In most cases, unless the employment contract states otherwise, architects are held to be agents with limited authority. An employer is liable for acts of an architect when they are within the scope of the architect's agency, although the contracting parties may further restrict the powers if they so desire.

Architects have a duty to exercise their personal skill and judgment in the performance of their work, and they may not delegate this duty without express authority to do so. They may, however, delegate responsibility to subordinates while performing their duties as agents.

A supervising architect does not have implied authority to perform work that has been assigned to a contractor or to employ or discharge workers. The supervising architect does, however, have authority to make decisions concerning proper workmanship, fitness of materials, and the manner of work.

Duties and liabilities Although the duties of architects generally depend on what is designated in the employment contract, some duties are carried out as a matter of custom, such as the duty to supervise construction.

Architects are in a FIDUCIARY relationship with their employers, and as such they must exercise good faith and loyalty towards them. As professionals, they are held to a standard of reasonable and ordinary care and skill in applying their knowledge and must conform to accepted architectural practices. The failure to exercise reasonable care and skill can result in liability for damages and the loss of the right to recover compensation for their services.

Compensation Architects have a right to compensation for their services unless there is an agreement that they shall work gratuitously. To be entitled to compensation they must carry out their contract with reasonable skill and care and without any substantial omissions or imperfections in performance. The employment contract usually fixes the amount of compensation. A standard payment scale created by the American Institute of Architects is customarily used to determine the amount of compensation.

In the event that an architect is refused payment for services, he or she may sue for the amount of compensation agreed upon in the employment contract or, in the absence of an agreement, for the reasonable value of the services under the theory of QUANTUM MERUIT.

ARCHITECT OF THE CAPITOL The first architect of the Capitol was appointed in 1793 by the president of the United States. During the period of the construction of the Capitol (1793–1865) appointments were made to the position of architect at such times and for such periods as the various stages of the construction work required. The office of architect has, however, been continuous from 1851 to date.

The functions of the office have changed materially through the years in accordance with the increased activities imposed upon it by Congress, due, principally, to the addition of new buildings and grounds. Originally, the duties of the architect of the Capitol were to plan and construct the Capitol building and, later, to supervise its care and maintenance.

Permanent authority for the care and maintenance of the Capitol building is provided by the act of August 15, 1876 (19 Stat. 147; 40 U.S.C. 162–163). This act has been amended from time to time to provide for the care and maintenance of the additional buildings and grounds placed under the jurisdiction of the architect of the Capitol by Congress in subsequent years.

The architect of the Capitol, acting as an agent of Congress, has charge of the structural and mechanical care of the United States Capitol building; makes arrangements with the proper authorities for ceremonies and ceremonials held in the building and on the grounds; is responsible for the care, maintenance, and improvement of the Capitol grounds, comprising approximately 190.5 acres; has the structural and mechanical care of the Library of Congress buildings and the United States Supreme Court building; and is responsible for the operation of the United States Senate restaurant.

In addition to these activities the architect has the following duties and responsibilities:

- Under the direction and approval of the House Office Building Commission, the structural, mechanical, and domestic care and maintenance of the House Office buildings, including the maintenance and operation of the mechanical, electrical, and electronic equipment, and the care, maintenance, and operation of the Capitol power plant, which supplies heat and air-conditioning refrigeration for the Capitol, Senate and House office buildings, Library of Congress buildings, and the United States Supreme Court building; heat for the United States Botanic Garden and the Senate and House garages; and steam heat for the Government Printing Office, Washington City Post Office, and steam heat and chilled water for the Folger Shakespeare Library;

- Subject to the approval of the Senate Committee on Rules and Administration as to matters of general policy, the structural, mechanical, and domestic care and maintenance of the Senate office buildings, including the maintenance and operation of the mechanical, electrical, and electronic equipment;

- The jurisdiction and control, including care and maintenance of the Senate garage, subject to such regulations respecting the use thereof as may be promulgated by the Senate Committee on Rules and Administration.

- The architect of the Capitol is also charged with the planning and construction of such buildings as may be committed to his or her care by Congress from time to time. Current projects include extension, reconstruction, alteration, and improvement of the United

States Capitol; construction and equipment of an extension to the Dirksen office building; construction and improvements under the additional House office building projects; construction of the Library of Congress James Madison Memorial building; and expansion, modification, and enlargement of the facilities of the Capitol power plant.

Under the direction and supervision of the Joint Committee on the Library, the architect of the Capitol serves as acting director of the United States Botanic Garden.

The architect of the Capitol also serves as a member of the Capitol Police Board, the Capitol Guide Board, the Advisory Council on Historic Preservation, the District of Columbia Zoning Commission, the Board of Directors of the Pennsylvania Avenue Development Corporation, the Art Advisory Committee to the Washington Metropolitan Area Transit Authority, and Coordinator of Civil Defense for the Capitol group of buildings.

Source: *The United States Government Manual 1981/82* and/or *1982/83.*

ARCTIC, LEGAL STATUS OF   Establishment of territorial sovereignty over portions of the Arctic and its seabed has become increasingly attractive to many nations for military purposes or as a source of minerals. Under international law, national claims of sovereignty over the Arctic traditionally were recognized only if accompanied by physical occupation. Consequently, two competing theories developed: (1) that no nation could achieve sovereignty over the Arctic (*res nullius*), and (2) that every nation shared in undivided sovereignty over the area (*res communes*). According to international law today, sovereignty is considered to be a derivative of the exercise of government functions and of notoriety over new territory. Therefore, national claims of sovereignty over portions of the Arctic that are supported by such governmental activity have become more plausible. Many such claims have rested on the sector principle, a version of the doctrine of contiguity, to define the area included in the claim. The sector principle traces longitudinal parallels from borders of countries adjacent to the Arctic Circle to the North Pole, assigning the sectors so formed to the neighboring nations. Claims resting solely on the sector principle have been denied legal force by many nations, including the United States, and it appears that only those claims of sovereignty accompanied by government control may be eventually accepted under international law.

ARGUENDO   □ In the course of the argument. □

When the phrase *in arguendo* is used by a judge during the course of a trial, it indicates that his or her comment is made as a matter of argument or illustration only. The statement does not bear directly upon the remainder of the discussion.

ARGUMENT   □ A form of expression consisting of a coherent set of reasons presenting or supporting a point of view; a series of reasons given for or against a matter under discussion that is intended to convince or persuade the listener. □

For example, an argument by counsel consists of a presentation of the facts or evidence and the inferences that may be drawn therefrom, which are aimed at persuading a judge or jury to render a verdict in favor of the attorney's client.

An attorney may begin to develop an argument in the OPENING STATEMENT, the initial discussion of the case in which the facts and the pertinent law are stated. In most cases, however, an attorney sets forth the main points of an argument in the CLOSING ARGUMENT, which is the attorney's final opportunity to comment on the case before a judge or jury retires to begin deliberation on a verdict.

ARGUMENTATIVE   □ Controversial; subject to argument. □

Pleading in which a point relied upon is not set out, but merely implied, is often labeled argumentative. Pleading that contains arguments that should be saved for trial, in addition to allegations establishing a cause of action or defense, is also called argumentative.

ARISTOTLE   Aristotle (*b.* 384 B.C., in Stagira, Greece; *d.* 322 B.C., in Chalcis, Greece) achieved prominence as an eminent philosopher who greatly influenced the basic principles of philosophy and whose ideologies are still practiced today.

Aristotle was a student of the renowned philosopher Plato and tutored Alexander the Great, who became King of Macedonia in 336 B.C.

Aristotle established his own school in the Lyceum, near Athens, in 335 B.C. He often lectured his students in the portico, or walking

Aristotle advocated the use of logic, reasoning, and factual explanations to interpret reality.

place, of the Lyceum. The school was subsequently called Peripatetic, after the Greek word *peripatos* for "walking place."

In 323 B.C., the reign of Alexander ended with his death, and Aristotle sought refuge at Chalcis.

Aristotle formulated numerous beliefs about the reasoning power of humans and the essence of being. He stressed the importance of nature and instructed his pupils to closely study natural phenomena. When teaching science, he believed that all ideas must be supported by explanations based upon facts.

Concerning the realm of politics, Aristotle propounded that humans are inherently political and demonstrate an essential part of their humanity when participating in civic affairs.

Philosophy was a subject of great interest to Aristotle, and he theorized that philosophy was the foundation of the ability to understand the basic axioms that comprise knowledge. In order to study and question completely, Aristotle viewed logic as the basic means of reasoning. To think logically, one had to apply the syllogism, which was a form of thought comprised of two premises that led to a conclusion; Aristotle taught that this form can be applied to all logical reasoning.

To understand reality, Aristotle theorized that it must be categorized as substance, quality, quantity, relation, determination in time and space, action, passion or passivity, position, and condition. To know and understand the reality of an object required an explanation of its material cause, which is why it exists or its composition; its formal cause, or its design; its efficient cause, or its creator; and its final cause, or its reason for being.

Aristotle agreed with his mentor, Plato, concerning the field of ethics. The goodness of a being depended upon the extent to which that being achieved its highest potential. For humans, the ultimate good is the continual use and development of their reasoning powers to fullest capacity. To effect fulfillment and contentment, humans must follow a life of contemplation, rather than pleasure.

The fundamental source of Aristotle's theories were his lectures to his students, which were compiled into several volumes. They include: *Organum,* which discusses logic; *Physics; Metaphysics; De Anima,* concerning the soul; *Rhetoric; Politics; Nichomachean Ethics and Eudemian Ethics,* involving principles of conduct; and *De Poetica,* or poetics.

Aristotle also wrote *Constitution of Athens,* a description of the foundations of the government of Athens. The work was discovered in the late nineteenth century.

ARMED MERCHANT SHIPS See Neutrality.

ARMED SERVICES ☐ The air, land, and naval forces, which are established and organized by the Federal government for national defense. ☐

The armed services refers to the military and those governmental agencies and personnel who deal with defense and war. The armed forces consist of the Army, Navy, Air Force, Marine Corps, Coast Guard, and the Reserves. Auxiliary forces include the National Guard and the militia of the individual states. A member of the National Guard serves both the National Guard of his or her home state and the National Guard of the United States, a reserve component of the Army. The state militia becomes part of the Federal service when called into action by the president.

The military is subordinate to the Constitution and the civil authority. Congress is empowered by the Constitution to raise, support, and regulate the armed services. The president, as commander in chief of the armed services, has exclusive and ultimate control of military matters unless restricted by law.

Military law　Military law is the collection of statutes, rules, and regulations enacted to govern the militia. It is separate and apart from CIVIL LAW, that law which governs the judicial branch of government. Military law is concerned with duty, discipline, and supervising the trials of military personnel.

Military law is based on the Constitution, statutes relating to the armed forces, military regulations, and customs of the particular service. Military orders, customs, or usages may not violate the Constitution, statutes, or any military law. Regulations, although not the law, have the effect of law when they conform with enacted statutes.

Military law and civil authority　Civil courts safeguard the constitutional rights of military personnel and exercise authority over statutory and regulatory violations. A civil court may properly decide whether the service has followed its own regulations and applicable statutes. Not every violation, however, is reviewable by a civil court, and the right to judicial intervention is limited to cases where regulations apply to the conduct of service personnel rather than to administrative procedures. The courts may review matters of internal military affairs to determine only if an official acted within the scope of his or her authority. Internal military affairs are not subject to judicial review in the absence of an alleged deprivation of a constitutional right or a claim that the military acted in violation of applicable statutes and regulations. Civil courts, therefore, show deference to a military agency's interpretation of an armed service regulation. The military, however, must follow the fundamental principle that no order may violate the Constitution, Federal statute, or military regulation, and such an order is reviewable to determine if it violates any of those three controlling areas of law. Generally, all military remedies must be exhausted before Federal courts will intervene unless the military action in issue affects civilians.

Military and martial law　Military law is not the same as MARTIAL LAW. Military law applies only to persons in the armed services. Martial law applies to all the people and property within the district subject to it. Military law is permanent and enforceable in both peace and war, while martial law is temporary and ceases with the necessity that brought it into existence. Military law is a well-defined set of rules and reg-

ulations that coexists with civil law. Martial law is not a recognized branch of jurisprudence but is merely the will of a military commander who issues laws and rules, which has the effect of suspending the civil government.

Court-martial　A court-martial is a military court responsible for the trial and punishment of specific offenses committed by service members. It is convened for a purely military crime and ceases to exist once a judgment and sentence, if warranted, has been pronounced. Once a person is no longer connected with the military, the court martial lacks jurisdiction over him or her, unless it was exercised prior to the individual leaving the service, such as by the commencement of proceedings.

All court-martial proceedings are required by law to undergo military review, first by the officer who convened the court-martial. The second review is by the JUDGE ADVOCATE GENERAL or he may establish a Court of Military Review to do so. Only serious convictions receive the latter review. The court of LAST RESORT is the Court of Military Appeals established by the president and composed of civilian judges. Death sentences and sentences involving a general or flag officer are also reviewable by the president. Although not all the constitutional safeguards available in civil courts must be observed in courts-martial, a fair trial and DUE PROCESS OF LAW are essential.

Military personnel　Members of the armed services join the service either voluntarily or involuntarily. Voluntary enlistment is the making of a CONTRACT to serve in the military for an agreed duration. An enlistee's rights depend on the terms of the contract and the statutes under which it was made. Minors may not avoid a valid enlistment if a parent's or guardian's permission is required and given. However, if a minor enlists without such permission, the parent or guardian may void the enlistment.

CONSCRIPTION is conducted under the provisions of the Military Selective Service Act (50 U.S.C.A. App. § 451 et seq. [1967]) which is still in effect. The power of a government to compel a citizen to enter military service is within the scope of its sovereignty. The act provides that if the induction of persons is discontinued, the Selective Service System shall maintain an active standby organization to reactivate registration in the event of a national emergency. The draft was last suspended on July 1, 1973. Male citizens between certain ages are, however, still required to report for registration. Noncompliance with the registration procedures of the Military Selective

Look at the great volume of human nature. They will foretell you that a defenceless country cannot be secure.

JOHN MARSHALL

A blindfolded Secretary of War, Henry L. Stimson, selects the first name in the U.S. draft lottery on October 29, 1940.

Library of Congress

Service Act is prosecutable as a criminal offense and upon conviction, a fine, term of imprisonment, or both, may be imposed.

The faculties and cadets of service academies are included among the personnel of the armed services. The service academies were created by statute. Cadets are nominated by their congressional representatives and appointed by the president. They must conform to an honor code, which establishes standards of behavior, discipline, and decorum. Gross violations of the honor code can constitute sufficient grounds for expulsion from a service academy. Expulsion entitles cadets to informal hearings where they do not have the right to COUNSEL but can offer evidence and witnesses on their own behalf.

The different grades and ranks of officers of the armed services are prescribed and governed by statute and include commissioned and warrant officers. The majority of officers are commissioned, which means that an officer holds a commission, or document, as evidence of the right to office, signed by the president, sealed with the seal of the United States, and attested by the proper official. Warrant officers are inferior officers who hold their rank by virtue of a warrant instead of a commission.

There is no property right with respect to promotion. Promotion is not automatic and does not arise from seniority status. Physical examinations and professional and moral qualifications operate as standards for promotion.

Officers may resign at the end of their tour of duty, although the resignation must be accepted before it is effective. Officers retire either voluntarily or involuntarily. Involuntary retirement is prompted by physical disability or being passed over in rank after a certain period of service. Generally, officers are dismissed only by sentence of a court-martial or, in time of war, by a presidential order. Grounds for an officer's dismissal include absence without leave for a designated period or the commission of a crime. An officer who states under oath that the dismissal pursuant to a presidential order was unjust is entitled to a trial by court-martial.

The discharge of enlisted personnel is an administrative matter. Physical disability, age, or moral and behavioral unsuitability are grounds for discharge.

Conscientious objection to participation in war is considered a valid reason for discharge. The objector must have an opposition to war in any form as a deeply held religious belief that must be genuine and sincere. A military board's skepticism as to the sincerity of the conscientious objector is not enough to deny a discharge; there must be some objective EVIDENCE.

An enlisted person is ordinarily entitled to a discharge after the expiration of the enlistment contract which restores that person to his or her former civilian status. An honorable discharge is regarded as a property right. Military boards exist to review discharges and to rectify mistakes. JUDICIAL REVIEW is available to determine if regulations were followed in the discharge and, generally, is restricted to deciding whether there was a good cause for the discharge.

Rights, duties, and liabilities   While a person is in the armed service, all fundamental rights and duties of citizens are retained but qualified by the peculiar requirements of military discipline and duty. Service members may initiate litigation in contract or personal injury cases, but they are immune from actions against them by fellow members of the military for an act performed within the scope of their duty. Civil remedies, when appropriate, are available. Individuals involved in court-martial proceedings cannot be sued as long as they act within their jurisdiction.

Service members are similarly liable to civilians as are other citizens but are exempt from fault for something done within the scope of duty. No personal liability arises when acting in accord with the lawful orders of a commanding officer, but liability will be imposed if a reasonable person would realize the illegality of the command. Criminal liability in performing a superior's order is determined by the same standards.

The Soldiers' and Sailors' Relief Act of 1940 (50 U.S.C.A. App. § 501 et seq.) is designed to protect the rights of persons entering the armed services who fail to attend to their personal affairs. The statute does not relieve members of the service of their civil liabilities, but temporarily suspends legal proceedings against them, thereby preventing the entry of default judgments against them for failure to appear before a court to defend themselves. Upon their discharge from the service, such persons lose this protection and become like any other citizen faced with legal matters.

The Soldiers' and Sailors' Relief Act prevails over state law. Protection is extended to armed services personnel, their dependents, and other specified persons, such as ENDORSERS of COMMERCIAL PAPER drawn by a service member. Payments on life INSURANCE policies, MORTGAGES, and installment contracts are some legal areas to which the law applies. A mortgage, however, must exist prior to the time of service, and military service must directly affect the ability to make payments. The law does not temporarily relieve the obligation to pay a mortgage executed while on active duty. Service in the military suspends the running of STATUTES OF LIMITATION governing civil actions by or against service members or their representatives.

Military status does not exempt persons from the responsibility of their criminal acts under Federal and state criminal statutes. Civil courts may exercise CONCURRENT JURISDICTION with military tribunals to punish crimes against either Federal or state laws, which are committed within the United States by persons subject to military law. In time of peace, crimes committed by a person in the military, which are not service connected, may be tried only by state courts and not by court-martial. For peacetime violations that are service connected, a military court and a civil court can both exercise jurisdiction. In time of war, however, military courts have the preference in the exercise of jurisdiction; all offenses committed by military personnel, whether service connected or not, are cognizable by court-martials or military commissions. If civil courts do exercise jurisdiction during war, it is done so out of COMITY or expediency. However, military courts do not have EXCLUSIVE JURISDICTION even in time of war over offenses by persons in the military against state laws. Civil courts still have concurrent jurisdiction over crimes against Federal or state laws committed within the United States and the District of Columbia. International agreements allow a foreign government to exercise criminal jurisdiction over offenses against its laws committed by a person in the military other than in the performance of official duties.

Congress enacted the UNIFORM CODE OF MILITARY JUSTICE to establish procedures for the investigation and punishment of military offenses. Besides enumerated offenses, the code covers disobedience of lawful orders and provides that minor infractions are punishable by the commanding officer.

Desertion from military service is a serious offense that involves absence without authority with no intent to return. A deserter is subject to military jurisdiction. In time of war, punishment is directed by a court-martial and can include death. There is no authority for the death penalty for desertion in time of peace. A prosecution for desertion is warranted for soliciting or advising another to desert when the other attempts to, or actually, deserts. If the offense is neither attempted nor committed, the court-martial directs the punishment.

Under the code, offenses are categorized as acts against good order, discipline, and conduct unbecoming an officer. An act against good order and discipline is undefined by the code but is determined by a court-martial on an individual basis using military custom, regulations, and case law as criteria for finding an offense. Officers are under a more demanding standard than enlisted personnel, not only to avoid violating any code provisions but also to conform to a higher standard of conduct.

The code regulates the administration of military justice and provides the rules for prosecution of alleged violators. The constitutional prohibition against self-incrimination is recognized. A court of inquiry does not make judicial decisions but functions as a GRAND JURY to determine whether further proceedings are necessary in a particular case. A second trial for the same offense is prohibited unless requested by the convicted party. The code provides for statutes of limitation but excludes such statutes for desertion in time of war, aiding the enemy, mutiny, and MURDER.

Civilians can be liable for offenses against the military. Impersonating an officer, obstructing recruitment, aiding desertion, and damaging military property are examples of some offenses civilians can commit against the armed services. Generally, civilians are not subject to trial by military courts, but Congress may, under its general war power, establish military courts authorized to try civilians who have acquired quasi-military status by accompanying the armed forces in the battlefield. In contrast, civil courts do not exercise jurisdiction over military courts, except for HABEAS CORPUS and when the military court lacks jurisdiction.

Compensation All pay, allowances, and allotments to service personnel and their dependents are regulated by Congress. The right to receive pay and allowances is dependent on statute. Pay is a fixed, statutory amount given to persons in the military in consideration for personal services rendered. Pay includes basic pay, special pay, retainer pay, incentive pay, retired pay, and equivalent pay, but does not include allowances. Congress has the authority to determine the amount of pay for military personnel. The president and commanding officers have no authority to increase or decrease pay unless the power to do so is conferred by statute.

Special pay is made for hazardous assignments and for reenlistment. Pay does not stop when a member is captured by the enemy or is missing in action but it is forfeited when a sentence of court-martial or a military offense conviction so provides. Aid and relief is also available to families and dependents of service members. Retired pay is not considered a pension but a property right, dependent on the office held and the years of service in the military. Federal statutes regulate the amount of retired pay that retired service personnel receive while they are subsequently employed in a Federal civilian government job. In addition to pay, allowances are made for medical expenses, uniforms, housing, food, and transportation. They are the fringe benefits that military personnel receive. Allowances are controlled by a statutory scheme. In the case of a housing allowance, for example, the allowance is determined by the particular pay grade of the service member.

Military personnel may also receive allotments to pay for support of dependents. Allotments are distributed according to a statutory scheme.

Allowances might also be forfeited under a sentence of court-martial or on conviction of some specified military offense. Pay is subject to GARNISHMENT when a member of the armed services is indebted to the United States.

Insurance Military insurance is offered in various forms to members of the armed services on active duty to protect service personnel and their dependents from financial difficulties. Recovery is automatic upon the death or the total and permanent disability of a person on active duty. The definition of total and permanent disability depends on the circumstances in each case, but it is generally defined as an impairment that makes it impossible for the insured to work regularly in any gainful position without risk to his or her health. A permanent disability is one that is expected to continue throughout the life of the insured without any reasonable hope of recovery. To receive payment, the death or disability must occur while the policy is in effect and the cause of either must be one designated in the policy.

Term insurance is temporary and easily converted into other forms of insurance offered by other insurers. In converting an insurance policy, the original policy is discharged to the extent that it is converted, although in cases of mistake, recovery under the original policy has been allowed even after conversion.

The policy may be canceled at the request of the insured or by the government in cases of FRAUD. Nonpayment of a premium causes the policy to lapse at the end of the GRACE PERIOD. Premiums might be waived in certain circumstances, such as total disability, and if a proper application is made. However, the failure to apply for a premium waiver is generally excused if such was caused by circumstances beyond the control of the insured. The waiver terminates when the disability ceases or if the insured does not cooperate by reporting for physical examinations.

The insurance policy matures upon the occurrence of a specified event, such as the death of the insured. A claim for benefits must be made in writing. When possible, beneficiaries are those named by the insured. Beneficiaries must be within the class of individuals enumerated in the statute. A spouse, parent, or child generally qualifies, but if other relatives or friends are named, the statute must be consulted. Within statutory limits, the insured may designate the beneficiary and change the selection at any time. A beneficiary must survive the insured to be entitled to any insurance proceeds. If there is fraud or if the beneficiary caused the death of the insured, no benefits are paid. If a claim under the policy is contested, an action may be commenced against the United States.

Veterans' rights Veterans' benefits include compensation and privileges given to former service members, their survivors, and dependents. Benefits are not a property right and Congress can withdraw them at any time. A veteran must apply for benefits within the time specified by statute. Benefits are lost when acts of fraud, treason, mutiny, or sabotage are committed. A dishonorable discharge results in the loss of benefits.

For those veterans receiving an honorable discharge, free hospitalization and medical facilities, rehabilitation services, job counseling, home and educational loans, and a burial plot in a national cemetery are among the benefits available. A veteran is eligible for educational assistance up to ten years after date of discharge. There is no time limit, however, to apply for a home loan as long as the veteran served more than 180 days with an honorable discharge or served any number of days with a discharge for a service-connected disability.

A claim for a benefit is filed with the VETERANS ADMINISTRATION, the Federal agency created to manage veteran affairs. These claims are confidential. Generally, the decisions of the administrator of Veterans Affairs are conclusive. Other agency officials and courts may not review them. Benefit payments are regulated by statute and, in suitable situations, are payable to a GUARDIAN. Improper payments are recoverable by the Federal government. A veteran cannot sue the Veterans Administration but can sue individual officials if they act beyond their authority.

Reemployment rights Upon returning to civilian status, veterans are entitled to their former position of employment or a position of similar seniority, status, and pay. This applies to employees of all Federal, state, and local governments, as well as private industry. Generally, veterans are entitled to job benefits that are automatic but not those that are discretionary. They are entitled to seniority rights as if they were in the continuous service of the employer including automatic wage increases in effect during the time in service. A veteran has no right to discretionary salary increases, such as those based on job performance. Promotions are treated similarly. If automatic, the veteran receives them; if discretionary, he or she does not. The returning veteran must be reemployed for at least one year as long as his or her conduct conforms to reasonable and ordinary standards.

Reemployment is premised on the veteran's ability to still perform the previous duties. The veteran must apply for reemployment within a specified time after discharge from training and service in the Armed Forces. The fact that a veteran did not desire at first to return to a former position is immaterial. A veteran may waive the reemployment right if such a waiver is clearly and unequivocally indicated.

A veteran is not entitled to reemployment if the employer's circumstances have changed so as to make it impossible or unreasonable to reemploy the veteran. The benefits due the returning veteran, however, are not lost. If the former position is not in existence, the employer, if able, must offer the veteran a similar position. See also, John De Barr's essay on Armed Services; Edward F. Sherman's essays on Military Government; and Military Law; Albert P. Blaustein's essay on Martial Law; and Eric L. Chase's essay on the Uniform Code of Military Justice.

The life of governments is like that of man. The latter has a right to kill in case of natural defence: the former have a right to wage war for their own preservation.

CHARLES DE MONTESQUIEU

John De Barr

Armed Services

The United States Constitution, Article I, Section 8, gives Congress the exclusive grant to establish and maintain the armed services. Under the United States Code, armed services is broadly defined as constituting the Army, Navy, Air Force, Marine Corps, and Coast Guard.

Army

The United States Army was created on July 14, 1775, when the Continental Congress conscripted the colonial militia besieging Boston, Massachusetts. In January 1776, a single standing force, distinct from the colonial militias, was raised by the Continental Congress. The army was disbanded following the Revolutionary War except for a small force to guard munitions. Thereafter, the strength of the army fluctuated, increasing in size with threats from Indian hostiles or other emergency situations and returning to previous low levels when the need subsided.

Today the reserve components of the army consist essentially of the Army National Guard and the Army Reserve. In addition, there is the Reserve Officers Training Corps (ROTC), with units at universities and colleges throughout the country.

Navy

The Marine Committee was created by the Continental Congress on October 13, 1775, to fit out ships and to subject all British vessels to capture and privateering. The Continental Navy comprised about sixty ships. Following the Revolutionary War, the first Congress disbanded the Navy in favor of an Army. Destruction of American commerce by the Barbary States influenced Congress to authorize the building of six frigates in 1794 and to establish the Navy Department in 1798.

The United States Navy did not participate in any sea battles during World War I, but it did expand multifold to provide essential antisubmarine, minefield, and convoy duty. A huge building program ensued after the start of World War II.

Air Force

The symbolic birth of the Air Force was with the establishment of the Aeronautical Division under the Signal Corps of the Army on August 1, 1907. The Army Air Service was formally established by Congress on June 4, 1920, and grew to strengths of 2.4 million persons and over eighty thousand aircraft during World War II.

The National Security Act of 1947 (61 Stat. 495) created the Department of the Air Force and the United States Air Force.

Marine Corps

The Continental Congress organized the U.S. Marine Corps on November 10, 1775. The Marines, like the Navy, were disbanded after the Revolutionary War but were reestablished on July 11, 1798, as a separate corps.

The primary mission of the Marines is to provide fleet marine forces for seizure and defense of advanced bases, to conduct land operations incident to naval campaigns and to develop doctrines, tactics, techniques, and equipment for amphibious landing operations.

The Fourth Marine Brigade fought in France during World War I, and played an essential part in the fight against the Germans. Over ninety percent of Marine Corps personnel served overseas in combat during World War II. Although the Corps has been compelled to accept draftees during certain periods of armed conflict, it is traditionally recruited from volunteers.

Coast Guard

The U.S. Coast Guard can trace its origin to ten small armed boats authorized by the first Congress on August 4, 1790. Its main function has been to guard the nation's coast against smuggling, to enforce customs laws, and to provide emergency assistance. The Coast Guard was officially created on January 28, 1915 (38 Stat. 800), and consisted essentially of the Revenue Cutter Service, the Lighthouse Service, and the Bureau of Marine Inspection and Navigation. The Act of 1915 made the Coast Guard a branch of the armed services and the military service. The Coast Guard was originally under the supervision of the Treasury Department except when operating as a service in the Navy during times of war. Since 1966, the Coast Guard has operated under the Department of Transportation.

Department of Defense

In 1947, the head of the reorganized National Military Establishment—the secretary of defense—became a cabinet member. The secretaries of the departments under his direction—Army, Navy and Air Force—were not given cabinet rank. Each service secretary, a civilian official, is appointed by the president and confirmed by the Senate. The secretary of defense supervises the Joint Chiefs of Staff, which serve as the principal advisors to the president, and the National Security Council.

The Joint Chiefs of Staff is composed of five members: the Army Chief of Staff, the Air Force Chief of Staff, the Chief of Naval Operations, the Commandant of the Marine Corps, and a Chairman selected from one of the armed services. The secretary of defense is immediately responsible to the president for all defense matters.

All armed services currently obtain personnel through voluntary enlistment. In 1980, a new draft registration act was passed; however, it has not yet been used to conscript.

Law pertaining to the armed services

The military service is governed by different laws, procedures, and considerations than those which govern civilians. The authority for this unique judicial system arises out of the Constitution (Art. I, § 8), the Uniform Code of Military Justice (10 U.S.C.A. § 801 et seq. [1956]), the custom and usage of the service, and congressional and executive regulation. The Uniform Code of Military Justice is not the same as the civilian criminal code, as it covers a larger segment of activities (*Parker v. Levy,* 417 U.S. 733, 94 S.Ct. 2547, 41 L.Ed.2d 439 [1974]). Civilian courts, therefore, supersede the jurisdiction of military courts where military personnel commit off-post, nonservice-connected crimes (*O'Callahan v. Parker,* 395 U.S. 258, 89 S.Ct. 1683, 23 L.Ed.2d 291 [1968]). However, a recent United States Supreme Court case now requires review of nonservice-related crimes by military personnel within the military court system before allowing review in the civilian court system (*Schlesinger v. Councilman,* 420 U.S. 738, 95 S.Ct. 1300, 43 L.Ed.2d 591 [1975]). See also, Edward S. Sherman's essay on Military Law; and Eric L. Chase's essay on the Uniform Code of Military Justice.

Bibliography: 6 C.J.S. *Armed Services* §§ 1–287; Edward M. Byrne, *Military Law,* 2d ed. (1975); 10 U.S.C.A. §§ 101–9840 (1975); 32 C.F.R. § 1 et seq. (1979).

. . . power must be lodged somewhere to prevent anarchy within and conquest from without . . . .

EARL WARREN

The Japanese delegation arrives on board the battleship USS *Missouri* on September 1, 1945, to sign the surrender documents ending hostilities in the Pacific.

National Archives

ARMISTICE □ A suspension or total stoppage of war or armed conflict between hostile nations for an extended period of time. □

An armistice is distinguishable from a suspension of arms, which takes place for extremely brief periods and for local military purposes only, since an armistice covers a longer period and is agreed upon for political purposes.

An armistice is general when it relates to the entire area of the war and partial when it relates to only a segment of such an area. The term *truce* is sometimes used interchangeably with partial armistice.

ARMS CONTROL AND DISARMAMENT

One of the major efforts to preserve international peace and security in the twentieth century has been to limit the number of weapons and the ways in which weapons can be used. Disarmament, which, for example, was imposed on Germany following World War I, refers to limitations or reductions in the number of weapons and troops maintained by a state. Arms control treaties, on the other hand, impose limitations on the types of weapons deployed and how they may be used. For instance, the development of nuclear weapons has been accompanied by efforts to control the number of nuclear weapons

National Archives

General Douglas MacArthur signs the Japanese surrender documents on board the USS *Missouri* in Tokyo Bay. Although this armistice effectively ended the war in the Pacific, the formal peace treaty concluding the war was not signed until September 8, 1951.

in existence—a form of disarmament—and restrictions on the deployment and testing of various nuclear devices—a means of controlling what kind of weapons are maintained.

For the complete text of the Treaty on the Non-Proliferation of Nuclear Weapons and the complete text of the 1972 Treaty on the Limitation of Antiballistic Missile Systems (SALT I), see the Appendix volume 11.

ARMS LENGTH □ The manner in which a commercial transaction is negotiated by unrelated parties, each motivated by individual self-interest. □

Arms-length negotiations bring about a contract between the parties for the exchange of property or services at their FAIR MARKET VALUE.

ARMS, RIGHT TO BEAR □ The privilege of the populace to possess arms as conferred by the Second Amendment to the United States Constitution. Arms have been defined by courts to mean any weapon or thing that can be used offensively or defensively by a militiaman in battle, such as guns of every kind, swords, bayonets, horseman's pistols, artillery, and mortar. This excludes weapons not used in civilized warfare. □

The Second Amendment provides "a well-regulated Militia, being necessary to the security of a free State, the right of the people to keep and bear Arms, shall not be infringed." The COMMON LAW does not recognize an unlimited right to bear arms. This guarantee was formulated in order to maintain a militia for the preservation of public safety and peace. Congress cannot infringe this constitutional right if a reasonable relationship exists between the possession and use of a firearm and the preservation of an efficient militia or state National Guard. The National Firearms Act and the 1968 Gun Control Act, which is also known as the Federal Firearms Act (26 U.S.C.A. § 5801 et seq. [1968]), have been enacted by Congress to regulate the interstate transportation of firearms.

State legislation can govern the possession and use of firearms, unless the provisions violate rights guaranteed by the state constitution. States, in the exercise of their POLICE POWER—the right to legislate for the protection of the health, safety, welfare, and morals of their citizens—can proscribe the possession or use of weapons under certain conditions. The controversy concerning state gun control laws pertains to whether a citizen has an absolute right to maintain and bear arms or whether this right must be reasonably related to the preservation of public peace. Courts have held that gun control laws, which generally require the investigation and fingerprinting of an applicant for a permit,

The United States has a long tradition of a citizen's right to bear arms, as seen in these two photos.

are a proper and reasonable exercise of a state's police power to protect its citizens from the hazards of illegal firearms, as long as the maintenance of a state militia is not impaired.

ARMY DEPARTMENT The American Continental Army, now called the United States Army, was established by the Continental Congress, June 14, 1775, more than a year before the Declaration of Independence.

The mission of the Department of the Army is to organize, train, and equip active duty and reserve forces for the preservation of peace, security, and the defense of our Nation. It serves as part of our national military team whose members include the Navy, Air Force, Marines, and Coast Guard. The Army's mission focuses on land operations; its soldiers must be trained with modern arms and equipment and be ready to respond quickly.

The Army also administers programs aimed at protecting the environment, improving waterway navigation, flood and beach erosion control, and water resource development. It supports the National Civil Defense Program, provides military assistance to Federal, State, and local government agencies, natural disaster relief assistance, and provides emergency medical air transportation services.

The Department of War was established as an executive department at the seat of government by an act approved August 7, 1789. The Secretary of War was established as its head and his powers were those entrusted to him by the President (1 Stat. 49; 5 U.S.C. 181).

The National Security Act of 1947 created the National Military Establishment and the Department of War was designated the Department of the Army and the title of its Secretary became Secretary of the Army (61 Stat. 499; 5 U.S.C. 171).

The National Security Act Amendments of 1949 established the Department of Defense as an executive department of Government and provided that the Department of the Army be a military department within the Department of Defense (63 Stat. 578; 5 U.S.C. 171).

The Army Organization Act provided the statutory basis for the internal organization of the Army and the Department of the Army. The act consolidated and revised the numerous earlier laws, incorporated various adjustments made necessary by the National Security Act of 1947 and other postwar enactments, and provided for the organization of the Department of the Army in a single comprehensive statute, with certain minor exceptions. In general, the act followed

the policy of vesting board organizational powers in the Secretary of the Army, subject to delegation by him, rather than specifying duties of subordinate officers (10 U.S.C. 3012, 3062 [1950]).

The Command of the Army is exercised by the President through the Secretary of Defense and the Secretary of the Army who directly represent him; and, under the law and decisions of the Supreme Court, their acts are the President's acts, and their directions and orders are the President's directions and orders.

OFFICE OF THE SECRETARY OF THE ARMY

Secretary The Secretary of the Army is the head of the Department of the Army. Subject to the direction, authority, and control of the President as Commander in Chief and of the Secretary of Defense, the Secretary of the Army is responsible for and has the authority to conduct all affairs of the Department of the Army, including its organization, administration, operation and efficiency, and such other activities as may be prescribed by the President or the Secretary of Defense as authorized by law.

The Secretary is also responsible for certain civil functions, such as oversight of the Panama Canal Commission, execution of the Panama Canal Treaty and sea-level canal affairs; the civil works program of the Corps of Engineers; Arlington and Soldiers' Home National Cemeteries; and such other activities of a civil nature as may be prescribed by higher authority or authorized by law.

Principal assistants Subject to the direction and control of the Secretary of the Army, the Under Secretary of the Army, Assistant Secretary of the Army (Civil Works), Assistant Secretary of the Army (Installation, Logistics and Financial Management), Assistant Secretary of the Army (Manpower and Reserve Affairs), Assistant Secretary of the Army (Research, Development and Acquisition), General Counsel, the Administrative Assistant, Deputy Under Secretary of the Army (Operations Research), Chief of Legislative Liaison, Chief of Public Affairs, and Director, Office of Small and Disadvantaged Business Utilization are authorized and directed to act for the Secretary of the Army within their respective fields of responsibility and as further directed by the Secretary.

This authority extends not only to actions within the Department of the Army but also to relationships and transactions with the Congress and other governmental and nongovernmental organizations and individuals. These officials are responsible for the exercise of direction and supervision over matters pertaining to the formulation, execution, and review of policies, plans and programs within their respective functional areas, including the establishment of objectives and appraisal of performance. Officers of the Army report to the Under Secretary of the Army, Assistant Secretaries of the Army, General Counsel, the Administrative Assistant, Deputy Under Secretary of the Army (Operations Research), Chief of Legislative Liaison, Chief of Public Affairs and the Director, Office of Small and Disadvantaged Business Utilization regarding matters within their respective fields of responsibility.

Army Policy Council   The Army Policy Council is the senior policy advisory council of the Department of the Army. It provides the Secretary of the Army and his principal civilian and military assistants with a forum for the discussion of Army subjects of significant policy interest and an opportunity for members to consult with other members on matters arising within their specific areas of responsibility.

Armed Forces Policy-Council   The Secretary of the Army serves as a member of the Armed Forces Policy Council, which advises the Secretary of Defense on broad policy matters relating to the Armed Forces.

ARMY STAFF

The Army Staff, presided over by the Chief of Staff, is the military staff of the Secretary of the Army. It includes a General Staff, a Special Staff, and a Personal Staff. The Army Staff renders professional advice and assistance to the Secretary of the Army, the Under Secretary of the Army, the Assistant Secretaries of the Army, and other officials of the Army Secretariat.

It is the duty of the Army Staff to: prepare for employment of the Army and for such recruiting, organizing, supplying, equipping, training, mobilizing, and demobilizing of the Army as will assist the execution of any power, duty, or function of the Secretary or the Chief of Staff; investigate and report upon the efficiency of the Army and its preparation for military operations; act as the agent of the Secretary of the Army and the Chief of Staff in coordinating the action of all organizations of the Department of the Army; and perform such other duties not otherwise assigned by law as may be prescribed by the Secretary of the Army.

Chief of Staff   The Chief of Staff is the principal military adviser to the Secretary of the Army and is charged by him with the planning, development, execution, review, and analysis of

the Army programs. The Chief of Staff, under the direction of the Secretary of the Army, supervises the members and organization of the Army and performs the duties prescribed for him by the National Security Act of 1947 and other laws. He is directly responsible to the Secretary of the Army for the efficiency of the Army, its state of preparation for military operations and plans therefor.

The Chief of Staff serves as the Army member of the Joint Chiefs of Staff and as a member of the Army Policy Council and the Armed Forces Policy Council. As a member of the Joint Chiefs of Staff, he is one of the principal advisers to the President, the National Security Council, and the Secretary of Defense.

Army General Staff   Under the direction of the Chief of Staff, the Army General Staff renders professional advice and assistance to the Secretary, the Under Secretary, and the Assistant Secretaries of the Army in providing broad basic policies and plans for the guidance of the Department of the Army. The Army General Staff specifically assists the Secretary in the preparation and issuance of directives to implement plans and policies and in the supervision of the execution and implementation of these directives.

Special Staff   The Special Staff provides advice and assistance to the Secretary of the Army, the Chief of Staff, other members of the Army Staff, and elements of the Department of the Army on specialized matters specifically within their respective fields of responsibility.

The heads of certain Special Staff agencies exercise dual functions of staff and command. These two functions, although vested in a single individual, are separate and distinct in that each involves different responsibilities and duties.

Personal Staff   The Personal Staff to the Chief of Staff includes aides, the Inspector General, the Chief of Chaplains, the Judge Advocate General, the Auditor General, and any other Army Staff member whose activities he desires to coordinate and administer directly.

Program areas

Military operations and plans   Determination of roles and missions of the Army and strategy formulation, plans, and application; Joint Service matters, plans, and operations; force and resource requirements; operational capabilities, priorities, and readiness; Army command and control system for military communications and operations; training concepts, policies, and programs for Army units and individuals; psychological operations and unconven-

It is, then, necessary to give the government that power, in time of peace, which the necessity of war will render indispensable, or else we shall be attacked unprepared.

JOHN MARSHALL

tional warfare; national security affairs; foreign internal defense policy; arms control, negotiations, and disarmament; international politico-military affairs; collective security; civil administration of certain foreign areas; civil affairs; audiovisual activities; and military support of civil defense.

Personnel Management of military and civilian personnel for overall integrated support of the Army, including personnel requirements, procurement, allocations and control, distribution, utilization, career development, equal opportunity, alcohol and drug abuse control, welfare and morale, promotion, retention, and separation; management of the program for law enforcement, correction and crime prevention for military members of the Army; management of civilian personnel training; manpower surveys; and safety.

Reserve components Management of individual and unit readiness and mobilization for Reserve Components, comprised of the Army National Guard and the U.S. Army Reserve.

Intelligence Management of Army intelligence and counterintelligence activities, personnel, equipment, systems, and organizations; Army cryptology, topography, and meteorology; coordination of Army requirements for mapping, charting, and geodesy; and Army industrial security.

Management-comptrollership Review and analysis of Army programs and major Army commands; management information systems, progress and statistical reporting, and reports control; financial management, budgeting, finance and accounting, cost analysis, economic analysis, military pay and allowances, resource management, productivity and value improvement; regulatory policies and programs pertaining to the overall management of the Army; and legislative policies and programs pertaining to appropriation acts affecting the Army.

Research, development, and materiel acquisition Management of Army research, development, development test and evaluation; planning, programming, and budgeting for the acquisition of materiel obtained by the procurement appropriations for the Army; materiel life cycle management from concept phase through acquisition; and research, development, and military standardization aspects of international military cooperative programs.

Logistics Management of Department of the Army logistical activities for the move-

ment and maintenance of forces; logistical planning and support of Army and Joint Service operations; materiel and supply management and maintenance; security assistance; transportation; and Army interservice supply operations.

Engineering Management of Army engineering, construction, installations, family housing, real estate, facilities requirements and stationing, and real property maintenance activities; environmental preservation and improvement activities; applicable research and development activities for engineer missions to include environmental sciences; Army topographic and military geographic information activities; and engineer aspects of Army strategic and operational plans.

Civil functions Civil functions of the Department of the Army include the Civil Works Program, the administration of Arlington and Soldiers' Home National Cemeteries, and other related matters. The Army's Civil Works Program, a responsibility of the Corps of Engineers under the direction and supervision of the Secretary of the Army, dates back to 1824 and is the Nation's major Federal water resources development activity and involves engineering works such as major dams, reservoirs, levees, harbors, waterways, locks, and many other types of structures. These works provide flood protection for cities and major river valleys, reduce the cost of transportation, supply water for municipal and industrial use, generate hydroelectric power, provide recreational opportunities for vast numbers of people, regulate the rivers for many purposes including the improvement of water quality and the enhancement of fish and wildlife, protect the shores of the oceans and lakes, and provide still other types of benefits. Planning assistance is also provided to states and other non-Federal entities for the comprehensive management of water resources, including pollution abatement works. In addition, through the Civil Works Program the Federal government protects the navigable waters of the United States under legislation empowering the Secretary of the Army to prohibit activities which would reduce the value of such waters to the Nation.

Medical Management of health services for the Army and, as directed for other services, agencies, and organizations; health standards for Army personnel; health professional education and training; career management authority over commissioned and warrant officer personnel of the Army Medical Department; medical research, materiel development, testing and evaluation; policies concerning health aspects of

Army environmental programs and prevention of disease; and planning, programing, and budgeting for Army-wide health services.

Inspection Management of inquiries, inspections, and reports on matters affecting the performance of mission and the state of discipline, efficiency, economy, and morale of the Department of the Army.

Religious Management of religious and moral leadership, and chaplain support activities Army-wide; religious ministrations, religious education, pastoral care and counseling for Army military personnel; liaison with the ecclesiastical agencies; chapel construction requirements and design approval; and career management of clergymen serving in the Chaplains Branch.

Legal Legal advisory services provided for all military personnel and agencies of the Army; review and take final action as designee of the Secretary of the Army on complaints of wrongs by service personnel submitted under the Uniform Code of Military Justice; administration of military justice and civil law matters pertaining to the Army; administration of Army claims and legal assistance services; operation of the legal system of appellate reviews of court-martial records as provided by the Uniform Code of Military Justice; general court-martial and real property records custodianship; records administration of proceedings of courts of inquiry and military commissions; liaison service with the Department of Justice and other Federal and State agencies on matters connected with litigation and legal proceedings concerning the Army; and career management of Judge Advocate General's Corps officers.

Information Public information, command information, and community relations services and preparation of information plans and programs in support of Army basic plans and programs.

History Advisory and coordination service provided on historical matters, including historical properties; formulation and execution of the Army Historical Program; and preparation and publication of histories required by the Army.

MAJOR ARMY COMMANDS

United States Army Forces Command The Commanding General, United States Army Forces Command, commands all assigned active Army forces in the continental United States, the Continental United States Armies, and the United States Army Reserve within the United States and serves as Commander in Chief, United States Army Forces, Readiness Command. He serves, for planning purposes, as Commander in Chief, United States Army Forces, Atlantic. He also commands those subordinate commands, installations, and activities assigned by Headquarters, Department of the Army and, as directed, provides administrative and logistical support through his subordinate installation commanders to other Department of the Army, Department of Defense, or other Government agencies. In addition, he supervises the training of Army National Guard units within the United States, the Commonwealth of Puerto Rico, and the U.S. Virgin Islands.

The Commanding General of each of the Continental United States Armies has the primary mission, under the Commanding General, United States Army Forces Command, to command the United States Army Reserve, plan for mobilization, coordinate domestic emergencies, and exercise training supervision over the Army National Guard. The three Army areas are as follows:

- First United States Army (Headquarters, Fort George G. Meade, Md.)—Maine, New Hampshire, Massachusetts, Connecticut, Rhode Island, New Jersey, New York, Vermont, Pennsylvania, Delaware, Maryland, Virginia, West Virginia, North Carolina, South Carolina, Georgia, Florida, Alabama, Mississippi, Tennessee, the District of Columbia, Puerto Rico, and the U.S. Virgin Islands.
- Fifth United States Army (Headquarters, Fort Sam Houston, Tex.)—Arkansas, Louisiana, Texas, Oklahoma, Michigan, Wisconsin, Illinois, Missouri, Indiana, Iowa, Minnesota, Ohio, and Kentucky.
- Sixth United States Army (Headquarters, Presidio of San Francisco, Calif.)—Montana, Washington, Oregon, Idaho, Utah, Nevada, Arizona, California, North Dakota, South Dakota, Wyoming, Colorado, New Mexico, Nebraska, and Kansas.

United States Army Training and Doctrine Command The Commanding General, United States Army Training and Doctrine Command, develops, manages, and supervises the training of individuals of the Active Army and Reserve Components. He also formulates and documents concepts, doctrine, materiel requirements, organizations, and appropriate training systems for the Army in all environments, tactical and nontactical.

He commands installations and activities as may be assigned by Headquarters, Department of the Army and, as directed, provides administrative and logistical support through his assigned installation commanders to elements and agencies of the Department of the Army, Department of Defense, or other Government agencies which are tenants or satellites of the installation.

United States Army Materiel Development and Readiness Command The Commanding General, United States Army Materiel Development and Readiness Command, develops and provides materiel and related services to the Army, to Army elements of unified commands and specified commands, and to other United States and foreign agencies as directed. His principal functions include research; development; product, production, and maintenance engineering; testing and evaluation of materiel; production and procurement of materiel; inventory management; and storage and distribution, maintenance, transportation, and disposal of materiel.

United States Army Communications Command The Commanding General, United States Army Communications Command, is responsible for the planning, engineering, installation, operation, and maintenance of the Army portion of the Defense Communications System, assigned Army communications, base communications, and Army air traffic control facilities. He provides Army communications support to other Federal agencies participating in civil disturbances or natural disasters.

United States Army Intelligence and Security Command The Commanding General, United States Army Intelligence and Security Command, is responsible for supporting the Army at echelons above Corps through counterintelligence, intelligence collection, production, and security operations performed by a worldwide command structure.

United States Army Health Services Command The Commanding General, United States Army Health Services Command, performs health services for the Army within the United States and, as directed, for other governmental agencies and activities. He commands the Army hospital system within the United States and other organizations, units, and facilities as may be directed. He is responsible for the conduct of medical professional education for Army personnel. He is further responsible, under the guidance of the Commanding General, United States Training and Doctrine Command, for the development of medical doctrine, concepts, organizations, materiel requirements, and systems in support of the Army.

. . . men unite into societies that they may have the united strength of the whole society to secure and defend their properties . . .

JOHN LOCKE

United States Army Criminal Investigation Command The Commanding General, United States Army Criminal Investigation Command, is responsible for exercising centralized command, authority, direction, and control of Army criminal investigative activities worldwide and for providing investigative support to all United States Army elements. He is charged with, and is responsible directly to the Secretary of the Army and the Chief of Staff for, conducting, controlling, and monitoring Army criminal investigations; developing investigative standards, procedures, and doctrinal policies; operating a criminal intelligence element; operating the United States Army Crime Records Repository; maintaining centralized records of criminal investigative agents; reviewing all investigative reports; operating investigative crime laboratories; planning and conducting protective service operations; and conducting the accreditation/certification program of investigative agents.

Military Traffic Management Command The Commanding General, Military Traffic Management Command (MTMC), is the Executive Director for military traffic management, land transportation, and common-user ocean terminal service within the United States, excluding Alaska and Hawaii, and for worldwide traffic management of the Department of Defense household goods moving and storage program. He administers Department of Defense activities pertaining to Highways for National Defense.

United States Army Military District of Washington The Commanding General, United States Army Military District of Washington (USAMDW), commands units, activities, and installations in the National Capital area as may be assigned by Headquarters Department of the Army (HQDA); provides base operation and other support to the Department of the Army, Department of Defense, or other Government activities which are tenants of or are located on USAMDW installations for such support; plans for and executes those missions peculiar to the needs of the seat of government as assigned by HQDA; and provides an organized and responsive defense of designated Department of Defense facilities.

United States Army Corps of Engineers The Commanding General, United States Army Corps of Engineers (CGUSACE) serves as the Army's Real Property Manager, performing the full cycle of real property activities (requirements, programing, acquisition, operation, maintenance and disposal); manages and executes engineering, construction, and real estate programs for the Army and the United States Air Force; and performs research and development in support of these programs. CGUSACE manages and executes Civil Works Programs. These programs include research and development, planning, design, construction, operation and maintenance, and real estate activities related to rivers, harbors and waterways; administration of laws for protection and preservation of navigable waters and related resources such as wetlands. CGUSACE assists in recovery from natural disasters.

Army components of unified commands   The missions of the commanding generals of the Army components of unified commands are set forth in directives of the Department of Defense. The Army components of unified commands are major commands of the Department of the Army and consist of such subordinate commands, units, activities, and installations as may be assigned to them by Headquarters, Department of the Army. In certain unified command areas—such as United States Southern Command and United States Atlantic Command—where the Army does not have a separate, single and distinct component headquarters or commander, a designated Army commander in the area will be responsible for certain Army "component" functions that must be performed at his location.

COMMANDS   United States Army, Europe; United States Army, Japan; Eighth United States Army; and United States Army, Western Command.

United States Military Academy   The United States Military Academy is located at West Point, N.Y. The course is of four years' duration, during which the cadets receive, besides a general education, theoretical and practical training as junior officers. Cadets who complete the course satisfactorily receive the degree of bachelor of science and a commission as second lieutenant in the Army.

Source: *The United States Government Manual 1981/ 82* and/or *1982/83.*

ARNOLD, Benedict   As an American general during the Revolutionary period, Benedict Arnold (*b.* January 14, 1741, in Norwich, Connecticut; *d.* June 14, 1801, in London, England) earned prominence in the military, but he ended his days in exile as a scorned traitor.

Arnold displayed a penchant for the military at an early age. The French and Indian War was fought between 1754 and 1763, and Arnold participated in battle while still a juvenile. By the Revolutionary War in 1775, Arnold was in

Library of Congress

Benedict Arnold

charge of a military campaign against Fort Ticonderoga and, with the aid of forces led by Ethan Allen, successfully captured the fort from English soldiers.

Arnold next attempted a conquest of Canada. By the time he reached Lake Champlain, he had successfully attacked a British military installation and several ships. He continued the rigorous Quebec Campaign and was wounded. Despite his injury, he continued to command his troops, but the British forced Arnold's army back to Lake Champlain. Undaunted, Arnold organized a group of ships and successfully stopped the advancement of the British.

Arnold received the first of a number of rebuffs in his military career in February 1777. Congress selected five brigadier generals for the rank of major general. Arnold, who had seniority, was passed over despite his war record and General George Washington's recommendations. Earlier in Arnold's career, accusations of misconduct had been alleged against him, but, after a delayed investigation, the charges were dropped on the grounds that they were false and malicious.

Arnold continued to serve valiantly in the militia, in spite of these upsets. He waged victorious campaigns in Connecticut and Saratoga and finally received his promotion.

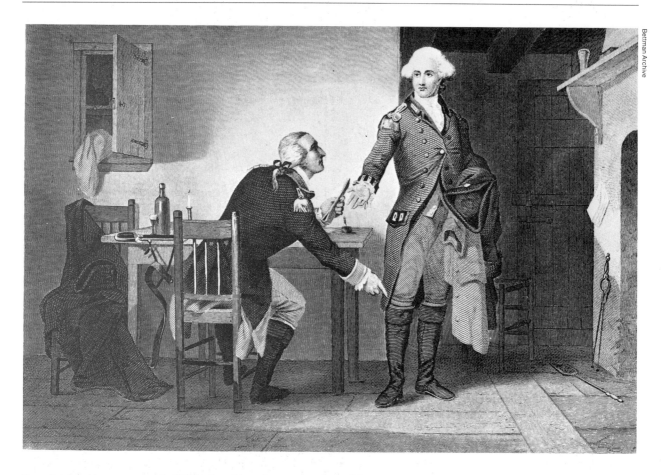

Bettman Archive

Benedict Arnold advises British spy John André to hide incriminating papers about the betrayal of West Point in his boot.

In 1778, Arnold took command of Philadelphia, and immediately became acclimated to the social lifestyle. He married Margaret Shippen, whose father had Loyalist sympathies. In 1779, Arnold was again charged with misconduct, this time by his rival, Joseph Reed of the Pennsylvania executive council. Congress dismissed four of the eight charges but reserved the remainder for a court-martial hearing. Arnold was again subject to a lengthy delay, and it is suspected that at this point he was considering joining the British militia and was secretly corresponding with Sir Henry Clinton, the senior British commander in the colonies at that time.

Arnold was finally acquitted of all major charges but received a slight reprimand from George Washington concerning several trivial charges.

By this time, Arnold's emotional state was one of anger, resentment, and bitterness; these feelings were heightened by the fact that Arnold was a sensitive man by nature and somewhat of an idealist. He felt his treatment had been unjust, and his subsequent actions were the result of his unchecked emotions.

In 1780, Arnold was in charge of the West Point Military Academy. Still desiring command in the British forces, Arnold agreed to betray West Point in return for a commission and money. Major John André, Sir Henry Clinton's adjutant general, met with Arnold to discuss terms. While returning to Clinton, André was taken prisoner, and papers exposing Arnold's plot were found on his person. Arnold learned of André's capture in time to escape. He joined the British army and, in 1781, waged two violent campaigns against colonial forces in Virginia and Connecticut.

Arnold's last years were spent in an attempt to gain more military commands. He went into exile in Canada and England but was regarded with contempt. He died in 1801, bitter and saddened over the failure of his undertakings.

ARNOLD, Thurman Wesley Thurman Wesley Arnold (*b.* June 2, 1891, in Laramie, Wyoming; *d.* November 7, 1969, in Alexandria, Virginia) was an eminent lawyer, judge, and author.

In 1911, Arnold received a bachelor of arts degree from Princeton, and three years later, a bachelor of laws degree from Harvard. In 1931, a bachelor of laws degree was bestowed upon Arnold by Yale, and in that year he became a professor of law, teaching at Yale until 1937.

Arnold became assistant United States attorney general in 1938 and specialized in antitrust cases during his five years of service. In 1943, Arnold entered the judicial phase of his career, presiding as associate justice of the United States Court of Appeals for the District of Columbia until 1945.

As an author, Arnold wrote several publications, including *The Folklore of Capitalism* (1937); and *Democracy and Free Enterprise* (1942).

ARRAIGNMENT □ A criminal procedure in which a person accused of a crime is brought before a judge to respond to the charges by pleading guilty, not guilty, or NOLO CONTENDERE. □

Thurman Arnold

Library of Congress

Bruno Richard Hauptmann was arraigned on September 21, 1934, for the kidnapping of the Lindbergh baby.

National Archives

ARRAY ☐ The entire group of jurors selected for a trial from which a smaller group is subsequently chosen to form a PETIT JURY or a GRAND JURY; the list of potential jurors. ☐

Virtually all states have enacted statutes delineating requirements for jury service. In most states, convicted felons and insane persons cannot be jurors. Professional persons such as judicial and government officials, lawyers, ministers, and medical personnel may be exempted by statute from jury service.

As a general rule, a group of local officials acting within the statutory framework select the persons who will make up the array.

ARREARS ☐ A sum of money that has not been paid or has only been paid in part at the time it is due. ☐

A person who is "in arrears" is behind in payments due and thus has outstanding debts or liabilities. For example, a tenant who has not paid rent on the day it is due is in arrears.

Arrears may also refer to the late distribution of the dividends of cumulative preferred stock.

ARREST

☐ To deprive a person of liberty of movement by detaining him or her pursuant to law.

☐ The seizure of a person by another, acting under real or apparent authority, to answer a civil demand or a criminal charge. ☐

Civil actions Arrest is a PROVISIONAL REMEDY used in civil lawsuits to prevent a defendant from fleeing the jurisdiction in which an action is brought against him or her in order to escape the power of the court. An arrest can also be made when it is believed that a defendant will try to conceal or dispose of assets or to transfer them to others in an attempt to deprive creditors of their rights to have the property sold to satisfy their outstanding claims. Civil arrest is considered a harsh remedy and is governed strictly by statute. It is virtually never used in CONTRACT actions but has been applied, to a limited extent, in cases involving TORTS. Only a plaintiff who has been directly injured by a defendant, not a third person, can have a person arrested in a civil action.

To obtain the civil arrest of an individual, the plaintiff or creditor ordinarily must put up a BOND, a conditional promise to pay money, which promises that if the arrest is unlawful, the defendant is entitled to a certain amount of DAMAGES. The posting of such security reduces the number of false allegations made to obtain a person's civil arrest. If a person is arrested on false charges, he or she can bring an action for FALSE ARREST against the person who caused the detention. BAIL is ordinarily set for a person who has been arrested. Once a bail bond is posted, the arrested person is released. If the arrested person is unable to pay the bond, he or she will be incarcerated until the time his or her performance is due. A defendant will be released from jail if it is subsequently discovered that there was no ground for the arrest, if the arrest was made illegally, if the defendant was under age or insane, or if the confinement causes undue financial hardship for the defendant's family.

Certain categories of persons, such as public and peace officers, judges, persons going to, attending, or returning from, court in connection with civil actions, and witnesss, are usually exempt from civil arrests.

Criminal arrest A criminal arrest is the seizure and detention of a person suspected of committing a crime by law enforcement officials, including PEACE OFFICERS, or in some

A rare nineteenth-century daguerreotype shows a police officer making an arrest.

cases, by private citizens. Depending upon the circumstances of the case, a person can be arrested with or without a warrant—a written order authorizing the seizure of the named individual—which is issued by a magistrate on behalf of the government and is based upon an allegation of criminal conduct in violation of a law or court ruling. A warrant empowers a law enforcement officer to make an arrest and to enter the home of the suspect to accomplish it. In the landmark case of *Payton v. New York,* 445 U.S. 573, 100 S.Ct. 1371, 63 L.Ed.2d 639 (1980), the Supreme Court clearly enunciated the need for an arrest warrant before police can enter a suspect's home to make a routine arrest. Prior to this decision, many states permitted arrests to be made in the home without a warrant, regardless of whether the officers had time to obtain one. The Court stated that its decision was based upon the Fourth Amendment, which provides for the "right of a man to retreat into his own home and there be free." It does not mean, however, that a warrant is necessary to arrest a person in a public place, such as a street or park, or if exigent circumstances exist that make it unreasonable to appear before a magistrate to obtain a warrant. Exigent circumstances traditionally include the possible escape of a defendant; the endangering of the life or safety of the officer or another; the destruction, damage, or concealment of material evidence; the commission of a FELONY in the presence of the person who is attempting the arrest; or the hot pursuit of a suspect. See also, Search and Seizure.

A citizen's arrest, the colloquial designation of an arrest made by a private citizen, is valid only if made during, or immediately following, the commisssion of a crime in the citizen's presence. Otherwise, the arrest is illegal, and the suspect can sue the citizen for false arrest to recover damages for wrongful detention.

Probable cause   In order to arrest a person for a crime not committed in a law enforcement officer's presence, the officer must obtain an arrest warrant by demonstrating probable cause to believe that the suspect has committed a crime. Probable or reasonable cause is present if the facts that the officer knows at the time of the arrest would lead a reasonable person of average intelligence to believe that the suspect has committed, or is committing, a crime. The belief that a crime is being or has been committed can be based on facts within an officer's knowledge, such as the past conduct, character, and reputation of the suspect. Mere hunches that a person has committed a crime are not enough, unless there are also facts that indicate that the suspect

An arrested man hides his face as he is taken into custody.

had the opportunity to commit the crime. If a suspect possesses, conceals, or lends another tools or the means to commit a crime, such as narcotics, stolen property, or firearms, probable cause is established, but a suspect's mere presence at the premises used for illegal activities is insufficient.

Frequently, probable cause is based upon statements made by eyewitnesses, victims, or persons who have participated in the crime. The reliability of the statements must be determined. If the statements are made by an informant, a person suspected of a crime who provides information in exchange for being charged with a lesser offense or immunity from prosecution, or a person convicted of a crime who cooperates in exchange for a reduction of his or her sentence, their reliability is evaluated in terms of past experience with information provided by the informant, receipt of similar information from other sources, and by personal observation of the police. Statements made by eyewitnesses or victims are usually considered more reliable than those of informants because they are not motivated by personal advantage. As a general rule, statements of informants require corroboration, but, in some states, so does information supplied by eyewitnesses or victims. Corroboration is confirmation of information by additional facts from independent sources, the suspect's conduct, or police observation.

Police observation must be done in a lawful manner, such as by looking through open doors or windows or noticing odors or sounds or by ob-

National Archives

Bruno Richard Hauptmann is fingerprinted by police following his arrest in the Lindbergh kidnapping case.

the circumstances, would cause an average person to believe that criminal activity is at hand and cause the peace officer to suspect that a crime has been, or is about to be, committed by the suspect. Intuition or hunches by the police are not enough to support a stop and frisk. The suspect need not be given the *Miranda* warnings since a stop and frisk is not the equivalent of a custodial interrogation. A valid arrest can be made pursuant to a properly conducted stop and frisk if the questioning of the suspect reveals probable cause.

Making an arrest   A law enforcement officer making an arrest must demonstrate the intention and authority to take the suspect into custody and act toward the suspect in a manner that deprives the suspect of liberty of movement, either voluntarily or through physical force exerted by the officer. In all cases, officers must identify themselves and their intentions. When an arrest is made pursuant to a warrant, the police must show the warrant to the suspect. If an arrest is made without a warrant, the police must state their authority to do so and the reasons for the arrest. Although this requirement is dispensed with when an offense is being committed in the officer's presence or when the suspect resists arrest, it must be satisfied after the suspect is subdued. Private citizens making a citizen's arrest must notify the person being arrested of the purpose and reasons for the arrest unless the circumstances are sufficient notice of it. A peace officer can order a bystander to assist in making an arrest. If a bystander fails to respond, his or her liability is determined by statute in the particular jurisdiction.

Force can be used in arresting a suspect only when it is necessary to overcome the resistance of the suspect. It must be reasonable, that is, in proportion to the amount of resistance offered by the suspect. An officer or citizen can use whatever force is necessary, even to the extent of killing the perpetrator if necessary to save his or her own life.

When the circumstances warrant it, force can be used to gain entry to a residence in which a suspect to be arrested is residing or hiding. This occurs usually in cases of a warrantless arrest of a person suspected of committing a felony or when a suspect for whom police have a warrant refuses to surrender to them. Officers must give notice of their authority and purpose and be refused entry prior to making a forcible entry. Notice is not necessary if it will endanger police or others, or permit the escape of the suspect or the concealment of evidence. Force is not justified,

taining consent from those authorized to give it. If done pursuant to an illegal search of premises in violation of the Fourth Amendment, any evidence obtained is inadmissible in court.

Probable cause is a mixed question of fact and law; the jury decides if the facts exist, and the magistrate determines if they constitute probable cause. In most situations, however, since no jury is present at a hearing for the issuance of an arrest warrant, the magistrate makes all determinations.

Stop and frisk   Depending upon the circumstances, a law enforcement officer can approach a person to investigate possible criminal activity even though there is no probable cause to justify an arrest. Under various statutes and case law, a peace officer can stop and frisk a person whom the officer reasonably suspects of criminal conduct. A stop and frisk is the temporary detention of the suspect by a police officer for the purpose of questioning the suspect's actions and, in some cases, searching for concealed weapons. The detention does not amount to an arrest since it is not based on probable cause but rather on reasonable suspicion—knowledge that, under however, when entry can be gained by consent, when there is time for police to get an arrest warrant, or when it is unlikely that the suspect will flee the jurisdiction.

An arrest warrant is valid only in the state where it is issued. An offense against the criminal statutes of one state does not justify an arrest in another state, but the second state can, by EXTRADITION, surrender the suspect to the state wherein the crime was committed. In some instances, peace officers do not have statewide authority but can arrest suspects only within their own local jurisdiction. Failure to object to an arrest made beyond an officer's jurisdiction waives the objection in a later proceeding to have a conviction of the suspect overturned.

As a general rule, once an arrest warrant has been used, it cannot be used again.

Rights of arrested persons A suspect who has been arrested maintains all constitutional rights, regardless of the offense allegedly committed. Once custodial interrogation begins, the suspect must be advised of the *Miranda* warnings and the decision to exercise them or not must be noted. A search of the suspect's person and property can be conducted incident to a lawful arrest or other exigent circumstances without a search warrant, but a warrant is necessary under all other circumstances. An arrested suspect can be placed in a lineup for identification by witnesses, physically examined, photographed, and fingerprinted. A preliminary hearing is held before a magistrate to determine whether the accused should be held liable for trial and bail set for the suspect's release pending the trial date.

Privileged persons Public policy exempts certain classes of persons from arrest. Members of Congress are immune from civil arrest during their attendance at legislative sessions, but this exclusion does not apply to criminal arrest. Foreign ministers and ambassadors and their households and staffs are exempt once they have been officially received and accredited in this country. State law must otherwise be consulted to determine if any other categories of persons are immune from arrest. See also, Joseph D. Grano's essay on the Miranda Warnings; and Stephen A. Saltzburg's essay on Custodial Interrogation.

ARREST OF JUDGMENT □ The postponement or stay of an official decision of a court, or the refusal to render such a determination, after a verdict has been reached in an action at law or a criminal prosecution, because some defect appears on the face of the record which, if a decision is made, would make it erroneous or REVERSIBLE. □

Although the FEDERAL RULES OF CIVIL PROCEDURE make no such provision, state codes of civil procedure should be consulted concerning the issuance of an arrest of judgment in actions at law.

In criminal proceedings, a defendant must make a MOTION for an arrest of judgment when the indictment or information fails to charge the accused with an offense or if the court lacks jurisdiction of the offense charged. State and federal rules of criminal procedure govern an arrest of judgment in criminal prosecutions.

ARREST WARRANT □ A written order issued by authority of the state and commanding the seizure of the person named. □

An arrest warrant must be based on a complaint that alleges probable cause that the person named has committed a specific offense, and it must be issued according to the formalities required by the rules of the court. The FEDERAL RULES OF CRIMINAL PROCEDURE specify that the warrant must be signed by the MAGISTRATE and must describe the offense charged. The defendant must be named or described in such a way that he or she can be identified with reasonable certainty. The warrant must also state that the defendant be arrested and brought before the nearest available magistrate.

For a sample arrest warrant, see the Appendix volume.

ARROGATION
□ Claiming or seizing something without justification; claiming something on behalf of another.
□ In civil law, the adoption of an adult who was legally capable of acting for himself or herself. □

ARSON □ At COMMON LAW, the malicious burning or exploding of the dwelling house of another, or the burning of a building within the CURTILAGE, the immediate surrounding space, of the dwelling of another. □

Modern legislation has extended the definition of arson to include the burning or exploding of commercial and public buildings—such as restaurants and schools—and structures—such as bridges. In many states, the act of burning any insured dwelling, regardless of whether it belongs to another, constitutes arson if it is done with an intent to defraud the insurer. Finally, the common-law rule that the property burned must

[t]he usual rule is that a police officer may arrest without warrant one believed by the officer upon reasonable cause to have been guilty of a felony . . .

WILLIAM HOWARD TAFT

A lynch mob set fire to the Bedford County Courthouse in Shelbyville, Tennessee, when its efforts to seize a Negro from jail were thwarted. Three rioters were killed by the National Guard; the Negro, who had allegedly attacked a white girl, was secretly taken to another town by the police; and the rioters destroyed the courthouse with fire and dynamite.

National Archives

Officials suspected arson to be the cause of a $40 million fire in an urban renewal area of Lynn, Massachusetts, in 1981. The fire destroyed 17 buildings, forced 600 people into the streets homeless, and left the neighborhood looking like a war zone.

UPI

belong to another person has been completely eliminated by statute in some states.

Elements of offense The main elements necessary to prove arson are evidence of a burning and evidence that a criminal act caused the fire. The accused must intend to burn a building or other structure. Absent a statutory description of the conduct required for arson, the conduct must be malicious, and not accidental. Malice, however, does not mean ill will. Intentional or outrageously reckless conduct is sufficient to constitute malice. Motive, on the other hand, is not an essential element of arson.

Unless a statute extends the crime to other property, only a house used as a residence, or buildings immediately surrounding it, can be the subject of arson. If a house is vacated, is closed up, or becomes unfit for human habitation, its burning will not constitute arson. A temporary absence from a dwelling will not negate its character as a residence.

Generally, the actual presence of a person within a dwelling at the moment it is burned is not necessary. It may, however, be required for a particular degree of the crime. The fact, and not the knowledge, of human occupancy is what is essential. If a dwelling is burned under the impression that it is uninhabited when people actually live in it, the crime is committed.

Absent a statute to the contrary, a person is innocent of arson if that individual burns his or her own property while living there. The common exception to this rule is the burning of one's own property with an intent to defraud or prejudice the property insurer. In addition, under statutes that punish the burning of a dwelling house without expressly requiring it to be the property of another, a person who burns his or her own property might be guilty of arson. An owner, for purposes of arson, is the person who possesses the house and has the care, control, and management of it. In those states that have maintained the common-law rule that the property burned must belong to another person, an owner who burns his or her house while it is in the possession of a lawful tenant is guilty of arson.

In many states arson is divided into degrees, depending sometimes on the value of the property but more commonly on its use and whether the crime was committed in the day or night. A typical statute might make the burning of an inhabited dwelling house at night first-degree arson, the burning of a building close enough to a dwelling so as to endanger it second-degree arson, and the burning of any structure with an intent to defraud an insurer thereof,

third-degree arson. Many statutes vary the degree of the crime according to the criminal intent of the accused.

Arson is a serious crime that was punishable by death under the common law. Presently, it is classified as a felony under most statutes, punishable by either imprisonment or death. Many jurisdictions impose prison sentences commensurate with the seriousness of the criminal intent of the accused. A finding, therefore, that the offense was committed intentionally will result in a longer prison sentence than a finding that it was done recklessly. When a human life is endangered, the penalty is most severe.

ARTHUR, Chester Alan   Chester Alan Arthur (*b.* October 5, 1830, in Fairfield, Vermont; *d.* November 18, 1886, in New York, New York) achieved prominence as a politician and as president of the United States.

An 1848 graduate of Union College, Arthur was admitted to the New York City bar in 1851, and he established a legal practice in New York City that same year.

With the onset of the Civil War, Arthur served as quartermaster general and inspector

Chester A. Arthur

Library of Congress

general of New York. After the war, from 1871 to 1878, he performed the duties of collector for the Port of New York. Although Arthur was a believer in the spoils system, a practice that rewards loyal political party members with jobs that require official appointment, he served his office as an honest administrator. President Rutherford B. Hayes was, however, an advocate of the civil service system, which provided that qualified people receive employment fairly based upon their qualifications, and removed Arthur from the office of collector.

Arthur returned to politics with his election as vice-president of the United States in March of 1880. In September 1881, he assumed the duties of president, after the assassination of President James Garfield.

As president, Arthur advocated the passage of the Pendleton Civil Service Reform Bill in 1883, adopting a view that was contrary to his previous support of the spoils system. He also signed laws allowing for the modernization of the United States Navy and supported the prosecution of the Star Route Trials, which exposed fraudulent activities in the United States Post Office Department. He also vetoed a Congressional bill, the Rivers and Harbours Bill of 1882, charging that the allotment of funds was too extravagant.

Arthur's presidential term ended in 1885; due to ill health, he did not seek renomination.

ARTICLES

☐ Series or subdivisions of individual and distinct sections of a document, statute, or other writing, such as the ARTICLES OF CONFEDERATION.

☐ Codes or systems of rules created by written agreements of parties or by statute that establish standards of legally acceptable behavior in a business relationship, such as ARTICLES OF INCORPORATION or ARTICLES OF PARTNERSHIP.

☐ Writings that embody contractual terms of agreements between parties. ☐

ARTICLES OF CONFEDERATION

☐ The name given to the document that memorializes the terms under which the original thirteen states agreed to participate in a centralized form of government, in addition to their self-rule, that was in effect from March 1, 1781, to March 4, 1789, prior to the adoption of the CONSTITUTION. ☐

The complete text of the Articles of Confederation follows.

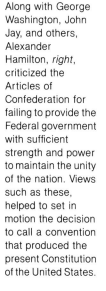

Along with George Washington, John Jay, and others, Alexander Hamilton, *right*, criticized the Articles of Confederation for failing to provide the Federal government with sufficient strength and power to maintain the unity of the nation. Views such as these, helped to set in motion the decision to call a convention that produced the present Constitution of the United States.

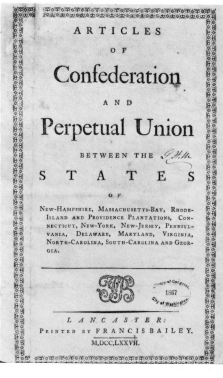

ARTICLES
OF
Confederation
AND
Perpetual Union
BETWEEN THE
STATES
OF
NEW-HAMPSHIRE, MASSACHUSETTS-BAY, RHODE-ISLAND AND PROVIDENCE PLANTATIONS, CONNECTICUT, NEW-YORK, NEW-JERSEY, PENNSYLVANIA, DELAWARE, MARYLAND, VIRGINIA, NORTH-CAROLINA, SOUTH-CAROLINA AND GEORGIA.

1867

LANCASTER:
PRINTED BY FRANCIS BAILEY.
M,DCC,LXXVII.

ARTICLES OF CONFEDERATION
(1777)

To all to whom these Presents shall come, we the undersigned Delegates of the States affixed to our Names send greeting

Whereas the Delegates of the United States of America in Congress assembled did on the fifteenth day of November in the Year of our Lord One Thousand Seven Hundred and Seventy-seven, and in the Second Year of the Independence of America agree to certain articles of Confederation and perpetual Union between the States of Newhampshire, Massachusetts-bay, Rhode-island, and Providence Plantations, Connecticut, New York, New Jersey, Pennsylvania, Delaware, Maryland, Virginia, North-Carolina, South-Carolina and Georgia in the Words following, viz.

> Articles of Confederation and perpetual Union between the States of Newhampshire, Massachusetts-bay, Rhodeisland and Providence Plantations, Connecticut, New-York, New-Jersey, Pennsylvania, Delaware, Maryland, Virginia, North-Carolina, South-Carolina and Georgia

Article I.   The stile of this confederacy shall be "The United States of America."

Article II.   Each State retains its sovereignty, freedom and independence, and every power, jurisdiction and right, which is not by this confederation expressly delegated to the United States, in Congress assembled.

Article III.   The said States hereby severally enter into a firm league of friendship with each other, for their common defense, the security of their liberties, and their mutual and general welfare, binding themselves to assist each other, against all force offered to, or attacks made upon them, or any of them, on account of religion, sovereignty trade or any other pretence whatever.

Article IV.   The better to secure and perpetuate mutual friendship and intercourse among the people of the different States in this Union, the free inhabitants of each of these States, paupers, vagabonds and fugitives from justice excepted, shall be entitled to all privileges and immunities of free citizens in the several States; and the people of each State shall have free ingress and regress to and from any other State, and shall enjoy therein all the privileges of trade and commerce, subject to the same duties, impositions and restrictions as the inhabitants thereof respectively, provided that such restrictions shall not extend so far as to prevent the removal of property imported into any State, to any other State of which the owner is an inhabitant; provided also that no imposition, duties or restriction shall be laid by any State, on the property of the United States, or either of them.

If any person guilty of, or charged with treason, felony, or other high misdemeanor in any State, shall flee from justice, and be found in any of the United States, he shall upon demand of the Governor or Executive power, of the State from which he fled, be delivered up and removed to the State having jurisdiction of his offense.

Full faith and credit shall be given in each of these States to the records, acts and judicial proceedings of the courts and magistrates of every other State.

Article V.   For the more convenient management of the general interests of the United States, delegates shall be annually appointed in such manner as the legislature of each State shall direct, to meet in Congress on the first Monday in November, in every year, with a power reserved to each State, to recall its delegates, or any of them, at any time within the year, and to send others in their stead, for the remainder of the year.

No State shall be represented in Congress by less than two, nor by more than seven members; and no person shall be capable of being a delegate for more than three years in any term of six years; nor shall any person, being a delegate, be capable of holding any office under the United States, for which he, or another for his benefit receives any salary, fees or emolument of any kind.

Each State shall maintain its own delegates in a meeting of the States, and while they act as members of the committee of the States.

In determining questions in the United States, in Congress assembled, each State shall have one vote.

Freedom of speech and debate in Congress shall not be impeached or questioned in any court, or place out of Congress, and the members of Congress shall be protected in their persons from arrests and imprisonments, during the time of their going to and from, and attendance on Congress, except for treason, felony, or breach of the peace.

Article VI. No State without the consent of the United States in Congress assembled, shall send any embassy to, or receive any embassy from, or enter into any conference, agreement, alliance or treaty with any king, prince or state; nor shall any person holding any office of profit or trust under the United States, or any of them, accept of any present, emolument, office or title of any kind whatever from any king, prince or foreign state; nor shall the United States in Congress assembled, or any of them, grant any title of nobility.

No two or more States shall enter into any treaty, confederation or alliance whatever between them, without the consent of the United States in Congress assembled, specifying accurately the purposes for which the same is to be entered into, and how long it shall continue.

No State shall lay any imposts or duties, which may interfere with any stipulations in treaties, entered into by the United States in Congress assembled, with any king, prince or state, in pursuance of any treaties already proposed by Congress, to the courts of France and Spain.

No vessels of war shall be kept up in time of peace by any State, except such number only, as shall be deemed necessary by the United States in Congress assembled, for the defence of such State, or its trade; nor shall any body of forces be kept up by any State, in time of peace, except such number only, as in the judgment of the United States, in Congress assembled, shall be deemed requisite to garrison the forts necessary for the defence of such State; but every State shall always keep up a well regulated and disciplined militia, sufficiently armed and accoutered, and shall provide and constantly have ready for use, in public stores, a due number of field pieces and tents, and a proper quantity of arms, ammunition and camp equipage.

No State shall engage in any war without the consent of the United States in Congress assembled, unless such State be actually invaded by enemies, or shall have received certain advice of a resolution being formed by some nation of Indians to invade such State, and the danger is so imminent as not to admit of a delay, till the United States in Congress assembled can be consulted: nor shall any State grant commissions to any ships or vessels of war, nor letters of marque or reprisal, except it be after a declaration of war by the United States in Congress assembled, and then only against the kingdom or state and the subjects thereof, against which war has been so declared and under such regulations as shall be established by the United States in Congress assembled, unless such State be infested by pirates, in which case vessels of war may be fitted out for that occasion, and kept so long as the danger shall continue, or until the United States in Congress assembled shall determine otherwise.

Article VII. When land-forces are raised by any State for the common defence, all officers of or under the rank of colonel, shall be appointed by the Legislature of each State respectively by whom such forces shall be raised, or in such manner as such State shall direct, and all vacancies shall be filled up by the State which first made the appointment.

Article VIII. All charges of war, and all other expenses that shall be incurred for the common defence or general welfare, and allowed by the United States in Congress assembled, shall be defrayed out of a common treasury, which shall be supplied by the several States, in proportion to the value of all land within each State, granted to or surveyed for any person, as such land and the buildings and improvements thereon shall be estimated according to such mode as the United States in Congress assembled, shall from time to time direct and appoint.

The taxes for paying that proportion shall be laid and levied by the authority and direction of the Legislatures of the several States within the time agreed upon by the United States in Congress Assembled.

Article IX. The United States in Congress assembled, shall have the sole and exclusive right and power of determining on peace and war, except in the cases mentioned in the sixth article—of sending and receiving ambassadors—entering into treaties and alliances, provided that no treaty of commerce shall be made whereby the legislative power of the respective States shall be restrained from imposing such imposts and duties on foreigners, as their own people are subjected to, or from prohibiting the exportation or importation of any species of goods or commodities whatsoever—of establishing rules for deciding in all cases, what captures on land or water shall be legal, and in what manner prizes taken by land or naval forces in the service of the United States shall be divided or appropriated—of granting letters of marque and reprisal in times of peace—appointing courts for the trial of piracies and felonies committed on the high seas and establishing courts for receiving and determining finally appeals in all cases of captures, provided that no member of Congress shall be appointed a judge of any of the said courts.

The United States in Congress assembled shall also be the last resort on appeal in all disputes and differences now subsisting or that hereafter may arise between two or more States concerning boundary, jurisdiction or any other cause whatever; which authority shall always be exercised in the manner following. Whenever the legislative or executive authority or lawful agent of any State in controversy with another shall present a petition to Congress, stating the matter in question and praying for a hearing, notice thereof shall be given by order of Congress to the legislative or executive authority of the other State in controversy, and a day assigned for the appearance of the parties by their lawful agents, who shall then be directed to appoint by joint consent, commissioners or judges to constitute a court for hearing and determining the matter in question: but if they cannot agree, Congress shall name three persons out of each of the United States, and from the list of such persons each party shall alternately strike out one, the petitioners beginning, until the number shall be reduced to thirteen; and from that number not less than seven, nor more than nine names as Congress shall direct, shall, in the presence of Congress be drawn out by lot, and the persons whose names shall be so drawn or any five of them, shall be commissioners or judges, to hear and finally determine the controversy, so always as a major part of the judges who shall hear the cause shall agree in the determination: and if either party shall neglect to attend at the day appointed, without showing reasons, which Congress shall judge sufficient, or being present shall refuse to strike, the Congress shall proceed to nominate three persons out of each State, and the Secretary of Congress shall strike in behalf of such party absent or refusing; and the judgment and sentence of the court to be appointed, in the manner before prescribed, shall be final and conclusive; and if any of the parties shall refuse to submit to the authority of such court, or to appear or defend their claim or cause, the court shall nevertheless proceed to pronounce sentence, or judgment, which shall in like manner be final and decisive, the judgment or sentence and other proceedings being in either case transmitted to Congress, and lodged among the acts of Congress for the security of the parties concerned: provided that every commissioner, before he sits in judgment, shall take an oath to be administered by one of the judges of the supreme or superior court of the State where the cause shall be tried, "well and truly to hear and determine the matter in question, according to the best of his judgment, without favour, affection or hope of reward:" provided also that no State shall be deprived of territory for the benefit of the United States.

All controversies concerning the private right of soil claimed under different grants of two or more States, whose jurisdiction as they may respect such lands, and the States which passed such grants are adjusted, the said grants or either of them being at the same time claimed to have originated antecedent to such settlement of jurisdiction, shall on the petition of either party to the Congress of the United States, be finally determined as near as may be in the same manner as is before prescribed for deciding disputes respecting territorial jurisdiction between different States.

The United States in Congress assembled shall also have the sole and exclusive right and power of regulating the alloy and value of coin struck by their own authority, or by that of the respective States.—fixing the standard of weights and measures throughout the United States.—regulating the trade and managing all affairs with the Indians, not members of any of the States, provided that the legislative right of any State within its own limits be not infringed or violated—establishing and regulating post-offices from one State to another, throughout all the United States, and exacting such postage on the papers passing thro' the same as may be requisite to defray the expenses of the said office—appointing all officers of the land forces, in the service of the United States, excepting regimental officers—appointing all the officers of the naval forces, and commissioning all officers whatever in the service of the United States—making rules for the government and regulation of the said land and naval forces, and directing their operations.

The United States in Congress assembled shall have authority to appoint a committee, to sit in the recess of Congress, to be denominated "a Committee of the States," and to consist of one delegate from each State; and to appoint such other committees and civil officers as may be necessary for managing the general affairs of the United States under their direction—to appoint one of their number to

The great end of men's entering into society being the enjoyment of their properties in peace and safety, and the great instrument and means of that being the laws established in that society.

JOHN LOCKE

preside, provided that no person be allowed to serve in the office of president more than one year in any term of three years; to ascertain the necessary sums of money to be raised for the service of the United States, and to appropriate and apply the same for defraying the public expenses—to borrow money or emit bills on the credit of the United States transmitting every half year to the respective States an account of the sums of money so borrowed or emitted,—to build and equip a navy—to agree upon the number of land forces, and to make requisitions from each State for its quota, in proportion to the number of white inhabitants in such State; which requisition shall be binding, and thereupon the Legislature of each State shall appoint the regimental officers, raise the men and cloath, arm and equip them in a soldier like manner, at the expense of the United States; and the officers and men so cloathed, armed and equipped shall march to the place appointed, and within the time agreed on by the United States in Congress assembled: but if the United States in Congress assembled shall, on consideration of circumstances judge proper that any State should not raise men, or should raise a smaller number than its quota, and that any other State should raise a greater number of men than the quota thereof, such extra number shall be raised, officered, cloathed, armed and equipped in the same manner as the quota of such State, unless the legislature of such State shall judge that such extra number cannot be safely spared out of the same, in which case they shall raise officer, cloath, arm and equip as many of such extra number as they judge can be safely spared. And the officers and men so cloathed, armed and equipped, shall march to the place appointed, and within the time agreed on by the United States in Congress assembled.

The United States in Congress assembled shall never engage in a war, nor grant letters of marque and reprisal in time of peace, nor enter into any treaties or alliances, nor coin money, nor regulate the value thereof, nor ascertain the sums and expenses necessary for the defence and welfare of the United States, or any of them, nor emit bills, nor borrow money on the credit of the United States, nor appropriate money, nor agree upon the number of vessels of war, to be built or purchased, or the number of land or sea forces to be raised, nor appoint a commander in chief of the army or navy, unless nine States assent to the same: nor shall a question on any other point, except for adjourning from day to day be determined, unless by the votes of a majority of the United States in Congress assembled.

The Congress of the United States shall have power to adjourn to any time within the year, and to any place within the United States, so that no period of adjournment be for a longer duration than the space of six months, and shall publish the journal of their proceedings monthly, except such parts thereof relating to treaties, alliances or military operations, as in their judgment require secrecy; and the yeas and nays of the delegates of each State on any question shall be entered on the journal, when it is desired by any delegate; and the delegates of a State, or any of them, at his or her request shall be furnished with a transcript of the said journal, except such parts as are above excepted, to lay before the Legislatures of the several States.

Article X. The committee of the States, or any nine of them, shall be authorized to execute in the recess of Congress, such of the powers of Congress as the United States in Congress assembled, by the consent of nine States, shall from time to time think expedient to vest them with; provided that no power be delegated to the said committee, for the exercise of which, by the articles of confederation, the voice of nine States in the Congress of the United States assembled is requisite.

Article XI. Canada acceding to this confederation, and joining in the measures of the United States, shall be admitted into, and entitled to all the advantages of this Union: but no other colony shall be admitted into the same, unless such admission be agreed to by nine States.

Article XII. All bills of credit emitted, monies borrowed and debts contracted by, or under the authority of Congress, before the assembling of the United States, in pursuance of the present confederation, shall be deemed and considered as a charge against the United States, for payment and satisfaction whereof the said United States, and the public faith are hereby solemnly pledged.

Article XIII. Every State shall abide by the determinations of the United States in Congress assembled, on all questions which by this confederation are submitted to them. And the articles of this confederation shall be inviolably observed by every State, and the Union shall be perpetual; nor shall any alteration at any time hereafter be made in any of them; unless such alteration be agreed to in a Congress of the United States, and be afterwards confirmed by the Legislatures of every State.

And whereas it has pleased the Great Governor of the world to incline the hearts of the Legislatures we respectively represent in Congress, to approve of, and to authorize us to ratify the said articles of confederation and perpetual union. Know ye that we the undersigned delegates, by virtue of the power and authority to us given for that purpose, do by these presents, in the name and in behalf of our respective constituents, fully and entirely ratify and confirm each and every of the said articles of confederation and perpetual union, and all and singular the matters and things therein contained: and we do further solemnly plight and engage the faith of our respective constituents, that they shall abide by the determinations of the United States in Congress assembled, on all questions, which by the said confederation are submitted to them. And that the articles thereof shall be inviolably observed by the States we re[s]pectively represent, and that the Union shall be perpetual.

In witness whereof we have hereunto set our hands in Congress.

Done at Philadelphia in the State of Pennsylvania the ninth day of July in the year of our Lord one thousand seven hundred and seventy-eight, and in the third year of the independence of America.

On the part and behalf of the State of New Hampshire

JOSIAH BARTLETT,   JOHN WENTWORTH, Junr.,
                              August 8th, 1778.

On the part and behalf of the State of Massachusetts Bay

JOHN HANCOCK,   FRANCIS DANA,
SAMUEL ADAMS,   JAMES LOVELL,
ELBRIDGE GERRY,   SAMUEL HOLTEN.

On the part and behalf of the State of Rhode Island
and Providence Plantations

WILLIAM ELLERY,   JOHN COLLINS.
HENRY MARCHANT,

On the part and behalf of the State of Connecticut

ROGER SHERMAN,   TITUS HOSMER,
SAMUEL HUNTINGTON,   ANDREW ADAMS.
OLIVER WOLCOTT,

On the part and behalf of the State of New York

JAS. DUANE,   WM. DUER,
FRA. LEWIS,   GOUV. MORRIS.

On the part and in behalf of the State of New Jersey, Novr. 26, 1778

JNO. WITHERSPOON,   NATHL. SCUDDER.

On the part and behalf of the State of Pennsylvania

ROBT. MORRIS,   WILLIAM CLINGAN,
DANIEL ROBERDEAU,   JOSEPH REED,
JONA. BAYARD SMITH,   22d July, 1778.

On the part & behalf of the State of Delaware

THO. M'KEAN, Feby. 12, 1779. NICHOLAS VAN DYKE.
JOHN DICKINSON, May 5th, 1779

On the part and behalf of the State of Maryland

JOHN HANSON,   DANIEL CARROLL,
   March 1, 1781.   Mar. 1, 1781.

On the part and behalf of the State of Virginia

RICHARD HENRY LEE,   JNO. HARVIE,
JOHN BANISTER,   FRANCIS LIGHTFOOT LEE.
THOMAS ADAMS,

On the part and behalf of the State of No. Carolina

JOHN PENN, July 21st, 1778.   JNO. WILLIAMS.
CORNS. HARNETT,

On the part & behalf of the State of South Carolina

HENRY LAURENS,   RICHD. HUTSON,
WILLIAM HENRY DRAYTON,   THOS. HEYWARD, Junr.
JNO. MATHEWS,

On the part & behalf of the State of Georgia

JNO. WALTON, 24th July, 1778.   EDWD. LANGWORTHY.
EDWD. TELFAIR,

ARTICLES OF IMPEACHMENT ☐ Formal written allegations of the causes that warrant the criminal trial of a public official before a quasi-political court. ☐

In cases of IMPEACHMENT, involving the president, vice-president, or other Federal officers, the HOUSE OF REPRESENTATIVES prepares the articles of impeachment, since it is endowed with the ". . . sole Power of Impeachment," under Article I, Section 2, Clause 5 of the Constitution. The articles are sent to the Senate, which has the exclusive power to ". . . try all Impeachments" by virtue of Article I, Section 3, Clause 6.

The use of articles of impeachment against state officials is governed by state constitutions and statutes.

Articles of impeachment are analogous to INDICTMENTS that initiate criminal prosecutions of private persons. See also, John D. Feerick's essay on Impeachment.

ARTICLES OF INCORPORATION

☐ The document that must be filed with an appropriate government agency, commonly the office of the secretary of state, if the owners of a business want it to be given legal recognition as a CORPORATION. ☐

Articles of incorporation, sometimes called a certificate of incorporation, must set forth certain information as mandated by statute. Although laws vary from state to state, the purposes of the corporation and the rights and liabilities of shareholders and directors are typical provisions required in the document. Official forms are prescribed in many states.

Once the articles of incorporation are filed with the secretary of state, corporate existence begins. In some jurisdictions, a formal certificate of incorporation attached to a duplicate of the articles must be issued to the applicant before the business will be given legal status as a corporation.

For a sample articles of incorporation, see the Appendix volume.

ARTICLES OF PARTNERSHIP ☐ A written compact by which parties agree to pool their money, labor, and/or skill to carry on a business for profit. The parties sign the compact with the understanding that they will share proportionally the losses and profits according to the provisions and conditions that they have mutually assented would govern their business relationship. ☐

See also, Partnership.

ARTICLES OF WAR ☐ Codes created to prescribe the manner in which the armed services of a nation are to be governed. ☐

For example, the UNIFORM CODE OF MILITARY JUSTICE is an article of war applied to the

Army, Navy, the Coast Guard, and the Air Force of the United States.

ARTIFICIAL INSEMINATION □ The medical procedure by which a female is impregnated through use of semen from a donor who is either her husband or a third party, usually anonymous, through means other than sexual intercourse. □

Artificial insemination using the husband's semen is sometimes used where conception is prevented by the husband's impotence or physical defect. The semen of a third-person donor is used in artificial insemination where the husband is sterile, where there is a risk of transmitting an inheritable disease, or where there is an Rh incompatability between the husband's and wife's blood that has resulted in repeated stillbirths. This procedure is known as *consensual* artificial insemination by donor.

Problems have arisen in many jurisdictions with respect to the legitimate status of a child conceived through artificial insemination by a third-party donor with the consent of the hus-

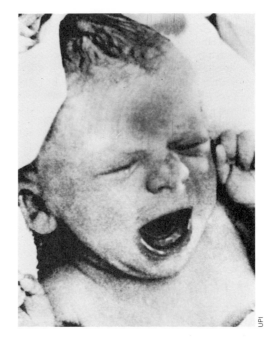

The first "test tube" baby, seen here shortly after birth, was a normal 5-pound, 12-ounce baby girl. Mrs. Lesley Brown of Oldham, England, gave birth to the baby, delivered by Caesarian section, on July 25, 1978, after she had been artificially impregnated because her blocked Fallopian tubes prevented normal conception.

The first artificially conceived baby, Louise Joy Brown, appeared on U.S. television with her parents when she was about one year old.

band. In some instances, the PRESUMPTION of legitimacy will protect the child if the artificial insemination procedure entails matching the husband's blood group with that of the donor and mingling the husband's semen with the donor's semen. Under such circumstances, it is difficult for the husband to rebut the presumption that the child is his. Courts have become more willing to recognize that husbands who consent to the artificial insemination of their wives by third-party donors are the natural fathers of legitimate offspring. See also, Illegitimacy.

ARTIFICIAL PERSON □ A legal entity that is not a human being but for certain purposes is considered by virtue of statute to be a natural person. □

A CORPORATION is considered an artificial person for SERVICE OF PROCESS.

AS IS □ A term used to describe a SALES transaction in which the seller offers goods in their present, existing condition to prospective buyers. □

The term *as is* gives notice to buyers that they are taking a risk on the quality of the goods. The buyer is free to inspect the goods before purchase; but if any hidden defects are discovered after purchase, the buyer has no recourse against the seller. Any implied or express WARRANTIES that usually accompany goods for sale are excluded in an "as is" sale.

CONTRACT law and the UNIFORM COMMERCIAL CODE regulate "as is" sales.

AS PER □ A phrase commonly recognized to mean "in accordance with the terms of" a particular document—such as a contract, deed, or affidavit—or "as authorized by the contract." □

ASPORTATION □ The removal of items from one place to another, such as carrying things away illegally. □

Asportation is one of the elements required to establish the crime of larceny. In order to prove that asportation has occurred, it is not necessary to show that the goods were moved a substantial distance, but only that they were moved.

Asportation was one of the elements necessary to establish common-law KIDNAPPING, and in many states it remains as an element of statutory kidnapping.

ASSASSINATION □ Murder committed by a perpetrator without the personal provocation of the victim who is usually a government official. □

It is a Federal crime to assassinate the president, vice-president, or person next in line to suc-

Three of the four United States presidents who were assassinated in office, are pictured alongside their assassins.

THREE PRESIDENTS WHO HAVE FALLEN VICTIMS TO ASSASSINS' BULLETS.

Abraham Lincoln, the first of the martyred Presidents, was shot and fatally wounded on the night of April 14, 1865, by John Wilkes Booth, an aberrated actor. James A. Garfield, the second President of the United States to be similarly stricken, was shot by Charles J. Guiteau, July 2, 1881. He died September 19th following.

The *New York Times* carried this banner headline following the assassination of President John F. Kennedy in 1963.

ceed to the presidency, or to advocate the overthrow of the government by assassination.

ASSAULT ☐ At COMMON LAW, an intentional act by one person that creates an apprehension in another of an imminent harmful or offensive contact. ☐

An assault is carried out by a threat of bodily harm coupled with an apparent, present ability to cause the harm. It is both a CRIME and a TORT and, therefore, may result in either criminal or civil liability. Generally, the common law definition is the same in criminal and tort law. There is, however, an additional criminal law category of assault consisting of an attempted but unsuccessful BATTERY.

Statutory definitions of assault in the various jurisdictions throughout the United States are not substantially different from the common-law definition.

Elements Generally, the essential elements of assault consist of an act intended to cause an apprehension of harmful or offensive contact that causes apprehension of such contact in the victim.

The act required for an assault must be overt. Although words alone are insufficient, they might create an assault when coupled with some action that indicates the ability to carry out the threat. A mere threat to harm is not an assault; however, a threat combined with a raised fist might be sufficient if it causes a reasonable apprehension of harm in the victim.

Intent is an essential element of assault. In tort law, the intent can be specific—if the assailant intends to cause the apprehension of harmful or offensive contact in the victim—or general—if he or she intends to do the act that causes such apprehension. In addition, the intent element is satisfied if it is substantially certain, to a reasonable person, that the act will cause the result. A defendant who holds a gun to a victim's head possesses the requisite intent, since it is substantially certain that this act will produce an apprehension in the victim. In all cases, intent to kill or harm is irrelevant.

In criminal law, the attempted battery type of assault requires a specific intent to commit battery. An intent to frighten will not suffice for this form of assault.

There can be no assault if the act does not produce a true apprehension of harm in the victim. There must be a reasonable fear of injury. The usual test applied is whether the act would induce such apprehension in the mind of a reasonable person. The status of the victim is taken into account. A threat made to a child might be sufficient to constitute an assault, while an identical threat made to an adult might not.

Virtually all jurisdictions agree that the victim must be aware of the danger. This element is not required, however, for the attempted battery type of assault. A defendant who throws a rock at a sleeping victim can only be guilty of the attempted battery assault, since the victim cannot be aware of the possible harm.

Aggravated assault An aggravated assault, punishable in all states as a FELONY, is committed when a defendant intends to do more than merely frighten the victim. Common types of aggravated assaults are those accompanied by an intent to kill, rob, or rape. An assault with a dangerous weapon is aggravated if there is an intent to cause serious harm. Pointing an unloaded gun at a victim to frighten the individual is not considered an aggravated assault.

Punishment A defendant adjudged to have committed civil assault is liable for DAMAGES. The question of the amount that should be awarded to the victim is determined by a jury. Compensatory damages, which are aimed at compensating the victim for the injury, are common. Nominal damages, a small sum awarded for the invasion of a right even though there has been no substantial injury, may be awarded. In some cases, courts allow punitive damages, which are designed to punish the defendant for the wrongful conduct.

The punishment for criminal assault is a fine, imprisonment, or both. Penalties are more severe when the assault is aggravated. Many states have statutes dividing criminal assault into various degrees. As in aggravated assault, the severity of the crime, the extent of violence and harm, and the criminal intent of the defendant are all factors considered in determining the sentence imposed.

ASSAULT AND BATTERY

☐ Two separate offenses against the person that when used in one expression may be defined as any unlawful and unpermitted touching of another.

☐ ASSAULT is an act that creates an apprehension in another of an imminent, harmful, or offensive contact. The act consists of a threat of harm accompanied by an apparent, present ability to carry out the threat. BATTERY is a harmful or offensive touching of another ☐

The main distinction between the two offenses is the existence or nonexistence of a touch-

ing or contact. While contact is an essential element of battery, there must be an absence of contact for assault. Sometimes assault is defined loosely to include battery; however, the expression *assault and battery* means battery.

Assault and battery are offenses in both criminal and tort law and, therefore, they can give rise to criminal or civil liability. In criminal law, an assault may additionally be defined as any attempt to commit a battery.

At COMMON LAW, both offenses were MISDEMEANORS. Today, under virtually all criminal codes, they are either misdemeanors or felonies. They are characterized as felonious when accompanied by a criminal intent, such as an intent to kill, rob, or rape, or when they are committed with a dangerous weapon.

Intent Intent is an essential element of both offenses. Generally, it is only necessary for the defendant to have an intent to do the act that causes the harm. In other words, the act must be done voluntarily. Although an intent to harm the victim is likely to exist, it is not a required element of either offense. There is an exception to this rule for the attempted battery type of criminal assault. If a defendant who commits this crime does not have an intent to harm the victim, the individual cannot be guilty of the offense.

Defenses

Consent In almost all states, consent is a defense to civil assault and battery. Some jurisdictions hold that in the case of mutual combat, consent will not suffice and either party may sue the other. Jurisdictions also differ on the question of whether consent is a defense to criminal assault and battery.

Consent must be given voluntarily in order to constitute a defense. If it is obtained by FRAUD or DURESS, or is otherwise unlawful, it will not suffice. When an act exceeds the scope of the given consent, the defense is not available. A person who participates in a football game impliedly consents to a certain amount of physical contact; however, the individual is not deemed to consent to contact beyond what is commonly permitted in the sport.

Self-defense Generally, a person may use whatever degree of force is reasonably necessary for protection from bodily harm. The question of whether or not this defense is valid is usually determined by a jury. A person who initiates a fight cannot claim self-defense unless the opponent responded with a greater and unforeseeable degree of force. When an aggressor retreats and is later attacked by the same opponent, the defense may be asserted.

Deadly force may be justified if initially used by the aggressor. The situation must be such

Self-defense is nature's eldest law.

DRYDEN

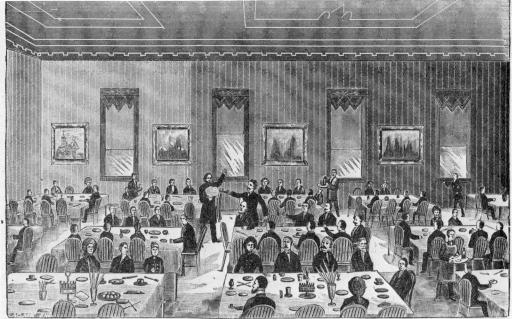

Library of Congress

JUDGE TERRY SLAPS JUSTICE FIELD IN THE FACE AND IS SHOT DEAD BY DEPUTY MARSHAL NEAGLE, AT LATHROP, AUGUST 14, 1889. TERRY SAT AT THE EAST END OF THE FIFTH TABLE, SAME ROW.

In August 1889 Judge David S. Terry assaulted Justice Stephen J. Field of the U.S. Supreme Court because of a ruling Field had made in the celebrated Sharon-Hill conspiracy case. This primitive woodcut shows a deputy U.S. marshal, who had been assigned to protect Field against Terry's often expressed threats, shooting the assailant.

that a reasonable person would likewise fear for his or her life. In some states, a person must retreat prior to using deadly force if the individual can do so in complete safety. A majority of states, however, allow a person to stand his or her ground even though there is a means of safe escape.

Whether the degree of force used is reasonable depends upon the circumstances. The usual test applied involves determining whether a reasonable person in a similar circumstance would respond with a similar amount of force. Factors such as age, size, and strength of the parties are also considered.

Defense of others Going to the aid of a person in distress is a valid defense, provided the defender is free from fault. In some states, the defender is treated as though he or she stands in the shoes of the person protected. The defender's right to claim defense of others depends upon whether the person protected had a justified claim of self-defense. In a minority of jurisdictions, the defense may be asserted if the defender reasonably believed the third party was in need of aid.

Defense of property Individuals may use a reasonable amount of force to protect their property. The privilege to defend one's property is more limited than that of self-defense because society places a lesser value on property than on

the integrity of human beings. Deadly force is usually not permitted. In most states, however, deadly force might be justified if it is used to prevent or stop a felony. An owner of real property or a person who rightfully possesses it, such as a tenant, may use force against a trespasser. Generally, a request to leave the property must be made before the application of force, unless the request would be futile. The amount of force used must be reasonable, and, unless it is necessary for self-defense, the infliction of bodily harm upon an intruder is improper. Courts have traditionally been more liberal in allowing the use of force to protect one's dwelling. Recent cases, however, have indicated that there must be a threat to the personal safety of the occupants.

The states are divided on the question of whether a person who is legally entitled to property may use force to recover possession of it. In most jurisdictions, a landowner is not liable for assault and battery if the owner forcibly expels someone who is wrongfully on the property. The owner must not, however, use excessive force; and the fact that the person may not be held civilly liable does not relieve the owner of criminal liability. In some states, the use of force against a person wrongfully in possession of land is not permitted unless such person has tortiously dispossessed the actor or the actor's predecessor in title.

Leslie's Illustrated Newspaper of March 9, 1861, carried an illustration of a knife attack on Congressman Van Wyck near the U.S. Capitol.

Library of Congress

If possession of real or personal property is in dispute, the universal rule is that force cannot be used. The dispute must be settled by a court.

With respect to personal property, the general view is that an owner may not commit an assault or battery upon the wrongdoer in order to recover property. A majority of jurisdictions recognize the right of an owner in HOT PURSUIT of stolen property to use a reasonable amount of force to retrieve it. In some states, stolen property may be taken back peaceably wherever it is found, even if it is necessary to enter another's premises. In all cases, the infliction of an unreasonable amount of harm will vitiate the defense.

Performance of duty and authority   A person may use reasonable force when it becomes necessary in the course of performing a duty. A police officer, for example, may use force when apprehending a criminal. Private citizens may also use reasonable force to stop a crime committed in their presence. Certain businesses, such as restaurants or nightclubs, are authorized to hire employees who may use rea-

sonable force to remove persons who disturb other patrons. Court officers, such as judges, may order the removal of disruptive persons who interfere with their duties.

Persons with authority in certain relationships, such as parents or teachers, may use force as a disciplinary measure, provided they do not exceed the scope of their authority. Punishment may not be cruel or excessive.

Punishment   The law considers an assault and battery to be an invasion of the personal security of the victim for which the wrongdoer is required to pay for DAMAGES. The determination of the amount of damages to which a victim might be entitled if a defendant is found civilly liable is usually made by a jury. Generally, a plaintiff is entitled to compensatory damages that compensate for injuries that are both directly and indirectly related to the wrong. Examples of compensatory damages include damages for pain and suffering, damages for medical expenses, and damages for lost earnings resulting from the victim's inability to work. NOMINAL

13 *Crime and Victim*
by Ruby Grady
acrylic and collage
41½ × 48

Art and the Law

The law has been a subject of artistic expression for many centuries. Art and the law are a vivid reflection of the individuals who produce them and the society from which they emerged.

The juxtaposition of these two seemingly unrelated disciplines is readily apparent in the reproductions that follow. They are eloquent testimony of the extent to which contemporary artists are drawn to the condition of the law in the United States. These paintings are reproduced by courtesy of The West Collection, West Publishing Company, from annual West/ART AND THE LAW exhibitions.

14 *The Bailiffs* by Barbara D. Hultmann
acrylic / 40 × 30

15　*Regulate the Water* by John Fitzgerald
watercolor　/　28¼ × 20¾

16　*Arraignment Court, Brooklyn*
by Harvey Dinnerstein　charcoal　/　24 × 19¼

17　*The Volunteer* by José S. Pérez
oil　/　90½ × 142

18   *At the Precinct* by Jack Levine
      oil / 21 × 24

19   *Moses "I Am That I Am"* by Abraham Rattner
      oil on paper / 24½ × 35

20 *The Lawyer* by R. C. Rothchild
    oil / 40 × 30

DAMAGES, given although there is no harm at all, or merely a slight one, may also be awarded in an assault and battery action. Some jurisdictions allow the award of PUNITIVE DAMAGES. They are often given when the offense was committed wantonly or maliciously to punish the defendant for the wrongful act, and to deter others from engaging in similar acts in the future. The defendant might additionally be subject to criminal liability.

If a defendant is found criminally liable, the punishment is imprisonment, a fine, or both. The amount of time a defendant must serve in prison depends upon the statute in the particular jurisdiction. When the offense is committed with an intent to murder or do serious harm, it is called aggravated assault and battery. An aggravated assault and battery is often committed with a dangerous weapon, and it is punishable as a felony in all states. See also, Richard G. Singer's essay on Deadly Force—Restrictions on Use.

ASSEMBLY □ The congregation of a number of persons at the same location. □

Political assemblies are those mandated by the Constitution and laws, such as the general assembly.

The lower, or more populous, arm of the legislature in several states is also known as the "House of Assembly" or the "Assembly."

ASSEMBLY AND PETITION □ The privilege guaranteed by the First Amendment to the United States Constitution, which permits people to congregate for any objective relating to government, especially for the protection of governmental actions and policies, and the promotion of ideas. □

The First Amendment permits a peaceful gathering of persons for nearly any lawful objective. The Supreme Court of the United States has held that participation in a Communist party political meeting cannot be a crime unless violence is advocated. Under the broad category of civil rights, demonstrations, picketing, and marches have been protected as lawful assemblages. Labor organizing meetings have also been deemed lawful exercises of the First Amendment right of assembly.

It is inconsequential whether a person is engaged in speech, association, assembly, or petition because all four rights are presently regarded as elements of a broad right to freedom of expression. The right of assembly encompasses

Library of Congress

Delegates to the National Equal Rights Convention convened in Washington, D.C., in 1873.

Brown Brothers

Members of the Women's Trade Union League of New York assembled to parade for better working conditions, particularly the eight-hour day and restrictions on child labor.

UPI

OPEC oil ministers assemble in Vienna to discuss production levels and pricing policies for member nations.

freedom of association, which is implied from the enumerated rights concerning free expression in the First Amendment. Association entails more than the right to attend a meeting, since it includes the right to express philosophies or opinions through group membership or by other lawful methods.

A corollary of this right is the right of an association to conceal from the state the names of its individual members, if it is probable that a deprivation of the personal liberty of the individuals would ensue that is not outweighed by the state demonstrating a controlling justification for the information.

The right to petition the government for redress of grievances has been the subject of appeals made to the Supreme Court. One group of these cases involved the attempts of various labor unions and civil rights groups to refer their members to attorneys after initially advising their members of their legal rights. States and state BAR ASSOCIATIONS asserted that this conduct constituted the unauthorized practice of law. The Court upheld the practice based in part on the First Amendment right of every person to petition for redress of grievances. In many instances, litigation is the only practical method available to minorities for redress of their grievances. With respect to union members, the Court acknowledged that engaging in collective activity to procure meaningful access to the courts is a fundamental right within the protection of the First Amendment.

The right to petition for the redress of grievances is not restricted exclusively to religious or political affairs but is applicable to any field of human enterprise, including business and economic activity. In the context of LABOR-MANAGEMENT RELATIONS, a state statute cannot compel labor union organizers to register with a state official before urging workers to join a union, since such a statute imposes PRIOR RESTRAINT on free speech and free assembly. Business interests may unite and lobby to influence the legislative, executive, or judicial branches of government, or the administrative agencies, without violating the antitrust laws, because such activities are protected by the right of petition. This right has been deemed a DEFENSE to criminal actions instituted for violation of various assembly laws. Restrictions cannot be imposed on a peaceful assembly to petition for redress of grievances if no violence is advocated.

Protection for the actions of groups or individuals is not absolute under the First Amendment rights of assembly and petition. Courts have justified limitations on those rights, ruling that they must be exercised in a lawful manner.

The rights cannot function as a shield to violate valid statutes or serve as a pretext for attaining substantive evil. The antitrust laws may be applied to groups that conspire to bar competitors from meaningful access to the agencies and the courts, or to a licensing authority that conspires to eliminate a competitor. A CONSPIRACY merits no First Amendment protection if its purpose is to achieve a criminal objective in the near future, rather than to advocate ideas to advance social or political reform. In general, when the state attempts to restrict the rights of assembly or petition, it must demonstrate a COMPELLING STATE INTEREST in an area in which it cannot otherwise lawfully regulate.

ASSENT □ An intentional approval of known facts that are offered by another for acceptance; agreement; consent. □

Express assent is manifest confirmation of a position for approval. *Implied assent* is that which the law presumes to exist because the conduct of the parties demonstrates their intentions. *Mutual assent*, sometimes called the meeting of the minds of the parties, is the reciprocal agreement of each party to accept all the terms and conditions in a CONTRACT.

ASSESS
□ To determine financial worth.
□ To ascertain the amount of DAMAGES.
□ To fix and adjust the individual shares to be contributed by several persons towards a common beneficial objective in proportion to the benefit each person will receive.
□ To tax by having qualified experts estimate the value of property by considering the nature of the property, its size, the value of other comparable property, and the proportionate share of services that is used by that property.
□ To levy a charge on the owner of property that has been improved at the expense of the local government unit, such as when sewers or sidewalks are installed. □

ASSESSED VALUATION □ The financial worth assigned to property by taxing authorities that is used as a basis or factor against which the tax rate is applied. □

A prescribed amount of the value of each unit must be paid as taxes in the future. In most cases, the assessed value is not representative of the FAIR MARKET VALUE of the property.

ASSESSMENT
□ The process by which the financial worth of property is determined.
□ The amount at which an item is valued.

. . . peaceable assembly for lawful discussion cannot be made a crime . . .

CHARLES EVANS HUGHES

□ A demand by the board of directors of a CORPORATION for the payment of any money that is still owed on the purchase of CAPITAL STOCK.

□ The determination of the amount of DAMAGES to be awarded to a plaintiff who has been successful in a lawsuit.

□ The ascertainment of the pro rata share of taxes to be paid by members of a group of taxpayers who have directly benefited from a particular common goal or project according to the benefit conferred upon the individual or his or her property. This is known as a SPECIAL ASSESSMENT.

□ The listing and valuation of property for purposes of fixing a tax upon it for which its owner will be liable.

□ The procedure by which the INTERNAL REVENUE SERVICE, or other government department of taxation, declares that a taxpayer owes additional tax because, for example, the individual has understated personal GROSS INCOME or has taken DEDUCTIONS to which he or she is not entitled. This process is also known as a *deficiency assessment.* □

ASSET □ Real or personal property, whether tangible or intangible, that has financial value and can be used for the payment of its owner's debts. □

An *accrued asset* is one that arises from revenue earned but not yet due. For example, an accrued dividend is a share of the net earnings of a corporation that has been declared but has not yet been paid out to its shareholder(s).

In BANKRUPTCY, an asset is any form of property owned by a debtor who is insolvent that is not exempt from being used to repay debts.

For INCOME TAX purposes, a *capital asset* is property held by a taxpayer for personal enjoyment or investment, such as a home, furniture, stocks and bonds, or an automobile, but does not include inventory, commercial accounts, and notes receivable, depreciable property, commercial property, copyrights, and short-term government obligations. When a capital asset is sold, any gain received is given preferential tax treatment.

A *current, liquid,* or *quick asset* is an item that can be readily converted to cash, such as stocks and bonds.

For many Americans, their most valuable capital asset is their home.

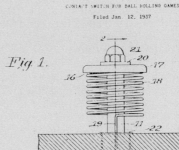

This patent for a contact switch for pinball games exemplifies an intangible asset.

Investment in fixed assets, such as this cranberry beater which churns the berries off the bushes, is often required in farming operations.

A *fixed asset* is one of a permanent or long-term nature used in the operation of a business and not intended for sale.

A *frozen asset* is one that cannot be easily converted into cash, such as real estate when there is no market, or that cannot be used because of a legal restriction, such as a spendthrift trust.

An *intangible asset* is one to which an arbitrary dollar value is attached because it has no intrinsic market value but represents financial value, such as the GOODWILL of a business, TRADEMARKS, or PATENTS.

ASSIGN

☐ To transfer to another, as to assign one's right to receive rental income from property to another.

☐ To designate for a particular function, as to assign an attorney to defend an indigent in a criminal prosecution.

☐ To specify or point out, as to assign errors in a lower court proceeding on a writ of error that is submitted to request a court to reverse the judgment of the lower court. ☐

ASSIGNED ACCOUNT □ A type of SE-CURED TRANSACTION whereby an ACCOUNT RE-CEIVABLE is pledged to a bank, factor, or other lender to secure the repayment of a loan. □

It is common commercial practice for a manufacturer or wholesaler to sell inventory on open account, a debt owed to the seller of inventory that is to be repaid by its buyer as the merchandise is sold. This arrangement creates an account receivable that the seller uses as collateral for a loan.

ASSIGNED RISK □ A danger or hazard of loss or injury that an insurer will not normally accept for coverage under a policy issued by the insurer, but that the insurance company is required by state law to offer protection against by participating in a pool of insurers who are also compelled to provide coverage. □

ASSIGNED RISK PLAN □ An INSURANCE plan created and imposed by state statute under which persons who normally would be denied insurance coverage as bad risks are permitted to purchase insurance from a pool of insurers who must offer coverage to such individuals. □

ASSIGNMENT □ A transfer of rights in real property or personal property to another that gives the recipient—the transferee—the rights that the owner or holder of the property—the transferor—had prior to the transfer. □

An *assignment of wages* is the transfer of the right to collect wages from the wage earner to his or her creditor. Statutes regulate the extent to which an assignment may be made.

ASSIGNMENT FOR BENEFIT OF CRED-ITORS □ The voluntary transfer of all or most of a debtor's property to another person in trust so that he or she will collect any money that is owed to the debtor, sell the debtor's property and apply the money received to the payment of the debts, returning any surplus to the debtor. □

The debtor is the *assignor,* the transferor; and the person who takes legal title to the property is the *assignee.*

Types There are three types of assignments that are categorized according to the limitations imposed upon the arrangement. A general assignment is one involving the transfer of all the debtor's property for the benefit of all his or her creditors. A partial assignment is one in which only part of a debtor's property is transferred to benefit all the creditors. When property is assigned to benefit only designated creditors, it is a special assignment.

The assignment results in the property being beyond the control of the debtor. It is different from AGENCY arrangements, PLEDGES, or MORTGAGES.

Trust law Unless otherwise expressly provided, TRUST law governs assignments for the benefit of creditors. The assignee is considered a trustee and his or her duties and responsibilities to the debtor's creditors are the same as a trustee's to the beneficiaries of a trust. The document that embodies the terms of the assignment authorizes the assignee to liquidate the debtor's property in satisfaction of the creditors' claims against the debtor as quickly as possible. Under COMMON LAW, this was the assignee's chief function. Even if the assignment instrument does not expressly empower an assignee to sell the property, the assignee still has the power to do so in order to pay the creditors.

Creation It is not necessary for a debtor to obtain the consent of creditors before making an assignment for their benefit. An owner of property has a right to transfer legal title to it by virtue of ownership. The limitation derived from common law that is placed upon its creation is that it cannot be done to dishonestly deprive a debtor's creditors of their rights to have property sold to repay debts. When an assignment for the benefit of creditors is intended by the debtor to place his or her property beyond the legal reach of creditors, it is called a fraudulent conveyance. This type of assignment is VOID, or legally ineffective, under statutes that prohibit such arrangements. An assignment by which the assignor-debtor retains any interest, benefit, or advantage from the conveyance, such as keeping the right to revoke the assignment, made to defraud creditors is also a fraudulent conveyance, as is an assignment by which the assignee is required to delay liquidation of the assets.

In some jurisdictions, a partial assignment is considered a fraudulent conveyance because the creditors are hindered and delayed in receiving payment if they must seek payment from the debtor after first being referred to the assignee. Other jurisdictions treat any assignment by a solvent debtor as fraudulent on the theory that such an arrangement prevents the immediate sale of the property so that creditors are delayed and hindered.

Deficiency A debtor is still liable to pay his or her creditors even if the proceeds from the sale of personal and real property pursuant to an assignment for the benefit of creditors are not sufficient to completely repay the debts. When, however, creditors agree to accept the proceeds in satisfaction of the debtor's obligations, such an agreement is called a COMPOSITION WITH

CREDITORS. For this reason, assignments for the benefit of creditors are used by corporate, rather than individual debtors.

Since preferences are permissible under common law, a common-law assignment for the benefit of creditors that provides for preferential payments to designated creditors is not a fraudulent conveyance. Most courts have held that debtors cannot use preferences to obtain discharges from creditors by conditioning preferences on their release from unpaid portions of their debts. To do so is considered a fraudulent conveyance, since a creditor would have to accept virtually any condition that the debtor decided upon if the creditor were to receive any money from the assignee.

Legality of assignments Most states have enacted statutes that regulate assignments for the benefit of creditors. Some states require that an assignment must comply with statutory requirements or be invalid, while in others the debtor may make a common-law assignment, which is regulated by common law, or a statutory assignment, which is controlled by applicable statutes.

The state statutes require that the assignment be recorded, schedules of assets and liabilities be filed, notice be given to the creditors, the assignee be bonded, and the assignor be supervised by the court. Almost every jurisdiction prohibits the granting of a preference. All creditors except those with liens or statutorily created priorities are treated equally. Some statutes empower an assignee to set aside prior fraudulent conveyances, and others authorize the assignee to set aside preferences made before the assignment.

If a debtor has made substantial preferences, fraudulent conveyances, or allowed liens VOIDABLE in BANKRUPTCY to attach to his or her property, then creditors might be able to force the debtor into bankruptcy if they decide that the assignment does not adequately protect their rights. An efficiently handled assignment for benefit of creditors is frequently more advantageous to creditors then bankruptcy because it usually brings about better liquidation prices and its less rigid and formal structure saves time and money.

For a sample assignment for benefit of creditors, see the Appendix volume 11.

ASSIGNS □ Individuals to whom property is, will, or may be transferred by CONVEYANCE, WILL, DESCENT AND DISTRIBUTION, or STATUTE; assignees. □

The term *assigns* is often found in deeds; for example, "heirs, administrators, and assigns

to denote the assignable nature of the interest or right created."

ASSISE, OR ASSIZE
□ A judicial procedure in early England whereby a certain number of men in a community were called together to hear and decide a dispute; a type of court.
□ A type of WRIT, commanding the convening of such a tribunal in order to determine disputed rights to possess land.
□ An edict or statute issued by an ancient assembly. □

For example, the Assize of Clarendon was a statute, or ordinance, passed in the tenth year of the reign of King Henry II (1164). It proclaimed that those who were accused of a heinous crime and were unable to exonerate themselves had forty days to gather provisions from friends to provide for their sustenance before they were sent into exile.

The word assize comes from the Latin *assideo*, which describes the fact that the men taking action sat together. An assize could be a number of citizens, eventually settled at the number twelve, called to hear cases. They decided not on the basis of evidence but from information they had or could gather in the community. This group of neighbors was presumed to know the facts well enough to determine who was entitled to possession of disputed lands. A writ of assize could be issued on behalf of the king to commission this body of twelve to hear a dispute.

Eventually, the writs gave birth to FORMS OF ACTION for lawsuits concerning real property. For example, the assise of novel disseisin was a form of action for the recovery of lands after the claimant had been wrongfully dispossessed (disseised). The assise of nuisance was proper to secure the abatement of a NUISANCE or for monetary damages to compensate for the harm done by the nuisance.

ASSISTANCE, WRIT OF □ A court order issued to enforce an existing judgment. □

See also, Stephen B. Presser's essay on the Writs of Assistance Case.

ASSOCIATE JUSTICE □ The designation given to a judge who is not the chief or presiding justice of the court on which he or she sits. □

An associate judge is usually a member of an appellate court.

ASSOCIATION □ A group of people who work together for the pursuit of some joint enterprise, without a CHARTER but subject to the same procedures and methods utilized by CORPORATIONS. □

An association is essentially a body of persons who band together for a particular purpose. It is created by contract without any grant from the state. The term *association* is often used synonymously with company or society. A CLUB is a specific type of association. The two general types of associations are those that are formed and organized for profit and those that are not-for-profit.

Unlike a corporation, however, an association is not a legal entity apart from the people who compose it, unless otherwise provided by statute. It can be considered a legal entity to the extent that statutes recognize the separate existence of associations for particular purposes, such as the right of a particular association to sue or be sued.

In some states, statutes provide for and regulate only limited PARTNERSHIPS and corporations. In such states, associations operate not under statutory regulations, protection, and restrictions but rather under the general law of the land.

As in the case of a club, an association is deemed effectual if its objectives are lawful. An association organized for unlawful purposes is a nullity.

Distinctions between associations and other organizations

Corporations A corporation is a separate legal entity that is a creature of the state, has the power of perpetual existence, the right to contract under a corporate name, and has the power to convey and dispose of property as a collective whole. An association, however, lacks such powers but is merely an unincorporated society rarely considered to be a distinct and separate legal entity.

Partnerships A partnership is similar to an association since it involves the combination of people for the purpose of entering into a joint venture. Unlike a partnership, there is no implication that one member of an association is an agent for another member.

Other relationships An association is not the same as a *joint stock company* because a voluntary organization cannot issue stock.

Similarly, an association is distinguishable from a *common-law trust*, since such a trust may have no element of association, or shared purpose, between its beneficiaries.

Organization Although the state may regulate the activities of associations to some extent under its POLICE POWER, unlike a corporation an association's organization does not generally depend upon statutory provisions. Its organization is within the discretion of its associates who are permitted to combine for any legal purpose for the advancement of their particular interests. Associations are usually formed by contract based upon voluntary affiliation of individuals. The contract is subsequently embodied in the articles of association or constitution.

A constitution of an association regulates its powers, rights, duties, and liabilities. Generally, it is designed to define the members' privileges and duties. An association has a considerable amount of latitude in rule making so that its objectives can be accomplished. Rules adopted are generally in accordance with the association's goal and purpose for existence.

A constitution and bylaws are an enforceable contract between the members of an association. The rules adopted are binding upon all members, but they confer no legal rights or duties on nonmembers. Articles of association and bylaws may be amended or repealed as provided by the constitution of the association or by a majority vote of its membership if no express provisions concerning amendment exists.

Rights, powers, and liabilities The rights, powers, and liabilities of an association may be governed either by statute or by its own bylaws or constitution. In the absence of statutory provision or articles, an association determines rights, powers, and liabilities by common law or common usage by its members.

Generally, no check exists upon an association's right to transact its business in the manner it deems appropriate, as long as it does not act unlawfully or contrary to public policy.

In addition to the powers an association has by virtue of statute and its charter, it possesses any and all incidental powers that are necessary to give the greatest effect to the expressed powers.

An association does not ordinarily have corporate powers, such as the power to issue stock or hold property as an organization.

Unless expressly authorized by statute, an association has no legal capacity to enter into contracts since it is not a legal entity. Officers of an association may, however, make contracts in the name of the association that will be enforceable against them personally. A person who deals with an association as though it were a legal entity with the capacity to engage in business transactions cannot subsequently deny its power to contract.

In the area of liability for TORTS, an association is held to the same standard of care as any individual. It will generally be held accountable for the wrongful acts of its members or employ-

[t]he First Amendment protects political association as well as political expression . . .

WILLIAM J. BRENNAN, JR.

ees acting collectively while conducting the association's business. Mere membership in an association does not render individual members liable for the torts of an association. Similarly, an association is not responsible for a wrongful act committed upon a third person while engaged in a member's individual business.

Unless a statute clearly provides otherwise, an association cannot be held criminally responsible. If an association is convicted of a crime, individual members will not be punished, but the association will usually be forced to pay a fine.

Officers, agents, and committees An association may appoint or elect officers if it so chooses, but it may also exist without officers. Courts will not regulate the internal management of associations unless there is an indication of fraud or unless the association has exhausted all internal remedies in a case.

The powers and duties of officers are created either by usage or by being specifically enumerated in the association's bylaws or constitution. Generally, officers act as custodians of the funds and records of the association.

When acting within the scope of their authority, the officers and agents of an association may legally obligate an association and its members to fulfill the provisions of a contract executed by them.

The duties and liabilities of officers are based upon the idea that they are bound to act for the best and common interests of all members. Officers and agents should not, therefore, reap secret profits at the association's expense; they will be held personally liable to the association's members if they do so.

Membership The bylaws of an association designate rules with respect to membership. Unless the constitution or bylaws otherwise provide, membership is not transferable.

An association has exclusive and total control as to who may become a member, but it must not exercise its power arbitrarily or capriciously.

Judicial review is not available if an individual has been denied membership in an association, except where monetary or property rights come into play, or where membership is a matter of economic or professional necessity. If a person is elected to membership and subsequently denied admission arbitrarily, that individual may obtain judicial relief. Unless otherwise indicated by statute or association law, a member may withdraw his or her membership at any time, subject to any and all financial obligations owed to the association.

If someone holds a membership of financial value, the person may not be expelled from an association except in compliance with its laws. An association may establish its own individual rules relating to the expulsion of members. Courts will generally intervene in expulsion cases where an expulsion is illegal or where property rights are involved.

Actions by associations An association might have STANDING to sue, not as a separate legal entity but in the names of its individual members. It lacks such standing where it has no property interest of its own that may be affected by the alleged wrongs or injury, distinct from that of individual members.

Some statutes authorize an association to bring suit in its own name rather than in the name of its officers.

Where a common interest exists in the subject matter of a suit, some of the members of an association may be permitted to sue as representatives or agents of all the members. See also, Beneficial Associations.

ASSOCIATION HENRI CAPITANT The Association Henri Capitant, named after the French legal scholar, was founded in 1935 to enhance the study of elements of legal systems derived from the French legal system and other jurisdictions. The association focuses on civil law.

In addition to its annual meetings, the group conducts seminars on topics of interest to its membership of attorneys, judges, and law professors. The association's annual publications are *Recueil des Travaux de l' Association Henri Capitant* and *Travaux Capitant*.

ASSOCIATION OF AMERICAN LAW SCHOOLS The Association of American Law Schools (AALS) is an association of schools and describes its purpose as "the improvement of the legal profession through legal education." It is the law teachers' learned society and legal education's principal representative to the Federal government and other national higher education and learned society organizations.

History The AALS has its beginnings in a meeting held on August 29, 1900, at Saratoga Springs, New York. Thirty-two law schools became charter members of the association. James B. Thayer was its first president. Professor Michael H. Cardozo of Cornell University Law School became the association's first executive director in the summer of 1963 and established the association's national office. After operating as an unincorporated association for 70 years, the association was incorporated under the laws of the District of Columbia on February 2, 1971.

Along with the American Bar Association (ABA), AALS is recognized as one of the two national accrediting agencies for law by the Council on Post Secondary Accreditation.

Membership AALS is literally an association of law schools; currently of the 171 ABA-approved law schools, 139 are AALS members. After a school has graduated at least three annual classes, it is eligible to apply for membership. Compliance with the rules of membership is determined through a three or four person inspection team. Recommendations for admission to membership are made by the Executive Committee, upon advice of the Accreditation Committee. Membership is attained by action of the House of Representatives.

Governance The plenary legislative body is the House of Representatives. Each member school has one vote and designates a member of its faculty to represent it in the House. The House customarily meets twice during the association's annual meeting.

The Executive Committee has the responsibility for conducting the affairs of the association in the interim between the annual meetings of the House of Representatives. The president, president-elect, immediate past-president and six elected committee members constitute the Executive Committee; they are elected by the House of Representatives. The term of the president is one year; the president-elect becomes the president on completion of a year's service as president-elect. Each year two faculty members of member schools are elected to serve three-year terms as members of the Executive Committee. The Executive Committee customarily meets five times each year—in February at the time and place of the ABA mid-year meeting; in June at the end of the Law School Admission Council's annual meeting; in August at the time and place of the annual meeting of the American Bar Association; in early to mid-November at a place of its own choosing; and in January at the time and place of the AALS annual meeting.

Staff The AALS full-time staff currently numbers eight, including the executive director, associate director and assistant director. During the summer months, two or three editors are employed to assist in the editing of the *Directory of Law Teachers.* All of the staff is based at the national office.

Finances About three-fourths of the association's income is derived from dues paid by member schools. Fees support certain services and functions, such as the annual meeting and Faculty Appointments Register. The dues paid by member schools are graduated on the basis of student enrollment.

Committee, section and other divisions Standing and other special committees are established by action of the Executive Committee and their membership appointed by the president. The traditionally active committees are Committee on Academic Freedom and Tenure, Accreditation Committee, Library Committee, Committee on Sections, Committee on Professional Development, and Government Relations Committee. The one standing joint committee is that with the Canadian Association of Law Teachers.

In 1972 the Executive Committee changed the operating structure so as to establish sections and to decrease greatly the number of committees and to eliminate entirely the Round Table Councils. There are forty-five sections, composed of members of the faculty of member schools who wish to join together to present a program at the annual meeting on a subject of common interest and to conduct other activities. Anyone may become an associate member. The membership of a section selects its own presiding officer and executive committee. The principal support for section activities are the general funds of the association; but several sections also collect dues from members. The association's assistant director and her administrative assistant staff the sections. Mailing lists for newsletters and other communications to section members are maintained at the national office.

Organizational affiliations The AALS is a member or has some other affiliation with the American Council on Education, American Council of Learned Societies, American Association for the Advancement of the Humanities, Council on Legal Education Opportunity, Council on Postsecondary Accreditation, Council on Specialized Accrediting Agencies, National Association of Bar Executives, and National Association of College and University Attorneys.

Annual meeting For the last half century the annual meetings of the association have been held between Christmas and New Year's Day. Since January 1979, the annual meeting is held during the first week in January. A number of deans, law teachers and librarians from member schools, nonmember ABA-approved schools, Canadian law schools and some other foreign law schools attend the association's annual meeting. The address at the annual association luncheon and the papers given at the association plenary session generally are highlights of the annual meeting program. Six half-day sessions are devoted to programs organized and presented by the association's forty-five sections. Many education-related organizations have a meeting or program or both during the association's annual meeting. In addition, a number of law schools hold alumni breakfasts, luncheons, dinners, or receptions.

Other meetings The association regularly schedules one other national event—the Faculty Recruitment Conference. Begun in 1974, this conference is held on the first Friday and Saturday in December. It is attended by the deans and members of the faculty of law schools seeking to interview potential candidates for their faculty and by persons who have registered in the Faculty Appointments Register their interest in considering appointment to a law faculty. The conference is under the management of the assistant director.

Workshops and teaching conferences Each year the AALS presents from four to six workshops and teaching conferences addressing the professional concerns of legal educators and administrators. These range in duration from two to five days and are held in various locations throughout the country.

Publications

Journal of Legal Education The *Journal of Legal Education* is in its fourth decade of publication. Through the courtesy of the West Publishing Company and Foundation Press, the *Journal* is made available without cost to the full-time members of the faculty of member schools who wish it. Editorial responsibility for the *Journal* is lodged with Dean John E. Murray, Jr. of the University of Pittsburgh. Professor Richard H. Seeburger of the University of Pittsburgh is the book review editor. An advisory committee of twelve deans and faculty gives general policy guidance. The quarterly publication is concerned largely with issues of legal education.

Proceedings The annual *Proceedings* of the association contain the reports of the committees and sections, the text of the address at the association luncheon, and the transcript of the sessions of the House of Representatives. From time to time, they contain the report of a project or research committee. The *Proceedings* also contain the audited financial report on the association, the current bylaws, the list of presidents of the association, the agenda memoranda for the House of Representatives' meetings and program of the annual meeting. The *Proceedings* are edited by the assistant director. They are distributed to member schools and are available on microfiche from Brookhaven Press.

AALS Newsletter The association newsletter is published four times a year—February, May, September, and November. Through the courtesy of Foundation Press, the newsletter is furnished without cost to the faculty of member schools. The *AALS Newsletter* is edited by the assistant director.

Research Bulletin In May 1976, the association launched the *Research Bulletin,* a newsletter that is published twice a year. It calls attention to the Federal government and foundation programs offering grants and fellowships of special interest to law schools and law teachers. The *Bulletin* is edited by the associate director, who interviews the grant officers at the various agencies to learn of their special interests as far as law and legal education are concerned so that law schools and law teachers making application may do so with knowledge of the special interests or emphases of the granting agency. The *Bulletin* is made available without charge to all full-time faculty of member schools.

Legal Affairs Manual In the fall of 1976, the Law School Admission Council and AALS joined in publishing the *Legal Affairs Manual*. It contains a checklist of the impact of Federal statutes and regulations affecting the operation of law schools, memoranda analyzing the impact of particular statutes and regulations on law schools and suggesting the ways in which these schools might respond, the text of pertinent Federal statutes and regulations, and a litigation bulletin summarizing state and Federal cases of particular interest to legal education. The *Manual* and its supplements are distributed without cost to schools that are members of the Law School Admission Council, which includes all AALS member schools.

Prelaw Handbook This *Handbook* is the publication of the Law School Admission Council and AALS. It contains general information on the legal profession and law schools, a description of the program of each ABA-approved law school and admissions profile for the most recently admitted class for the great majority of these schools.

Placement Bulletin In the fall of 1976, the association established the *Placement Bulletin*. This *Bulletin,* published six times a year, carries the listing of openings for law teaching and professional administrative positions and also announces dean searches at accredited law schools, other law schools and other schools and colleges within the universities. The assistant director edits this *Bulletin*.

Services

Faculty Appointments Register Upon the payment of a fee a person interested in a full-time faculty or a full-time professional staff position with a law school may register that interest by completing a structured one-page resumé. These resumés are duplicated and distributed to

Through our great good fortune, in our youth our hearts were touched with fire. The Law, wherein, as in a magic mirror, we see reflected not only our own lives, but the lives of all men that have been! When I think on this majestic theme, my eyes dazzle.

OLIVER WENDELL HOLMES, JR.

the law schools, which use them as a basis for re-cruiting additions to the faculty. The registrants receive a copy of the *Placement Bulletin* without additional cost. Supplementing this service is the register for faculty who wish to consider invitations as visiting faculty during the coming school year, the register of full-time faculty members who will retire from teaching at the end of the current school year, and the register of those foreign law teachers who wish to consider invitations to be a visiting member of a United States law faculty. The information gathered for these three registers is distributed in the form of memoranda to the deans of all member and non-member service fee paid schools.

ASSOCIATION OF AMERICAN TRIAL LAWYERS
See Association of Trial Lawyers of America.

ASSOCIATION OF IMMIGRATION AND NATIONALITY LAWYERS
The Association of Immigration and Nationality Lawyers (AINL) was formed in 1946 to enhance the administration of justice in the United States in the areas of immigration and nationality law. Its 975 members are lawyers specializing in the field.

The association has twenty local groups. It has the following committees: American Citizenship, Amicus Curiae, Ethics, Grievances, Immigration Legislation, Unlawful Practice of the Law, and Visa Practice. It publishes the *AINL Immigration Newsletter* (bimonthly) and holds meetings in January and May.

ASSOCIATION OF INSURANCE ATTORNEYS
Founded in 1937, the Association of Insurance Attorneys (AIA) is an organization of trial lawyers who have at least five years of experience in the field of insurance law and who meet the association's standards for knowledge and ability to provide quality services. The association maintains current biographical data on each of its members.

The association publishes an annual roster, a newsletter, and monographs. It holds annual meetings in the spring.

ASSOCIATION OF INTERSTATE COMMERCE COMMISSION PRACTITIONERS
The Association of Interstate Commerce Commission (ICC) Practitioners was founded in 1929 to promote the proper administration of the Interstate Commerce Act and related legislation; to uphold the honor of practice before the Interstate Commerce Commission; to cooperate in fostering increased educational opportu-

nities and maintaining high standards of professional conduct; and to encourage cordial intercourse among the practitioners. Its members are lawyers and transportation and traffic specialists who have been admitted to practice before the ICC. The association has thirteen standing committees, thirty-three local chapters, and a staff of six. Committees include Admission to Practice, Appointment of ICC Commissioners, Budget of the ICC, Education for Practice, Legislation, and Professional Ethics and Grievances. The association publishes the *ICC Practitioners Journal* (bimonthly), *Association Highlights* (bimonthly), *Transportation Law Seminar Papers and Proceedings* (semiannually), and a *Directory of Members and Constitution and Bylaws* (biyearly). Periodically, the association also publishes a *Code of Ethics, Abstracts of Supreme Court Decisions Interpreting the Interstate Commerce Act,* and *Consolidated Index to Decisions of the Interstate Commerce Commission.*

The association holds annual meetings as well as annual transportation law seminars in the spring and fall.

ASSOCIATION OF LEGAL ADMINISTRATORS
The Association of Legal Administrators (ALA) was formed in 1971 to promote the exchange of information regarding the administration and management problems peculiar to legal organizations, including private law offices, corporate legal departments, governmental legal and judicial organizations, and public service legal groups; to provide information on the value and availability of professional administrators; to improve the standards and qualifications for such administrators; to develop continuing-education programs; and to participate in any other way in the advancement of the art of legal administration.

The association compiles statistics, operates a placement service, provides a speakers bureau, and publishes *The Legal Administrator* (monthly) and a semiannual directory. It holds annual meetings in the spring.

ASSOCIATION OF LIFE INSURANCE COUNSEL
The Association of Life Insurance Counsel was founded in 1913 to further the education of its members; to increase the members' knowledge of those areas of the law that affect insurance by undertaking the research, preparation, and dissemination to its members of legal studies in such areas; to promote efficiency in legal service to life insurance companies; and to encourage cordial relations among the legal representatives of life insurance companies.

The members of the association are attorneys who provide general legal services to life insurance companies. The association holds its annual meetings in May.

ASSOCIATION OF STUDENT INTERNATIONAL LAW SOCIETIES

The Association of Student International Law Societies (ASILS) is an association of autonomous student international law societies, each with its own schedule of activities in addition to those of the association. The ASILS was founded in 1962 by five charter member schools, "believing that the principles of international law should be more fully understood and recognized" and "determined to educate ourselves and our fellow students in the principles and purposes of international law, international organizations and institutions, and comparison of legal systems." Membership has grown to include international law societies at over 100 law schools throughout the world.

The association's varied activities include the publication of a newsletter, assistance in locating employment opportunities, publication of an international law journal, and the collection and dissemination of program information for the benefit of member societies. The association links the editors of twenty-five student international law journals and participates in the regional meetings of the American Society of International Law, many of which are organized and administered by individual student societies.

An important goal of the association is to develop clear ties with foreign law students and schools, with a view to integrating the student societies abroad into one international association. It hopes in this way to foster cooperation between the world's future lawyers and public officials. Its most noteworthy activity in this connection is the Philip C. Jessup International Law Moot Court Competition. See also, Philip C. Jessup International Law Moot Court Competition.

The association publishes the *Directory of Student International Law Journals* (annually), the *Handbook for Student International Law Societies*, and a quarterly newsletter. It holds an annual meeting in April in Washington, DC. with the American Society of International Law. See also, American Society of International Law.

ASSOCIATION OF THE CUSTOMS BAR

Founded in 1917, the Association of the Customs Bar (ACB) is an association of attorneys admitted to practice before the U.S. Court of Customs and Patent Appeals. The association is affiliated with the International Bar Association and the Inter-American Bar Association.

The association has committees on Ethics, Practice, Procedure, Legislation, and the Unlawful Practice of the Law. It holds semiannual meetings.

ASSOCIATION OF TRIAL LAWYERS OF AMERICA

The Association of Trial Lawyers of America (ATLA) was founded in 1946 to help protect the interests of people who seek redress for injury and to protect individuals from abuses of power. To this end, the association promotes the fair administration of justice by advancing the science of jurisprudence, by training attorneys in the skills of advocacy, by upholding and improving the adversary system and trial by jury, by promoting the honor and dignity of the legal profession, and by fostering a feeling of brotherhood among the members of the bar. Association activities include seminars and conferences; the presentation of awards; an environmental law essay contest; and research on topics, such as insurance, product liability, and medical malpractice. Services provided by the association include a specialization certification program for trial skills, statistical compilation, a placement service, and the Roscoe Pound Library of law, philosophy, and history. The members are lawyers, judges, law professors, and students involved in a phase of advocacy.

The association has fifty-one state groups, thirty local groups, and a staff of more than seventy-five. Association sections include Admiralty Law, Aviation Law, Commercial Law, Criminal Law, Environmental Law, Family Law, Labor Law, Military Law, Railroad Law, Tort Law, and Worker's Compensation Law.

The association publishes *Trial* magazine (monthly), *ATLA Law Reporter Journal* (biennially), an annual directory, and monographs on various legal topics.

ASSOCIATION OF U.S. MEMBERS OF THE INTERNATIONAL INSTITUTE OF SPACE LAW

The Association of U.S. Members of the International Institute of Space Law supports the participation of U.S. members of the institute so as to better contribute to the handling of legal problems that have arisen in the context of the exploration of outer space. The institute is a component of the International Astronautical Federation.

The association holds two meetings each year: one in the spring in conjunction with the American Society of International Law, and the other in the fall, usually abroad in conjunction with the institute's annual Space Law colloquium held during the Congress of the International Astronautical Federation.

ASSUMPSIT   [*Latin, "He undertook" or "he promised."*]

☐ A promise by which someone assumes or undertakes an obligation to another person. The promise may be oral or in writing, but it is not under SEAL. It is express when the person making the promise puts it into distinct and specific language, but it may also be implied because the law sometimes imposes obligations based on the conduct of the parties or the circumstances of their dealings. ☐

Action of assumpsit *Assumpsit* was one of the common-law FORMS OF ACTION. It determined the right to sue and the relief available for someone who claimed that a contract had been breached.

When the common law was developing in England, there was no legal remedy for the breach of a contract. Glanvill, a famous legal scholar, wrote just before the year 1200 that "[i]t is not the custom of the court of the lord king to protect private agreements, nor does it concern itself with such contracts as can be considered private agreements." Ordinary lawsuits could be heard in local courts, but the king was primarily interested in royal rights and the disputes of his noblemen. As commerce began to develop, the king's courts did allow two forms of action for breach of contract—the actions of COVENANT and DEBT. Covenant could be maintained only if the agreement had been made in writing and under seal and only if the action of debt was not available. One could sue on the debt only if the obligations in the contract had been fully performed and the breach was no more than a failure to pay a specific sum of money.

Finally, in 1370, a plaintiff sought to sue a defendant who had undertaken to cure his horse but treated it so negligently that the horse died, and the action was allowed. In 1375, another man was permitted to sue a surgeon who had maimed him while trying to cure him. These cases showed a new willingness to permit a lawsuit for monetary damages arising directly from the failure to live up to an agreement. For the next hundred years the courts began to allow lawsuits for badly performed obligations but not for a complete failure to perform what was required by contract. Unexpectedly, this restriction was abandoned also, and a new form of action was recognized by the courts, an action in *special assumpsit* for breach of an express agreement.

Special assumpsit gave a new legal right to parties who could not sue on a debt. Gradually, it became possible to sue in *assumpsit* if the defendant owed a debt and then violated a fresh promise to pay it. This action came to be known as *indebitatus assumpsit*, which means "being indebted, he promised."

As time passed, courts were willing to assume that the fresh promise had been made and to impose obligations as if it had. This allowed lawsuits for a whole range of contract breaches, not just those recognized by an action on the debt or in *special assumpsit*. If the plaintiff could claim that services had been performed or goods had been delivered to the defendant, then the law would assume that the defendant had promised to pay for them. Any failure to do so gave the plaintiff the right to sue in *assumpsit*. This development allowed such a wide range of lawsuits based on promises to private parties that it came to be known as *general assumpsit*.

Eventually, the right to sue was extended even to situations where the defendant had no intention to pay but it was only fair that he or she be made to do so. This form was called *assumpsit on quantum meruit*. *Special assumpsit, general assumpsit* (or *indebitatus assumpsit*), and *quantum meruit* are all *ex contractu*, arising out of a contract. Their development is the foundation of our modern law of CONTRACTS.

ASSUMPTION   ☐ The undertaking of the repayment of a debt or the performance of an obligation owed by another. ☐

When a purchaser of real property assumes the MORTGAGE of the seller, he or she agrees to adopt the mortgage debt, becoming personally liable for its full repayment in case of default. If a FORECLOSURE sale of the mortgaged property does not satisfy the debt, the purchaser remains financially responsible for the outstanding balance.

In contrast, a purchaser who takes subject to the seller's mortgage agrees to repay the mortgage debt, but that person's liability is limited only to the amount that the mortgaged property is sold for in the case of foreclosure. If the property is sold for less than the mortgage debt, the mortgagee must seek the remaining balance due from the seller, the original mortgagor.

ASSUMPTION OF RISK   ☐ A DEFENSE, facts offered by a party against whom proceedings have been instituted to diminish a plaintiff's cause of action or defeat recovery to an action in NEGLIGENCE, which entails proving that the

When men are pure, laws are useless; when men are corrupt, laws are broken.

BENJAMIN DISRAELI

plaintiff knew of a dangerous condition and voluntarily exposed himself or herself to it. □

Under the rules of FEDERAL CIVIL PROCEDURE, assumption of the risk is an AFFIRMATIVE DEFENSE that the defendant in a negligence action must plead and prove. The doctrine of assumption of risk is also known as VOLENTI NON FIT INJURIA.

Situations that encompass assumption of the risk have been classified into three broad categories. In its principal sense, assumption of the risk signifies that the plaintiff, in advance, has consented to relieve the defendant of an obligation of conduct toward him or her, and to take a chance of injury from a known risk ensuing from what the defendant is to do or leave undone. The consequence is that the defendant is unburdened of all legal duty to the plaintiff, and, therefore, cannot be held liable in negligence.

A second situation occurs when the plaintiff voluntarily enters into some relation with the defendant, knowing that the defendant will not safeguard the plaintiff against the risk. The plaintiff can then be viewed as tacitly or implicitly consenting to the negligence, as in the case of riding in a car with knowledge that the steering apparatus is defective, which relieves the defendant of the duty that would ordinarily exist.

In the third type of situation, the plaintiff, cognizant of a risk previously created by the negligence of the defendant, proceeds voluntarily to confront it, as where he or she has been provided with an article that the plaintiff knows to be hazardous, and continues to use it after the danger has been detected. If this is a voluntary choice, the plaintiff is deemed to have accepted the situation and assented to free the defendant of all obligations.

In all three situations, the plaintiff might be acting in a reasonable manner, and not be negligent in the venture, because the advantages of his or her conduct outweigh the peril. The plaintiff's decision might be correct, and he or she might even act with unusual circumspection because he or she is cognizant of the danger that will be encountered. If that is the case, the defense operates to refute the defendant's negligence by denying the duty of care that would invoke this liability, and the plaintiff does not recover because the defendant's conduct was not wrongful towards the plaintiff.

With respect to the second and third situations, however, the plaintiff's conduct in confronting a known risk might be in itself unreasonable, because the danger is disproportionate to the advantage the plaintiff is pursuing, as where, with other transportation available, the individual chooses to ride with an intoxicated driver. If this occurs, the plaintiff's conduct is a type of CONTRIBUTORY NEGLIGENCE, an act or omission by the plaintiff that constitutes a deficiency in ordinary CARE, which concurs with the defendant's negligence to comprise the direct or PROXIMATE CAUSE of injury. In such cases, the defenses of assumption of risk and contributory negligence overlap.

In this area of intersection, the courts have held that the defendant can employ either defense, or both. Since ordinarily either is sufficient to bar the action, the defenses have been distinguished on the theory that assumption of risk consists of awareness of the peril and intelligent submission to it, while contributory negligence entails some deviation from the standard of conduct of the REASONABLE PERSON, irrespective of any remonstration or unawareness displayed by the plaintiff. The two concepts can coexist when the plaintiff unreasonably decides to incur the risk, or can exist independently of each other. The distinction, when one exists, is likely to be one between risks that were in fact known to the plaintiff, and risks that the individual merely might have discovered by the exercise of ordinary care.

Express agreement The parties can enter into a written agreement absolving the defendant from any obligation of care for the benefit of the plaintiff, and liability for the consequence of conduct that would otherwise constitute negligence. In the ordinary case, PUBLIC POLICY does not prevent the parties from contracting in regard to whether the plaintiff will be responsible for the maintenance of personal safety. A person who enters into a lease, or rents an animal, or enters into a variety of similar relations entailing free and open bargaining between the parties, can assent to relieving the defendant of the obligation to take precautions, and thereby render the defendant free from liability for negligence.

The courts have refused to uphold such agreements, however, if one party possesses a patent disadvantage in bargaining power. For example, a contract exempting an employer from all liability for negligence toward employees is VOID as against public policy. A CARRIER transporting cargo or passengers for hire cannot evade its public responsibility in this manner, even though the agreement limits recovery to an amount less than the probable DAMAGES. The contract has been upheld, however, where it represents a realistic attempt to assess a value as liquidated or ascertained damages in advance, and the carrier graduates its rates in accordance with such value, so that complete protection would be available to the plaintiff upon paying a higher rate. The same principles apply to innkeepers, public warehousemen, and other professional BAILEES—such as garage, parking lot, and checkroom attendants—on the basis that the indispensable necessity for their services deprives the customer of all meaningful equal bargaining power.

An express agreement can relieve the defendant from liability for negligence only if the plaintiff comprehends its terms. If the plaintiff is not cognizant of the provision in his or her contract, and a reasonable person in the same position would not have known of it, it is not binding upon the individual, and the agreement fails for lack of mutual assent. The expressed terms of the agreement must apply to the particular misconduct of the defendant. Such contracts generally do not encompass gross, willful, wanton, or reckless negligence or any conduct that constitutes an intentional tort.

Implied acceptance of risk In a majority of cases, the consent to assume the risk is implied from the conduct of the plaintiff under the circumstances. The basis of the defense is not contract, but consent, and it is available in many cases where no express agreement exists.

By entering voluntarily into any relationship or transaction where the negligence of the defendant is evident, the plaintiff is deemed to accept and consent to it, to assume responsibility for personal safety, and unburden the defendant of the obligation. Spectators at certain sports events assume all the known risks of injury from flying objects. Plaintiffs who enter business premises as INVITEES and detect dangerous conditions can be deemed to assume the risks when they continue voluntarily to encounter them.

Knowledge of risk The plaintiff will not normally be regarded as assuming any risk of either conditions or activities of which he or she has no knowledge. The plaintiff must not merely create the danger but must comprehend and appreciate the danger itself.

The applicable standard is basically subjective in nature, tailored to the particular plaintiff and his or her situation, as opposed to the objective standard of the reasonable person of ordinary prudence, which is employed in contributory negligence. If, because of age, lack of information, or experience, the plaintiff does not comprehend the risk entailed in a known situation, the individual will not be regarded as consenting to assume it. Failure to exercise ordinary care to discover the danger is not encompassed within assumption of risk, but in the defense of contributory negligence.

An entirely subjective standard, however, allows the plaintiff considerable latitude in testifying that he or she did not know or comprehend the risk. To counteract the adverse effects of the application of this liberal standard, courts have interjected an objective element by holding that a plaintiff cannot evade responsibility by alleging that he or she did not comprehend a risk that must have been obvious.

A denial of cognizance of certain matters that are common knowledge in the community is not credible, unless a satisfactory explanation exists. As in the case of negligence itself, there are particular risks that any adult must appreciate, such as falling on ice, lifting heavy objects, and driving a defective vehicle. In addition, a plaintiff situated for a considerable length of time in the immediate vicinity of a hazardous condition is deemed to have detected and to comprehend the ordinary risks entailed in that situation. If the person completely understands the risk, the fact that or she has temporarily forgotten it does not provide protection.

Even where there is knowledge and appreciation of a risk, the plaintiff might not be prohibited from recovery where the circumstances introduce a new factor. The fact that the plaintiff is totally cognizant of one risk, such as the speed of a vehicle, does not signify that he or she assumes another of which he or she is unaware, such as the intoxication of the driver.

Although knowledge and understanding of the risk incurred are encompassed within the concept of assumption of the risk, it is possible for the plaintiff to assume risks of whose specific existence he or she is unaware—to consent to venture into unknown conditions. In a majority of instances, the undertaking is express, although it can arise by implication in a few cases. A guest who accepts a gratuitous ride in an automobile has been regarded as assuming the risk of defects in the vehicle, unknown to the driver.

Voluntary assumption The doctrine of assumption of risk does not bar the plaintiff from recovery unless the individual's decision is free and voluntary. There must be some manifestation of consent to relieve the defendant of the obligation of reasonable conduct. A risk is not viewed as assumed if it appears from the plaintiff's words, or from the circumstances, that he or she does not actually consent. If the plaintiff relinquishes his or her better judgment upon assurances that the situation is safe, or that it will be remedied, or upon a promise of protection, the plaintiff does not assume the risk, unless the danger is so patent and so extreme that there can be no reasonable reliance upon the assurance.

Even where the plaintiff does not protest, the risk is not assumed where the conduct of the defendant has provided the individual with no reasonable alternative, causing him or her to act under DURESS. Where the defendant creates a peril, such as a burning building, those who dash into it to save their own property or the lives or property of others do not assume the risk where the alternative is to permit the threatened injury to occur. If, however, the danger is disproportionate to the value of the interest to be protected, the plaintiff might be charged with contributory negligence in regard to his or her own unreasonable conduct. Where a reasonably safe alternative exists, the plaintiff's selection of the hazardous route is free and can constitute both contributory negligence and assumption of risk.

The defendant has a legal duty, which he or she is not at liberty to refuse to perform, to exercise reasonable care for the plaintiff's safety, so that the plaintiff has a parallel legal right to demand that care. The plaintiff does not assume the risk while using the defendant's services or facilities, notwithstanding knowledge of the peril, where he or she acts reasonably, and the defendant has provided no reasonable alternative other than to refrain completely from exercising the right. A common carrier, or other public utility, which has negligently furnished a dangerously defective set of steps, cannot assert assumption of risk against a patron who uses the steps as the sole convenient means of access to the company's premises. The same principle applies to a city maintaining a public roadway or sidewalk, or other public area that the plaintiff has a right to use, and premises onto which the plaintiff has a contractual right to enter. Where a reasonable alternative is available, the plaintiff's recalcitrance in unreasonably encountering danger constitutes contributory negligence, as well as assumption of risk.

Violation of statute The plaintiff still assumes the risk where the defendant's negligence consists of the violation of a statute. A guest who accepts a nighttime ride in a vehicle with inoperative lights has been regarded as consenting to relieve the defendant of the duty of complying with the standard established by the statute for protection, and cannot recover for injuries. Particular statutes, however, such as child labor acts and safety statutes for the benefit of employees, safeguard the plaintiff against personal inability to protect himself or herself due to improvident judgment or incapability to resist certain pressures. Since the basic objective of such states would be frustrated if the plaintiff were allowed to assume the risk, it is generally held that the plaintiff cannot do so, either expressly or impliedly.

Abolition of the defense Numerous states have abrogated the defense of assumption of risk in automobile cases through the enactment of no-fault INSURANCE legislation or COMPARATIVE NEGLIGENCE acts. The theories underlying its abolition are that it serves no purpose that is not completely disposed of by the other doctrines, it increases the likelihood of confusion, and it bars recovery in meritorious cases.

Assumption of risk is not a defense under state WORKER'S COMPENSATION laws or in Federal Employer's Liability Act actions. The worker's compensation laws abolished the defense in recognition of the severe economic pressure a threatened loss of employment exerted upon workers. A worker was deemed to have assumed the risk even when acting under a direct order that conveyed an explicit or implicit threat of discharge for insubordination.

The Federal Employers' Liability Act (45 U.S.C.A. § 51 et seq. [1908]) was intended to furnish an equitable method of compensation for railroad workers injured within the scope of their employment. The act provides that an employee is not deemed to have assumed the risks of employment where injury or death ensued totally or partially from the negligence of the carrier's officers, agents, or employees, or from the carrier's violation of any statute enacted for the safety of employees, where the infraction contributed to the employee's injury or death. This doctrine was abolished because of the extreme hardship it imposed on workers who frequently encountered the hazards inherent in this line of employment.

ASSURED ☐ A person protected by INSURANCE coverage against loss or damage stipulated by the provisions of a policy purchased from an insurance company or an UNDERWRITER. ☐

Assured is synonymous with insured.

ASYLUM ☐ The offer by a country of a place of refuge or protection within its borders or under its jurisdiction to an individual who is not a citizen. ☐

Political asylum is the discretionary power of a nation to provide shelter and protection to an individual who defects from his or her native land for political reasons. No nation has a legally enforceable duty to anyone to provide political asylum. *Territorial asylum* refers to that protection afforded within the sheltering nation's geographical borders. *Diplomatic asylum* is protection that is extended beyond the physical

UPI

Joseph Stalin's daughter, Svetlana Alliluyeva, sought asylum in the United States in 1967 because she wanted "to seek the self-expression" that had been denied to her "for so long in Russia."

boundaries of the sheltering nation, but within its embassies, consulates, legations, and warships.

Ordinarily, only political fugitives, not fugitives from criminal justice are afforded asylum. See also, entry on International Law and John H. Jackson's essay on International Law.

ASYLUM, DIPLOMATIC ☐ Individuals seeking refuge within the confines of foreign embassies and legations, if permitted to stay, obtain what is known as diplomatic asylum. In contrast, political or territorial asylum is found when a state acts to receive into its own territory persons seeking refuge from the judicial power of another state. Those individuals securing diplomatic asylum are forced to remain within the compound until safe passage out of the local state is arranged through diplomatic negotiations. ☐

Because diplomatic asylum represents a limitation of the territorial jurisdiction of the local state, the existence of such a right under international law is subject to much controversy. For instance, the United States and the United Kingdom recognize such a right only for humanitarian reasons. Similarly, few states accord diplomatic asylum to common criminals. Outside of Latin America, the right exists primarily because of treaty law protecting the inviolability of diplomatic premises, such as that established by the Vienna Convention on Diplomatic Relations. See also, John H. Jackson's essay on International Law.

ASYLUMS ☐ Establishments that exist for the aid and protection of individuals in need of assistance due to disability, such as INSANE PERSONS, those who are physically handicapped, or persons who are unable to properly care for themselves, such as orphans. ☐

The term *asylum* has been used, in constitutional and legislative provisions, to encompass all institutions that are established and supported by the general public.

An *insane asylum* is one in which custody and care is provided for people with mental problems. An orphanage is an asylum set up as a shelter or refuge for INFANTS and children who do not have parents or guardians.

Establishment and maintenance In the absence of constitutional restrictions, the state is permitted to fulfill its obligation to aid or support individuals in need of care by contributions to care facilities established or maintained by political subdivisions and private charity. In addition, the state may inaugurate a state asylum, delegating the management responsibility thereof to a private CORPORATION. Some authorities view contributions to asylums of religious organizations or private enterprises as violative of constitutional prohibitions of government aid to parochial institutions or individuals. Express exceptions can be made by state statute or constitution for the payment of funds for designated purposes to specific types of asylums. In situations that are embraced by such exceptions, the contribution that the state makes to the maintenance of the asylum is not regarded as a charity but as part of the state's duty to aid its citizens who cannot do so themselves.

Public asylums

Ownership and status An asylum founded and supported by the state has the status of a public institution. The state has the true ownership of the property that a state asylum occupies, and the character of the state's interest in such property is dependent upon the terms of the DEED or CONTRACT under which it is held for the institution.

When a county conveys property to a board of directors of an insane asylum acting as TRUSTEES, title is not vested in the state to the extent that the power to reconvey the land to the county is restricted. In a situation where property has been conveyed for a particular purpose connected to the operation of the asylum, it has been held that the trustees are permitted to reconvey the property to the county for the establishment of a general hospital.

Location and support Where no constitutional provision prescribing the location of

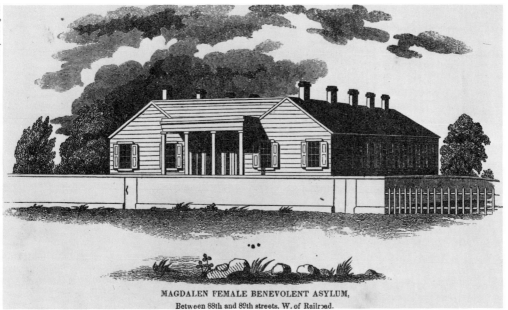

MAGDALEN FEMALE BENEVOLENT ASYLUM,
Between 88th and 89th streets, W. of Railroad.

This 1844 engraving of the Magdalen Female Benevolent Asylum in New York characteristically shows the asylum of that period as physically removed from the rest of society by its location and wall.

public institutions exists, the state may designate a location or arrange for a place to be found by a specially appointed committee or commission.

A state asylum may be funded either by general state taxation or through an allocation of a portion or all of the costs among political subdivisions or to the inmates of the asylum.

Regulation Under the POLICE POWER of the state, the establishment and regulation of private asylums are subject to the state legislative authority. Such powers may be delegated to political subdivisions and administrative agencies. If legislative authority is delegated in such situations, guidelines and standards for regulatory enforcement must be present.

In order for a regulation to be valid, it must be reasonable, applied uniformly, and it must not infringe upon constitutional rights. A state or political subdivision cannot proscribe the lawful operation of an asylum or care facility, or create or enforce unreasonable or arbitrary requirements regarding its construction or physical location. Similarly, it cannot make capricious requirements relating to the classification and nature of individuals to be admitted. Regulations and practices must comply with constitutional and statutory provisions.

The governing board of an asylum or institutional care facility is empowered to create all necessary rules and BYLAWS and is responsible for its policies and general administration. The courts will neither prescribe rules nor alter those created by the authorities, unless they are unreasonable or inappropriate.

Investigation and inspection The legislature has the exclusive power to order an investigation of the management of an asylum or care facility. Private individuals may not conduct an investigation. When an investigation is initiated, the institution's governing board has the power to set forth regulations regarding relations with employees and patients and access to the records. A nursing home operator must make records kept pursuant to a public health statute available for inspection by authorized public officials. In addition, a private facility can be required to turn over annual fiscal reports to a regulatory agency.

Statutory requirements for the safety of individuals in institutions are imposed and must be observed. Similarly, standards concerning the type of personnel needed to care for the patients are usually set forth, but they must not be unreasonable.

Licenses Ordinarily, a LICENSE is required to operate an asylum or institutional care facility to ensure that minimal health and safety requirements imposed by law are observed. When a license is necessary, operation of a facility without one may be enjoined and, under certain statutes, a contract made by an unlicensed person is void, which would bar recovery for NECESSARIES provided for individuals. The procedure for procuring a license is governed by statute, and the state licensing authorities have the discretion concerning whether or not it should be granted. Where there is a final decision, determinations in licensing proceedings may be subject to judicial review. The proceedings on judicial review are generally regulated by statutory provisions that limit the proceedings to those initiated by aggrieved individuals.

Under some statutes, before an institutional care facility can be built, a certificate of need, which establishes approval of its construction by a public agency, is required.

Officers and employees   The rules that generally apply to public service employees govern the status of officers and employees of institutions. Statutory provisions may provide for the termination of such officers and employees.

Inmates, patients, and residents
Statutory provisions, administrative regulations, and discretion of its administrator govern the admission of inmates or patients to a public institution. When a public asylum is founded for the reception of a specific class of individuals, anyone in the designated class may be admitted.

The law is for the protection of the weak more than the strong.

SIR WILLIAM ERLE

A constitutional provision that requires the advancement and support of certain specified institutions does not mandate that the state incur the total cost of maintaining institutionalized individuals. The expedience of soliciting repayment from responsible people for the expense of care, support, and maintenance of a patient cannot be based exclusively upon whether the commitment is voluntary or involuntary. In addition, recovery might be permitted for services actually rendered.

The individual in charge of an asylum that stands IN LOCO PARENTIS to infants upon their admission has custody of the children who are committed to its care. Unless otherwise prohibited by statute, qualified people may examine the records of children in private institutions when so authorized by its administrators. Where a statute exists that guarantees the adult residents of proprietary adult homes the right to manage their own financial affairs, their handling of such matters cannot be subject to judicial challenge. An institution may be mandated to meet the individual needs of its patients under rules that monitor the operation of private care facilities for the purpose of the Medicaid program.

Appropriate regulations may govern the visitation rights of individuals in an asylum.

An individual may be dismissed from the institution for conduct proscribed by the bylaws under penalty of expulsion, provided the person is first afforded notice and an opportunity to be heard.

Contracts for care and occupancy
The admission of an individual to a public institution for care can be the subject of a contract between the patient and the institution concerning the transfer of property to the institution. Even without an express agreement, however, the circumstances may bring about a quasi contract to provide for services rendered.

An individual may not rescind an occupancy agreement and regain an admission fee without proof of a breach of contract by the institution.

Management   The management of public institutions is usually entrusted to specific governing bodies or officers. The appropriate body can hire employees to operate the asylum but cannot relinquish its management responsibilities. Physicians who wish to visit patients in private nursing homes can be excluded. If an institution does not provide reasons at the time of the exclusion, it does not preclude the institution from excluding the physician, provided that valid reasons exist and are communicated upon request.

Generally, the governing body of an asylum has the power to decide how funds appropriated for its support shall be spent, in the absence of contrary legislative provision. Funds appropriated by a legislature for specific purposes cannot, however, be diverted, and the governing body of the asylum does not have the power to compel the state to provide funding for services other than those for which the money was appropriated. Similarly, they are not empowered to borrow money or incur debts beyond allotments made for the support of institutions.

It is proper procedure to make a provision that an asylum may only accept as many inmates for admission as the facilities can adequately accommodate.

An institution may not initiate a visitation plan that limits a patient's right to allocate his or her visiting time among particular people, unless such limitation bears a rational relationship to the patient's treatment or security.

Liabilities   An asylum or institutional care facility has the obligation to exercise reasonable care toward patients, and can be held liable for a breach of this duty of care. The care taken toward inmates should be in the light of their mental and physical condition.

Recovery for injuries precipitated by an institution's NEGLIGENCE can be barred or limited by the CONTRIBUTORY NEGLIGENCE of the injured party. The defense of contributory negligence cannot, however, be used when an individual is physically or mentally incapable of self-care.

AT ISSUE ☐ A phrase that describes the status of parties in a lawsuit when they make contradictory statements about a point specified in their PLEADINGS. ☐

ATKYNS, Sir Robert Sir Robert Atkyns (*b.* in 1621, in Gloucestershire, England; *d.* February 18, 1709, at Sapperton Hall, Gloucestershire, England) was an eminent English lawyer whose reputation was based on his brilliance and honesty in the courtroom during an era of widespread corruption in the English court system. He achieved acclaim for his defense of William Russell, a leader of the Whig party who was accused of treason.

In addition to his legal career, Atkyns served as chief lord of the Exchequer, the English equivalent of the United States Treasury, and wrote many publications, including *Parliamentary and Political Tracts.*

Library of Congress

Sir Robert Atkyns

AT LARGE
☐ Not limited to any place, person, or topic; for example, a representative at large is elected by the voters of the state as a whole rather than voters of a particular district.
☐ Free from control or restraint, such as a criminal at large. ☐

AT LAW
☐ According to law; by, for, or in the law, as in the professional title attorney at law.
☐ Within or arising from the traditions of the COMMON LAW as opposed to EQUITY, the system of law that developed alongside the common law and emphasized fairness and justice rather than enforcement of technical rules. ☐

ATTACHMENT ☐ The legal process of seizing property to ensure satisfaction of a judgment. ☐

The document by which a court orders such a seizure may be called a WRIT OF ATTACHMENT or an order of attachment.

Originally, the main purpose of attachment was to coerce a defendant into appearing in court and answering the plaintiff's claim. The court's order pressured the sheriff to take the defendant's property into custody, depriving the individual of the right to use or sell it. If the defendant obstinately refused to appear, the property could be sold by the court to pay off any monetary judgment entered against him or her. Today, the process of attachment has two functions, as a jurisdictional predicate and as a provisional remedy.

Attachment of property within reach of the court's jurisdiction gives the court authority over the defendant to the extent of that property's value even if the court cannot reach the defendant personally. For example, a court must have some connection with the defendant in order to require that person to appear and defend himself or herself in an action before that court.

A variety of different facts are sufficient to give the court jurisdiction over the defendant's person; for example, the defendant's residence within the state, the defendant's commission of a wrongful act within the state, or the defendant's doing business within the state.

If none of these kinds of facts exist to give the court jurisdiction over the defendant's person, the court may nevertheless assert its authority over property that the defendant owns within the state. In such a case, the plaintiff cannot recover a monetary judgment for an amount larger than the value of the proeprty nor can the individual reach the defendant's property outside the state, but this sort of jurisdiction, called jurisdiction IN REM or QUASI IN REM, may be the best the plaintiff can get. Before the court can exercise jurisdiction over the property, the plaintiff must obtain a writ of attachment to bring it into custody of the court.

Attachment may also be a PROVISIONAL REMEDY, that is, relief that temporarily offers the plaintiff some security while pursuing a final judgment in the lawsuit. For example, a plaintiff who has good reason to believe that the person he or she is suing is about to pack up and leave the state will want the court to prevent this until the plaintiff has a chance to win the action and collect on the judgment. The plaintiff can apply for an order of attachment that brings the property into the custody of the court and takes away the defendant's right to remove it or dispose of it.

Attachment is considered a very harsh remedy because it substantially interferes with the defendant's property rights before final resolution of the overall dispute. For this reason, there have been a number of challenges to the attachment procedures in different states, and the Supreme Court has established standards that are the least that DUE PROCESS requires. For example, for centuries attachment of a defendant's property was granted EX PARTE, that is, without first allowing the defendant to argue against it. The theory was that any defendant was likely to leave the state if he or she knew beforehand that his or her property was about to be attached. This collides with the individual's right to be free of interference with his or her rights unless the individual is given notice and an opportunity to be heard in the matter. States, therefore, now generally provide that notice must be given to the defendant before the seizure of property whenever practical, and the defendant must be given a hearing promptly after the seizure. Furthermore, a court cannot sanction a seizure that is made without a court order of attachment. To obtain the order, the plaintiff must swear to a set of facts that justify such a drastic interference with the defendant's property.

The process of attachment varies in detail from state to state, but it is not overly complicated. The plaintiff submits an application to the court describing the cause of action against the defendant and the grounds for seeking an attachment. The plaintiff may have to include documents or other evidence to support the claim that he or she will probably win the lawsuit, and the individual usually is required to make the application under oath. States generally require that the plaintiff post a BOND or UNDERTAKING in an amount sufficient to secure payment of damages to the defendant if it turns out that the plaintiff was not in fact entitled to the attachment.

The court issues a writ of attachment directing the sheriff or other law enforcement officer to serve a copy of the order on the defendant and to seize property equal in value to the sum specified in the writ. This is called a LEVY of attachment. The defendant then has a right to challenge the seizure or to post bond for the release of the property, in effect substituting the bond for the property in the court's custody. The order of attachment is effective only for a limited period, the time necessary to wind up the lawsuit between plaintiff and defendant or a specified period intended to permit resolution of the controversy. Provisions are usually made for special circumstances or extreme hardship.

Not every kind of property owned by the defendant is subject to attachment. The laws of a state may provide EXEMPTIONS for certain household items, clothing, tools, and other essentials. The defendant's salary may be subject to attachment, but a certain amount is exempt in order to allow for personal support or for family support. Property belonging to the defendant but in the hands of someone else, such as salary owed or a debt not yet paid, may also be seized, but this procedure is usually called GARNISHMENT rather than attachment.

Courts always have the discretion to exempt more property than that specified in a statute or to deny the attachment altogether under the proper circumstances. This may be done, for example, when the court believes that the property sought to be attached is worth much more than any judgment the plaintiff could hope to win, or where the property is an ongoing business that would be destroyed by attachment.

For a sample writ of attachment, see the Appendix volume 11.

ATTAINDER

☐ A legislative act, known as a BILL OF ATTAINDER, that sentenced a person to death for commission of a serious crime without a trial.

☐ Under COMMON LAW, the extinguishment of a person's civil rights and the forfeiture of all the property the individual owned that took effect immediately after he or she was sentenced to death upon conviction of TREASON or a FELONY. ☐

The term *attainder* is derived from *attincta,* Latin for stained or blackened. When attainder occurred, the condemned person was considered to bear a mark of infamy that corrupted his or her blood. Attainder was eventually abolished in England by statute.

In the United States, attainder is scarcely known today, although several states enacted acts of attainder during the Revolutionary War period. A few states consider the disqualification of a person impeached and convicted to hold any government office to be a type of attainder. Attainder is akin to the concept of CIVIL DEATH, the forefeiture of certain rights and privileges upon conviction of a serious crime.

ATTEMPT ☐ An undertaking to do an act that entails more than mere preparation but does not result in the successful completion of the act. ☐

In criminal law, an attempt to commit a crime is an offense when an accused makes a substantial but unsuccessful effort to commit a crime. The elements of attempt vary, although generally, there must be an intent to commit the crime, an overt act beyond mere preparation, and an apparent ability to complete the crime.

Generally, attempts are punishable by imprisonment, with sentence lengths that vary in time, depending upon the severity of the offense attempted.

ATTENUATE ☐ To reduce the force or severity; to lessen a relationship or connection between two objects. ☐

In criminal procedure, the relationship between an illegal search and a confession may be sufficiently attenuated as to remove the confession from the protection afforded by the FRUIT OF THE POISONOUS TREE DOCTRINE, thereby making it admissible as evidence in a criminal prosecution depending upon the facts of the case.

ATTEST
☐ To solemnly declare verbally or in writing that a particular document or testimony about an event is a true and accurate representation of the facts; to bear witness to.
☐ To formally certify by a signature that the signer has been present at the execution of a particular writing so as to rebut any potential challenges to its authenticity. ☐

ATTESTATION ☐ The act of attending the execution of a document and bearing witness to its authenticity, by signing one's name to it to affirm that it is genuine. ☐

An attestation is a declaration by a witness that an instrument has been executed in his or her presence according to the formalities required by law. It is not the same as an ACKNOWLEDGMENT, a statement by the maker of a document that verifies its authenticity.

An attestation clause is frequently found in legal documents that must be witnessed if they are to be valid, for example, a WILL or a DEED. It states that the instrument has been completed in the manner required by law in the presence of the witness who places his or her signature in the designated space.
☐ The certification by a custodian of records that a copy of an original document is a true copy that is demonstrated by his or her signature on a CERTIFICATE. ☐

ATTORN
☐ To turn over money, rent, or goods to another.
☐ To assign to a specific function or service. ☐

ATTORNEY ☐ A person admitted to practice law in his or her respective state and authorized to perform criminal and civil legal functions on behalf of CLIENTS. These functions include providing legal counsel, drafting legal documents, and representing clients before courts, administrative agencies, and other tribunals. ☐

Unless a contrary meaning is plainly indicated this term is synonymous with "attorney at law," "lawyer," or "counselor at law."

In order to become an attorney, a person must obtain a JURIS DOCTOR degree from an accredited law school, although this requirement may vary in some states where the apprenticeship method of studying law is permitted. Attendance at law school usually entails three years of full-time study, or four years of study in evening classes, where available. A bachelor's degree is generally a prerequisite to admission to law school.

A person must pass the bar examination of his or her respective state in order to be ADMITTED to practice law. After passing a bar examination and practicing law for a specified period, a person may be admitted to the bars of other states, pursuant to their own court rules.

Although an attorney might be required by law to render some services PRO BONO (free of charge), the individual is ordinarily entitled to compensation for the reasonable value of services performed. He or she has a right, called an ATTORNEY'S LIEN, to retain the property or money of a client until payment has been received for all services. An attorney must generally obtain court permission, however, to discontinue representation of a client during the course of a trial or criminal proceedings.

Certain discourse between attorney and client is protected by the ATTORNEY-CLIENT PRIVILEGE. In the law of EVIDENCE, the client can refuse to divulge and prohibit anyone else from disclosing, confidential communications transmitted to and from the attorney. See also, Charles R. McKirdy's essay on Apprenticeship; and Francis H. Musselman's essay on Attorney and Client.

Francis H. Musselman

Attorney and Client

The relationship between a client and a client's attorney is complex. The most important aspect in the relationship is that of "trust." Trust is the very foundation of the attorney-client relationship. Without the client's trust in his or her attorney, the relationship is unsatisfactory to each. Without the attorney's trust in his or her client, the attorney's representation of the client might very well result in failure.

Action by an attorney that is inconsistent with the client's trust in his or her attorney is not only destructive to the relationship, it is punishable by law. The most common punishment inflicted upon an attorney for an act that seriously violates the trust placed in the attorney by a client is the revocation of the attorney's license.

In recognition of the importance of the need for trust in the attorney-client relationship, several states and the District of Columbia have adopted uniform rules under which lawyers conduct the practice of law. The rules are called the "Code of Professional Responsibility." The Code of Professional Responsibility requires lawyers to maintain the highest standards of ethics and conduct, especially with respect to clients' matters and clients' property. Lawyers are required to hold clients' money and property in trust and not to commingle them with their own. Lawyers are required to preserve the confidence and secrets of clients. Lawyers are required to exercise professional judgment on behalf of clients and to represent clients competently. Lawyers are required to represent clients zealously within the bounds of the law. If a lawyer fails in any respect to handle clients' matters as required by the code, the lawyer can be subjected to disciplinary proceedings.

One might ask how to go about finding a lawyer in whom to place complete trust. How can one be sure of selecting a lawyer who is trustworthy as well as one who is competent concerning a particular problem, who will be zealous in taking care of the problem, who will exercise professional judgment of the highest order, who will keep inviolate the client's confidences and secrets and, at the same time, who can be afforded? Among the best sources of this kind of information are personal friends who have used the services of lawyers. Others in the community such as clergy, bankers, and doctors can also be good sources. If one is new to a community, one can consult the local bar association or an attorney in one's former community about the reputation of lawyers in the new community.

An attorney representing a client needs to be well-informed about a client's problem or matter. The attorney must know all of the facts as well as the relevant law. To encourage clients to disclose to their lawyers all of the facts concerning their legal problems, the law cloaks communications between attorneys and their clients with a privilege, known as the *attorney-client privilege*.

Unless a client consents to waive the attorney-client privilege, the content of communications between an attorney and a client may not be disclosed to anyone. There are very few exceptions to this rule where limited disclosure is permitted. For instance, if a client discloses to an attorney that the client is going to commit a serious crime, the attorney may warn the authorities to prevent its commission. Of course, the attorney should first try to persuade the client not to engage in illegal activity. In nearly every other circumstance the lawyer must remain silent. Communications about prior events, including prior crimes, are protected by the attorney-client privilege.

The attorney-client privilege may be waived, but only by the client. The client may waive, indeed unwittingly waive, the privilege by disclosing to other people the content of communications intended to be covered by the privilege. To prevent a waiver, a client should keep secret everything said to the attorney and everything said to the client by the attorney. This rule should be followed with respect to written communications as well as spoken communications. Indeed, written communications from one's attorney should be kept in a place where other people are unlikely to find and read them.

Lawyers and clients should not confuse their respective roles. Generally speaking, lawyers should avoid assuming the role of the client and vice versa. It is a proper role of lawyers to give advice on the basis of which clients make decisions respecting the clients' affairs. When there is a choice to be made, the client should make the choice. By the same token a client should not make choices involving serious legal consequences without first obtaining the advice of a competent lawyer. To avoid confusing the roles, a good lawyer will not act as his own lawyer in a matter involving serious legal consequences. It has been often said that a lawyer who does so "has a fool for a client." See also, entry on Code of Professional Responsibility.

The good lawyer is not the man who has an eye to every side and angle of contingency, and qualifies all his qualifications, but who throws himself on your part so heartily, that he can get you out of a scrape.

RALPH WALDO EMERSON

Bibliography: John A. Carnahan, "Do You Hate Your Clients, and Is the Feeling Mutual?" 65 *American Bar Association Journal* (March 1979): 29A–31A; David Goldberger, "Unpopular Clients Have a Right to Counsel," 3 *Bar Leader* (May–June 1978): 2–4.

ATTORNEY-CLIENT PRIVILEGE □ A rule of law, at COMMON LAW and under current statutes, that CONFIDENTIAL COMMUNICATIONS between an ATTORNEY and client, during the course of their professional relationship, may not be revealed by the attorney without the client's consent. □

The attorney-client privilege is ordinarily applicable if (1) the individual asserting the privilege is currently, or is seeking to become, a client; (2) the attorney is a member of the bar, and acting in a professional capacity in receiving the communication; or (3) the information is revealed in order for the client to obtain an opinion on the law or a specific legal proceeding, and not for the purpose of committing a TORT or crime.

The attorney-client privilege is an exception to the general rule that every individual must testify as to all facts within his or her knowledge if such information is sought in a court of justice, provided that his or her constitutional right against SELF-INCRIMINATION is protected. It protects the client, by ensuring that disclosures cannot be used against him or her in disputes with third parties. The purpose of this rule is to foster the free and open communications between attorney and client that are essential for an attorney to act with a complete understanding of the matters for which he or she is employed. The privilege is not dependent upon any affirmative request for secrecy by the client. It is effective even if the client is unaware of it.

The attorney-client privilege does not automatically render every communication made to an attorney privileged. There must be a relationship of attorney and client at the time of the communication, or the party relaying the communication must have believed such relationship existed. If the prospective client does not regard the attorney as his or her lawyer, the communication is not confidential. When an attorney is consulted and acting in a professional capacity, communications to the attorney are privileged, regardless of whether he or she is paid a RETAINER, charges a fee for his or her advice, or provides gratuitous counsel.

When no professional relationship exists between the attorney and the individual by whom the statements are made, the statements are not privileged merely because the individual subsequently hires the attorney in the matter to which the communications relate. If an individual consults an attorney with the intent of employing him or her, any information acquired by the attorney during the interview is privileged, even in the event that the attorney is not hired. Information given to an attorney after he tells a prospective client that he will not represent him, however, is not privileged.

A communication made between attorney and client in the presence of a third party, who is not the AGENT of either the attorney or client, is not protected by the privilege. This is also true in regard to a conversation in the attorney's presence between a client and a third person, or between two clients whose legal problems are unrelated. Even in a situation in which the attorney and client are speaking confidentially, and do not intend to have anyone overhear them, anyone who does overhear the conversation may testify as to what was said.

In certain situations, however, the circumstances concerning the presence of the third party might be such that the communication acquires a confidential character, such as when the third person who is present is the attorney's or the client's confidential agent, such as a private detective, or his or her associate. Neither the attorney's confidential secretary nor stenographer may disclose matters learned because of the position, when the attorney employing the individual would be INCOMPETENT to testify. In addition, the privilege safeguards communications between the attorney and the spouse of the client.

In order for a communication between an attorney and client to be regarded as privileged, it must concern the subject matter of the employment. A client may refuse to state whether he or she communicated certain facts to the attorney, however, the fact that the communication took place and the date that it did, are not privileged. Generally, statements made by a client to his or her attorney that are intended to be communicated to others are not privileged. An attorney's statements to a client made at the request of the adverse party or his or her attorney are not within the scope of the privilege.

Documents that arise as confidential communications between attorney and client are privileged, and not subject to production or disclosure by either the attorney or client. Documents not initially privileged while in the client's possession cannot later become privileged by a client placing them with the attorney. An attorney can be ordered to produce any paper, record, or document in his or her possession if the client could be forced to do so. He or she can also properly be forced to identify a document prepared or witnessed by him or her. The attorney may, however, be protected from disclosing its contents pursuant to the privilege.

The attorney-client privilege is not applicable to communications that relate to proposed infractions of the law, since it is not intended to serve as a cloak or shield for the perpetration of a CRIME or a tort. Communications concerning an alleged crime or FRAUD which has been committed, are privileged.

The termination of the relationship, even in the event that the client dies, does not destroy the attorney-client privilege. See also, Francis H. Musselman's essay on Attorney and Client.

ATTORNEY GENERAL'S OPINION □ A written memorandum submitted by the attorney general of the United States to the president, members of the executive branch, or officials of Federal regulatory agencies in response to questions of law that have arisen during the performance of such positions. □

The powers of the attorney general to issue such opinions are limited by Federal statute. The attorney general cannot render opinions to Congress. Any matters dealing with the question of government revenues must be referred to the comptroller of the treasury for a decision. The attorney general cannot advise an agency official on the course of action to be taken, since that is a matter of policy. Neither can the attorney general examine evidence to determine questions of fact nor can he or she decide questions that should be raised in judicial proceedings. Criminal matters are not the proper subject of an attorney general's opinion.

Attorney General Homer Cummings (left) congratulates Melvin H. Purvis of the FBI for his part in the 1934 capture of John Dillinger, who was then considered to be "Public Enemy No. 1."

Questions submitted for an opinion must be precise and specifically formulated. There must be a statement of facts that establishes how the question of law actually arose during the administration of the duties of a particular position. This requirement may be waived if public and private interests warrant immediate action.

An attorney general's opinion is persuasive and provides guidance to the official who requested it. Although not legally binding on them, most courts will take JUDICIAL NOTICE of such an opinion in a lawsuit. The attorney general may withdraw an opinion or it can be overruled by a court decision. The opinion may be reviewed by a subsequent attorney general only if extraordinary circumstances warrant it.

Similarly, a state attorney general issues an opinion on his or her interpretation of a law that has been requested by the governor or state administrative agencies.

ATTORNEY'S LIEN □ The right of a lawyer to hold a client's property or money until payment has been made for legal aid and advice given. □

In general, a lien is a security interest used by a creditor to ensure payment by a debtor for money owed. Since an attorney is entitled to payment for services performed, the attorney has a claim on a client's property until compensation is duly made.

A *charging lien* is an attorney's right to a portion of the judgment that was won for the client through professional services. It is a specific lien and only covers a lawyer's claim on money obtained in a particular action.

A *retaining lien* is more general in its scope. It extends to all of a client's property that an attorney might come into possession of during the course of a lawsuit. Until an attorney is compensated for services, he or she has a claim or interest in such property. See also, Francis H. Musselman's essay on Attorney and Client.

ATTRACTIVE NUISANCE □ In the law of TORTS, the doctrine that holds a person who has or creates a condition upon his or her own premises, the premises of another, or in a public place, which can reasonably be comprehended to be perilous to children, has a duty to take reasonable precautions to prevent harm to children when he or she knows, or has reason to know, that they are likely to TRESPASS thereupon. □

Children, by virtue of their immaturity, deficiency in judgment, and inexperience, frequently do not recognize and comprehend the perils in their environment. The arbitrary and in-

James L. Shaffer

A fence erected around a swimming pool by a homeowner helps keep children who might be attracted to the pool out of danger.

flexible limitations on the possessor's duty to trespassers would lead to inequitable results if applied to trespassing children. Most courts have adopted special liability rules that impose on landowners and occupiers a greater duty of care in regard to children. Although these rules apply equally to children who are trespassers, LICENSEES, and INVITEES, the cases invariably involve trespassing youngsters.

The attractive nuisance doctrine is a misnomer. Nuisance is a tort that entails the interference with the use and enjoyment of the property of another. Most jurisdictions have abolished the requirement that the condition must have "attracted" or lured the child onto the premises in order for him or her to recover. An increasing number of courts employs a four-part test to determine whether a possessor of land is liable for physical harm to trespassing children caused by an artificial condition upon the land.

The first requirement is that the place where the condition exists must be one upon which the possessor knows or has reason to know that children are likely to trespass. It is insufficient that trespasses by children are merely foreseeable, but the possessor is not required to have actual knowledge that children are entering upon the premises. This requirement is satisfied if the possessor has such knowledge, or if the individual has actual knowledge of facts from which he or she should infer that such trespasses are likely to occur. The possessor need not inspect the premises to ascertain whether children are present or whether the conditions are conducive to their trespasses, but he or she is chargeable with what he or she actually knows about the premises and what he or she can reasonably anticipate based upon that knowledge.

The second requirement is that the condition must be one which the possessor knows, or has reason to know, and which he or she realizes, or should realize, will entail an unreasonable risk of death or serious bodily harm to such children. The doctrine applies only to conditions on the land, not to activities; with respect to the latter, the child is granted the same protection as all other trespassers.

The possessor need not have created the condition. It is sufficient that he or she maintains it or allows it to exist. As a general rule, the doctrine applies only to artificial, man-made conditions, such as machinery and equipment, excavations, and swimming pools, and not to natural conditions, such as trees, bodies of water, and land formations. The hazards presented by natural conditions usually do not create unreasonable risks because nearly all children can be expected to appreciate them, and the burden of changing or guarding them is disproportionately great.

This limitation is derived from the broader rule that the hazard must be unusually dangerous. The significant phrase is "unreasonable risk," since not every condition on the land presents a foreseeable risk of harm to a child that will subject the possessor to liability. The condition must create a risk of serious bodily injury to a child that is unreasonable in light of the usefulness of the condition and the burden to the possessor of decreasing or eliminating the danger to the child. In addition, the risk is not unreasonable if the child whose trespass is to be anticipated can be expected to observe and totally comprehend the peril and evade it. Some cases deny liability where a trespassing youngster injures himself or herself or another child while recklessly using an object or condition which, in and of itself, presents no extraordinary danger. The possessor is not liable because the risk was not unreasonable, provided the possessor could expect the child to perceive and understand the consequences of reckless misuse. The possessor is not required to make the premises "child-proof."

Some courts have created arbitrary categories of conditions for which there is no liability. A possessor is not liable for "common hazards" but is liable only for "dangerous instrumentalities." Some courts have ruled that any child of sufficient age to be permitted to roam is, as a matter of law, capable of comprehending such perils as fire, drowning, and falling from a height. These inflexible rules, however, have been inapplicable to certain cases, as where the possessor knows or has reason to know that the children who are likely to trespass are so young that they cannot appreciate the danger, or where there is some extraordinary or increased hazard associated with the condition that is not evident to the children.

The third requirement is that the children, because of their youth, must not discover the condition or realize the risk involved in intermeddling with it or in coming within the area made dangerous by it. It must be proved that the child did not recognize and completely comprehend the risk, by virtue of inexperience and age, which is to be distinguished from unreasonable conduct. The child might have been too young to be capable of such conduct, or might have acted reasonably for a child of a similar age, but the youngster cannot recover if he or she knew of the condition, totally understood the peril, and continued to encounter it.

Most of the cases have involved children under twelve years of age, and a few courts have established an arbitrary age limit for the application of the doctrine. Theoretically, however, there is no reason why it should not apply to older children if the peril is especially complex; however, the older the child, the fewer the dangers he or she is deemed not to understand and appreciate.

The fourth requirement is that the utility to the possessor of maintaining the condition must be slight as compared with the risk to children. As a general rule, the public interest in unencumbered land use is of such importance that the possessor need not take precautions that are so burdensome or expensive as to be unreasonable in light of the risk, or to render the premises "child-proof." The defendant is liable only for NEGLIGENCE. The individual is required to exercise only reasonable care and to take only those precautions that would be taken by a reasonable person under the circumstances. A warning to the child might be all that is required, especially where other precautions are difficult or impossible.

AUCTIONS □ A sale open to the general public and conducted by an auctioneer, a person empowered to conduct such a sale, at which property is sold to the highest bidder. □

A *bid* is an offer by a *bidder,* a prospective purchaser, to pay a designated amount for the property on sale.

A Dutch auction is a method of sale that entails the public offer of the property at a price in excess of its value, accompanied by a gradual reduction in price until the item is purchased.

According to the UNIFORM COMMERCIAL CODE (UCC), a body of law governing commercial transactions that has been adopted by the states, the auction sale of any item concludes with the fall of the hammer or in any other customary manner. Such a sale is "with reserve," which denotes that the goods can be withdrawn at any time, until the auctioneer announces the

But the character of every act depends upon the circumstances in which it is done.

OLIVER WENDELL HOLMES, JR.

A slave is sold by public auction in the antebellum South.

completion of the sale, unless the goods are explicitly put up "without reserve," which signifies that the article cannot be withdrawn after the call for bids unless no bid is made within a reasonable time. In both types of auctions, the bidder can withdraw a bid prior to the auctioneer's announcement that the sale has been completed.

Regulation As a legitimate business enterprise, auctions cannot be proscribed. They are not above reasonable regulation by both state and local authorities. Some states subject auction sales to taxation.

In the absence of statutes, any person can act as an auctioneer, but a LICENSE which usually restricts his or her authority to a certain region is often required. Licensing officers can refuse to issue a license, but only if done reasonably, impartially, and to promote the interest of the community.

Agency of auctioneer An auctioneer serves as the AGENT of the seller who employs him or her, and the auctioneer must act in GOOD FAITH, advance the interest of the seller, and conduct the sale in accordance with the seller's instructions. If real property or goods priced at

$500 or more are sold at auction, a written agreement is necessary to satisfy the STATUTE OF FRAUDS, an old English law adopted in the United States that requires certain contracts to be in writing. The auctioneer is authorized to sign a memorandum of sale on behalf of both parties, but this authority is limited and expires shortly after the sale has been concluded. Both the buyer and the seller are bound by the announcement of the auctioneer concerning the identity of the property and the terms and conditions of the sale.

In the absence of a statutory provision requiring authority to be in writing, an agent, pursuant to oral authorization, can execute any contract required to be in writing. The statutory provisions vary, however, in regard to the execution of contracts to purchase real property.

Because of the trust and confidence the seller reposes in an auctioneer, the individual cannot delegate the power to sell without special authority from the seller. The delegation of insignificant duties, such as the striking of the hammer and the announcement of the sale, is allowable if conducted pursuant to the auctioneer's immediate supervision and direction.

An auctioneer's authority normally terminates upon the completion of the sale and the collection of the purchase price, but the seller can revoke the authority at any time prior to the sale. According to some authorities, the buyer or seller can end the auctioneer's authority to sign a memorandum on his or her behalf between the time of the fall of the hammer and the signing of the memorandum, but the prevailing view deems the auctioneer's authority to be irrevocable. Private sales by an auctioneer are generally impermissible.

Conduct and validity of sale The owner of the property has the right to control the sale until its conclusion. Unless conditions are imposed by the seller, the auctioneer is free to conduct the sale in any manner chosen, in order to bar fraudulent bidders and to earn the confidence of honest purchasers. The auctioneer cannot amend the printed terms and conditions of the auction, but he or she is empowered to postpone the sale, if that is the desire. The auctioneer can modify the sale terms of goods advertised in a catalog at any time during the sale, if announced publicly and all of the bidders present are cognizant of it. The auctioneer may also retain the right to resell should there be an error or a dispute concerning the sale property. The description of the property in the catalog must be unambiguous. A significant error in a descrip-

tion might cause the cancellation of the sale, although trivial discrepancies between the property and the description are not problematic. The seller can withdraw property until the acceptance of a bid by an auctioneer.

A bid is an offer to purchase, and no obligations are imposed upon the seller until the bid is accepted. It can be made in any manner that demonstrates the bidder's willingness to pay a particular price for the auctioned property, whether orally, or in writing, or through bodily movements, such as a wave of the hand. Secret signals between the bidder and the auctioneer militate against equality in bidding and are thereby prohibited. The auctioneer accepts a bid by the fall of the hammer or by any other perceptible method that advises the bidder that the property is his or hers upon tendering the amount of the bid in accordance with the terms of the sale. An auctioneer can reject a bid on various grounds, such as where it is combined with terms or conditions other than those of the sale, or is below the minimum price acceptable to the owner.

As a general rule, any act of the auctioneer, seller, or buyer that prevents an impartial, free, and open sale or that reduces competition in the bidding is contrary to PUBLIC POLICY. An agreement among prospective buyers not to bid has been held to VOID the sale to any buyer within this group. A purchase by a person who has not participated in the illegal agreement remains in effect. A *puffer* is a person who has no intention of buying but is hired by the seller to place fictitious bids in order to raise the bidding of genuine purchasers. In general, if a purchaser at an auction can prove that a puffer was employed, he or she can void the sale. Some jurisdictions require the buyer to have been financially hurt by the puffer, but others permit an individual to void a sale even if no harm occurred. Puffing and *by-bidding* are synonymous.

A deposit is not a pledge but a partial payment of the purchase price, usually made pay-

A sign advertises an Ohio farm for sale at public auction in 1938.

Library of Congress

A street auction scene in New York in 1868

able to the auctioneer who retains it until the completion of the sale.

The property of one person should not be commingled and sold with the property of another by the auctioneer unless notice is furnished to all interested parties, or it might constitute FRAUD.

An auctioneer is not entitled to bid on property that he or she has been hired to sell, but the auctioneer can, however, bid a particular sum for a purchaser without violating any duties to the seller or even to other prospective bidders.

An auctioneer who does not have the required license but who executes a sale can be penalized, but the sale remains valid; an auction is void, however, when it is conducted without the owner's consent.

Right and liabilities of buyer and seller In an unconditional sale, title passes to the bidder when the auctioneer's hammer falls. If conditions exist, title passes upon their fulfill-

ment or through their WAIVER, the intentional relinquishment of a known right. The bidder is ordinarily entitled to possession when he or she pays the amount bid.

A person who bids on behalf of another is personally liable for the bid unless the person discloses this relationship to the auctioneer.

Fraud, or a misrepresentation of a material fact on which the buyer detrimentally relied, or the seller's failure to provide good title furnishes a basis for setting aside the sale.

The seller has a LIEN, a security interest, on the property until the price is paid. If the purchaser fails to comply with the conditions of a sale, the seller can regard the sale as abandoned and sue for DAMAGES. Where a resale occurs, and the price is lower than the contract price, the defaulting buyer in some jurisdictions is liable to the seller for the difference between what he or she had agreed to pay and what the seller receives on the resale. In general, whether a deposit or a partial payment must be repaid depends upon which party was responsible for the incompleted sale. If the buyer is responsible, he or she cannot recover either the deposit or partial payment.

Compensation The party employing the auctioneer pays a commission regardless of whether he or she procures a sale, unless the auctioneer is responsible for the failure of the sale. The auctioneer is entitled to a reasonable sum unless a statute or contract provision determines the amount.

Liabilities of auctioneer An auctioneer is usually liable to the seller for monetary losses attributable to his or her NEGLIGENCE in failing to follow the seller's instructions. The auctioneer can also be responsible to the buyer for fraud, conduct in excess of authority, and failure to deliver the goods. Since the auctioneer is a stakeholder, a third party designated by two or more persons to retain on deposit money or property that is the subject of a dispute, the auctioneer is liable to the buyer in those instances where the buyer is entitled to the return of the deposit. An auctioneer who sells property on behalf of one who does not own it, and delivers the proceeds to that person, is personally liable to the rightful owner even though the auctioneer acted in good faith and without knowledge of the absence of title. He or she can recover his or her losses from the person who received the proceeds in the form of damages that he or she was ordered to pay to the actual owner.

AUDIT

☐ A systematic examination of financial or accounting records by a specialized inspector, called an auditor, to verify their accuracy and truthfulness.

☐ A hearing during which financial data are investigated for purposes of authentication. ☐

AUDITA QUERELA

☐ A common-law WRIT for an action brought by a defendant against whom a judgment was rendered for relief against the judgment on the basis of some matter or defense that arose since it was rendered. ☐

When matters arise before judgment that the defendant did not have the opportunity to raise in his or her defense, the writ may also be used to obtain relief from the judgment.

In most states that have adopted the rules of FEDERAL CIVIL PROCEDURE, the writ has been superseded by a motion for relief from judgment.

AUGUSTINE

Augustine (*b*. November 13, 354, in Tagaste, North Africa; *d*. August 28, 430, in Hippo, North Africa) achieved prominence as

Augustine

a scholar, teacher, philosopher, and religious leader and is considered by many to be the founder of theology.

The son of a pagan father, Augustine was strongly affected by the beliefs of his Christian mother. He rejected his faith at age seventeen when he became a student at Carthage, where he excelled in rhetorical studies. While at Carthage, Augustine followed a life of pleasure and licentiousness; he began a relationship with a mistress that would last for fourteen years, resulting in the birth of his illegitimate son, Adeodatus. He concluded his education, and subsequently taught grammar for two years. In 375, he established a school of rhetoric at Carthage.

During this time, Augustine again turned towards religion and became a follower of Manichaeism, a sect founded by Mani. Mani, believed to be Persian by birth, incorporated aspects of several ideologies, including Christianity, into his religion. He believed that God represented goodness and light, and Satan was the embodiment of evil and darkness; man was constantly involved in the power play between the two forces.

In 383, Augustine relocated to Rome where he again taught rhetoric. One year later, the Manichaeans requested that he teach at Milan, which proved to be a turning point in his life. He studied the teachings of Plato and became critical of Manichaeism. Augustine was searching for a deeper meaning and found the answer in the lectures of Ambrose, bishop of Milan. Two years later, he returned to his native faith of Christianity and was baptized on Easter, 387.

After his conversion, Augustine lived quietly in Tagaste for four years. In 391, he traveled to nearby Hippo and was selected as a Christian priest. He spent the rest of his life at Hippo, serving as auxiliary bishop in 395 and as bishop in 396. During this time, he concentrated his efforts on reorganizing and strengthening the Catholic church.

Augustine is the author of many classic works that reveal his philosophical and theological beliefs. Perhaps the most prominent is *Confessions,* written circa 400, which is an autobiographical study wherein Augustine examines his life and deplores the wildness of his youth.

During the years from 413 to 426, Augustine wrote the *City of God,* which contrasts the ideologies of Christianity and paganism. The cults, superstitions, and idols of paganism are examined as is Christianity, which has its basis in the Old Testament. The book is a defense of Christianity against the worldly values of materialism and pleasure.

Augustine wrote two other works concerning theology: *On the Trinity* (c. 400–c. 420), which presents an account of Christian doctrine, and *Against Faustus* (c. 400), which is a denial of his former religion, Manichaeism.

On Baptism (c. 400) and *On the Correction of the Donatists* (c. 405) are two studies directed against Donatism, a Christian schism that espoused the beliefs that only people totally without sin could be church members and that the goodness of the priest bestowing a sacrament determined the quality of that sacrament. Augustine argued that the authority of the church safeguards the right of Christians to practice their faith and such authority is due to apostolic succession, the authority vested in the original apostles by Christ that is passed down to future church officials.

In addition to his campaign against the Donatists, Augustine became embroiled in a controversy against Pelagianism, another Christian schism. The Pelagianists opposed Augustine's views of grace by declaring that man is born innocent, does not need to be baptized, and therefore, does not require God's grace for redemption. Augustine argued that man is inherently helpless and sinful and needs God's help and grace to achieve salvation. The disagreement that ensued prompted Augustine to compose several important treatises concerning his theories on grace.

One of the last works of Augustine is *Retractions* (426), wherein the author reviews his previous works and offers some changes concerning his earlier views.

AUGUSTUS, John   During the nineteenth century, U.S. law was still undergoing a process of development. Criminal law, in particular, was slowly evolving towards a more humanistic and equitable approach than had previously been taken. One man in Massachusetts, through an act of compassion, initiated a procedure that was the forerunner of the probation system.

John Augustus (*b.* 1785; *d.* June 21, 1859, in Boston, Massachusetts) was a cobbler in Boston during the 1840s. He was interested in the legal process and often visited the criminal courts in Boston. In 1841, he was especially touched by the plight of a person convicted of public intoxication who begged the court not to incarcerate him and promised to give up alcohol in return for his freedom. Augustus, sensing hope for the man's rehabilitation, paid the man's bail; three weeks later, he returned to court with his sober charge. The judge was favorably moved, and the man was allowed to go free.

After his initial success, John Augustus continued to take custody of convicted criminals. By the time he died in 1859, he had helped nearly 2,000 prisoners. He used his own money for bail or received financial aid from other residents of Boston who believed in his cause; several of these followers continued the program after his death.

Augustus' benevolence was made an official practice in 1878 when a law was enacted assigning a regular probation officer to the Boston criminal courts. In 1891, the commonwealth of Massachusetts adopted a similar program, and during the next nine years, other states began to provide for probationary programs based on the humanitarian actions of John Augustus.

AUSTIN, John   John Austin (*b.* March 3, 1790, in Creeting Mill, Suffolk, England; *d.* December 17, 1859, in Weybridge, Surrey, England) achieved a reputation as an eminent jurist, legal author, and teacher.

From 1826 to 1832, he taught as a professor of jurisprudence at the University of London. His series of instructional lectures were incorporated into two volumes titled *The Province of Jurisprudence Determined,* which was published in 1832, and *Lectures on Jurisprudence,* published in 1869. Austin, who is credited with the definition of many legal terms and ideas, believed that law represented the highest authority, not to be equated with religion and ethics. One of Austin's students was John Stuart Mill, who gained fame as a philosopher and economics expert. See also, Thomas M. Feldstein and Stephen B. Presser's essay on John Austin; and Stephen B. Presser's essay on John Stuart Mill.

Thomas M. Feldstein & Stephen B. Presser

John Austin

Though never able to achieve marked professional success either as a lawyer or teacher during his life, John Austin (*b.* March 3, 1790, in Creeting Mill, Suffolk, England; *d.* December 17, 1859, in Weybridge, Surrey, England) proved to be one of the most influential legal philosophers of nineteenth-century England. Austin was closely associated with and strongly influenced by Jeremy Bentham, and was himself a strong influence on his friend John Stuart Mill. Austin's ideas were drawn from those of John Locke, Thomas Hobbes, George Berkeley, Bentham, and other philosophers, and thus could not be said to be original. Since Austin was the first to state his analytical precepts in language somewhat removed from that of philosophy and closer to that of the law, he is properly regarded as the man who established the modern study of jurisprudence in England.

Austin was born in Suffolk in 1790, the son of a wealthy miller who had made his fortune contracting with the government during the French War. John Austin was a lifelong believer in the military virtues of honor, strength, and patriotism. He joined the British Army at the age of sixteen and served as a lieutenant before resigning his commission in 1812 to begin the study of law. Like America's Oliver Wendell Holmes, Jr., who was reported to have read Austin's works five times, Austin's military experience and sympathies probably made it easier for him to conceive of the law as a mandatory command from the sovereign, to which obedience was owed in the line of patriotic duty.

Austin was called to the bar at the Inner Temple and became an equity pleader. He was soon made uncomfortable by the meticulous thoroughness he thought was required of him and by the pressures and anxieties generally attendant upon the profession. Suffering from both exhaustion and financial failure, Austin abandoned the practice of law in 1825. Following the creation of the University of London in 1826, Austin was appointed to the new chair of jurisprudence.

Convinced that Germany was the most important scholarly center to prepare his lectures, Austin spent two years in Bonn, reading the newly discovered Institutes of Gaius; the Pandicts; and the works of Gustav Hugo, Frederich Karl von Savigny, and Anton Friedrich Justus Thibaut. Returning in 1828, Austin began his lectures at the University. They were enthusiastically attended initially, especially by Benthamites, but Austin's classes eventually dwindled; and, in 1832, with only five students remaining, a disheartened Austin resigned his chair.

That year, based on his lectures, Austin published *The Province of Jurisprudence Determined,* the only complete work on jurisprudence he ever published and the best known of his writings. The following year Austin received an appointment as a member of the Criminal Law Commission, an experience Austin's wife described as one that left her husband disturbed and agitated. He reportedly abhorred the notion of receiving money from the public treasury "for work [from]

Nor is it enough the law be written and published, but also that there be manifest signs that it proceedeth from the will of the sovereign.

THOMAS HOBBES

373

which he thought the public would derive little or no benefit." Austin soon resigned his commission; in 1834 he attempted again to lecture on jurisprudence, this time before the Society of the Inner Temple. Again Austin's lectures were abandoned.

One of his few professional successes was his 1836 appointment, along with his former student Sir George Cornwall Lewis, as a commissioner to examine the administration and government of Malta. Austin performed his usual meticulous job, and one of his recommendations—a tariff reform proposal—was termed by Sir James Stephen, the Under-Secretary of the Colonial Office, as "the most successful legislative experiment he had seen in his time." Austin spent the remaining years of his life both in England and on the continent, using his wife's earnings as a writer and translator for support. Austin died in 1859, in Weybridge, after living what he regarded as a misplaced life: "I was born out of time and place. I ought to have been a schoolman of the twelfth century or a German professor."

Austin's lifelong habit of demanding of himself the most rigorous effort and perfection appears to have usually resulted in frustration at his own shortcomings. John Stuart Mill reported in his autobiography that Austin's high standards and analytic power were inspirations to his friends and associates, and Austin's meticulousness did allow him to create a much more dispassionate and systematic approach to jurisprudence than had existed before. An essential part of this jurisprudence was Austin's conception that there existed certain principles, notions, and distinctions that were necessarily part of every advanced system of law.

At the heart of Austin's theory was his definition of "law properly so-called" as the express or tacit command of the sovereign—the command that can be enforced through the use of official sanctions to which a duty of obedience is owed by the subject. As H.L.A. Hart explained, Austin's objective was "to identify the distinguishing characteristics of positive law and so to free it from the perennial confusion with the precepts of religion and morality which had been encouraged by natural law theorists and exploited by the opponents of legal reform." Austin thus shared with his friend Bentham a distaste for the superstitious reverence in which the chaotic and confused English common-law rules were held by conservatives, such as Sir William Blackstone, and a desire that the law might be changed and used more effectively to promote the greatest happiness for the greatest number.

Austin believed that a legislator could intelligently profit from study, clarification, and classification of features that existed in every refined legal system, such as concepts of "duty, right, liberty, injury, punishment, redress, law, sovereignty, and independent political society." (Rumble, below at 994). Nevertheless, while Austin did advocate intelligent and sytematic legal reform, he did not share Bentham's romatic notion that radical reform could be prompted by the lower classes. Austin also believed that shaping of the law ought to be dictated by the representatives of the holders of inherited or acquired property.

While the conservative premises of Austin's politics were thus similar to those of Blackstone, he differed with him over the best means of securing conservative goals. Blackstone often appeared to advocate the recognition that the English common law incorporated the dictates of morality and religion, and thus ought not to be tampered with by man. Austin carefully distinguished what *was* law, that is the existing commands of the sovereign, from idealized conceptions of what *ought* to be law. Austin held out the possibility that a better understanding of

THE

PROVINCE OF JURISPRUDENCE

DETERMINED.

By JOHN AUSTIN, Esq.

BARRISTER AT LAW.

LONDON:

JOHN MURRAY, ALBEMARLE STREET.

———

1832.

Courtesy of the University of Minnesota Law School

The title page of the first edition of John Austin's *The Province of Jurisprudence Determined*

the nature of existing law could lead men intelligently and actively to alter it in the best interests of society. In this reforming spirit, and in his recognition of the separation between positive law and morality, Austin's jurisprudence bears marked similarities to the thought of Holmes and of the American legal realists.

Like these American jurists, and unlike Blackstone, Austin made clear his belief that judges, as well as legislators, did not simply discover preexisting rules but actually made law. Moreover, while he believed that "judiciary law" was inherently uncertain and that codification was a better means of reform, Austin suggested that reform by judicial legislation had long been the means of the common laws to keep the law responsive to the needs of a changing society.

According to his wife's harsh assessment, Austin's life had been one of "unbroken disappointment and failure." As the progenitor of the American legal positivists and realists, however, Austin's spirit still animates much of American legal analysis. The dominant note in Austinian jurisprudence is the malleability of the law in the hands of the sovereign, and American academics, lawyers, judges, and legislators show no signs of ceasing self-consciously to seek to mold the law. See also, Catherine Gilbert and Stephen B. Presser's essay on Thomas Hobbes as well as Stephen B. Presser's essays on Jeremy Bentham; John Stuart Mill; and Sir William Blackstone.

For the laws of nature, which consist in equity, justice, gratitude, and other moral virtues on these depending, in the condition of mere nature . . . are not properly laws, but qualities that dispose men to peace and to obedience.

THOMAS HOBBES

Bibliography: John Austin, *The Province of Jurisprudence Determined* (Introduction by H.L.A. Hart) (1954); John Austin, *Lectures on Jurisprudence* (1970); R. A. Eastwood and G. W. Keeton, *The Austinian Theories of Law and Sovereignty* (1929); Wilfred E. Rumble, "The Legal Positivism of John Austin and the Realist Movement in American Jurisprudence," 66 *Cornell Law Review* (June 1981): 986–1031.

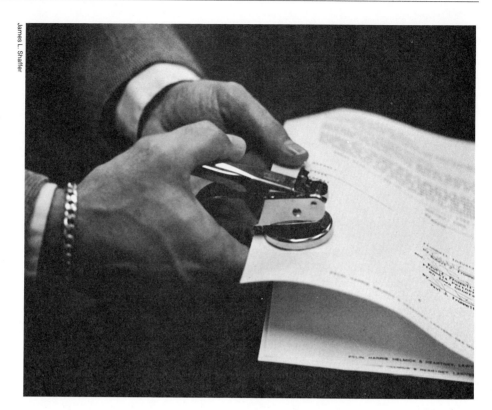

James L. Shaffer

By impressing his seal on this legal form, the notary public authenticates the validity of the content of the document.

AUTHENTICATION
- The confirmation rendered by an officer of a court that a CERTIFIED COPY of a JUDGMENT is what it purports to be, an accurate duplicate of the original judgment.
- In the law of EVIDENCE, the act of establishing a statute, record, or other document, or a certified copy of such an instrument as genuine and official so that it can be used in a lawsuit to prove an issue in dispute. □

Self-authentication of particular categories of documents is provided by federal and state rules of evidence. A deed or conveyance that has been acknowledged by its signers before a notary public, a certified copy of a public record, or an official publication of the government are examples of self-authenticating documents.

AUTHENTIC INTERPRETATION   See Interpretation of Treaties.

AUTHORITIES
- Legal powers.
- Governmental agencies created by statute for specific public purposes, such as a county highway authority.

- References to statutes, precedents, judicial decision, and legal textbooks that support the position of a party to a lawsuit made in the BRIEFS submitted by the attorneys for the parties to the court that is to hear the case or during the trial in the oral arguments. □

Primary authorities are citations to statutes, court decisions, and government regulations that, if having the force of law, must be applied by the court to dispose of the issue in dispute if they are relevant to the matter. *Secondary authorities* are references to treatises, textbooks, or RESTATEMENTS that explain and review general principles of law that buttress a party's position in a lawsuit. Such authorities have no legal effect and can be disregarded by the court.

Authorities are also cited by scholars in legal treatises, HORNBOOKS, and restatements to establish the bases of the statements and conclusions contained in the works.

AUTHORIZE □ To empower another with the legal right to perform an action. □

The Constitution authorizes Congress to regulate interstate commerce.

Joseph D. Grano

"Automobile Exception" to Search Warrant Requirement

The Fourth Amendment of the U.S. Constitution protects the people against unreasonable searches and seizures. Interpreting this provision, the Supreme Court has indicated that a search conducted without a search warrant is presumptively unreasonable. The warrant requirement enables a neutral, disinterested magistrate to determine that the police really have probable cause (a legal term descriptive of something more than mere suspicion) to conduct the search. The warrant requirement, however, has several exceptions; one is the "automobile exception."

The title of this exception to the warrant requirement is somewhat misleading because the Supreme Court has never held that a warrantless search is permissible merely because an automobile is involved. While the exception often will permit a warrantless search, its precise scope is uncertain, and the Supreme Court has sharply divided over the issue. Further complicating the matter, the exception may not apply to certain containers carried in the car. In one case, for example, the Court held that while the police lawfully searched the trunk of a cab without a warrant, they should have obtained a warrant before searching the defendant's suitcase, taken from the trunk.

The "automobile exception" is based on several considerations. First, because cars are mobile, the police often will not have time to obtain a warrant before the search. Second, in the view of the Court, an individual's expectation of privacy in a car is substantially less than in other places, such as a home. In other words, people have considerably less Fourth Amendment protection in their cars than in their homes, and accordingly the Court will permit warrantless searches of cars under circumstances where it would not permit warrantless searches of homes. Third, because of a car's size, the police cannot easily hold and safeguard a car while seeking a warrant from a magistrate. A suitcase, by way of contrast, can be taken into the police station and safeguarded while a magistrate is consulted.

While any statement of the rule risks inaccuracy, it generally may be said that the police may stop and search a moving vehicle without a search warrant when they have probable cause to believe it contains instrumentalities or evidence of crime. The exception does not permit the police to search without probable cause; the exception merely removes the additional safeguard of having a magistrate determine before the search whether probable cause is present. Hence, the police may not search an automobile merely because they have stopped the driver for speeding. If probable cause develops after such a lawful stop (for example, the officer smells marijuana), the "automobile exception" would permit a warrantless search.

. . . the guaranty of freedom from unreasonable searches and seizures by the Fourth Amendment has been construed, practically since the beginning of the government, as recognizing a necessary difference between a search of a store, dwelling house, or other structure in respect of which a proper official warrant readily may be obtained and a search of a ship, motor boat, wagon, or automobile for contraband goods, where it is not practicable to secure a warrant, because the vehicle can be quickly moved out of the locality or jurisdiction in which the warrant must be sought.

WILLIAM HOWARD TAFT

In order to conduct a warrantless search of this automobile, the police officer must have probable cause to believe the car contains evidence of a crime.

If the police take custody of a car that they could have searched on the street after stopping it, a later warrantless search at the police station is still permissible. Even though it would seem that getting a warrant is no longer impractical, the owner's lesser expectation of privacy and the difficulties of safeguarding the car support a warrantless search. The exception has other dimensions, but further consideration would require an extended analysis of several judicial opinions. See also, Stephen A. Saltzburg's essay on Search Warrant; and Craig R. Ducat's essay on Privacy, Right of.

Bibliography: Y. Kamisar, J. Grano, and J. Haddad, *Sum and Substance of Criminal Procedure* (1977); W. La Fave, *Search and Seizure*, vol. 2 (1978).

AUTOMOBILE LEGAL ASSOCIATION

The Automobile Legal Association, founded in 1907, provides a wide range of travel and emergency services, including bail bond and legal services for its members. The association is affiliated with the Automobile Touring Alliance.

AUTOPSY □ The dissection of a dead body by a local medical examiner or physician authorized by law to do so in order to determine the cause and time of a death that appears to have resulted from other than natural causes. □

This postmortem examination, required by law, is ordered by the local CORONER when a person is suspected to have died by violent or unnatural means. The consent of the decedent's next of kin is not necessary for an authorized autopsy to be held. The medical findings must be presented at an INQUEST and might be used as evidence in a police investigation and a subsequent criminal prosecution.

The Autopsy

Let those who interdict the opening of bodies well understand their errors. When the cause of a disease is obscure, in opposing the dissection of a corpse which must soon become the food of worms, they do no good to the inanimate mass, and they cause a grave damage to the rest of mankind; for they prevent the physicians from acquiring a knowledge which may afford the means of great relief, eventually, to individuals attacked by a similar disease. No less blame is applicable to those delicate physicians, who, from laziness or repugnance, love better to remain in the darkness of ignorance than to scrutinize, laboriously, the truth; not reflecting that by such conduct they render themselves culpable toward God, toward themselves and toward society at large.

—*Theophilus Bonetus (1620-1689)*

This quotation from Theophilus Bonetus, a Swiss physician and early student of morbid anatomy, hangs on a wall outside the autopsy room in a medical examiner's building.

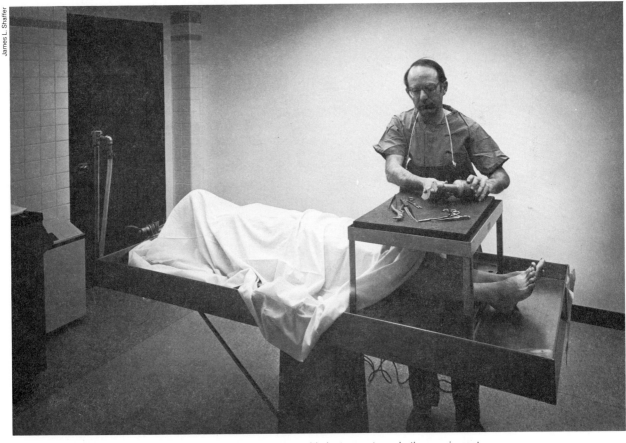

Prior to performing an autopsy the medical examiner arranges his instruments and other equipment.

AUTRE   [*French, "Another."*]
☐ A descriptive term used to denote the existence of another object or standard that is comparable with, or related to, a particular item or action. ☐

An *autre action pendant* is a phrase used in common-law pleading to indicate that another action is pending.

AUTREFOIS ACQUIT   [*French, "Formerly acquitted."*]
☐ The name of a historic defense sometimes asserted in cases raising the issue of DOUBLE JEOPARDY to bar a subsequent prosecution of a defendant for the same crime for which he had already been indicted, tried, and found not guilty (acquitted). ☐

AUTREFOIS CONVICT   [*French, "Formerly convicted."*]
☐ Similar to *autrefois acquit*, the name of a defense asserted in DOUBLE JEOPARDY cases to prevent a successive prosecution of a defendant for a crime for which he has been indicted, tried, and found guilty (convicted). ☐

AUTRE VIE   [*French, "Another's life."*]
☐ A term used to denote a time period measured by the life of another specified person. ☐

An individual who is given the right to use and enjoy property during the lifetime of another is called a tenant *pur autre vie*. A LIFE TENANT is one who holds property for the period of his or her own life or that of another specific person.

AUXILIARY   ☐ Aiding; ANCILLARY; subordinate; subsidiary. ☐

Auxiliary or ancillary administration is the management and settlement of property belonging to a decedent that is not located where he or she was domiciled. It is subordinate to the principal or domiciliary administration of the decedent's property that occurs in the state where the individual was domiciled. Auxiliary administration ensures that any local creditors will be paid before the out-of-state property will be transferred for distribution under domiciliary administration.

AVAILS   ☐ An archaic term for proceeds or profits. ☐

When a provision in a WILL states that the avails from the sale of property shall be equally divided among the testator's children after all debts have been paid, avails is synonymous with the profits from the sale.

Law is the crystallization of the habit and thought of society.

WOODROW WILSON

AVER   ☐ To specifically allege certain facts or claims in a PLEADING. ☐

AVERMENT   ☐ The allegation of facts or claims in a PLEADING. ☐

The FEDERAL RULES OF CIVIL PROCEDURE require that averments be simple, concise, and direct.

A VINCULO MATRIMONII
  [*Latin, "From the bond of matrimony."*]
☐ A phrase used in some states to describe a DIVORCE that is complete and final, relieving the husband and wife from the duties and obligations of marriage and entitling them to remarry. ☐

A divorce *a vinculo matrimonii* differs from a divorce A MENSA ET THORO obtainable in some states that is akin to a legal SEPARATION, giving the parties only a legal right to live apart. The marriage is not dissolved nor can the parties remarry.

AVOIDABLE CONSEQUENCES   ☐ The doctrine that places the responsibility of minimizing DAMAGES upon the person who has been injured. ☐

The major function of the doctrine is to reduce the damages brought about by the defendant's misconduct. Ordinarily, an individual cannot recover for losses that might have been prevented through reasonable effort by the person particularly where the conduct causing the loss or injury is not willful, intentional, or perpetuated in bad faith. The rule of avoidable consequences applies to both CONTRACT and TORT actions, but is not applicable in cases involving willful injury or where the plaintiff could not possibly have circumvented any of the harm for which he or she claims damages.

The efforts that the person who has been injured must take to avoid the consequences of the misconduct are required to be reasonable, based upon the circumstances of the particular case, and subject to the rules of common sense and fair dealing. That which is reasonably required is contingent upon the extent of the potential injury as compared with the cost of rectifying the situation, and the realistic likelihood of success in the protective effort. A plaintiff who neglects to mitigate damages will not be entirely barred from recovering such damages that he or she might have circumvented through reasonable efforts.

Included in the effort that the law requires is the payment of reasonable expenditures. The injured party need not, however, make extraordinary payments to prevent the consequences of the wrongdoer's conduct. The plaintiff's inabil-

Because this woman has sustained a whiplash injury to her neck in an automobile accident and her physician has recommended that she wear a protective neck brace, she has fulfilled the basic requirements of the doctrine of avoidable consequences by wearing the brace to avoid further injury.

ity to produce funds to meet the situation presented can excuse efforts to reduce the injury.

Breach of contract   A party injured by the breach of contract generally must exercise reasonable efforts to lessen the damages. This rule has no application in an action on a contract for an agreed compensation. Upon the breach of a contract to supply personal service or the use of some type of specific equipment or instrumentality, the individual who agrees to furnish such service or items must attempt to acquire a replacement contract if one can reasonably be found. The defendant can then prove, in attempting to reduce damages, that the plaintiff has procured other employment as well as the amount he or she earned or might have earned by exercising reasonable care and diligence. The test of the applicability of this rule is whether the employment or services of the plaintiff were personal in nature. The rule is not applicable in contracts that do not require all, or a significant portion, of the plaintiff's time, or those that do not preclude the plaintiff from becoming engaged in simultaneous performance of other contracts.

Torts   A party who suffers a personal injury is required to exercise ordinary care and perseverance to find a cure, thereby reducing the damages to the most practicable extent. Such an individual should seek reasonable medical care if so required by the injury. It is not necessary for the person to undergo excessively painful treatment or that which involves a significant hazard of death or injury or offers a mere possibility of a cure. The pain inherent in the necessary medical care and treatment may be taken into consideration in assessing whether the plaintiff acted rea-

sonably in declining to submit to it. Although submission to treatment is not a prerequisite to an award of damages, recovery cannot be obtained for increased damages that stem from the failure to submit to necessary medical treatment. Conversely, the mere fact that medical attention was not sought immediately, or at all, will not proscribe an award of damages where the circumstances did not reasonably indicate that medical aid and attention was necessary.

In addition, an injured party has no absolute duty to subscribe to a physician's advice to mitigate damages. The party might, however, under some circumstances, be under an obligation to exercise ordinary care in following such advice.

AVOIDANCE ☐ An escape from the consequences of a specific course of action through the use of legally acceptable means. ☐

A taxpaper may take all legally recognized DEDUCTIONS in order to minimize the INCOME TAX liability. This conduct is called TAX AVOIDANCE and is legal. If, however, a taxpayer claims deductions to which he or she is not entitled so that the individual pays less income tax than is actually owed, then the taxpayer has committed TAX EVASION, a crime punishable by a fine, imprisonment, or both.

☐ Cancellation; the act of rendering something useless or legally ineffective. ☐

A plea in CONFESSION AND AVOIDANCE is one that admits the truth of allegations made in former pleading but presents new information that neutralizes or avoids the legal ramifications of those admitted facts.

William M. Beaney

Avoiding Constitutional Questions

The Constitution (Article III) vests judicial power in the Supreme Court and those lesser Federal courts that Congress chooses to establish. The important jurisdictional authority (authority to hear and determine a case) of all Federal courts is limited to "cases and controversies" and further confined to those arising under the Constitution, law, and treaties of the United States. In addition, the Eleventh Amendment bars suit against states. Upon this meager framework the Supreme Court has built an elaborate structure of rules and principles defining the roles that it and the lower Federal courts will play in our governmental system of separated and shared powers at the national level, and relationships between the nation and states.

The avoidance of constitutional issues is one way in which the Court, by refusing to extend its own powers, shows deference to the legislative and executive branches. As the umpire of federalism, it can favor or disfavor a state or the nation by leaving the resolution of conflicts to the political processes. It is the Supreme Court justices' way of reiterating the limitations of the Court's role: to decide only those cases where it is appropriate and necessary for the judicial process to operate in order to maintain the supremacy of the Constitution while avoiding the character of a super-legislature.

This "modest" guise that the Court frequently assumes should not be taken wholly at face value. The rules and principles developed over the years are of the Court's own making. In addition, there are exceptions, also devised by the Court, which allow it to sidestep its own rules. Frequently, the invocation of a rule of avoidance represents a concealed decision on the merits of a case. On other occasions, the Court may simply be grasping for a postponement of resolution of an issue that must be faced at some future time.

The justification for rules of avoidance lies in some instances in Article III itself. A real "case or controversy" must exist, according to the Court (*Muskrat v. United States,* 219 U.S. 346, 31 S.Ct. 250, 55 L.Ed. 246 [1911]). Two or more actual parties in a situation where existing or threatened harm can be shown are necessary to show "standing" to sue (*Frothingham v. Mellon*, 262 U.S. 447, 43 S.Ct. 597, 67 L.Ed. 1078 [1923]). The controversy must be "ripe" and remain so throughout the legal action (*United Public Workers v. Mitchell*, 330 U.S. 75, 67 S.Ct. 556, 91 L.Ed. 754 [1947]). It must not be a controversy that no longer exists, thus "moot" (*DeFunis v. Odegaard,* 416 U.S. 312, 94 S.Ct. 1704, 40 L.Ed.2d 164 [1974]). It cannot involve a question that has been entrusted to the disposition by one or both of the other branches—hence, a "political question" (Compare *Colegrove v. Green,* 328 U.S. 549, 66 S.Ct. 1198, 90 L.Ed. 1432 [1946] with *Baker v. Carr,* 369 U.S. 186, 82 S.Ct. 691, 7 L.Ed.2d 663 [1962]).

But there are other self-denying rules that do not have a clear constitutional basis. Prudential reasons explain the justices' stance in cases where they refuse to reach a decision on the merits, but do not regard themselves restricted by the Constitution itself. Some of these principles were listed by Justice Louis Brandeis, in his concurrence in *Ashwander v. Tennessee Valley Authority,* 297 U.S. 288, 341–356, 56 S.Ct. 466, 80 L.Ed. 688 (1936). Examples are rules that forbid consideration of constitutional issues affecting legislation in friendly, nonadversary proceedings, in advance of the necessity of deciding them, in broader terms than are required by the precise facts to which the ruling is to be applied; and if the record presents some other ground upon which the case can be disposed. The latter principle is extremely important in the numerous cases where the Court determines that a question of statutory interpretation allows avoidance of a constitutional question.

A quite different type of avoidance arises from the justices' refusal to decide a case coming from the state courts where, although a Federal question is involved, an adequate and independent state ground justifies the result (*Murdock v. City of Memphis,* 87 U.S. [20 Wall.] 590, 22 L.Ed. 429 [1875]). This is true even when the state court has made an erroneous interpretation of a United States constitutional provision in the course of its decision. Here the Court displays deference toward state court interpretations of state law, ignoring the decision-making potentiality presented by the fact that a Federal issue does exist in these cases. Similarly, the Court embraces a doctrine of abstention where a case admittedly within its jurisdiction presents a constitutional question that turns on an unsettled interpretation of state law.

Bibliography: J. Nowak, R. Rotunda, J. Young, *Constitutional Law* (1978); A. Mason and W. Beaney, *American Constitutional Law,* 6th ed. (1978).

AVOWAL ☐ An open declaration by an attorney representing a party in a lawsuit, made after the jury has been removed from the courtroom, that requests the admission of particular testimony from a witness that would otherwise be inadmissible because it has been successfully objected to during the trial. ☐

An avowal serves two purposes. It enables an attorney to have the court learn what a witness would have replied to a question that opposing counsel had objected and which the trial judge sustained. It also provides the interrogator with an opportunity to offer evidence that contradicts the disputed testimony. If, upon appeal, an appellate court decides that a witness should have been allowed to respond to such questions before a jury, an avowal will be a record of the witness' response.

AVULSION ☐ The immediate and noticeable addition to land caused by its removal from the property of another, by a sudden change in a water bed or in the course of a stream. ☐

When a stream that is a boundary suddenly abandons its bed and seeks a new bed, the boundary line does not change. It remains in the center of the original bed even if water no longer flows through it. This is known as the *rule of avulsion*.

Avulsion is not the same as accretion or alluvion, the gradual and imperceptible buildup of land by the continuous activity of the sea, a river, or by other natural causes. See also, Charles H. McLaughlin's essay on Territory, National.

AWARD ☐ To concede; to give by judicial determination; to rule in favor of after an evaluation of the facts, EVIDENCE, or merits. ☐

A jury awards DAMAGES; a municipal corporation awards a PUBLIC CONTRACT to a bidder. ☐ The decision made by a panel of arbitrators or commissioners, a jury, or other authorized individuals in a controversy that has been presented for resolution. ☐ A document that memorializes the determination reached in a dispute. ☐

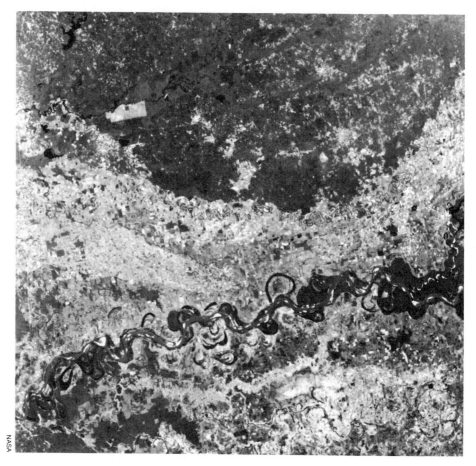

This NASA satellite photograph shows that the serpentine course of the Mississippi River makes it difficult for surveyors to fix an unchanging boundary on one of the river's banks.

NASA

West® Publications
Used to Prepare Volume 1

Abernathy, Charles F. *Civil Rights: Cases and Materials* (1980).

Atkinson, Thomas Edgar. *Handbook of the Law of Wills and Other Principles of Succession,* 2nd ed. (1953).

Averill, Lawrence. *Uniform Probate Code in a Nutshell* (1978).

Bailey, Henry J. III. *Secured Transactions in a Nutshell,* 2nd ed. (1981).

Bator, Paul M.; Mishkin, Paul J.; Shapiro, David L.; and Wechsler, Herbert. *Hart and Wechsler's the Federal Courts and the Federal System,* 2nd ed. (1973).

Bernhardt, Roger. *Real Property in a Nutshell,* 2nd ed. (1981).

Black, Henry Campbell. *Black's Law Dictionary,* 4th ed. (1951).

———. *Black's Law Dictionary,* 5th ed. (1979).

Bodenheimer, Edgar; Oakley, John Bilyeu; and Love, Jean C. *An Introduction to the Anglo-American Legal System: Readings and Cases* (1980).

Bogert, George Gleason. *Handbook of the Law of Trusts,* 5th ed. (1973).

Boyer, Ralph E. *Survey of the Law of Property,* 3rd ed. (1981).

Bruce, Jon W. *Real Estate Finance in a Nutshell* (1979).

Burby, William Edward. *Handbook of the Law of Real Property,* 3rd ed. (1965).

Calamari, John D., and Perillo, Joseph M. *The Law of Contracts,* 2nd ed. (1977).

Casad, Robert C. *Res Judicata in a Nutshell* (1976).

Choate, Robert A., and Francis, William H. *Cases and Materials on Patent Law,* 2nd ed. (1981).

Clark, Charles Edward. *Cases on Modern Pleading* (1952).

———. *Handbook of the Law of Code Pleading* (1928).

Clark, Elias; Lusky, Louis; and Murphy, Arthur W. *Cases and Materials on Gratuitous Transfers: Wills, Intestate Succession, Trusts, Gifts, and Future Interests,* 2nd ed. (1977).

Clark, Homer Harrison, Jr. *The Law of Domestic Relations in the United States* (1968).

Corbin, Arthur Linton. *Cases on the Law of Contracts,* 3rd ed. (1947).

———. *Corbin on Contracts: A Comprehensive Treatise on the Working Rules of Contracts Law* (1950).

Cound, John J.; Friedenthal, Jack H.; and Miller, Arthur R. *Civil Procedure: Cases and Materials,* 3rd ed. (1980).

Cound, John J.; Friedenthal, Jack H.; and Miller, Arthur R. *Pleading, Joinder, and Discovery: Cases and Materials* (1968).

Currie, David P. *Federal Jurisdiction in a Nutshell,* 2nd ed. (1981).

———. *Pollution: Cases and Materials* (1975).

Davies, Jack. *Legislative Law and Process in a Nutshell* (1975).

Davis, Kenneth C. *Administrative Law,* 3rd ed. (1972).

———. *Administrative Law: Cases—Text—Problems,* 6th ed. (1977).

———. *Administrative Law Treatise,* 2nd ed. (1980).

Devitt, Edward James, and Blackmar, Charles B. *Federal Jury Practice and Instructions: Civil and Criminal,* 3rd ed. (1977).

Dobbs, Dan B. *Handbook on the Law of Remedies: Damages—Equity—Restitution* (1973).

Dobbyn, John F. *Injunctions in a Nutshell* (1974).

Dionisopoulos, P. Allan, and Ducat, Craig R. *The Right to Privacy: Essays and Cases* (1976).

Dolgin, Erica L., and Guilbert, Thomas G. P. *Federal Environmental Law* (1974).

Ducat, Craig R. *Modes of Constitutional Interpretation* (1978).

Dvorkin, Elizabeth; Himmelstein, Jack; and Lesnick, Howard. *Becoming a Lawyer: A Humanistic Perspective on Legal Education and Professionalism* (1981).

Ehrenzweig, Albert Armin. *Conflicts in a Nutshell,* 3rd ed. (1974).

Ehrenzweig, Albert Armin; Louisell, David W.; and Hazard, Geoffrey C. *Jurisdiction in a Nutshell: State and Federal,* 4th ed. (1980).

Emanuel, Steven L.; Rossen, Howard M.; and Sogg, Wilton S. *Civil Procedure, for Law School and Bar Examination* (1977).

Epstein, David G. *Debtor-Creditor Relations in a Nutshell,* 2nd ed. (1980).

Epstein, David G., and Landers, Jonathan M. *Debtors and Creditors: Cases and Materials* (1978).

Epstein, David G., and Nickles, Steve H. *Consumer Law in a Nutshell,* 2nd ed. (1981).

Findley, Roger W., and Farber, Daniel A. *Environmental Law: Cases and Materials* (1981).

Forrester, Ray, and Moye, John E. *Cases and Materials on Federal Jurisdiction and Procedure,* 3rd ed. (1977).

Fox, Sanford J. *The Law of Juvenile Courts in a Nutshell,* 2nd ed. (1977).

Freedman, Monroe H. *Cases and Materials on Contracts* (1973).

Fuller, Lon L., and Eisenberg, Melvin Aron. *Basic Contract Law,* 4th ed. (1981).

Gellhorn, Ernest. *Antitrust Law and Economics in a Nutshell,* 2nd ed. (1981).

Gellhorn, Ernest, and Boyer, Barry B. *Administrative Law and Process in a Nutshell,* 2nd ed. (1981).

Gilmore, Grant, and Black, Charles L., Jr. *The Law of Admiralty,* 2nd ed. (1975).

Ginsburg, Douglas H. *Regulation of Broadcasting: Law and Policy Towards Radio, Television, and Cable Communications* (1979).

Ginsburg, Ruth Bader. *Constitutional Aspects of Sex-Based Discrimination,* pamphlet (1974).

Gorman, Robert A. *Basic Text on Labor Law: Unionization and Collective Bargaining* (1976).

Graham, Michael H. *Federal Rules of Evidence in a Nutshell* (1981).

Green, Leon, et al. *Advanced Torts: Injuries to Business, Political, and Family Interests* (1977).

Gulliver, Ashbel Green. *Cases and Materials on the Law of Future Interests* (1959).

Gunther, Gerald. *Constitutional Law: Cases and Materials,* 9th ed. (1975).

Hamilton, Robert W. *Law of Corporations in a Nutshell* (1980).

Hanks, Eva H.; Tarlock, A. Dan; and Hanks, John L. *Cases and Materials on Environmental Law and Policy* (1974).

Hemingway, Richard W. *The Law of Oil and Gas* (1971), pocket part (1979).

Henkin, Louis. *Foreign Affairs and the Constitution* (1972).

Henkin, Louis, et al. *International Law: Cases and Materials* (1980).

Henn, Harry G. *Agency, Partnership, and Other Unincorporated Business Enterprises* (1972).

———. *Cases and Materials on the Laws of Corporations* (1974).

———. *Handbook of the Law of Corporations and Other Business Enterprises,* 2nd ed. (1970).

Hill, David S. *Landlord and Tenant Law in a Nutshell* (1979).

Hill, Myron G., Jr.; Rossen, Howard M.; and Sogg, Wilton S. *Administrative Law, for Law School and Bar Examinations,* 2nd ed. (1977).

Hill, Myron G., Jr.; Rossen, Howard M.; and Sogg, Wilton S. *Agency and Partnership, for Law School, Bar, and College Examinations,* 3rd ed. (1979).

Hill, Myron G., Jr.; Rossen, Howard M.; and Sogg, Wilton S. *Constitutional Law, for Law School, Bar, and College Examinations,* 4th ed. (1982).

Hill, Myron G., Jr.; Rossen, Howard M.; and Sogg, Wilton S. *Contracts, for Law School, Bar, and College Examinations,* 3rd ed. (1976).

Hill, Myron G., Jr.; Rossen, Howard M.; and Sogg, Wilton S. *Criminal Law, for Law Schools and Bar Examinations* (1977).

Hill, Myron G., Jr.; Rossen, Howard M.; and Sogg, Wilton S. *Criminal Procedure, for Law School and Bar Examinations,* 4th ed. (1982).

Hill, Myron G., Jr.; Rossen, Howard M.; and Sogg, Wilton S. *Evidence, for Law School, Bar, and College Examinations,* 3rd ed. (1978).

Hill, Myron G., Jr.; Rossen, Howard M.; and Sogg, Wilton S. *Family Law: For Law School, Bar, and College Examinations,* 2nd ed. (1981).

Hill, Myron G., Jr.; Rossen, Howard M.; and Sogg, Wilton S. *Remedies: Equity— Damages—Restitution for Law School and Bar Examinations* (1974).

Hill, Myron G., Jr.; Rossen, Howard M.; and Sogg, Wilton S. *Torts, for Law School and Bar Examinations,* 3rd ed. (1975).

Israel, Jerold H., and LaFave, Wayne R. *Criminal Procedure in a Nutshell: Constitutional Limitations,* 3rd ed. (1980).

Jackson, John Howard. *Legal Problems of International Economic Relations: Cases, Materials, and Text on the National and International Regulation of Transnational Economic Relations* (1977).

Kamisar, Yale; LaFave, Wayne; and Israel, Jerold H. *Modern Criminal Procedure: Cases, Comments, Questions,* 5th ed. (1980).

Kane, Mary K. *Civil Procedure in a Nutshell* (1979).

Karlen, Delmar. *Civil Procedure: Cases and Materials* (1975).

———. *Procedure Before Trial in a Nutshell* (1972).

Keeton, Page, and Keeton, Robert E. *Cases and Materials on the Law of Torts,* 2nd ed. (1977).

Keeton, Robert E. *Basic Text on Insurance Law* (1971).

———. *Cases and Materials on Basic Insurance Law,* 2nd ed. (1977).

———. *Case Supplement to Keeton's Basic Text on Insurance Law* (1978).

Kempin, Frederick G., Jr. *Historical Introduction to Anglo-American Law in a Nutshell,* 2nd ed. (1973).

Keyes, W. Noel. *Government Contracts in a Nutshell* (1979).

Kimball, Spencer L. *Historical Introduction to the Legal System* (1966).

King, Joseph H. *The Law of Medical Malpractice in a Nutshell* (1977).

Kionka, Edward J. *Torts in a Nutshell: Injuries to Persons and Property* (1977).

Kirgis, Frederic L., Jr. *International Organizations in Their Legal Setting: Documents, Comments, and Questions* (1977).

Krantz, Sheldon. *Cases and Materials on the Law of Corrections and Prisoners' Rights,* 2nd ed. (1981).

———. *The Law of Corrections and Prisoners' Rights in a Nutshell* (1976).

Krause, Harry D. *Family Law: Cases and Materials* (1976).

———. *Family Law in a Nutshell* (1977).

LaFave, Wayne R. *Modern Criminal Law: Cases, Comments, and Questions* (1978).

———. *Search and Seizure: A Treatise on the Fourth Amendment* (1978).

LaFave, Wayne R., and Scott, Austin W., Jr. *Handbook on Criminal Law* (1972).

LaFrance, Arthur B. *Welfare Law: Structure and Entitlement in a Nutshell* (1979).

LaFrance, Arthur B., et al. *Law of the Poor* (1973).

Leavell, Robert N.; Love, Jean C.; and Nelson, Grant S. *Cases and Materials on Equitable Remedies and Restitutions,* 3rd ed. (1980).

Leslie, Douglas L. *Labor Law in a Nutshell* (1979).

Lockhart, William B.; Kamisar, Yale; and Choper, Jesse H. *Constitutional Law: Cases, Comments, Questions,* 5th ed. (1980).

Loewy, Arnold H. *Criminal Law in a Nutshell* (1975).

Lynn, Robert J. *Introduction to Estate Planning in a Nutshell,* 2nd ed. (1978).

McBaine, James Patterson. *Introduction to Civil Procedure: Common Law Actions and Pleading* (1950).

McCall, James R. *Consumer Protection: Cases, Notes, and Materials* (1977).

———. *Statutory Supplement to Consumer Protection* (1977).

McCarthy, David J. *Local Government Law in a Nutshell* (1975).

McCoid, John C. II. *Civil Procedure: Cases and Materials* (1974).

McCormick, Charles Tilford. *Handbook on the Law of Damages* (1935).

McCormick, Charles Tilford, et al. *McCormick's Handbook of the Law of Evidence,* 2nd ed. (1972).

Mack, William, et al. *Corpus Juris Secundum* (1936–).

McNulty, John K. *Federal Estate and Gift Taxation in a Nutshell,* 2nd ed. (1979).

———. *Federal Income Taxation of Individuals in a Nutshell,* 2nd ed. (1978).

Malone, Wex S. *Torts in a Nutshell: Injuries to Family, Social, and Trade Relations* (1979).

Mashaw, Jerry L., and Merrill, Richard A. *Introduction to the American Public Law System: Cases and Materials* (1975).

Mennell, Robert L. *Wills and Trusts in a Nutshell* (1979).

Miller, Arthur Selwyn. *Presidential Power in a Nutshell* (1977).

Moody, Lizabeth A.; Rossen, Howard M.; and Sogg, Wilton S. *Corporations: For Law School and Bar Examinations,* 3rd ed. (1976).

Moody, Lizabeth A.; Rossen, Howard M.; and Sogg, Wilton S. *Wills, Trusts, Probate, Administration, and the Fiduciary: For Law School, Bar, and Bar Examinations, Trust Officers, and Life Underwriters,* 3rd ed. (1982).

Morris, Arval A. *The Constitution and American Education,* 2nd ed. (1980).

Nimmer, Melville B. *Cases and Materials on Copyright and Other Aspects of Law Pertaining to Literary, Musical, and Artistic Works,* 2nd ed. (1979).

Noel, Dix W., and Phillips, Jerry J. *Products Liability in a Nutshell,* 2nd ed. (1981).

Nolan, Dennis R. *Labor Arbitration Law and Practice in a Nutshell* (1979).

Nowak, John E.; Rotunda, Ronald D.; and Young, J. Nelson. *Handbook on Constitutional Law* (1978).

Oberer, Walter E.; Hanslowe, Kurt L.; and Andersen, Jerry R. *Cases and Materials on Labor Law: Collective Bargaining in a Free Society,* 2nd ed. (1979).

O'Connell, John F. *Remedies in a Nutshell* (1977).

Oppenheim, S. Chesterfield; Weston, Glen A.; and McCarthy, J. Thomas. *Federal Antitrust Laws: Cases, Text, and Commentary,* 4th ed. (1981).

Perkins, Rollin M. *Criminal Law,* 2nd ed. (1969).

Phipps, Oval A. *Titles in a Nutshell: The Calculus of Interests* (1968).

Player, Mack A. *Federal Law of Employment Discrimination in a Nutshell,* 2nd ed. (1980).

Popper, Robert. *Post-Conviction Remedies in a Nutshell* (1978).

Posner, Richard A.; and Easterbrook, Frank H. *Antitrust Cases, Economic Notes, and Other Materials,* 2nd ed. (1981).

Pound, Roscoe. *The Lawyer from Antiquity to Modern Times* (1953).

Presser, Stephen B., and Zainaldin, Jamil S. *Law and American History: Cases and Materials* (1980).

Prosser, William L. *Handbook of the Law of Torts,* 4th ed. (1971).

Ratner, David L. *Securities Regulation in a Nutshell* (1978).

Reynolds, William L. *Judicial Process in a Nutshell* (1980).

Riesenfeld, Stefan Albrecht. *Cases and Materials on Creditors' Remedies and Debtors' Protection,* 3rd ed. (1979).

Robertson, David W. *Admiralty and Federalism: History and Analysis of Problems of Federal-State Relations in the Maritime Law of the United States* (1970).

Robinson, Glen O.; Gellhorn, Ernest; and Bruff, Harold H. *The Administrative Process,* 2nd ed. (1980).

Rodgers, William H. *Cases and Materials on Energy and Natural Resources* (1979).

———. *Handbook on Environmental Law* (1977).

Rothstein, Paul F. *Evidence in a Nutshell: State and Federal Rules,* 2nd ed. (1981).

Saltzburg, Stephen. *American Criminal Procedure: Cases and Commentary* (1980).

Schaber, Gordon D., and Rohwer, Claude D. *Contracts in a Nutshell* (1975).

Schlesinger, Rudolf B. *Comparative Law: Cases, Texts, Materials,* 4th ed. (1980).

Seavey, Warren A., *Handbook of the Law of Agency* (1964).

Seavey, Warren A. Reuschlein, Harold Gill; and Hall, Livingston. *Cases on Agency and Partnership* (1962).

Shanor, Charles A., and Terrell, Timothy P. *Military Law in a Nutshell* (1980).

Simes, Lewis Mallalieu. *Handbook of the Law of Future Interests,* 2nd ed. (1966).

Spanogle, John A., Jr., and Rohner, Ralph J. *Consumer Law: Cases and Materials* (1979).

Speidel, Richard E.; Summers, Robert S.; and White, James J. *Teaching Materials on Commercial and Consumer Law,* 3rd ed. (1981).

Steffen, Roscoe Turner. *Agency and Partnership in a Nutshell* (1977).

Steffen, Roscoe Turner, and Kerr, Thomas R. *Agency-Partnership: Cases and Materials,* 4th ed. (1980).

Stockton, John M. *Sales in a Nutshell,* 2nd ed. (1981).

Stone, Bradford. *Uniform Commercial Code in a Nutshell* (1974).

Sullivan, Lawrence Anthony. *Handbook of the Law of Antitrust* (1977).

Tomain, Joseph P. *Energy Law in a Nutshell* (1981).

Tribe, Laurence H. *American Constitutional Law* (1978), supplement (1979).

Vieira, Norman, *Civil Rights in a Nutshell* (1978).

Waggoner, Lawrence W. *Future Interests in a Nutshell* (1980).

Weber, Charles M., and Speidel, Richard E. *Commercial Paper in a Nutshell,* 3rd ed. (1982).

Weintraub, Russell J. *Commentary on the Conflict of Laws,* 2nd ed. (1980).

West Publishing Company. *Corpus Juris Secundum.*

———. *United States Code Annotated.*

Weston, Burns H.; Falk, Richard A.; and D'Amato, Anthony A. *Basic Documents in International Law and World Order* (1980).

Weston, Burns H.; Falk, Richard A.; and D'Amato, Anthony A. *International Law and World Order: An Introductory Problem-Oriented Coursebook* (1980).

White, James J. *Statutory Supplement to Teaching Materials on Banking Law* (1980).

———. *Teaching Materials on Banking Law* (1976).

White, James J., and Summers, Robert S. *Handbook of the Law Under the Uniform Commercial Code* (1980).

Wilson, Donald T. *International Business Transactions in a Nutshell* (1981).

Wright, Charles Alan. *Handbook of the Law of Federal Courts,* 3rd ed. (1976).

Wright, Robert, and Webber, Susan. *Land Use in a Nutshell* (1978).

Zuckman, Harvey L., and Gaynes, Martin J. *Mass Communications Law in a Nutshell* (1977).

Appendix

Table of Cases Cited

389

Appendix

Table of Popular Name Acts

Table of Legal Documents
in Appendix Volume 11

Act of Settlement of 1701
Antarctic Treaty
Articles of Confederation
Bill of Rights
Charter of the Organization of American States
Code of Judicial Conduct
Code of Professional Responsibility
Compromise of 1850
Constitution
Covenant of the League of Nations
Declaration of Independence
Emancipation Proclamation
English Bill of Rights
European Convention for the Protection of
   Human Rights and Freedoms
Kansas-Nebraska Act
Lincoln's Gettysburg Address
Lincoln's Second Inaugural Address
Magna Charta
Marshall Plan
Mayflower Compact
Missouri Compromise
Monroe Doctrine
NATO
Northwest Ordinance
Nuremberg War Crimes Trial Judgment
Peace Treaty of 1783

Pennsylvania Constitution of 1776
Petition of Right of 1628
Preamble to the Constitution   *See* Constitution
SALT I
SALT II
SEATO
Stamp Act
Statute of Frauds of 1677
Statute of Gloucester
Statute of the International Court of Justice
Statutes of Westminster
Summa Theologica excerpts
Ten Commandments
Townshend Acts
Tonkin Gulf Resolution
Treaty of London of August 8, 1945, regarding
   the prosecution and punishment of war
   criminals
Treaty on the Non-Proliferation of Nuclear
   Weapons
Truman Doctrine
United Nations Charter
Universal Declaration of Human Rights
Virginia Declaration of Rights of 1776
Washington's Farewell Address
Wilmot Proviso

Appendix

Table of Legal Forms
in Appendix Volume 11

393

Savings clause
Search warrant
Secured transaction
Separation agreement
Settlement statement
Sight draft
Single name partnership
Slip law
Stipulation
Stop payment order
Subordination agreement
Subpoena
Summons

Surety agreements
Temporary restraining order
Time draft
Title insurance policy
Totten trust
Trademark
Trust
Visa
Voting trust
Warehouse receipts
Warranty
Weapons—gun permit
Will

Volume 1

Special Topics Lists

Jurisprudence

Legal Education

Legal Organizations

Index by Topic

Index entries are cited by both volume number and page number. Thus, 1:123 means Volume 1, page 123.

Index by Author

Index entries are cited by both volume number and page number. Thus, 1:123 means Volume 1, page 123.

Index

Index entries are cited by both volume number and
page number. Thus, 1:123 means Volume 1, page 123.

Index

Index entries are cited by both volume number and
page number. Thus, 1:123 means Volume 1, page 123.

Index

Index entries are cited by both volume number and
page number. Thus, 1: 123 means Volume 1, page 123.

†